Reading and pondering over Kazi's writings, I am reminded of my personal journeys and learnings. Architecture is not merely a static dumb built form but is a cosmos in itself. Not merely produced theoretically but created through varied moods and activities of life, place, space, and ecosystems. Theoretically — arguably and rationally — functions or activities or appearances are organisms, but only if seen holistically. Hence, Vastu is not only an environment and not merely an object but has an all-pervading soul, and this is what Kazi conveys through his travels and experiences.

—Balkrishna Doshi on *The Mother Tongue of Architecture*

Kazi Ashraf is that rare contribution of a critical intellectual, well versed in the mores of Indian culture of both the distant and the recent past and, at the same time, an experienced largely academic architect who is profoundly engaged with the vicissitudes of contemporary practice.

—Kenneth Frampton, from the text in the book

The anthology of Kazi Ashraf's essays on a wide spectrum of topics, is a stimulating collection of facts, observations, interpretations and ideas. The essays valorize the cultural, philosophical and experiential grounding of architecture through Indian, Bangladeshi and Western examples. There are also thought-provoking essays on the hidden mental meanings in architecture. Ashraf's essays are grounded in decades of wide erudition and independent thinking. This is a humanist's look at the mental dimensions of the art of building in today's complex world.

—Juhani Pallasmaa

THE MOTHER TONGUE OF ARCHITECTURE

The Mother Tongue of Architecture
Essays on Architecture, Urbanism, and Culture
Selected Writings of Kazi Khaleed Ashraf

ORO Editions
Publishers of Architecture, Art, and Design
Gordon Goff: Publisher

Bengal Institute for Architecture, Landscape and Settlements
45 Kemal Ataturk Avenue
Dhaka 1213, Bangladesh
http://bengal.institute/

www.oroeditions.com
info@oroeditions.com

Published by ORO Editions and Bengal Institute for Architecture, Landscape and Settlements

Book Design: Irteza Ameen
Project Manager: Jake Anderson

10 9 8 7 6 5 4 3 2 1 First Edition

ISBN: 978-1-957183-59-6

Prepress and Print work by ORO Editions Inc
Printed in China

ORO Editions makes a continuous effort to minimize the overall carbon footprint of its publications. As part of this goal, ORO, in association with Global ReLeaf, arranges to plant trees to replace those used in the manufacturing of the paper produced for its books. Global ReLeaf is an international campaign run by American Forests, one of the world's oldest nonprofit conservation organizations. Global ReLeaf is American Forests' education and action program that helps individuals, organizations, agencies, and corporations improve the local and global environment by planting and caring for trees.

THE MOTHER TONGUE OF ARCHITECTURE

Essays on Architecture, Urbanism, and Culture

SELECTED WRITINGS OF
KAZI KHALEED ASHRAF

Published by
ORO Editions and
Bengal Institute for Architecture, Landscape and Settlementts

Contents

Architecture in India

Cityness

Conversations

Introduction

Architecture in Place

Kazi Khaleed Ashraf

I have often heard it said that it is not easy being both an architect and a writer. Writing belongs to everyone but somehow becomes questionable for an architect. Making clear where he stands on this, the Finnish master architect Alvar Aalto declared that God invented paper to draw on, not write. In critical times, which these days are almost every day, I think some architects also need to work through writing. In defense of my newspaper columns, I once wrote:

> Yes, I write – not just about Dhaka but architecture in the country – because it has to be written, not so much thinking what will come out of it, and nothing much is coming out of it, but one writes because it has to be written. As if, if one keeps on writing on this pixilated screen, or sheaf of paper, if one keeps on mounting words after words, laying words over words, incessantly and relentlessly, that words will become bricks and semi-colons will become mortars, and texts will have become buildings and spaces, that then can be inhabited and furnish a space for experience. That's all an architect *who writes* can hope for. (2019)

An architect should be singularly devoted to the role of a designer, as is commonly expected, and an undertaking such as writing is often seen either as a deviation from or devaluation of that reified role. As an architect I am beholden to the domain of design, but my writing action is not a replacement of the design act – writing intensifies the motives of design while admitting and laying bare some of the quandaries of doing: Why am I doing this? Where am I doing this? Writing is a reflective practice for an architect. Taking it another step forward, writing can also be a critical engagement.

Reviewing this anthology, it is not surprising to see how my writings have circled around the notion of place, no matter how both predictable and obscure the notion remains. I see how I have tried to tether architecture to that notion even when the architectural object has remained largely a thing in itself. My effort in this case has been evolutionary. Whether I reflected on the pavilionated structure of the tropics or the minimalist ascetic hut in the forest, each made better sense in its setting.

It took me a while to arrive at the understanding of architecture as a *situated art*, at a kind of quasi-philosophy of what it means to be situated. It did begin with a naïve understanding of regionalism as the notion circulated when we were young students in the late 1970s. But like a stubborn shadow, the idea of "regionalism" never left me. Rather it followed me throughout my career in different reckonings, in my first years being an architect, later as an aspiring scholar, as a professor, and as an architect maneuvering with a little better understanding of the scheme of things.

While going through the collection of writings once more, I notice that I have maintained a kind of fidelity to the "geographical-climatical" theme. This needs an explanation.

First, the geographical-climatical issue is not considered in a techno-functional way, as in the pragmatic practices of "tropical architecture" or "science of comfort," but as a fundament of existence. I tried to develop an ontology of location out of readings of Maurice Merleau-Ponty, especially through his difficult notion of "chiasm," the intertwining of the lived-body and the world. I am still trying to work that towards architecture.

Even if a vague sense of "placeness" pervaded my thinking as an undergraduate student in Dhaka, it acquired a more historical and conceptual depth as a member of Chetana Research Society in the early 1980s under the Bengali master architect Muzharul Islam. His avowed modernist position rooted in a socialist internationalism was also modulated by a deep commitment to a Bengali ethos. Muzharul Islam's *Bengaliness* ran the gamut of political nationalism and locational ethics. The latter remained a foundational point of view for me.

The situational orientation was vastly motivated by new ideas around critical regionalism that we received in the then intellectual barrenness of Dhaka of the early 1980s, but most memorably by the Aga Khan Award for Architecture Seminar in Dhaka in 1986 when we saw the best of Geoffrey Bawa, Charles Correa, Minnette de Silva, and Paul Rudolph. Looking back at that historic event, I now find it momentous that I would be assigned to accompany Kenneth Frampton, who was also speaking at the seminar, to visit Kahn's Capital Complex. A careful conversation on my part during that visit led to a mentorship and friendship that have continued up to now. All of those – a discourse on identity in our circle in Dhaka, the constant cajoling of Muzharul Islam for a locational ethics, the focused turn towards regionalist ideas as the Aga Khan Seminar and the award program demonstrated, and a direct encounter with the most compelling framer of the topic, Kenneth Frampton – led "critical regionalism" to usher a new arc of thinking.

Arguing that the term was still tied to a fidelity to modernist ideology, if not a Euroamerican-centrism ("universal civilization"), I looked for a revision. I argued that the English term "place" was a better notion than regionalism – it did not carry the possible burden of region as inherently parochial or being subservient to a larger whole. When Frampton proposed that "the fundamental strategy of Critical Regionalism is to mediate the impact of universal civilization with elements derived indirectly from the *peculiarities* of a particular place," [italics mine] I thought framing the lines as "*particularities* of place" would be a better description in which a place would be understood on its own definitional terms.

Regionalism led to an interest in "place," in turn leading to an obvious investigation of *genius loci*. Continuing a conceptual kinship, I arrived at the notion of "loka" in Vedic culture, which was a key turning point facilitated by my conversations and classes with Wilhelm Halbfass, the venerable professor of philosophy and ancient India at the University of Pennsylvania. "Loka," the domain of ancient forest spaces, would serendipitously bring me closer to the citizens of the Vedic forest, the renunciants and ascetics, and their reductive architecture. It was quite a bit of circumambulation before I was able to reach a threshold of understanding that linked an ancient practice with modern ideas.

From the rather innocuous question "how do you produce an appropriate architecture?" arose a sustained query on the obligations of locationality. Muzharul Islam raised that issue from political and ethical obligations of location that could be advanced as nationalism, or in a more scientific frame, as an ecological ethics. The veracity of architecture, in terms of its locational purposefulness, whether national, regional, technical, ethical, ecological or ontological, remained a part of the open and sustained query.

Raising a critical issue in his essay, "The mother tongue of architecture," Rabiul Hussain, an important architect and poet in Dhaka, lamented the weak use of Bangla language in education and professional practice, and how that is related to a frail local architectural language. The topic triggered for me a set of provocations around that intimate pair, architecture and culture, and developed as a question: "Is there a mother tongue in architecture?"

I wondered what is the relationship between language and architecture when, in most cultural discourse, "mother tongue" is perceived as the original condition of naturalness and belonging (notwithstanding architecture is also an expressive system)? Despite an implied provocation, Rabiul Husain's essay remains within a predictable nationalistic orientation in which language (speech) is the epicenter of cultural production. It was clear in Husain's suggestion for an original belongingness, language precedes architecture.

A geographic reflection – the relationship between language and land – was missing in Hussain's discussion. Considering the complex terrain of political history, race, and religion, and, most importantly, migration and mutation, the relationship between language and land is quite unstable, and language appears as far more portable and amoebic than one realizes.

Although architecture itself is not an unchanging phenomenon, it has a more enduring relationship with land. Being more intimately and materially tied with the fabric of the land, architecture is a primal juncture of the human existential struggle in a specific locality where the first collective intentionalities are discovered, expressed, and possibly given name. I stress that the naming – converting into a word or a literalization – follows the material formation. It is not that someone said "let us build a hut" and they proceeded to build one. Material conditions and shared habits led to some kind of formation that was given a name that then entered the practice of language.

Contemporary politics of cultural identity has relegated architecture to a mostly marginalized position, at best a technical operation, when it is possible that between architecture and language, the former is a comparatively more durable and geographically anchored, and much prior to national and cultural identities. Writing about contemporary architecture in Bangladesh, I wrote in 2009:

> Over twenty years ago, I described the work of a small group of architects in Bangladesh as being "place-responsive," that is, the architecture responded to a deltaic place-situation, which perhaps now can be called "Bengali." With the paralysis of a Bengali architectural sensibility in the last hundred years or so, it seemed to me that it has become morally imperative and culturally urgent that a significant section of contemporary architecture in Bangladesh be "archaeological," that is, excavate from the historical layers of contradictory and imposed ideologies a more "place-responsive" architecture. The archaeological inquiry is not in the sense of uncovering fossils, nor is it in the sense of trips to exotica, but rather with the objective of restoring cultural archetypes which still have deep existential significance, and be a beginning for fresh trajectories.

My writing comes from a need for a theoretical articulation for practice and production in place. Despite the many circumambulations that have helped me reorient, I have not strayed too much from that position articulated some thirty years ago. But what is clear now is that in understanding the nature of a located architecture, I needed the help of words.

I am very fortunate for the closeness with some incredible stalwarts in the thinking and making of architecture: Muzharul Islam, Stanley Tigerman, Stan Anderson, Bill Porter, Joseph Rykwert, Ivan Illich, and Balkrishna Doshi. It is only natural to be affected by the wide array of ideologies and views as this grand ensemble of thinking represents. Receiving clarity from Muzharul Islam and Rykwert, for both of whom there is no sacred cow, although Islam would be suspicious of anything sacred, and Rykwert would be very interested in how it originates and is maintained, is an indication of a contrapuntal thinking I inherited.

The impetus for the anthology comes from Adnan Morshed, a colleague and friend, and a co-rider in the journey of writing. Although I was initially reluctant about such an anthology, fearing a pretension, I finally realized the importance of gathering the variously distributed writings together in a volume now accessible to many. I am thankful to Adnan for convincing me. I am grateful to many friends and colleagues who have over the years read, critiqued, questioned, supported and often collaborated with my writing tasks. I list them in no particular order: Saif Ul Haque, Jyoti Puri, Salauddin Ahmed, Ehsan Khan, William Whitaker, and Nusrat Sumaiya. I also thank the many editors who have invited me to think and write for various publications, the products of which are here.

I also thank all the publishers and editors who provided permission for reprinting essays and texts here that were originally published in various books and journals.

In the acknowledgment page of *The Hermit's Hut* (2012), I wrote: "Works as these are produced under the immense, sustaining canopy of a family even if its members are at times bewildered by the content. I treasure the patience and support, as well as samplings of irreverence, offered by Neelu, Oona, and Amit, and family in Dhaka. To Neelu, spouse, partner, and companion, verbal thanks are obviously not enough for suffering my quasi-ascetic wanderings. In the end, the book, or the story here, is for her." Nothing much has changed since then, only the debt has increased.

A note on the text: All essays are arranged chronologically within a particular section. Except for some minor edits, all texts retain their original form. Some unpublished pieces are also included in the anthology – while the pieces may appear a bit out of tune now, they make sense in the evolutionary frame of the anthology. There are some repetitions with certain sections appearing in more than one essay. What the essays and articles document are thoughts in motion along with provisional assumptions and occasional presumptions. They are all here.

Dhaka and Philadelphia
2019 and 2022

On *The Mother Tongue*

Writing Architecture: Kazi Khaleed Ashraf's Critical Practice

Adnan Zillur Morshed

The decades following the independence of Bangladesh in 1971 were a time of uncertainty. The country was embroiled in, among other things, an acrimonious political battle about its national identity, oscillating between the ethno-linguistic identity of Bangali and the national citizenship of Bangladeshi. Challenged by the ongoing identity politics, further exacerbated by an alleged loss of national purpose, many believed that architecture as a cultural endeavor had an instrumental role to play in inspiring society.

When Kazi Khaleed Ashraf graduated from the Bangladesh University of Engineering and Technology (BUET) in 1983 with his first degree in architecture, Bangladesh had just entered into its second decade as an independent country. The country's only school of architecture, established in the 1960s with the technical assistance of Texas A&M University, advanced a conformist curriculum based on a technically-oriented, watered-down version of the Bauhaus. Many observers considered the prevailing architecture culture moribund, immersed only in the nitty-gritty of professional practice, unperturbed by any broader cultural and anthropological inquiries. For many members of Ashraf's generation, there was no committed search for what he later called "place-evocative" architecture. Perceptive practitioners also felt that architecture was far removed from any shared values of Bengal's history, modernist ethos, and broader social missions. Despite architect Muzharul Islam's path-breaking modernist work in the 1950s and the flourishing of an architectural "golden age" in the then East Pakistan during the 1960s with the advent of such globally recognized architects as Louis Kahn, Paul Rudolph, Constantinos Doxiadis, and Stanley Tigerman, the discipline of architecture continued to be viewed mostly as part of the construction industry in the post-independence period.

Chetana Study Group, founded in Dhaka in 1981, was an exception. Spearheaded by Muzharul Islam, and involving a multidisciplinary group of architects, artists, writers, poets, journalists, and historians, Chetana advocated a discursive conversation on architecture, art, and history. The study group offered a critical vantage point to examine the roles of architecture in building a new nation, while analyzing history as a crucial repository of knowledge and addressing such immediate problems as resource constraints and urban conditions. In many ways, the early 1980s was a Dickensian "best of times ... worst of times" moment for architecture in Bangladesh.

The architect, researcher, and writer Kazi Khaleed Ashraf took shape in this context. Committedly participating in the activities of Chetana from 1983 onward and perhaps inspired by Muzharul Islam and his intrinsic ability to prod young architects to look at life from alternative angles, Ashraf not only understood the urgency of integrating Bengal's history with modernist architectural thinking but also sought to expand the very definition of architecture beyond an utilitarianist view. An awareness that architecture needed to be more than mere construction gradually became an impetus for Ashraf to research and write. The theoretical foundation of a lifelong researcher was laid, for whom critical historiography was not merely an investigative task or an academic obligation but a necessary intellectual activism. Ashraf's interest in reimagining architectural pedagogy in a cross-disciplinary panorama and an informed professional practice that could result from it received much boost from Chetana's intellectual programs during the 1980s, as well as what was happening theoretically within architectural circles around the world. The critique of modernism's alleged positivistic worldview, the advent of postmodernist criticism and semiotic interpretation of buildings, and a phenomenology of embodied place-making led to much curricular rethinking in architecture schools. These "radical" ideas have been percolating in the humanities studies since the 1960s. The cultural theorist Frederic Jameson wrote: "The 1960s are in many ways the key transitional period, a period in which the new international order (neocolonialism, the Green Revolution, computerization, and electronic information) is at one and the same time in place and is swept and shaken by its own internal contradictions and by external resistance."[1] Kenneth Frampton related the situation to architecture by noting that "there is little doubt that by the mid-sixties, we were increasingly bereft of a realistic theoretical basis on which to work."[2]

Postmodernist "nihilism" notwithstanding, for Ashraf, one of the key contentions in these developments was how architecture and place interfaced. Architecture's promise of being situated in a place and embodying its essential "spirit" as potential antidotes to modernism's purported homogenization of the building culture across geographies appealed to new generations of architects in Bangladesh. A search for "regional identity," "critical regionalism," and "genius loci," among other theoretical concerns, motivated their architectural pursuits. In this context, in Asia, one cannot overlook the pedagogical impact of the Aga Khan Award for Architecture (established in 1977) and its advocacy of building practices invested in local norms, customs, and traditions, without being atavistic and sentimentally vernacular. Founded in 1981, *Mimar: Architecture in Development*, the only international architectural magazine that examined and championed the built environment of developing countries, inspired architects in Asia, including Bangladesh, to seek what was dubbed variously as "indigenous or hybrid modernities."

During this time, as a young researcher and architectural practitioner, Ashraf developed an empathy for what he termed as an architecture of place. But his notion of place was neither regionalist nor nostalgic. His place transcended the immobility of the ground, without undermining the primacy of its rootedness. He always carried his place with him, in his imagination, in the choreography of his peripatetic self, and in his steadfast commitment to the multiplicity of the meaning of place. Since 1988, when he went to MIT to pursue his master's degree in architecture and, in the early 1990s, a PhD at the University of Pennsylvania, he has been in and out of Dhaka, the city in which he grew up and for which he developed a lifelong interest. His relationship with this city was somewhat existential. Every time he would return to Dhaka from the US, his mother would ask, "When are you coming back?" Ashraf would reply, "I never left." This spartan mother-son dialogue offers a poignant foil for a metaphysics of affiliation, attachment, and detachment. In many ways, Ashraf's ability to dwell in his city became possible only when he left it. Paraphrasing cultural theorist Edward Said, one may argue that his very departure enabled his introspection into the city he grew up. Ashraf's pithy answer to his mother highlighted his conceptualization of place through the tension of a covered, uncovered, and unseverable umbilical cord, revealing an intriguing tapestry of maternity, place, and human conditions. The title of Ashraf's anthology—*The Mother Tongue of Architecture*—should be understood in this context. As Ashraf would argue, mother and place share an ontological bond by a common thread of nurturing. When architecture speaks in the mother tongue, it is possible to truly inhabit a place.

[1] Frederic Jameson, "Postmodernism and Consumer Society," in Hal Foster, ed., *The Anti-Aesthetic*, (Seattle: Bay Press, 1983), p. 113.

[2] Kenneth Frampton, "Place-form and Cultural Identity," in John Thackara, ed., *Design after Modernism: Beyond the Object* (New York: Thames and Hudson, 1988), pp. 51-52.

This was Kazi Khaleed Ashraf's quintessential story, a "citizen of the world," who viewed himself simultaneously rooted in and uprooted from multiple places. And that very transience provided him with Cubist perspectives on things and life. He found himself capable of inhabiting three cities at the same time: Dhaka, Philadelphia, and Honolulu (where his tenured academic career flourished). Yet Dhaka recurred in his writing and thinking as a perennial anchor, a perpetual experiment in how a place becomes home, and home an embodied place. This was Ashraf's enduring Merleau-Pontyan probe into the phenomenological consciousness of a body-home-perception matrix. This has been his journey.

This journey was buttressed along the way by many key figures of architecture and architectural history and theory while Ashraf was attending universities in the US. At MIT, Bill Porter, Stanford Anderson, and Ron Lewcock helped him start on the journey. While at the University of Pennsylvania, Joseph Rykwert had much influence on his ideational and anthropological direction in architecture. Rykwert's *On Adam's House in Paradise* became the conceptual fodder for Ashraf's *The Hermit's Hut*, "a significant site for reflecting on the scope and limits of renunciation, on its external, ritual, and aporetic dimensions." Ivan Illich, William Gass, and Barbara Duden, scholars who would visit Rykwert's seminars at Penn, enriched Ashraf's theoretical foundation. Wilhelm Halbfass, a Sanskrit scholar, and Michael Meister, an art historian, both at Penn, were important influences on his developing work. A mentor since 1987, Kenneth Frampton has maintained a long-lasting conversation with Ashraf. Various friends and colleagues became interlocutors in a shared journey of architecture, culture, geography, and history. Architect Saif Ul Haque, sociologist Jyoti Puri, Penn landscape architects Anuradha Mathur and Dilip da Cunha, and his partner architect Hasina Choudhury prompted and shared Ashraf's passion for adda, debate, discussion, and "dissection of unresolved things."

Ashraf's writing discloses the aggregate intellectual footprints of his professors, mentors, colleagues, and friends who crossed paths with him and shared his interests. His oeuvre revolves around a number of key themes: (a) the signification of place, (b) cities and urbanism, (c) modern and contemporary architecture in India and Bangladesh, (d) Louis Kahn, and (e) water and "wet urbanism." What cuts across all these themes is his perceptive inquiry into the nature and meaning of place, in all its contextual, theoretical, phenomenological, and epistemological complexities and contradictions. To understand place, for Ashraf, is to explain the perils and promises of architecture and, ultimately, to inquire into an ontology of human endeavors. This is evident in his latest foray into location as a fundamental underpinning of architecture and revision of the perennial theme of place, represented in his publication series *Locations: An Anthology of Architecture and Urbanism*.

Ashraf's etymological investigation of *sthapatya* (a locus of inhabitation; architecture), *sthapana* (to establish), and *sthana* (locality, place)—with their common root *stha*—offers a poignant parallel to Heidegger's notions of *bauen* (to build) and *buan* (to dwell or to be). Through an intertwined narrative of *sthapana* and *sthana*, architecture or *sthapatya* invokes embodied and empathetic stories of *sthaniya* (local) through climate, material, custom, tradition, manner, etc. But the production of an architecture invested in *sthaniya* is not merely a matter of being place-based or site-specific. It is, in a Heideggerian vein, to inhabit a microcosmic universe, or to cherish and preserve what we inhabit and how we are located. Ashraf identifies a conceptual bridge between the ideas of *sthapana* and *buan*, linguistic cousins related by a shared desire for an ontological multi-existence. Ashraf is a close reader of the Japanese thinker Tetsuro Watsuji's *Climate: A Philosophical Study*, a lyrical exploration of how climate is, and should be, "the basis of how we see ourselves and how we see the world." Climate is architecture's epic premise, but architecture makes climate visible and comprehensible, as "Louis Kahn reflected, the sun never knew how beautiful it was until it touched the wall."[3] It is not surprising that Ashraf was intrigued when a Japanese architect, visiting Penn, asked his students to "draw the wind."

If place and climate are architecture's primary conditions and revelations, water is its ubiquitous yet ignored alter ego. Ashraf laments how current architectural practices suppress and deny an ecology of water, or what he calls "waterness" or "water ethos" in both the manifest and conceptual spaces of architecture. In many ways, he echoes philosopher Ivan Illich's melancholic evocation of the modern abstraction of reverential water into chemical H2O. This way Ashraf questions the denial of water in architectural and urban imaginations, revealing how canonical epistemological methodologies favor land as the secure foundation of architectural knowledge. In the case of the city he grew up in, "Dhaka and the delta appear increasingly as two separate entities, antithetical and stranger to each other."[4]

Ashraf often looks at his native Bangladesh through the prism of its riverine geography and the literary repertoire of classic Bengali novels that portray it. He often refers to Manik Bandhyopadhyay's *Padma Nadir Majhi* (1936) and Advaita Malla Berman's *A River Called Titash* (1973) as frames for understanding the cultural meanings of Bengal's deltaic nature. He writes: "There are hundreds of stories for hundreds of rivers and their hundreds of twists and turns. The floods and emergent courses impart to the delta a corrugation of flat plains, ponds, muddy enclaves and lowlands."[5] The hydraulic morphology of Bengal, he claims, calls for a "liquid or wet urbanism" that warrants an epistemological shift from land-centrism to a land-water ecology. Ashraf's central thesis is that the need to look at architecture and cities from a "wet perspective" has now become an ethical imperative, especially in the age of global water stress and Anthropocene. The iconic modernist mantra—form follows function—should now transition into a twenty-first century one: form follows (hydraulic) flow. He credits Kahn for understanding the aquatic *genius loci* of Bengal:

> Louis Kahn intuitively recognized the dynamics of water when he received the commission for the National Capitol Complex in Dhaka in 1963. Although water was a powerful compositional thematic in the design of the assembly complex, with the whole layout seen as a mirror of a delta topography, Kahn moved beyond compositional engagement after he received the commission for a large housing project in a functional floodplain. Kahn's unrealized sketches show a new investigation of water as ground, in which bridge-like housing hovers above fields and floodplains allowing the passage of water. Without naming it so, Kahn had already inaugurated the foundation of what we now call wet urbanism.[6]

If Louis Kahn was a quintessential practitioner of a wet perspective, he developed that, Ashraf claims, while working in Bangladesh.

Ashraf's protagonists—from Rabindranath Tagore to Muzharul Islam, from the Buddha to Louis Kahn, from Maurice Merleau-Ponty to Ivan Illich—express more about the kind of architecture and its pedagogy that he advocates than the protagonists themselves. The seed of his activist and analytical mindset was sown early on, sometimes at his family dinner table, the essential theater

[3] Kazi Khaleed Ashraf, "Placing Architecture, Presencing Architecture," (2001).

[4] Kazi Khaleed Ashraf, "Water as Ground," in Anuradha Mathur and Dilip da Cunha, eds., *Design in the Terrain of Water* (Applied Research + Design Publishing, 2014).

[5] Ashraf, "Water as Ground."

[6] Kazi Khaleed Ashraf, "Fluid Space," in *Architectural Review* (June 2017).

of "argumentative Bengalis." His was a "typical" middle-class Bengali family, with both of his politically progressive parents deeply aligned with the Bengali nationalist movement that marked the 1960s. His father was a lawyer and mother a professor of history at Eden and Badrunnessa College in Dhaka. The family appreciated travels to India, especially the picturesque Kashmir. Music was a mainstay of the family's cultural universe, particularly Rabindra Sangeet by acclaimed singers Pankaj Mullick and Debabrata Biswas. Ashraf was drawn to the music of, among others, Paul Simon and Bob Dylan, and, in an adolescent zeal, would often try to convince his father to listen to them, as if to expand the family's musical horizon or to examine how accepting a parent was of western influences. The family's bibliophilia was evident in household bookcases, and no topic would be off limits during familial conversations. When in high school, Ashraf aspired to be an astronomer. He even took his O-Level examination in Astronomy, a rather unusual subject selection during the 1970s in Bangladesh, because parents typically would have liked their children to pursue more employable careers. And, during college, he wanted to be an astrophysicist. One wonders what his interests in two cosmoses—the macro/astronomic and micro/particles—portend for his eventual pursuit of architecture as a discipline and its multidisciplinary interpretation in revealing how the world, our *sthana*, our *vastu*, works at many scales and dimensions.

The multifaceted writings of Ashraf on cultural identity, delta, Dhaka, wet perspective, city, Muzharul Islam, home, hermit's hut, Louis Kahn, forest, the Buddha, and the "citizen of the world," all loop back to one question: How do we imagine, create, and inhabit a place, and, in turn, how place shapes us? In his lifelong deliberation of this vexing question, he recalls Aldo Rossi, who once enigmatically stated that as one approaches place, it recedes. Yet Ashraf does not approach place. He circles it. He crisscrosses it with intellectual nuance and empathy with a view to being in it. His place is tangible, imaginary, haunting, climatic, elusive, ideational, revelatory, and a condenser of culture and values. Like Plato's "bastard reasoning," his place is ultimately many things, all at the same time, and can only be made sense of by not letting go. And, architecture's beauty, strength, tragedy, and triumph reside in its ability to search perpetually for the meaning of place.

Kazi Khaleed Ashraf is a pioneer of critical writing on architecture in South Asia. A trailblazer, he helped broaden the scope of architecture beyond construction and utility by embracing writing as a critical practice of architecture. I recall, in the second half of the 1980s, as an undergraduate in architecture in Bangladesh, our textbooks were almost exclusively written by people from the West: from O. H. Koenigsberger to Banister Fletcher to Amos Rapoport. The only exception was Indian architect Charles Correa's *The New Landscape* (1985), which presented a perceptive analysis of how cities were, and should be, conceived and developed in South Asia. While I don't want to argue that curricular reliance on Western textbooks was necessarily a problem of epistemology, we hardly read any reflective and analytical literature that posited Bengal or even Asia within a discursive, global, and multidisciplinary framing of architecture. There were two architecture magazines that endeavored to make a difference: *Mimar* and *Architecture+Design*. The latter was inaugurated in 1986 in Mumbai as one of the earliest magazines in India that sought to develop a critical conversation on South Asian architecture and design. Yet our curriculum hardly drew anything from those valuable magazines. Those publications were merely our private interests.

It is in these conditions Ashraf's scholarship inspired a new generation of architects in Bangladesh to introspect and rediscover themselves, as they

[7] Manfredo Tafuri, *Theories and History of Architecture*, trans. Giorgio Verrecchia (New York: Harper & Row, 1980), iii, quoted in Thomas A. Dutton and Lian Hurst Mann, "Introduction: Modernism, Postmodernism, and Architecture's Social Project," in *Reconstructing Architecture: Critical Discourses and Social Practices*, ed. Thomas A. Dutton and Lian Hurst Mann (Minneapolis: University of Minnesota Press, 1996), p.17.

attempted to reimagine architecture's broader mission and the discipline's pedagogical scope. Ashraf's writing was panoramic. He published in scholarly journals and popular design magazines, contributed opinion pieces to newspapers, guest-edited magazines on special themes, and authored books. Before him nobody in Bangladesh championed how the relationship between Bengal's "braided matrix of land and water" and architecture entailed an understanding of the spirituality of the mystic, singer, and folk philosopher Lalon Shah, "avowedly neither Muslim nor Hindu, but both, and more … deeply embedded in the ethos of rural Bengal." Ashraf hinted at a potential parallel between Lalon's rejection of social hierarchies and religious chasms by using the power of folk music and Tagore's indebtedness to *jari*, *shari*, and *bhatiali* folksongs of the Padma landscape in creating a universalist ethos. Ashraf employed this type of anthropological reading of rural Bengal to unpack the ideological modernity of Muzharul Islam and the "wet urbanism" of Louis Kahn.

In my view, Ashraf's belief in the possibility of an experiential inquiry into place, location, and geography somewhat went against the dominant theoretical currents of the 1990s, when French poststructuralist criticism and postcolonial theories swept through the academia in the US and Europe. Foucault's panopticon, Derrida's *différance*, and Said's orientalism, among other key theoretical positions, highlighted the inscrutability of knowledge and its inalienable complicity with the hegemonic structures of power, often leaving little room for subjective experience, authenticity, empathy, and cognitive freedom. As a doctoral student of architectural history, theory, and criticism at MIT during the second half of the 1990s, I myself experienced the radical attraction of poststructuralism and postcolonialism in our methodological approach to architectural scholarship. The Italian architectural theorist Manfredo Tafuri's "nihilism" had already convinced many of my peers that as an instrument of the capitalist plot, architecture had become pointless, a failed project, since it was no longer able to emancipate society from ideology's stranglehold. There was no escape. Architecture was doomed. Tafuri wrote: "One cannot anticipate … an architecture for a liberated society; what is possible is the introduction of class criticism into architecture."[7] In this scenario I found refreshing Ashraf's commitment to architecture's ability to situate, orient, locate, and even liberate us. Ashraf's scholarship filled a gaping hole in the multidisciplinary reading of Bangladesh's architectural culture. Just as Muzharul Islam motivated the first generation of practicing architects in Bangladesh, Ashraf inspired the first generation of architectural historians and theorists, including me, who embraced critical historiography as a form of their architectural practice.

I knew of Ashraf since the mid-1980s, but I first met him in 1994 when I went to the University of Pennsylvania to carry out a research project on Louis Kahn. Since then we remain friends and collaborators, sharing a common anthropological interest in the architecture and urbanism of Bangladesh. I recall spending much fun-filled times with him in Dhaka, Philadelphia, and Honolulu. It has been a pleasure and privilege knowing Kazi Khaleed Ashraf, scholar and a good human being. I proposed the creation of this anthology to him out of admiration.

Washington, DC
January 2020

Adnan Zillur Morshed is an architect, architectural historian, and urbanist, and currently professor of architecture and architectural history at the Catholic University of America in Washington, DC, US.

The Forest, the City, and the Delta: Kazi Khaleed Ashraf's Architectural Journeys

Sonia Nishat Amin

It was fitting and in harmony with the order of things that one day on my way to class around 2009, I should chance upon Kazi Khaleed Ashraf, sitting in the shade beneath a sprawling banyan tree in the idyllic campus of the University of Hawaii at Manoa, with laptop open in front of him and a sheaf of notes beside it. On enquiring, he said he was working on the manuscript for his forthcoming book on asceticism and architecture in ancient India, the special focus of which would be the Buddha's hut. Reading the surprise on my face he mused, "I know most people think the Buddha and other ascetics spent their entire lives in clement weather and fair conditions under trees and vines, when the reality is they did have abodes of a kind. In the case of the Buddha, it even had a beautiful name – the *gandhakuti* (the fragrant hut)."

Thus started my own journey through the pages of the manuscript that I subsequently read (published in 2013 as *The Hermit's Hut: Asceticism and Architecture in India* by the University of Hawai'i Press). Consumed by curiosity, I embarked on a journey into India's ancient past when *sannyasins* or ascetics roamed the fields and forests, seeking truth, building the most basic abodes to shelter themselves from the weather and wild beasts.

At the center of the study stood the enigmatic "house" of one of India's most fascinating and timeless figures – the Buddha. Aided by the methodology used in iconography, the ascetic's hut was reconstructed from stone sculpture and friezes – featuring pre-Buddhist, primitive ones built from leaves, branches, and clay to the more habitable and aesthetic gandhakuti. From the floor plan of the single room, to the simple pillars and wall supporting it, to the ornamented *chaita* and *harmika* at the apex, the reading of the now petrified *gandhakuti(s)* in the light of Buddhist philosophy turned out to be an engrossing experience. While turning the pages one never strayed far from the history that surrounded the ascetics' quests, the context in which this took place over centuries. As a historian, I developed an admiration for a scholar who believed in delving into the past and weaving in the rich hue and texture of historicism – the belief that understanding peoples and cultures requires an understanding of their historical events – into stone and mortar.

It must have taken a mind of rare curiosity to investigate the habitats of those who had left homes, to unravel the relationship between asceticism and architecture, and to study the nature of the Buddha's shelter. This going back to the roots informs much of Khaleed's oeuvre and enables him to enter the present and the future, equipped with a clear vision of the continuity and "grounded-ness" that lies at the heart of genuine architectural thought and practice.

Khaleed (as I call him) brought these qualities of scholarship and insight with him when he decided to return to *his* own roots in Dhaka around 2015. Once back to the city where he grew up, he set about blazing new pathways. As an architectural theorist, he excavated the contribution of the first modern architect of Bangladesh, Muzharul Islam, through the publication of conversations that had lain buried and forgotten for decades. Along with a handful of other scholars, Khaleed is a key figure in building the foundation for a systematic architectural and urban theory in our country. He made it his special calling to awaken specialists and laypersons to the need to rethink our architectural legacy and the environment in which it developed and possibilities for the future.

To preserve and enrich this legacy, Khaleed moved towards building up a concrete institution that would "house" the ideas and ideals nurtured by him and his cohorts, and transmit them to the next generation. Thus was born in 2015, with a team of dedicated architects and students, the Bengal Institute for Architecture, Landscapes and Settlements.

The Institute was set up with the purpose of providing "a unique trans-disciplinary forum for the study and design of the environment… a post-graduate platform on architecture, landscapes and settlements in Bangladesh." Structured around seminars, lecture series, design studios, research, and publications, it has opened up a space for students and young architects who are caught up in the completion of degrees requiring rigorous training and who cannot afford to engage much with what falls outside the curriculum, yet that which completes the whole. It is here that students and practitioners can gather around the gurus of their discipline and get insights into the wonders of architecture from the ancient *Vastushastra* to the latest in theory and practice.

While rethinking modernity and its ancient linkages, minimalism and the grotesque excesses of architecture that surround us, Khaleed's eyes fall on what many consider the dystopian city of his homeland – Dhaka. His writings weave a region, a city, a site, a locality into an entirety, a holistic tapestry of time and topography. So, Dhaka is viewed as part of the Bengal Delta, the Delta as part of the Indian subcontinent, the latter is placed within the history and geography of building in Asia, and so forth. Very little falls outside this purview – be it Muzharul Islam, Doshi, Corbusier, Louis Kahn, or Alvar Aalto. Thus, he takes his readers along on the long journey of his ceaseless quest. The lay reader/listener and the specialist alike get an insight into the unity (and diversity) that characterizes architecture through the ages – from the past to the future and vice-versa.

This was well exemplified in the three public lectures Khaleed delivered in Dhaka recently (August 29 – September 4, 2019): "Bengali Modernism (in Architecture)"; "Architecture is a Landscape Event"; and, "The Pursuit of 'Nothingness'". The three lectures embodied much of his intellectual pursuits to date.

Through a relentless reexamination of Dhaka's past and future in newspaper articles, learned papers, and books about a city almost given up as comatose and dysfunctional by its residents, Khaleed compels his readers and listeners to think again about the city and its future. Any account of the urban historiography of Dhaka will have his name right up there at the top as a pioneering scholar. His work will be considered "seminal in exploring new territory in a nascent discipline."

With a single invocation "Dhaka, once the Garden City on the bank of the Buriganga, has turned its back on the river," he has shown us the city's past glory and present dilapidation. By tracing the downward trajectory since the river formed the backbone of the city, he lays bare the havoc wreaked by humans on a viable and green environment. However, the reader/listener leaves with a feeling that redemption is yet possible. When city dwellers are devastated by the utter chaos that confronts them day after day, Khaleed opens windows of possibilities, however narrow, through his expositions. He excavates the extant beauty and order that the city contains and the possibilities of renewal. This is borne out by the titles of his work (sometimes in collaboration with others): *Pundranagar to Sherebanglanagar; Sherebanglanagar: Louis Kahn and the Making of a Capital Complex; Louis Kahn: House of the Nation* and *Designing Dhaka*.

Khaleed's study of water and the city, specially in the hydrological reality of Bangladesh, land of the delta, leads him to a profound admiration for the work of Louis Kahn in Bangladesh – the Parliament Complex in the enclave within Dhaka known as Sher e Bangla Nagar – and Kahn's own understanding and assimilation of the deltaic topography.

This theoretical position of incorporating 'water' of the deltaic land into architectural practice and imagination evolved over the years and is evident in Khaleed's recent writings and lectures. The solutions he proposes are outside the purview of my essay. I wish only to highlight the problematic of the present praxis as he views it, and the theoretical approach which needs to be undertaken as a resolution of the matter. He dwells on this again on a recent article: "An urbanism for Dhaka has to be conceptualized from the hydrological property of the delta, the foundational basis of our existence." (*Daily Star*, September 15, 2019)

Sometimes, on my own trips outside Dhaka, when I see the lowlands, the water bodies, the floodplains, and agricultural fields that comprise our lifeline, being thoughtlessly and greedily filled up by sand for multi-storied buildings and complexes, I am reminded of these words. For, to Kazi Khaleed Ashraf: "A city is not mere building, streets, and spaces; it is a theatre of social actions. And it is in that theatre, according to the American urbanist Lewis Mumford, that man's more purposive activities work out… into more significant culminations. I see the city as an existential theatre of our actions, practices, dreams and imaginations." (*Daily Star*, September 15, 2019)

And like that revelation about the Buddha's abode under the banyan tree in the University of Hawai'i, Manoa, long ago, Kazi Khaleed Ashraf has made many of us re-imagine the history and environment that we inherit and act upon.

Sonia Amin is an eminent historian and formerly Chairperson and Professor at the Department of History of Dhaka University. She is a recipient of the Atawar Hussain Gold Medal from the Asiatic Society of Bangladesh and the Anannya Sahitya Puraskar.

Kazi Khaleed Ashraf and the Presence of Architecture

Kenneth Frampton

It is symptomatic of Ashraf's sensibility that in his 2007 essay on the American architect Louis Kahn, he would attach particular importance to Kahn's use of the term 'land architect,' as opposed to the professional convention of landscape architecture regarded as a separate discipline. For Ashraf as for Kahn, the concept of landscape, as its etymological origin suggests, is too picturesque to match the telluric character of land as the ultimate magma out of which everything eventually emerges. For Ashraf as a Bengali, land or rather more fundamentally earth, in the Heideggerian sense, also presupposes the antithetical presence of water, which in the case of the Bengal is so ubiquitous and unruly as to make a perpetual mockery out of the 'land-filled', terra firma on which much of Dhaka has been and is still being built. This disturbing perverse presence haunts Ashraf's purview of the city as with that of his closest colleague, the architect Saif Ul Haque, who has long since recognized that sooner or later we shall have to get used to the construction of buildings that float, given relentless climate change and the rising elevation of the sea.

In the interim, the Bangladeshi capital of Dhaka, the ninth largest city in the world with a current population of fifteen million, increasing at the rate of one million every three years and surrounded on all sides by water, is still engaged in the vicious circle of odorant landfill not to mention the other dysfunctional aspects such as the ever-expanding ramshackle slum areas and its inadequate provision for the disposal of waste. It is the latent hydrological aspect of Dhaka that preoccupies Ashraf in his meditations on the anachronistic dimensions of architecture, above all surely the inevitable destiny of all buildings to fall eventually into ruin. Such concerns remind one of Kahn's somewhat romantic observation that there are two moments in the life of a building when it will be guaranteed a modicum of beauty; first, when it is under construction and second when it has become a ruin. For Kahn it is the initial Piranesian moment of putting a building into the ground that is seminal not only for the stability of the structure but also for its cosmogonic significance of the earthwork. Hence the dialectic between underlying earthwork and water work, which in Kahn's case possibly account for the drainage channels that line the perimeter of his Salk Institute in San Diego, as it emerges from the ground; these all but mythical channels for the discharge of water which are equally present in the work of the Venetian architect Carlo Scarpa. It is possibly no accident in this regard that Venice would serve as the site of Kahn's most ambitious and contradictory project; his Congress Center of 1969 suspended like a bridge well above the Venetian *aqua alta*. A key figure in the development of this work was Kahn's most structurally adept and trusted assistant, the Catalan architect Carlos Vallhonrat, who played an equally salient role in the design of the Bangladeshi Parliament complex, of which he would write at length as to the difficulties of grounding such a heavy structure on a terrain extensively permeated by water.

Ashraf's critical late modern overview was perhaps first most clearly set forth in a brilliant paper that he gave to the 2001 ACSA meeting in Baltimore under the title, "Placing Architecture, Presencing Architecture" wherein he insisted on architecture as a lived experience and argued that:

> *If architecture is an art it is an existential art, perhaps best approximated by an Indian term for architecture, Vastushilpa. I translate Vastushilpa as the art of existence, the root word 'vas'*

> *belonging to a family of Indo-European terms having to do with existence or presence in some form of other, such as the German 'wesen,' the English 'was.' Architecture and existence are inextricably mixed, and if any criterion of thinking best addresses this condition, it is the anthropological approach. I am describing the approach as an anthropological one for the lack of better terminology. It refers to a diverse body of thinking – hermeneutical, existential, phenomenological. The approach is existential in the sense that it readdresses architecture as the elemental and foundational way of being. It is phenomenological in the way it reviews architecture as opening up the receptivity "to the full ontological potential of human experience." The anthropological approach exposes a possible disjunction between architectural practices that rely on a retinal primacy (as the terms image, drawing, analytic, desk crits, etc. convey in academic conversation) and the concrete lived experience of architecture. This divergence is exposed in two ways: (1) "placing architecture," in the fissure that lies between the ideology of architectonic autonomy and the inevitability of situatednesss, and (2) "presencing architecture" in the distance that has emerged between the presence and representation of architecture.*

The millennium returned Ashraf to Heidegger's characterization of place, as opposed to space, as that which is determined by the Greek concept of *peras*, meaning boundary. From a different vantage point, Ashraf combined the idea of place with the notion of the "lived body" as formulated by the phenomenologist Maurice Merleau-Ponty. Thus we find him writing: "For the lived body, the environment is an indefinite extension of it, and not distinguished as standing over and against the living body." Ashraf notes, according to Merleau-Ponty in *The Phenomenology of Perception*:

> *The environment is a "manipulated area" for the lived-body. On the other side, the environment directly and indirectly regulates the lived-body. The environment conditions the body in such a way that the body is the expression or reflection of the environment. In living the body not only lives itself but also lives the environment. This is what Merleau-Ponty calls a "'reciprocal insertion and intertwining'" of the lived-body and the environment.*

For Ashraf as for the Japanese philosopher Tetsuro Watsuji, whose book Climate: *A Philosophical Study* was first published in 1936, climate is just as vitally experienced by the lived body as one's ontological awareness of place. As Ashraf writes:

> *Architecture in this sense may be seen not merely as shelter from climate, as if architecture and climate are confronting each other, but as the inevitable intertwining of the architectural body and climate; it is where climate is revealed. Architecture is the trace of wind, water and rain.*

Ashraf's criticism has been at its most prescient in his writing about the evolution of modern architecture in India, as is evident in the various appraisals that he has made over some twenty-five years of commentary; initially in his appreciation of the fundamental contributions made by Le Corbusier and Kahn to the timeless architectonic culture of the South Asia, above all ultimately via the legacy of the Moghul Empire, as this makes itself manifest in the silhouettes of Le Corbusier's Capitol in Chandigarh and in the metaphorically 'fortified' rotund concrete mass-forms of the Dhaka parliament complex, the Sher-e-Bangla Nagar. From his initial recognition of the founding character of these monumental set-pieces, Ashraf entered into the project of recording and reviewing the salient contributions of the first post-independence Indian architects ranging from Nehru's favorite state-architect of Achyut Kanvinde to Charles Correa working in Bombay, Balkrishna Doshi in Ahmedabad, Raj Rewal in Delhi and, finally, perhaps given his own formation in Dhaka, Ashraf's own immediate teacher, the Bangladeshi master architect Muzharul Islam. The initial pioneering works of each of these architects were first represented collectively in an omnibus exhibition curated by Ashraf in New York in 1997. This exhibition was already a manifestation of Ashraf's drive to launch a critical discourse about the evolution of South Asian modern architecture, a discourse which he has continued to elaborate to this day, as recently evident in the analysis he has made of such architects as Balkrishna Doshi and Bijoy Jain; above all perhaps through his revelations about the deeper ramifications of Doshi's Sangath establishment and the elegant, luxurious residences that Jain has recently built within the palm-laden, coastal territories of Maharashtra state. In both instances, it is the land-form in the Kahnian sense that Ashraf emphasizes. Thus of Doshi's office on the outskirts of Ahmedabad we find him writing:

> *Sangath as a turning point that marks both a crystallization of earlier experiments and deliberate movement towards a new stage, three principal terms stand out: an intimate conversation between architecture and landscape, a constructional assembly derived from a climatic imperative, and a choreographed movement in a spatial matrix.*

This, exceptionally sensitive analysis focused on the threshold of Doshi's initial maturity will be followed by another equally insightful, paragraph which clinches, as it were the underlying tectonic of Doshi's work.

> *The dominant imagery of Sangath is a group of vaulted shapes oriented in one direction that rises from a constructed landscape of planes, terraces, walls and steps. Water runs along the interstices of the vault, on channels and troughs, often cascading down to create a pool. While the interior of the building is a mystery from the exterior, a subterranean possibility is already indicated in the overall ensemble.*

This is a synthetic appraisal that which we in the Eurocentric world are now barely capable of, neither at the level of *post facto* critique nor at the level of everyday professional conversation in either offices or architectural schools. It is as though the decadence of the commodified spectacle totally dominates the neoliberal occidental scene, in the name of a false originality, when in contrast Ashraf's vital discourse is as rich and intertwined in its references as the architecture on which he happens to be focused. This is particularly evident say in his sensitive critique of the work of Bijoy Jain wherein he writes:

> *The principle of land architecture suggests a complex dialogue between the grounding and a rising of a building – a fact of constructedness – rising from the ambiguous earth into a precise form even if the earth is still the material and the genealogical source of the unfolding. Such a reasoned consideration of the simultaneity of distinctiveness and seamlessness – of architecture and landscape – is expressed in the articulation of subterranean gravitas and atmospheric lightness in Jain's work. Palmyra records the architect's*

earliest articulation of an architecture of porosity formed simply by slatted envelopes or an analogue of a filigree of coconut tree leaves. Formed over and along low basalt walls rising from the ground, the tectonic assemblage of the Utsay House in Satirje, Maharashtra (2008), utilizes the porous property to complete the intertwined relationship.

Kazi Ashraf is that rare contribution of a critical intellectual, well versed in the mores of Indian culture of both the distant and the recent past and, at the same time, an experienced largely academic architect who is profoundly engaged with the vicissitudes of contemporary practice, most particularly of recent date in that of the South Asian continent. This apart from his evident talent as a writer of exceptional fluidity and depth, he has also increasingly become an environmental activist, particularly with regard to the emerging predicament of the capital city of Dhaka where he is now residing in his capacity as the director of the Bengal Institute, the mandate of which is dedicated to furthering the quality of local architectural practice combined with meeting the needs of education and research. This undertaking and Ashraf's involvement with it is well represented by the insightful and committed essay he contributed recently to the publication *Bengal Stream: The Vibrant Architecture Scene of Bangladesh*, which is the outsized and beautiful assembled catalog that accompanied the blockbuster exhibition featuring the architecture of Bangladesh, staged at the Swiss Architecture Museum in Basel in 2017. In this essay, Ashraf was to focus on the longstanding Bengali trope of the pavilion as kind of a canopied open-ended, provisional structure which possesses a particular kind of adaptability, appropriate to the monsoon climate of the country constantly subject to unpredictable flood patterns that demand that tectonic interventions remain open to the demands of continual challenge.

Ware Professor at Columbia University's School of Architecture, and author of numerous influential books, Kenneth Frampton is arguably the leading architectural historian and critic of the present time.

Finding Kazi Khaleed Ashraf

Marina Tabassum

I am not much of a writer. Words in my mind fail to manifest in the same manner as space and form. I am conscious of this weakness and try to avoid it in every possible way. But it would be a missed opportunity if I do not attempt to talk about one person whose contribution has been immense in my shaping as an architect.

Now, where to begin with Kazi Khaleed Ashraf? The first time I saw him was in the Nandan Architects office of Uttam Kumar Saha. I was then a third year student in architecture and working on a model in the office. "Do you know him?" asked Shaha after Ashraf left. My blank look obliged him to give a long detailed account of accomplishments of this distinguished, very impressive young professor who was visiting Bangladesh from the US. The name was known to me not through architecture but because of *Unmad*, the Bengali version of the famous *MAD* magazine. As teenagers in the 1980s we all enjoyed the humor of the humble black and white publication. Reading *Unmad* was a family event and my father was a big fan. Ashraf was one of the founder-editors of the magazine.

"Why do all the brilliant accomplished architects leave Bangladesh?" was going through my mind while Uttam Kumar Shaha continued explaining Ashraf's visit. It was a disappointment, perhaps a bit of frustration, imagining what was I missing in not being Ashraf's student. Self-esteem was usually shaky growing up in a country ravaged by war and poverty, and challenged climatically and politically. Few talked about patriotism when we grew up in the late nineteen seventies and eighties. "If you can manage a pair of wings, you fly out of uncertainty to a secure land in the west" was a tacit motto of many graduates of our time. With Ashraf, it was different. When asked when he was coming back, he would reply "I never left," and quite rightly so.

Physical presence in a location does not always guarantee one's participation in the greater good. Ashraf's writings and publications bear proof of how he embodied Bangladesh irrespective of his geographical location. His searches in architectural thinking kept Bangladesh in focus while living and teaching abroad. Ashraf's Dhaka visits never went unnoticed. The visits were all planned and lined up with activities, whether with an exhibition, workshop or seminar. The architecture community in Dhaka eagerly awaited his home-coming in the summer. And some of us looked forward to taking part in the events and activities he planned. There was always something fresh to experience, something new to learn. It was during one such occasion – a theory workshop – that I first read "Towards a Critical Regionalism: Six Points of an Architecture of Resistance" by Kenneth Frampton, an essay that in many ways shaped my consciousness and compelled me to look deeper into the land where I belong. "Bangladesh is composed of a fluidity of land and water: how is it relevant to architecture?" During our formative years in architecture, while mastering the manipulation of space and form, this was not a question that was addressed with any rigor or significance. I must acknowledge that is a window that Ashraf opened up for me and my generation of architects, and installed an insight into place that brought relevance to an otherwise banal pursuit of form-making. Ashraf taught us to "think like a farmer," as he loved saying quoting Wharton Esherick.

Ashraf's contribution to the architecture culture of Bangladesh is unparalleled by any individual other that Muzharul Islam. While Islam's architecture shows a definitive and deep understanding of place with an informed awareness of world culture, Ashraf builds up his research from a similar standpoint but linking Islam's legacy. Through his books and writings that are now indispensable resource in pedagogy, there is a slow and silent transformation taking place manifested throughout contemporary architecture of Bangladesh.

With the formation of Bengal Institute in 2015 and Ashraf assuming the role as director-general, we have been working closely in shaping a multidisciplinary platform that we believe is a necessity to address the environmental challenges of rapid unplanned urbanization. Understanding the relationship of water and land is critical in living in the delta, as it is crucial to acknowledge water as resource and to plan around it. This is a lesson learnt from Ashraf and which has produced the commitment that Bengal Institute follows wholeheartedly. *Designing Dhaka: A Manifesto for a Better City* (2012) a time appropriate publication by Kazi Khaleed Ashraf encouraged Abul Khair, a lifetime patron of arts and literature, to persuade him to return to Bangladesh fully.

Within the four years of Ashraf's *latest* homecoming and Bengal Institute's committed pursuits, I can proudly claim that we have been able to make a wider impact through engaging with leading academics, researchers, and practitioners from all around the globe. The achievement would not be possible without the unwavering pursuit, passion and belief that Ashraf imbued us with. He is not only a prolific writer, thinker, teacher and influencer of the academic discourse, but also a passionate architect and urbanist, something I have discovered fairly recently with the planning and intervention projects that Bengal Institute has undertaken. Research and large-scale design operations and strategies on cities, small towns and settlements produced by Bengal Institute under Ashraf's guidance are now being presented through exhibitions, publications and symposiums to a wider audience including politicians, mayors, and civic leaders.

In the last four years of working closely, Ashraf never ceases to amaze us in handling every challenge that came our way, and in being relentless in reinventing and evolving as a person and professional. Not only is he an inspiration of whom I can speak with great admiration and immense respect, but also someone I look up to for guidance and wisdom. I hope our journey in the pursuit of architecture, which we believe is much larger than architecture itself, continues through thick and thin and our contribution to the society at large can make some difference to a better life and living.

Marina Tabassum is a leading architect of Bangladesh and a winner of the Aga Khan Award for Architecture.

Kazi Khaleed Ashraf: The Future-Maker

Syed Manzoorul Islam

My interest in architecture grew after I heard the legendary Muzharul Islam speak on a few occasions on architecture, tradition and modernity, and then had the privilege of meeting and talking with him at his residence a couple of times – all in the early 1970s. Islam put forward a vision of modernity that valued tradition and continuity and promoted the local and the organic over the spectacular and the purely functional. I could see the virtue of Islam's architectural philosophy when Dhaka began to expand since the mid-1980s like a monster that feeds on its own entrails. Canals and *jheels*, including the fabled Dholai Khal were gone, filled up or paved over; children's parks and playing fields disappeared; and concrete and glass buildings, many of them high rise, began to spring up, crowding Dhaka's once serene skyline. The buildings, which housed apartment blocks, were like some abysmal and faulty machines for living. Despite a shift from the earlier builder-planned houses to architect-designed ones, the clutter and the mess continued until Dhaka (and other cities that follow Dhaka as a model) became a thoroughly dysfunctional city, bursting, quite literally, at the seams.

My reading of cultural studies had introduced me to urban historians, theorists and Marxist geographers like Henri Lefebvre, Marc Auge and Edward Soja, among others, who taught me the importance of reimagining the city and human geography away from, what Soja described as 'the spatio-temporal rhythm of capitalist development' (*Postmodern Geographies*, London: Verso, 1989:3). When I looked at Dhaka through their theoretical lens, I found a serious lack of understanding among policy makers, planners and designers of history, theory, the environment – particularly hydrology—and urban aesthetics. I kept looking for a newer breed of architects who would rescue the city from the brutality of mindless expansion, reintroduce the importance of semiotics, contextualism, and imagination, and ensure a critical engagement with history and culture in designing buildings and neighborhoods. Soon enough I found a group of young architects who had started to challenge the way architecture here was made to serve money and the makeshift. The run of the mill and eclectic assemblage of buildings erected all over the city showed an acute failure of imagination and a total disregard to environmental ethics. Some of the new breed architects began to revisit areas that had been glossed over or neglected by our city planners and developers which included morphology or the physical fabric of the city, hydrology, the socio-spatial systems and their interface with culture and tradition, landscape and environment, transportation and civic amenities, housing for the poor and the internally displaced and so on. One of the vigorous and consistent advocates for a sea change in our urban planning and design has been Kazi Khaleed Ashraf, known by his first name Khaleed to friends and colleagues.

Educated at Bangladesh University of Engineering and Technology and Massachusetts Institute of Technology with a PhD from University of Pennsylvania, US, Khaleed Ashraf has been teaching in the US and Bangladesh, curating architectural shows, theorizing on and writing about architecture and, most importantly, presenting holistic and realistic yet visionary plans that, if implemented, could see a radical change in the way we imagine, plan, build, live in, relate to and own the city. Ashraf is an urbanist with a keen sense of history and a commitment to the environment who foregrounds a transformational ethics and new technologies of collaborative architecture in which land, water, and the environment are fused together.

I came to know about Khaleed Ashraf from Saif Ul Haque, himself a talented architect who was quite enthusiastic about what his friend was doing. Khaleed's reputation thus preceded him. When I met him and began to get acquainted with his thought and work, I found him much like Marco Polo of Italo Calvino's *Invisible Cities* (New York: Harcourt, 1974), a traveler who imagines his city, Venice, in fifty-five different incarnations and describes them to the Tartar emperor Kublai Khan. Ashraf too imagines and plans Dhaka as a city of signs, of memory, dreams and desires and visualizes space for everyone, including daydreamers and travelers amid the network of settlements, gardens, parks, rivers, canals, pavements and pathways, markets, the heterotopias and even non-places that ideally mark a metropolis. Anyone who wants an elaboration on this may read his book *Designing Dhaka: A Manifesto for a Better City* (Dhaka: Loka Press, 2012) which, in my opinion, should rank as a primer for urban planning in our country.

Ashraf has written on a range of topics that are considered important in context specific study of architecture and takes a broad-based approach to discuss and debate the core areas of architectural practice in our time. When he took charge of the Bengal Institute for Architecture, Landscapes and Settlements, he began to pursue a truly multidisciplinary framework that includes such subjects as innovative agriculture, habitat management and cultural studies. When he invited me to give a few lectures on the city, I chose the soft city as my area of focus. Ashraf not only gave his enthusiastic approval, he often sat in my class, contributing to the discussion with his insights and theoretical views. I have always been amazed by the breadth and depth of his knowledge and the effortless way he tackles the complex issues that contribute to a cognitive and ideological mapping of modern (and postmodern) trends in contemporary architectural debates.

Having read his work, particularly on Louis Kahn, Muzharul Islam, South Asian architecture, modernity and urban renewal, and listening to his perceptive discussions on topics ranging from urban morphology to social ecology and cultural geography I believe I have a fairly broad understanding of what constitutes Ashraf's architectural philosophy. Here is a brief account of some of the core ideas that inform that philosophy:

Imagine/Reimagine: Ashraf sees a lack of imagination as the primary challenge in our urban planning and design. He finds it disappointing that urban planning increasingly focuses on class and economic/corporate interests, neglecting the larger human issues. He wants a revitalized imagination that will not only energize urban processes, forms and functions as well as the entire eco-system, but also inspire a reimagining of the city to make it more inclusive, humane and livable.

Rethink: Rethink modernity, for example, or even postmodernity which challenges its grand theories and narratives and emphasizes the values of the local and the peripheral. Khaleed has been inspired by Muzharul Islam's reconfiguration of modernism and his urge to 'return home' which is not only a re-evaluation of the space called home, but is also an assessment of all that is nourishing in tradition and human connectivity. It is much like reliving, what Ashish Nandy calls 'the village of the mind' which he believes 'shapes the city of the mind' (*An Ambiguous Journey to the City*, Oxford University Press, 2001:19). Ashraf expects us to go beyond the amalgamations of structures and normative models of planning to discover the hidden structures that make human relationship dynamic such as the ethos of interactive *paras* and *mahallas*, or the older household designs that eliminate or reduce the distance between neighbors. He wants a renewal of community living where spaces are shared and cultivated with care and compassion. He is against isolationism of the kind practiced by gated communities that are a common feature now in our cityscapes. Rethink the city, Ashraf says, connect it with history, tradition, the elements of nature and the network of small towns within commuting distance. Rethink, in other words, the phenomenon known as conurbation.

Space as liberation: Much like Lefebvre, space for Ashraf is liberation: liberation from immobility and the rigid – and hugely claustrophobic – built environment. He believes spatiality should show a radical shift towards a redistribution of space in keeping with the flow of human movement, the need for sites of action and activities, leisure and social interaction – in other words a new socio-spatial dialectic that includes every group and individual inhabitants of the city.

Future is fluid: Ashraf is a great promoter of hydrology as a key element in urban planning and design. Most cities and towns in Bangladesh have rivers flowing past, or through them, but these are mostly used for transportation and trade and for discharging municipal and industrial waste and effluents. Ashraf wants to make them and other water bodies integral parts of urban planning so that they may serve as transportation passages but also become sources of drinking water and rich aquatic life and ecosystems. Without any encroachments they may become perennial open spaces supporting – and interacting with – waterfronts, recreational sites, urban settlements, playing fields and parks. He envisions a future where rivers and water bodies will define urban and human ecology.

Convergence design: Ashraf believes that urban design should flawlessly converge family and community life and work. Community, he feels, should be valued more than the design. A city should not promote divergence which is what characterizes our big cities now, where power and control lie with the class that believes in its separateness. He expects an end to this practice.

Cities are a million stories: Ashraf considers the city as a 'theatre of social action' and not a site dominated by technical and economic notions. To a large extent like Calvino's Marco, he visualizes the city as a receptacle of our collective history, memories and dreams. In describing a particular incarnation of Venice, Marco says, 'the city however does not tell its past, but contains it like the lines of a hand.' Ashraf wants us to read those lines and revive memories of green, of kites flying over canals, fields that separate and humanize building blocks, pictures of storytellers animating groups of listeners, the smell of food wafting into the streets or the sound of music across neighborhoods. He imagines a soft city vibrant to the core, like Marco's honeycomb that contains all our memories and stories.

Listening to Marco, Kublai said, 'Your cities do not exist …. Why do you amuse yourself with consolatory fables?' Ashraf's city also does not exist, but he refuses to consider it a fable. He believes one day the city we all imagine will rise through our collective effort and the power of our imagination. This prompts me to consider him a dreamer and a future-maker.

Syed Manzoorul Islam is an eminent Bangladeshi academic, writer, columnist, and a literary critic, and recipient of the Bangla Academy Award.

… in these same societies. It is this tension – created from drawing lessons from worldwide sources in order to transform

… The parasol as *chattri* (umbrella) had also a symbolic significance in earlier Buddhist architecture and

… rhetoric of the avant-garde. Nietzsche is invoked.

… opted for further study in architecture, and went to the University of Oregon in the United States and to Yale University where he received a Masters degree

… in theological term, a resurrection, or in ascetical sense, an alchemical transformation, leaving one body for another. There is always something else.

The Eventful 1960s

… silhouette – the way human artefacts touched the sky – had remained registered in Corbusier's mind since his trip to Istanbul, and now in India, in the world of *chattris* and domes, he finds an analogous condition. In most

… a cosmological significance, or in the extension of the wheel motif "a metaphor

… too in the architectural realm. A development spree (often as part of "foreign aid package") saw a profusion of building activities. "There was chaos in architecture, but

… important foreign architects like Louis I. Kahn, Paul Rudolph, Constantin

… clear that India prompted this definitive attitude.

Destruction is a beginning. The enactment of destruction has a contractual relationship with pre-established norms and practices. As with Edward Said's meditation on beginnings, one would suggest that there is intention and method in

… if today we are a living soul that is sensitive to ideas and to beauty of form, let it prove its capacity by

climax of the composition – linear and centralised in the classical model but deliberately asymmetric and displaced in the Assembly – and, finally, the climactic space itself, consciously dramatic and overtly expressive, with the dome for

… had to be rebuilt so it could be burned again). In Tarkovsky's driven meditation on the macrocosmic scope of human annihilation (in the film, nuclear catastrophe), and its microscopic reach into the lives

… many times before and she will survive."

—Jawaharlal Nehru

… leadership that foresaw the future in the treasury of modernity: industrial progress, democracy and international fraternity.

… colonial consternations, that fanned contemporary progressive thinking in people like Jawaharlal Nehru, the first prime minister of India. In being invited to plan for Chandigarh by Nehru, Le Corbusier was thrust into the heart of that contradiction.

Why Did Amelia Burn the Temple?"

… working forth more acutely the ideological polarity, and at the same time an approach to a reconcilement.

… purely Corbusian, the works jeopardise the homogeneity of that body of work called

… ("a pact with nature"), Corbusier not only reverts his ambiguous conception of nature, but attempts to tap a earth-hugging sensibility, which he does more unequivocally

Le Corbusier's "Prehistory"

… Secondly, unlike his earlier work like Villa Savoye, where the spatial and organisational complexity is camouflaged behind a comparatively restrained exterior, Shodhan House makes explicit its internal tension and

… Shodhan House, it is the brazen animation, busy and diverse as a bazaar under a sheltering umbrella, the various brise-soleil and complex organisation of the terraces, which creates a distinct identity.

at a number of levels in which the Acropolis and Istanbul remain as perceptual sources, and the Apollonian and Dionysian notions as intellectual motives. A tension of the "pair" of concepts" may operate at the broadest scale, in the

PLACING ARCHITETURE

Confronting the climatic conditions of hot-tropical regions was not new to Corbusier. In his long and inspirational relationship with North Africa, he had already developed the fundamental notions of control, and "invented" their architectural-typological counterpart: the brise-soleil and the roof as an umbrella. From a tentative expression as in Villa Bezeau in Carthage, Tunisia (1928), the brise-soleil becomes a highly articulated "element poetique" in the office tower for Algiers (1939 1942). The separation of the roof from the more used volume of the building also dates as early as 1928 in the first sketch for Villa Bezeau, and 1939 in the pavilion at the exposition at Liege where the consideration was purely plastic.[17]

Corbusier thus is already equipped in his personal typological cache to work with climate control in India. His association with Maxwell Fry, who more than anyone else was concerned with the tropical conditions of creating architecture,

An urban building at Ananda Coomaraswamy. *La scripture de Bodhgaya.*

On *Vastushilpa* and the Art of Dwelling

Written December 1994, published in *EARTH* magazine, Volume 2, 1995.

The idea of architecture continues to be articulated within the three well-trodden themes of visual aesthetics, mechanistic functionalism and constructional technology,[1] often reduced into the binary of aesthetics and functionalism. Derived from Vitruvian ideas, the themes found a strong base in the classicism of Renaissance Europe, and were carried through to the modern architectural profession despite its anti-historical stance.

In the delta of the Ganges, far from Florence and Milan, in spite of the clamors of regionalism and other anti-modern protestations, we are still operating in large part, or in the most basic formulation, within Vitruvian-Albertian concepts.

Although we use the Bangla word *sthapatya*, the significance and meaning of the discipline is derived from the term "architecture." The Bangla word is a mere transliteration, carrying in it the full force of current connotations of the English term. *Architecture* however is a derivation of the Greek word *architecton*, meaning a chief builder or artificer, the emphasis being on the term *tekton* (*tekton* is the builder, *archi-tekton* is the chief builder, and *architectonic* is the art of building).

The key term is *tekton*. Derived from an archaic Greek verb, *teucho*, the term is found in the poetical texts of Homer (presumably eighth century BCE), meaning (1) to fabricate, to produce, to construct, and (2) tool, instrument. In ancient Greek, *tekton* meant a carpenter, a builder, which is closely allied to the Sanskrit word for carpenter, *takshan*. The meaning of *tekton* as carpenter broadened to include the artisan-craftsman, and finally the builder-architect. The closely related derivative *techne* (from which we get technical, technological, etc.) comes to mean "material fabrication," or the manner of making/doing something effectively.

What is crucial is the shift that occurs in the meaning of *techne*, even in Homeric texts, from the sense of "material fabrication" to "causing, bringing about, bringing into existence." While *tekton* as architect carried more the notion of building well, the later Homeric meaning is also embedded in it. By the idea of "bringing into existence," *techne* comes closer to the notion of *poiesis,* creation. In Plato's *Symposium*, *poeisis* is seen as any

[1]A distinctly twentieth-century category is architecture-as-process, considered especially in the case of housing developments as phrased by John F.C. Turner as "housing as verb."

action that is the cause of a thing emerging from non-being into being. What earlier seemed to be a limitation of *techne*, that is, material fabrication, is seen in the sense of *poeisis* of bringing into existence something other than what already existed.

In its current usage, *techne* as the technical or the technological serves the purpose of only material fabrication or mechanics of construction. The sense of *poeisis*, with which techne was originally aligned, is hardly addressed in contemporary understanding of architecture.[2]

Moving from Greece to the Ganges, we find architecture approximated in Sanskritic conceptions by two terms: *sthapatya* and *vastushilpa*. In contemporary coinage, the ancient term *sthapatya* is used as a direct transliteration (*paribhasha*) of the current sense of architecture, but remaining a stranger to its own original richer meanings. It is this world of meanings, carried by *sthapatya* and *vastushilpa*, which we may have lost that I intend to uncover here.

The Concept of Vastu

In India, a collection of treatises on architecture called the *Vastusastras* – the canons of *Vastu* – was compiled, from roughly the ninth century CE and onwards, that formed the discipline of "*vastuvidya*." The Vastusastras was a systematization of diverse architectural and planning ideas strewn all over in ritual treatises and mythological literature extending back to the Vedic period.[3]

But what are we to do with *Vastusastras* in our times? Even though the *Vastusastras* may be used as principles for temple-building by *sthapati-pundits* in some parts of South Asia, the ancient texts hardly help the modernized and secularized consciousness of current times. There is still a possibility that, with conceptual imagination, we can still be edified by the *Vastusastras* for our most fundamental practices.

All treatises have a more or less a common understanding of *vastu*. The texts define *vastu* as a place of residence, a house-site, or a house-proper. In the *Arthasastra* (composed around third century BCE), the philosopher-economist Kautilya includes building sites, gardens, *setubandhas*, and tanks as *vastus*. Later, the architectural treatise *Manasara* (ninth century CE), in repeating earlier texts, includes as *vastu* such objects as furniture, conveyances and sculpture, primarily a "seat," a place where men or gods reside. *Manasara* makes the following classification of *vastu*: (1) ground, *dhara*, (2) building, *harmya*, (3) conveyance, *yana*, and (4) "seat," *paryanka*. In certain treatises, there is a more direct reference to *vastu* and the gods. In the *Tantrasamuccaya*, an eleventh-century text, *vastu* is regarded as a deity, as revealed in the chapter on "Digging of the Foundation-Pit": "After having dug this earth in the auspicious time either to the depth of the man's height or till the water on rock (in the bottom) is reached, and then having filled the same till one-fourth of the depth is left, on the 'Isana' corner of a purified vedi constructed therein, let him, when the night falls, offer homage to Vastu."

[2] Kenneth Frampton laments the tectonic loss in architecture seen in the shift from a material base, where architecture presents itself in structural and constructional form, to something "scenographic" and thus degenerative. However, the tectonic does not refer to merely "the mechanical revelation of construction, but rather to a potentially poetic manifestation of structure in the original Greek sense of *poeisis* as an act of making and revealing." Frampton's essay "*Rappel a l'Ordre*: The Case for the Tectonic" in *Constancy and Change in Architecture* (Texas A&M Press, 1991).

[3] Tarapada Bhattacharya, who worked at the Varendra Museum at Rajshahi in the 1930s, gives a comprehensive summary of the Vastusastra literature in *A Study on Vastuvidya Or Canons of Indian Architecture* (Calcutta: United Press, 1948).

A more well-known image of divine personification is that of Vastupurusa caged in the grid of the mandala. As retold by Stella Kramrisch, the most perceptive scholar of Indian art, architecture and mythology, a myth of how things may have begun lies behind this personification and the production of the mandala.[4] In brief: An unwholesomeness prevailed in the world as an amorphous being (Purusa) hovered above. The gods brought the being down to earth pinning it to the ground in the formation of a grid (in fact, murdering/sacrificing the being). The site where the being lay sacrificed on the ground became available for dwelling; it is the Vastupurusamandala.

If for a second we can suspend our disbelief in the fabulous world of mythology, and see through it to the human's struggle in critical life-situations when it is felt that a sense of wholeness remains disrupted, moments that require a new edification, we understand the crucial role of *vastu* in re-establishing that lost sense.

A basic idea of *vastu* may be unearthed from the accumulation of religious ideas, rituals and doctrines. Ancient religious rituals and practices may be seen as obvert edifices hiding under their foundations a more elemental task: the human preoccupation to construct a stabilizing point or a sense of wholeness in the face of critical existential situations. We should also recall that some of those practices bear problematic histories of violence and suppression, of one group by another, or one gender by another.

A preliminary task can be a study of words and terms associated with those ancient rituals. *Vas*, as the root of *vastu*, is linked to a wide-ranging family of Indo-European words with equally wide significance. Noting the philosophical implication of *vas*, the Sanskritist Wilhelm Halbfass sees the term, along with a group of other word roots, such as *as* (from which we have *sat*, *satya*, *astitva*, etc.), *bhu* (*bhava, bhavana, bhuta*, etc.) and *vrt* (*vrtti*), as constituting an ontological vocabulary for the query "what there is."[5]

Vas is traced further back to two more archaic Indo-European root meanings: to *burn* and to *shine* (from the version *wes-*). *Wes-* is closely linked to a number of ontological terms: the German *Wesen, essence*, and the English *was*. The relationship to *as*, and therefore to Sanskrit *asana* (seat) and *astitva* (existence) is possible. Beyond an ontological significance, *wes-*, in alignment with *vas*, offers terms for dwelling, inhabitation, homestead, site and place: principally, the Sanskrit *vastu*, and possibly the Greek *asti*, a town. Other derivations include *vasa, vasati, vasaghara,* the Prakrit *vatthu-* (object), and the Bangla *basa* (abode).[6]

Such a close alignment of ontology (an understanding of "existence," "what there is," "to be") and inhabitation ("dwelling," "to take place") is not a coincidence. The closeness implies the intertwining of *to dwell* (to be) and *dwelling* (abode). An ontological understanding of *vastu* reveals dwelling as a durable presence, as 'taking place,' a seat. This may be further

[4] Stella Kramrisch, *The Hindu Temple* (Calcutta: The University of Calcutta, 1946).

[5] Wilhelm Halbfass in *On Being and What There Is: Classical Vaisesika and the History of Indian Ontology* (Albany: SUNY Press, 1992).

[6] M. Mayrhofer, *Etymologisches Worterbuch des Altindoarischen* (Heidelberg: Universitaetsverlag Winter, 1996).

understood through the anthro-geometrical metaphor of "center." One could see why "seat," "couch," and other such sitting apparatuses, were conceived as *vastu* in the *Vastusastras*. It would appear that sitting, often more than standing, is a deep-rooted human act. Joseph Rykwert points to the association of sitting with the womb and the earth (the two coincides within the notion of "mother earth"); it is this association that gives the (unconscious) sense of stability to a sitting equipment.[7]

"Seat," or taking a place, is the ontological basis of making a center. When *vastu* was seen as the "seat" of a divinity, as in the placing of a religious icon, it can be understood as the exteriorizing of a basic human mode of being, that of conceptualizing sitting as "center." The term "making" or "constructing" a center is to be understood in two ways. On the one hand, it may be a notional, mental, or psychological act without any physical attribute. On the other hand, it might be manifested physically or spatially through architecture.

An important Greek-Roman parallel may be invoked here. Among the Greek gods and goddesses, Hestia (known among the Romans as Vesta) is the most significant architecturally and spatially. Hestia is the goddess of the hearth, the home-fire, found in every household as the guardian and the center of family life. Every Greek town also had its state hearth that symbolized the town as a family with the altar of Hestia as its central point. When the Greeks went out to establish colonies, they would take portion of the fire from the mother-town to establish the new one.

Being the conceptualization of stability and continuity, and the articulation of a permanent center, Hestia stood out both in character and form from other gods. In a Greek (or Roman) house, she was personified in the hearth where the fire burnt at the gravitational center of the house. The hearth signified the establishing of a center around which the life of the household rotated, and from which the family sought the assurance of its basis, permanence, and continuity. Hestia's status as a virgin goddess tending the flames not only defined the rigmaroles of domesticity but also the status of women in a patriarchal system.

In Rome, Hestia's temple was the only one circular in plan referring to her relationship to the earth or ground and her primary task of grounding and establishing. In modern Western architecture, it is probably Frank Lloyd Wright who reestablishes the spirit of Hestia through the architectural glorification of the fireplace.

An etymological connection and semantic correspondence among the Greek Hestia (the Roman Vesta) and *vastu* remain a matter of significance. Georges Dumezil, the eminent French scholar, points to the strong parallel in the ritual of Roman Vesta and Vedic Vivasvat, and the importance of the common word-root *vas*.[8] What is common in those rituals of two distinct cultures is the building and maintenance of a stable center carried out by the hearth with its perpetually burning fire in

[7] Joseph Rykwert, in the essays "Building and Meaning" and "The Sitting Position: A Question of Method," in *On the Necessity of Artifice* (London: Academy Editions, 1982), investigates the phenomenology of sitting. Referring, for example, to the popularity of the so-called Hardoy Chair in England in the 1930s, Rykwert describes how its 'discomfort' at the ergonomic/rational/ functional level was overridden by its offering of comfort at an emotional and symbolic level. The emotional content, which is translated into the association with womb and earth, is analyzed from various anthropological information, from the status of sitting in various cultures, the symbolism of chairs as burial utensils, the prevalence of the "sitting" position in burial rituals, etc.

[8] Georges Dumezil, *Rituels Indo-Europeens a Rome* (Paris: Librairie C. Klincksieck, 1954).

which the hearth is further anchored, physically, ritually and conceptually, to the earth.

Sthapatya and *sthapana*: To establish

The idea of establishing stability is available more unambiguously from the word *sthapatya*. Through *sthapana* (to establish) and *sthana* (locality, place), a "sthaniya" or localized architecture is implied, one that relates to locality through climate, material, manners, etc., but more importantly, establishes or affirms *sthana*, the space of inhabitation.

Used in an everyday context in a prosaic manner, un-thoughtfully and intuitively, *sthana* does not provide its full connotations immediately. Often times, things and words of common usage, those that form the grains of our day-to-day existence, remain too close at hand, and are consumed unreflectively, are the ones more difficult to grasp in a conceptual sense.

The root of both *sthapatya* and *sthana* is *stha-*. A constellation of meanings cluster around *stha-*:[9] To stand, stand upon, station one's self, to take up a position; to stand up against an enemy (concerning *pura*, the city); to stay, remain, continue in any condition or action; to continue to be or exist, to endure; to stand still, stay quiet, remain stationary, linger, hesitate, etc.; to cause to stand, place, locate, fix, establish; to set up, erect, raise, build; make durable, strengthen, prop up, support; to fix, settle, determine.

A review of *stha-* derivatives further highlights its conceptual significance and foundational purpose. *Sthapana* would suggest causing to stand, establish, found, erect, preserve, etc. *Sthayi* would suggest constancy, stability, permanency, durableness, invariableness. *Sthiti* would take this a little further to suggest a condition of well-being through a continuing existence. *Sthavara*, besides the meanings suggested by *sthayi*, further denotes immovable properties, real estate, heir-loom and other such family-possessions by which one is literally grounded. *Sthira* is related to firmness, solidity and an unfluctuating condition. However, a pejorative sense denoting stagnation and immobility, would also gather around *stha-* through such words as *sthavira* (old age, senility) and *sthula* (massive, bulky, coarse).

The root *stha-* is also related, through the Indo-European language system, to a number of European words, such as the German *stehen*, *stuhl* (chair, pillar), the English *stand, stability, statics, stare, store, establish* (all these stemming from a number of Latin and Greek words).

Such a proliferation of the meanings of *stha-* is not surprising, but all point to "standing, staying, being situated in, existing, being in or among." The primary task of ancient thinkers was to assure stability – psychological and existential – of their world, a stability that was not found naturally or given to them as a divine gift. All ancient religious rituals, ceremonies and mythological thoughts exhibited an underlying essence: that of establishing in

[9] This is mostly identified in Vedic literature from a period roughly covering 1500 to 100 BCE. Sir Monier-Williams, *A Sanskrit-English Dictionary* (Oxford: The Clarendon Press, 1899).

a shifting, turbulent and unpredictable world, a fixity as opposed to a wandering and fluctuating existence.

Among Sanskrit derivatives, the most architectonic is *sthambha* and *sthuna*, meaning a post, pillar, column or beam, often of a house, or the trunk of a tree.[10] The development of the symbolism of the post-column-tree, especially as a "Cosmic Pillar," has been the topic of a vast scholarship. Mircea Eliade has spoken about the wide cultural distribution of this idea. The Pillar as *axis mundi* (the axis of the universe) in North European cosmologies, the Buddhist Tree of Life as the center of the universe, the Chinese *Kien-Mu* as the miraculous tree growing at the center of the universe uniting the Nine Springs with the Nine Heavens, the Irminsul of the Saxons: All represent the Cosmic Pillar upholding the world, and a "communication with heaven can be effected only near it or by means of it."[11] Another way to understand the proliferation of the ultra-symbolic Pillar is the human desire to establish order and stability to the world.

To Dwell

What can a renewed thinking on *vastu* do for current practices in architecture? Nothing much if it is expected to be a tool for form-making.

The concept of *vastu* directs us to a more basic and graver task of architecture beyond the limiting themes of aesthetics and functionalism. As real-estate developers ponder over square-footage, as engineers calibrate the correct shear, as concerned scientists plot the sun-path, and as decorators decide between blue or purple tiles on the bathroom wall, the task of architecture remains as elementary as the first fire: How to dwell, as some philosophers ponder? How to establish an "existential foothold" on the earth?

To dwell is to be. This is the most fundamental and "un-thoughtful" aspect of humanity, always with us with an immediateness that makes it difficult to conceptualize. It is for this very reason that philosophical inquiry has been directed towards it. In recent times, the German philosopher Martin Heidegger (1889–1976), by speaking on dwelling, has oriented attention to this topic. In Heidegger's now classic essay "Building Dwelling Thinking," *building*, in the sense of both noun and verb, becomes the locus of understanding what it means *to dwell*, and what does it mean *to be*.[12]

In Heidegger's reflection on dwelling, architecture is invoked as a significant element that affects architectural thinking irrevocably. He states explicitly: "The nature of building is letting dwell. Only if we are capable of dwelling, only then can we build." From within the architectural discipline itself, the theorist Christian Norberg-Schulz has attempted, sometimes ambiguously but sometimes with insight, to reinvigorate the idea of dwelling, and rediscover a purposefulness of architecture distinct from aesthetics and functionalism.[13]

As the scope of this essay is inadequate in addressing extensively the notion "what is dwelling" in the context of

[10] Sir Monier-Williams, *A Sanskrit-English Dictionary*.

[11] Mircea Eliade, *Patterns in Comparative Religion* (Sheed and Ward, 1958).

[12] Martin Heidegger, "Building Dwelling Thinking," in *Basic Writings* (New York: Harper & Row, 1977), translation.

[13] Christian Norberg-Schulz, *The Concept of Dwelling: On the Way to Figurative Architecture* (New York: Rizzoli, 1985).

[14] Karsten Harries, in his essay "Time, Death and Building," and Norberg-Schulz, in his essay "Order and Change," in *Constancy and Change in Architecture*.

architecture, a sweeping description is offered here.[14] Three central ideas may be abstracted from Heidegger's intense thinking (although, often chastised for being esoteric): (1) Dwelling is deeply tied to earth. "Dwelling is the manner mortals are on earth," and "The buildings bring the earth as inhabited landscape close to man and at the same time place the nearness of neighborly dwelling under the expanse of the sky." In other words, a dwelling "gathers the world"; in an architectonic sense, that would mean that a building in its making discloses the landscape, shows where and how it stands, and makes the sun and the rain reappear before us, say for example, in the drooping eaves of the roof. (2) Dwelling is about the "presencing" of things rather than a referral to absent things as in the form of symbols, signs or other abstract tools. A building as dwelling represents nothing; it simply is, so to speak. Heidegger says about a Greek temple that just by standing there "it reveals the properties of the earth and the things and beings that inhabit the earth." (3) A building as dwelling is not only an artifact in space but also something that embraces time. Karsten Harries, an American philosopher, explains that such a building must embrace "the rhythm of the seasons, of the passing generations, of birth, and of death." In short, it captures under one roof the journey of different generations through time, or as Heidegger was to say, in a kind of oracular tone: "Let earth and heaven, divinities and mortals enter in one simple oneness into things." And what does dwelling achieve? To Norberg-Schulz, when dwelling is accomplished, our wish for belonging and participation is fulfilled. Harries condenses it in one statement: Dwelling is the general purpose of architecture.

While Norberg-Schulz highlights the inadequacy of current architectural concepts, and seeks a rethinking through Heidegger from the Western tradition, it seems that, here, close to us, the concept of *vastu* may provide the possibility of rethinking architecture. Yet, *vastu* remains unexamined and hence elusive. The main reason for that is the prejudice of modernity. What can an archaic term such as *vastu*, loaded with seemingly superstitious rites and rituals, offer us in an age of reason and progress? Secondly, there is the bigotry around religious practices and ideologies. What can the materials of one religious system offer to others outside its pale? Quite a bit, if one is willing to listen.

Jean Baudrillard's *America.*

Looking for America

The text is adapted from the paper, "Main Street is Almost Alright: Post-Modernism in American Art and Architecture," read at the Regional American Studies Conference organized by the Bangladesh Association of American Studies and the United States Information Service, in Dhaka, March, 1999.

Myths, fables, and fairy tales are the stock of every culture. They are, what the mythologist Joseph Campbell terms, the engines of society. Whether they are true or not, factual or sensible, is irrelevant; what is important is that they provide the mystical impetus for collective life, and keep the societal machine going. (It is in this sense the term "myth" has a double meaning, considered a falsehood, on the one hand, and a cultural engine, on the other hand).

Few things keep the American machinery moving as rapidly and gustily as the car. You might ask where is it going, but that's another thing. Mobility is the most powerful American fable, expressed in the euphoria of the automobile, in the dream of the road to be taken. Cars are everything, as evident from ubiquitous and relentless advertisements. One announced recently, "Life is a journey… in the Main Street of America," Main Street being the mythic place of happenings in American life. The mythology is expressed in popular culture, as in the lines of a blues song: "I don't have a place to go, I sleep in my car."

America finds rootedness in mobility. From this paradoxical longing for stability and mobility, anchoring and speeding, America invented new dwelling types: the trailer home and the suburb. The trailer is the reinvention of the home on wheel. Although its genealogy is in the frontier and the cabin – the rolling wagon becoming the little house on the prairie – it has spawned a whole new way of living: the trailer communities (although, arguably, it is also the home of society's poorest). It is present in the lifestyle of the romanticized motor-cycle gangs, who re-enact nothing less than the spirit of ancient nomads and their world of boundless mobility. It also generates that obsessive theme that has flavoured so many films and fictional work: searching for America, that mysterious longing for taking to the roads (I am thinking especially of the 1969 film *Easy Rider*).

The suburb is a modern condition of dwelling, realizing its fullest potential in the United States by dint of the car. The car makes everything accessible, and consequently living in an isolated location poses no problem for the motorized mortal. In fact, the premodern site of dwelling – the city – is now deemed unfit for a civilized living. In areas ringing New York City and Washington

DC, and all the small cities in New Jersey, there are these liminal zones, hard to give a category to, those miles and miles of land pockmarked with apartment buildings, whose inhabitants form a sort of "bedroom community". People drive in and out from these places to go to work in the big cities. Locationality is easily abandoned. One can, and many do, just pack and leave, wholesale, for another town. This immense practice of mobility has totally redefined rootedness and the sense of place in the United States.

Jean Baudrillard, the noted French philosopher, sees the American continent as a desert milieu (as Bangladesh might be seen as a hydraulic one). And when you combine the "desert" milieu with the phenomenon of speeding, you get what Paul Virillio, another French man of ideas, describes as the "aesthetics of disappearance," that incandescent act of disappearing depicted in the last scene of the 1991 film *Thelma and Louise.*

In describing the psychology of the desert milieu, Baudrillard thinks pure speed can be attained in the geography of the desert, and it is in the barrenness of speed that "disaffection" finds its pure form. In that space "the transpolitical finds its generic, mental space" and "the inhumanity of our ulterior, asocial superficial world immediately finds its aesthetic and ecstatic form." It does not matter where you are, whether in the actual desert of Arizona and California, or the swamps of Florida, or the pine forests of New England, America is in essence a desert matrix where one can discover that ecstatic form.

Scene from the film *Thelma and Louise*.

Elvis Presley in a publicity photo for "Jailhouse Rock." From Metro-Goldwyn-Mayer, Inc.

The desert milieu is also an ecstatic critique of culture, as defined in two thousand years of European history with its sense of proximity, collectivity, and sociality. The desert invites solitary existence, a sort of ascetic indulgence and a-sociality. A-sociality is still part of human reality; it finds its truest expression and greatest glorification in that special American milieu.

This incandescent act of speeding and disappearing is in some way related to the other pervasive American theme – a resistance to authority. The distrust of authority has historical, political, and mythical roots—the struggle with Europe, the rejection of European Classicism, and the lure of the frontier inhabitation, that is, the urge to be oneself, to be one's own arbiter in a sort of elemental democracy.

All of America's finest icons emerge from this myth: from John Wayne to Clint Eastwood via Elvis Presley in the area of the most powerful icon-making machinery, the movies. There is Henry David Thoreau and Ernest Hemingway in literature. And, of course, the grandest of them all is the architect Frank Lloyd Wright, who built a legend around his flamboyant rejection of authority, and creating and living his own in the "hermitage" he built in Arizona desert.

Elvis Presley is a serious matter. The culture of "teenagers" had not arrived until Elvis, around 1955 or so. This pelvis-swaggering mesmerizer ushered in a whole new generation. Before that time, teenagers were just young adults. With Elvis, one could say, teenagers emerged; they either found themselves or reinvented themselves. From then on, "rebellion" became an aesthetic form. MTV is just a commodified and modulated version of that.

There are also extreme manifestations of the business of "rebellion." One may find that in the Oklahoma bombing, the Unabomber case, or in that enigmatic story of Christopher McCandless (retold by Jon Krakauer in a recent best seller *Into the Wild*). McCandless came from a well-to-do family, and was raised and educated in the Washington DC area. One day, he simply walked away, giving away his $25,000 savings to charity, abandoning his car, and rejecting the love of family. He was taken so much by the lure of "pure freedom" that he literally walked into the wilderness of America, travelling from state to state. He was found dead in a "shed" (actually, an abandoned bus) in a desolate area of Alaska. McCandless was quite determined not to go through any kind of social mediation, neither a university life, nor a career, nor even family. The irony is that an anti-urban recluse meets his end in an invalid motor vehicle.

Every culture has its ambiguities, its oppositions and contradictions, by which it tries to negotiate with diverse desires and dreams. America has its own. Here, one of the most consumptive culture of the world finds the most ascetic values (the Quakers, Thoreau, artists like Esherick and O' Keefe), where the most private becomes the most public (TV showman Jerry Springer and Geraldo Rivera), where the most venerable becomes the most trite (the Bill Clinton affair), and where the most mundane becomes the most theatrical (TV show *Cops*, where domestic violence becomes a spectacle).

I am not quite sure whether all these are not paradoxes spun out of the television, out of the "spectacular" dimension that also pervades America. But Baudrillard does write about how the wealthiest place on earth suffers and passionately struggles with contradictory things like recycling, solar heating, minimal living, etc., that is, a struggle between ascetic compulsion and consumptive urges.

The city is another big theme in American life. In fact, the American city is now the global perception of what an urban culture is like. Two cities frame American urbanity, two cities like gigantic beacons locking the continent at the either end: New York, in the east coast, and Los Angeles, in the west.
In the 1920s, when the French-Swiss architect and prophet of the modern city, Le Corbusier, came for the first time to New York, the city of tall buildings, he declared in his characteristic irony, "The New York buildings are not tall enough." The remark only highlights the world's, even Le Corbusier's, dream of New York. It is the mother city of all modern cities, and yet it does not fulfil its own expectation. The tallest city in the world is not tall enough.

The other Frenchman, Baudrillard, rhapsodizes poetically in the 1990s:

"(H)eir to all other cities at once… Heir to Athens, Alexandria, Persepolis: New York. All the game – all games – get more intense. It's always like this when you are getting near the center of the world. New York. It is a world completely rotten with wealth, power, senility, indifference, puritanism, and mental hygiene, poverty and waste, technological futility and aimless violence, and yet I cannot help but feel it has about it something of the dawning of the universe. Perhaps because the entire world continues to dream of New York, even as New York dominates and exploits it."

Los Angeles is at the same time the denial of European heritage, and the culmination of western urbanity, that fatal "break" where the "other" is embraced – Mexican, Chinese, Vietnamese. Los Angeles is where the baggage of European sociality breaks down, and the desert milieu takes over. The film *Blade Runner* could not have been visualized anywhere other than LA.

It is this dawning of a new universe combined with the image of these cities as impending doom that makes them compelling dreams. There is something deeply menacing in the fascination for blowing up New York architectural icons, specially the Empire State Building, in a crop of films made in the last two years: *Independence Day, Armageddon, Godzilla*, and *Deep Impact* (I heard movie crowds gasp in awe when the alien ship blows up the White House in *Independence Day*). New York in the East Coast and LA in the West Coast suffer the same expectation. They are the future dream of the world, as well as the vortex of

Los Angeles in the film *Blade Runner* (1982).

New York City in the film *Independence Day, Resurgence* (2016).

the coming apocalypse. They are archetypal and apocalyptic at the same time.

There is also the melting pot scenario, or what radio personality Studs Terkel prefers to call, the "salad bowl" situation. The salad bowl brings about the most sensitive and volatile question of races and cultures, of integrity and ethnicity, of unity and distinction. It involves the philosophy of amalgamation, juxtaposition and synthesis in a curiously American way. The best emblem to understand that is jazz music, a quintessential American production.

In a concert at Prospect Park in Brooklyn some years ago, the jazz artist Branford Marsalis played along with a Chinese musician who was playing a thousand-year-old string instrument in a traditional Chinese mode. In Philip Glass's recent production "Monsters of Grace," a high-tech digital-aural presentation of opera, he weaved in the work of the Persian Sufi poet Rumi, avant-garde music, along with his own experience in Indian classical and African music. One could say the same thing for Paul Simon's experimental extravaganza, where he brought musical forms from South Africa and South America into the rock-pop genre. Old and new, east and west, or north and south, amalgamated and distinct in the cauldron of jazz.

Jazz is the unmistakable signature of America, its sound and aesthetics, its history and vigor, and its dark side. It is the rejection of the oppressive "father," of Europe, and the forgetfulness of Africa, of moving onto new grounds. Jazz is modern in so far as it forms no (direct) lineage with any tradition – it is (almost) its own tradition – modernism only dreamt of that, but jazz is supremely postmodern in the sense that it is constantly transforming, constantly moving, not apprehensive to reinvent itself. Jazz is embrace-ful, it is urban and it is rural, it is suave and it is tragic. It is the autobiography of America.

Diana, the Greek godess of the hunt.
http://www.theglobaldispatches.com/articles/lake-nemi-the-sacred-grove-of-diana.

From Sacred Groves to Architectural Paradigms: The Forest in Greek and Indian Imagination

Presented at a meeting of the Society of Architectural Historians, Philadelphia, November 1994.

The forest is a place of awe; it is awesome, awe-striking, and awful. It is through these realizations I will try to rekindle the idea of the forest in Greek and Indian imagination in order to consider concepts of sacred space.

With an enduring presence in human thought, the space of the forest – the deep forest, the sacred grove, and the clearing – led to diverse experiences and conceptualizations. Those experiences were foundational not only for the earliest speculations on sacred space, but also for metaphysical thoughts and fabrications of architectural paradigms. Giambattista Vico writes: "This was the order of human institutions: first, the forests, after the huts, then the villages, next the cities, and finally the academies." Vitruvius attributes the origin of society in a forest fire.

The forest was an overwhelming phenomenon in the ancient environment. Mountains and forests, and their significations, defined the earth, and were not yet converted to abstractions. It was in the "naturalness" of the mountains and forests that the sacred was articulated, and a religious-mythological-cosmological system produced. The mountains are still here, but forests have progressively dwindled, making the forest an idea, thus making it doubly significant.

In architectural contexts, the forest has appeared and reappeared in many ways. For example, the construction of temples has been foreshadowed by the awesome power of sacred groves in any ancient cultures. Temples and sanctuaries have been interpreted as the "lithification" of forest space. Cathedrals have been seen as representing the forest. As we proceed backwards, architecture becomes increasingly indistinguishable from other phenomenal experiences. We may have to sort through mythological ideas and religious rituals as the foundation of architecture is intertwined with those practices. My talk is about this nexus of pre-architecture and architecture.

Before proceeding to the temple precinct, I would like to enter the depth of the forest. The forest is many things as far as human experiences are concerned – it is a space for asylum, exile, enlightenment, wildness, ascetic renunciation and erotic indulgence.

In a primary sense, the forest is wilderness, the domain of things afar and set apart from human society. These ideas cohere strongly around the ancient Greek goddess Artemis. If any deity represents best what lies outside humanity, and what is truly uncultivated nature, it is Artemis. She is beyond regular reason and control, and enigmatically, both a virgin and goddess of sexual power. She is also the pre-cultivation aspect of the great goddess. Earlier to agriculture, the forest is a space that both provided and threatened. It is this tension-filled aspect that characterizes Artemis, or Diana, as she was known to the Romans.

The forest is a space for the outcast and the outlawed. Roman historian Tacitus mentions the grove of the Asylum, where Romulus wishing to gather foreigners into his new state made a sanctuary. At the famous sanctuary of Diana Nemorensis, the high priest, called the king of the grove, was a fugitive slave who always obtained the position by killing his predecessor. While in any sacred grove, the breaking of a branch was sacrilege, at that sanctuary a runaway slave was allowed to break a branch before he engaged in a combat with the incumbent priest.

Scene of a forest hermitage, from Sanchi, India.

As a site for metamorphosis, the forest appears in fictional forms, as in fairy tales, when the protagonist goes off into the forest seeking adventure meeting dragons and other antisocial creatures. This can happen in a mythic sense when the Pandava brothers in the epic *Mahabharata*, and Rama and Sita in the *Ramayana* live in the forest a life of exile but fulfilment. The forest can become an actual space for "spiritual transformation" as it happened for the Buddha and many other sages in ancient India.

Invoking an oppositional orientation, the forest harbours both asceticism and eroticism. Indian tradition is replete with the figure of the hermit and the world-renouncer, who in almost all occasions takes up abode in the forest. It is in the forest that various Vedic texts were composed; a key Upanisadic text was named after the forest. The art historian Ananda Coomaraswamy argues that the hermit's hut in the forest provided the constructional and notional paradigm for built temples. The hut in the forest epitomized the secluded hermit, who in turn served as the approximation of the divine. In Indic traditions, the hut in the forest and the body of the hermit coalesced into a singular connotation of the sacred.

The forest also is the site of "play," a space of tryst and divine revelry. This can be seen in a variety of forms in Greek and Indian traditions: in the charming sexual encounter between Radha and Krishna in Vrindavana, the frenzied sexuality of the Maenads in Dionysism, and the eroticism of the women in the cult of Adonis. Indo-European mythologies are filled with sexual encounters, chases, and consummations in the forest. A host of godly figures participate in this theophanic sexuality: Siva, Krishna, Dionysos, Adonis. The gods are not alone. The gods are

often accompanied or emulated by various forest spirits; in India by *yaksas* and *gandharvas*, and in Greece by satyrs, centaurs, nymphs, pans, and silenus.

This array of attributes of the forest may be summed up in the idea of the "other." Etymology supports this. The Latin *foris*, meaning "outside," out of doors, provides a perceptual polarity between the city and the forest. Being constructed and as a pure human inscription, the city is artificial; it is "invented." The forest is *found*, where significances reveal themselves to human experience – the nature of the forest spatiality is 'discovered,' so to speak. This oppositional nature is also confirmed by the Roman dual term *domi-fori*, in which *domi* implied in-dwelling and *fori* "outside." The spatial meaning of domus as home and forum as a public space is also derived from that duality. Another term for sacred grove, *lucus*, also implied "outside in the field."

Vana, the forest in Sanskrit, does not imply the explicit inside-outside polarity of the Roman *domi-fori*. For ancient Indians, unlike the Greeks, the forest was not really an "other;" it was an "another," an *another* existential space that could be inhabited. In India, the idea of another is codified in the doctrine of four *asramas* of life: being a student, householder (*grhysta*), forest-dweller (*vanaprastha*), and renouncer, in which *vana*, the forest, is considered the space of a necessary stage. The horizon of the "world" includes both the city and the forest.

It is because of the many shades of "otherness" that we can term the forest a heterotopia, to appropriate something from Michel Foucault. "Heterotopia" are those sites which, Foucault writes, "have the curious property of being in relation to other sites, but in such a way as to suspect, neutralize, or invert the set of relations that they happen to designate, mirror or reflect. ... There are also, probably in every culture, in every civilization,

A forest scene from the *Ramayana* (from *Pahari Masters*).

Bodhighara as tree shrine from Ananda Coomaraswamy, *Indian Art*.

real places – places that do exist and that are formed in the very founding of society which are something like counter-sites, a kind of effectively enacted utopia in which the real sites ... are simultaneously represented, contested, and inverted." It is in the sense of a "heterotopia," that is, they "suspect, neutralize, or invert the set of relations that they happen to designate, mirror or reflect" that the forest might be approached.

To talk about the other is also to speak about the sacred, which is truly the "wholly other," in a religious phenomenological sense. There is a close tie between conceptualizing the sacred and constructing sacred space. It is this relationship that can clarify why forest groves may be considered the basis of temples.

The concept of the sacred emerges from a lived-experience of the forest. Deriving from *sacer*, the word sacred describes that which is set apart and reserved, especially for the gods. In Germanic languages there are two orientations of the idea of the sacred: *weihen* and *heilig*. *Weihen* suggests the sacredness of separation – that which has been cut off from ordinary usage and belongs to a god towards which man's attitude is one of reserve and awe. In Rome, *sacer* was akin to *weihen*. In his philological studies, Jakob Grimm notes that the meaning of *weihen* alternates between *templum* and *idolum*, on the one hand, and wood, grove, and numen, on the other hand, which is to say, the same term suggested wood and temple.

Lucus mentioned earlier is another important term. As the Roman term for sacred grove, *lucus*, and its Sanskrit equivalent loka, allow us to map the horizon of this sacred world. Both *lucus* and *loka* denote a variety of conditions: "a wood, grove or thicket of trees sacred to a deity," "a clearance in the forest," and "outside, in the country." The word root *louko-* essentially suggests 'light' and 'clearance,' an open place to which the day of light has access. *Lucus* gives us locus, location and locality.

Roman classical writings abound in the mention of *lucus*, including the psychological experiences of being there. Many ancient poets and writers have documented the "fearful shudder," "awe-inspiring presence" of unknown gods, and "occult nature" of the experience of a wanderer who ventures near sacred groves. Seneca mentions: "If ever you have come upon a grove that is full of ancient trees, which have grown to an unusual height, shutting out a view of the sky by a veil of pleached and intertwining branches, then the loftiness of the forest, the seclusion of the spot, and your marvel at the thick unbroken shade in the midst of the open spaces, will prove to you the presence of deity." In more recent times, Vico sees *lucus* as one of the original moments of a "terrifying" situation that needed to be domesticated within the human fold. Domestication took place through cult activities and constructing spaces.

Two proto-architectural conditions may be noted: the manner by which the actual forest space was enclosed, tectonically and ritually, and how a notional space was encapsulated.

Temples are relatively late productions. Before temples, there were sacred trees or sacred groves (and, of course, caves and hill spots) where things were found "as they are." Those sites were special, often making them indistinguishable from the gods. Rituals animated those sites which may be considered as moments between pre-architecture and architecture. Before an architectural paradigm is instituted, it is preceded by a particular myth and ritual, be it the sinister figure of the priest at Diana Nemorensis, votaries arriving in procession and dancing ecstatically around the sacred tree, or the conflation of the body of the hermit, the hut and the divine in Vedic forests. The architectonics of the bowery is not enough. Rituals complete the paradigm.

Two themes embody the act of enclosure: the tree shrine and the grove. Tree shrines are the most compelling examples for considering the origins of temples. While tree shrines housed various deities, it is not surprising that, in Greece, the most potent would be related to Artemis. No other deity has such an intrinsic relation to the tree and to the forest at the same time. Artemis/Diana rules the woodland, her "true color" is explained in the forest situation — she is the goddess of nature, of both wild beasts and fecund vegetation, but she is also embodied in a tree that becomes her sanctuary. The tree shrine reverberates with a number of meanings: as a pillar cult, it is a cosmic axis; as a valorised tree, it signifies fecundity, growth and genealogy; and, as a sacred tree, it suggests the presence of the god. The tree-sanctuary is the condensation of the forest.

With few archaeological evidence for sacred enclosures, representational art on various relics and monuments is the next best document. It appears, from such representations, that forest clearings or rocky spots with trees were once cult places that were mostly enclosed, often by low walls, made mostly by rough, unhewn stones. Thicker and higher walls with imposing gateways may have encircled important sacred enclosures. Walls around the sacred enclosures were often crowned with horns of consecration that later became translated into architectural elements, as some scholars argue. A necessity for increasingly elaborate buildings arose with the growth of rituals and attendance of worshippers. The successive development of temple buildings at Dodona in Greece is a vivid example.

The Indian context furnishes an important genre of tree shrines: the *bodhigharas*. Depicted on second-century BCE Buddhist structures, the *bodhi* tree with its accessories are shown surrounded by a two- or three-storied wooden structure. The construction around the tree served the purpose of a gallery and platform for the "lustration of the tree." While the tree is an important aspect of Buddhist symbolism, part of the *bodhighara* tradition is drawn from earlier non-Buddhist ideas, such as the perception of the tree as a cosmic axis, and as abode of forest deities.

To consider encapsulation of a forest space or its "lithification" in an architectural form, I would like to cite the hermit's hut, the pillared temples of India and the Greek Ionic temples. Examples of the hermit's hut are from India. At Sudama cave, excavated in the third c. BCE, the outer doorway or entrance leads to a barrel-vaulted hall. A circular cell in stone with a hemispherical domed roof is situated at the end of the ante-chamber. The stone cell displays an over-hanging eave as in a thatched hut, and walls with grooves in imitation of upright battens or bamboo. In line with Coomaraswamy's explanation, this cell then replicates and reifies the ascetic's hut. If the cell replicates the hut in the forest, then the "hall" of the cave may be understood as encapsulating the clearing in front of the hut.

Certain stone temples from central India built around the seventh c. CE provide another example. A simple conception of a pillared pavilion governed the form of those temples. Pillared pavilions have been interpreted as originating from wooden prototypes and not stone ones, wood being "the material of forests" and stone of caves. The forest paradigm is reinforced by the vegetal iconography in those temples, with broad swirls of foliage between pillars at Mahua, and vase-and-foliage motifs on the pillars at Chandrabhaga. Studying these temples, Michael Meister suggests that when stone is used like wood, in the case of these temples, "it petrifies the forest, turning the grove of Siva into a womb, a stone shell, like the edge of the Universe, enclosing all the cosmos."

In Greece, Ionic temples have particularly been considered as grove-like or lithified form of the grove. In fact the primary intentions may have been to form a grove. From a distance, such a temple might seem to be a single gleaming object, but at close range it is "an inner landscape," distinct from the more "sculpturesque" Doric structures. Vincent Scully writes that the Ionic columns formed the ambient of a human-made grove, within which the sacred cave was set.

To summarize: In the western imagination, the forest constitutes the topos of the "other," a necessary other to the space of society. This otherness is generally translated as an opposition: forest-city, and therefore, nature-culture. In the ancient Indian imagination, the heterotopic forest is not necessarily an opposition to the space of society, but actually another societally sanctioned space.

In either situation, the forest is the space of metamorphosis, of being taken to a different "reality," be it the sacred or what is otherwise not possible in normative society. The metamorphosis occurs either in the actual space of the forest, as in the case of Buddha, or in a representational space, as when sylvan elements interact with societal conditions, subverting for a moment societal norms, as in the Roman Lupercalian ritual, or when Dionysos enters Thebes, or in the Hindu festival of Holi.

This distinction between actual and representational space has architectural implications. The ensemble of the sacred enclosure, formed by the sacred tree, the enclosing wall, the gateway, a column with the statue of a deity, and various other assortments appear as a motif in many Hellenistic and Roman paintings. By the representation of this ensemble we know that a particular tree and a particular spot is sacred or special. The first act of creating this ensemble is of "enclosing" whereby a "natural" sacrality is architecturally demarcated; elements are next added to create a typology of the cult place. The ensemble then becomes an architectural embodiment of the original *lucus*. When the sacred enclosure can be represented, that is, when the representation signifies the sacred, it is roughly from that point the actual ensemble, detached from the particular originating location, becomes an idea. It then enters the repertoire of autonomous (portable) architectural conventions. From then on, the architectural task is not one of "enclosing" an actual forest space, but one of "encapsulating" a notion.

Finally, we may consider the theoretical divide: Is the forest space the origin of architectural form-space, or are architectural configurations interpreted only as analogous to or metaphors of the forest? If origin theories are placed in the foreground, we are asking: Can we understand, ruptured as we are from the original moment, something about the originating condition of architecture? And if origin theories seem dubious, and if a sylvan narrative of architecture appear only metaphorical and representational, we might also ask: Why is this metaphor evoked, and so persistently? Are we right in calling this a metaphor, in an aesthetical sense, or can we suggest a deeper psychological and existential basis for its necessity?

References

Ananda Coomaraswamy, *Selected Papers: Traditional Art and Symbolism* (Princeton University Press, 1986).

James Frazer, *The Golden Bough* (Macmillan Publishers, 1890).

Jan Gonda, *Loka: World and Heaven in the Veda* (N Noord-Hollandsche Uitgevers Maatschappij, 1966).

Jakob Grimm, *Teutonic Mythology* (published as Deutsche Mythologie, 1835).

Giles Gunn, *The Interpretation of Otherness: Literature, Religion and the American Imagination* (New York: Oxford University Press, 1979).

Vincent Scully, *The Earth, the Temple and the Gods: Greek Sacred Architecture* (Trinity University Press, 1962).

Jean-Pierre Vernant, *Myth and Society in Ancient Greece* (Sussex: Harvester Press; Atlantic Highlands, NJ: Humanities Press, 1980), originally *Mythe et société en Grèce ancienne* (Paris, 1974).

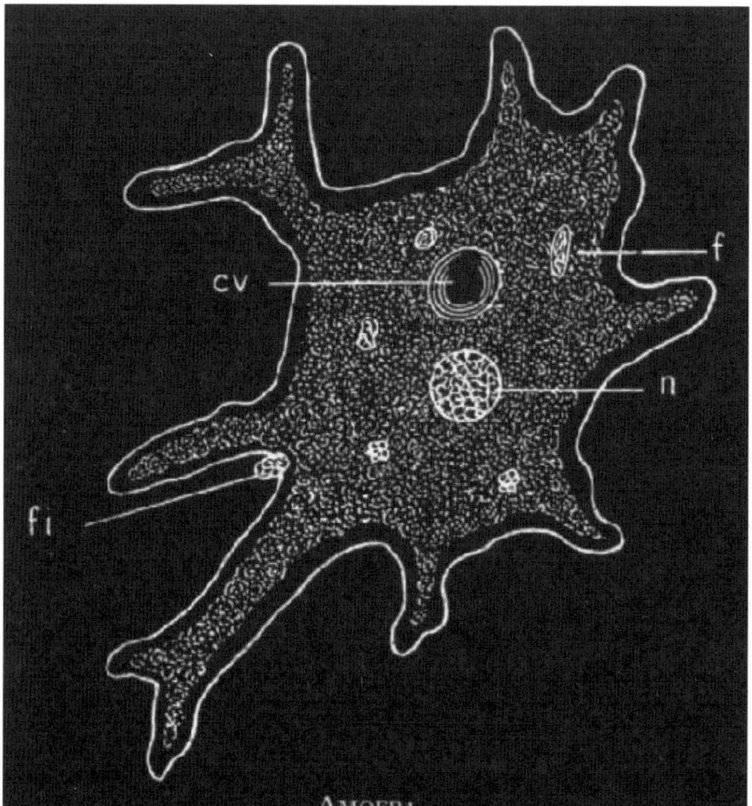

AMOEBA

fi, in the process of engulfing a particle of food; *n*, nucleus; *cv*, the contractile vacuole; *f*, several food particles already engulfed.

Placing Architecture, Presencing Architecture

Published in the proceedings of the Association of Collegiate Schools of Architecture Annual Meeting, Baltimore, USA, 2001.

A weather-exposed skeleton
haunts my mind:
how the wind penetrates my body.
–Matsuo Basho (1644–1694)

Drawing the Wind

Kinya Maruyama, a visiting Japanese architect at the University of Pennsylvania, once sent out his students with their sketchbooks to "draw the wind," an exercise that elicited much skepticism and frustration. The event represents to me two symptoms about current architecture culture: (1) the limits of the representational project, and (2) a consideration for returning "to the things themselves."

Architecture is more than a discipline; it is above all, a "lived-experience." If architecture is an art, it is an existential art, perhaps best approximated by an Indian term for architecture, *vastushilpa*. I translate *vastushilpa* as the art of existence, the word root *vas* belonging to a family of Indo-European terms having to do with existence or presence in some form or other, such as the German *wesen,* the English *was*.[1] Architecture and existence are inextricably intertwined, and if any criterion of thinking best addresses this condition, it is the "anthropological" approach.

The discipline of architecture has undergone a major transformation in the last few decades, both in the nature of its production, and in the way it thinks about itself. One aspect of that is a deeper realignment of architecture and architectural theory with other disciplines. This is a new nexus, in which the discourse has proceeded beyond the well-known triad of the aesthetical/visual, social/political, and technological/functional. The anthropological dimension is a major part of the new nexus.

I am describing the approach as an anthropological one for lack of a better terminology. It refers to a diverse body of thinking – hermeneutical, existential, and phenomenological. It would be presumptuous to claim a human dimension for architecture all over again, and yet the new anthropological project renews or deepens the question of the human situation via architecture. The approach is existential in the sense that it re-addresses

[1] Wilhlem Halbfass, *On Being and What There Is: Classical Vaisesika and the History of Indian Ontology* (Albany: SUNY Press, 1992).

architecture as the elemental and foundational way of being. It is phenomenological in the way it re-views architecture as opening up the receptivity "to the full ontological potential of human experience." What is involved here is the direct investigation and description of phenomena as experienced free as possible from unexamined preconceptions and presuppositions, in a heightened reception of all the senses. Mistrusted faculties – sensorial, kinesthetic, haptic, oneiric – are no longer considered merely irrational, but authentic data for the investigation of the human experience.

The anthropological approach exposes a possible disjunction between architectural practices that rely on a retinal primacy (as the terms image, drawing, analytique, desk crit, etc., convey in academic conversation), and the concrete "lived-experience" of architecture. This divergence is exposed in two major ways: (1) "placing architecture," in the fissure that lies between the ideology of architectonic autonomy and the inevitability of situatedness, and (2) "presencing architecture," in the distance that has emerged between the presence and re-presentation of architecture.

It is the situatedness of architecture – the business of placing architecture – that I wish to ponder on a bit inordinately. The question that arises is basic but critical: What does it mean for architecture to be situated? Is not architecture by its very nature situated? What more can we mean by *being situated*? What I am trying to argue here is that the inevitable situatedness of architecture involves a phenomenological understanding of place and placing, and the relationship between body and the environment.

The anthropological project becomes significant here for a renewed understanding of situatedness as it presents new thoughts on corporeal "actuality." In the euphoric age of disembodied (virtual) realities and mediated connectivities, the approach returns to and amplifies the fundamental intimacy of the body to architectural conditions, and vice versa. What the enigmatic exercise of Maruyama provokes is the necessity of architectural thinking to confront the primal and the phenomenal (Husserl's "back to the things"), and to reconsider the architectural presence prior to and beyond the representational strata, no matter how compulsive and persuasive the latter may be.

What Is This Thing Called "Place"?

A "place" is something durable and yet flimsy. As Aldo Rossi once remarked that as you approach place, it recedes. Much earlier, Plato noted in his distinction of *topos* and *chora* that the latter, what may be translated as "place," is hard to grasp, approachable only by what he called "bastard reasoning."[2]

"Place" is flimsy because it is hard to take its measure. A region can be measured by a cadastral survey, demographic data, or taxation statistics. A nation can be enumerated by all sorts of literature and narratives, both serious and spurious. But "place"

[2] The English sense is a translation of a phrase from Plato's *Timaeus* that expresses the limits of human discourse.

[3] Fredric Jameson, *The Cultural Turn: Selected Writings on Post-Modernism* 1983-1998 (London: Verso, 1998).

is not just a region, and not a nation either. Place, region, and nation are not necessarily commensurable terms. Provisionally, let me say that place is both a given and a construct.

The notion "place," in its English usage, remains particularly suspect, despite or perhaps because of the extensive literature on it. There is the possibility that the notion survives or thrives beyond the English usage, or for that matter, beyond linguistic usage. Yet, how to write place, literally, as "place," Place, *Place*? The symbol "place" invites thoughts; the notation ["] is a *zone* of interweaving not unlike the Greek sense of the word zone, a liminal condition between two kinds of spaces. There is both distinction and continuity. *Place*, with the capital P, implies a reified object, as something conceptual and abstracted, and Place has the implication of being too disjunctive and aberrant.

It should be admitted that re-writing "place" in the twenty-first century often has a retrogressive intonation, especially with the implication of an ultra-green ideology, landscape romanticism, regional chauvinism, or as something stable and perennial. It is also particularly challenging when the opposite of "place"– placelessness – begins to be apotheosized. Many critics think that much of what we understand by place is now outmoded, and one has to recognize placelessness as a new space that is slowly proliferating before us. It is not the kind of placelessness often glorified by modernism, the one that was a sort of a utopian, prescriptive space. One now confronts placelessness as another kind of existent space, perhaps as a heterotopia, the paradigms for which are hotels and airports.

In the *The Cultural Turn: Selected Writings on the Postmodern*,[3] Fredric Jameson presents and discusses the Westin Bonaventure Hotel in Los Angeles as the epitome of this new space – what he calls a hyperspace – a space that we can now enter and experience. A similar characterization may be made about the unfolding nature of airport spaces. Studs Terkel, the celebrated radio personality, gives a humorous account of it: While trying to get to Cleveland from Detroit, Terkel rushed to the counter to board his plane only to receive the answer: "But, sir, you are in Cleveland!" I had a similar "border" experience. Once (among a number of times), while riding a terminal bus at Dubai Airport to catch a connecting flight, for a fleeting but intensely disorienting second, I wasn't sure whether I was traveling to Philadelphia or Dhaka. The feeling was slightly unnerving.

A more poignant case is that of Mehran Nasseri Kasini, an Iranian "stranded" at Charles de Gaulle airport for more than eleven years while trying to enter France unsuccessfully after fleeing Iran. The newspapers described him being seen inside the terminal "sitting at a table, perhaps smoking a pipe, taking stroll, stopping to pick up his mail at the post office or lunch at the in-house McDonald's... he will be looking very much at home." Kasini is ironically caught between the juridical notion of two countries. Following Jameson, one can say that this between space (hyperspace) can now be fully experienced, and therefore needs to be taken seriously. Jameson thinks that we still do not possess the "perceptual equipment" to face this new hyperspace; in fact, this new conditions require that we "grow new organs to expand our sensoria and our bodies to some new, as yet unimaginable, perhaps ultimately impossible, dimensions."[4]

While new kinds of spatiality are emerging around us, challenging our "perceptual equipment," one is not convinced that a more elemental understanding of "place" has been exhausted despite the profusion of literature on it.[5] Such an understanding, I would like to argue and emphasize, is still a foundational condition for architecture, but something that has not been sufficiently addressed from within the standpoint of the discipline itself.

I would like to suggest that "place," culture and nation are distinct concepts, even when they seem interchangeable. The most obvious distinction is that "place" is the one that is least portable. On the other hand, culture (and perhaps, nation) is now perfectly transportable and immensely commodifiable. It can be mailed, shipped, faxed, beamed, and very soon will have nothing to do with any originary location. With MTV, diasporic movements, e-commerce and electronic transfer of capital, the geographic rootedness of culture and community is increasingly becoming irrelevant.

"Place," on the other hand, is formed primarily by a locational underpinning – this place. "Place" is now poised against culture, so that one can pose the phrase: "place versus culture." But what kind of place am I talking about? I am aware that an examination of placement requires a position on place that I will withhold for the time being. More than inquiring directly what is place, I am interested in expanding the internment of the body in space/place, and the primacy of embodiment and placement. Going back to the airport paradigm, I reflect on the phenomenon of air travel as it underscores the primacy of placement experienced in the form of jet-lag – the nagging revelation of a dis-placement, how place-specific biological and diurnal rhythms are incarnated in us, and before adjustments to a new place can be made remain as aberrant traces in the physiological system.

In summation (as a kind of presumption), I would like to say that the human, first and foremost, is a place-conscious being, even if it happens unselfconsciously, and that despite the evangelical persuasion of "global span" (Saskia Sassen), the often chimerical nature of "there" (Gertrude Stein), and the existential anguish of being thrust into this world without a clue of how we may dwell here (Jean-Paul Sartre). In short, the human is inherently an emplaced being.

Chiasm: Body and Place
I wish to enter the realm of place from a very unexpected but finally understandable vantage point: the body. More precisely, the body as articulated by the French philosopher Maurice Merleau-Ponty as the "lived-body," the perceptually sentient organism that by its very definition is implicated with/in the world.

[4] Jameson, *The Cultural Turn*.

[5] A number of authors from diverse disciplines has written about the nature and structure of place; it includes most notably Yi-Fu Tuan, Christian Norberg-Schulz, Relph and Edward Casey.

[6] See interview with Andres Serrano by Anna Blume in *BOMB Magazine* (April 1, 1993).

[7] Eugene Minkowski, *Lived Time: Phenomenological and Psychopathological Studies* (Evanston, IL: Northwestern University, 1970), pp. 400-406.

How is the human emplaced? By being a body. And how does a body achieve body-ness? By being emplaced. Is this a simple syllogism, or is there room for reflection here?

Geographically, or objectively, the environment is distinguished as standing over and against the living body. Andre Serrano's macabre photographs of lacerated, mutilated or punctured bodies drive home the point of the body's fragile existence as a container of fluids.[6] The polarity of nature and culture which is taken for granted in classical European epistemology, and which serves as the foundation for the modern worldview, is primarily an Indo-European construct. This particular conceptualization may be questioned from two quarters: the phenomenological concept of the "lived-body," and the Japanese notion of *fudo*, where distinctions are articulated in a less mutually exclusive way, and where one does not face the other, so that I am here and space is there, or as Heidegger might say that one is revealed through the other.

Eugene Minkowski, through his clinical studies of spatiality and temporality, points out that there is lived space as there is lived time. It is worthwhile to quote him at length:

> I look in front of me: I then see objects or people or people more or less distant from me. But I also see life unfolding around me… it is the clarity of this visual space which forms the backdrop against which my own life and the life of other living beings come to unfold. But clarity is not the only substance of life; we also live in the night. But I no longer have the black night, complete obscurity *before* me; instead it covers me completely, it penetrates my whole being, it *touches* me in a much more intimate way than the clarity of visual space. Certainly, the dark night is not taken here in the sense of absence of light or the impossibility of seeing; it is taken in its positive value – in its materiality, we would almost like to say – and as such it is much more material, much more tangible, and even more penetrating than the limpid clarity of visual space… it will be given to it in a particular way, completely different from the way in which clear space is given, and the words "distance" and "touch" seem to bring out this difference very well. The dark night also has something more personal about it in relation to the ego: I remain face to face with it; it is more "mine" than clear space… [also] auditory space envelops me and penetrates like black space; there will be neither free space nor a "next to," neither perspective, nor horizon, nor distance in it, as there is in lived space.[7]
> (italics are Minkowski's)

Through a number of concepts – "chiasm," "flesh" – Merleau-Ponty would carry out the most substantial philosophical inquiry of the body's presenceness in space. Merleau-Ponty remarks that "our body is not in space like things; it inhabits or haunts space." This is the core idea of the "lived-body." One could think the same for architecture and the environment in which architecture corresponds to a lived-body, as a revision of the pervasive analogy of body and building.

For the lived-body, the environment is an indefinite extension of it, and not distinguished as standing over and against the living body. According to Merleau-Ponty, in *The Phenomenology of Perception*, the environment is a "manipulatory area" for the lived-body, something potentially to be taken and incorporated. The lived-body appropriates certain objects in the world to the extent that these objects cease to be objects and become "incorporated," become part of the lived-body. On the other side, the environment directly and indirectly regulates the lived-body. The environment conditions the body in such a way that the body is the expression or reflection of the environment. In living, the body not only lives itself but also lives the environment. This is what Merleau-Ponty calls a "reciprocal insertion and intertwining" of the lived-body and the environment. As another writer explains it: "the limits of one are lost in the other."

The sense of place takes a different turn in this context. If the human is an emplaced being, and if emplacement is another way of saying that body and world are in an inscrutable intertwining, then carrying the analogy further, I see building as an emplaced and essentially situated object, and situated with all the conditional features of the "lived-body." One can perhaps talk about situated architecture as "lived" architecture. What may be discerned from here is at least a theoretical possibility that architecture and environment are inseparable concepts, they form a "chiasm," at least in the *actual* physical, material sense, and as a consequence, and by extension, in an ideational sense.

Climate and Gravity

The irreversible indictment of the modern age, that societal and cultural norms can no longer be written in purely regional or local terms, produces euphoric claims for a global civilization. At the same time, the specificity of particular places continues to vitiate the homogenizing project of globalism. The specificity is derived not so much from cultural criteria (culture having become a portable and commodifiable schema), as much from more elemental "realities," or conditions that both openly and surreptitiously affect the life and form of architecture, and constitute the nature of its situatedness.

What are then the primal features of architecture's situatedness? Situatedeness involves, above other things, the following three conditions: (1) A telluric "reality" which indicates that the earth is the ultimate ground-basis for architecture, in which architecture can be seen as another topographical manipulation of the earth's surface. (2) A climatic "reality" that is the most direct evidence of architecture's chiasmic relation with the elements. And, (3) a geo-logic "reality" that stresses that architecture is a phenomenon of gravity, not so much in a technical sense but in a visceral way.

Climate and gravity impinge on us imperceptibly, two things we take for granted as being given, and yet are essential for

[8] Tetsuro Watsuji, *Climate: A Philosophical Study* (Tokyo: Government of Japan, 1961).

where and *how we are*. What distinguishes lived and actualized architecture from say ideational ones, or digitized ones, is that it is literally and perceptually embedded in climate and gravity in a seamless manner, in the way Minkowski's "night" envelops the body.

Still, the question of climate remains suspect in architectural discourse. It is considered either as a dry prosaic technicality coming under the rubric of climatology, or a sentimental balderdash about nature. Or worse, it could be considered, again not enthusiastically, as a sort of climatic determinism. The issue, I believe, goes beyond these considerations.

The Japanese thinker Tetsuro Watsuji sees space, environment, and climate as synonymous terms. In his book *Climate: A Philosophical Study*, Watsuji places premium on climate, how climate is the basis of *how we see ourselves* and *how we see the world*.[8] He wishes to rephrase the phenomenological notion of how "we discover ourselves in space" by how "we discover ourselves in climate," that is, how we find ourselves, always, in a concrete climatic and geographic envelope. Notwithstanding allusion to climatic determinism for cultures and risky links to fascist fascination for the soil, Watsuji's arguments have implications for a rephrasing of architecture and environment. First, Watsuji may claim that terms like space and environment are abstract notions (that is, saying that architecture has to contend with environment is not enough), that they make sense only when they have been particularized by climatic specifics. Second, Watsuji offers the Japanese term "fudo" where space and climate (or, culture and nature, or by extension, architecture and environment) are seen in a conjoined sense such that it is hard to distinguish the two. It is in the sense of an "ontological inseparability" between two entities that Watsuji's notions correspond to Merleau-Ponty's ideas of intertwining.

Architecture, in this sense, may be seen not merely as a shelter from climate, as if climate and architecture are confronting each other, but as the inevitable intertwining of the architectural body and climate; it is where climate is revealed. Architecture is the trace of wind, water, sun, and rain. As Louis Kahn reflected, the sun never knew how beautiful it was until it touched the wall.

In the sweep of diverse rhetorics and ideologies, the weathering narrative of many modern buildings has been either glossed over or relegated to a technical prosody. The parasol and the brise-soleil in Le Corbusier's buildings, the marble strips of Kahn's Assembly Building in Dhaka, or more recently, Peter Zumthor's weathered church, or Herzog and de Meuron's winery project, all have a weathering narrative. Diller and Scofidio's Blur Building is the closest approximation, perhaps a bit theatrically, of Merleau-Ponty's "flesh."

Gravity is the other bane of architecture. It is after all the metaphor of limit and death; as is often said, sleep is the complete surrender of the body to gravity. In the film *The Matrix*, the first thing that is attempted is to overcome the reality of gravity. There are comparable anti-gravitational desires all throughout architectural history, particularly in the modern period, from the incredible peripatetic architecture of Archigram to the coordinateless configuration of deconstructivism.

But gravity persists, and continues to interject an ambivalence to the architectural dream. There is the story of Kahn and Vincent Scully on a visit to Moscow. Scully pointed to the famous church spires there, and exclaimed: "See, Lou, how they touch the sky." Kahn replied, possibly looking at the foundations: "See how they rise from the ground." Kahn's architecture, more than others in contemporary times, has been an unabashed reflection on gravity asserting that architecture on earth is firmly gravity-bound. This is perhaps what makes the work of Kahn appear to many critics ponderous and retrogressive.

Tectonics is actually the *poeisis* of gravity. Tectonics is no mere expression of making, but making the geo-logic presence of earth and gravity tangible; it is the human's dialogue with gravity. Even if architectonic configuration is veiled by scenographics, gravity remains as an unperturbed ontological condition. Gravity is also a phantom dynamic in spatial embodiment, in establishing the pre-conceptual modes of left and right, and up and down. There are other vectors of gravity with architectural implications: horizontality and verticality, heaviness and lightness, ascent and descent, wetness and dryness, and seating and standing.

Take for example the task of making a platform. It may seem like a pedestrian exercise – making a flat, horizontal surface – but is actually fraught with primal urgency (the only place where the need for a horizontal datum is diminished is in zero-gravity). Some current works present and problematize the phenomenon of gravity through literally a tilt in architectural elements. The return of the ramp – an instrument of movement or pause? – as a slanted inhabited plane (as in Rem Koolhaas proposed library in Seattle going back to Le Corbusier's Strasbourg project) is one such example. In Balkrishna Doshi's Husain-Doshi Goofa in Ahmedabad, a semi-underground art gallery in a serpentine configuration, there is an excruciating absence of the flat plane, either the horizontal or the vertical. All "planes," including the floor, slant, curve, and undulate. Attempts to stand still or stay stationary remind one how much we take standing or sitting for granted, and how precious is the horizontal datum. While sitting on that mean floor during an exhibition opening, constantly trying to adjust to an elusive position of comfort, the thought that came to my mind was the quiet presence of gravity.

Senses and Presences

The situatedness of architecture is a tectonic, physical and material event. In other words, it is a phenomenal engagement with climate, gravity, and the earth. Steven Holl, echoing an Albertian theme, notes: "An architecture is born when actual phenomena and the idea that drives it intersect." Idea is a matter of the mind, so to speak, while phenomenon involves sensations, perceptions, and visceral feelings. The former implies "design" as modern architecture culture has come to know and practice it, and phenomenon points to the opening up of a work to a full corporeal and environmental engagement. It is siting, tectonics and materiality that give a building a presence. At that point, the building is both part of the collective realm and part of the earth's strata; in both cases, de-moored from the mind of the creator. It then becomes an engaged and engaging phenomenon, and has presence.

There are different modes of "presencing architecture," that is, different ways and degrees of visualization, representation, and experience. There is a clear distinctiveness between the dominantly ocular mode, and the whole range of spatial, pneumatic, visceral, tactile, aural, and peripatetic/kinesthetic conditions, which also enables a disjunction on which the modern discipline and the transaction of architectural knowledge are substantially based. It would be fruitful to investigate how the visual mode informs and forms, describes and inscribes, expands and limits the perimeter of the discipline.

Sound, smell, shadow, tactility, and temperature, along with sight, attune us to place, and to emplaced or sited architecture. One hears a city in the call of the muezzin, in the tolling of the church bell (in some places), and perhaps today, in the scream of the police siren (what Yehudi Menuhin calls the aural environment). In distinction to the olfactorily neutral places such as Boston and Minneapolis, one can still smell Istanbul, Venice, Delhi, and perhaps New York. Architectural tactility is present everywhere, in the textures of the pavement we walk on, in the grass in the park, or in the smooth surface of a hospital corridor. The non-visual dimensions of architecture have been addressed in the writings of Kenneth Frampton, Juhani Palaasma, and David Leatherbarrow. Few recent projects stand as a proclamation of this theme, especially in the work of Peter Zumthor and Kengo Kuma.

As a final remark, let me point to light that the ocular dimension has not yet exhausted. While light and lightness have enjoyed an exalted status in much of western modern architecture, as in the crystal metaphor, Mediterranean light, or the "the magnificent play of masses brought together in light," there is still much to say about shades, shadows, and darkness. The construction of shadows, not just as comforting conditions but as mythopoeic elements, may be seen in Arab courtyards, sanctums of Hindu temples, stepwells of Gujarat, and in the Japanese aesthetics of darkness. Place and placing are also about how shadows are made.

The aesthetical articulation of shadows and darkness may be seen most significantly in Japanese tea-houses and other artifacts as written about by Junichiro Tanizaki. A masterful construction of darkness is Tadao Ando's Japanese Gallery at the Chicago Institute of Art. On entering the gallery, one is immediately confronted with a dusky atmosphere, not an expectation in a museum setting. One sees only a vague apparition of a set of columns (trees in a forest?) beyond which there is a somewhat more lighted area appearing to contain some objects. One navigates through and beyond the dark forest (it is, one realizes afterwards, a grid of nine square wooden posts), and arrives at the semi-lighted area. The area contains glass cases displaying Japanese artifacts; the light seems insufficient to examine the pieces. There is a long and heavy wooden bench on one side on which one sits and lets the eyes slowly adjust to the dimness. The effect is almost epiphanous: The artifacts slowly begin to appear amidst the haze of a visible darkness. The whole experience is one of a delayed visibility. For certain things to appear, one has to wait; for certain things to prosper, one has to delay. It is no wonder that the term "dwelling" is cognate with "delaying."

References

Edward S Casey, *Getting Back into Place: Toward a Renewed Understanding of the Place-World* (Bloomington: Indiana University Press, 1993).

Fredric Jameson, *The Cultural Turn: Selected Writings on Post-Modernism 1983-1998* (London: Verso, 1998).

David Leatherbarrow, *Uncommon Ground: Architecture, Technology and Topography* (Cambridge: The MIT Press, 2000).

Henri Lefebvre, *The Production of Space* (Oxford: Basil Blackwell, English trans. 1991).

Maurice Merleau-Ponty, *The Phenomenology of Perception* (London: Routledge and Kegan Paul, 1962).

Eugene Minkowski, *Lived Time: Phenomenological and Psychopathological Studies* (Evanston, IL: Northwestern University, 1970).

Mohsen Mostafavi and David Leatherbarrow, *On Weathering: The Life of Buildings in Time* (Cambridge: MIT Press, 1993).

Robert Mugerauer, *Interpretations on Behalf of Place: Environmental Displacements and Alternative Responses* (Albany: State University of New York Press, 1994).

Junichiro Tanizaki, *In Praise of Shadows* (originally published 1933, translation Leete's Island Books, 1977).

Tetsuro Watsuji, *Climate: A Philosophical Study* (Tokyo: Government of Japan, 1961).

Mehran Karim Nasseri at Charles de Gaulle Airport. Photo: from internet.

Terminal Places

Unpublished text, Philadelphia, 2004.

At Bangkok Airport, date unknown.
Photo: Ashraf.

The airport is a strange place.
—Dixon, airport manager in the film The Terminal.

"Unhomely" is a term urban sociologists, and literary and architectural theorists sometimes use to describe the alien and unsettling nature of certain aspects of contemporary life. The architectural historian Anthony Vidler, who has written about the modern unhomely in his book *The Architectural Uncanny*, notes that such a phenomenon did not exist prior to the nineteenth century. Instances of the unhomely or uncanny, the terrifying and anxiety-filled are now quite routine and are often actually designed for experience. Something as ordinary as being stuck inside an airport terminal could become the closest experience of the unhomely or the uncanny.

Viktor Navorski was stuck at JFK international airport for a year. Mehran Karimi Nasseri was trapped at Paris Charles de Gaulle Airport for eleven years. Navorski, from an unknown Eastern European country of Krakozhia, arrives at JFK to find that his country has erupted in a civil war and incredibly does not exist anymore, and neither does the validity of his passport. Nasseri flees Iran in 1988 with the intention of seeking asylum in London, but on his way, in Paris, has his documents stolen. A man without papers is a man without a country. Immigration officers at London airport send him back to Paris, and officers in Paris will not let him enter the "official" soil of France, and since Nasseri had no papers and therefore no valid country to send him back to, he is stuck at the airport. For over eleven years.

Navorksi, played by Tom Hanks, is from the fictitious country of Krakozhia in Steven Spielberg's recently released film *The Terminal*. Mehran Karimi Nasseri is a real life refuge seeker from Iran whose strange plight has inspired a number of documentary and feature films (*Sir Alfred of CDG Airport* by Hamid Rahmanian and Melissa Hibbard, *Waiting for Godot at de Gaulle* by Alexis Couros, and the French film *Tombés du Ciel* by Philippe Lioret), and in the latest rash, into a Hollywood film. The difference is that the new terminal citizen is east European, his terminal duration is for one year, and he gets to fall in love with the lovely Catherine Zeta-Jones. Clearly, Nasseri's terminal life is a tad bit more tragic than what Spielberg can make of Tom Hanks latest cast away.

Spielberg falls short with his movie not because of the comedic and actually rapturous turns of Navorski's experience (one was almost expecting he and his terminal pals bursting out in an uproarious musical), but the fictionalization he resorts to. The poignancy of a terminal existence increases against the nuanced context of a real homeland that one is bound for, abandons, or pines for. Stranded at JFK because of an imaginary Krakozhia that no longer exists only heightens the fairy-tale-like predicament complete with monsters at the gate and a jazz finale in Manhattan. JFK airport, in its internationalized makeover as a three-storey steel and glass structure with sixty-five thousand square feet of granite floor (all built in a hangar in Palmdale, California) seemed quite incredulous considering its typical disarray.

And how real did Krakozhia seem? Although nations in Eastern Europe have been torn asunder in civil strife, inventing a country that vanishes into thin air makes Navorski's predicament quite concocted. Tom Hanks contrived accent and mannerism, no matter how endearing, only added to the business of enactment.

Nasseri, on the other hand, has an actual past, and an authentic reason to flee from a real place. Turned away by immigration, Nasseri soon becomes a figure of media attention. Newspaper stories, magazine articles, academic essays, documentaries, feature films trail the man without a country, a homeless celebrity who gives lounging a profundity never seen before. One newspaper report describes him in the terminal "sitting at a table, perhaps smoking a pipe, taking a stroll, stopping to pick his mail at the post office or lunch at the McDonalds's… he will be looking very much at home." The fact of being very much at home in the enigmatic space of an airport terminal that wants us to figure out the puzzle of a man's home.

2

Nasseri was a mathematics student in Iran when he left for London in 1988 to seek asylum. This was precipitated after the fall of the Shah and Nasseri's continued requests for political asylum that was finally granted in 1981 by the United Nations High Commission for Refugees in Belgium. Since one of his parents was British, England was his choice for residence. When he loses his documents during the short stopover at the Charles de Gaulle Airport, Nasseri decides to fly on to London, but immigration officials there finding no paper on him sends him back to Paris. He is however not allowed to enter France even as a refugee, or even given a transit visa. Neither can he be returned to his original homeland because it appears that he has no proof of where that is. Thus begins Nasseri's entry into a phantom zone.

The zone is made complex by an intractable bureaucratic paradox and Nasseri's own enigmatic attitudes. When Nasseri and his French lawyer wrote to Belgium for the refugee documents, the Belgian authorities refused to mail them as Nasseri had to be present in person to receive the papers. At the same time, Belgium did not allow Nasseri to come there pointing out a law that a refugee who voluntarily leaves a country that has accepted him cannot return. But when in 1995, Belgium offered Nasseri his documents and a residence in Belgium, Nasseri refused saying that he wished to go only to England. While his status is reviewed by Belgian and French authorities, Nasseri remains confined within the passenger lounge of the terminal.

He makes himself at home, if we can say that, in Terminal 1 of Charles de Gaulle Airport. He sleeps on the red plastic chairs of the terminal, wakes up at 5:30 in the morning so that he could use the men's room before passengers arrive. He keeps himself clean and dignified. He eats at the restaurants where he receives food offered by people at the airport. He befriends the shopkeepers, the airport workers, the airline people and passersby. It would seem that there is no real need for money in the phantom zone. He hangs his blazer wrapped in plastic in an airport cart next to his old suitcase. All day long, he listens to the radio, writes in his diary, and frequently talks to journalists and visitors. He reads regularly; he is seen reading Hillary Clinton's *It Takes a Village*. Sometimes, he will stand at a certain spot from where he can catch a stealthy whiff of fresh air when a nearby door opens and closes to the outside.

Homeless? Stateless? Placeless? Identityless? Nasseri's predicament compounds as every regularized spatial attestation as we have come to know is denied. Nasseri soon no longer responds to the name Mehran, he wishes to be called by the adopted name of Alfred or Sir Alfred. Hamid Naficy, professor at Rice University and scholar on exilic and diasporic experiences, feels that Nasseri may actually resent his own Iranian background, and was using every ploy – "engaging in various games of ethnic camouflage, denial, and passing" – to present a European origin. When Hamid Rahmanian and his wife were making the documentary *Sir Alfred*, Nasseri refused to speak to Rahmanian in Farsi, preferring to talk to his English-speaking wife. When his French residency permit finally arrived in 1999, Nasseri actually hesitated leaving the terminal of Charles de Gaulle airport. He would rather make the limbo his home than go out to a space of normality. A *Boston Globe* report quotes Danielle Yzerman, spokeswoman for the Charles de Gaulle Airport, "An airport is kind of a place between heaven and earth. He has found a home here."

Why is Nasseri's story that I have described at length so engrossing and disturbing at the same time when people have lived life in exile and abandonment in far less congenial conditions? Is it because of the terror that we think he experiences that is quite alien to us, something that we can only imagine? Is it because of the political and ethical question placed on the rigorous nature of the modern state, on the construction of its steadfast boundaries and their simultaneous fluidities? Is it because we are unaware of the interstitial zones that are created in unimaginable places? We can think of the strange nature of certain modern spaces that require new requisites on what we do. Is Nasseri, to put it in academic terms, a case of modern human's experiential limit, politically, ethically, legalistically, and spatially?

3
Eleven years at an airport terminal, even if it be Paris, is an astonishing epic. We develop genuine anguish even when we are stuck for a day or so with a delayed or missed flight at an international terminal. After the aura of the swanky space and twinkle of the duty-free shops and bars fade out, the only landmarks of meaning are to be found in the panorama of anonymous chairs, the coming and going of people through a tiny portal, the digital bulletin board, the bank of telephones, and the occasional trip to the restrooms. Things take on a different orientation in the enclosure of the terminal.

Studs Terkel, the radio personality, once trying to get to Cleveland from Detroit rushed to the counter to board his plane only to receive the answer: "But, sir, you are in Cleveland!" I had a similar terminal experience once on one of my regular flights between Philadelphia and Dhaka. At Dubai Airport, on the bus taking the passengers to the terminal from the just landed plane, for a brief second, I wasn't sure whether I was going to Philadelphia or Dhaka. It was, even for an angstrom moment, strangely unnerving.

Last December, I was at Taipei Airport to catch an onward flight to Bangkok. Being in a foreign airport for the first time can present a bewildering landscape of signs and symbols. Most often, we take some of those things for granted as we apply a familiar and cultural logic to how they are placed, structured, and to be read. I thought the television monitors at Taipei are in odd places, to begin with. Next, I discovered that the signs for the restrooms do not necessarily take you to your destination. You see it finally, behind some columns, the door with the ubiquitous sign of the rounded off Vitruvian man ready for a pee. Going from one terminal to another can be an anxious journey of its own. I go from Terminal A to Terminal B to catch my flight to Bangkok by traversing corridors of infinite perspective that only aggravates my anxiety about how long the walk will take. The walk is interrupted only by undulating floor planes, ubiquitous construction sites, and surrealistic advertising graphics. I arrive at B3 but I clearly see that the lounge to the plane is two stories below the corridor where passengers are already mulling around. I am with two bags and look for an elevator. I go into one and push the button "1." The door opens and I find myself in a desolate lounge with one old cleaning woman. Clearly "1" is not the lounge I saw from above. I speak and gesticulate to the woman, how do I go up. No comprehension. I climb back into the elevator, and hey, I didn't notice, there is no button for "2" or "3." How do I go up? Mild panic. A security guard suddenly materializes. Before I can explain or ask, he demands my boarding pass. He then opens a door and takes me to another elevator and up to the floor I am looking for. I walk in but it is the departure corridor. A China Airlines staff tells me I am in the wrong space and that I should go all the way back to security, back to where I started from. Another panic. I give a semiological argument, insisting on variable interpretations of the sign system. He finally lets me in. My own little Nasserian moment.

Nasseri's experience is a heightened emblem of the space that he unwittingly inhabits for eleven years: the terminal of an international airport. All of a sudden the space of the airport presents itself as a new paradigm of human experience. The airport is no longer just a functionally charged communication node but a space opened up in the juridical fissure of the laws of nations and states. Like a parking garage, the terminal is certainly not a destination, but a point of perpetual departure, and when that is made ambiguous, a Nasserian moment inevitably ensues. But it is also a space of its own with its own physiognomy where one can fully survey the topography of placelessness. I am assuming that Fredric Jameson, the Marxist philosopher of postmodern life, would have no problem in designating this as a postmodern space, one kind of spatial experience in our multitude of experiences that characterize the modern existence, and something over which we do not, yet, have a full intellectual and perceptual grasp.

4

I mentioned placelessness in designating the space of the terminal, but not in any kind of pejorative way, that is, as a space that stands hopelessly in contrast to the familiar spaces of unequivocal meanings that affirm what we do normally and prosaically. Placelessness is a new modern configuration.

If placelessness has acquired a new status, it is not surprising in a postmodern cosmos. The notion of "place" in the twenty-first century has come under increasing questions, especially when it is seen as romanticism about landscape, chauvinism around regional or territorial affiliation, or as something stable and perennial in a world of perpetual flux and denuded fixities. Placelessness as a possibility has proliferated in the context of new globalization and mediatization with the unencumbered transfer of capital and information, or in the spaces "discovered" or "invented" in new urban and architectural conditions. Placelessness is no longer the condition of vapid wandering or the residue of assuring spaces. One now confronts placelessness as another kind of existent space. Placelessness is now a place.

The philosopher Michel Foucault labeled those spaces as "heterotopias" that are located in the midst of our normative life but that neutralize or invert the meaning of that normativity; he was thinking of cemeteries and hospitals for example. But what about the terminal of an airport, the parking garage, the space without a name under a freeway, or the various other spatial debris of the modern city? What do they reflect or mirror? Perhaps the space of the terminal does none of these. In its swanky, squeaky clean air, and antiseptic glamour, the space makes us feel sheer uncanniness, something borne out of an incomprehension of these spaces, of being completely outside of anything we have experienced so far. Like a monad, the terminal space is not umbilically connected to any continuum, either historical or geographical, thus nothing in our collective imagination predisposes us to that experience.

O'Hare Airport, Chicago. Photo: Ashraf.

The realm of the terminal is a kind of an extruded space, cleaved open from the multitude of existent spaces. From a large hallway for a new building type that the airport began as, it has become a landscape of infinite and unexpected possibilities. Since this extruded space is now here and can be experienced, it needs to be taken seriously. In his essay "Postmodernism and the Consumer Society" (1988), Jameson presents the Westin Bonaventure Hotel in Los Angeles as the epitome of "hyperspace," a new kind of space that we can now enter and encounter. It is really a new paradigm of experience, asking from us nothing less than spatial and perceptual re-orientations.

5

What is true for the Westin Bonaventure Hotel in Jameson's observation is quite relevant for the airport terminal. Both are instances of "postmodern hyperspace," a new kind of spatial concatenation, arrived at partly consciously, cumulatively, and serendipitously, but are now upon us when we are still floundering in an older and familiar space frame and have no clue yet how to orient ourselves in those spaces. There is a space lag.

Jameson describes these spaces as a mutation in built space, and that we, as the human subject, who happen to be in that space, have not kept pace with that evolution, that is, we have not acquired an equal degree of (perceptual) mutation or orientation, and as such "do not yet possess the perceptual equipment to match this new hyperspace." This is in part because our spatial orientation and perceptual habits were formed in an older kind of space over a long period of time. Jameson thinks that something extraordinarily surprising is happening with these new spaces and architecture. The Westin Bonaventure Hotel, as an example of this new architecture, "stands as something like an imperative to grow new organs to expand our sensorial and our bodies to some new, as yet unimaginable, perhaps ultimately impossible, dimensions." While such lessons of a spatial recoding and sensorial reconfiguration will come rather smoothly or innocuously for visitors breezing through the atrium of the Bonaventure, for others, like Nasseri, it will arrive with a nearly indecipherable trauma. The matter is broader than we care to think. Such an experience, Jameson argues, is "a symbol and analogue of a larger decentering in which we find ourselves caught" in which the individual is no longer capable of organizing itself in a "mappable external world." Anthony Vidler, in cataloging the varieties of unsettling spaces in his book *Warped Space* (2000), regards this as an emblem of "the conditions of a less than settled everyday life" that characterize contemporary production of art and architecture.

The first striking thing about the Bonaventure is that it is a totally disjunctive space; it lays no claim to making any meaningful link with the continuum it otherwise is in – Los Angeles. Unlike Foucault's "heterotopia," those spaces have no conversation with spaces outside them; they do not invert, neutralize, mirror or do any such thing the world outside it. Those new spaces are a complete world by themselves, as Jameson characterizes, being categorically disjunctive from the surrounding environment, and being neither the shadow nor microcosm of it. I would describe those spaces as monadic, completely oblivious to anything beyond itself, like the self-centrism of a mercury globule. What is visible in the far distance, the vistas of LA from the hotel, and the surreal landscape of the tarmac in the terminal with the goings in and out of the lumbering planes and the fleeting service cars, seems strangely inaccessible.

A new typology of enclosure characterizes the space inside, as at lobbies at the Bonaventure and atriums in airport terminals. The point of contact or porosity between these spaces and the space outside them is hopelessly asymptotic. In the case of the hotel, they are curiously unmarked, and in the case of the terminal they are deceptively controlled. And once inside the terminal, you are in a complete befuddlement about where you are, where the plane of the earth is, where the geographical north is, and where the building opens to the outside. The array of escalators, elevators and people movers further confound any proper sense of orientation to the earth or outside. Movement seems to be the enduring phenomenon here. As with the motion outside, there is an endless movement within this hermetic zone; it's not, however, a stroll down a promenade.

6
The airport terminal is neither city nor country in its characterization; it is an empty volume – pure emptiness – suffused with the flicker of monitors, signs and signage. More properly, it is a semiologically charged space where meanings and bearings are found only by reading and interpreting signs in a milieu of endless arriving and departing. The additional element is aural, of the crisp announcement of flights delayed, passengers recalled, with the hum and drone of those incredible flying machines lumbering to and fro from the thin pane of glass that seems to separate here and there.

The massing of people is only spectacular; it is a congregation without community, a proximity without intimacy. The density is only reminiscent of a village fair or the quasi-urban shopping mall with its increasingly stunning and equally increasing sameness of retail units. Perhaps, at best, it is a pseudo-community in a propped-up plaza where everything is public with its particular social codes and etiquettes about how people should move around in its surveilled environment to do the only thing allowed: wait. Vidler has noted the photographic documentation of the spaces of airport terminals by Martha Rosler (1997) that seems to give evidence to "the combined discomfort of demoralized waiting and anonymous passage" associated with these spaces.

With the airport "community" forever changing, for whom no second day is animated with the same constituency, the anonymity of passage and waiting is exacerbated. The change is precipitated by passages – a double bind that is the leitmotif of the airport.

Roland Barthes described the train stations in Japan as a big void and, at the same time, the foci of Japanese cities. The stations are voids because they are not a destination for staying but a space where droves of people arrive endlessly only with the intention to depart. Those train stations, as in Shinjuku and Shibuya in Tokyo, where shops after shops line the corridors as in a pilgrimage route going nowhere, create de facto urban intersections that still maintain a certain continuum with the rest of the city.

The terminal of the airport is a void without a continuity; it is unilaterally self-referential like a zone in the ancient Greek sense of the term. As Jean Francois Lyotard explains, the zone means "a belt, neither country nor city, but another site, one not mentioned in the registry of places." But it is not a wasteland either – such a space is an interim realm between here and there, between departing and arriving (as cryptically coded in the term "transfer"), between nowhere and everywhere, and increasingly between nations. None of the older co-ordinates are meaningful here, east, west, north, south, mountain-side, sea view. Terminal buildings, by their sheer nature, show what Rem Koolhaas, Frank Gehry, Zaha Hadid, and Daniel Liebeskind and other architects of a similar persuasion are trying: to get rid of all the regular geographical, territorial, and environmental co-ordinates in a building.

7

Nasseri sits there, motionless and somewhat bewildered, in the haze of interminable movements and motions. For eleven years, when everything is moving, everyone is departing, Nasseri goes nowhere, a stasis in sea of endless movements, a Hestia among the airborne Hermeses.

If placelessness is a new place in the postmodern cosmos, homelessness is a new home. The Greek goddess Hestia was the epitome of home, of things that are stable and immobile. She represented the hearth around which the family and therefore the individual gravitated. Terminus was another character who never moved from the place he occupied. The Romans considered him as the god who presided over boundaries and landmarks, and because of his immobility represented him with just the human head without feet or arms. Nasseri is immobile as those ancient gods and yet perfectly homeless.

Homelessness in the modern world has now reached epic proportion – there are delinquents from home of all sorts, such as the migrant workers, the sophisticated cosmopolite, the anguished exilee, the asylum seekers, the transnational traveler, the multinational employee, and people who unwittingly fall into unpredictable spatial fissures. The terminal – the airport terminal more than other terminals like the train station and bus depot – has become an unwarranted space of asylum providing a new kind of refuge for the international homeless.

One could be homeless by being perfectly immobile as Nasseri, or one could generally acquire homelessness by being mobile as evidenced by Walter Faber in Max Frisch's existentialist and quasi-ethical novel *Homo Faber* (1954). There is a long tradition in Japan of a calibrated homelessness in which a man of means would renounce the objects of a socialized life to take up residence in the forest or wilderness. He would build his own little hut from whatever materials are at his disposal in that desolate space and spend the rest of his life with minimal possessions meditating on the transitoriness of life. The classic text of this tradition is The *Hojo-ki* (The Hut) written by Kamo no Chomei in the thirteenth century. Chomei was an urban courtier, who after realizing the transience and fluctuation of social life, decides to abandon it for the life of a hermit. After leaving the city, Chomei takes up residence in a mountain forest where he builds a simple, elemental hut, evoking the transience of his "dew like life." All the joints of the structure are such that if the situation no longer pleased Chomei, he could easily take the whole thing down and transport it elsewhere. Chomei explains that the hut is like a "shelter that some hunter might build for a night's lodging in the hills, or like the cocoon some old silkworm might spin." It is not only Chomei who is peripatetic, his home is too.

Could one be at home and territorially rooted, and yet be completely adrift as the Portuguese writer Jose Saramago ponders in his work *The Stone Raft* (1986)? Saramago questions the inviolable stability of land, and at the same time exposes unforeseen consequences when a destabilization occurs. In the book, the whole Iberian peninsula breaks off from the continent and starts drifting, like a gigantic raft, towards the ocean, taking people, places, mountains, horses and dogs, all with it. The work is fantastical but it points to the possibility that it is not just the human who is subject to the phenomenon of placelessness but place itself. The whole terra firma that is considered an infallible thing of fixity can behave otherwise; motility can also come to what is considered a fixed geography.

Perhaps still sitting impassively in Terminal 1 and reading once more *It Takes A Village*, the enigmatic Nasseri reminds us that motility, fixity, stability and identity are all undergoing paroxysmic changes. As Nasseri makes the totally unhomely his home, the distance between home and the unhomely seems uncannily narrow. If the homely becomes the *unheimlich* according to Freud, thus creating modern neuroses and psychoses, now the decidedly unhomely becomes home.

Where Is Architecture

Introduction to *Jamini: International Arts Quarterly* issue on "New Architecture," 2007.

Christo's installation in New York City. Photo: Jyoti Puri.

Chashistsu at Kodaiji Temple, Kyotô. Photo: Ashraf.

In the Swiss writer Max Frisch's novel *Homo Faber* (1954), the protagonist Walter Faber is a UNESCO engineer, a quintessential modern man, for whom only the "tangible, calculable, verifiable" exists, and who lives for the service of a technological omnipotence. For *homo faber*, man the maker, the imperative is "life can be mastered by technology." As an emblematic figure befitting a world body as UNESCO, Faber moves from one location to another, his uprootedness seen as liberative. The architect-turned-novelist Max Frisch, in this existentialist and quasi-ethical work that made a stir when it was published, charts the enigmatic quandary of such a modern nomad. On a cruise liner – the ubiquitous trope of placelessness – Faber meets a young woman and falls in love with her. It's not certain if they consummate their relationship or not, but in a twist reminiscent of Oedipus and his exile from his place of origin and his devastating forgetfulness (that leads to killing his father and marrying his mother), Faber finds out that the young woman is actually his daughter (the syndrome is more Electra than Oedipus). It's then the novel takes on the aura of a classic Greek tragedy.

Would it be an exaggeration to say that being modern is to be bequeathed with that exhilarating and burdensome nomadism, the promise to transcend the terror of territory but face the terrifying consequence of the Oedipal dislocation and forgetfulness?

Modern architecture and its various incarnations are still perceived as bearers of the imaginary that architecture need not be encumbered by territory and geography. This idea was best circulated through such high architectural polemics as Archigram's 1964 architectural vision of literal world mobility, visualized as tentacled mega-machines poised for traveling the globe. The contemporary phenomenon in which specific places have retreated in the face of an euphoric globalization and planetary transmutation shares with the earlier universalist aspiration of modernity a suspicion of place, or to say in an obverse way an unabashed glorification of "placelessness." While nomadism is not really placeless but a moving from place to place without fixity, a celebration of that often comes with its quandary, as Walter Faber discovers.

Peter Zumthtor, Saint Benedict Chapel, Sumvitg, Graubunden, Switzerland. Photo: Saif Ul Haque.

Patrick Doughtery, Na Hale O' Waiawi, Contemporary Museum of Art, Honululu, 2003. Photo: Ashraf.

I was in my own quandary when invited to edit an issue of *Jamini* on architecture, about what to present from the brilliant diversity of architecture today, from new and newer form-generating principles (Shuhei Endo, whose work is discussed here) to highly poetic constructional innovations (Renzo Piano), from models of eco-architecture (Ken Yeang) to radical visions of urban form (Rem Koolhaas). I wanted to return to the stubborn themes of nomadism and rootedness that still constitute the human drama, and wonder how they are played out in architecture and urbanism today. While new dynamics such as transnational, digital, and "free-flow" modalities constitute new calculi and imaginations for architecture, most of the works presented in this issue are also a demonstration that they are always *somewhere*. And there are many such somewheres.

"Where Is Architecture"
Some years ago, at a seminar on contemporary architecture in Dhaka, I invoked the invisible genius – the enduring presence of wind, water and clay – in describing the architecture of the Bengal delta even as it positions itself in a transnational niche. A colleague at the seminar interpreted this as my muddy orientation, a rather romantic urge to proceed backwards, when valiant figures in architecture are no longer looking to some crumbling monument or ossified form, but galloping towards a buoyant, flamboyant future. My point was neither about what is old and what is new, nor about the over-indulged opposition between modernity and tradition, but that architecture, if it can be called an art, is a *situated* art. I wanted to stress that a persistent and obstinate condition in architecture is the geographical-climatical one, which is far more significant than what is authentically historical, what is flashingly modern, or what is cleverly deconstructivist, or some other ideologued postures.

The bottom line is: *where do I work as an architect*. From *where* do I get my architectural response, and *where* do I situate my work. One can design in an autonomous manner anywhere, but one always builds somewhere. One could give a clever argument that somewhere is anywhere, or nowhere for that matter, or in the manner of Gertrude Stein, that there is no there *there*, and so why linger. The first argument comes from the cartography of "free-flow," either the electronic mode of digitization or the fluid capital of global economy, and the latter is an indictment of the sociological and cultural void of the modern metropolis (in Stein's case, Los Angeles). Yet, if one cares to detect, there is a certain wistfulness in Stein's poignant lines.

"Where is architecture" is not a question, but it could be one, about the position and role of architecture in cultural and economic production today. What I actually propose is to orient focus away from "what is architecture" to "where" and try to unravel what that "where" might mean, whether we have been making inordinate demands on the "what," and how far the question of "where" remains unexamined. In any case, the question of "what" is intimately tied to the matter of "where": to architecture and its place in the world, to the making of the flesh of the architectural body. "Where" refers to a zone of inevitability, be it geographical, cultural, temporal, or some combination of it. Yet, zones and boundaries are never fixed things; their fluidity makes it difficult to maintain a precise overlap of the political, cultural, and geographical, and that is the conceptual challenge. If from the bustle of the modern metropolis, in its phantasmagoric setting, these reflections seem dubious, then to what premise can architecture respond to?

Building in Tokyo by Kengo Kuma. Photo: Ashraf.

The Mother Tongue of Architecture
Rabiul Husain, an architect and poet in Dhaka, posed a query in an essay few years back: "Is there a mother tongue in architecture?" The question triggers a whole set of intriguing and provocative issues around that intimate pair: architecture and culture.

First, what is the relationship of language and architecture when language as a "mother tongue" is often perceived as the original site of naturalness and belonging? What significance does architecture bear when it is also considered as an expressive system, a language? Second (following the previous point), can there be different levels of operation within architecture, from a kind of primordial and originary state, comparable to a mother tongue, to a whole variety of appropriated, imported, modified, and contaminated (and, possibly, more exciting!) mode of expression? And, third, most importantly perhaps, what results from the triadic relationship of (literary) language, architecture, and land? Is there an ontological divide here between language and architecture in the context of geography?

The obsessive notion here is "rootedness," referring to some original condition of arising and belonging, thus the highly charged maternal metaphor. And it is not without its fiction and prejudice. Mother language receives an extraordinary importance in modern Bengali cultural context because it is equated with, or what is perceived to be, the most authentic and natural state of being that appears to have been with us forever. After all, it is the *raison d'etre* of the nation-state of Bangladesh. It is for this reason, along with recent historical and political events, language has been the principal medium for articulating the cultural universe in Bangladesh. Everything else seems to follow that unquestionably, including the formation of the idea of nation and identity. Rabiul Husain's essay, despite the implied provocations, remains within a predictable and particular nationalistic orientation in which language is at the center of cultural discourse.

And, yet, when juxtaposed with architecture and land, language might have a more debatable status when it comes to the question of an original belongingness. It seems the relationship of language with land is quite unstable, and language is a far more portable and malleable material than one would like to wish. In any case, Bengali derives its primary root from an Indo-European language source, whose geographic origin, despite its deep and now quite ancient re-rooting in India, is nomadic. The question of mother tongue must address the complex terrain of political history, race, religion, region, and, most importantly, migration and mutation.

Michael Sorkin, Amsterdam Avenue Transformed, New York.

Konjian Yu, Qiaoyuan Wetland Park, Tianjin City (Photo: Turenscape).

Relatively speaking, architecture has a more basic and enduring relationship with land. Mediating diverse fluctuating contingencies, architecture is not an unchanging phenomenon; however, it is more deeply sited, that is, more intimately and irrevocably tied with the weather and fabric of the land. It is the primal site of human's existential struggle in a specific locality where the first collective intentionalities are discovered, articulated, expressed, and possibly given name. The dialogue and politics of cultural identity have relegated architecture to a mostly marginalized position, when it is possible that between architecture and language, the former is comparatively more durable and geographically anchored, and relatively a more foundational site of those existential moments.

Placing Architecture

"Place" is at the heart of architecture. "The architect's task is more than the manipulation of materials and the molding of space, it is the definition and possession of place." The American architect Charles Moore said that more than thirty years ago. The possessing of place as an intimate and existential need is a basic human inclination; it engages a wide range of human thinking, imagination, and feeling, and has not become passé in the thunderous roll of new epistemologies.

seship near downtown Honolulu. Photo: Ashraf.

se Construction, Honolulu. Photo: Ashraf.

Although the idea of a definite and definable space could lead to ideological deadends, place does not immediately promote a nationalistic or identity-laden rhetoric. What is immediately implied by a place-situation is not so much identity in the sense of nationalistic ideologies or cultural chauvinism as the persistent presence of the "real." People will dwell in definite places, in real localized situations. In the context of architecture that translates into the obviousness of being situated, the inevitable existence of a work in a palpable condition of wind, water, sun, soil, and time.

Even though there is a complex relationship between culture and place, I make a subtle distinction between the two, not too dissimilar from the parting between language and architecture. It is possible to question culture as the permanent premise of architecture, for culture, as it stands today, cannot fully account for the tumultuous societal transformations, and is certainly no longer capable of sustaining singular authority for architecture. Culture itself has become portable, malleable, and commodifiable. On the other hand, it is possible that the situatedness of architecture involves comparatively more enduring and resilient conditions or "realities." These "realities" – primarily of a geological, climatical, and terrestrial nature – constitute a place-situation that tacitly, surreptitiously and inevitably affect the life and form of architecture there. The best analogy is the amoeba, how its form and function are an expression of its inevitable, intimate and dissociable relationship with its place-situation. The old conception about building is similarly valid: it is established in relation to a specific place, and it too establishes our place in the world. The riotous growth of cities and the undeniable pressure to build in a triumphant consumerist culture should not delude one into thinking that a building is only a commodity, a product of space necessity and real-estate equation.

82. RELIEF WITH BUDDHA ENTHRONED.
Found at Muhammad Nâri in Yûsufzâï. Cole, *Pr. N. Monts.* pl. 1.

The Buddha under a distended lintel with bodhisattvas in pavillions, Gandhara.

The Buddha's House

Published in *RES: Aesthetics and Anthropology*, Vol. 53/54, Spring/Autumn, 2008.

The Buddha's house is an enigma. Even though there is no clear, single image of the house, and Buddhist traditions do not describe it with any precision or unanimity, the shadow of the house exerts a tremendous influence on pragmatic, didactic and symbolic deliberations of the various tenets of Buddhism. If the Buddha's house acquires a larger than life status, it is not because of the house itself, but because of the stature of the dweller of the house, the Buddha. The purpose of this essay is to draw the outline of that house.[1]

Why should one be interested in the Buddha's house other than the reason that the house belonged to a world-moving teacher? If Buddhism and its various practices are ascetical in nature, dwelling is a key locus in that tradition.[2] If an architectural exegesis is sought in that ascetical culture, it must begin with the house of the Buddha.

The Buddha's house appears in manifold ways within the Buddhist traditions, depending on the various schools that emerged since the First Council held immediately after the passing away of the Buddha, and the various accounts and concepts of the Buddha that developed soon after.[3] Conversations in the traditions are not so much about the literal architecture of the house as much as employing the architectural structure for a deliberation on asceticism, on describing, explaining and encoding the dimensions of renunciation. This is the principal reason for an elementary structure as the Buddha's house to emerge with a kind of paradigmatic value. Joseph Rykwert, in establishing the significance of Adam's House, writes how the image of a clearly imaginary house becomes the locus of a compelling religious, sociological, and philosophical imagination.[4] The aim of the production of such a paradigm is the reform of society that is envisioned in a kind of "purer" architecture which society somehow would follow as a model.[5] It seems many cultures assign reified properties to a certain architectural image that will charge the lives of people, forming expectations broader than prosaic architecture.

The Buddha's house becomes a significant site for reflecting on the scope and limits of renunciation, on its existential, ritual, and aporetic dimensions. After all, the Buddha – Gautama Śākyamuni

[1] I am in pursuit of a house that does not exist *per se*. No single literary, archaeological, anthropological or epigraphic account – the tools of reconstruction – can fully build this house. By the "Buddha's House," I am referring to the wide-range of architectural references made in the context of Buddha's habitation, from purely pragmatic ones to those that play more than domiciliary roles in the Budhhist cosmos. The sources of this architectural image are literary descriptions and commentaries, pictorial and three-dimensional representations, and ritual texts. The house starts to appear through an hermeneutical treatment of the materials, and for me that also includes the so-called secondary literature, that is, comments and essays written in our times, for I consider that many of the essays significantly hinted at the plan of the house, so to speak, but none attempted to erect it *in toto*. I am aware of the discrepancies in the account of Buddhist past where often literary accounts do not match with archaeological or epigraphic ones, as Gregory Schopen demonstrates in his essays in *Bones, Stones and Buddhist Monks* (Honolulu: University of Hawaii Press, 1997), on the one hand, and where sometimes epigraphic accounts are held to be unreliable, as commented upon by Maurizio Taddei, "Recent Archaeological Research in Gandhara: The New Evidence," in Pia Branacaccio and Kurt Behrendt (eds.), *Gandhāran Buddhism* (Vancouver: UBC Press, 2006), on the other hand. I cannot quite participate in that debate as I am not writing with Buddhistic scholarship but as a historian of (architectural) ideas adopting, I am admitting, certain latitude.

[2] While it might appear that the Buddha might have distanced himself from asceticism at the moment of his awakening by adopting the so-called "middle-path," he was actually rejecting the extreme forms of practices prevalent among various ascetic groups at that time. The Buddhist monastic tradition can still be described as a combination of renunciatory and ascetic practices.

[3] The term "Buddha" has acquired multiple meanings in conjunction with the emergence of various sects, schools and traditions, the principal ones that have continued are the Theravāda and Mahāyāna. While the notion of the Buddha is not limited to the historical figure of Gautama Śākyamuni as it took on a universal aspect in most conceptualizations, the proliferation of the idea is still predicated upon the known life-story of Gautama. In elaborating the idea of the Buddha, from an historically specific Buddha (Gautama) to non-specific Buddhas, texts in all schools adopt various methods whereby legends

– was an arch-ascetic whose life practice and teaching were about the critical relinquishment of "home," and the various re-formations thereafter. Within Buddhist traditions, the house appears diversely, from practical considerations to didactic, metaphorical and symbolic treatments. There are descriptions, in both literary forms and visual representations, of the house that the Buddha dwelled in prosaic ways. The house also appears in various fabulous narratives, as we shall see, where it acquires an extraordinary dimension in itself, from being a repository of something miraculous to signifying the invisible. However, in Buddhist ascetical thinking, the final encounter of renunciation takes place within the frame of the human body which is visualized, in many Buddhist narratives, as a dwelling, thus bringing an intimacy to two aspects of existence: building and body. The house is homologized with the ascetic's body so that a metaphysical or mystical understanding of the supra-human figure is embodied in the architecture. All these ideas emerged from the facts around the life of the historical Buddha and the regards accorded to him then and after as the "perfected ascetic," or as he was described, the *mahāsāmanā* (arch-ascetic), or *mahāpurusa* (superman).[6]

The Architecture of the House

Jetavana is a special place in the life of the historical Buddha, Gautama Siddhārta (543-483 BCE). The place was a garden retreat outside the city of Śrāvastī (still an extant city in present day Uttar Pradesh in northern India). In around the sixth century BCE, when the Buddha was roaming the Gangetic plain, going from one city to another with his ardent project of transforming oneself, he would station himself in a secluded area inside or just outside the city. The area could be a garden (*ārama*) as part of the estate of a wealthy person, an established retreat, or part of a forested site. During his visits to Śrāvastī, he stayed at Jetavana for a total of over twenty-five years. The site of Jetavana fares very significantly in Buddhist art and hagiography where it is depicted with what are known to be dwellings especially constructed for the Buddha.[7]

We can assume that prior to the dwellings in the Jetavana, the Buddha had experienced various architectural spaces. When the Buddha was about twenty-nine years old and known as Siddhārta, a prince in the northern kingdom of Kapilavastu (in modern Nepal), he abandoned his palatial home and left in the dead of the night for his now celebrated quest and culmination under a tree in Gayā (present day Bodhgayā in Bihar). The story has been told and retold, one that primarily focuses on the Buddha's teachings and exemplary life that combines self-abnegation, ascetical discipline and contemplation, and finally a self-transformative illumination about the course of life (a phenomenon that came to be characterized as "enlightenment").

But what remains rather elusive is how the Buddha lived and carried on his day to day routines, first, in his life of wandering in the wilderness after renouncing his princely home, and second, in his life of post-nirvanic traveling in more urban settings. It would be important to know how the great teacher and practitioner of renunciation dealt with the

and fables surround even the historical figure.

[4] Joseph Rykwert, *On Adam's House in Paradise: The Idea of the Primitive Hut in Architectural History* (Cambridge: MIT Press, 1984).

[5] Joseph Rykwert, The First Moderns (Cambridge: MIT Press, 1980), p. 299.

[6] In the history and tradition of ascetic practice, the full development of the idealized ascetic figure occurs around the sixth-fifth century BCE within the particular socio-economic context and theological-religious background, where the Buddha represents one "perfected ascetic," preceded by an extensive tradition of wanderers, renouncers, and ascetics. In defining the "perfected ascetic," the hermit or the ascetic of that momentous period is considered the most idealized human figure in Indian imagination. In Louis Dumont's view, that figure is the true individual, the person standing outside or against the world, see Louis Dumont, "World Renunciation in Indian Religions," in *Contributions to Indian Sociology 4* (1960). To Mircea Eliade, he is the one who is considered to define and challenge the limits of civilization, and consequently reveal the domain beyond the ordinary and the mundane. He is also the one who articulates an individuated path for the transformation of the self, which is nothing less than gaining "immortality" and "freedom," see Mircea Eliade, *Yoga: Freedom and Immortality* (Princeton: Bollingen Press, 1958), pp. xx, 118.

[7] One reason for Jetavana's prominence in visual and literary narratives is because of the well-known story of its building by the merchant Anathapindika, especially the laying of gold pieces on the ground as the price of the place. The narrative is found in many Buddhist texts, including the *Vinayas*.

The Buddha visiting a seated Brahmanic ascetic in a woven hut, Gandhara (Ingholt, *Gandharan Art in Pakistan*).

The Buddha inside a shrine structure, Gandhara (Museum of Art and Archeology, University of Missouri-Columbia).

mundane but necessary aspects of dwelling after the moment of enlightenment. The Buddha, in an ideological move, may have repudiated the normative house as the prime symbol of domestic and social ensnarement (*samsāra*), but he did require and acquire some sort of dwelling even in his life as a great teacher. We know only spottily about the actual residence of the Buddha (the Jetavana structures being a case), of the various huts or pavilion-like structures he might have used in the gardens of cities that he visited in his itinerant life. Images start appearing in Buddhist literature and iconography from around the third to second century BCE, a few centuries after the Buddha's own time.

The earliest dwelling of Siddhārta, in his life of wandering in the forest in the pre-enlightenment phase, may be regarded as an elemental shelter. Buddhist texts written few centuries after his death describe such an elemental condition variously as being under a tree, seating on a cushion of grass, or being in a cave.[8] Such primitive conditions were part and parcel of the renunciatory life styles of various hermits and ascetics in India that go back to Vedic times.[9] The ascetical movements of Buddhism and Jainism in the sixth century BCE considered those conditions in a more formalized and organized manner that

[8] The description is ascribed to the Buddha in the "Mahā-Assapura Sutta" (39.12), in the Pali Therāvada text *The Majjhima Nikāya*.

[9] See comments on various kinds of arboreal structures such as *kutī* (plain hut of the peasant or forest recluses), *pannasālā* (leaf hut), *nalāgāra* (reed hut), in Ananda K. Coomaraswamy, "Early Indian Architecture" (1930, 31), *Essays in Early Indian Architecture*, reprinted and edited with an introduction by Michael W. Meister (New Delhi: Oxford University Press, 1992), pp. 105-108.

[10] While it is beyond the scope of this essay to even briefly discuss the psychological, philosophical or religious issues of "nirvāna," I am simply describing it as a climactic moment, the *telos* in the ascetic-meditative practice of Buddhism.

also came to constitute or define the ideology of renunciation.

In any case, the tree fares prominently in early Buddhist universe. Next to the cave, the tree is the archetypal site of ascetic practice despite their marked phenomenological differences. It was actually the tree at Gayā that becomes the critical site and "structure" associated both in actuality and metaphorically (and soon metaphysically) with the climactic moment of *nirvāna* or "awakening."[10] It is not surprising that the tree becomes the prevalent sanctioned "dwelling" in Buddhist monastic literature, and soon a multivalent motif in the representation, explanation, and elaboration of the Buddha's "abode." Although the reified tree is a widespread and ancient phenomenon, it becomes an emblem par excellence within Buddhist symbolism and its ascetic practices. The tree is simultaneously the site of enlightenment, and an emblem of Buddhist metaphysics (such as "Cosmic Tree" and the "Tree of Wisdom").[11] It is both an abode and a temple: The tree is both a symbol of the actual site of Buddha's enlightenment, and therefore an actual spatial location, and of the more abstract notion of yogic enlightenment. This is best exemplified architecturally by the creation of the hypaethral temples, the *bodhigharas*.[12] The *bodhighara*, coming a little later after the Buddha but certainly imbued with pre-Buddhist significance, is basically a sacred tree associated with the Buddha around which is constructed an elaborate structure for carrying out rituals.[13]

The tree, as the Indologist Heinrich Zimmer remarks, is very much like a hut.[14] The tree and the cave are not only naturalistic conditions of dwelling, as distinct from a constructed artifact, but are also archaic sources of a vast metaphysical and mythological imagination. In the ascetic realm, there is reciprocal significance between the tree, the cave, and the hut when approaching the architecture of the ascetic. Some of that significance comes from an earlier source such as the *yaksa* imagery that has substantially influenced the build-up of the image of the hermit under a tree. The *yaksa* is an archaic tree or water spirit, the veneration of which was present as a devotional cult in almost all villages, a practice that predates Buddhism in India but was apparently co-opted into the Buddhist worldview.[15] In any case, the abode of the *yaksa* is an important feature: it is a tree, most often located in a forest. The *yaksa* and the tree are, however, virtually interchangeable;[16] specific trees are abodes of the *yaksa* beings that often develop into a locus of venerable activities, creating a ritual ensemble of tree, altar, seat and enclosure[17] that would come to be known as a *cetiya* or *caitya*.[18] It is this ensemble that informs the site of the Buddha's enlightenment to such an extent that the village girl Sujata mistakes the contemplative Siddhārta for a *yaksa*.[19] There is a conflation here between the property of a dwelling (*bhavanām*, as the *yaksa* abode was known), and an honorific locus (*caitya*). In both Buddhist and Jaina narratives, the *yaksa caityas* are used as resorts, or halting places (temporary abodes) for itinerant monks.[20] Stories abound about the Buddha taking brief residence under a *yaksa* tree and resting on its altar slab or seat.[21]

[11] Mircea Eliade notes, like others before him, "The Cosmic Tree is at the center of the world; it unites the three cosmic regions, for it sends its roots down into the underworld, and its top touches the sky," *A History of Religious Ideas* (Chicago: University of Chicago Press, 1982), Vol. 1, p. 42.

[12] Coomaraswamy, *Essays*, p. 19-29.

[13] Ibid.

[14] Heinrich Zimmer, "Trees, Huts and Temples," in *Journal of the Indian Society of Oriental Art*, Vol. 5 (1937).

[15] Coomaraswamy, *Yaksas* (1928-31, reprinted by Munshilal Manoharlal, 1971), p. 18-22, and Moti Chandra "Some Aspects of the Yaksa Cult in India," *The Bulletin of the Prince of Wales Museum* 3 (1952): 43-62.

[16] Coomaraswamy, *Yaksas*, p. 11.

[17] Cited in such texts as the *Dhammapada Atthakathā*, noted by Coomaraswamy, Yaksas, p. 22. See Moti Chandra, "Some Aspects of the Yaksa Cult in India.

[18] The word *caitya* is possibly derived from the root ci meaning to build or heap up, but by the time of the Epics and Buddhist and Jaina literature came to mean any holystead, altar, shrine grove, temple, etc. Coomaraswamy, *Yaksas*, p. 24, ff. 2. In some cases, *caitya* overlaps with the term *stūpa*.

[19] Pali traditions hold the view that every Buddha was offered milk-rice from a maiden just before his enlightenment. In the case of Gautama Buddha, he was offered that by Sujata, a woman from the nearby village of Uruvela. In *Dīgha Nikāya* ii.135.

[20] Coomaraswamy, *Yaksas*, p. 23.

[21] Ibid.

[22] Dietrich Seckel notes that in the *Divyāvadāna*, the Buddha describes the bodhi-tree as his "permanent residence" *(mana nibaddhavaso viya)*, and during his absence a bodhi-tree may be planted as his representative. See Seckel, *Before and Beyond the Image: Aniconic Symbolism in Buddhist Art* (Zurich: Artibus Asiae, 2004).

[23] The Vinayas is the key Pali canonical text, being one of the *Tripitakas*, that contains codes, injunctions and rules for Buddhist monastic life, and specific commentaries on monastic inhabitations. The monastic codes are collected together in what is known as "Pratimoksa" rules. Also, the "Mahāvagga" and the "Cullavagga" are two important sections in the *Vinayas* that elaborate upon the monastic life.

All these means is that living under a tree came to be reified in a special way in Buddhist ascetic thought.[22] The *Vinayas*,[23] a compendium of rules put together for the monks, and supposedly passed down from the Buddha, announces: "In the matter of housing, the śramana's life is based on dwelling at the foot of a tree. Thus you must endeavor to live all your life. Cells, houses, mansions, and huts are extras."[24] The Buddha on occasions encouraged living under trees and in caves, giving at the same time its efficacy for ascetic purpose.[25] At around 400 CE, the prolific commentator Buddhaghosa writes in the *Visudhhimagga*[26] that there are thirteen ascetic practices known as *dhutángas*[27] that are conducive to the pursuit of ascetic virtues. Of the thirteen practices, one is the "tree-root dweller's practice." This conforms to the *Vinaya* suggestion of "depending on the root of a tree as an abode," in which the ascetic begins his renunciatory practice by declaring: "I refuse a roof." The root of a tree is clearly a dwelling recommended by the Buddha because it is "valueless, easy to get, and blameless."[28] Buddhaghosa lists the following benefits for living at the root of a tree: (1) the perception of impermanence is aroused through seeing the continual alteration of young leaves, (2) avarice of abodes and love of (building) work are absent, (3) one dwells in the company of deities, and (4) lives in conformity with (the principles of) fewness of wishes.[29]

There is also the post-enlightenment wandering of the Buddha when he would travel, always with a retinue of followers, from city to city, teaching and discoursing. On such journeys, he would generally reside in a forested site near a city, or a large garden such as at Jetavana. Sometimes the garden, often belonging to a wealthy patron sympathetic to the Buddha's teachings, would be dedicated for the sole use of the Buddha, whence the site from being a pleasure-garden would become a retreat (*ārāma*) for hallowed, meditational purposes.[30] The large site would also be a residence for the group of people accompanying the Buddha, including fellow elders and fresh initiates. There were not yet the regularized monastic establishments that happened soon afterwards and remain the evidence of Buddhist architecture today.

The huts at Jetavana are the most significant constructions made for the Buddha. The huts depicted in both the reliefs in Bhārhut and Sāncī (both from around the 3rd c. BCE) are shown as refined construction of thatch and possibly wattle and daub walls. The relief from Bhārhut shows two huts, one a square or circular hut, and another an oblong, vaulted one. An elaborate *caitya* doorway with wooden end-beams forms the entry for both. The *caitya* frames several arched motifs with decorative patterns, the latter could be some kind of lattice-work to let air and light in. The roof, adorned with pinnacles, is well-formed with an elegant curved shape in section that follows the contour of the *caitya*-arch. Such an architectural profile is recalled in full scale as either a gateway or compressed building volume at the front of the Lomas Rsi cave that was carved out by the Ājīvika ascetics not too far from Gayā, at about 260 BCE.

[24] The *Vinayas* I, 58.

[25] In the *Majjhima Nikāya*, translated by Lord Chalmers as *Further Dialogues of the Buddha* (1926). The *Majjhima Nikāya* is a text belonging to the *Sutta Pitaka*, one of the three components of the Pali *Tripitaka*. The *Sutta Pitakas* contains various teachings (*sutta*) attributed to the Buddha.

[26] *Visudhhimagga* is a comprehensive manual written by the 5th century Theravadin commentator and scholar Buddhaghosa. Buddhaghosa, *Visuddhimagga: The Path of Purification*, translated by Bhikkhu Nyanamoli (Colombo: A. Semage, 1964).

[27] The "dhutánga" practice is distinct from the general cenobitic practice of the monks. The "dhutánga" covers a stricter and individualized ascetic mode, something that may be practiced by individuals in remote places, in distinction to the collective and public practice in the monastery. See *Visuddhimagga*.

[28] Noted in the *Anguttara Nikāya* (ii, 26).

[29] *Visuddhimagga*, Chapter II, pp. 56-59.

[30] Gustaf Roth discusses how pleasure gardens (*udayana*) were converted to monastic retreats (*ārāmas*) through certain simple rituals, in Roth, *Ārāma*, *Vihāra* and *Mahāvihāra* (Patna: Buddha Sanskriti Kendra, 1997), p. 71.

It is not clear yet whether the hut dedicated for the Buddha in the Jetavana relief is an actual representation of a structure the Buddha lived in, a simple adaptation from common dwellings of that time, or more possibly, a stylized convention for important buildings (the Bhārhut and Sāncī reliefs were produced about two hundred years after the time of the Buddha). Early representations of residential architecture of that time, as in the art of Gandhāra and sites like Bhārhut, do show some with resemblances to the huts at Jetavana. What is significant is that the profile of the Jetavana huts depicted in the Bhārhut and Sāncī reliefs takes on a codified character making it possibly a mark of the Buddha. Among the few examples that may be cited, the most striking one is the image of a hut within a *bodhighara*-ensemble from a medallion from Mathurā.[31] Another is a statue from a site in Gandhāra of what is known as a female donor with a votive object that seems to be a cross-section of a "triple-arched building" bearing close resemblance to the profile of Jetavana hut.[32] A fragment of a statue from Gandhāra shows compressed scenes of Buddha at the fire-temple in Uruvilvā. A structure on the right, possibly the fire-temple, depicts the Buddha inside, and the same structure on the left with the "tri-lobed arch" opening shows an empty space.[33]

In the period of Buddhist art, from perhaps the time of the Buddha to the second century BCE, the Buddha was not represented directly, and was conveyed in the so-called aniconic manner through visual marks of which the more established ones included footprints, the wheel of teaching, the *bodhi* tree or the stūpa. In the repertoire of signs or marks of the aniconic Buddha, I would provisionally like to include the hut motif, something that has to await a closer inspection later. The hut motif is certainly not as wide spread as the established ones, yet there are many examples as above that have been overlooked by scholars studying aniconic representations.[34]

In the case of the structures at Jetavana, the identifying "mark" of a hut being the Buddha's dwelling is not only visual, but also olfactory. The structures there were called *gandhakuti*, or fragrant or perfumed hut, and that term *gandhakuti* came to refer to the abode of the Buddha in more than one ways. It is through the *gandhakuti* that the space of the Buddha's habitation has been reified in early Buddhist circles.

Gandhakuti, the House of Fragrance

The *gandhakuti* was always considered a very special "place of the Buddha," a structure prepared for him either during or after his life. While the building of the *gandhakuti* at Jetavana seems to be most known, it was not unique to that site alone. It was part of the importance accorded to the accommodation of the Buddha whenever he arrived at some city with his retinue.[35]

Fragrant architecture was particularly highlighted in early Buddhist tradition. In Jetavana itself, there were structures other than the *gandhakuti* that were also described as being fragrant buildings: *kosambakuti*, also meaning a fragrant hut, was one of them,[36] and *candanamālā*, the sandalwood pavilion, is one

[31] Plate XIV (a), in Jean Philippe Vogel, *La Sculpture de Mathurā* (Paris: Ars Asiatica, 1930).

[32] Plate 400, in Harold Ingholt, *Gandhāran Art in Pakistan* (New York: Pantheon Books, 1957).

[33] Plate 84, in Ingholt, *Gandhāran Art in Pakistan*

[34] Dietrich Seckel discusses the broad range of marks of the aniconic Buddha, where only a "cupola pavilion" (from Nāgārjunikonda is mentioned, pp. 35-36. See Seckel, *Before and Beyond the Image: Aniconic Symbolism in Buddhist Art* (Zurich: Artibus Asiae, 2004, first published 1976).

[35] The *gandhakuti* is mentioned in numerous *Jātakas*, and other Buddhist texts such as Pali commentary literature and Sanskrit *avadānas*. T.W. Rhys Davids and other scholars of the Pali school think that the *gandhakuti* was a specific building in a particular monastery, referring especially to the one at Jetavana, while Eugene Burnouf, Monier Monier-Williams, and H.C. Norman hold the opinion that the *gandhakuti* was not specific to a single monastery but referred to a house for the Buddha wherever he went. See discussion by H.C. Norman, "Gandhakuti – The Buddha's Private Abode," in *Journal of the Asiatic Society of Bengal* (Vol. 4, 1908); John G. Strong, "Gandhakuti: The Perfumed Chamber of the Buddha," in *History of Religions* (Vol. 16, 1977), and Gregory Schopen, "Buddha as an Owner of Property and Resident in Medieval Indian Monasteries," in his *Bones, Stones, and Buddhist Monks* (Honolulu: University of Hawai'i Press, 1997). Schopen, citing epigraphic evidence, observes that the *gandhakuti* referred to both the specific structure at Śrāvastī and also various other monastic sites where a particular space was designated as a *gandhakuti*, pp. 268-269. Some texts mention the building of *gandhakutis* for Buddhas other than Gautama, in Buddhaghosa's commentary on the *Dhammapada* and the *Anguttara Nikāya*.

[36] B. Barua and K.S. Sinha, *Bārhut Inscriptions* (Calcutta: University of Calcutta 1926), p. 60. The term is found in inscriptions in Bārhut, and the authors think that the term refers to a "perfumed cottage," and not to the place-name Kausambi. The term is a Pali counterpart to the Skt. *kausumbha*, meaning sweet-scented, or literally bearing the perfume of *kusumbha* flower.

[37] Joel Tatelman, *The Glorious Deeds of Purna: A Translation and Study of the Purnavādana* (Surrey: Curzon Press, 2000), p. 143.

of the several dwellings that were created for the Buddha in a number of cities.[37] *Kārerimandalamālā* or musk-rose pavilion, *puspamandapa* or the flower pavilion, and *mālā-vihāra* or the garland pavilion are mentioned in various literatures.[38]

The strongest reason for calling the house of the Buddha a fragrant or perfumed one is the offering of perfumes and flowers during his time. The *gandhakuti* was then not only the private dwelling place of the Buddha but also "the repository of floral offerings which gave its sweet perfume and its Pali name."[39] The fifth century CE text *Dhammapada Attakathā*, in one instance, describes the *gandhakuti* as having pillars, three great windows, gem-set roofing tiles, a golden bowl on the roof, and pinnacles of coral.[40] Coomaraswamy thinks that the golden bowl is located inside the roof and is some kind of device for sprinkling perfume on the Buddha seated within, and it is this that gave the name *gandhakuti*.[41] The *Dhammapada*, an important text compiled as the Buddha's sayings, assembled after his death, mention the nature of flower and fragrance, and the sage being like a bee. The tropical climatic setting is certainly a factor here. The role of smell as signifier came about because of the greater abundance of plants with fragrant flowers and the more porous relationship of the house with the outside.[42]

When the hut becomes a site for devotional offerings by laypeople, the *gandhakuti* assumes more the status of, what John Strong calls, a "cultic abode" than a pragmatic house of the ascetic. A cultic characterization implies that the house was oriented more for the devotional activity of the broader community of monks and laypeople, in which the association of flowers with the hut came to be an honorific trope for the Buddha.[43] Flowers were often treated in a much more architectural way in connection to spaces for the Buddha. In this sense, two types of *gandhakutis* are identifiable. The main type is the constructed hut that was very likely functionally lived in by the Buddha.[44] The second type is a flowery pavilion that is not a space of inhabitation but a "new space" that either shelters the Buddha ceremonially or invokes his presence during absent conditions.

It is highly likely that these flowery pavilions were erected as temporary structures wherever the Buddha went for visits, and were used to frame the platform from where he spoke and taught, and also most likely, meditated. In any case, both types – the functional hut and the flowery pavilion – shared the fragrant aspect of the Buddha's presence, and both came to be reified as such.

The flowers in the fragrant hut were given as simple offerings, but were also used to create a bower or pavilion of flowers around the Buddha, delineating a space around him. That would be the most literal architectural sense of a floral pavilion. The image of the flowery pavilion is depicted in a number of sculptures that show the Buddha under a form of arboreal, floral, or garland-decked canopy.[45] This is also corroborated in certain texts. There is a striking imagery in the *Dhammapada Atthakathā* where a

[38] Tatelman, *Glorious Deeds*, p. 143-145. The *Mahāvastu* mentions a *malavihāra*, translated as the "garland building" or "booth of festoons" put up over the relics of the Buddha, noted by Roth, *Ārāma*, p. 36.

[39] There were also other fragrant huts with different names, and possibly with different characterizations. There was another hut at Jetavana for the residence of the Buddha that was called *kosambakuti*, also meaning a perfumed hut. Norman, "Gandhakuti."

[40] Noted by Coomaraswamy, "Early Indian Architecture," *Essays*, p. 110.

[41] Ibid.

[42] The offering of flowers, not uncommonly, developed into a cluster of important notions in Buddhist narratives and practices that are depicted in numerous Buddhist art. It is also not surprising that floral offerings were an important aspect of the *yaksa* cult, a practice noted in many Buddhist texts, see Coomaraswamy, *Yaksas*, p. 25, 28.

[43] The *Mahāvastu* mentions the high purpose of the use of a "booth of festoons": "After having made festoons at a Vihara (with a shrine inside), he shall turn his mind towards enlightenment," *Mahāvastu* II.333.21 (Translated by J.J. Jones. London: Pali Text Soceity, 1973), noted by Roth, *Ārāmā*, p. 36.

[44] Buddhaghosa in his *Sumangalavilāsinī* describes what is known to be the daily routine of the Buddha in and around the *gandhakuti*. Excerpts in Henry Clarke Wilson, *Buddhism in Translations* (Cambridge: Harvard University Press, 1896).

gardener after meeting the Buddha offers him flowers.[46] The gardener first threw a handful of flowers over the Buddha that remained suspended over his head like a canopy. The next handful that was thrown created a curtain on the Buddha's right side, eventually creating a curtain wall all around him. The flowery pavilion accompanies the Buddha as a sort of mobile *gandhakuti* wherever he moves until he reaches the actual fragrant hut, and once he goes inside the hut, the flowers suddenly fall off all around him.[47]

Even if this is a fabulous story, it describes the creation of an architectural space through floral means. John S. Strong describes these as "creating a new space" around the Buddha,[48] a space that also may be seen as coterminous with the body of the arch-ascetic. It is because of this correspondence between the body and the space delineated around it that reverential followers could visualize a scenario of a mobile floral canopy as the Buddha moved around.

Once that correspondence – between body and pavilion – emerges, it is natural to come up with moments when a flowery space is created to represent or commemorate a missing Buddha, who may either be in a distant place when alive, or after his passing may no longer be bodily available. The effect in either case was to "make a space in which the absent Buddha can be present here and now."[49]

The House of Absence

The house of fragrance is also the house of absence. I have already mentioned how fragrance becomes a cue for invoking absent bodies such that a powerful meaning is assigned to smell over visual signals. There is an interesting passage in an *Avadāna text* where the protagonist Purna suggests to a group of merchants that they build a sweet-smelling pavilion to invoke the Buddha, when apparently the Buddha is far away and the merchants have never seen him. As Purna recommends: "use this [sandalwood] to build a circular pavilion (*mandalamālā*) for the Teacher and then you shall see him." Purna actually donates towards the building of an elaborate structure made out of sandalwood called the *candanamālā* (the sandalwood pavilion) with the intention of inviting the Buddha there. After the pavilion was completed, the *avadāna* narrates:

> Purna climbed onto the roof of [the pavilion], that place of refuge, and stood facing the Jeta[vana] grove [where the Buddha was staying at that time in Śrāvastī]. He knelt down, strewed flowers, waved incense. Then, through the spiritual power of the Buddhas and the divine power of the gods, the flowers fashioned themselves into an airborne pavilion and were transported to the Jeta Grove.[52]

In elaborating the idea of "new" space, John S. Strong gives examples of floral offerings, such as those of later and present times in front of the statue of the Buddha in Buddhist image halls, and of the established practice of "sweeping the *gandhakuti*":[53]

[45] A number of Gandhāra sculptures show the Buddha under such a canopy where the fragrant moment is further amplified by the presence of spiritual or human figures offering or strewing flowers at the Buddha. There is one image in which a standing Buddha is seen under a suspended floral canopy with monks and worshippers around him while a devotee on his left is seen tossing flowers at him. The image is part of a larger composition in relief, being divided from the upper half by what appears to be some kind of arboreal or vegetal gateway or pavilion. See Plate 188, in Ingholt, *Gandhāran Art in Pakistan*.

[46] In Buddhaghosa's *Dhammapada Atthakathā*, mentioned by Strong, "Gandhakuti."

[47] There are images of standing Buddha with a floral canopy or garland over him. See Plate 188, in Ingholt, *Gandhāran Art,* and Plates 117, 290, in W. Zwalf, A Catalogue of the *Gandhāra Sculpture in the British Museum* (London: British Museum Press, 1996).

[48] Strong notes that the theme of a floral pavilion, and thus the motif of a "new space," occurs repeatedly throughout avadāna literature. *Avadānas* narrate the religious deeds of an individual with the intention to "illustrate the workings of karma and the values of faith and devotion."

[49] Strong, "Gandhakuti."

[50] Tatelman, *Glorious Deeds*, p. 183. For note on *avadāna*, see ff. 48.

[51] Ibid.

[52] Tatelman, *Glorious Deeds,* pp. 67-68.

[53] It seems that the practice of "sweeping the *gandhakuti*," as if preparing a space for the arrival of the Buddha, was initiated by Anathapindika just after the death of the Buddha, which becomes one more aspect of the identity of the Buddha and his space. See Strong, "Gandhakuti."

> What this effects ritually is the construction in the image hall itself of a floral perfumed chamber in which the presence of the Buddha can be realized here and now, even though he is in Nirvāna. The Buddha, of course, is to a certain extent "present" already in his image. Presumably the gift of the devotee and the spirit in which it is arranged create a new psycho-physical environment which brings that presence out even more.[54]

Such symbolic *gandhakutis* of later times in the form of floral offerings and flowery structures created a "new" space in order to invoke an absent figure. One could describe these symbolic *gandhakuti* as mimetic, surrogate or associative spaces, that is, they evoke in one form or another the original, living space of the Buddha's dwelling. So from a place prepared as an abode for the living Buddha, the *gandhakuti* in its various later forms came to be "a special place in which the Buddha's presence could be recaptured" for and by the devotees.[55] From a special dwelling place, the significance of the *gandhakuti* quickly ramified symbolically especially after the passing away of the Buddha. The most important representational aspect of the *gandhakuti* is the identification of the architectural structure with its dweller, whereby the flowery "new space" becomes coterminous with the figure of the Buddha.

In further ramification of the *gandhakuti*, it is spoken of as a glorious house or as a large and elaborate temple,[56] sometimes with an extra-ordinary quality. This is understandable in the context of devotional tradition where the *gandhakuti* is seen as the residence of a supra-human being. The *Purnavadāna*, mentioned earlier, describes the scene of the Buddha's inhabiting the *gandhakuti* in the following fabulous terms:

> Meanwhile, [in Jetavana outside Śrāvastī], the Lord washed his feet, entered his personal cell, sat on the specially appointed seat, assumed an upright posture, and established himself in full mindfulness. As soon as the Lord, with fixed determination of mind, set foot in his perfumed chamber (*gandhakuti*), the earth shook in six different ways: the great earth stirred, quivered and quaked; it shook, trembled and shuddered… The nadir rose up, the zenith sank down. The zenith rose up, the nadir sank down… Then, from his body the Lord radiated an effulgent stream of golden light.[57]

The Buddha's house becomes the basis for morphological configurations of later structures and campuses when Buddhism becomes an organized religion. Originally, in the Buddha's lifetime, the residential *gandhakuti* was understandably located in the middle of a retreat surrounded by huts of other elders and monks and various monastic facilities. This is perhaps the proto-monastic configuration for the later elaborate monasteries built after the death of the Buddha where the central position in the campus was taken up by a temple-stūpa bearing the designation of a *gandhakuti*. It is highly possible, as Coomaraswamy observes, that after the death of the Buddha,

[54] Strong, "Gandhakuti."

[55] Strong, "Gandhakuti."

[56] Coomaraswamy, "Early Indian Architecture," Essays, pp. 112-113. Coomaraswamy mentions an inscription at Bodhgaya temple describing it as "the great *gandhakuti* of the *vajrāsana*."

[57] *Purnavadāna*, translated by Tatelman as *The Glorious Deed*, p. 71.

[58] Coomaraswamy, "Early Indian Architecture: Huts," *Essays*, pp. 109-110. This is consonant with Coomaraswamy's important thesis of the original prototype of Indic temple architecture being the ascetic shrine which itself was a derivation of the ascetic hut.

[59] Gregory Schopen provides epigraphical and archaeological records of the symbolic use of *gandhakuti* in 10th century monasteries where the Buddha was considered a "current resident" in terms of proprietorships, *Bones, Stones and Buddhist Monks: Collected Papers on Archaeology, Epigraphy, and Texts of Monastic Buddhism in India* (Honolulu, 1997), pp. 270-271.

[60] Op. cit.

[61] The *Bhagāvata Purāna* x, 60, 20, mentioned by Monier-Williams in A *Sanskrit-English Dictionary* in note to "geha." The *Bhagāvata Purāna* may have written around the ninth to tenth century CE.

[62] Modern literature on this homology is vast, but the principal scholarships include the following: Heinrich Zimmer, *Kunstform und Yoga im indichsen Kultbild*, 1926; and, Stella Kramsrich, "Marks of the Great Being: Mahāpurusa-laksana" (1931). Coomaraswamy discusses the relationship on a number of occasions: "Mahā Purusa: Supreme Identity" (1935), reprinted in *Metaphysics* (Princeton: Bollingen, 1977), "Symbolism of the Dome" (1938), reprinted in *Selected Papers: Traditional Art and Symbolism* (Princeton: Bollingen, 1977); "Ātmayajna: Self-Sacrifice" (1942), reprinted in *Metaphysics*, p. 129-130; "Usnīsa and Chatra," The Poona Orientalist III:1 (April, 1938): 1-19, and " Svayāmatrnnā: Janua Coeli" (1939), reprinted in *Selected Papers. Mircea Eliade discusses the theme* in his essay "Cosmical Homology and Yoga," *Journal of the Indian Society of Oriental Art 5* (1937): 188-203, and *Yoga: Freedom and Immortality* (Princeton: Bollingen, 1958), p. 139, 327. Also, J.C. Heesterman, *The Broken World of Sacrifice: An Essay in Ancient Indian Ritual* (Chicago: University of Chicago Press, 1993).

[63] Joseph Rykwert, *On Adam's House in Paradise: The Idea of the Primitive Hut in Architectural History* (Cambridge: MIT Press, 1984), p. 184, 190. Also, *The Dancing Column: On Order in Architecture* (Cambridge: MIT Press, 1996).

the residential *gandhakuti* became the first shrine or temple.[58] Gregory Schopen, in analyzing epigraphic evidence for certain tenth century monasteries, notes that the idea of *gandhakuti* was continued by designating and maintaining a space as a gandhakuti where the Buddha was thought to have been "a current resident and an abiding presence."[59] Some of these practices were facilitated by the already established idea of the homology of the Buddha and the *gandhakuti* described above. In brief, the essence of the *gandhakuti* was quickly magnified and expanded in both literature and architecture to characterize Buddhist temples, a morphological development that proceeded from the dwelling to a shrine.[60]

The Body of the Building

When the Brahmanical text *Bhāgavata Purāna* talks of two habitations of humanity – the house and the body – it ascribes for architecture a role far wider than plain functionality.[61] A homology between builder/dweller (the sacrificer) and the built-object (altar) is an ancient theme in India.[62] Joseph Rykwert, in discussing an analogy of body and building in the Graeco-Roman, Jewish and Christian traditions, explains "Adam's house" as being not really a shelter against the weather, but a volume that the human could interpret in terms of its own body. The house is also an ideologue of the paradisal plan, the center of which where the human establishes himself.[63] The analogy of the body and building also invokes a third element, the cosmos, uniting in a schema all three: the larger universe, the microcosm of the body, and the building as a mediational mesocosm. As Coomaraswamy writes, "The human frame, the constructed temple, and the universe being analogical equivalents, the parts of the temple correspond to those of the human body no less to those of the universe itself."[64] The correspondence between the human figure and an architectural body is a trope present abundantly in phenomenal, mystical or metaphysical terms in many cultural productions.

The relationship between the ascetic dweller and his dwelling is a particular category in the discourse of body and building. At an immediate level, the ascetic establishes a spatial association with his elemental structure or space. With the Buddha, the relationship takes on multiple significances. An associative relationship between building and body is witnessed in the Buddha's house of fragrance where the presence of one signals the other. This is possible because the house belongs to the dweller in a sort of spatial intimacy. The intimacy is metrical, phenomenal, and figural.

Part of the Vinaya canons that represents a list of rules for Buddhist monastic living, the "Prātimoksa,"[65] states that: "When a monk himself is begging to have a hut built which has no donor, being intended for himself, it should be made [according to measure]. This is the measure: twelve spans of the Sugata-span;[66] in width, seven spans inside."[67] The *sugata*-measure represents an idealized physical dimension of the Buddha's body. The "Pratimoksa" rules not only prescribe sugata-measure for the hut of the monk, but also for his robe, couch, rug, etc.;

[64] Coomaraswamy, "An Indian Temple: Kandarya Mahadeo" (1947), reprinted in Selected Papers: *Traditional Art and Symbolism* (Princeton: Bollingen, 1977).

[65] The "Prātimoksa," or the Pali "Patimokkha," represents a list of confessional rules and degrees of punishment for Buddhist monastic living. It is an important part of the Buddhist monastic ritual and practice, perhaps the oldest text in the Buddhist canon, presumably handed down orally from the time of the Buddha, enunciated regularly at the assembly of monks, and maintained as the code of living. Any deviation from the rules incurred penalties. See Thanissaro Bhikkhu, *The Buddhist Monastic Code: The Sanskrit Prātimoksa Sūtras of the Mahāsāṃghikas and Mūlasarvāstivādins* (Valley Center, 1994), p. 19. Also, Charles S. Prebish, *Buddhist Monastic Discipline* (University Park: Pennsylvania State University Press, 1975).

[66] "Sugata" is one of the common epithets for the Buddha, meaning literally "one who has gone well," suggesting a sublime quality. The fourth century commentator Buddhaghosa proposes that the Buddha is called the "sugata" because of the manner of going that is good, being gone to an excellent place (*sundaram thanam gatatta*), having gone rightly, and enunciating rightly. In Buddhaghosa's *Visudhhimagga*, VII 33, p. 215.

[67] From the "Prātimoksa Sūtras" of the Mahāsāṃghikas, in Prebish, *Buddhist Monastic Discipline*, p. 54.

any deviation from that measure resulted in an offense. The actual measure of the *sugata* dimension has not been without controversy for different texts suggest different measures for the Buddha, often making it absurdly high. However, a reasonable estimation of the dimensions of the Buddha makes the sugata span 25 cm. such that "applied to the various rules, this would give us a hut 3 x 1.75 meters – small, but adequate…"[68] The dimension corresponds very well with the well-known ten-square-feet hut of the thirteenth-century Japanese writer Kamo-no-Chōmei in his *Hōjōki* that further recalls the dimension of the magical house of the Mahāyāna figure Vimalakīrti.[69]

The house of fragrance establishes an identity between the ascetic and his dwelling by the fact that the two coexist in the same space in which one may be substituted by the other. An intimacy, and thus an interchangeability, between body and building is generated by the fact that the dweller is the only occupant of the space that is unmediated by others. The intimacy is established by the dimensional property of the space, in which the space does not seem to be an ensemble of places creating a topography of here and there. The space could be seen as the projection of the body, like a garment, that in its closest proximity as a layer, sheathes or envelops the body. A dimensional proximity is crucial for strengthening the intimacy, and for the space to be associative of the dweller. In many images, especially from Buddhist Gandhāra, Brahmanic hermits and ascetics are depicted outside their dwellings that are, in dimension and size, not much larger than a robe they might wear.

This primal intimacy is the basis for a fundamental anthropological exchange between a dweller and his dwelling. It is fundamental because we are considering a single subject, not immediately obligated to the exigency of the family, the next level of normative socialized association. I am not proposing the correspondence as a mystical unity of some sort, but as a vivid illustration of an ontological intertwining of corporeality and spatiality, in which each can still articulate the other. It is in this sense that dwelling, along with clothing, becomes the critical zone of intimacy between the ascetic and the world.[70] The *digambara* ascetics among the Jainas are described as sky-clad since they go about fully naked, and consider the wide space as their garment such that the zone of intimacy is totally unmediated.

It is this ontological intimacy that forms the basis of a heightened symbolic articulation of the ascetic figure through architectural means. One recurrent motif in Buddhist representational art is the framing of a Buddha figure by a "caitya" arch. There are sculptures of the Buddha, mostly from the Gandhāra region from around the third to first century BCE, where a seated Buddha figure is placed within an architectural frame in which the shape of the frame follows closely the contour of the Buddha body. There are a number of versions of this frame, from a somewhat rectilinear configuration to a simple pointed arch or a particular form that looks like a "tri-lobed arch."[71] The latter is the shape of

[68] Thanissaro Bhikkhu, *The Buddhist Monastic Code*, p. 529.

[69] Vimalakīrti's house forms a core of the narrative in the very influential 1st c. CE Mahāyāna text, the *Vimalakīrtinirdeśasūtra*, translated by Robert A. F. Thurman as *The Holy Teaching of Vimalakīrti* (University Park: Pennsylvania State University Press, 1976). *The Hōjōki* is a well-known Japanese thirteenth century CE text by Kamo-no-Chomei, translated by A. L. Sadler (Westport: Greenwood Press, 1971).

[70] Lodging and clothing, along with food and medicine, are considered the nissayas, the four essential elements by which the monks (*bhikkhus*) negotiate the world. The *nissayas* are described in the *Vīnayapitakas* as part of the monastic codes, something that are resources for sustenance. Literally, the *nissayas* are something on which "anything depends," that is, the necessities of life upon which the life of a Buddhist monk depended. See *The Pali-English Dictionary*.

[71] *Alfred Foucher, Les Bas-Reliefs gréco-Bouddhique du Gandhāra* (Paris: Imprimerie Nationale, 1904), p. 129.

[72] Coomaraswamy notes how the caitya shape is quite widespread in the description and representation of early Indian architecture. He also discusses the overlap and differentiations between *caitya*-window, *candraśālā*, and *gavāksa* window. See Coomaraswamy, "Indian Architectural Terms" (1927), reprinted in *Essays in Early Indian Architecture*, p. 76.

The Mughal emperor Akbar visiting Baba Bilas, Mughal miniature painting (Chester Beatty Library, Dublin).

Harmika atop a votive stupa with chaitya-arch openings, Bhaja (from J. Burgess, *Report on Buddhist Cave Temples*).

The Buddha under a distended lintel in a domed pavillion (drawing by Raphael Tran based on an image from Gandhara).

The two *gandhikutis* at Jetavana arama, from a stele, Bharhut.

the so-called *caitya* façade that characterizes the architectural physiognomy of many Buddhist architecture, including the gandhakuti at Jetavana depicted on the Bhārhut relief.[72] In Gandhāra art, besides being used to sheath the figure of the seated Buddha, the arches are used to frame significant icons or even pictorial narratives from various Buddhistic themes. In any case, it appears that the shape of the seated figure "fits" perfectly the contour of the arch, the lower segment enclosing the splayed legs of the seated ascetic, and the upper segment bulges out to sheath the head and the upper body. The *caitya* arch, contoured by the figure of the seated ascetic as it were, appears in various forms in cultic practices often without the literal representation of the Buddha.[73]

The intimacy suggested by the framing device also indicates a paradox when considering the house of an arch-ascetic as the Buddha. Although the framing device does not lead immediately to an understanding of the hut/house, it nonetheless suggests an elementary architectural system that corresponds to the profile of a hut. Among the framing devices, images show either an orthogonal frame in which the topmost horizontal lintel is deformed or distended, or an arched shape where the central "peak" makes room for the intercepting head of the Buddha (or, in some pieces, other important figures). One possible interpretation of the "distended lintel" is that it seems to be on the verge of being deformed by the potent and supra-human ascetic who can no longer be contained within the sheltering structure. It would seem that as much as the sheltering space is a necessity, the framing is finally challenged by the greater reality of an "enlightened," larger than life figure. This is the paradox that may have haunted Buddhist artists: How to in-frame (shelter) an arch-ascetic, a superman, who no longer can be contained within it?

The "distended lintel" is particularly illustrative of the inherent paradoxical nature of asceticism. Without a textual explanation it would be convenient to describe it as a conventional decorative device, but it would be an oversight not to remark, even in a speculative manner, on this rather odd architectonic frame that appears frequently in Buddhist art. The trapezoidal frame initially performs as some kind of shelter that demarcates a special zone for sacral objects or images. But, in its distended condition, the framing represents or visualizes the aporetic nature of the super-ascetic – the "perfected" one who has gained enlightenment, as someone of this world but who can no longer be contained within it. The distended architectural frame serves a dual purpose, and by doing so negotiates the ascetic paradox: it signifies the world, and at the same time a transcendence from it. The representation is then simultaneously of a shelter that is being superseded by a superman. The lintel, like the *ushnīsha*, is thus a sign of the *excessive* nature of the enlightened human being, of his breaking forth.

Harmikā: The Zero Point

With the passing away of the Buddha, a new set of symbolic and representational imperatives arise in Buddhist traditions

[73] See above, ff. 31-33.

[74] Although there was a tradition of making funerary mounds before the time of the Buddha, it was after his passing away that the construction of stūpas as hemispherical relic or funerary mound gained momentum within Buddhism.

[75] In the seventh century CE Ashrafpur Bronze Chaitya (found in present-day Bangladesh), the Buddha is actually seen sitting in a hut. For image, see *Eastern Indian School of Medieval Sculpture*, published as *The Archaeological Survey of India*, Vol. XLVII (1933).

(some of which have started at his own time). The stūpa as a commemorative structure is one of the most important edifices of early Buddhism, a building practice that began immediately after the passing away of the Buddha.[74]

On top of most Buddhist stūpas there is a cubical structure known as the *harmikā* whose significance, although not fully deciphered, makes it the most polysemic and enigmatic object in Buddhist architecture. In fact, the *harmikā* and the stūpa form a highly charged symbolic ensemble in Buddhism. The harmikā is a distinctive feature of the Buddhist stūpa: it adorns the apex of stūpas, in most cases, as a cubical structure through which arises a vertical post (*yasti*) with a series of parasols. The form of the *harmikā* varies from a simple enclosure (without the post-parasol ensemble) to fully enclosed "boxes," to unequivocal depiction of a dwelling. There are instances of smaller votive stūpas in which the *harmikā* is clearly an architectonic structure, depicted sometimes as a hut-like piece,[75] and even as an elaborate multi-storied mansion.[76] One of the votive stūpas at Bhaja is remarkable in that two of the levels in the multi-leveled stūpa show what I have described as the "*chaitya*-arch." It is plausible that this representation was derived from conventional houses of that time, and then conveyed in a stylized way. But the *chaitya*-arch is also a motif that has been used for the *gandhakuti* in various representations of Jetavana offering a possible link to the Buddha's house. If the *harmikā* is also the Buddha's house, what kind of a house is this?

While the literal meaning of the term *harmikā* is a "little dwelling,"[77] there is no unanimity as to what extant the *harmikā* may be regarded as a dwelling, or as to what it signifies in the elaborate symbolical scheme of the stūpa, even when some *harmikās* depict the profile of a Jetavana *gandhakuti*. The *harmikā* refers not so much to a pragmatic residence but to a notional dwelling of the Buddha, something that may be seen as a final halting place in conceptualizing the ascetical itinerary.

Among the various connotations of the *harmikā*, it has been considered as a tomb, coffin or sarcophagus, all of which perhaps refer to the pre-Buddhist practice of creating a mound or some kind of edifice over the remains of a special person. It is first by referring to the symbolism of the dwelling of "death" that the *harmikā* might be described as the final or last abode.[78] *Dhātugarbha*, or womb chamber, is a term that was applied to the *harmikā* before it was used for the stūpa where a funerary idea and an abode become conflated.[79] The notion of the dwelling of "death" is further supported by considering the *harmikā* as a *kūtāgāra*, the initiation hut, or a house in which one dies in order to be reborn.[80] A funerary purpose enters here not in the sense of a literal death but rather in the sense of one who dies only to be "born" as a transformed self. The ascetic finality of receiving "enlightenment" or gaining "awakening" is interpreted as the penultimate transformation of the meditative ascetic, also understood as a climactic dying to this world. This dual meaning of attaining "awakening" and "dying" to the world is poignantly carried by the term *samādhi*. *Samādhi* is the yogic term for the

[76] The stūpas at Sāncī, Bhārhut and Amrāvatī show the *harmikā* in the form of a simple enclosure of vedikā railings. There are more elaborate *harmikās*, as in certain stūpas in interior *caitya*-halls, votive stūpas and represented stūpas in relief art. The one in Bhājā [date unknown] mentioned here is far the most elaborate, showing a mansion of sort with details like the *caitya*-arch windows.

[77] *Harmya* in Sanskrit is a dwelling (*Atharva Veda*), "a beautiful palace," see Coomaraswamy "Indian Architectural Terms," in *Early Indian*, p. 80. The *Divyādāna* describes the *hārmika* simply as "a little structure on the stūpa," noted by H. Sarkar, *Studies in Early Buddhist Architecture of India* (Delhi: Munshilal Manoharlal, 1966), p. 12. Sarkar also echoes the words of the 5th century commentator Buddhaghosa by comparing the *hārmika* to the *kūtāgāra*, a sort of sky-room or lookout space on the top level of a multi-terraced building.

[78] J. Przyluski identifies the *hārmika* as continuing the practice of Brahmanic square tombs; it may be noted that it was only the hermit who was given a befitting burial, in "The Hārmika and the Origin of Buddhist Stūpas" in *The Indian Historical Quarterly*, Vol. 11 (June 1935). James Fergusson's opinion was that the hārmika is the location of a physical relic of an arahant, either in a coffin or a vessel, see John Irwin, "The Axial Symbolism of the Early Stupa: An Exegesis," in Anna Dallapiccola (ed.), *The Stupa* (Wisebaden: Franz Steiner Verlag, 1980).

[79] A. Snodgrass, *The Symbolism of the Stupa* (Ithaca: SEAP, 1985), p. 254. Snodgrass cites the work of Anagarika Govinda, Stella Kramrisch, and James Fergusson. Snodgrass especially comments on the correspondence between the *harmikā* and the *āmalaka* on the Hindu temple, and the common theme of the "Cosmic Egg."

[80] The Mahāyāna text *Lalita Vistara*, Ch. 7 (possibly from the third century CE) mentions that the pavilion occupied by the Bodhisattva while in his mother's womb is called a *kūtāgāra*, as noted by Coomaraswamy in "Indian Architectural Terms," Essays, p. 86-87. But Coomaraswamy goes on to note that *kūtāgāra* may ultimately suggest an "honorable building," or simply "a house with a finial (or finials)." Coomaraswamy discusses the *kūtāgāra* as a room at the top or something as "soaring," in "Early Indian Architecture: III. Palaces," *Essays*, pp. 43-44. Symbolically, the *kūtāgāra* refers to the structure of metamorphosis, in which one enters, dies to this world, and is born anew.

[81] Eliade, *Yoga*, p. 77.

[82] In that sense, the harmika is like the *āmalaka*, the fluted melon-shaped object, placed as a coping stone on the peak of North Indian Hindu temples. The symbolism here, as in the *harmikā* and

last stage for meditational practice; it is also the tomb of a holy person.[81]

The locational relationship of the *harmikā* in the geography of the stupa provides a more contextual understanding of this penultimate condition.[82] Echoing the words of the 13th century commentator Buddhaghosa, H. Sarkar compares the *harmikā* to the literal meaning of *kūtāgāra*, a sort of sky-room or lookout space in a multi-terraced building, or more simply described, a piece located at the apex of a larger ensemble that.[83] Paul Mus takes that image up in more symbolic terms by seeing it as a "hut on a mountain top," where the stūpa signifies a world-mountain.[84] To Stella Kramrisch, the image of a structure on the mountain-top refers to the "high temple," and such a locational structure marks the point of a potent transition. Kramrisch describes the "high temple" as representing "the zenithal pole of realization where this world ends and that world begins," and, by doing so marks "the point limit of the manifest and the unmanifest, the Bindu."[85] The *harmikā* is also likened to a caitya-vrksa at the top of the world-mountain, whereupon the *harmikā -yasti* ensemble becomes analogous to the "world tree" and the "cosmic axis,"[86] and by doing so demarcates a sacred space (*bodhimanda*).[87]

With the stupa interpreted as an embodiment of the structure of ascetic meditation, the *harmikā* is also seen as a crucial mark, a very particular moment in the rising planes of yogic or ascetic consciousness.[88] The meditational symbolism is rendered in corporeal terms in certain Nepalese stūpa in which the *hārmika* is decorated with painted human eyes, "thus suggesting a human figure in the posture of meditation hidden in the stūpa: the crossed legs in the base, the body up to the shoulders in the hemisphere, the head in the *harmikā*."[89]

With the apex of the stūpa as a transformative and dynamic marker, the significance of the stūpa is amplified through further analogy with the idealized body of the Buddha, especially in iconic representations. In mapping ascetic physiology, Kramrisch identifies the *ushnīsha*, the cranial protuberance that purportedly occurs at the climax of ascetic meditation, as the "zero point of Nirvāna." The *ushnīsha* signifies both the limit and rupture of the anthropomorphic figure, and represents all that is "non-representable" in the physiological experience of the engaged ascetic. In other words, it is an *excess*. "At the zero-point, there can be no identity of any extent. Still, if this is to be conveyed by the image, a symbol, a no-thing may do it: the Usnisa."[90] Similarly, Ananda Coomaraswamy interprets the *harmikā* as the liminality of understanding, the very edge of production, proliferation and expression that makes up our cognitive, experiential, and normative world. Coomaraswamy remarks about the stūpa that: "All that is mortal [is] contained within, and all that is immortal exceed[s] the structure."[91] Clearly, the *harmikā* visibly marks that tenuous point, the threshold of embodiment, and it's excess.

In this symbolically charged scenario, the innocuous little dwelling presents a vibrant polysemy: The *harmikā* is both an image and

the *āmalaka*, is that of an egg, bringing up association with the sun, the sun being Brahma in Vedic symbolism having been born from a "Cosmic Egg." See Snodgrass, *Stupa*, p. 254, ff. 75.

[83] H. Sarkar, *Studies,* p. 12.

[84] Paul Mus, "Barabadur," in *Bulletin de l'Ecole Francaise d'Extreme-Orient* 32 (1932).

[85] Stella Kramrisch, *The Hindu Temple* (Calcutta: University of Calcutta, 1946).

[86] Snodgrass, *Stupa*, p. 256.

[87] Snodgrass, *Stupa*, p. 257.

[88] As Roth notes in tune with other commentators, the *harmikā* signifies the Eightfold Path in "Stūpa-laksana," and marks the constituent of enlightenment known as "born on the fourth ground of meditation" which results in not returning to this existence. Gustav Roth, *Ārāma, Vihāra and Mahāvihāra* (Patna, 1997), p. 194. This is a based on a broader application of the identification of the stūpa with the body of the Buddha as mentioned in the Lalitavistara, noted by Benisti, *Etude sur le Stupe*, p. 51.

[89] Lama Angarika Govinda, *Pyscho-Cosmic Symbolism of the Buddhist Stūpa* (Emeryville, CA: Dharma Publications, 1976), p. 6.

[90] S. Kramrisch, "Note on Usnisa," *Journal of the Indian Society of Oriental Art* 4 (1936).

[91] Coomaraswamy, "Symbolism of the Dome," reprinted in *Selected Papers*, p. 437.

structure of "awakening," a locus of the final transformation of the ascetic. Akin to the condition of dying and being born anew, "awakening" corresponds to a critical initiation in certain ascetic interpretation. The phenomenon is emblematized when the *harmikā* is placed in its critical spatial location either in the geography of the stūpa, or analogically, as *ushnīsha*, in the physiognomy of the iconic Buddha. Both conditions point to the *harmikā* as a heightened moment, as nirvāna embodied, and as paradoxical as this may seem, as an embodiment of which cannot be visually realized. In other words, the *harmikā* is the last vestige of embodiment or incorporation, or as Stella Kramrisch describes the *ushnīsha*, the *harmikā* is the "zero point."[92]

Despite the profusion of symbolisms, the *harmikā* refers to something close at hand: a finality. The *harmikā* as the house of "enlightenment" is the final dwelling that is metaphorically constructed on the body of the stūpa, or analogized on the figure of the Buddha that can *still* be envisioned as part of the ascetic journey. It is the image of the last vestige of things that binds one corporeally and cognitively to the world; it is, in fact, the *last* thing. The *harmikā* is a glimpse of the "last" hut before the unspeakable nothingness.

The Last Hut

"The rafters are shattered, the ridge-pole is destroyed, and the house-builder will no longer be able to erect the house again."
- *The Dhammapada* [93]

If a sense of finality is conveyed by the *hārmika*, it appears in a much more cataclysmic manner in the language employed to account for the penultimate experience of the ascetic: enlightenment. The most literal and volatile imagery of the end of architecture may be found in a statement attributed to the Buddha when he reached an ascetic climax at the end of his arduous meditation. The description from the *Dhammapada* is a compelling evidence of the conceptual conflation of body and building.

In many ascetic narratives, the body is a hut whose existing lineaments and ligaments must be shattered before the enlightened life can begin.[94] The shattering of the roof-rafters (*vivata chado*) is the most cataclysmic expression in visualizing the transformative termination of the ascetic practice.[95]

The concept of "awakening" is undoubtedly the goal of Indic ascetic labor, including Buddhism.[96] Even though "awakening" is a precise climactic moment, it is preceded by a sequence of renunciatory rites (*samnyas*), and disciplined labor (*ascesis*, *srama*). The sequence is both sociological and physiological. The sociological sequence represents the literal renunciation of society and family, and the initiation into the ascetic mode. The physiological sequence represents a psycho-physiological transformation that begins with corporeal exertions (*ascesis*) towards a both subtle and cataclysmic transformation of the normative body.[97] The finality of "awakening" is conceived of in volatile terms. And when that moment is to be represented, either in literary, iconographic or architectural form, there is a

[92] S. Kramrisch, "Emblems of the Universal Being," *Journal of the Indian Society of Oriental Art* III (1935).

[93] *Dhammapada*, Verse 154: "Looking for the maker of this tabernacle I ran to no avail through a round of many births; and wearisome is birth again and again. But now, maker of the tabernacle, thou hast been seen; thou shalt not rear this tabernacle again. All thy rafters are broken, thy ridge-pole is shattered; the mind approaching the Eternal, has attained to the extinction of all desires."

[94] On numerous occasions, yogic ascesis itself is spoken of in architectural terms. The *Milindapanhā* mentions that the five skilled mental states – the five cardinal virtues – are moral habit, faith, energy, mindfulness, and concentration, the last being the chief among them. "As in a house with a ridge-pole all the rafters go to the ridge-pole, lean towards it and join it, and the ridge-pole is pointed to as their chief, even so all those mental states that are skilled have concentration (*samādhi*) as the chief, they lean, tend, and incline towards concentration." Similarly, the *Majjhima-Nikāya* mentions: "Just as the roof plate of a domed mansion is the peak that ties together and holds together, just so the sheltering roof of the skilful habits (is the peak that ties together and holds together) the six states of consciousness." (*Majjhima Nikāya* I.,322-23, cited by Snodgrass, *The Symbolism of the Stupa*, p. 281.) It is this architectural analogy that will facilitate the equation of the attainment of final "awakening" with the dramatic shattering of the roof-plate or ridge-pole.

[95] Various parables echo this theme, as when the Buddha uses the story of breaking the shell to enter a transformed life, a "second birth," described in the *Suttavibanga*, and discussed by Paul Mus, "La notion de temps reversible dans la mythologique bouddhique," extracts in *l'Annuaire de l'Ecole Pratique des hautes Etudes* (1938), p. 13; and, *Eliade, Images and Symbols: Studies in Religious Symbolism* (New York: Sheed and Ward, 1961, paperback 1969), pp. 77-78.

[96] The English term "awakening" along with "liberation," "enlightenment," "transparency," or "emptiness," falls in the cluster of terms suggestive of the ascetic goal. The Buddhist concept is expounded through two Sanskrit terms: "nirvāna" and "sunnyata." There are different explanations within Buddhism itself, but it can be said that a principal difference with other ascetic ideologies is that the Buddhist achievement is a completely human endeavor and devoid of any supernatural or divine component, and metaphysical import.

[97] See Julius Evola on "the phenomenology of liberation," in *The Doctrine of Awakening* (London: Luzac Press, 1951), pp. 191-202.

[98] The Pali term *gāha* (Sanskrit *grihá*,

challenge in expressing that peculiarly ineffable moment.

The nirvanic moment, articulated as freedom from the so-called fetters of the world, precipitates an architectural destruction, in which the body of the aspirant ascetic uses the hut as a trope, and the moment as a climactic and dramatic shattering of the rafters. The villain in the larger ascetic narrative is *gāha*,[98] the house in its most immediate sense of being-in-the-world, socially, familially and phenomenally. It is the primordial means of rootedness, and one of the principal foundations and causes for craving, be it biological or societal. It is craving, in one form or another, that generates the cycle of activities sheltered in a dwelling – birth, life, death. The Buddha identified the presence of being in this world with being in a dwelling, that is, being within a confined, enclosed, and defined space as *gāha*.[99] No doubt, a whole world of sociological, political, familial, and ritual dimensions are implicated in that sense of being in a *gāha*.

While the Buddha needs a real house for his dwelling, ideationally he is saying that the moment of enlightenment means that the need for dwelling is over, that is, social dwelling as a condensation of suffering, impermanence, and desire. From then on the relationship to the pragmatic dwelling is one of detachment. From the Buddha's perspective, the hut/house is not something to be adored; it is regarded as the last vestige of attachment. When the Buddha employs the hut as a metaphor for ascetic liberation, it is only a metaphor; there are no real equivalents to it. The volatile, destructive imagery of *vivata-chado*, is one of resurrective death, of dying to this world, and being born again in order to create another "human," a body more purified and superior.[100]

Prkarit *ghara*) in its root meaning refers to girdling and encirclement, as a means of defining territory and at the same time marking the edge that protects the central area. *Grihá* is house, habitation, home in Vedic texts, and forms various compound words. *Geha* is a corrupted form of *grihá*, still meaning house, dwelling, habitation in later texts, including the *Mahābhārata*. Etymology suggests a possible link between *gāha* and *ghere*, to surround, to bound. Monier-Williams, *A Sanskrit-English Dictionary*.

99 *The Majjhima Nikāya* I, 241. The Buddha describes that state of being as a confinement: "[it] occurred to me that life in the home is cramped and dirty, while the life gone forth into homelessness is wide open; it is difficult to live a spiritual life completely perfect and pure in all its parts while cabined inside."

100 Mircea Eliade, "Cosmical Homology and Yoga," in *Journal of the Indian Society of Oriental Art* 5 (1937). Eliade writes: "It is known that the characteristic of yoga practices, and chiefly of Patanjali's *Yoga*, is to create another "man," more purified, more unitary, who in his turn is being destroyed and replaced by another one, a superior one."

Inside of Gandhi's Bapu Kuti in Wardha, Nagpur.

Interior of a Japanese teahouse.

The Architecture of Asceticism

Introduction from the book, *The Hermit's Hut: Architecture and Asceticism in India* (University of Hawai'i Press, 2013), written 2010 (partially reproduced here).

He looks at his house with (the words): 'Give us a house, O Fathers!'
—Gobila Gṛhya Sūtra[1]

I refuse a roof.
—Dhutaṇga practitioner[2]

With the declaration, "Architect, you shall not build your house again," Gautama Siddhārtha[3] announces his arrival at the critical destination called nirvāṇa, and acquires the qualities of a *mahāsamana*, a super-ascetic.[4] Siddhārtha, likening his ascetically charged body to a building, describes the inconceivable and ineffable moment of becoming the Buddha. In that pairing between body and building, architecture is positioned for a portentous destiny in Buddhist imagination. This is made evident when the Buddha provides a cataclysmic scenario for the momentous turn of the building-body. "The roof rafters are shattered," he announces, and "the roof is destroyed." The metaphor, while narrating the engineering of the ascetic body, is also an evidence of the deeply imbricated significance of architecture in ascetic discourse and practices. The image of a building has already come to haunt the imagination of asceticism.

Six years earlier, the Buddha, then known as Siddhārtha, had awakened in his magnificent palace in Kapilavāstu, and like so many others before him motivated by a similar compulsion, stole in the middle of the night to leave home and family, the core of dwelling. Thus ensues the operatic process of renunciation and asceticism. Searching for answers to some burning existential questions and looking for pathways for a liberation from suffering as he saw them, Siddhārtha wandered through forests and glades, living under trees or in some basic shelters, and visiting the āśramas of sages and hermits. While the ascetic Siddhārtha will eventually find his climactic answer, as conveyed in the narrative of the destroyed house-body, and go on to propound a world turning philosophy and disciplined institution of monastic practices, he, as well as his disciples and followers after him, will continue to be vexed by the fundament that he began with, the matter of dwelling.

[1] *Gobila Gṛhya Sūtra*, IV.3.24.

[2] A declaration of the *dhutaṇga* practitioner, an isolated type of ascetic active in the earliest period of Buddhism, as described by the fifth-century Buddhist commentator and scholar Buddhaghosa in his *Visuddhimagga* (The Path of Purification).

[3] The Pali form of the name is Gotama Siddhattha. The Buddha refers here to the historical figure of Gautama Siddhārtha who presumably lived between 543 and 483 BCE, having been born and raised as a prince in the northern city-state of Kapilavāstu (now in present day-Nepal).

[4] These lines are from the *Dhammapada*, Verse 154. Part of the Pali canon, the *Dhammapada* is a collection of statements and sayings attributed to the Buddha. Different translations give different terms for "gahakāraka," from house-builder, house-maker, maker of tabernacle to architect. Similarly, the word "geha" has been translated as house, home, and tabernacle.

After having renounced house and home, even the Buddha will require some form of lodging. So will his followers. Dwelling for the super-ascetic will include living under a tree, in a cave, or a simple shelter. Each of these conditions, prosaic as may seem, will be occasions for a continuous debate and struggle in various ascetic circles on the nature of dwelling, its minimal requirements and implications in the life of an ascetic. Some of these deliberations, continuing for well hundreds of years after the Buddha, will form the core of ritual and regulatory texts for monks. Prescribed with an ideal life of wandering and alms-collecting, the earliest group of Buddhist monks encountered the exigency of dwelling during the rainy seasons of north India. Stalling the practice of wandering, the monks were urged to take up temporary residence for the wet period. The matter of temporary dwellings in the rain led to the formation of stable and permanent monasteries. Even the Buddha is assigned an address and lodging. He may be moving from city to city, teaching and preaching, but he stayed in particular compounds in each city and lived in a dedicated building. From what we know, such buildings were simple and unassuming compared to elaborate houses in the city, but the house of the Buddha, known as the *gandhakuṭī* or the fragrant hut, came to receive a focused attention from monks and laypeople, and remains a source of didactic and philosophical reflection in Buddhist asceticism.

It appears that the matter of dwelling, addressed as a house or hut, is a critical factor in the trajectory of the ascetic project. Or to see it in another way, the narratives of asceticism are deeply etched by the profile of a hut. In the Mahāyāna story of Vimalakīrti, a transformation of a mansion emblematizes the profound and subtle notions around "emptiness." The story relates how the ascetically empowered merchant Vimalakīrti, upon learning the impending arrival of a large emissary from the Buddha to his mansion-like house, divests it of all things, that is, makes it empty so that it can hold multitudes.[5] Vimalakīrti is most likely an apocryphal figure, and so is the narrative of the transformation of the house, but in the *Vimalakīrti Nirdeśa Sūtra*, the story of the magical mutation of the house from fullness to emptiness becomes a discourse on ascetic prerogatives and motivations. Little was anticipated how the story of a well-to-do man of the world transforming his mansion in the city to a plain, empty house, might impact the fabrication of dwelling. Vimalakīrti's emptied house is neither a hut nor a hovel, but it imbues all such structures with a resolute significance that belongs to a very particular human type, the hermit, the ascetic, or the recluse.[6]

With the *gandhakuṭī* or Vimalakīrti's emptied house, we are already deep in ascetic territory where the hut comes to represent the inner nature of the practice. We can never know when the hut – the dwelling – comes into focus in the ascetic consciousness, and becomes an object of intense deliberation and narrativization for the first time. Before it becomes codified in doctrines and practices, and subsequently gets subsumed in the building of monasteries, the hut-dwelling is part of an existential experience. Food and clothing are also two critical, existential categories that define the parameter and practice of

[5] This particular narrative is found in the *Vimalakīrti Nirdeśa Sūtra*, an important Mahāyāna text composed around 100 CE that expounds on the notion of "emptiness" or *śūnyatā* through conversations with the bodhisattva lay figure Vimalakīrti. A Tibetan version has been translated as *The Holy Teachings of Vimalakīrti* by Robert A.F. Thurman (University Park: Pennsylvania State University Press, 1976).

[6] Vimalakīrti's mythopoeic mansion rematerializes, in Japan, in the shack the twelfth-century courtier-turned-renunciant Kamo no Chōmei built for himself in a forest outside Kyoto, and the teahouse fashioned and codified by the sixteenth-century tea-master Sen no Rikyū.

Gandhi's Bapu Kuti, Wardha. Photo: Ashraf.

Votive stupa, from the Indian Museum, Kolkata.

asceticism but neither receives the wide range of discursive and conceptual treatment as the plain hut. The ascetic hut becomes critical because it is no mere object of reflection but a metonym of that reflection; the hut stands for how asceticism structures its intentions and practices.

All these experiences began earlier, in the historical and sometimes fabulous period in time when people left home and society for a journey into the disciplined world of asceticism. Buildings belonging to hermits and ascetics have actually appeared in the horizon since the first human walked out of home to reconfigure one's relationship to the world, and understanding of oneself. Since then, these simple structures – huts, hovels, shacks and other forms of reductive structures – have played a critical, yet paradoxical, role in cultural imagination. While asceticism is understood as a practice of renunciation and reduction, it also involves quite intrinsically an architectural project with immediate implications of spatial rootedness and material embellishment. In fact, the ascetic hut, despite an inherent image of plainness and reduction, is implicated in the development of grand and monumental architecture. The magisterial cathedrals of Gothic Europe, the exquisite temples and gardens of Buddhist Japan, and the elaborate Hindu temples of India, all have evolved, in one way or another, from a meditation on reductive dwellings. The minimal, ascetic hut seems to be, rather intriguingly, a source for an amplified architecture.

The essays in this book investigate how a hut belonging to the ascetic structures the world of elaboration. The geographical, historical, and phenomenological site of the study is ancient India, and its traditions of asceticism especially in the practices of Buddhism.[7] With pragmatic practices and ideological deliberations of asceticism centered on the hut, as noted earlier, the structure remains as a repository of significances. However, in the historiography of Indian architecture, the ascetic hut has for most part vanished from the horizon; there is little discussion of possible originary connections between elaborate temples and this mundane, nondescript structure. Far less discussed is how that connection may have augmented venerated architectural ideas or anthropological paradigms. The lacuna seems troubling when there is sufficient evidence that a simple building such as the hut formed the morphology and character of monumental architecture; it can be shown that an unremarkable space such as the ascetic dwelling informed the anthropological and symbolic content of elaborate buildings. The act of disappearance of the hut also indicates that it has been absorbed in an increasingly refined architectural scheme or diffused in a world of ideas and imagination. With the presence of the hut confined to allusions and fragments in architectural, literary and ritual repositories, the recovery of the plan and profile of that hut requires a process akin to an archaeological excavation.

[partial text]

[7] The traditions of Buddhism, despite the identity of heterogeneity and distinctiveness, maintain an intricate link with both pre-Buddhist and non-Buddhist practices. A discussion of Buddhist architecture and ideology invariably invokes the other traditions.

Kinkakuji, The Temple of the Golden Pavilion, now and after the fire in 1950. Source: author and http://maizuru-walker.hp.infoseek.co.jp/zatsugaku/047/index.htm.

Postmortem: Building Destruction

Published in *Architecture Post Mortem: The Diastolic Architecture of Decline, Dystopia and Death,* edited by Donald Kunze, David Bertolini, and Simone Brott (Ashgate Studies in Architecture, Routledge, Oxfordshire, 2013).

The art of building contains the finer art of destruction.

To build is to be human may appear axiomatic, but human beings also bear an enigmatic impulse for the destruction of their own fabrications. The incendiary beauty of a burning building is both awful and awesome, making us beholden in a kind of a catatonic grip to something we understand vaguely. And whatever we seem to understand, we hardly acknowledge.

The demolition of Veterans Stadium in Philadelphia in 2004 was not only a spectacular event but a demonstration of an intractable lure for the coming down of a construction. Televised for two whole days, the implosion was presented as a magnificent theater of dismantling. "It was so cool," many spectators exclaimed, while nearby residents bemoaned the vanishing of a familiar landmark. Perhaps such obliteration is destined as the life-cycle or utility of a building runs out. But buildings have been marked for an episodic downfall so that new wonders may arise. The iconic demolition of Pruitt-Igoe Housing in St. Louis (1972) and the patricidal drowning of Mies van der Rohe's Crown Hall in Stanley Tigerman's photo-montage marked the passing away of a regime in anticipation of a new one. From the sacrificial ashes and rubbles rises the unashamed rhetoric of the avant-garde. Nietzsche is invoked.

Presented at the outset, a provisional typology of building destructions suggests the following: *nihilistic* (most famously, the apocryphal scene of Nero playing the lyre while the city burnt, or Pompeii or Fukushima ravaged by a natural disaster), *tactical* (triumphal destruction of cities from Alexander to Genghiz Khan, the blitzkrieg of Second World War, or the demolition of Babri Masjid in India in 1992), and *transitional*, one that leads to the release of a new epoch (Pruitt-Igoe or Philadelphia's Veterans Stadium). The tilt of this essay is neither towards the nihilistic nor the tactical mode although one cannot completely escape either in a narrative on destruction. Transition is perhaps an endemic condition in the phenomenon of destruction but something that needs to be analyzed as a thing in itself. Instead of offering a sociological or pathological explanation for all building catastrophes, one is drawn here, like moth to fire, to provide a risky metaphor, to meditations on a fourth type: contrived or ritualized destructions.

Even if building ends with construction, the story is not completely over as something begins anew from annihilation. This essay is a narrative on ritualized destruction, how various practices and performances of de-construction convey a significance contrary to the immediate or literal phenomenon of destruction. If tectonics (in its original link to techne/poeisis) is about appearing and making appear, destruction is about the presencing of an absence; it is not simply an antinomy, but making an otherwise appear. A vivid example is the blowing away of a Tibetan sand-mandala after its meticulous construction, or the weaving of baskets by Abba Paul, a Desert Father, and burning them at the end each year. Such a phenomenon may be approached by a number of concept-heavy terms: sacrifice, death, dismemberment, disappearance, "un-building," or what Gordon Matta-Clark called "anarchitecture." In any of these conceptual horizons, there is a narratival or ritual continuity to what may appear to be an abrupt end. Destruction means a second chance, or in theological term, a resurrection, or in ascetical sense, an alchemical transformation, leaving one body for another. There is always something else.

Destruction is always mobilized around a figural substance, often bringing a convergence of the anthropological and architectural body. A contrived destruction of the building-body is one of the oldest and recurrent tropes in architecture. Whether it is the body constructed in the tectonic framework of a building, or the building formed in the ligaments of a body, both fall victim to a homicide or *bauicide*, as the case may be. Body and building are bound together in a bond of violence that re- or de-form each other. The ritual destruction of buildings is found in diverse situations: Many emblems and elements on Greek temples are lithified versions of sacrificial objects. The Ise Shrine in Japan is taken apart and rebuilt every twenty years. The Hindu mandala is created on the dismembered body of a mysterious being (Vastupurusa) upon which arises temples or cities. Rituals for gaining adulthood in certain tribal cultures were performed through breaking down special huts. The roof is a favorite trope of destruction: Shamans or Buddhist arhats conceived illuminative ecstasy as breaking through the roof.

James Frazer notes how Dieris of Australia tore through the roof of a special hut to initiate the arrival of rain. There is, in short, blood on the body of architecture.

The following sections present five post-mortems performed on departed bodies of architecture. The narratives intend not only to expand the significance of demolition, dismemberment and disappearance, but invoke the epistemic question of whether destruction can be studied. If we are to pursue a theory for building destruction, the narratives suggest both a preliminary horizon for that mysterious event and provisional mapping of architectural violence. There are few questions that are left suspended for a later analysis: Does destruction precede construction? Or, is construction always followed by destruction? Is destruction implicit in construction? Is destruction antithetical to construction? The following anticipatory observations are proposed for reading the post-mortem reports:

The drowning of Mies van der Rohe's Crown Hall, by Stanley Tigerman.

Destruction is a beginning. The enactment of destruction has a contractual relationship with pre-established norms and practices. As with Edward Said's meditation on beginnings, one would suggest that there is intention and method in such systematized mayhem. In other words, there is a method to the madness. Every beginning is an occasion of violence, and it is embedded in the very ritual of building.

Destruction disrupts normativity; it involves a transgression or transcendence for which normativity is a required benchmark. Destruction triggers, as in Jacques Derrida's reflection on death, a "rhetoric of borders," a conversation on border making and limit condition. The sense of destruction as an end – final limit – invites an analogy with death. "Seneca describes the absolute imminence, the imminence of death at every instant. The imminence of a disappearance that is by essence premature seals the union of the possible and the impossible, of fear and desire, and of mortality and immortality, in being-to-death." Thus, re-citing Seneca via Derrida, one could say destruction is imminent in building.

Destruction is purposeful. Andrei Tarkovsky's film *Offret* (*The Sacrifice*, 1986) ends with a fiery destruction of a house. (In fact, the end does not begin well in the making of the film. During the final shoot, the camera jams while the house-set is burning. The house had to be rebuilt so it could be burned again). In Tarkovsky's driven meditation on the macrocosmic scope of human annihilation (in the film, nuclear catastrophe), and its microscopic reach into the lives of the individual, the father figure in the film pulls together the material possessions of the family and burns the house down as a kind of barter to save the family. Is this cataclysmic or cathartic? Is it a sacrifice or surrender? Compared to Michelangelo Antonioni's nihilistic and ecstatic destruction of the consumerist house in *Zabriskie Point* (1970), the burning of the dwelling in the eponymous *Sacrifice* is an Abrahamic gift.

As with Siva's bipolar cosmic dance, *destruction is ambiguous*. Destruction is implicated in a doubleness: it is both a silencing and an emergence, a depletion and a regeneration. Its paradoxical kinship with creation is not only non-extractable, but also necessary, as many artists have noted how an oscillation between creation/constructivity and destruction is present ubiquitously in the rhythms or proceedings of nature. The prosaic destiny of the deterioration of buildings receives a discursive doubleness in David Leatherbarrow and Mohsen Mostafavi's notion of "weathering" when they proclaim: "Finishing ends construction, weathering constructs finishes."

Destruction is performative, and as such is materially tenuous (although it needs materiality for that very performance), making the event both unsettled and unsettling. That is why the artworks of Matta-Clark or Andy Goldsworthy which are literally performed for deterioration rely on the photographic medium for their rhetorical reproduction. The ontology of destruction requires a human agency in the performance and practice.

"Why Did the Monk Burn the Temple?"

The writer Yukio Mishima wondered, as did millions of people, when the news spread that a monk at Kyoto's wondrous temple had burnt it down: "why did the monk do that?" One sultry summer night in 1950, an acolyte priest Hayashi Yoken struck a match to a bundle of dry sticks and threw it at the most beautiful edifice on earth, Kinkakuji, or the Temple of the Golden Pavilion. The building burnt to ashes. Few things are known about Hayashi. The club-footed monk stammered, and before proceeding to burn the temple, went on a drinking binge and visiting prostitutes. But that did not explain why he torched Kyoto's sacred monument.

Mishima was induced to reflect on the mystery of destruction through writing a fictionalized version of events that led to the climactic incendiary moment. Mishima's story, *The Temple of the Golden Pavilion* (1956), recreates the stammering priest Yoken as the fictional Mizoguchi. The book is finally an essay on the question of beauty and the beautiful, and what is one to do when beholden to a thing of beauty that not only confounds a visual apprehension but also challenges a conceptual comprehension. But if beauty is here, can its shadow be far behind. Mizoguchi was both ugly and irresistible. He stuttered, dragged his foot, and presented himself as a miserable creature, a kind of hunchback of Kinkakuji. And that also, as Mizoguchi began to observe, made him an object of people's attention even if it was surreptitious or unacknowledged. In a chain of actions that are both contemplative and concatenated, Mizoguchi homologizes himself with the Golden Pavilion. The object of veneration and the subject of revulsion become alter egos.

Such a homology is however fraught with perplexity. Mizoguchi wondered which one was the "real" Kinkakuji, the temple that his father had described so lovingly when he was a child, the model of the temple that he had seen in another precinct, the Kinkakuji that he serves as an acolyte monk, or the idea of that temple that sediments in the soul of a beholder? And if the destination of a thing of perfect beauty is annihilation, as Mizoguchi arrives at that realization, which one is to be destroyed?

The golden phoenix that perches on the roof of Kinkakuji, as well as the supposed ashes of the Buddha kept in the pavilion, is both a poignant and ironic reminder of the temple's burning destiny, and its convulsive history of destruction and rebuilding (but not quite like the ritual dismantling and reconstruction of Ise Shrine). Kinkakuji was rebuilt after Yoken/Mizoguchi destroyed it in 1950. It was destroyed during a war in the fifteenth century and rebuilt after that.

Yukio Mishima's own life parallels an itinerary of careful construction towards a ritualized annihilation. Identifying his own body as the national/ist ethic, Mishima built up his corporeal body, athletically and militaristically (and auto-erotically), to represent a perfect vision of the nationalist destination. But, in 1970, thwarted by the course of the body politic to give credence to his nationalist vision or to enact a theatrical termination of such edification, or a combination of

Scene of the burning house from Andrei Tarkovsky's *Offret* (1986).

both, Mishima committed *seppuku*, a self-ritualized suicide. In *The Temple of the Golden Pavilion*, Mishima makes complex conjunctions of Buddhist ideas of transitoriness with social and nationalist ethics, all of which comes at a particular historical moment in war-torn Japan. The ambivalence of post-war chaos of Japan and an incendiary illumination of social pathology was reflected in Mishima's first staged play *Kataku* (*The Burning House*, 1948). Drawn from a Buddhist fable in the *Lotus Sutra*, the burning house becomes a metaphor for immersion in and release from a troubled world of sufferings and defilements.

Mishima as the martyred Saint Sebastian.
Photo: Kishin Shinoyama.

"The Rafters Are Shattered"

The young man, emaciated but resolute, sits under the fig tree in a forest, determined not to move until he has found the light. He sits cross-legged but erect, eyes closed but focused, with only one objective: the truth. For eight years he has roamed the forest in search of that elusive target. He had subjected his body to various trials if only truth would show. He remained standing on one leg as a form of penance. He went without food for weeks, his skin and bones were indistinguishable, and yet truth remained concealed and unavailable.

Eight years earlier, he was a prince in a palace, a lucky guy who had it all. Yet, he left home, renounced as people would say, so home or gaha could be abolished forever. Home has not left him; it clung to his body like a leech after one has come out from bathing in an ancient pond.

While young leaves twinkled like green stars at the gentle breeze, he sat under the bo tree determined not to stand up or open his eyes until what he sought has been found. Then at the end comes the brilliant moment, something that would signify the ultimate episode in an operatic journey. At a point in the meditation, a deep realization dawns on him, and he exclaims: "The rafters are shattered, the ridge-pole is destroyed, and the architect will no longer erect the house (*gaha*) again." That is when the young man known as Gautama Siddhartha becomes the Buddha.

That is the only statement attributed to the Buddha describing himself at the highly enigmatic and ineffable event of attaining nirvana. Literary and artistic representations will struggle with recreating that condition, but the verses describe arriving at the ascetic telos in cataclysmic terms, as a dramatic destruction of the body. And what is also significant is that the destruction is carried out in the tectonic framework of a building.

Two notions are embedded in that cryptic statement. First, there is the body and building reference where the body is conceived of as gaha, home or house. And, second, there is the ushering of the dismantling of that structure. Two consequential questions emerge here: Why a building imagery for the body? And, why is the event rendered in a cataclysmic manner?

Gaha is the villain in the description. *Gaha* is home in its normative sense, implying being in the world, socially, familially and phenomenally. The Buddha's statement is the most vivid expression of the violent destruction of *gaha*. And what is the consequence of this climactic condition? The moment coincides with the final goal of asceticism, or freeing oneself from the tethers of the world. But this is part of a series of key episodes in the ascetic journey. The climactic nature of this event is premised by an ascetic conceptualization where the body is like a hut, whose existing lineaments and ligaments must be shattered before the enlightened life can begin. Clearly this is a vivid body and building association in which the body-building is conceived of particularly as a "final" hut. The house-body stands as the last bastion in what appears to be a single minded pursuit of the ascetic to literally de-construct the existing structure of life. That is the truth the young prince was seeking.

In Buddhist sense, the destruction of the "last" hut is an ideograph of nirvana, the climax of renunciation. The cataclysm, using the trope of the shattered hut, basically inaugurates a new life in the teleological narrative where the old parameters are nullified. The narratival content is based on, first, the ascetic body being homologous to a building, and second, the body being primarily conditioned by socialization, must now be transformed radically.

The great ascetic experiment works through a simultaneity of the occupation and "destruction" of the body-building. It is not truly a destruction, however the rhetoric may be, but a radical reconstitution or transformation, in which "something" remains, although the old measures of identity are no longer valid. The so-called destruction of the hut is comparable to attaining a "non-conditioned" mode of existence, akin to a "second birth," of dying to this world and being born again in order to create another "human," a body more purified and superior. The Buddha once used the example of a chick breaking out of the egg-shell as a "second birth." "To break the shell of the egg is equivalent," Mircea Eliade explains "to breaking out of the samsara, out of the wheel of existence." After the shattered *gaha*, there is nothing, for it is coeval to a condition that is totally ineffable, or as one text mentions, *asamskrata*, or unconstructed. The art historian Stella Kramrisch describes that un-constructed condition as arriving at "zero-point."

The Buddha under a distended lintel. Image from Albert Foucher, *L'art Greco-bouddhique*.

The Temple of Doom and Enthusiasm

The town was a luminous artifact, an ideal representation of upright citizens, celestial gods and the institutions of man. Emblem of Apollonian Virtues, the town was an embodiment of Laws and Principles. On the liminal side of that illustrious town, on a site at the far outskirts where tall, green trees surrounded a dank, marshy land, lay the temple. It was a wooden temple, with stocky columns and tiled roof on a wooden frame held together by rope lashings. The temple lay untended and overgrown with vines, waiting quietly for the god to come.

The women in town waited for the day when he would come. The women represented wives, mothers and whores: wife of a senator, mother of a general, sister to a noble person, or just a plain prostitute from the shadier part of town. They waited for the arrival of the god who comes from Elsewhere, the god who drives them mad.

The god arrives and the city is tense. It's a time when the regular remains suspended and challenged. The official gods, the gods from the sky, look elsewhere, and generals, senators and merchants appear helpless as the women grow tenser. It's a time of the violence of "wellborn ladies," as Marcel Detienne describes.

Dancing around the idol of Dionysos. Image from Staatliche Museen zu Berlin.

Riding a leopard, the brazen god comes accompanied by prancing satyrs and maenads making music and flaunting various kinds of intoxicants. The god dances through the streets, from one neighborhood to another, followed by his raucous retinue. The women run to the windows for a glimpse. Some run out of their houses, from their kitchen, from their afternoon nap, from attending to their children in the aulae. Some are young, some are old, dutiful wife of a senator, venerable mother of a general, chaste sister to a noble person, or just a plain whore. They run out of their houses and follow the god.

The party turns bigger and bigger. Satyrs, maenads, and wellborn ladies. They follow the gridded frame of the city streets, and after leaving the gates, take to the winding path that leads to the liminal location. The party arrives at the site of the temple, the old, sad temple waiting patiently for something. Wine is drunk, dresses are loosened, bodies sway and swing. A goat is sacrificed, blood is mixed with drinks. The women shout the name of the god. The untying begins.

In a trance, in the name of the god, Dio-Nysos the Liberator, who came from nowhere and elsewhere, the women pounce on the temple. They climb and grab at the ropes tying the bundle of wooden posts that hold the roof rafters, they shake and pull in frenzy, their palms bruised and bloody in no time. The ropes come apart, and one by one, the purlins fall, crashing to the ground, and soon the roof tiles, often one by one and often in the loud rumble of a bundle. There are ecstatic shouts, the roof is gone, the temple is no more.

As soon as the temple is dismantled, it had to be put together again before sunset. The women, a little weary by now, had to work harder to gather up the materials again, and climb the precarious scaffolds prepared to rebuild the temple. One woman or another, a little dazed by the drink and the euphoria of enthusiasm, and the strain of carrying building materials, trip from an upper level of the platform and come tumbling down. And in a frenzy that is as ferocious as before when they began, the other women would jump down and pounce on the poor, fallen woman, and pull and tug at her until her limbs are severed. Thus the temple and its builders and un-builders would enter a curious and volatile relationship of building and mayhem, of death and birthing, recalling the genealogy of the god himself, whether it is the mother figure Semele impregnated after drinking a potion made of the heart of Dionysis torn apart by Titans, or dying

before giving birth to baby Dionysos whence the impregnator Zeus sews the fetus to his leg for a paternal birth.
The whole ritual of sacrifice is structured around designed death and demolition, and consequent reconstruction. At the root of the bacchanalian destruction of the temple is "ecstasy" or "enthusiasm." "The Bacchic ritual produced what was called 'enthusiasm'," Bertrand Russell notes, "which means etymologically having the god enter the worshipper, who believed that he became one with the god." The intoxicating drink facilitated the enthusiasm but more than that it was a rapturous oneness with the spirit of the god who transgressed the customs of the city and inverted the roles of citizenship and duty, ecstasy and responsibility, and the sacred and the sacrilegious.
[The above tale is a collage of many Dionysian narratives. Marcel Detienne discusses the ritual practice of the roof destruction and its rebuilding from an island at the mouth of the Loire from a description by the geographer Strabo.]

The Origin of Architecture Is in a Slaughter
History begins with monstrosity. Architectural narratives wrestle with it: From the paintings at Altamira to the lithified parts of sacrificed bulls on Greek temples, from the genetically hybrid Minotaur at Knossos to Le Corbusler's animal sketches for Chandigarh. That the space of architecture is bestowed with the carcasses of beautiful beasts and unnamed monsters, hidden in its basement or concealed behind its walls, is a secret story told only around a camp-fire or by a brooding Poe. Monstrosities demonstrate, as Marco Frascari claims, or remonstrate.

The story takes place in a geography that can no longer be located and a time that cannot be recalled with any precision: Unnamed and unidentified, the thing appeared suddenly over a cerulean sky. The perturbed gods ganged up and brought the thing down on earth. They laid him/her/it on the ground, each god holding a limb or an organ. The thing had no chance. Then the gods slaughtered the thing. The poor thing must have twitched a little for it put up little resistance, and then it was no more. That is, no more than what it was. The gods did not even bother to ask the thing its name. They simply proceeded to dismember it. After the deed was done, then they had a name for it. They called it Vastupurusa, the Cosmic Man.

Those gods assigned for measurement and survey brought out their instruments, the thread, the chalk powder, the theodolites, and the tripods. On the ground where Vastupurusa lay slaughtered and dismembered, with each anatomical piece strewn around, the gods drew calcified lines that caged each dismembered piece within a fine geometric grid. For each grid, the gods gave a name, a name that represented the property of that organ. Moreover, each god was given the task of presiding over a grid. A forelimb for one god, an elbow for another, one eye for one god, a foot for another. So the thing that did not have a name, and could not be described, now upon its demise received not only names and locations for its various severed parts, but also a designated divinity.

The navel was in the central grid, the source of things to come. It was the point of emergence for Brahma, the master deity of creation. The navel connected to the origin. The navel was the mundus, the omphalos, center of the earth, the point of the axis mundi around which things to come manifest. Thus on the dismembered body of the poor thing emerged a grid of order and measure, and for each grid appeared property and character, and upon that superimposed system arose the mountain of finely cut stones and porphyry that was called a work of art, architecture. A city with a handsome temple. Or, a temple with a beautiful tower. From the murderous earth it rose once more to touch the sky.

Such is the origin of a mandala, of the making of a worlding.

The place of beginning as a site of slaughter and blood sacrifice, and eventual construction, is central to many ancient practices. Marcel Detienne describes such a cosmogonic murder scene, an infanticide from an Orphic account of the death of Dionysus. The child Dionysus was slaughtered by the Titans, his body was dismembered, and the parts were thrown over a fire and roasted. The Titans were preparing to devour the victim's flesh. "They just have time to gobble it down, all except the heart, before Zeus' lightning comes to punish their crime and reduce the Titan party to smoke and ashes, out of which was born the human species."

Awesome monsters and un-nameable creatures were given lesser understanding than gods, for they formed a convenient group of dissonant and perplexing elements. But the demonstration of monsters was a crucial creative act, and if creation on earth is to be considered a dwelling act, the making of a world, it was first and foremost existential. "I call monsters all original inexhaustible beauty," writes Alfred Jarry. Marco Frascari traces the designation of mostri sacri in the Etruscan-Roman tradition of divination that considered monsters as "extraordinary events, celestial novelties, untouchable sacred signs of a possible future." They are enigmas that can be interpreted only with a vague precision, and understood only with apprehensive distance. But Frascari proposes another destination for such mysterious creatures. "Architectural monsters… are the extraordinary signs of an imaginative production based on perception and knowledge." The highest function of a poet, or for that matter an artist or architect, or anybody involved in the act of production, is the invention of monsters. "An architect must subject the reality presented by nature to a host of legitimate deformations and unnatural relationships to produce monsters that are enigmas which express precisions." There is then always the possibility of a minotaur in the cabinet, wild things under the bed. To paraphrase Einstein arguing for another extraordinary being, even if there were no monsters, we had every reason to invent one.

The Lost House
The Barcelona Pavilion was destined to be lost before it was built. It was already a ruin before it was history. Architecture, for Mies van der Rohe, was a gradual and relentless progression to almost nothing. *Beinahe nichts*. Not nothing, but almost nothing.

The Barcelona Pavilion is/was a house, "the house of the German spirit," and an emblem of the modern house to come. In 1929, one is already in a quandary with the modern house for such a house comes to terrorize the present, or as Jose Quetglas ruminates, the modern is a machine that anachronises the present. "The modern house is the house where I don't belong," Quetglas continues, "which I cannot claim as mine, where neither I nor my imagination may venture." The modern house dethrones the fundamental citizen of the house, the dweller, for "the modern house… excludes me, because I am radically absent from it, because it is the house of the Other." And Rudolf Otto has pointed out earlier that the Other is either a divinity or monstrosity, or some kind of bewildering phenomenon.

The Barcelona Pavilion, or the Miesian house, is a house that cannot be lived for it perpetrates a domestic violence. It is a forbidden house, un-dwellable, a house destined to dematerialize before it can be domesticated, but not before our domestic imagination has been terrorized forever. Designed for dematerialization, the pavilion/house was built in stone, glass and steel with sheer planes that floated and stood precariously in "free" space. The unbridled space, the material minimalism, the constructive reduction, and the polished pillars were all decisive elements in the Miesian vanishing act. Polished many times over, the chrome plated columns not only concealed the joints but also perpetuated the dematerializing effect of reflection from polished surfaces. Polishing presented an act of mutilation: the array of reflections and transparencies hastened the disappearance of any tectonic logic or structural order. First, domesticity is denied, and then all architectural habits and conveniences are confounded. And finally the interior has been emptied out. It is a house of absence where bodies have been devoured.

Mies' house, in effect, is not made of stone, glass and steel; it is, as Quetglas realizes, made of reflections. All that is solid is reflected back to oblivion. "The entire pavilion is a mirror." The whole house is a great disappearing act. Mirrors produce a hopeless desire, it reflects back an image and inverts desires by dissolving them in the space over there where none can enter. Quetglas invokes Rilke: "You mirrors, who go on emptying the empty rooms." Mirrors conjure the spirit of Narcissus, suffering the anguish of a split, and Medusa, self-reflecting itself back into an inert form.

Barcelona Pavilion, 1929. Photo: from the collection of the University of California, San Diego.

The house has no doors, and space flows in and out unheeded, and yet it is a resolute labyrinth made of many reflective glass and marble that perpetually decenters and disorients. There is a constant anxiety in the visitor as all movements, materials and mirroring reflections hasten a perpetual dissolution. "In the pavilion, Mies was to stimulate the spectator to the utmost degree. Shall we go in then?" Where is this going? Rilke is invoked by Quetglas: "Above us there's a house without doors. Is it open or closed? There are two paths. Neither of them leads anywhere." This is far more perplexing than Hercules's ambiguous bivium.

Representing a struggle between excess and less, the house of mirror sits equivocally between the ordinariness of excess and the exquisite excessiveness of less. Is the house of absence about an infinite enrichment or systematic impoverishment, or more disconcertingly, the horror of emptiness, a horror vacui?

Mies has devoted a sustained contemplative and constructive energy to a dialogical relationship between excess and less, and between appearance and absence. He is certainly the most ascetic of all modern architects who has articulated the theme of "nothingness" with its complex conjunctions of excess and less, reduction and selectivity, and exquisiteness and exclusiveness. The idea of *beinahe nichts* suggests two immediate readings: a reductive aesthetical and architectural expression that could be characterized by the vogue notion of minimalism, and a more intellectual understanding of reductivism analogous to the ideology and practice of asceticism.

In an architectural sense, Mies' path towards "almost nothing," the art of disappearance, is made possible by two procedures: the minimalization in structure and materials, and further "dematerialization" of the materials one is left to work with. In any case, both procedures are attempts at dematerializing either physically (by reduction) or virtually (by visual effects) the very fundamental conditions of architecture: materiality and presence.

A house such as that can only be dismantled and dispatched off. The pavilion is dismantled, Quetglas argues, because the modern house is empty, and the presentation of emptiness is the object of the representation. Since the modern house is but a mirror, it inverses all that it stands for including inverting itself. Finally, in a great disappearing act, the house itself disappears. The actual house was dismantled after the exhibition in 1929 and placed in crates, put on a train and shipped back to Germany. En route, the crates containing the dismembered house were lost in toto. A house that begins in disappearing can only disappear in full. No trace. And what is left are apparitions and haunting images.

A structure was rebuilt on the same site in 1986. The original does not exist. The imagination is pervaded by the ruins of the original. What exists is a simulacrum. Or, a sarcophagus.

The essay began with anticipating a method to the madness. But what conclusions can we draw with the Buddha, Dionysos, Mishima and Mies as protagonists on the same stage? To speak of these names in one breath is a challenge. Hastening to elaborate what we already know – that destruction is a necessary condition for a spiritual rebirth or material transformation, or as Piet Mondrian wished, "ascension away from matter" – is not enough.

All the above narratives can be considered from a metamorphic perspective. This is fundamentally an evolutionary scheme involving change and Nietzschean "transvaluation" in which "destruction of old forms [is] a condition of higher forms" and where dissolution is directed at the limitations posed either by matter, conventions or values. But where actually is the location of destruction in the metamorphic scheme? Is destruction about the violence of origin (Vastupurusa)? Is destruction the telos of a project (Buddha/Mies)? Or, is destruction a point of reversibility (Dionysos and Mizoguchi/Mishima)?

But also what is revealed as a subtle strand in the narratives is a kind of domestic violence, where domus or dwelling is the object of a relentless onslaught, whether it is as obvious and literal as the modern house, or analogical as the body, or metaphorical as the temple. As house, temple or body, home suggests a universe condensed and contained. But the constructed containment is not quite stable. Domus is a terrible destination: it is a primordial and perpetual site of the need to build and frame and enclose, and an equal need to transgress and transcend. They invite construction, yet we know they are temptingly tenuous and fragile requiring a frequent revision and reformation.

Destruction is therefore not simply a point of transition but a necessary complement, an active and calculated counterpart. Dwelling becomes an aporia precisely in its location between construction and destruction. Home and body seem to be the repeated site of ritualized destruction as both require meticulous construction, nurturing of the body and fabrication of home, being at the same time susceptible to rupture and tremor. Andres Serrano's photographs of bodies in morgues with stab or burn injuries captures the tenuous nature of the "living" body. The images convey not so much the macabre and grisly but the fragile containment of the built body, with its fluids and organs. One could, in reference to "weathering," say the same thing for architectural bodies.

Dwelling as a term returns us to burning, a clearly destructive phenomenon that lends itself to a discursive propagation. To burn is *to be*, as the ancient sacrificial ritual in the Indo-European traditions conveyed. The sacrificial act around the sacred fire is one of humanity's most ancient existential activities. It brought humanity, divinity, earth and sky into a precarious and precious conversation. The burning temple too is a "fourfold," as the famous philosophical reflection on the four-folding bridge, for burning is the most ancient instrument available for dwelling. This is conveyed as much as in the phenomenology of fire as the technology of language, and reproduced in rituals and narratives. The name of the goddess of the hearth, Hesta for the Greeks, Vesta for the Romans, and vastu for Vedic Indians (meaning a "thing," a "building"), all had roots in the word as, which literally means 'to burn.' More importantly, the root is related to such existential terms as the German wesen, the English word *was*, and the Indian word that directly means existence, *astitwa*. The Indian word for architecture, *vastushilpa*, which in its congenial connotation means the art of architecture, or literally the art of existence, is in a more equivocal sense, the art of burning.

References

Kazi K. Ashraf, "The Buddha's House," *RES: Anthropology and Aesthetics*, 53/54 (2008): 225–243; and, *The Hermit's Hut: Architecture and Asceticism in India* (Honolulu: University of Hawai'i Press, 2013).

Carel Blotkamp, *Mondrian: The Art of Destruction* (New York: Harry N. Abrams, 1995).

Adrian Del Caro, *Dionysian Aesthetics: The Role of Destruction in Creation as Reflected in the Life and Works of Friedrich Nietzsche* (Frankfurt am Main: Peter Lang, 1981).

Jacques Derrida, *The Gift of Death,* trans. David Willis (Chicago: University of Chicago Press, 1995).

Marcel Detienne, *Dionysos at Large*, trans. Arthur Goldhammer (Cambridge, MA: Harvard University Press, 1989).

Marcel Detienne and Jean-Pierre Vernant, *Cuisine of Sacrifice among the Greeks*, trans. Paula Wissing (Chicago: University of Chicago Press, 1989).

Marco Frascari, *Monsters of Architecture: Anthropomorphism in Architectural Theory* (Savage, MD: Rowman & Littlefield, 1991).

Carl Kerenyi, *Dionysos: Archetypal Image of the Indestructible Life*, trans. Ralph Manheim (Princeton, NJ: Princeton University Press, 1976).

Stella Kramrisch, *The Presence of Siva* (Princeton, NJ: Princeton University Press, 1981).

Yukio Mishima, *The Temple of the Golden Pavilion*, trans. Ivan Morris (New York: Knopf, 1959).

Josep Quetglas, *Fear of Glass: Mies van der Rohe's Pavilion in Barcelona*, trans. John Stone and Rosa Roig (Basel and Boston: Birkhäuser, 2001).

Mrs. Oikawa Shiyuko sits among the remains of what was once her home, Otsuchi, Japan, after the 2011 tsunami. Photo: Alejandro Chaskieberg.

Architecture's Anxiety

Introduction to *Locations: Anthology of Architecture and Urbanism*, Volume 1, 2016.

1
One always arrives at a building, and that perhaps already makes the building an *other*. We are more or less on a slippery slope in our understanding.

Describing a building is a bigger challenge than interpreting one. It's a passage to a deception in which we all participate unwittingly. The process almost always begins outside of that building; it accepts a separation in which a deeply intertwined condition is formatted into conceptual islands. Consciousness and intellect begin when bodies and things are already differentiated and over there. Understanding and description simply follow from a splintered world.

Visually legible and easily available objects present themselves as dominant in such a normative reality. And among those things that recede from the horizon of understanding —an irony there —are topography and terrain. That perhaps is the source of architecture's primary anxiety: an uncertain and queasy relationship with location. Architectural thoughts and descriptions need to rescript this topographical counter-predication, and regain the primitive contact with the here.

2
Usually registered as a disjunction, anxieties can be projective and productive in architecture. Rafael Moneo, in his commentary on the work of eight Euro-American architects in *Theoretical Anxiety and Design Strategies* (2004), considers theoretical anxiety a kind of "caustic reflection" and critical discourse, and ultimately generative of design strategies. That the productive capacity of architecture is hinged to wider social disturbances describes the nature of modern architecture. The disquiet over the nineteenth century city, its incapacity to deal with the emerging age led some architects to organize new methods for addressing housing, city frame and social conditions in totally new ways that came to be known as "modern."

In a psychosomatic sense, anxiety is *being modern*, a condition that for W. H. Auden (1948) describes a whole age. Does the "age of anxiety" continue now as an inheritance of the original modernist agitation, or is it more a consequence of a neoliberal world-order, what the sociologist Ulrich Beck describes as a “second modernity”? Is the latter, a “geo-liberated economy,” an inherent aspect of nouveau middle-class aspirations spurring stresses and strains borne out of unfulfilled desires that lead to more desires and anxieties? In the rumble-tumble of economic globalization to which all have succumbed, from nation-states to corporations and agencies, and to the individual psyche, and in the furious proliferation of buildings and cities, a single thought haunts us: “What makes for significant architecture?”

High Line, New York. Photo: Ashraf.

3

There are compelling reasons why we should talk about spatial anxieties while addressing architectural significance. In the Portuguese writer José Saramago’s novel *The Stone Raft* (1986), the Iberian Peninsula dislodges itself from the European continent and begins drifting away in the Atlantic Ocean. Disturbances ensue when parameters—coordinates, orientation, position and bearing—that direct our corporeal operations in the lived-world alter. When George Clooney’s character Bingham, in the film *Up in the Air*, is asked by a flight attendant on an airborne airplane where he is from, he replies, “Here.” Location has a greater human hue; it is more than a simple geographic coordinate.

The Swiss writer Max Frisch, in his novel Homo Faber (1954), presents the protagonist Walter Faber as a UNESCO engineer, a quintessential modern man who lives for the service of a purely technological realm, and for whom only the “tangible, calculable, verifiable” exists. As an emblematic figure befitting such a world body as UNESCO, Faber moves from one location to another allowing himself to be uprooted in a liberative way. Frisch, in this existentialist and quasi-ethical novel, charts the enigmatic quandary of such a modern nomad. On a cruise liner—travel being the ubiquitous trope of place-liberation—Faber meets a young woman and falls in love with her consummating the relationship. In a twist reminiscent of Oedipus and his exile from his place of origin and his devastating forgetfulness, Faber finds out that the young woman is actually his daughter. The novel then proceeds towards a tragic Greek destiny.

Sometimes, place remains as it is, but the terms of location changes. In “The Other Side of Silence” (2007), writing about the Indian subcontinent’s partition in 1947, Urvashi Butalia recounts her trip from Delhi to Lahore (in Pakistan) to locate an uncle who did not migrate to India with his other Hindu family members following the violence and dislocations of partition. The uncle, Ranamama, opts to stay back in Lahore with his aging mother with the purpose of retaining their ancestral home until the trouble died down. Ranamama promised that he would join the relocated family later but after about thirty years he is still in Lahore, while the other family members live in Delhi. Butalia locates him in the same city that belonged to them for generations, and to which they belonged. Ranamama is in the same house, has converted to Islam, married, raised daughters, and buried his old mother per Muslim customs. Although the uncle has remained in the same spatial coordinates, he himself has become the other.

Mehran Karimi Nasseri's real story positions airport spaces as the most vivid site of modern dislocations. Nasseri, fleeing Iran in 1988 was "stranded" at Charles de Gaulle Airport for more than eleven years while trying to enter France unsuccessfully. While waiting at the airport, he made the terminal his home. Newspapers describe him in the terminal "siting at a table, perhaps smoking a pipe, taking a stroll, stopping to pick up his mail at the post office or lunch at the McDonalds's… he will be looking very much at home."

Being "at home" in this improbable space can now be experienced by those who cannot even imagine such a space. Following Frederick Jameson, in *Postmodernism, or, the Cultural Logic of Late Capitalism* (1991), we can say that this extruded or cleaved open space —Jameson's "hyperspace"—can now be experienced, and therefore needs to be taken seriously. Many of us will be struggling to look very much at home in this warped world. Jameson thinks that we have not yet developed the "perceptual equipment" to face this spatial convolution, this new hyperspace; in fact, the new conditions require that we "grow new organs to expand our sensoria and our bodies to some new, as yet unimaginable perhaps ultimately impossible dimensions."

4

Would it be a hyperbole to declare that being modern is to be bequeathed with that exhilarating and burdensome nomadism, the promise to transcend the terror of territory but face the terrifying consequence of the Oedipal flight?

The anxiety that we developed with place and location is now thrust on buildings. Modern architecture and its incarnations are bearers of a world-view that architecture need not be encumbered by territory and geography. This was perhaps presented provocatively in Archigram's 1964 architectural vision of literal world mobility, with tentacled mega-machines poised for globe-trotting. Specific places—call them what you may, nation, locality, or region—have taken a bit of a beating to the euphoria offered by new globalization, economization, and more lately, digitization. And what that shares with the old universalist aspiration of modernity is a suspicion of place, or to say it in an obverse way, an unabashed glorification of "placelessness." However, that celebration does not come without its attendant quandary, as the stories of Walter Faber or Nasseri demonstrate.

A basic locational question in architecture begins with: Where do I work as an architect? From where do I get my architectural responses, and where do I situate my work. One can design in a situationally independent manner anywhere, but one always builds somewhere. A clever argument could be made that somewhere is anywhere, or nowhere for that matter, or in the voice of Gertrude Stein, that "there is no there there," and so why linger. The first point comes out from the cartography of "free-flow," either the electronic mode of digitization or the fluid capital of globalization, and the latter as an indictment of the sociological and cultural void of the modern city (in Stein's case, Oakland in California). Yet, if one cares to detect, there is a certain wistfulness in Stein's captivating lines. "Where is architecture" is not a question, but it could trigger reflections about the role of architecture in cultural and economic production, and about its situation in the world. In orienting focus away from "what is architecture" to "where," we need to accept that we have been making inordinate demands on the "what," and have left the question of "where" largely unexamined.

Yet, the question of "what" is intimately tied to the matter of "where"—to architecture and its place in the world. "Where" refers to a zone of inevitability, be it geographical or cultural, or some combination of it. Zones and boundaries are never fixed things; their fluidity makes it difficult to maintain a precise overlap of the political, cultural, and geographical, and that is both a charm and challenge. If flux is now the reality, then to what boundedness can architecture respond to?

A reflection on "where is architecture" is either subsumed or found unimportant in the glamorous and spectacular pursuit of the "what." With "where is architecture," the debate may deflect from form to situation, from ideation to sensation, and from the asymptotic present to a phenomenal presence.

5

"The architect's task is more than the manipulation of materials and the molding of space, it is the definition and possession of place," the American architect Charles Moore said more than fifty years ago, and it continues to matter for architectural operations today. While beginning his work at Chandigarh, Le Corbusier's biggest predicament concerned place and territory, on how to begin on that site, and how to relate to the geographic surrounds. Louis Kahn's first meditation on beginning in Dhaka was not quite directed towards cultural associations, but rather toward how the buildings are to take their place there. It is in this taking place that a work of architecture, from Corbusier's Ronchamp to Kahn's Kimbell Art Museum, to speak of grand gestures, or even an anonymous building in Honolulu, literally finds substantiality and significance. Humans are geographic beings; the possessing of place is a basic existential impetus, and has not become passé in the onslaught of new epistemologies and technologies.

Invoking the notion of "place" in the twenty-first century often has a retrogressive implication, especially with the intonation of romanticism about landscape, of a chauvinism around regional or territorial affiliation, or of something just stable and perennial in the (post)modern world of perpetual flux and denuded fixities. At the same time, the obverse of place —"placelessness"—is increasingly apotheosized as another kind of existent space.

Although place, culture, region, and nation are often used interchangeably, they are distinct concepts; place does not immediately promote a nationalistic or identity-laden rhetoric, or a cultural foundation. Place and culture, once homological, soon became alter egos, and are now currently at such tangents that

Farming carrots in Havana. Photo: Carey Clouse.

Le Corbusier's Ronchamp Chapel in 2015. Photo: Saif Ul Haque.

we can now pose the phrase: "place versus culture." With culture becoming portable, malleable, and commodifiable, and the geographic rootedness of culture and community increasingly becoming tenuous, it is possible to question it as a reliable premise for architecture. On the other hand, it is possible that the situatedness of architecture involves comparatively more enduring conditions, or "realities." These "earth-realities"—primarily of a meteorological and terrestrial nature—constitute a place-situation that tacitly and inevitably affects the life and form of architecture there.

6

Identity, with its vexing questions, is the other side of location. An anxiety over identity follows from that of location; it is the locational ontology that conditions the formation of identity and the production of tradition. With tradition now in turmoil, and a fixed pattern of life uncertain, how is the significance of architecture to be considered? Heinrich Hübsch's self-reflection posed in the context of nineteenth century disquiet in Germany —"In what style should we build?"—returns again as a question to any reflective architect embarking on a project.

Framed in the 1980s within a regionalist discourse in architecture, and earlier in the political sphere of the nation, identity remains a stubborn topic, even while stumbling from one kind of articulation to another and encountering newer practices and critiques. While identity may appear as a natural issue for autochthons, it also brings up the question of the other. Transnational exchanges disrupt many of the precepts that have informed regionalist or nationalistic practices. At the same time, an unprecedented wave of migration—intra- and international—creates new definitions of far and near, and ours and theirs, in which identity is constantly being reconstituted.

It is critical for an architect, or a writer or an artist, wherever she or he is geographically, to locate her or his work in this horizon of identity. In his essay "Die Weltliteratur" (2007), the Czech-born writer Milan Kundera considers the place of a work of art in tension between two contexts: On the one hand, a writer, as well as the work, is obligated to the historical process of the nation. Such an emplacement brings up the matter of national identity—as things stand today, one is invariably described/identified within the legal parameter of a nation. Kundera calls this "the small context." On the other hand, the work finds itself placed and categorized in "the supranational history of that art" – what, according to Kundera is the large context, the *weltliteratur*.

The ambiguity of placement is relevant to architecture. Transferring the question of *weltliteratur* to architecture, we wonder: Is Antonin Raymond's elegant ashram in Pondicherry (1936), for example, a European modernist work in India refracted by climate, a Czech-American architect's production inflected by Japan, or by dint of being in India, an Indian work? Similarly, does Chandigarh belong to India, to Le Corbusier, or to European modernism?

Kundera's quandary is a European one: how a work is to be situated within the diverse and porous context of Europe, where there is also a disproportionate status to each nation. How a work is read and positioned on a world stage, whether in the smaller context of a nation or the larger universe of a world art, is still decidedly a Euro-American dispensation. Kundera describes the vexation of writing from Czechoslovakia in the shadow of Europe whence the writer's identity is marked, without the writer's say in the matter, in the small or bigger context, as provincial or worldly. In fact, the politics of placement and the identity of the artist, writer, or architect become particularly fraught outside the Euro-American orbit. In that condition, one has to contend with a more dubious politics of identity categories.

Kundera's double context within which the appreciation of a work of art oscillates is not quite the same as Paul Ricoeur's much discussed dichotomy between a universal civilization and local culture. Consider India, whose nationhood began with a struggle to define cultural identity through the works of artists in Bengal in the late nineteenth century. This was the period when identity arose as a contentious theme as part of and reaction to the colonial system in British India. With art as the site of a nationalist discourse, artists, writers, and intellectuals debated on what constitutes Indian art. While many argued for a nationalist position, the Bengali poet-philosopher Rabindranath Tagore (1861-1941) rejected a nationalist identity for art, and argued more for an individual creativity in the service of a larger humanity. The art critic Benoy Sarkar, writing from Paris in the 1920s, stated that one doesn't produce "Indian" art just by painting in India. Today, in India as in anywhere else, a singular identity is under severe critique and is being replaced by ideologies of hybridity, multiplicity, and fluctuating formations. In shaking up the foundation of a unitary nation, the postcolonial critic Homi Bhabha positions hybridity towards dissolving "coherent identities, conceptual purity and cultural unity." The British-Bangladeshi choreographer Akram Khan's oscillation among various obligations and affiliations is a more recent reminder of this ongoing strife.

How to engage this discussion in architecture? With national identity considered suspect, and cultural identity despatialized, the basis of architecture may have to return to something more fundamental and prosaic, such as climate. However, climatic reflections do not excite most social and political scientists engaged in the critique of identity and culture (Bhabha, for example, has nothing to say about it). In that debate, there is no room for weather, and no philosophy of climate.

In the conjunction of climate and architecture, I am not immediately recalling Otto Koenigsberger, Maxwell Fry and Jane Drew, and Victor Olgyay, and their metrics of tropical architecture, as useful as they are, but remembering a lesser known work, the Japanese writer Watsuji Tetsuro's *Climate and Culture: A Philosophical Study* (1961). Notwithstanding controversies around essentialist links between types of climate and the nature of culture, Watsuji's work presents an ineluctable position of climate in our lived experiences, and to our profoundest beings. Place is a surrogate for climate in which the latter is not simply a geographic condition but a particular milieu—literally an environment of molecular continuum in agitation.

In the spectrum of culture and climate, an architectural work remains beholden to the latter. Wherever it is positioned in the interpretive scheme of critique and historiography, an architectural work is still there in a specific locale. And it is to that locational ontology that a work of architecture, unlike a book or painting, or a musical work or performance, or a critique for that matter, must eventually turn to. In fact, interpreted or not, described or otherwise, it is already there in that milieu.

7
Poised between disaster and promise, the contemporary city makes architects teeter. A new city is emerging in the landscapes of Asia, Africa, and South America whose contours remain unmapped and whose nature close to being explosive. Powerless to comprehend the scope of the new urban landscape, and unable to figure out a point of entry into the enigma, architects are content in their allocated lots and plots to be ironic or phantasmagoric. Where once architecture and the city formed a twinness, the parameters of one informing the other, there is now a contention. While architects make stunning architecture, the city goes to hell. The production of architecture, thus liberated, seems either unable to deal with the furious city or prescribe ways of negotiations. That remains as a challenge and third anxiety for most architects.

Better understood as economic engines, ecological footprints, and social intensities, cities are poorly comprehended in their humanistic or existential dimensions. Writers and film-makers have done better in drawing the contour of this new city. Whether in the alternative reality of Haruki Murakami's *1Q84*, transnational movement in Wong Kar-Wai's films *Chungking Express* and *2046*, or the ultra-real narrative (of Mumbai) in Gregory David Roberts's *Shantaram* and Suketu Mehta's *Maximum City*, the city once again is the site of new collective consciousness.

In *Memories of Istanbul* (2009), Orhan Pamuk describes the slow but sure disappearance of a deeply sedimented city, lending to Istanbul a melancholia, or *hüzün*, that is particular to that city. But not all cities are shedding their old selves with such wistfulness. Most cities in Asia and South America are transforming with a fury and forwardness in which investment supersedes the environment, and architecture finds itself in an adversarial relationship with the city.

Tokyo provides earlier instances for architecture's edgy relationship with the city. In response to Tokyo's corrugated and discordant morphology, some architects declared their inability to converse with the city and resorted to introverted buildings. Examples are Toyo Ito's U-House (1976) and Tadao Ando's

House in Daikanyama (1991). On the other hand, Fumihiko Maki whose work is known for a restrained and elegant language, conceived a dynamic facade for the Spiral 10 11 Building (1985) as a condensation of the city's ensemble nature. Drawing up a conclusion after analyzing Tokyo, the maverick thinker Kazuo Shinohara (1925-2006) went a step further arguing for a new approach of violent and disjunctional assembly in a manner he called "savage architecture."

When architects do engage the city now, they produce phantasmagorias—edifices of elsewhere in response to the powerful middle-class desires. The "longing for elsewhere" is now embodied in new building configurations that are radically affecting the urban landscape, constituting a new "hyperspace": malls and shopping centers, cineplexes and flyovers, and exclusive apartment and residential complexes.

In writing about the new Indian city ten years ago, I described the mall as urban space par excellence borne out of a transnational exchange that, on the one hand, mimics the shopping culture of America, and on the other hand embodies the surreal city of "elsewhere." "While the American mall is a populist destination, the mall in India and South Asia has taken on a unique and exclusive aura that architecture helps codify. As an alternative to the older streets and bazaars, from where the aspirant class has fled, the mall holds the city at arm's length through a series of barriers—by the curtailed interaction with the surrounding city, by the inevitable motorized access, and by the spectacular security befitting an airport terminal—all of which works towards intimidating people. The residential gated enclaves are similarly policed and truncated from the continuum of the city. The metrosexual citizen can now travel from home to mall, bypassing the rest of India." (2009)

8

Despite a glib consumerism marked by luxury malls and raunchy residences, towards which most architects are understandably rushing to, architecture broadly faces some formidable issues: How best to reconfigure the city, humanistically and ecologically, in the climate of rushed development? What urban types to innovate to meet rising levels of middle-class requirements? How to mobilize the resources of the new economy to raise millions out of poverty, especially in vulnerable regions? And how to rephrase the questions of identity and locality without being parochial or dogmatic?

What, then, makes for significant architecture? It does not have to call out for an ancient name, nor does it have to be abrasively modern to attract attention, as the ancient Indian poet Kalidasa said some 2,000 years ago. To be significant, architecture does not have to be large, monumental, or overwhelming. Some of the finest examples of architecture produced today come from many small-scale projects demonstrating the dense presence of poetics and tectonics even in a low-key situation—for example, the railway Signal Box by Herzog and de Meuron, a quiet courtyard by Anjalendran or Channa Daswatte, a village church

Cover of *Locations*, Volume 1.

by Peter Zumthor, a quirky teahouse by Terunobu Fujimori, a visitors' center in a remote region of Australia by Greg Burgess. Responding to the anxiety over food and energy security, architecture can be projective of an alternative urban future, as in Michael Sorkin's vegetal plan for feeding Manhattan. Again, architecture does not necessarily have to be urban to be significant, and certainly not the graphical hodge-podge that makes up the metropolitan landscape. Significant architecture need not even be buildings. In an expanded field, architecture now includes the much featured High-Line project, Kongjian Yu's ecological park, and urban parks in Havana. At the same time, mobilizing a community project in Curitiba or Medellin, building a settlement in a raw landscape in Bangladesh, or restoring of a wetland in Saudi Arabia that receives the Aga Khan Award—all certify as fine works of architecture. Significance calls for substance. With much of the earlier assurances in tatters—whether the grandiose humanism of modernity or the ethnocentrism of a regional architecture—many architects seek a basis of their work in the fundamental ontology of material formation and site entrenchment, or the reality of lived communities. Whether carried out in a neomodernist or paratraditional vein, making and building are opportunities for architects to create a phenomenal and sensual ensemble, with a social enterprise to support it.

The publication *Locations* presents the art of building that demonstrate both the substantiality and sustainability of architecture in an age of new anxieties. Works represented here embody a tectonic clarity, landscape consciousness, humanitarian ethics, constructional elegance, and material sensuality without seeking validation in symbols and signs (even though they may be visually powerful and socially persuasive at times). The works presented or discussed in *Locations* invoke neither the tottering certainty of archaism nor the inevitability of excess, but instead the challenge of the assuredness of a fine built work. Such acts of building are deployed toward the obligations of habitation and well-being rather than a spectacular presence.

...of a possible future." They are enigmas that can be interpreted only with a vague precision,

...further study in architecture, and went to the University of Oregon in the United States and to Yale University where he received a Masters

The Lost House

...supervision of Paul Rudolph. It was upon his return to East Pakistan, and as part of his responsibilities within the ubiquitous Public Works Department (as no private architectural firms existed at the time) that

...radically absent from it, because it is the house of the Other." And Rudolf Otto has pointed

The Eventful 1960s

...Other is either a divinity or monstrosity, or some kind of bewildering phenomenon.

...grooves of certain common characteristics. But today that range

...at every instant. The imminence of a disappearance

house-set is burning. The house had to be rebuilt so it could be burned again). In Tarkovsky's driven meditation on the macrocosmic scope of human annihilation (in the film, nuclear catastrophe), and its microscopic reach into the lives

...materiality and presence.

...apparitions and haunting images.

...contradiction.

The essay began with anticipating a method to the madness. But what conclusions can we draw with the Buddha, Dionysos, Mishima and Mies as protagonists on the same stage? To speak of these names in one breath is a challenge.

...in verancular means, and perpetuating ancient myths, remained quite operative in

Le Corbusier's Prehistory

...and complex organisation of the terraces, which creates a distinct identity.

...the Shodhan House, it is the brazen animation, busy and diverse as a bazaar under a sheltering umbrella, the various brise-soleil and complex organisation of the terraces, which creates a distinct identity.

ARCHITECTURE IN BANGLADESH

India and Le Corbusier: The Open Hand

"This prodigious spectacle has been produced by the interplay of two elements, one male, and one female: sun and water. Two

operatic journey. At a point in the meditation, a deep realization dawns on him, and he exclaims: "The rafters are shattered, the ridge-pole is destroyed, and the architect will no longer erect the

Europe to Africa, from "high classical" to vernacular, from machine imagery to folk

'meaning transposed' before becoming an architectural reality in the Corbusian schemata.[5] As a rule, the appropriated source

India the Humane and Profound Civilisation

important cultural manifestation of fascism."[33]

the world, socially, familially and phenomenally. The Buddha's statement is the most vivid expression of the violent destruction of *gaha*. And what

life can begin. Clearly this is a vivid body and building association in which the body-building is conceived of particularly as a "final" hut. The house-body stands as the last bastion in what appears to be a single minded pursuit of the ascetic to literally de-construct the existing structure of life. That is the

although the old measures of identity are no longer valid. The so-called destruction of the hut is comparable to attaining a "non-conditioned" mode of existence, akin to a "second birth," of dying to this world and being born again in order to create another "human," a body more purified and superior. The Buddha once used the example of a chick breaking out of the egg-shell as a "second birth." "To break the shell of the egg is equivalent,"

The Temple of Doom and Enthusiasm

that many perceive as a positive alternative.[9] In claiming the city as a social and urban disaster, some people have demanded: "Leave Chandigarh alone!"

Virtues, the town was an embodiment of Laws and Principles. On the liminal side of that

The god arrives and the city is tense. It's a time when the regular remains suspended and challenged. The official gods, the gods from the sky, look elsewhere, and generals, senators and merchants appear helpless as the women grow

Measures of Water

five years of research through continuous attempts in his life to give expression to the collective ethos of "the new epoch" through its various

venerable mother of a general, chaste sister to a noble person, or just a plain whore. They run out of their houses and follow the god.

the roof is gone, the temple is no more.

The Matrix of the Delta

Semele impregnated after drinking a potion made of the heart of Dionysis torn apart by Titans,

The Origin of Architecture is in a Slaughter

the restless Meghna, dancing along her way, slipped into a careless moment

finding and molding soft alluvium, cutting and twisting through hard ground. After making a broad sweep that

the ground, each god holding a limb or an organ. The thing had

nor French, nor American but Indian of the second half of the twentieth century."[16]

Those gods assigned for measurement and survey brought out their instruments, the thread, the chalk powder, the theodolites, and the tripods. On the ground where Vastupurusa lay slaughtered and dismembered, with each anatomical

Parasols and Silhouettes

It is the current of air, it is the shade, and yet the sun must penetrate at the proper time, in the favourable seasons. The conditions of the problem are

easily, the point of the axis mundi around which things to come manifest. Thus on the dismembered body of the poor thing emerged a grid of order and measure, and for each grid appeared property and character, and upon that

architecturally typological counterpart: the brise-soleil and the roof as an umbrella. From a tentative expression as in Villa Bezeau in Carthage, Tunisia (1928), the brise-soleil becomes a highly articulated "element poetique" in the office tower for Algiers (1939-1942). The separation of the roof from the more used volume of the building also dates as early as 1928 in the first sketch for Villa Bezeau, and 1939 in the pavilion at the exposition at Liege where the

of the making of a worlding.

Muzharul Islam, Dhaka University Library, Dhaka, 1952-1955.

Architecture in Bangladesh

Published as "Muzharul Islam, Kahn and Architecture in Bangladesh," in *MIMAR*, Volume 31, 1989.

While the role of British colonialism in the Indian subcontinent has been widely debated, it is difficult to ignore its overwhelming spectre even in contemporary times. Colonial rule constituted a great rupture in Indian societies, yet it is equally true that an exposure to European institutions also revealed some of the more repressive conditions existing in these same societies. It is this tension—created from drawing lessons from worldwide sources in order to transform what appeared to be obsolete systems, yet at the same time rediscovering the essence of an ancient culture—which has charged the core of Bengali intellectuals under foreign domination and since.

From the beginning of this century almost all aspects of societal existence in Bengal, particularly stimulated by movements in political and literary fields, have been informed by a duality of articulating and aligning with a Bengali cultural identity and appropriating things from a global repository. There continues to reign a complex situation of *acceptance* and *resistance*—a resistance to both the traumatising aspects of colonialism *and* repressive "traditional" conditions, and an acceptance albeit critical of trans-cultural techniques and norms that promise new avenues for exploration. While the poet Rabindranath Tagore, through his varied intellectual pursuits, had been the most heroic figure in taming this duality, others were less successful in areas like painting and especially architecture, where a Eurocentric sensibility held sway. The problem was compounded because of the amnesia into which architectural culture had lapsed into during the colonial period, and the vacuum in thinking that prevailed in this realm of the arts.

onstantin Doxiadis, Teachers Students Center, haka University, 1963-1964, Photo: F Binte Zaman, /ikimedia.

In architecture, there were no comparable efforts to the Bengal School of Arts for example, which attempted to synthesize the imagery and symbolism of Bengali (Indian) culture with European representational methods. In fact, the Public Works Department, manned primarily by engineers and draftsmen, became the exclusive authority for construction, and devastatingly, synonymous with architecture.

Muzharul Islam, the leading figure in architecture of the region, began his lonely yet committed struggle under these conditions, by designing two buildings in Dhaka in 1955 that, it might be said, initiated a movement in contemporary architecture in East Pakistan. Having trained first as an engineer, Muzharul Islam opted for further study in architecture, and went to the University of Oregon in the United States and to Yale University where he received a Masters degree under the supervision of Paul Rudolph. It was upon his return to East Pakistan, and as part of his responsibilities within the ubiquitous Public Works Department (as no private architectural firms existed at the time) that he designed two edifices that are landmark in terms of the recent history of the profession: Dhaka Public Library (now Dhaka University Library) and the College of Arts and Crafts. The former was clearly organised in a Corbusian mode—a cubic volume on stilts, complete with ramps, sun-breakers and pristine white colour—but it indicated for Dhaka then fresh qualities of an urbanism and environment. The western wing of the project, with its climate control devices such as shell roofs and brick louvers for the openings, was an original articulation by the architect. It was, however, the College for Arts and Crafts that came closer to mediating with the conditions of the place and programme. Sprawling, low building volumes, the use of exposed fired brick that always has such a magical resonance with the "green" of Bengal, the natural garden setting on an urban site, all went to form the atmosphere of a campus ideal for the contemplation and learning of the arts, and, more importantly, a spatial environment evoking the architectural poetics of the land.

The Eventful 1960s

In the political arena, the 1950s registered the first tremor of a rift between the two wings of Pakistan. The Language Movement of 1952, when lives were lost to establish Bengali as an official language, indicated the inability of Pakistani leaders then to comprehend the spiritual depth of cultures, and signalled the beginning of the struggle for Bengali self-identity that would explode into the War of Liberation of 1971. The dominant political consciousness in East Pakistan, particularly in the 1960s, motivated by the issue of economic disparities between the two wings, and fuelled by the manipulative use of religion by the central government, would polarize most Bengali intellectual towards secular, socialist thinking.

Turbulent as this period was politically, the 1960s was significant too in the architectural realm. A development spree (often as part of "foreign aid package") saw a profusion of building activities. "There was chaos in architecture, but there were achievements too," Shamsul Wares writes. "It was in this decade that formal architectural education was established. And it was in this decade that important foreign architects like Louis I. Kahn, Paul Rudolph, Constantin Doxiadis, Richard Neutra, Stanley Tigerman produced their works here. It was at Dhaka, in 1968, that the most important conference of the Institute of Architects Pakistan was organised, proclaiming a new spirit of architecture. In the 60s, there were very few practising architects, there were gaps in architectural sensibility, and inadequately trained people with vested interests were operating within the profession, yet there was an agreement among the architects to offer their very best to society."[1]

[1] Shamsul Wares, "Architecture in the 50s and 60s in Bangladesh," *Architecture and Planning 1982*, (Bangladesh University of Engineering and Technology, 1982).

Louis Kahn, Parliament building and Secretariet's Housing, Sher e Bangla Nagar, Dhaka, 1962-82, Photo: Ashraf.

The involvement of the American trio—Kahn, Rudolph and Tigerman—was due to a great degree to Muzharul Islam who saw a need in the vacuous contemporary situation to provide visual and provocative paradigms in the Bengali landscape. The intention was not too dissimilar to the still-fresh, high adventure of Le Corbusier at Chandigarh— Nehru's "jolt" to Indians. Paul Rudolph was Muzharul Islam's teacher at Yale, and Stanley Tigerman was a close class-friend in the same institution. While students both Tigerman and Muzharul Islam had resolved to work together someday, and this was accomplished through the commission of five polytechnic institutes in Bangladesh. Rudolph was invited in 1966 to prepare a master plan and design important buildings of the Agricultural University at Mymensingh. In the overwhelming atmosphere of national development through primarily Western models then prevalent, the work of these otherwise deeply sensitive architects provides interesting insights into the encounter between architectural morphology basically developed in the West and conditions that are often totally different from their original milieu. The most perceptible zones of this encounter were the architectonic and spatial solutions by which specific climatic conditions were tackled, the intelligent exploiting of available materials and technology, and the subsequent abstract sculptural rendering of the artefact in the brilliant, tropical light.

However, the most poignant event would be to invite Louis Kahn to design the Capital Complex at Shere Bangla Nagar in Dhaka. The decision to make Dhaka a "second" capital, and install the National Parliament there, was taken at the Governor's Conference in 1959 by Pakistan's president Ayub Khan, not out of an overwhelming reverence for democratic institutions but as a bid to placate the growing discontent among the Bengalis. Kahn worked on the project from 1965 to until his death in 1973. Construction continued slowly, with a number of interruptions, but was substantially finished by 1982. The Sangsad Bhaban (Assembly) has begun to be used for the parliamentary assemblies, although democracy hangs somewhere between a charade and a genuine national aspiration in the murky political circumstances of Bangladesh.

Kahn's involvement at Dhaka is of epic proportion in itself. The Shere Bangla Nagar project eludes categorical statements of economic and cultural impropriety often made by some critics; the project continues to provoke an inspirational dialogue on the fundamental nature of architecture and of human institutions. The force of Kahn's ensemble is not merely formal, but emotional too; its genesis has become inextricably linked with the national struggle of the Bengalis. And this is what many people outside the Bengali domain fail to comprehend. Of course, Kahn never intended this consciously, and whether the work of any other architect would have performed the same role is an open question (although a number of internationally reputed architects were operating in Pakistan then), yet it is possible that Kahn's particular philosophical speculation about universal qualities in architecture — to mediate between global and specific culture, and "ancestral voice" and contemporaneity – found in the Dhaka project a coincidental significance.

Kahn's project has the capacity to engage a conversation with an emerging collective manifesto. The "ruinous" architecture that transcends recognisable styles despite a Piranesian inspiration coincided with the rise of Bengali identity, and the two formed an unforeseeable empathy with one another. Both contemplated the metaphorical glory of a lost time, and triggered what Charles Correa would describe as our latent, architectonic sense. Moreover, both reflect a new collective vision stratified by a complex layering of images and events.

Although originally commissioned with a political motive by a basically exploitative government, the meaning of Kahn's ultimate imagery has never been perceived in Bangladesh as a haughty imposition comparable to Lutyen's government complex in New Delhi. Although the planning of Shere Bangla Nagar is informed by Beaux Arts sensibilities and its architectonic character by a Roman aura, it nonetheless creates a spiritual communion with certain aspects of Mughal planning, and even the architectural order of monastic complexes such as Nalanda (in Bihar, India) and Paharpur (in northern Bangladesh). This gives meaning to a still open search for archetypal, timeless dimensions in human enterprises. In spite of the debatable issue of economy and those abrupt circular cut-outs, Kahn's work for a long time will stir and elucidate, as well as inspire generations of architects, in Bangladesh and India, to take up architecture as a serious, spiritual mission unlike the short-lived visual titillation in which so many architects today are engrossed in.

Monumental Muzharul Islam

It is Muzharul Islam's work that, in addition to Kahn's capital buildings, has dominated the early architectural scene in Bangladesh. His practice has been discontinuous in time, with periods of greater or lesser intensity of production, but it has always been multisided from the late 1950s and onwards. Muzharul Islam created the nascent architectural culture of Bangladesh, carrying out a struggle against government bureaucracy, against political domination by engineers, and against academic sterility. He incarnated honourable practice in Bangladesh (and Pakistan before 1971) and "progressively" enlightened architectural endeavour. Despite the arguable results since, the commissions for the American trio in Bangladesh was initiated in sincere faith by Muzharul Islam, primarily in order to instil an international level of awareness and inquiry locally. Hardly involved with the school of architecture in Dhaka, Muzharul Islam offered his office Vastukalabid more than once as a springboard for passionate movements by committed young architects.

Although Muzharul Islam's notion of architecture, as "the creation and arrangement of physical objects in a total, natural and social design,"[2] aligned him with an non-traditional and progressivist ideology in architecture, represented by certain attitudes of modernism, his crucial contribution was in his persistence in formulating a Bengali sense of identity that permeates more than just architecture. His essential point is that

[2] Muzharul Islam, "Regional Planning in East Pakistan," proceedings of the Conference Institute of Architects Pakistan (1968).

Muzharul Islam, Housing for the Joypurhat Limestone Factory, 1969. Photo: Rashidul Hasan.

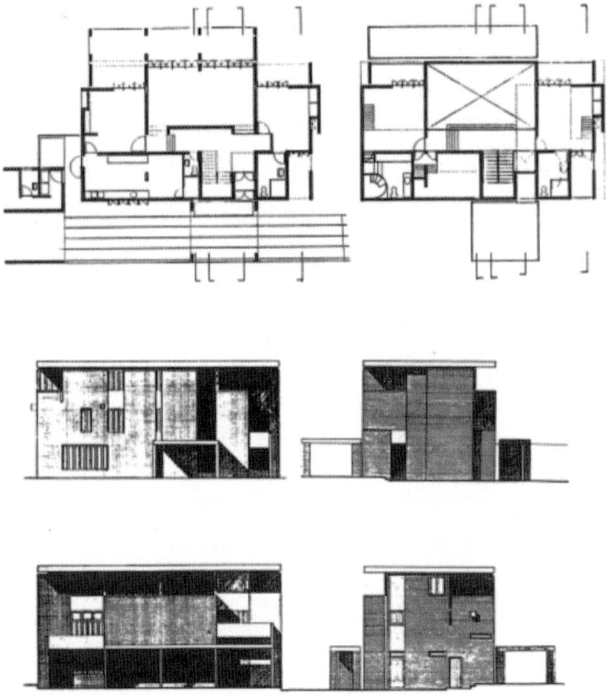

Muzharul Islam, Own Residence, Drawings, 1969.

if the psyche has transcended the dilemmas and contradictions of identity, architecture will find its own natural expression. It was this concern that, in the urgency of political and cultural consciousness of the 1960s, moved him gradually from a purely architectural performance to political activism as a more immediate role to confront social conditions. The Liberation War of 1971 created the first major discontinuity in his career and that was to recur in the unstable political and professional conditions of the post-independence years. In the chaotic situation of the profession in the 1970s, the bulk of architects, lacking any legal or ethical basis for practice, submitted totally to mere profit-making, and thus completely severed the building task from real social needs and cultural imperatives. In that condition, Muzharul Islam was ironically edged into isolation. What started as a highly-charged beginning in his architecture could not, unfortunately, be carried to a more paradigmatic phase.

Despite the discontinuities in his practice, the work of Muzharul Islam does reveal a progression of research from a clear reference to the language of certain contemporary Western masters towards a more personal formulation. His early projects from the late 1950s to works like N.I.P.A. and his own house constitute a first phase in which, through his own experimentation, there is an unmistakable continuation of certain Corbusian-Rudolphian devices. They are evident in the innovation of climate control (the umbrella roof of his own house recalling Shodhan Villa); in the sculptural animation made by varying reliefs, deep shadows and juxtaposition of materials; in the spatial composition (again, as in the multi-levelled organisation of his own house); and, finally, in the manner the artifact confronted the setting, more as an assertive and self-referential stance than a mediative one. In the late 1960s, with the commission of two university projects, involving large-scale organisation, began his later phase. While the pervading order, as in Jahangirnagar University and the housing for Jaipurhat Limestone Factory, is an a priori geometry, the concern is to generate an "urbanised" order by the formation of community spatial enclosures, streets and continuous facades. The individual buildings are of exposed brickwork, in which spaces and voids seem to be carved out of masonry solids that, despite their often-curious geometrical purity and unlike the skeletal nature of his earlier projects, form a more earth-hugging ambience.

It was in the National Library at Dhaka, his most recent work (1979-84), that "distortion" of the idealised form itself become the generator of architecture; the ultimate artifact acknowledges more explicitly the conditions of the "place"— the context and the contradictions. The building, by its geometry, solidity and spatial order, makes a convincing dialogue with the neighbouring ensemble by Kahn that by now has formed an important context or fabric in the north of Dhaka. While geometric abstraction and a consummate skill for physiognomic articulation provide a continuity in all his work, the urbanity of National Library is a world removed from the Public Library of 1955.

Muzharul Islam singly motivated the first generation of contemporary architects and laid the basis of a profession and an intellectual discipline. His work ultimately seemed too reserved however in proposing an iconography that would be evocative of a Bengali sensibility. This is the concern that seems to engage a group of small but conscientious architects today and that is where the significant thrust of thoughtful production will lie in the future.

Unfortunately, the important promoters of building activity — the state and the upper-middle class clientele groups – still adhere to an image of progress set in machine aesthetics and industrialisation. The largest group of architects, in quick and easy responses, have continued a fallacious interpretation of the rationality and aesthetics of functionalism and technology, evident in the monolithic expressions, uncritical use of materials and technology, and nonchalance towards the figurative aspect of architecture.

Architectural strategies in Bangladesh are locked, to a great degree, within the global politico-economic conditions of today, and within these transitional times when the country is again at a loss for a collective vision. Under such conditions, it is probable that design propositions will still be shaped by a Eurocentric language, but what is really disconcerting is the still uncritical, and overt allegiance to it by the majority of the practitioners.

There is a far more undesirable tendency, seemingly liberated from the early clutches of international "modernism," which has found its modus operandi in the worst form of hybridisation. By remorselessly implanting neo-Classical devices on Bengali cityscapes, or grafting pseudo-Islamic motifs on European

Bashirul Haq, Residence, 1983. Photo: Ashraf.

Rabiul Husain and Shaheedullah and Associates, Bangladesh Agricultural Research Council (BARC), Dhaka, 1982. Photo: Zulfiqar Hyder.

Bashirul Haq, Residence interior.

Uttam Kumar Saha, SOS Social Center, Khulna.

Raziul Ahsan and Nahas Khalil (CAPE), Youth Village, Dhaka, 1984.

planimetric organisation, this attitude forms the most self-interested group of commercial practitioners, and the more likely agent of trumped-up state ideology. In short, absolved more from the rigours and responsibilities than from stylistic constraints, this group is apt to do the least service, and most damage, to evolving architectural principles.

Finally, within the overbearing presence of the two tendencies just cited, there is a maturing, committed trend that encompasses an investigative architecture. The central thrust of this group is to evoke the myth and poesis of the land within the tension of archaism and contemporaneity, and global and local pressures. With the paralysis of Bengali architectural sensibility in the last hundred years or so, it has become morally imperative and culturally urgent that a significant portion of contemporary architecture in Bangladesh become "archaeological": to excavate from the historical layers of contradictory and imposed ideologies a more "place-responsive" architecture. The archaeological inquiry is not in the sense of uncovering fossils, nor is it in the sense of a trip to "exotica," but rather with the objective of restoring cultural archetypes that still have deep existential significance, and will be a beginning point for fresh trajectories.

Doruk Pamir, Islamic Center, Tongi, 1986. Photo: Zulfiqar Hyder.

Kallman, McKinell and Wood, US Embassy, Dhaka, 1989. Photo: US National Archive.

Some of the works of Rabiul Husain (of Shaheedullah Associates) and Bashirul Haq, while employing culturally syncretic devices, mark the tentative beginning of this research. Bashirul Haq has particularly endeared himself for his notable rendition of private houses—quiet, unobtrusive masonry volumes in close affiliation with the setting. His special sensitivity for the domestic realm is meticulously articulated in his own house and studio—light, plantation and construction materials as tactile sensation—and the crafting of space—hierarchical, exterior-interior, private-public, diversely volumed—all create a memorable experience of living. Rabiul Husain, once a close member of Muzharul Islam's studio, has used the idiom of abstract geometric configurations creatively to confront the Bengali sun and rain, the ambience of light and shade, and the sensitiveness of use. His association with S.M. Shaheedullah, a highly creative engineer, has often evolved into fruitful architectural-engineering coalitions, from the experiment with vaults at Begumganj to the more notable BARC building in Dhaka. The office for Bangladesh Agricultural Research Council (BARC), with its unique use of brick even in major structural members, takes available materials and constructional techniques to greater lengths and suggests unforeseen potential for what has always appeared to be limited resources and conventions.

Interestingly, it is some of the work of much younger architects that takes the "archaeological" exploration of evocative types and complex formation to a new level of discourse. This is apparent in some of the work of Uttam Kumar Saha, and the offices of C.A.P.E and Diagram. The S.O.S. Youth Village at Dhaka designed by C.A.P.E. (architects: Raziul Ahsan and Nahas Khalil), completed in 1984, and the more recent Hermann Gmeiner Social Centre at Khulna by Uttam Kumar Saha (of Consociates Ltd.), completed in 1987, both indicate a tentative beginning in this new direction. While the former is located on an urban site and the latter on a rural one, both projects engage in similar strategies: fragmentation of volumes instead of a single, cubic monolith, and the resulting creation of contained exterior spaces. The permeability of the space, as in the *uthan* (courtyard) of traditional spatial organisation, forms a link with the public realm and allows pavilion-like settings for the individual volumes. Both projects are convincing responses to their geo-physical location: the Dhaka project is consciously articulated, in its relationship to the street and in its formal "impurity," to play its (sub)urban role, and the Khulna project makes a sensitive interjection in the idyllic Bengali landscape. Again, both the projects employ contemporary constructional means to form their specific roofscapes of remembered shapes.

Some recent projects carried out by foreign architects are also likely to generate debate on the nature of large complexes involving certain architectonic elements and external compositional norms, as the Islamic Centre for Vocational Training and Research at Tongi by Turkish architect Doruk Pamir, completed in 1986. This is true also for the potency of remembered iconology as boldly expressed in the U.S. Chancery Building, designed between 1983-86 by the Boston firm of Kallman, McKinell and Woods.

Besides investigation through real buildings, another important domain that the architectural culture in this region has lacked is a more committed inquiry into the nature and significance of "place-evocative" architecture through academic and research programmes. "Chetana," a group founded in Dhaka in 1981, within the overwhelming gloom of the profession and the incapacity of the academy to foster deeper inquiry, has initiated a significant discourse, involving not only architects but also artists, writers, poets, journalists and historians.

While these small emerging architectural events promise a new watershed in evolving a "place-evocative" architectural strategy within contemporary conditions, more formidable issues remain to be confronted: How can architecture, as a profession and discipline, attain a more responsible role in this vulnerable land-water mass inhabited by an incredible number of people? While phenomenal rural exodus requires a closer scrutiny of unprecedented changes in the urban domain, how can the urban-based architects of Bangladesh focus their energies and services when nearly 80% of the people still live in villages? How can architecture be socially responsive at all in the present political and economic instability engendered more than anything by a lack of collective vision? What immediate roles can, and should, architects play, given the range of resources available and political-societal constraints, in order to confront the daunting dilemma of housing and organisation of the human environment?

Muzharul Islam, as early as 1968, spoke about the special task of architecture and architects in this critical situation: "When the activities of man eventuate in the creation of either natural or

Muzharul Islam, Hostel for Jahangirnagar University. Photo: Ashraf.

[3] Ibid.

man-made objects on the surface of the earth, they become the concern of the architect. The architect's traditional activities have been in the realm of small-scale structures, but he now feels that without rational and large-scale designing of physical space and objects, it is not possible for him to function fully even within his own discipline. He feels that it is through regional planning alone it is possible to change nature and create the most favourable conditions for his small-scale activities."[3] It seems that the situation in Bangladesh, instead of relegating architecture to an elitist and peripheral role, demands precisely the total involvement of architects and the broadest scope of visionary and architectural thinking.

Drawing by Quamrul Hasan, 1963.

Vastukala: The Architecture of Muzharul Islam

Written in Philadelphia, November 17, 1993. A shorter version appeared in *The India International Centre Quarterly*, New Delhi, 1996. Also published as main essay in *Muzharul Islam Architect*, edited by Zainab Faruqui Ali and Fuad H. Mallick, (BRAC University Press, 2011).

Muzharul Islam (1923-2012). Photo: Muzharul Islam Archive.

The work of Muzharul Islam, coming from a single figure, frames the contours of recent Bengali cultural history. In fact, the work is an intense registration of post-colonial dynamics, engaging all the issues of contemporary existence: modernization, westernization, nation-building, "world dialogue," cultural amnesia, and the more tenuous "return home."

Muzharul Islam does not offer an easy access to his world. While his architecture owes much to the language of modernism, there is a more complex relationship with modernity. Furthermore, his buildings, not produced for photographic purposes, are more than what they appear; they are organizational and constructional. Finally, the buildings constitute only an aspect of Muzharul Islam's broader relation to architecture culture. This includes his role as teacher, mentor, activist and plainly the enfant terrible. This is further complicated by his political consciousness and, in the last twenty-five years (written in 1993), by his direct political involvements, spilling the scope and substance of architecture beyond its conventional boundary.

Architectural modernism might have begun in Bangladesh with Muzharul Islam, but modernity has a long lineage and deep strata in Bengal. Muzharul Islam emerges from this condition, and it is against that his output can be situated. It is however necessary to rethink the relationship beyond the demonization of modernity that characterizes most contemporary architectural criticism. For most Asian societies, modernism is often conveniently seen as the perpetrator of cultural ruptures, pitting it against a "pre-modern" condition, that is, tradition. The reverse claim, present in the work and thinking of Muzharul Islam, needs to be examined too. It might be seen that Muzharul Islam adopts and employs the principles of modernity in order to overcome what was perceived as colonialist rupture. Modernism, in this sense, becomes an attempt to "return home."

The Return Home

"How do we enter the twenty-first century?" wonders Muzharul Islam. The oft-raised question throws us immediately in the throes of modernity. The generality of the question leads to more concrete reflections: on the idea of the nation ("we"), on the political and economic nature of society, and on its spatial manifestation. One also senses in that query a degree of hesitation, a momentary stalling. The question, as much as it is about propelling forward, takes in by that hesitation and that collective "we," a glance at the other direction, the past. All the issues that recur in Muzharul Islam's thinking are in this query: what to hold on to, what to abandon, what to take.

The idea of modernity in Bangladesh, and by extension the ideology of Muzharul Islam, can best be understood by that broad sweep of cultural and intellectual upheavals ushered in Bengal by the nineteenth-century movement often described as the "Bengal Renaissance." As the basis of modern Bengali society, the movement was a complex intertwining of acceptance and resistance; a resistance to both the traumatic experience of colonialism and the tyranny of tradition. The condition of acceptance was also two-fold but more complex: it involved an outward voyage to embrace from a global repository anything that assured a new degree of social and intellectual liberation (as for example, the scientific, progressive and humanistic institutions of Europe *seem* to promise), and, an inward journey, a conscious "archaeological" excavation, so to say, of one's own uncharted and taken-for-granted cultural strata.

The inward journey involves the process of understanding oneself. This is important, for this implies that one is suddenly made aware of oneself, and, as often understood, self-awareness is double-edged: it is a moment of self-discovery, it is also a moment of a distancing from the familiar. The search of self-discovery presupposes a sense of alienation and remoteness from tradition and does not arise so long as, as Jaravalal Mehta comments, "we *unreflectively* live under its domination, or fail to see the novel present as it actually is and claims us." Both Charulata and Bimala, characters from two Rabindranath novels, signify that at the moment of self-awareness the familiar is made foreign, or conversely, one is made a stranger to the comfort of familiar setting. And, yet, it is within this condition of self-awareness, *where tradition is no longer available unreflectively*, that the idea of identity–cultural, gender, or national–can arise.

In essence, it is this paradox that creates the project of *return home*. "Return home" is a metaphor, even if an exaggerated one, by which we can name the the struggle encountered particularly by the "Bengal Renaissance," the movement to articulate an identity when tradition is no longer available uncritically. This leads to, on one hand, the appropriation of foreign ideas in the very core of society, and, on the other hand, zealous efforts to resolve what it means to be Bengali. As often, the words of Rabindranath Tagore poetically encapsulate the *Zeitgeist:* the inevitability of the journey, and the exilic anguish of departing. In "Probash," Rabindranath speaks of the thousand bonds binding one to the ancestral home (*bhita*). Yet, he realizes that "the vast universe is beckoning me from every shore/there is a thousand knock of the world at my door."

It is by way of attempting to "return home," and not by a stylistic or a rhetorical sense of progress and development, that I would like to pose Muzharul Islam's alignment with modernism. This encompasses the work, the political commitment and the personality of Muzharul Islam. Such an estimation may appear dubious, and I have a feeling to Muzharul Islam himself, but it is by this one can understand the apparent distance between his rootedness in Bengali culture and the modernistic forms of his architecture.

What is the historic root of this alienation from "home," the point of departure, so to speak? In Muzharul Islam, the question of "return" emerges because of the colonial experience, through interpreting colonialism as a "rupture," as a fatal and irreversible condition created by its disruptive mechanisms. In the context of Bangladesh, the "rupture" is compounded, since the time of Pakistan, by the added pressure to undermine "Bengaliness" by a pan-Islamic ideology. These disruptions urge Muzharul Islam to speak of "mone-prane-karmokande khati bangali houa," that is, to be a "true" Bengali in mind, spirit and *praxis*. This is another sense of the "return" metaphor, taken up particularly as a political agenda, that one is displaced from where one was once *mone-prane-karmokande bangali*, and the return to that site is prior to any ethical and creative behaviour.

Modernity, for Muzharul Islam, is as much a returning as going away. It is a going away from the immediate colonial past, and a returning to an "essentialist" condition that seems free from specific religious ideologies or traumatic inheritance. It is this which might distinguish it from the radicalizing motive of European modernism. For most Asian societies, colonialism is still *the* datum. When Franz Fanon speaks of "defamiliarization" as the immediate project of post-colonial culture it is not difficult to see why modernity was adopted with such ease. Muzharul Islam wishes to use modernity as a way of critiquing colonialism, particularly what he sees as the nature of colonial "rupture," and to use architectural modernism, as the term suggests in its formal and spatial characteristics, as a way of overcoming the rupture. The rupture cannot be overcome by the adoption of traditional motifs, although that partially helps. As much politically avowed to a Bengali identity and a suspicion of Western domination, he would not immediately transfer this onto architectural making. It is this overcoming, which is not to go away further, but to go forward to an essentialist condition encircling both the past and the present, that may be understood as the metaphor of "return."

But, one can no longer return to what once was. Actually, one can no longer know what once was. Overt traditionalism, in most cases, is a sentimental return hiding behind it a consumerist intention (as in the interior decorations of five-star hotels) and a lack of critical and intellectual rigour. Or worse, traditionalism could, and does, slip towards national chauvinism. When Romi Khosla proposes an "Asian consciousness" poised obviously against the "West," it verges close to an old "us-versus-them" theme, never clarifying what consciousness means, or questioning the validity of this pan-Asian monolith.

College of Arts and Crafts, now Faculty of Fine Arts, Dhaka. Photo: Saif Ul Haque.

College of Arts and Crafts, now Faculty of Fine Arts, 1953, Dhaka. Photo: Muzharul Islam Archive.

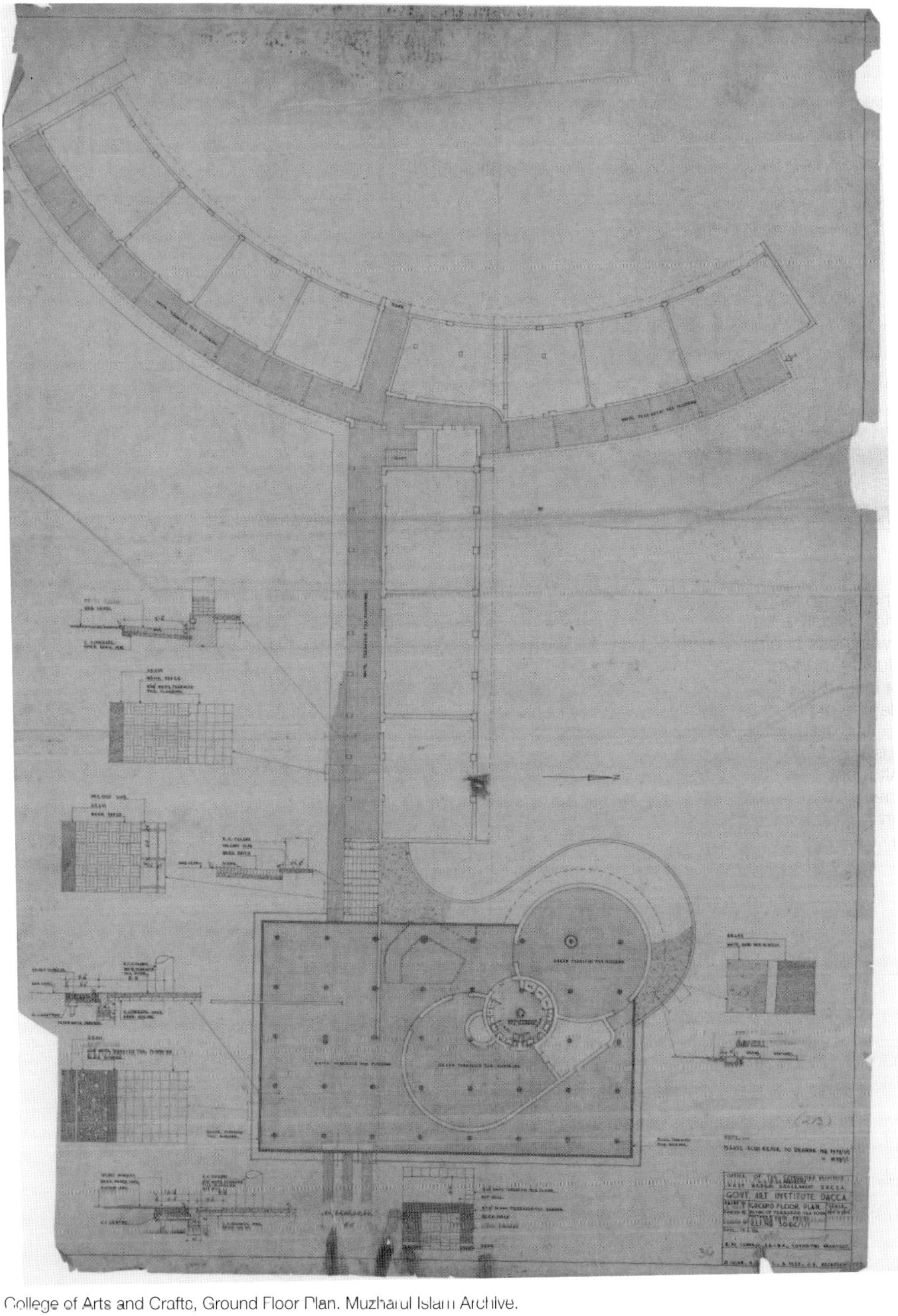

College of Arts and Crafts, Ground Floor Plan. Muzharul Islam Archive.

Public Library, present Dhaka University Library, 1963. Photo: Unknown.

There is no longer *the* return. One can now only return critically, there is only a transformed or a "constructed" return. Once self-awareness begins, we are forever fated to a "re-construction." But what distinguishes this construction from the facile method of instant traditionalism? What might give the former a greater degree of authenticity?

It is this: Muzharul Islam's position is dialogical and dialectical. Although hinged to a specific place – its socio-cultural milieu – the position does not falter in engaging in a "world dialogue," and is not daunted that such engagement might necessitate a different, or a *new* way of making. Muzharul Islam wants to operate within the nexus of cultural particularness and the humanist idea of "the-world-as-my-village." This is what brings him close to a Rabindrik ethos, and to the central tenet of the "Renaissance" movement.

In fact, Muzharul Islam grew up within the intellectual and spiritual shadow of the idea that living in the twentieth century is *living in a nexus*; one can no longer escape this, no matter what ideological posturing one adopts, and no matter if V.S. Naipaul calls it the "burden" of the middle-class. That one can no longer live in ethnic, racial or national "purity" is pretty much certain.

Architecture and Nation-Building

The American architect Stanley Tigerman, who has been a close friend of Muzharul Islam, relates how he found Louis Kahn very disturbed when they met at Heathrow Airport in 1974. Tigerman was on his way to Dhaka for the Polytechnique projects, which he was designing with Muzharul Islam, and Kahn was going back to the United States from India (and to his tragic death). Tigerman remembers that the only thing that was bothering Kahn was the thought of Muzharul Islam and "how could he leave architecture for politics?" Kahn conceded that he could never do that, and yet, as Tigerman recalls, did not seem relieved by his own statement.

To begin to understand Kahn's query is to be lead to the problematic juncture of architecture and nation-building. This is highlighted in Muzharul Islam by two strands of inheritance: the Rabindrik and the Marxian, in other words, the contradictory commitments of artistic detachment and political engagement. The antipodal strands of Marx and Rabindranath form an illuminating intersection that can be mentioned only fleetingly here. While Marxism would tend to flatten out the topography of cultural differences leading to ideas of a radical humanism, Rabindranath would universalize a local experience such that reading lines from his work would make a W.B. Yeats quiver on a London omnibus, or a Victoria Ocampo weep in distant Argentina.

In Bengal, "aesthetics" and the idea of nation have always constituted a critical (and problematic) intorcoction. In fact, the articulation of the nation may be understood, and the recent political and cultural history of Bangladesh may be made clearer, by bringing up the debate on "national" style in aesthetics. This took placo from the 1900 to 1930s as a direct outcome of the "Renaissance" movement.

The most vivid record of the triangular tension of tradition, nationalism, and modernisation is seen in the development of "modern" Indian art. It was primarily through the writings of E. Havell and the work of Abanindranth Tagore that art becomes a site for nationalist discourse. Abanindranath's work was seen by critics and his supporters as the rediscovery project of the aesthetic ideal of India. The implication was broader; it was no less than the political project of national rediscovery, it came to symbolize the recovery of tradition and lost identity. Through the Havell-Abanindranath discourse, art – Indian art as well as Indian ethos – came to be regarded as "essentially idealistic, mystic, symbolic and transcendental."

Abanindranth's attempt to forge a link with Mughal miniature schools, and later Japanese and Chinese traditions, with a view towards "aesthetic and national recovery" was countered by two other camps. One was the Academic tradition, which in the name of progress as understood through colonial training, was contented with doing realistic rendering of Hindu mythological scenes.

The third position attacked both pro-colonial Academism and the pathos-filled "national" art of Abanindranath. The protagonists of this position were suspicious of the Hindu exclusivism of the Academicts, but more than that, were apprehensive of both the pretentiousness of "Indianness" and the exclusiviness of the ideal and spiritual art as envisioned by Havell, Coomaraswamy and Abanindranath. Various thoughts can be claimed as forming this third camp: from the historian Akshay Maitreya, who had said that just by painting in India one does not produce Indian painting, to Benoy Sarkar who, writing from Paris in 1922 in his path-breaking essay, extolled the necessity if not the inevitability of a "truly International modern style of art." The exhibition of the work of Paul Klee, Kandinsky and other German artists organized in Calcutta in 1922 by Rabindranath and Gaganendranth was a major event. Furthermore, there emerged a group of younger Calcutta artists who declared in their manifesto that the "Bengal School paintings lacked vitality and that the false sense of Indian art and the propaganda for the eastern art should be resisted." These artists were referring to the idealized, but sentimental themes of Abanindranath, and also to the more politically-motivated program of a pan-Asian ethos urged by the Japanese writer Okakura and Sister Nivedita. The analysis of the third camp was significant: In their attempt to confront the colonizer, the "traditionalists" took refuge in a "recovered" pre-colonial past, or more correctly, in a fabricated past, never questioning which or whose past was being recovered. This invariably lead to eulogizing "a pre-capitalist social order ... rather than the grim realities of a people striving under sub-human conditions." Such moves lead to the recovery of a specific past at the cost of excluding others.

The most important figure in this debate is Rabindranath Tagore. Although he appears like his nephew Abanindranath disengaged from social realities, and actually comes close to the idea of Havell and others of the spiritual artistic persona, he is sharply critical of the "narrow-mindedness" of an 'Indian' art. "I strongly urge our artists vehemently," Rabindranath wrote, "to deny their obligation carefully to produce something that can be labelled as Indian Art by conforming to some old world mannerisms. Let them proudly refuse to be herded into a pen like branded beasts that are treated as cattle and not as cows." Further, he said, "when we speak of Indian Art it indicates some truth based upon the Indian tradition and temperament. At the same time we must know that there is no such thing as absolute caste restriction in human cultures; they even have the power to combine and produce new variations, and such combinations have been going on for ages, proving the truth of the deep unity of human psychology." A "world dialogue" is seen as fundamental to a modern existence.

Although these two strands – commitment to the idea of a nation and to the realm of architecture – are tied up in Muzharul Islam's thinking, his architecture remains consciously distant from nationalistic polemics. He understands that nationalistic posturing does not automatically lead to a 'regional' architecture. Here, political ideology and architectural fabrication enter an impasse. But even if unresolved, architecture and politics lie inextricably intertwined. The intertwining raises questions about understanding the premise of architectural production, about the subtle thread of creation and vested interests, and about the nature of social engagement of architecture.

The dilemma brings to focus, on the one hand, the figure of the truly artistic persona, as Rabindranath and the architect Louis Kahn, who are suspicious of political arguments, and, on the other hand, the impossibility of political aloofness particularly

PA Building, Dhaka University, 1967. Photo: Ashraf.

in nations like Bangladesh and India. Political engagement however has convinced Muzharul Islam about the insufficiency of architectural form to address social conditions, and that has gradually shifted him towards a more politicized role.

Search for Architectural Paradigms

In his 1944 essay "Our Heritage," Humayun Kabir notes that "in all modern manifestations of Indian art, the one form which is absent is architecture." If literature, painting, and somewhat later, film, were thematically confronting the existential question of "what it means to be a Bengali in the twentieth century," architecture remained far behind as a mere construction activity. An architectural discourse was clearly missing from the Renaissance movement, despite the intellectual strides of its early period, and the stimulating debates on aesthetics. Even Rabindranath, who had reflected on almost all spheres of human existence, and who had actually experimented with some houses at Santiniketan, had little to say directly about it. Pointing to colonialism, Humayun Kabir insists that the ensuing fragmentation of social collectivity was responsible for a deficiency in architecture culture. It was the individualist art – painting, poetry and literature – that flourished even within the fractured condition of colonial society.

The leadership of the building activity was taken up by engineers, earlier by the corps of British army engineers, and inherited later by the new cadre of civilianized personnel, the "civil" engineers. Even after independence from colonial rule in 1947, architecture remained within the hegemony of the "civil" engineering profession. Building activity was reduced to a mundane functional manipulation of the box, far removed from an investigation of the spatial, experiential or symbolic dimension of architecture. The principles and typologies of the Bengali building tradition also remained uninvestigated.

It was in 1953, in this imbalanced condition of cultural energy and architectural amnesia that Muzharul Islam began his career. For a thirty-year old working single-handedly, the task was immense: his architectural production involved, at one level, a resistance to the entrenched practice of the engineers, and, at another level, the formulation of a Bengali building paradigm. From the very first projects, the formulation of a paradigm is addressed through a two-fold concern: the question of the house, and the question of the city.

The paradigm of the modern house in the subcontinent is constituted by a chain of developments that originates in the colonial bungalow. Derived from the *bangla* hut of rural Bengal (and hence *bungalow*), the bungalow itself is adopted by the English as a model of dwelling in the pavilion, from where "one could see the sunset and the horizon," and no doubt, from where one could keep a watchful eye on restive natives too. It was the latter reason framed within an imperial imperative that lead to the classicizing of the bungalow. The Bengali elites continued the classicized bungalow, caricaturing its details or applying ornate decorations. The ultimate twist to the bungalow came from modern architecture, and the 'scientism' of tropical architecture, that involved filtering the stigma of colonial architecture to produce the modern model of dwelling. Principles of tropical architecture gave a climatic rationale to the bungalow in the hot-humid zone, while architectural modernism introduced an abstract asymmetrical disposition, jettisonning the classical-colonial imagery and breaking the cuboid geometry of the bungalow into a lyrical composition of planes. Architecturally, the pavilion model was seen as a machine for living in the hot-humid zone, as pictured in certain *pata* paintings. Sociologically, the modern house responded to the emerging aspirations of an altogether new urban group: the middle class.

Throughout the 1950s and most part of 1960s, Muzharul Islam experimented with a number of house types and techniques: the courtyard house for O.R. Jaigirder, the vaulted residence for a government executive engineer, the house-on-stilts, and the parasol house for himself at Dhanmondi. There were also experiments with various techniques: the vault, the brick-and-concrete composite wall, and brick construction. But, fundamentally the early houses, in articulating the paradigm of the modern bungalow, incorporated the spatial and the planar dimension of the classic houses of early modernism. In this period, Muzharul Islam also developed his crafting of architecture that became vivid in such signature details as the somewhat

Section through own residence, Dhaka, 1968. Muzharul Islam Archive.

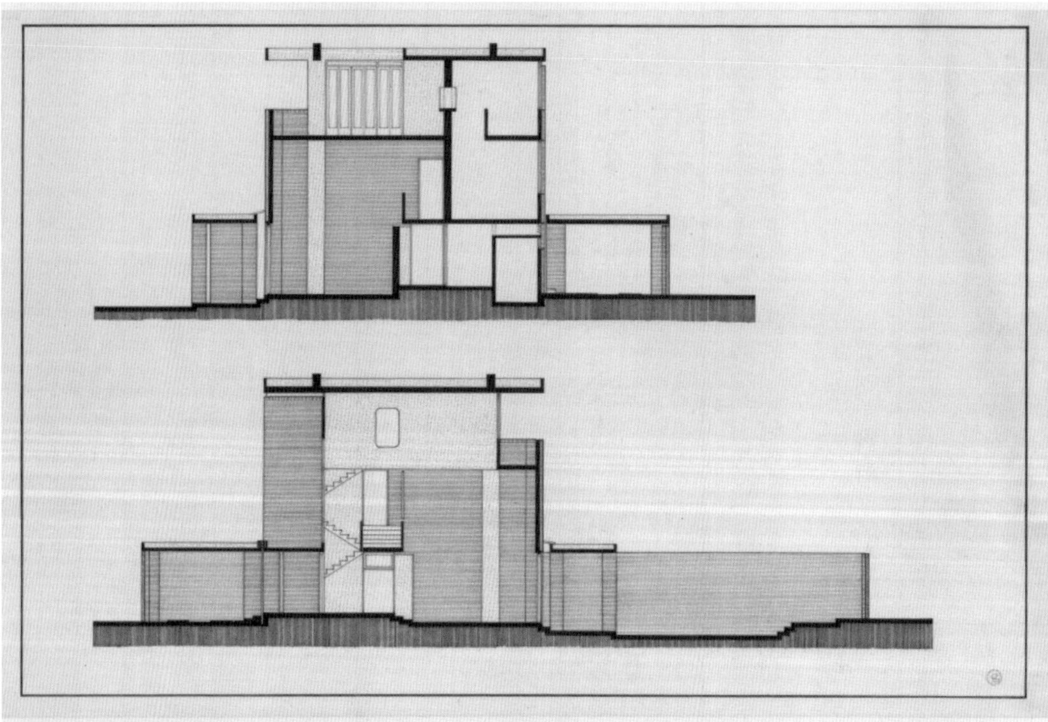

Wrightian proportion of windows, columns, and openings, and always, in the spatial character of the entrance porch.

The idea of the pavilion was also behind large projects, from the Public Library and the Science Laboratory to the NIPA building at Dhaka University. The Public Library (1953) was organized in a clearly Corbusian mode – a cubic volume on stilts, complete with ramps, sun-breakers and pristine white colors – but it indicated for Dhaka then a fresh approach to urbanism. With its climate control devices of shell roofs and brick louvers for openings, the western wing was an original articulation. With its array of concrete piers girding the building, and programmatic spaces recessed further behind, the NIPA building (1967) signified a pavilion. The hovering plane of the roof as a *chattri* (parasol) completed the imagery. The Art College, designed at the same time as the Public Library, stands apart from this group. It came much closer to mediating with the conditions of the place in a sensorial and evocative manner. Sprawling, low building volumes unlike the monolithic Public Library, the use of exposed fire brick which always has such a magical resonance with the "greenness" of Bengal, the natural garden setting on an urban site, all went to form the atmosphere of a campus that was ideal for the contemplation and learning of the arts, and more importantly, to indicate a spatial environment that evoked the architectural poetics of the land.

Despite discontinuities which affected his practice, the works of Muzharul Islam reveal a progression from a reference to the language of certain western masters towards a more personal formulation. The 1960s remain his most prolific period of building. He was also involved at this time in the development of the professional institute of the architects, and was influential in drafting its constitution, for which architects in Pakistan still remember him admiringly. Besides his own contribution to the architecture culture, he was also instrumental in bringing Louis Kahn, Paul Rudolph and Stanley Tigerman to Bangladesh. The involvement of the American trio was seen by Muzharul Islam as a necessary occasion for providing visual and provocative examples in the vacuous contemporary situation.

His early projects from the 1950s up to works like NIPA and his own house in the late 60s owe much to Frank Lloyd Wright, Le Corbusier and Paul Rudolph. This is evident, in varying degrees, in the basic skeletal configuration of the works, in the innovation of climate control (the umbrella roof of his own house recalling Shodhan Villa); in the sculptural animation made by varying reliefs, deep shadows and juxtaposition of materials; in the spatial composition (as in the multi-levelled organization of his own house); and, finally, in the manner the buildings engage with the landscape with an assertive and self-referential stance (again, with the exception of Arts College).

In the late 60s, with the commission of two university projects, involving large-scale organization, began his later phase. The presence of Louis Kahn in Dhaka, ensuing into a dialogue with Muzharul Islam, is more than incidental for this shift. While the pervading order, as in Jahangirnagar University and the housing for Jaipurhat Limestone Factory, is an a *priori* geometry, the concern is to generate an 'urbanised' order by the formation of communal spatial enclosures, streets and continuous facades, qualities which are not explicit in earlier projects. Individual buildings are clearly of masonry, where spaces and voids seem to be carved out of masonry solids that, despite their often curious geometrical purity and unlike the skeletal nature of his earlier projects, form a more earth-hugging ambience.

The shift is most explicit in the National Library project (1978). It is here that "distortion" of the idealized form itself becomes the generator of architecture; the final form acknowledges more explicitly the contradictory conditions of the place and the programme. Gone is the stark clarity of his earlier skeletal work, there is now a ponderous massive presence accentuated both by the centralized form and the use of brick. The building presents a convincing response to the neighbouring ensemble by Kahn which has by now formed an important context in the north of Dhaka. While geometric abstraction and a consummate skill for crafting constitute a continuity in all his work, the iconography of National Library is a world removed from the Public Library of 1955. The Library is a surreptitious triumph, almost against Muzharul Islam's own rational rigor, of the empirical over the rational, of the accidental over the planned, of the a *posteriori over the a priori*. Moreover, what has been a materialist constant in his work, that is, the privileging of reason that has lead to a suspicion of mystery and the "unconscious," is somewhat undermined. One can begin to talk now of the reification of the mysterious, and of such anti-Marxist stuff as wonder and amazement.

Thinking the City

All along in Muzharul Islam's work there is a thinking or rather a rethinking of the city. This is implicit in the typology of the early houses and projects, present analogously in the plans for the Polytechnique Institutes and the universities, and then directly in the sketches for the future of Dhaka city.

The concern for the city has deep roots. In the post-colonial situation of most Asian societies, two interconnected conditions have become crucial: the collapse of the structure of generally self-sufficient rural communities, and the institutional vacuum of burgeoning cities. It is too simplistic to think that the moral responsibilities for one should supercede the other despite the demographical tip towards the village. If the rural situation demands visions for retaining existing institutions, the urban situation requires new models, a totally new setting for an unprecedented urban condition. In social and political leadership, Gandhi represented the former, Kemal Ataturk and Nehru the latter. The Egyptian architect Hassan Fathy, in his experiments at New Gourna, provides an architectural example of the Gandhian variety. Still, what of the city?

The question is: What is the Bengali city *to be*? Also, what has been the nature of the city in Bengal (before it was destroyed in

Hostel, Jahangirnagar University, 1967. Muzharul Islam Archive.

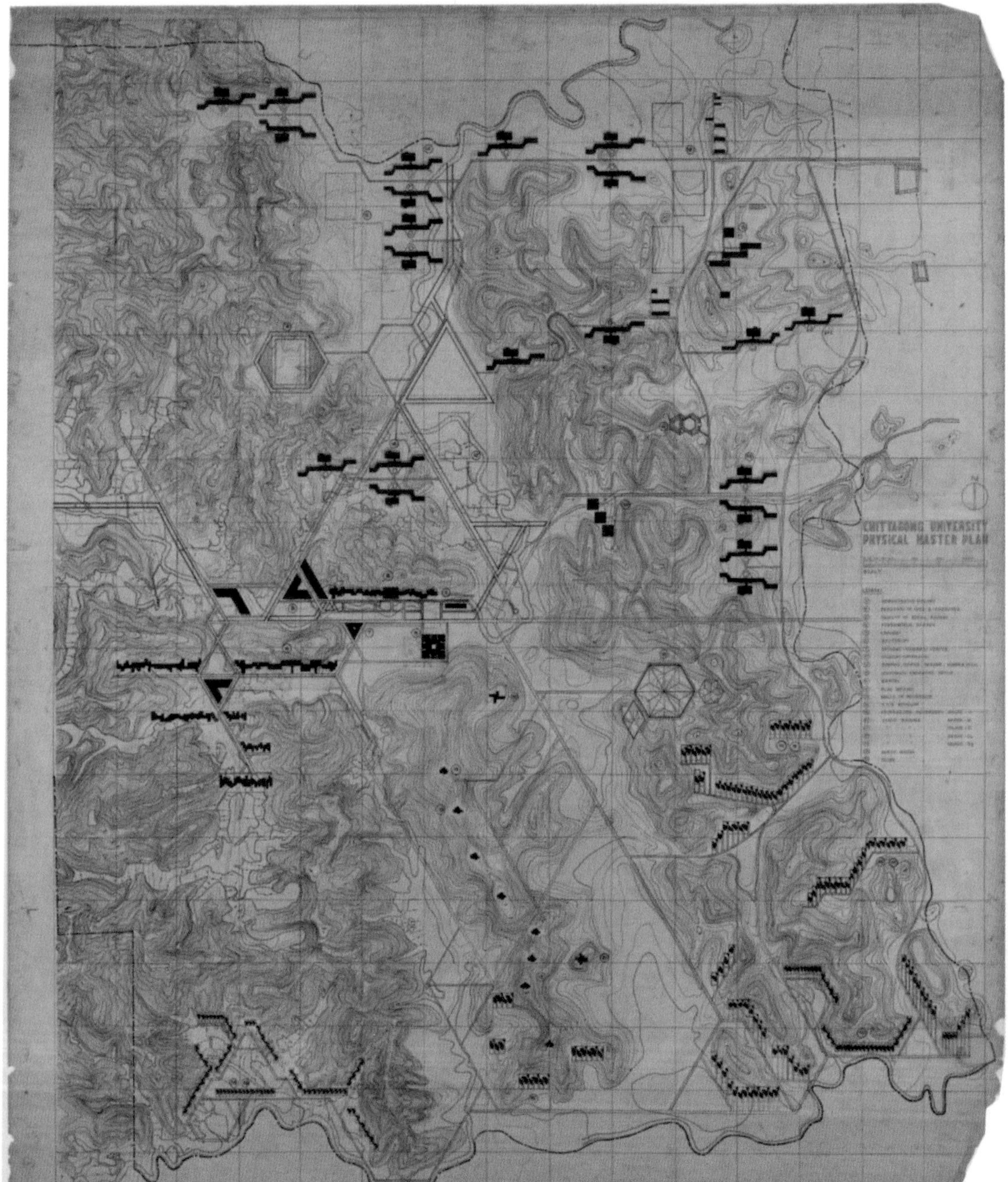

Plan for Chittagong University, 1965-1971. Muzharul Islam Archive.

Hostel, Chittagong University, 1965-1971. Muzharul Islam Archive.

the name of development, as when the historic canals of Dhaka were filled over to make roads, or before it was reconfigured by mushroom growth due to sheer economic imperatives)? The Bengali city can never be imagined through the morphology of Jaipur and Udaipur, or Sienna and Cairo. If the Bengali city is to be rearticulated again, one has to look eastwards, in the spatiality of Chinese, Japanese or Javanese cities. The layout of Sherebanglanagar by Louis Kahn, or the master plans for the Polytechnique Institutes, by Muzharul Islam and Stanley Tigerman, suggest a paradigmatic Bengali city. This is an "alternative" city, derived neither from the romanticized image of the dense, interiorized Middle Eastern city nor from the randomly dispersed village homesteads of Bengal.

Muzharul Islam has arrived at the "alternative" city through a Marxian reading of the difference between the city and the so-called rural hinterland, seeing a spatial representation of oppression and social disparity. Here, a Marxian perspective comes to an agreement with a Rabindrik vision. Echoing Rabindranath's 1928 essay "City and Village," Muzharul Islam finds the difference unacceptable, he believes that "old ideas of society divided into haves and have-nots are no longer valid... The world has advanced sufficiently in science and technology to help remove the differences between the city and the so-called rural hinterland." He recognizes that "the problem of designing, re-designing, building, and re-building of cities have become one of the most pressing problems facing our countries," and "cities must be re-designed and re-built," but this must proceed with the intention of obliterating the topos of the city-country difference. While the vision of this city has a strong moral and economic underpinning, Muzharul Islam recognizes that "the cities should provide the environment for civilized life within the context of our own culture." Moreover, "the city can develop only as a part of the physical environment of the country – with the

Clinic, Joypurhat Housing, 1974. Muzharul Islam Archive.

ultimate aim of abolishing all differences between the city and the rural areas. The traditional relationship with nature (still existing to a certain extent in the villages of Bangladesh) should be continued in the cities." One way that the traditional relationship can be interpreted is through the modernist slogan of "light, green and air" for the city.

Plans for Jaipurhat and Jahangirnagar are Muzharul Islam's closest effort to move away from the conventional morphology of either the city or the country. Although the plans incorporate a certain collectivity, they have less to do with the city as we have come to know it. The plans respond to the nature of dwelling in the delta; the buildings are arrayed in the plan and architecturally articulated to be receptacles for "light, green and air."

*

Architect, teacher, mentor, activist, provocateur, Muzharul Islam is an institution by himself. Life at his office-abode Vastukalabid has been a setting for all these possibilities for a number of generations.

Flat Type A, B, and C, Joypurhat Housing, 1974. Muzharul Islam Archive.

Working as an architect in *Vastukalabid* is not easy. Muzharul Islam demands a lot from the tense initiates: a particular commitment to architecture, a knowledge of how things come together, sharpness of response, a hand in drawing, an eye for details, but, most of all, a patience for his own impatience. Vastukalabid in the evening assumes a semi-Socratic atmosphere, when the drudgery of the day's work has been left aside, when Muzharul Islam takes on a more amiable disposition, when age bar collapses, and senior architects, young beginners, and students mingle, and tea arrives in the gigantic tottering white cup, and where nothing is holy and nothing is left unquestioned. Politics and the recent turmoil on the streets of Dhaka are discussed, manifestos are written to launch this new venture or another to salvage architecture, and petitions are drafted to protest some bureaucratic mismanagement. On some architecturally propitious evening the slide projector would be set up for a talk by someone important passing through Dhaka: the art historian Michael Meister, a French video-film team, a researcher from Columbia University, a professor from a Canadian university, the Italian architect Atillio Petruciolli; or, the whole drafting area cleared of desks and chairs to lay *satranjis* on the floor for an evening of songs.

Yet, institutional architecture keeps him at a distance, always trying hard to marginalize his impact. A result of the apolitical nature of current architectural practice, certainly not in the sense of Kahn and Rabindranath, this is partially due to the result of the post-modern critique of ideological positions, and mainly a consequence of economic self-interest. From the vantage point of current architecture culture, Muzharul Islam appears as an annoyance in the placid comfort of a non-ideological existence. His ethical exhortation sounds shrill in the ears of architectural opportunism.

And then there are unresolved tensions, between idealization and the "real" incongruities of existence, between social engagement and artistic autonomy, between political ideology and architectural production. Architecturally speaking, what was arrived at in the National Library – the co-existence of the contingent and the idealized – is missing in the large-scale plans. The *essential* plan still awaits incorporation of the texture of our concretely lived life.

Muzharul Islam remains a "tragic" artist, the quintessential modern figure who is no longer a tool, a manifestation of the collectivity (as in traditional conditions). The artist now is a reformer; he has a critical mind. More than being a mouthpiece, he is now a social critic. More than being a representation, he *re-presents*. Every piece he produces, every thought he thinks, is no more mere reflection on society than locating what, in his mind, is lagging in it, and what is usurpable in it. He is more an iconoclast than an iconist. It is this largely self-appointed role – the usurper of the social strongholds – that inevitably results in futility, lending tragicality to the modern artist. Yet what counts is not the fruits borne, but the seeds sown.

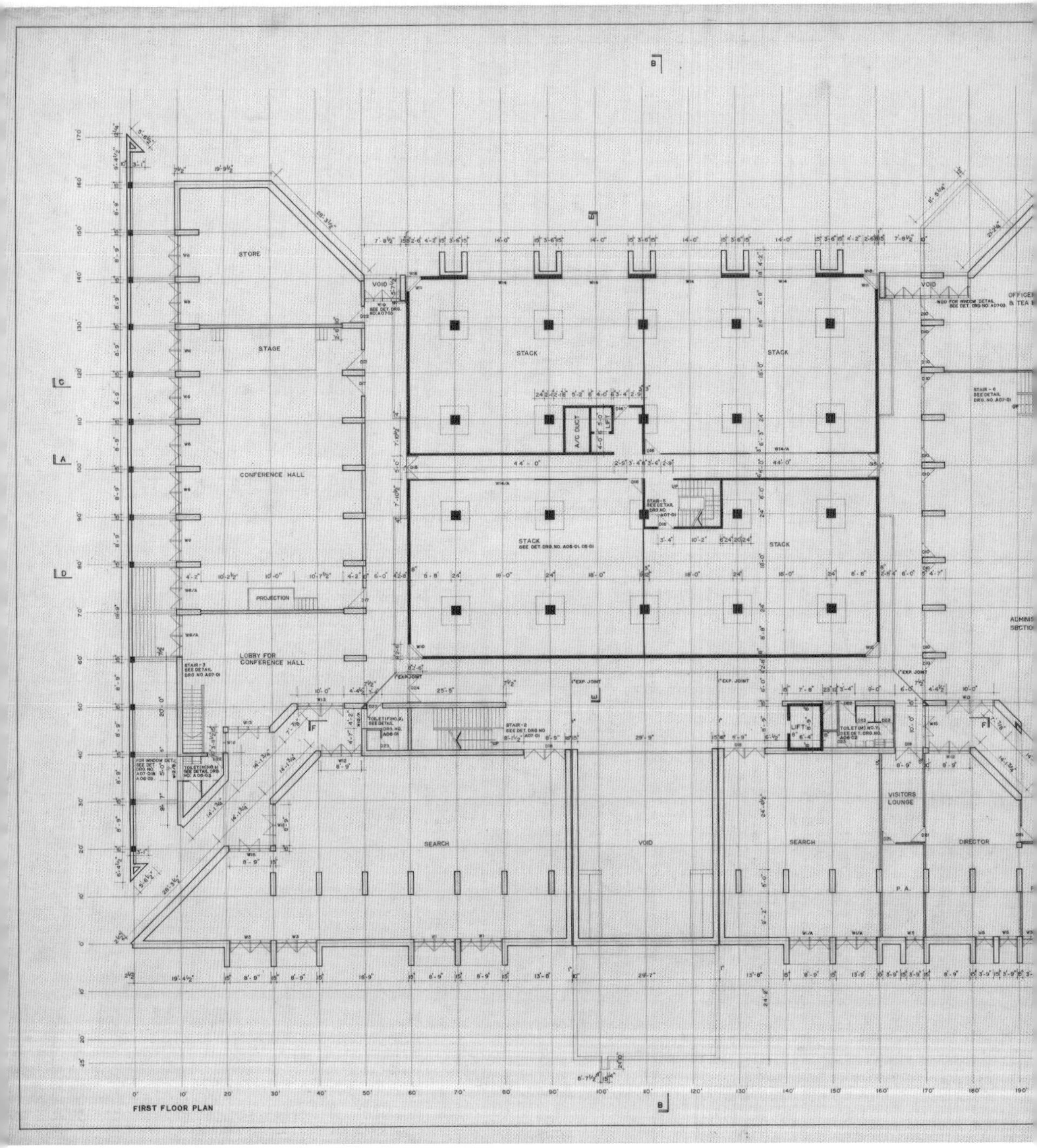

National Library, Dhaka, First floor plan.

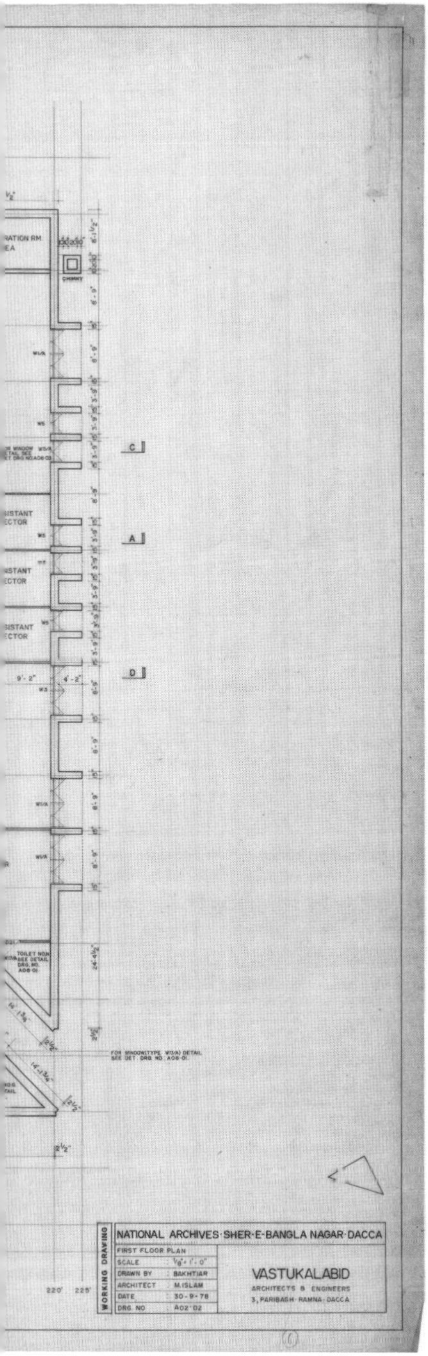

National Library, Dhaka, 1980-1984. Photo: Ashraf.

Even if it seems idealized, Muzharul Islam is concerned with the wholeness of life, the horizon of existence. It is significant that he names his office *Vastukalabid*, recalling the ancient practice of *vastushilpa*, literally the "art of existing," and not just the craft of making as implied in the Latin sense of architecture (*archi*, chief; *tecton*, making, while the root vas is connected to astitwa, the German *wesen*, essence, the English *was*). *Vastu* is not an aesthetical category, but an existential one if by that we can mean the way we situate ourselves in the world, and the way we are in the world. This is not something given to us, or we find ourselves in, but is a conscious effort of *construction*.

Bangala Ragini, A Ragmala Painting, Bundi School, eighteenth century.

Land, Water, and People in Bengal: Themes for a Deltaic Architecture

Published in *Contemporary Architecture and City Form: The South Asian Paradigm*, edited by Farooq Ameen Bombay: MARG Publications, 1997.

Rice and Identity

Comprising of Bangladesh and most of West Bengal, the Bengal delta is crucially located between two geo-cultural matrices. On the one hand, it has always been considered part of a western orbit formed by the larger Indian culture, but one that extends towards Persia, Arabia, and ultimately Europe. This aspect is seen in most explicit levels of culture: language, liturgies, institutions, and the laws. On the other hand, at a more primordial or foundational level, there is an irreducible stratum that is linked to an eastern matrix, that of South-East Asia.[1]

Predominantly a water-based civilization, this eastern matrix is a world of moistness, fecundity, and lushness where cosmological and valorized concepts are generated from riverine dynamics and agricultural life patterns. This matrix is also one of "rice culture," where rice is not something merely consumed but forms the basis of value-construction of a collective *ethos* and *mythos*, and of the articulation of self-identity. In the Bengal delta, rice cultivation is an existential occupation; the production of rice is "the production of a world-view."

The Bengal delta is a pure chemistry of land and water; it is in fact land on lease from water. Formed by the silt, and then constantly shaped and reshaped by the rivers that themselves are perpetually shifting and changing, the land has a certain amorphous character. Advaita Malla Burman, in his novel *A River Called Titash*, captures the human equation of this land-water environment in two paradigmatic figures: the fisherman and the peasant, the man with the net (*jaal*) and the man with the plough (*langol*). Besides the life-sustaining occupation around rice and fish, the Bengal delta is characterized by the life-enhancing occupation around bamboo-weaving and clay-moulding, that is, basketry and pottery. The art of weaving may be seen in the objects of daily life, and in the fabrication of bamboo mats and other architectural elements. Clay kneading has led to the art of pottery, and to the magnificent production of terracotta art and brick construction. The fundamental fact is that, from wet-rice production to material fabrication and to cultivating dwelling, living in the delta still means a deep tie to the land and the climate.

Form Reveals Climate

"The Mother Tongue of Architecture" is a rather tantalizing title of an essay by Rabiul Husain, an architect who is more known as a poet. Concerned with the rehabilitation of "localness" in architecture, Husain invites an analogy between language and architecture: Is there, as in language, a "mother tongue" in architecture, an irreducible substratum that defines identity? If there is, where is that substratum? And what is the relationship between language as mother tongue and "mother tongue" in architecture?

Citing the current atmosphere of Euro-American-centric globalization and the loss of local cultures, Husain wonders if it is possible to recover the "mother tongue" of architecture if we have yielded, for example, to an English-centrism in language. Quatremere de Quincy, the eighteenth-century French theorist, would say that architecture and language originate from the same cultural junction. In Bangladesh specifically, the language over which people have laid down their lives (a nationalist symbolization) is however preceded by an architecture that is phenomenally more rooted to nature. There is possibly a rupture between architecture and language; while architecture still remains bound to place, site, and situation, that is, a matrix of nature-climate, language has assumed the contrary character of portability. Bengali is spoken with the same ease in Begumganj as in Bricklane and Brooklyn.

Climate then is more fundamental than language. It may not be simply that "form follows climate," as Charles Correa suggests, but more significantly climate is the basis of how we see ourselves and how we see the world. The old Japanese notion of *fudo* offers an illuminating nexus of climate and architecture. *Fudo*, which literally means wind and earth, conceptually suggests the intertwining of the idea of climate (nature) and culture, a conjoined sense of the two. The singular notion of fudo challenges the Indo-European polarized sense of culture and nature, of *songskriti and prokriti*, the basis of the modern world-view.

Like *fudo*, the phenomenological concept of "lived-body" also questions the conceptual separation, of how the environment is distinguished as standing over and against the living body, while it actually may be considered as an indefinite extension of the "lived-body." There is, as the French philosopher Maurice Merleau-Ponty sees it, a "reciprocal insertion and intertwining" of the "lived-body" and the environment. In living, the body not only lives itself but also the environment. The boundary of one overlaps with the other.

The Japanese thinker Tetsuro Watsuji, who has developed the notion of *fudo* in contemporary thoughts, qualifies the generalized terms space and environment by characterizing the environment primarily as climate. Thus the "intertwining" becomes specific. The phenomenological notion of how "we discover ourselves in space" is rephrased as how "we discover ourselves in climate," that is, we find ourselves in a concrete

Atiya Masjid, Tangail, 1679 CE. Photo: Anup Saha Raju, Chetana Sthapatya Bangladesh Project.

Govinda Temple, Puthia, nineteenth century. Photo: Anup Saha Raju, Chetana Sthapatya Bangladesh Project.

A pata painting from Murshidabad, nineteenth century, from *Pata Art*.

climatic and geographic envelope. In this sense, nature-climate is the foundational aspect of culture. "Climate is the agent by which human life is objectivized, and it is here that man comprehends himself: there is self-discovery in climate."[6]

Architecture may then be seen not merely as a shelter *from* climate, as if climate and architecture are confronting each other. Fundamentally speaking, architecture is the "presencing" of the intertwining of climate and culture; it is where climate is revealed. As Martin Heidegger was to say about the Greek temple, it portrays nothing, it simply *is*. By standing there on the rocky ground, the temple shows the ground's spontaneous support, makes manifest the storm raging above, brings to radiance the light of the day and breadth of the sky, and makes visible the invisible space of the air.[7]

The Pavilion Paradigm

The most pervasive architectural presence in the delta is the pavilion structure: the rustic Bengali hut is a primal pavilion, *a machine for living in a hot-humid milieu*, so to speak. The hut is essentially a roof characterized by the uniquely swooping canopy or *chhad* that makes "visible" the presence of the intense sun and the torrential rain (*chhad* is cognate with *chhatri*, parasol, and *chhaya*, shadow). What holds the roof up is secondary; whether mud walls or bamboo posts, they are always placed well within the perimeter of the roof. But it is important that the enclosure be permeable, as in the ideal Laugerian structure on columns. The seventeenth-century Bundi painting *Bangala Ragini* is an illuminating depiction of the deltaic pavilion. Historical evidence of the idealization of the hut in Bengal – as a tiered shrine serving cosmological purposes – may be seen in representations in the eighth century Ashrafpur Bronze Caitya, and in the eleventh-century Buddhist manuscript *Ashtasahasrika Prajnaparamita*.[9]

Noting how the desert has shaped the Arab house and cosmology, the Egyptian architect Hassan Fathy writes: "Because the desert during the day is burning, glaring and productive of sand-storms, the Arab does not find any comfort in opening his house to nature at ground level. The only kindly aspect of nature for him is the sky, promising him coolness in the night and dwarfing even the expanse of the desert with the starry infinitude of the universe. So the Arab tries to shut out the desert with its suffocating sand and open his house on to the *sahn* or internal courtyard." Fathy further cosmologizes the *sahn*, seeing its walls as props for the dome of the sky.[10]

Fathy's glorified description of the Arab courtyard house is also illuminating for the Bengali pavilion house, for the two are typologically opposed. A pata painting from Murshidabad illustrates this well. Where the courtyard house puts up a blank wall to shut off the desert, the pavilion house dematerializes it's walls, making them permeable thus diffusing the distinction between exterior and interior. And, where the courtyard house opens up its central space to the sky, the pavilion puts up a shadow-giving roof. Unlike the intention of shutting out the elements as in the interiorized courtyard-houses of hot-arid places, and the sealed-off spaces of colder climates, the pavilion is completely *with the plein air*.

The pavilion is a locus from where one looks outwards horizontally, or, as the Filipino architect Leandro Locsin would imply, one sees sunsets and moonlight. On a more sociological note, Anthony D. King points to the centrifugal nature of the pavilion house in which the movement of activity is "outward, on to the verandah, and further into the compound," unlike the courtyard house, where it is centripetal, towards the courtyard.[11] Terraces and verandahs, by extending this quality, become natural appurtenances of the pavilion.

To be *with the plein air* thus translates into a continuum of the external/natural world and the architectural space into establishing a visual, spatial, and sensorial interpenetration of "nature" and architecture. It would appear that the concept of fudo finds a suitable elaboration in a deltaic situation. It is for this reason the Bengali dwelling is always idealized with its setting. The territory of the house is much wider than the "room" under the roof. A *khanar bachan* (popular folk proverb) describes such a dwelling as having "Ducks to the East/Bamboo to the West/ Banana to the North/Open to the South," that is, a pond towards the east of the house, and orchards and gardens around it. This has been the perennial image of the Bengali landscape: modest-scaled detached structures among foliage and ponds.

Manifested diversely, the idea of the pavilion takes many forms. The bamboo-woven hut on stilts and the thatch hut on earth platform (*bhita*) are straightforward examples in which the plan-form may be rectangular or square. The solid centralized mass, constructed in brick or stone out of social needs and monumental urges, is a more arguable elaboration of the pavilion idea (not all centralized mass in the delta participates in the pavilion). For example, the brick-earth stupa with the symbolic Buddhist *chhatri* at the pinnacle is a sort of combination of the pavilion emblem and masonry mass in which the latter may aspire towards a pavilion condition in a more phenomenal way by the character of its openings.

From simple clustering to a deltaic city-form, the pavilion is also a key to complex organization. Clusters are formed by grouping pavilion "units" in a series or around an amorphously interiorized space. Deltaic morphology implies the disposition of isolated buildings in a fabric of paddyfields, gardens, orchards, lakes, and ponds. An understanding of deltaic city-form or urbanism lies, not in the dense labyrinthine fabric of cities like Jaipur and Lahore – the "city of figure ground," but in city-forms east of the Bengal delta, in the "rice culture" matrix, described by the Japanese architect Fumihiko Maki as the "city of figure-nature" in which the distinction between urban and rural morphology is not so oppositional. In summation, the deltaic pavilion may be seen as an independent form with a centrifugal spatiality creating a continuum with the surrounding. The nature of the pavilion is manifested in the parasol roof, the permeable wall, and the verandahs.

From Bangladar to Bungalows
Occurring between the fourteenth and sixteenth century, the Sultanate rule in Bengal was crucial and productive in engaging Bengali architectural themes, especially in restating the idea of the deltaic pavilion in a *new* mosque form. This particular architectural phenomenon reflects a conflict between a universalist Islam and a territorial ideal.

Temple with a bangla roof. Photo SN Maitra (collected).

Adina Masjid (in Pandua, built 1375) points to the rather monumental failure of the large, interiorized courtyard model in the deltaic environment. In following a greater Islamic ideology, the inspiration for Adina must have been the Great Mosque in Damascus with its high vaulted space and large courtyard. The impressive Damascus model never continued through as neither huge congregation nor interiorized courtyards of a hot-dry condition was the reality in the waterlogged delta.

Sultanate architecture in Bengal, as other cultural aspects, grew from a territorial condition. Constructed in the regional brick and terracotta idiom, the architecture of the place was characterized by detached cubic volumes. The interiorized courtyard was dropped altogether. Many buildings instead "opened" their walls by multiple doors on all sides; in the case of a mosque, all sides had doors except the *Qibla* wall where niches represented the door. In some mosques, the symbolic dome itself was replaced by the monumentalized *bangla* roof.[14]

Louis Kahn, ambulatory, Assembly Building, Photo: Ashraf.

Sultanate architects learned their lessons from the common hut, and also, as Perween Hasan demonstrates, from contemporary temples that too developed from the hut.[15] The transfer of the uniquely curved roof of the bangla hut, from bamboo and thatch to masonry, was a Sultanate contribution. And when the swooping *chattri* was not possible, a softly curving cornice still evoked the original hut. Most Sultanate mosques, and concurrent Hindu temples, employed this element as the single most important feature. The combination of the centralized cubic form and multiplication of the bangla roof would generate a distinct genre of temples.[16] The Mughals, and then the Rajputs, fascinated by the *bangla* roof, would incorporate it as *bangladar* in their architectural repertoire.

Extending to the idea of the bungalow and the urban detached house, the deltaic pavilion continued to be a dominant theme in more recent times. In colonial Bengal, the bungalow began by monumentalizing the rural hut, but soon spurred by imperialist agendas took an unabashed neoclassical appearance. Modern architecture, by filtering out the stigma of colonial imageries, provided another twist to the bungalow. While the principles of "tropical architecture" gave a climatic rationale to the bungalow in hot-humid zones, modernist themes provided an abstract and asymmetrical configuration. The bungalow turned from a cuboid geometry into a lyrical composition of planes, the lessons of which could be found in the architecture of Frank Lloyd Wright.

The Parasol and the *Jali* Wall

In Le Corbusier's architecture for India, the parasol was a central theme although conceived for hot-arid Ahmedabad and Chandigarh. The parasol is the dominant roof on the High Court, the entrance canopy for the Assembly, the symbolic *chhatri* in front of the governor's chamber in the Secretariat, and a surrogate-dome on the unbuilt Governor's Palace and the Mill-Owners' Building. The Shodhan Villa (1956) is a masterful essay of the parasol concept.

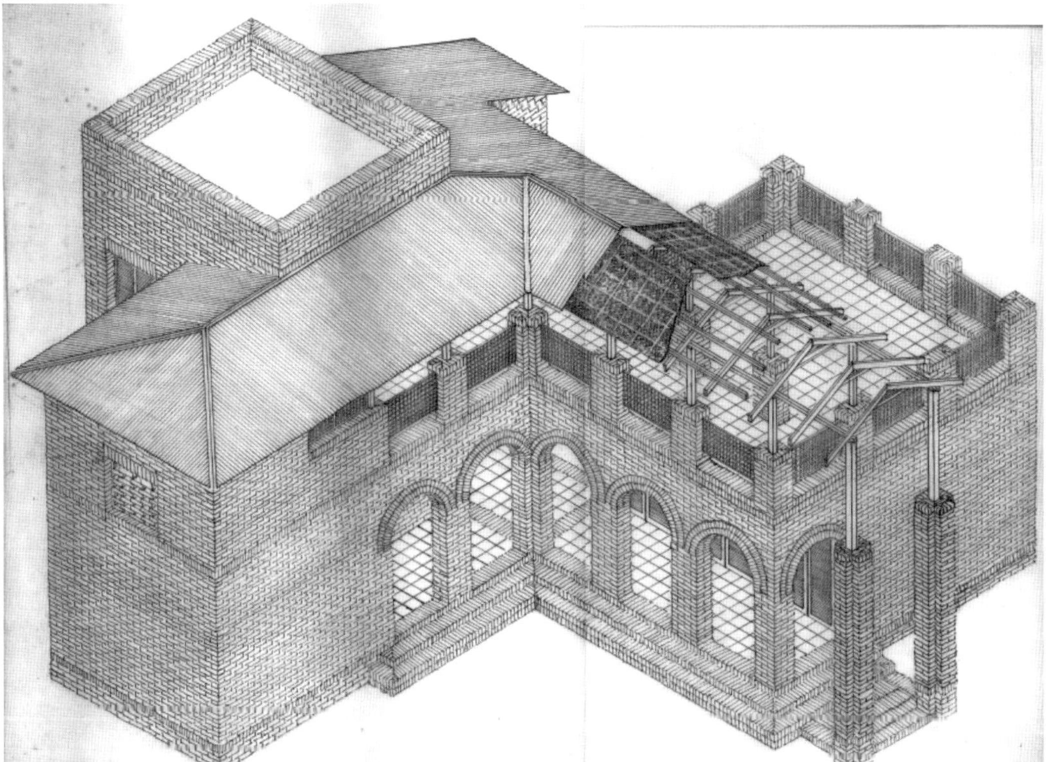

Bashirul Haq, architect's family house, Bhatshala, Brahmanbaria, 1991.

Timmy Zamir Aziz, addition to house, Dhanmondi, Dhaka, 1993. Photo: Aziz.

Bruno Lang Quang, Buddhist Children's Monastery, Mirpur, 1994. Photo: Ashraf.

In Bangladesh, the earliest modernist realizations of the parasol idea are Constantin Doxiadis's Teachers-Students' Centre (1963) and Muzharul Islam's NIPA building (1969), both for Dhaka University. Both projects are important for considering pavilion themes in a non-domestic realm. The inwardly-slanted parasol over the Teachers-Students' Centre is however more gestural compared to the brooding presence of the monumental parasol of NIPA that hovers majestically on free-standing columns casting a deep shadow on the multiple functions tucked behind the ring of columns. In his own house (1969), Muzharul Islam conceived a free-floating concrete plane under which brick walls articulated complex layers of spaces. A more recent version is Bruno Lang Duan's Buddhist monastery in Dhaka (1994), where a single concrete canopy shelters discrete brick volumes. In more abstract form, Uttam Kumar Saha has conceived a number of residences as three-dimensional compositions of largely horizontal planes.

When it comes to the wall, to be *with the plein air*, is not so natural as suggested in the elemental condition of the rural hut or the idealization in *Bangala Ragini*. More durable enclosures are necessitated by practical needs, economic status, or new urban conditions. While bamboo screens establish a degree of balance between the need for permeability and the necessity of enclosure, the paradox is heightened with a mud, brick, or concrete walls: how to make the wall both solid and porous.

The filigree screen at the Tomb of Salim Chisti in Fatehpur Sikri is a classic example of a permeable wall. Antonin Raymond's dormitory at Pondicherry (1936) and Laurie Baker's Centre for Development Studies at Trivandrum (1972) are more recent articulations of the *jali* wall. The *jali* was an important feature in Muzharul Islam's Dhaka University Library (1954), Science Laboratories (1960), and other projects. The wooden blind (*khorkhori*) is another way of making a surface alternately open and closed, as in the Polytechnic projects (1966), designed jointly by Stanley Tigerman and Muzharul Islam. Louis Kahn conceived the double wall, in which an inner private wall of regular openings is preceded by an outer wall of large geometric openings: it would seem that the envelope of a taut geometric solid has been "eroded" by natural elements.

Saif Ul Haque and Jalal Ahmed (Diagram Architects), BRAC Centre, Faridpur, 1993. Photo: Ashraf.

Timmy Aziz in his mother's house (1993) takes up the issue more squarely but with some ingenuity. He literally perforated the solid brick wall and celebrated those perforations by introducing hollow glazed tiles with wirenet inserts.

Clusters and Courts

The delta has emerged with modernism also. In fact, the rationalist abstraction of modernism, as in Muzharul Islam's essentialism, has filtered the lessons of the delta to a fundamental core (seen in another way, the delta has put modernism in its *place*), Deltaic themes are addressed in new building programmes without referring to historical motifs or traditional symbolisms.

Uttam Kumar Saha, Herman Gmeiner Social Center, Khulna, 1986. Photo: Architect's office.

In more recent times, themes of the pavilion and how pavilions are to be grouped together appear within a more traditional iconography and planning. The issue of grouping has been inseparable from the pavilion idea. Once the modernist monolith, in which diverse functions are subsumed within a single form, has been disintegrated into entities approaching autonomous pavilions, the next critical issue is how to group these together. Most recent projects evoke the traditional *uthaan* – the semi-enclosed courtyard in Bengali dwellings formed by isolated volumes where corners of the courtyard sort of "leak" to the outside.

Raziul Ahsan of CAPE, in his SOS Youth Village at Mirpur (1984), arranged clustered but disaggregated volumes, formed of vaults and slanted overhangs around semi-interiorized spaces. Uttam Kumar Saha, in his Children's Village at Khulna (1986), arranged crisp volumes around a stark courtyard. Diagram Architects (Saif Ul Haque and Jalal Ahmed) in a number of projects have created a rich grid of spaces by a seemingly disarrayed clustering of diverse pavilions jostling each other. Their concern is also about the traditional iconography of buildings, especially with pitched roofs, corbelled windows, and the relationship with water and vegetation.

In organizing his building volumes around an enclosed or semi-enclosed courtyard, Bashirul Haq has evolved a distinct typology: a solid mass at ground level, characterized by a brick structure, of arched openings and wooden shutters, with dark nooks and crannies, and a skeletal structure at the upper level, creating a partially canopied airy terrace from where one has a breath taking view of the endless paddyfields.

Raziul Ahsan has also displayed his concern for another aspect of the delta: *building with* the land. At the Children's Village in Bogra (1994), he expanded and elaborated the *bhita* – the solid earth platform on which the house rises into varieties of land configurations: mounds, embankments, terraces, etc. In certain ways, Ahsan has taken a hesitant attitude towards the buildings themselves, keeping them rather straight-forward, while concentrating on and expanding this liminal condition, the grounding of the house.

Large-scale visions in recent times that would incorporate the form of landwater have so far been schematic. In a hypothetical plan for Dhaka (1987), Muzharul Islam suggested reconfiguring the land-water mesh that grids the city, and exploiting the seasonal exchange of water by land terraces with different levels and different uses.[17] Earlier, Louis Kahn suggested the creation of "land" by brick roads and arched bridges *for* a large wetland area north of the Capital Complex in Dhaka (1973). During drier seasons, the area beneath could be used for cultivation, while during the monsoon, the bridges would provide a safe and dry platform for building houses. Observing the nature of the deltaic topography and its basic architectural principle of "dig-and-mound" – earth excavated to create both a pond and a mound upon which rises the house – Kahn condensed the realities of the delta as "an architecture of the land." In the delta, land could be reshaped to give architectural configurations, and conversely, buildings configured to approximate the form of land.

References:

1. See Paul Wheatley, *Nagora and Commondery: Origin of the Southeast Asian Urban Traditions* (Chicago: University of Chicago, 1983), for a socio-cultural and urban contiguity in the area lying to the east of India and the south of China; and Sumet Jumsai, *Nago: Cultural Origins in Siam and the West Pacific,* (Singapore: Oxford University Press, 1988), for an architectural commonality in the region between Burma and Indonesia. Curiously, in both studies, the western edge of the matrix stops in Bengal. The matrix actually dips down from Bengal towards Sri Lanka and most of South India.

2. See Emiko Ohnuki-Tierney, *Rice as Identity: Japanese Identities Through Time* (Princeton: Princeton University Press, 1993).

3. See Richard Eaton, *The Rise of Islam and the Bengal Frontier 1204- 1760*, (University of California Press, 1993). Eaton suggests that the transformation of the (eastern) delta from forest- to-cultivation occurs with Islamization.

But the cosmology of cultivation is still very much indigenous, for wet-rice production had started in the western Bengal delta by the sixth century BC.

4. See Rabiul Husain, *Bangladesher Sthapatyasanskrti* (Dhaka: Sahitya Samabaya, 1987) (in Bengali).

5. See Maurice Merleau-Ponty, *Phenomenology of Perception*, (London: Routledge & Kegan Paul, 1962).

6. See Tetsuro Watsuji, *Climate: A Philosophical Study* (a translated version published by the Government of Japan in 1930).

7. See Martin Heidegger, "On the Origin of the Work of Art," reprinted in *Martin Heidegger: Basic Writings* (New York: Harper and Row, 1977).

8. Although the pavilion-type is quite widespread all across India, the deltaic one is distinct from the predominant usage in the north as "pleasure-pavilions" and kiosks for inclement weather. In the north, it is often an idealization, as depicted in so many lyrical scenes in miniature paintings. The deltaic pavilion has a rather "existential" necessity; it operates as a paradigm of dwelling, circulating with consistency from the common hut and rich dwellings to religious and public buildings.

9. See S. K. Saraswati, *Architecture of Bengal*, Vol.1, (Calcutta: Bharadwaj & Co., 1976), pp. 64-65.

10. See Hassan Fathy, "The Qa'a of the Cairene Arab House, Its Development and Some Usages for Its Design Concepts," in *Colloque International sur l'Histoire du Caire*, 1969, Proceedings (Cairo: Ministry of Culture, Arab Republic of Egypt, 1972), pp. 135-52.

11. See Nicholas Polites, *The Architecture of Leandro V. Locsin*, (New York: Weatherhill, 1977); and Anthony D. King, *The Bungalow: The Production of a Global Culture*, (London: Routledge & Kegan Paul, 1984), p. 35.

12. See Rafiuddin Ahmad, "Conflict and Contradictions in Bengali Islam: Problems of Change and Adjustment," in Katherine P. Ewing, ed., *Shariat and Ambiguity in South Asian Islam* (University of California Press, 1988).

13. The Great Mosque of Baghdad is a more likely model for Adina considering the importance of both the city and the mosque in the Islamic domain, although Richard Eaton argues that Adina is directly influenced by Ctesiphon. The common elements are the rectangular perimeter with the main hall and the courtyard, and the tripartite division of the hall with a central nave. See R. Ettinghausen and O. Grabar, *The Art and Architecture of Islam 650-1250*, (Harmondsworth: Penguin, 1987).

14. See Perween Hasan, "Sultanate Mosque and Continuity in Bengal Architecture," *Muqarnas, An Annual on Islamic Art and Architecture,* (Leiden: E. J. Brill, 1989), pp. 58-74, for the Bengali characteristics of Sultanate mosques against a broader continuity of vernacular, historical, and "high" architecture that transcends specific religious expressions.

15. Ibid., for a correspondence between Bengali mosque forms and temples in Pagan.

16. See George Michell, editor, *Brick Temples in Bengal: From the Archives of David McCutchion* (Princeton; Princeton University Press, 1983).

17. Presented at a workshop on "Architecture and the City" in Dhaka (1987), organized by Chetana Architecture Research Group and sponsored by the Aga Khan Program for Islamic Architecture at Harvard and MIT.

Village landscape, from a nineteenth-century publication.

Wind, Water, and Clay: The Architecture of Bangladesh

The essay is excerpted from a book that accompanied the exhibition *"Pundranagar to Sherebanglanagar: The Architecture of Bangladesh,"* organized by Chetana Sthapatya Unnoyon Society at the National Museum in Dhaka in 1997. The exhibition was curated and the book edited by Raziul Ahsan, Kazi Khaleed Ashraf, and Saif Ul Haque.

The challenge for the twenty-first century is manifold. While the new, exploding urban dimension must be faced, and while the pressures of modernity, modernization, and the market must be met, it is well to remember that there is always the power of place and the features of locality. The architecture of the last two thousand years or so records a continuous contest between universal and local traditions, but it is the character of the Bengal delta that has persisted and re-emerged in the form and force of the undeniable delta with its wind, water, and clay.

Uncontrolled growth of cities and massive pressures to build in a global consumerist culture should not delude one into thinking that a building is only a commodity, a product of space necessity and economic urgency. The old conception about building is as valid as ever: it establishes our place on earth, becoming a visual manifestation of a much deeper relationship between human life and nature.

It is a curious thing that while the issue of identity has been foremost in Bengali cultural consciousness, architecture, which is the most profound site of identity-making, has been poorly addressed in cultural discourse. Yet, only an investigation of architecture can adequately reveal the depth of our culture and the concealed layers of our heritage. Architecture is a crucial source for understanding where we are and who we are.

The Bengal Delta

The architecture of Bangladesh constitutes a very distinctive character, much as Bengal defines a distinguishable cultural entity. Such distinctiveness rests primarily on two things: the deltaic condition of the region, and its critical location in a wider geographical and cultural context.

Comprising of Bangladesh and part of West Bengal, the delta is located between two geo-cultural matrices. On the one hand, it has always been considered part of a western domain formed mostly by the larger Indian culture, but also extending towards Persia, Arabia, and ultimately Europe. This aspect is seen in most explicit levels of culture: language, liturgies, institutions and laws. On the other hand, at a more primary or foundational level, an unnoticed layer links it with an eastern matrix formed mostly by the cultures of South-East Asia.

As a world of moistness, fecundity and lushness, this eastern matrix is predominantly a water-based civilization where life-enhancing ideals are generated from riverine dynamics and agricultural rituals. It is also a matrix of "rice-culture," where rice is not something merely consumed but is the basis of a collective ideology, and the articulation of self-identity.

The most prevalent architectural model in the delta is the "pavilion" structure. And the most elemental pavilion is the rustic Bengali hut, which is essentially a roof, a canopy or *chhad*, meant to thwart the intense sun and the torrential rain, and secondarily, the walls, permeable to the movement of the air and placed well within the perimeter of the roof. Expressed primarily by the parasol roof and porous walls, the hut is a free-standing form whose pavilion-like quality is emphasized by verandahs, terraces, and semi-enclosures. The hut is also the basic living unit of the universe of the Bengali peasant, and the household the unit of production. Both are tied intimately to the spatial context formed by the hut, the *uthan* (a court) and the wider paddy fields.

An integral relationship between the pavilion and the deltaic geography may be observed in complex organization, from simple clustering to large settlement, and to a city. The relationship implies the arrangement of isolated buildings in a fabric of paddyfields, gardens, orchards, lakes, and ponds. In such arrangements, building clusters are formed by grouping pavilion units in a series or around a loosely interiorized space (the *uthan)*. An understanding of a deltaic city lies, not in the dense labyrinthine fabric of cities like Jaipur and Lahore, but in city-forms east of the Bengal delta, in the so-called "rice-culture" matrix, where the distinction between urban and rural morphology has not been so oppositional.

Stupas, Temples, and Monasteries

The earliest evidence of historical monumental architecture in Bengal comes primarily from the Buddhist tradition and includes stupas, temples, and monasteries, the remains of some of which extend from Paharpur in the north to Mainamati in the south-east. Adopting a more metaphorical and symbolic construction, early monumental architecture represents a conscious deliberation of architectural creation. This deliberateness was the result of a more consolidated political and social structure, that is, the long and fairly stable reign of the Palas (750-1160 AD) and their architectural and artistic maturity, and to the strong cultural links between Bengal, Bihar and Northern India.

Important cities and settlements characterized the "janapadas" in the eastern region at that time. Pundranagar in Paundrabhukti was one of the most important cities in the region, now identified with the current site of Mahasthan. It was a vibrant administrative, religious, and cultural center from the third century BC to the twelfth century. Archaeological remains and literary descriptions speak of a planned and magnificent city.

The 8th century monastic complex at Paharpur was the largest in the Pala domain, and presumably the largest in the sub-continent. The complex is a unique combination of the *vihara* (monastery) and temple, consisting of a vast courtyard, nearly a thousand feet wide, with votive stupas, minor chapels, water tank and other structures. Enclosed by a quadrangular ring of one hundred and seventy-five cells, the center of the complex is described by the impressive cruciform temple-structure that even in its ruinous state stands seventy feet above the ground. It has been suggested that the unique plan of Paharpur – a cruciform multi-leveled central volume with a low-lying monastic perimeter, that is, the combination of *vihara* and temple-stupa in a single configuration – is the forerunner of well-known temple complexes in South-East Asia, including Borobudur and Angkor Wat.

Remains of temple architecture, particularly Brahmanical, are scanty. Motifs and representations in the sculptural art of the Palas and Senas and certain eleventh-century manuscript illustrations give indirect evidence of the form and shape of religious structures. Extant temples in Pagan in Burma built in the tenth and the eleventh centuries are another important clue to the building tradition of Bengal. According to roof shapes two distinct temple types have been identified: the *sikhara* (tower) type and the *bhadra* (tiered) and combinations of the two. Here, a certain tension between the North Indian category, the *sikhara* type, and the delta-based *bhadra* type may be noticed, pointing to a difference between the verticality of the sky-soaring *sikhara* and horizontality of the low-massed structure.

Islam in the Delta

The arrival of the Turks in the thirteenth century marked a major event in Bengal's political and social life: the introduction of a Turko-Persian culture, but most importantly, the beginning of the compelling influence of Islam. The new religion was introduced primarily through the mediatory practices of Sufi *shaikhs* and *pirs* during the Sultani period, transforming the delta environment in two hundred years into an ambience of mosques and shrines. While later Islam or its orthodox aspect developed a resilience towards local cultures, it is not often acknowledged that the dynamic relationship between Sultani and *sthaniya* (local) experiences created the efflorescence of a Bengali culture distinct from and often opposed to the North India-centered Sanskritism.

Sultani architecture is generally characterized by the introduction of new building types – mosque, mazar, and madrasa – and of renewed building techniques – the arch and the dome. The most important architectural phenomenon of this period is the introduction of the mosque as a new building type; what is more significant is the development of a "Bengali" mosque type. The "Bengali" mosques elaborate the pavilion idea – the singular, free-standing volume, the walls with real or suggested perforations, and the roof as a canopy similar to the village hut. The expressive quality of brick, and the prolific use of terracotta further strengthen a local quality. Art historian Perween Hasan

The Ashrafpur Bronze Chaitya, seventh century CE.

Image of a shrine, drawn after an eleventh-century illustration.

Terracotta details, from Atiya Mosque 1609 CE.

An interior of the Chala vault, Lattan Mosc
late fifteenth century CE.

The Nawab's Palace, Murshidabad, 1829-1837, architect Duncan MacLeod.

The now destroyed eleven-spired ten

ighi Mosque, Nawabganj, fifteenth century CE.

Cornice over central doorway, Shait Gumbad Mosque, Bagerhat, fifteenth century CE.

Terracotta ddepiction of a hut, from Kantanagar Temple, 1752 CE.

nagar, drrwan by Joseph Phillips, 1883.

Kantaji Temple, Dinajpur, eighteenth-century photograph.

has written about the uniqueness of the Bengali mosque and how little it relates to the characteristic mosques of the Middle-East and North India, with their cloister, the *liwan*, the elaborate ablution fountain, the minaret and the ceremonial gate. The courtyard of the hot-dry climate was generally rejected in the Bengali mosque, although courtyards were created by putting boundary walls that were never enclosed or too high but were open visually to the surrounding landscape. The walls of the mosque were opened out on all sides; on the *qibla* side, niches on the wall mirrored the openings on the opposite walls.

The Rise of *Laukik* Culture

The fifteenth and sixteenth centuries saw the upsurge of a truly *laukik* (vernacular/folk) Bengali culture. Broadly speaking, two streams characterized the culture of the region: the Sanskritic stream, the domain of the *pundits* and *acharyas* whose authority came primarily from the Vedic sastras, and the vernacular stream, the world of the river and village dwellers, whose practices relied mostly on localized beliefs and rituals. Even Pala culture, splendorous as it was, was largely articulated through the Sanskritic culture of Magadha and Central India. The distinct architecture of Paharpur was tied in an evolutionary chain to earlier Buddhist architecture at Ellora, Taxila and Nalanda. Until the 15th century, Brahmanical temples were either in the North Indian *Nagara* mode or the Southern *Dravida*.

A remarkable thing about this period was the way in which Islam deeply affected the cultural matrix of Bengal, and yet at the same time sparked off the efflorescence of a Bengali *laukik* culture. While historians argue about the possible cause of the rise of Bengali vernacular literature and culture – a *laukik* tradition opposed to the classical Sanskritic culture – it is clear that the political and social change brought about by the Pathans and Turks, particularly the disruption of the hegemony of the Brahmins, had a broad and deep effect. Sufi sages were also able to make deep inroads in the villages and into the heartland of Bengal. At the same time, Chaitanya and his devotional Vaisnavism ushered a resurgence of popular traditions as a counterpoint to Brahmanic ritualism. The net result was the flourishing of Bengali language and literature, and certainly architecture: the monumentalized "bangla" roof is a clear sign of that efflorescence.

Sultani architecture is best understood by a triangular relationship of the hut, temple, and mosque, in which the hut was the basis of the development of a Bengali mosque type. While the hut, or the free-standing pavilion, might have been the conceptual idea for building Sultani mosques, it also appeared more literally through various adaptations of the *chala* form. At the Shait Gumbad mosque in Bagerhat, the Darash Bari mosque and the Choto Sona mosque, both in Rajshahi, the central aisle of each mosque was covered by *chau-chala* vaults while the rest of the mosque was spanned by domes. If the dome is the icon par excellence of Turko-Persian architecture, or for that matter, the symbol of Muslim architecture, then its replacement by *chala* shapes, particularly over the main aisle of a mosque, is truly an extraordinary intervention.

"Khurdah Temples," West Bengal, from a nineteenth-century engraving.

Mughal Subah-e-Bangla

By 1596 Mughal rule was consolidated all over Bengal. The formation of the Subah-e-Bangla, the province of Bengal, marked a renewed tension between a Delhi-centered empire and the provincial status of the region. The continuity of a *laukik* character that had developed and been promoted during the Sultani period was interrupted to a great degree.

Mughal power was interested in the provinces primarily for economic reasons, and to some extent for their exoticism. Abul Faz'l, in the *Ain-i-Akbari*, mentions the popularity in Agra of the architecture of two provinces, Gujarat and Bengal. An example of it is the privilege given to the uniquely curved "bangla" roof, seen in Delhi in the marble canopy on the emperor's throne, and in Agra and Lahore on the roof of the emperor's audience pavilion (the *naulakha*), and in the emperor's private mosque, the Moti Masjid.

On the other hand, Mughal architecture in Bengal itself was quite perfunctory. The brick and terracotta tradition was ignored for a plain plastered look that was a feeble shadow of the opulent marble buildings in Delhi and Agra. The result was the waning of *laukik* iconography evolved from local considerations for more Delhi-centered imageries.

Concentrating more on establishing an efficient imperial administrative system, the Mughals focused more on the construction of forts, roads and *serais* than building memorable and awe-inspiring buildings. Although there was a reasonable number of modest-scaled mosques, mausoleums, madrasas and other buildings, especially in and around Rajmahal, Burdwan, Murshidabad and Dhaka, and while fragments of some palatial complexes survive from Rajmahal and Murshidabad, most Mughal buildings were rather unremarkable.

Principles of large-scale planning in Mughal architecture were exhibited, although feebly, in Shah Shuja's Palace in Rajmahal (1740s), the Khwaja-i-Shahid Complex in Burdwan (late 17th century), and the incomplete Lalbagh Fort in Dhaka (1680s). Formal gardens and pools, gateways and enclosures, and various buildings like mosques, tombs and madrasas, and sometimes a pavilion in the water, were organized in the characteristic Mughal axial relationship. An important aspect of the late Mughal period is a flurry of temple-building that continued even more prolifically during the British rule. Many temples continued the tradition of earlier centuries, with elaborate brick and terra-cotta work, and glorified *bangla* roof, but many began to adopt elements from Turko-Persian and later British colonial architecture.

Bengal and Europe

The late eighteenth century, coinciding with the decline of Mughal power, marked another profound turning point: the arrival of the Europeans. Bengal became the gateway of European ascendancy in India; what initially began as trading lead to the usurpation of political power and the complete subjugation of Bengal to English political and cultural dominance.

British colonialism resulted in an overwhelming contact with European culture that eventually coincided with global modernization. A complete overhaul of the social, cultural and urban system resulted through the themes of science, rationalism and technology. New "civic" institutions were introduced, along with the structure of a segregated dual city: the European city and the so-called "native" city. The former came to represent ideas of progress and development, while the latter a congested and chaotic condition. The new economic and administrative structure led naturally to an unprecedented level of building activities with a completely new range of building types: office buildings, railway structures, bungalows, warehouses, hospitals, colleges, etc.

Architectural strategies of the colonial system, as shadows of larger cultural policies, ranged from the haughty neoclassical presence as the Viceroy's Residence (later the High Court) in Dhaka, to the more climatically and iconographically suitable Curzon Hall. While most buildings followed European models in some way or another, an original architectural event was the production of the "bungalow." The bungalow epitomized the idea of dwelling in an independent structure in the landscape under the assured shelter of a big roof from where one could

The "drawing room," site of the public-domestic encounter, from a nineteenth-century publication.

"Roodapoore Bungalow," from a nineteenth-century engraving.

look out into the distant horizon. Various forms and techniques were employed for the bungalow but always derived from lessons learnt from climate and local idioms. However, within the colonial ideology of racial segregation, the bungalow also came to encourage spatial distancing and separation. It was soon transplanted as an architectural idea all across the subcontinent and later in many parts of the world.

Within Bengali society, a fresh breed of elite was created by the mid-nineteenth century with a completely new set of ideologies and viewpoints, setting off an elaborate dynamics with colonial culture. It was in essence a complex relationship of resistance and acceptance: a resistance to the traumatising aspects of colonialism and to repressive "traditions," and an acceptance of trans-cultural ideas and techniques promising new avenues of cultural explorations. Architecture soon reflected this panoply of contradictory and compromising values, tastes and aspirations. This was most evident in the mansions of the zamindars – the *zamindarbaris* and *rajbaris* – strewn all across the delta.

The *zamindarbaris* are an intricate condition of "publicity" and "domesticity." While the public embracing and practice of European form, mannerism and language were more predominant among the Hindu elite, the Muslim gentry vacillated between European manner and Persian *adab*. The public "front," the entry facade of the main building was in an Europeanized architecture, very much in keeping with the public life of the zamindar, while the "drawing room," a new space type in Bengali domestic world became the site of confrontation between "publicity" and "domesticity," between the display of public life and the restrictions of the domestic world. In the inner domain of the house, where women prevailed, the practice in both communities was more "Bengali": in the language spoken, in many of the rituals practiced, in the way space was inhabited, and generally in the way tradition was carried on.

Bengali Modernism

The modern period included both the political movement for independence of the subcontinental nations, and the increasing influence of the international modernist ideology. Bengal's relation with the "modern project" – the social vision of recreating the world anew – is quite intensive. It had been triggered earlier in the 19th century by colonial dynamics leading towards what came to be known as the "Bengal Renaissance" movement. The radical social and cultural programs of "Bengal Renaissance" generated unprecedented experimentations in literature and art, and in social and cultural institutions (with the only exception of architecture). All these pointed to Bengal's new eagerness for a civilizational exchange, or in other words, a deep commitment to both world civilization and *sthaniya* culture.

Two architectural phenomena stand out as strong examples of the modern period: the pioneering work of Muzharul Islam, and the powerful creation of the American architect Louis I. Kahn. Muzharul Islam single-handedly established a modern architectural culture in the country. While architecture was a missing component in the "Bengal Renaissance" experimentations, Muzharul Islam's work can be seen as its late architectural blooming. A modernist language was practiced purposefully to announce a new promising vision, away from both stigmatized colonial forms and hybrid concoctions. At the Art College and Public Library, both built in 1953, the lessons of European modernism were mediated and manipulated by the rationale of place and climate. His early work of a skeletal nature – sweeping parasols supported by thin columns as witnessed in the NIPA Building of Dhaka University – certainly characterized the deltaic pavilion. His later work, like Jahangirnagar University and National Archives, gave way to a more ponderous expression: earth-hugging volumes geometrically arranged in exposed brick from which openings seen to have been carved out.

Louis Kahn's Capital Complex project has been considered as one of the most astounding group of buildings of the twentieth century. The architecture of the Assembly – the crown of the group – evokes many traditions, harkening, it may seem, to some classic paradigm. The possibility of a relationship between the form-diagram of the Paharpur monastery-temple complex and Kahn's Assembly group has been suggested in Chetana's manifesto of 1981. The rationale lay in the nature of the centralized configuration – low, subservient volumes arranged geometrically and volumetrically to accentuate the central form, the most honorific space at the center.

Kahn's architecture effectively suggested that sthaniyata and modernism are not incompatible. While programmatically and symbolically, the Assembly houses the highest institution of the country, architecturally it is a thoughtful essay on building in the delta. While Kahn's modernist architecture offered a new architectural language in Bangladesh, his work in response to the landscape also showed how buildings, gardens and, lakes could form an indivisible unity, how brick could again form a renewed idiom, and how the age-old but straightforward deltaic practice of "dig-and-mound" could generate a modern expression.

But what have received lesser attention are Kahn's overall master plan and his deep reflection on "how the buildings are to take their place on the land," that is, in what ways can the buildings be grouped together so that they reveal the qualities of the place. This is suggestively answered in Kahn's composition of the buildings in an environment of parks, gardens, orchards and lakes. Kahn understood and wanted to heighten the idea that buildings also come together in a particular way in the delta. This issue of grouping buildings can finally be stretched to the overall form of the city. Cities in the delta, or in what has earlier been termed the "rice-culture" matrix, stretching from Bengal to Burma and further to Vietnam, dipping on the other side towards South India and Sri Lanka, have unique urban morphologies, distinct from the interiorized tightly clustered cities of hot-dry cultures. Kahn's plan – the siting of independent pavilion-like buildings amidst gardens, orchards, lakes – reflects such a deltaic milieu.

Agricultural University, site plan.

Tropical Trysts: An American Architect in the Bengal Delta

Published in *Reassessing Rudolph*, edited by Timothy Rohan (Yale University Press, New Haven, 2017).

Model of site, Agricultural University, Mymensingh (Paul Rudolph Foundation).

In 1965, Paul Rudolph was commissioned to make a campus plan for the East Pakistan Agricultural University outside the small town of Mymensingh in the northern part of Bangladesh. Over the next five years he produced a master plan and designs for key buildings on the campus, which in 1971 was renamed Bangladesh Agricultural University. The project is little known and little spoken about when considering Rudolph's work; even the architect himself had little to say about it. He visited the site only a few times, and never went to see it after its completion. One of the associates on the project, William Grindereng, has commented on Rudolph's strange ambivalence about the project, the commission for which may have coincided with a particularly busy professional time for Rudolph. I, too, mentioned the project only in passing when writing about architecture in Bangladesh, but I realize now that it is neither minor nor without significance in the narrative of a cultural encounter.

First, the project in Mymensingh is significant for its scale and scope. It involved the master plan of a new agricultural university and designs for most of its key buildings, including academic buildings, dormitories, faculty housing, an auditorium, a gymnasium, and a stadium – that is, all of the critical facilities required for a full-fledged residential university. The scope and complexity of a university is like that of a micro-city with all its institutions, groupings of buildings, and range of social constituencies and their interactions. Notably, the university at Mymensingh came on the heels of a similar project with similar prospects: Rudolph's plan for the University of Massachusetts at

Dartmouth, formerly Southeastern Massachusetts Technological Institute (1963–1966).

The Mymensingh project also raised issues about the development of an educational institution in a country that was beginning to organize its national priorities, having achieved political independence after nearly two hundred years of British rule. Located in the eastern province of the new state of Pakistan, which was carved out of India following the British withdrawal from the Indian subcontinent in 1947, the university would continue to be critical after the formation of the independent nation of Bangladesh following the brutal liberation war from Pakistan in 1971.

Richard Neutra, Administrative Building, Agricultural University.

The project is thus deeply imbricated with the developmental history of Pakistan and with the United States' involvement in the political and economic life of that nation. The development initiatives included modernizing the sectors that were identified as part of the economic backbone of Pakistan, of which agriculture was the most significant in both provinces of the country. It became imperative to organize the agricultural sector into a modern and more productive institution, for which foreign, and especially American, aid was sought. The USAID, through Texas A & M University, sponsored the establishment of an agricultural university in each province of Pakistan, Mymensingh in East Pakistan (now Bangladesh), and Lyallpur in West Pakistan (now Pakistan).

Sports Pavillion at stadium, Agricultural University.

If the founding of an agricultural university provided a national narrative of modernization and Westernization, and furthermore, an encounter between a new global power and an abiding Asian nation, the place of the project in Rudolph's own architectural itinerary provided another story of encounter. The university in Mymensingh represented Rudolph's first tropical adventure outside the US (besides his unbuilt proposal for the US Embassy in a "less tropical" Amman, Jordan, in 1955). From a climatic sense, Mymensingh was as remote as could be from New Haven, where Rudolph was living in 1965, but the climatic conditions and the architectural responses they elicited in Mymensingh were not alien to him. The successful innovations of modern buildings in Sarasota, Florida, had already attuned Rudolph to the specific architectural demands of the tropics.

Is there an arc between Sarasota and Mymensingh – Sarasota as the site of Rudolph's brilliant articulation of a modern tropical typology, and Mymensingh as a location of its exotic other? Or, is there a difference that Rudolph never reconciled, or perhaps even recognized? With the geographical shift from Florida to Mymensingh, does Rudolph veer towards a Kiplingesque quandary in the shadow of a post- (or neo?) colonial darkness, where the twain failed to meet? These were Rudolph's tropical trysts, which distinguished him more than any other architect of his generation – the group that came out of the cold, so to speak, from the hallways in Cambridge or Chicago, to test the métier of modernism under the mesmerizing sun and furious rain of the tropics, and in the cultural politics of the "other." For Rudolph, Mymensingh was both familiar and different.

Even if Rudolph appeared to be an accidental tourist in 1960s Asia, unlike some of the architects who were already exploring the question of a tropical modernism, his work remains important in the related discourse of tropical modernism and regionalism in architecture. There is a distinction to be made between the exigencies of a tropical architecture as a kind of localized, or emplaced, modernism, and the emerging discourse of regionalism in architecture which sought alternatives to modernism and not merely its inflection. From Otto Koenigsberger to Maxwell Fry, by way of Le Corbusier, the notion of a tropical modern architecture was already embedded in the Asian context, but Rudolph's work brought an American twist to the discourse. I say American because Rudolph's innovations in tropical Florida had found little recognition in the discourse of tropical architecture that some European architects had taken on a lead and expanded that in various continents.

2

The 1960s was both a dynamic and volatile time in the emergence of Bangladesh, as well as a rather ebullient moment of American presence in Pakistan. Considered a critical geo-political location in the theater of the Cold War, an economically impoverished Pakistan was seen as a strategic partner by the United States, and was propped up as a bulwark against the Soviet presence in Asia. This was carried out through huge supplies of aid, mostly in the form of defense, but also in social programs such as food, education, health, and institution building for that developing nation. Many of the technical institutions that were vital to the development of a modern Pakistan were created by American financial and logistical support through the agencies of USAID, the Ford Foundation, and the World Bank. Part of the package involved establishing, and training people for a series of engineering and agricultural universities, which also included planning the universities and producing their facilities. The agricultural university at Mymensingh was one such venture.

That is how Rudolph found himself in the Bengal delta at the height of a nation-building program under considerable US patronage. He was not, however, the only traveling architect in the 1960s working in the mission of social and national development in then East Pakistan. The first foreigner to receive major commissions in then East Pakistan (now Bangladesh) was the prolific Greek architect and planner Constantine Doxiadis, who by the late 1950s had already evolved an idiom suited to the tropics. The Austria-born California architect Richard Neutra was invited to design a number of educational buildings throughout Pakistan beginning in 1963, which also included the first building for the agricultural university at Mymensingh. When Rudolph arrived there, he made a master plan that ambivalently engaged the set of administrative and academic buildings that Neutra had designed. It appears that even in a remote corner of Asia, Rudolph found himself face-to-face with a European modernist. With Neutra's planar architecture and Rudolph's skeletal expressionism, it was a kind of encounter between a California modernism and a Florida tropicalism.

Alexander Lodge, Mymensingh, nineteenth century.

Academic Building with experimental gardens.

In the wake of the American development initiatives, three American architects were invited to Bangladesh through the intervention of the Bengali architect Muzharul Islam. The lives of the three architects intersected both in the US, and in their independent itineraries in Bangladesh. Following Rudolph's 1965 commission, Stanley Tigerman teamed up with his Yale colleague Muzharul Islam in 1966 to design five polytechnic institutes. Earlier, in 1962, Louis Kahn, once a visiting professor at Yale but by that time working and teaching in Philadelphia, had been invited to design the National Capital Complex, which turned out to be an epic venture, a narrative that is much better known.

Through the work of these architects, Bangladesh became a rather fertile zone for architectural investigations. As Tigerman has commented, "Bangladesh was loaded with poignancy for Kahn and Rudolph," meaning that the encounter is meant to bring a new alchemy or acuity to their own work rather than a progression of the same (which was far more actual as far as Tigerman's work was concerned). In the rapid and even overwhelming presence of Western models of development then prevalent the world over, the work of these leading figures in architectural thought and culturally perceptive productions provides fresh insights into the encounter between architectural ideologies basically developed in the West and conditions that are often totally different from their original milieu.

It is important to note here Muzharul Islam's discerning leadership in bringing the American trio to Bangladesh. Islam had been a student of Rudolph in the Yale master's program in 1961. Tigerman was a classmate with whom he established a life-long friendship and architectural camaraderie. As students, Tigerman and Islam resolved to work together someday, a vow that materialized in the polytechnic projects. While at Yale, Islam came to know Kahn's work and heard him speak on

Academic Building.

Academic Building, courtyard.

several occasions. After returning from the US in 1962 with a master's degree in architecture, Islam became a key architect in the Public Works Department of the Pakistan Government. At the age of 30, he was entrusted with the design of a number of significant institutional and civic buildings that came to be recognized as inaugurating a Bengali modernism in architecture. His engagement of the American architects, as well as his own involvement, was triggered by a need to create both a principled practice and modernist paradigms for what was then seen as a vacuous architectural landscape. Islam was seeking a better option than what was presented in the US foreign-aid package, which sometimes brought in expertise from lesser-known technical institutions in the US. Islam's intent was not dissimilar from the still-vivid high adventure of Le Corbusier in Chandigarh, which was seen as a jolt to Indians, as Nehru himself declared, made to wake them from the turgidity of tradition and move towards the liberating potentials of modernity.

[partial text]

Muzharul Islam at the jury of the Aga Khan Award for Architecture, 1980. Photos: AKAA.

What Now? The Perpetual Vigilance of Muzharul Islam

Published as introduction to the book *An Architect in Bangladesh: Conversations with Muzharul Islam* (Loka Press, Dhaka, 2014).

Holding a copy of Manfredo Tafuri's *Architecture and Utopia*, Muzharul Islam greeted me one day sometime in the early 1990s at his house in Paribag. It was quite significant to see Muzharul Islam with Tafuri's book. I thought if there was someone who can engage in a dialog with Islam, it had to be the Marxist intellectual and architectural historian Tafuri. In that incisive book, Tafuri analyzes the tragic turn of modern architecture, and how its avant-garde stance has been compromised if not co-opted by capitalist development. Considering Tafuri's book made me wonder how the Italian Marxist scholar may incite Islam to reflect on the nexus of architecture, politics and society.

Whether Muzharul Islam agreed with Tafuri's cynicism about the salvationary role of modern architecture is something to ponder upon especially when he continued to believe in its role in the context of Bangladesh far from the European theater. When Islam greeted me on the steps of his house with the book in his hand, I came to appreciate, once again, his razor sharp intellect, his keen understanding of architecture, culture and politics, and their critical intersections. At the same time, I came to realize that despite work in various spheres – architectural profession, design education, cultural activism, political engagement – little is known about the depth of Islam's thoughts.

As young students of architecture in the late 1970s, we had often wondered: "Who is Muzharul Islam?" It was ironic that the most important architect of the country remained invisible in the mainstream architectural arena in Bangladesh, whether it was in education or in the profession. Detractors kept him at bay from the community of architects and students, weaving uncharitable tales of his being a 'controversial person.' Little was written about him and his work at that time, and much less was known about his own views on architecture and culture despite the fact that Muzharul Islam embodied the most progressive side of Bengali modernity.

Knowing Muzharul Islam

Despite his immense influence on the architectural culture in Bangladesh, and close interactions with many prominent artists, writers and intellectuals of the country, few documents are available on Islam's thoughts and views. Interviews published sporadically in different newspapers and periodicals have remained mostly inaccessible. Other than criticisms of the general condition of architecture and the frustrating political culture in the country, and regular outbursts against unethical practices, and on special occasions, insights into the world of architecture, of stories about Paul Rudolph, Louis Kahn, and other architectural stalwarts, Islam was largely silent about himself. His own philosophy of architecture remained opaque to most people other than emerging in oblique ways during unscheduled conversations. Even though the buildings were always there for us to interpret we needed to hear from the architect who designed them.

Chetana, the architectural research and study group that grew around and was mentored by Muzharul Islam, provided a special access for those willing to know him. Through many dedicated discussions, presentations, events, and informal conversations, Chetana provided a closeness with the architect-teacher beyond formal conditions of the classroom or the office.

An Architect in Bangladesh: Conversations with Muzharul Islam provides a window for a view on modernity in Bangladesh, and the place of architecture there in the views of the foremost architect of the time. Recorded some twenty years ago over a period of one week, the conversations testify to Islam's deeply felt thoughts on architecture, art, culture and politics.

At the time of recording this conversation in 1992, we were younger and a lot more naïve with our questions to a man who, even if less active as a practicing architect, remained a formidable figure in the world of culture and politics. *Who were your influences? Why is your architecture of the 1980s different from the 1950s?* Islam entertained these questions with surprising frankness and keenness. But it took us a while to get there, and to ask unhesitant questions, as it was for Islam to take time in opening up from his usual reserve and reach out to us. It seemed he was waiting for that moment, for an extended conversation. To publish this document about twenty years later may seem a bit tardy but in some ways it is more relevant with the passing away of the architect and evolving architectural and political conditions, both globally and locally.

The conversations took place at his renowned house in Paribagh – his residence and office, and a lot of other things. Part of the house served as Islam's slowed down architectural practice and more as a de facto laboratory for critical thinking. Few times a week, since 1982, members of Chetana met to consider the state of architecture, and come up with renewed principles of action. On other days, strictly distinct from architectural programs, members of his left leaning political circle met to consider the condition of the nation. And, on some other evenings, desks in the drafting section of the office would be cleared or the garden in front organized for a musical soiree. Although the content in this book highlights architecture, there could be separate conversations on politics and culture.

Design shapes the way we live

Conversation with Islam was always an intense and continuous lesson in Bangladesh's cultural modernity, and its promises and anxieties. If the idea of a Bengali modernity could be transferred into the personality and dynamic output of a person, it unequivocally had to be Muzharul Islam. He also makes us understand that conditions of modernity come with its attendant complexities and challenges that one must take up nonetheless.

At the foreground of Islam's close analytique is the realization that architectural practice will get intertwined with political thoughts, particularly in a place like Bangladesh where capitalist motivation, economic inequity, and cultural confrontations have swayed ground conditions. In echoing the thoughts of Tafuri, Islam would insist that entering the field of political theory is necessary in order to understand "the precise identification of those tasks which capitalist development has taken away from architecture." While most architects in the 1970s and 80s preferred to bypass such a realization and its ethical and form-making consequences, Islam increasingly came to see politico-cultural engagement superseding aesthetical motivation for architecture.

The nexus of architecture and politics is best conveyed by Stanley Tigerman's experience in Bangladesh. Tigerman, the "bad boy" of Chicago architecture, a close friend of Muzharul Islam since their time together at Yale University (1961), and a colleague in the Polytechnic projects designed for the then East Pakistan (1968-1971), relates how when he met Louis Kahn at Heathrow Airport in 1974, the latter had one question: "Why did Muzharul Islam leave architecture for politics? I could never do that." Kahn was on his way from Ahmedabad, India, to Philadelphia, and his tragic death in New York's Penn Station. To Tigerman, Kahn seemed disheveled and rather disoriented, and was perhaps considering what constitutes the value of an architect. How does one really contribute to society?

Designing and building of the polytechnic projects brought Tigerman to Bangladesh many times, and to a closer contact with Islam and conditions in the country. Describing it as an "extraordinary episode" in his life, Tigerman attributes his own transformation as an architect in Chicago to his experience in Bangladesh and association with Islam. The process involved a move from a kind of functional pragmatism or hermetic aesthetics to a socially and morally responsive practice.

"The polytechnic projects," admits Tigerman, "had perhaps its greatest effect on me as a consequence of Muzharul Islam's insisting that I live with the Bengalis and spend as little time as possible with the American community in Dacca [Dhaka]. I ate the Bengalis' food and drank their water, got dysentery and was cured and became acclimated to the local conditions. Islam also made sure that I approached the problem of designing for his people in a way that would bring lessons of Western logic to the young architects of East Pakistan well beyond those inherent in the buildings themselves. This in turn prompted me to become aware of the needs of my own people and of the way architecture is practiced in America. It was an enormously rewarding experience that even now influences my thinking." Tigerman would eventually establish Archeworks (1994) as an institute of innovative architectural pedagogy with a social and community focus. The fundamentals of Islam's thoughts seem to echo in Archeworks' mission: "Design shapes the way we live. The fewer resources communities and individuals have, the more they need great design solutions to enhance their quality of life."

When Tigerman was ousted from the country by the Pakistan Army during one of his professional visits in 1971, he protested at a press conference in Kolkata: "I am an architect. I am not a political person." Clearly, the architect has been imbued with a political urgency. Chastising the Pakistan government for its atrocities, Tigerman concluded the press conference by stating: "I am an architect. I am also a human being."

How to be a human being comes neither naturally nor effortlessly. All throughout his life, as a professional architect, dedicated teacher, culturally and politically engaged person, as a family man, conducting it without pause or compromise, carrying out the sharpest critique of social, religious and traditional norms, Islam wished for himself and those who came in contact with him, to be just that: a decent human being. No matter how simple it may appear, the nobility of a decent life remained at the forefront of Islam's thinking.

Bangaliana

Our conversation with Muzharul Islam began with a provocation: *What is the necessity of architects in Bangladesh?* A kind of impatience, brought about by conditions in the 1980s and 90s, when the practice of architecture was undergoing a creative anemia and social purposelessness, produced this question. It was followed by another: If one were to be beholden to a Bengali ethic, what kind of an architect would one be?

To be deeply Bengali and precisely modern constitutes the motto of Muzharul Islam. He would expect the same of others in his circle. An oscillation – between pride in being Bengali, and being an "internationalist" in the socialist sense – also manifested in Islam's orientation for a Rabindrik ethos and a Marxist ideology, or a conviction for being "established on my own soil" and a belief in a socialist teleology.

Many writers, including myself while introducing an essay on Islam, have noted that he singlehandedly brought architectural modernism to Bangladesh. He was not just a modernist but he was modernism, a single man institution who embodied the norms of a new ideal and production. Since the 1950s, following the world-wide proliferation of the principles of modern architecture, many master architects, from Balkrishna Doshi in India to Oscar Niemeyer in Brazil, were engaged in a similar project of modernist reconstitution. What distinguishes Islam's position is his attempt for aligning modernism with what one could describe as "Bangaliana," a deeply abiding sense of Bengali culture and history. This could be observed in such aesthetical practice as Islam's wearing white cotton kurta, maintaining a Gandhian sparseness in his office, and carrying on close relationships with all the major writers and intellectuals of his time articulating a Bengali cultural nationalism. Islam always noted: "The people who first started here [referring to leaders of Bengali social and political movements] had their source in an incredible love for the country. The basis of the movement was: I am a Bengali, I have a language, I have things to tell my people, I want to build a decent society, everyone in the society has the capability and the right to what is available in it." He attempted to carry this ethic into his architecture.

Premised on the fundamental fact of cultivating a Bengaliness, his commitment to an ethical practice, equitable social system, and cultural basis for architectural practice never diminished. Anyone who has "interacted" with Muzharul Islam knows the many thresholds that need to be crossed to access the depth of his enigma. It took us many years to reach that point where we could claim we were having a conversation with Islam Saheb, or "sir," as is the custom to address one who taught without being a teacher in the formal sense.

There were many stages to that induction. One had to be divested of any ambiguity or confusion in one's dedication to the Bengali cause, and, as an architect, in one's devotion to the tasks of the profession. What often impeded a frank interaction with Islam was his predictable intolerance of a frigid academism or distrust of professional double-talk. He was never at a loss for pointing out the foibles of these two architectural institutions and he never shifted from – what Aldo Rossi described regarding the work of his fellow Italian architect Ettore Sottsass – "the search for a higher level of recomposition."

Islam believed a dedication to the Bengali cause must be unequivocal, yet something not quite nationalistic rather hovering somewhere between an unwavering sense of Bengaliness and a creative mission for a "recomposition." Secondly, architectural aspirations must be realized through an intellectual foundation supported by vigilance about how things behave in the political and economic spectrum of society. One needed to recognize that there is a deeply intertwined relationship between cultural nationalism and forms of architecture, and between politico-economic structure and architectural production. After 1975, the purist that he was, Islam began to notice a cultural devaluation in which many were complicit, and most, it appeared to him, were tainted until proven otherwise. For such reasons, it required a few stages, and evidence of an unfaltering dedication, to get close to him and entertain the possibility of a free discussion. Islam's purist position must be read against the general ambience of easy compromise and petty accommodation he perceived all around him in that contested time in the history of Bangladesh.

Political analytiques can produce tricky moments in architecture. Despite his invitations to Paul Rudolph, Louis Kahn and Stanley Tigerman to work in Bangladesh, Islam had no patience – only a disdain – for Euro-American paternalism, considering it a subterfuge for a new imperium. His incisive understanding of political events since the 19th century, both in the Indian subcontinent and Europe, and experience of independence movement from the British were too deeply ingrained in his personality. At the same time, Islam had no sympathy with a parochialism that went in the name of tradition. He continued to conduct a vigorous critique of plans of the imperium as well as the pitfalls of parochialism.

What Now?

Often described as an unapologetic and uncompromising idealist, Islam remains part ideologist, part utopian and part visionary while also devoted to pragmatism and rationality. In his own aspiration in this regard as well as expectation from those around him, he could be obstinate and resolute. He required of those claiming to tread the path of architecture to practice constant vigilance and criticism. His sheer presence would often make one aware of that elevated mission, of the weight of the "winged eye." As the emblem of the 16th century Renaissance architect and humanist Alberti (such emblems were common to Renaissance intellectuals), the winged eye was also Manfredo Tafuri's favorite trope. While various meanings are associated with that enigmatic sign, it is mostly understood as indicating a sentient human being who with critical knowledge and alertness is prepared to counter obstacles in order arrive at a higher moral or spiritual ground. If Islam is to be associated with any emblem, I see him sharing Alberti's winged eye and the associated Latin motto: *Quid tum? What now?*

If ideology and utopia are fundamental to the thinking of Muzharul Islam through which we may penetrate the enigma of the man, it is precisely these that Tafuri critiqued in *Architecture and Utopia*. In his analysis of the state of architecture until the 1970s, Tafuri notes how ideology has become useless to capitalist development giving a fatal twist to the nobler goals of modern architecture. Consequently, lack of ideology or critical framing produces a pure but impotent architecture, a "form without utopia, a sublime uselessness," a scenario very evident in the 1980s and 90s. It is this troubled relationship between intellectual work and capitalist development, in which most architects have abandoned the former to the force-field of the latter that had situated Muzharul Islam in an anachronistic place by the early 1980s. His political alignment did not help either amidst the risen or rising reactionary forces in the country. How an architect of vigilance would have fared now, in the sweep of a liberal economy, to the spectacular architectural drama of "sublime uselessness," is open to question.

When architects had abrogated their tasks to "the merciless commercialization of the human environment," Muzharul Islam remained fairly persistent in his call for producing a "decent architecture" and in the making of a "decent society." In his formulation for architecture and society for Bangladesh, he abhorred symbolic apparatuses and what he described as "flourish," the convenient tools of contemporary architecture. The topic of symbol was particularly an anathema for him.

"Symbol for what?" he would retort sharply at a suggestion for such practices. "Symbol of what? Symbol for whom? You raise the issue of symbols. I feel that human society has been kept in darkness for thousands of years by the use of symbols. I revolt against it. By raising the issue of symbols, in the name of symbols, my perspective has been kept limited." A subtle and restrained vision for the future, for an ideal Bangladesh that is decent and enlightened ("bhadra samaj"), was a constant refrain with Muzharul Islam.

If the crisis in European architecture in the 19th century led to the task of a continual invention of advanced solutions, as a political process as Tafuri noted, then the architect's role as idealist became critical. Islam believed it is far more important in a place like Bangladesh with scarce resources and environmental fallibility to be a political visionary (I describe that as "pragmatic utopia"). His idea of an equitable and decent social condition, *bhadra samaj*, translates into thinking about new types of settlement morphology in which the lopsided differentia between the city and the village would be erased. Islam's thought on new villages is radical and provisional, but remain a provocation that has not been picked up by the next generation. New thinking on settlements is particularly critical when land and landscape are the crux in the great game of capitalist development, much more so now than what was anticipated in the 1980s.

A ferocious intellect represented in the emblem of the winged eye often creates an ironic predicament making its bearer a kind of a tragic hero. Such vigilance against a relentless and wily opposition that could wear down anyone lends an heroic aura to Muzharul Islam. It also results in a solitary struggle with increasingly few compatriots. Even family members, admits his daughter Dalia Nausheen, found it hard to cope with Islam's forward-oriented thinking. At the same time, as a kind of redemption, Nausheen writes: "He could comprehend the future beautifully." The evidence is here in this book.

Building Bangladesh: From Pavilion-Form to Landscape-Form

Published in *Bengal Stream: The Vibrant Architecture Scene of Bangladesh*, edited by Niklaus Graber, Andreas Ruby and Viviane Ehrensberger (Christoph Merian Verlag, Basel, 2017).

Bangladesh played a critical role in the history of mid modern architecture but it is a story that is poorly narrated and also less known. The building of the new city Chandigarh in India, planned and designed by Le Corbusier, and the parliament complex of Sherebanglanagar in Dhaka, designed by Louis Kahn, had a profound impact on the trajectory of modern architecture in the 1960s as it swayed between corporatization and banality.

Louis Kahn's work in Dhaka, Bangladesh, played a key role in the evolution of modernism towards more humanistic dimensions. His engagement with some of the taboo topics of modernism – landscape and geography, spirituality and sacrality – found inspiration and reciprocal significance in Bangladesh. While the robust geometry of Kahn's Capital Complex has received greater attention from architects and critics, with some hesitant acknowledgment of architecture's psycho-spiritual dimensions, it's urban and landscape themes remain largely unexplored.

It should also be recalled – another story that is also poorly known – that starting in the eighteenth century, a major architectural idea emerged from Bangladesh (known as Bengal then) that eventually became a global paradigm of dwelling: the bungalow. The production and circulation of the bungalow type followed the English adaptation of the bangla, the rural hut of Bengal, as a climatic paradigm for the tropics. As an intersection of ecology and sociology, there was much to learn from the primal bangla hut. A techno-utilitarian aspect generated from the diminutive bangla hut subsequently informed the content of modern "tropical architecture," and its metrics of comfort and wellbeing.

Early modern architecture in Bangladesh, in the works of the pioneering modernist architect Muzharul Islam (1923-2012), was framed primarily by meteorological and ecological themes, befitting topics of the tropics, and an utilitarian ethic that coincided with post colonial nation-building. Following Muzharul Islam's seminal projects in the 1950s, examples of a "tropical modernism" were realized in the works of Constantine Doxiadis, Robert Bouighy, Paul Rudolph, Richard Neutra, Stanley Tigerman, and other foreign architects working in then Bangladesh. While all these works established the language

Aerial photograph of the Bengal delta by Shamim Shorif Susom.

Muzharul Islam, NIPA Building, Dhaka University, 1967. Photo: Brian Brace Taylor.

of a new architecture, they also heralded an early version of sustainable ethic that combined climate, ecology and functionalism in which an argument for "regionalist" architecture was framed in a climatic logic – angle of the sun, direction of the wind, measures of thermal comfort, and material propriety.

The Pavilion Paradigm

While the pavilion model was central in developing the ideas of "tropical architecture," and the subsequent discourse of "architectural regionalism," it also underlined the fact that the pavilion type is not to be considered as an isolated object but rather in its intimate intertwining with its setting and landscape.

In a series of essays written since 1987, I noted that with "the paralysis of a Bengali architectural sensibility in the last hundred years or so, it has become morally imperative and culturally urgent that a significant section of contemporary architecture in Bangladesh be "archaeological," that is, excavate from the historical layers of contradictory and imposed ideologies [produced in colonial encounters] a more "place-responsive" architecture. An archaeological inquiry was not propositioned in the sense of uncovering fossils, nor as a way of trips to exotica, but rather with the objective of restoring cultural archetypes which still have deep existential significance, and be a beginning for fresh trajectories."

I also argued that revisiting the pavilion-like hut, the *bangla*, was central to understanding what constituted a recurrent type-form in the Bengal delta. The Bengali hut-type is a primal pavilion, a machine for living in a hot-humid milieu. There are broader implications of the pavilion structure, particularly in the relationship between architecture and "nature." By turning its walls permeable, the pavilion-form makes the distinction between exterior and interior ambiguous. Unlike the intention of shutting out the elements as in the interiorized courtyard-houses of hot-arid places, and the sealed-off spaces of colder climates, the pavilion is completely with the atmosphere. This creates, what Anthony D. King describes, the centrifugal nature of the pavilion house, generating a movement of activity "outward, on to the verandah, and further into the compound."

To be with the atmosphere translates into a continuum of the external/natural world and the architectural space, and establishing a visual, spatial and sensorial interpenetration of architecture and "nature," in this case, the deltaic geography. It is for this reason, the Bengali dwelling is always idealized with its setting. The perennial image of the Bengali landscape is that of modest-scaled detached structures amidst foliage and ponds. The pavilion-form need not be considered for only idyllic settings. While it has sustained the idea of dwelling in an agrarian landscape, it can, with analogical translation, be the premise for urban categories (both residential and non-residential), and even whole urban fabrics.

There has been experimentation in recreating the pavilion within a modern and urban vocabulary in the early works of Muzharul Islam. The Art College (1953) and the NIPA Building in Dhaka University (1964) are two distinguished expressions of the pavilion idea, the former as a whole campus and the latter as a building type. An analogical sense of the pavilion can be detected in most notable works of the 1960s, from Stanley Tigerman and Muzharul Islam's five Polytechique projects to Paul Rudolph's buildings for the Mymensingh Agricultural University and Robert Bouighy's Railway Station at Kamlapur. A remarkable report on building in then East Pakistan, produced by Tigerman and Islam, prescribed the constructional, spatial and climatic behavior of buildings in the region.

Nahas, Khalil, residence, Sarabo.

A later reinterpretation of the pavilion type, resonating with a more compelling regionalist and cultural character, is Bashirul Haq's village home at Bhatsala in Comilla (1991). The building is a two-storied structure built around an existing courtyard ("uthan") with older huts. The lower floor of the new building is built in ordinary exposed brick, a heavy mass containing small enclosed rooms. The upper level, on the other hand, is an open skeletal structure forming a partially-canopied airy terrace from where there is a breathtaking view of paddy fields. Even if it employs contemporary methods of construction, the project demonstrates the special sensitivity for working in a rural setting – the existing "uthan" around which the new house is organised, and the village, with its pattern of independent huts, ponds, orchards, pathways, and paddyfields.

The pavilion form also provides clues to creating complex organization, from simple clusterings to urbanistic fabrics. Clusters could be formed by lining pavilion "units" in a series or grouping around an amorphously interiorized space. A deltaic morphology for rural areas implies the disposition of isolated buildings in a fabric of paddyfields, gardens, orchards, lakes and ponds. Notable projects that thoughtfully tackle the issue of grouping with such a milieu in mind are the SOS Village in Dhaka by Raziul Ahsan (1984), the Herman Gmeiner Centre in Khulna by Uttam Kumar Saha (1986), the BRAC Centre in Faridpur by Saif Ul Haque and Jalal Ahmad (1993), and the "Bacchte Shekha" Centre by Saif Ul Haque (1994).

Saif Ul Haque has been particularly attentive to the placing and grouping of his buildings, designed for and built mostly in a rural context. He has developed a theme for organising his complexes that appears to be an extrapolation of the familiar rambling village homesteads but redefined in a disciplined architectural format. The complexes are formed by a fabric of buildings and spaces in which different independent volumes are arrayed around interlocking courtyards, some of which are enclosed and some semi-enclosed. The new fabric is sometimes intimately engaged with existing ponds and orchards. One can meander from one area to another through a variety of spatial experiences that are further heightened by semi-traditional architectural elements. The deliberately subdued nature of the elements, the intimate texture of materials, and the modulation of light and shadow also give a sense of belongingness, a feeling of "having been there."

Dhaka as a Theorem

While the pavilion-form provided a tool for engagement for architects in rural or open areas, the challenge lay elsewhere. What would be a greater issue, something that has not yet been taken up substantially, is to consider the pavilion-form in the dense and complex matrix of the city. And no narrative of Bangladesh is complete without Dhaka in the story.

Dhaka is a deltaic city where water forms a delicate nexus. Symptomatic of most cities located in powerful hydrological milieux but undergoing furious urbanization, planning practices have succumbed to the regime of a dry ideology. Since the 1960s, a new development ethos has prevailed in the organization of cities in that part of the delta. Landfills, embankments, bridges and roadways have supported the technology and ideology of a dry culture, pitting the city against the moisture-laden delta. Conventional urban planning has basically become the production of land, or manufacture of dryness. Much of the current crises of Dhaka, especially the perception of lack of land, stems from the inability to incorporate the processes of a dynamic aquatic landscape into planning thinking and action. In the meantime, water is pushed away, disastrously, through large-scale engineering operations in the form of embankments and landfills in which strategic terms such "land-use" continues to privilege the production of dryness.

From the heart of the present city, Dhaka and the delta appear as two separate entities, antithetical and stranger to each other. Fed on dry ideas, planners and policy-makers remain befuddled about envisioning or even managing a city in such a nuanced terrain; any deliberation begins with an assumption that such a watery behavior is unreliable to the city and must be resisted. In the horizon of the contemporary city, the delta does not even appear in the consciousness until a deluge comes, with clockwork, seasonally and unmistakably. In the schism between dry and wet, dominant planning practices have not only obscured immersive world-views but also enforced a kind of limiting measure on an otherwise prodigious and unruly landscape that a delta represents, whether it be the Gangetic,

Kashef Mahboob Chowdhury, Friendship Center, Gaibandha. Photo: AKAA.

Saif Ul Haque Sthapati, Arcadia school project, near Dhaka. Photo: AKAA.

Mohammad Rizwan, floating school, different locations.

Mohammad Rizwan, floating school.

Yves Marre and Runa Khan, restoring boat project.

Yves Marre and Runa Khan, boats realized.

the Mekong or the Mississippi. How to find a contemporary relevance for such a fluid dynamic? That is the challenge for architects in Bangladesh.

A deltaic geography is an immense force of nature. Borne out of the hydrological chemistry of rivers, land in the delta is formed primarily by silt deposits, that is constantly shaped and reshaped by the rivers and their distributaries, which themselves are perpetually shifting and changing. This dynamic gives the land an amorphous nature, and characterizes the region's climate, topography, ecology, and sociology. Floods and overflow impart to this landscape a corrugation of flat plains, ponds, muddy enclaves and "lowlands," all of which constitute a topography of habitation and occupation. In a great alchemy that is both mystical and cosmogonic, land-forms rise in an annual rhythm in unexpected waters, and inaugurates a new micro universe. In such an excruciatingly flat terrain, a few centimeters matter in defining what is wet and what is dry, as the 'delta urbanist' Kelly Shannon observes, and often the ground is water.

In the delta, the householder knows how to build a house on a mound next to a pond, or how to tether the house to a slope, a farmer knows when to plant his crop of mustard or eggplant, what variety of rice paddy at the onset of the monsoon or during, the farmer knows how to become a fisherman when the water does not recede, and the villager knows "the river is now an empty vessel, and they cannot cast their nets." Such a

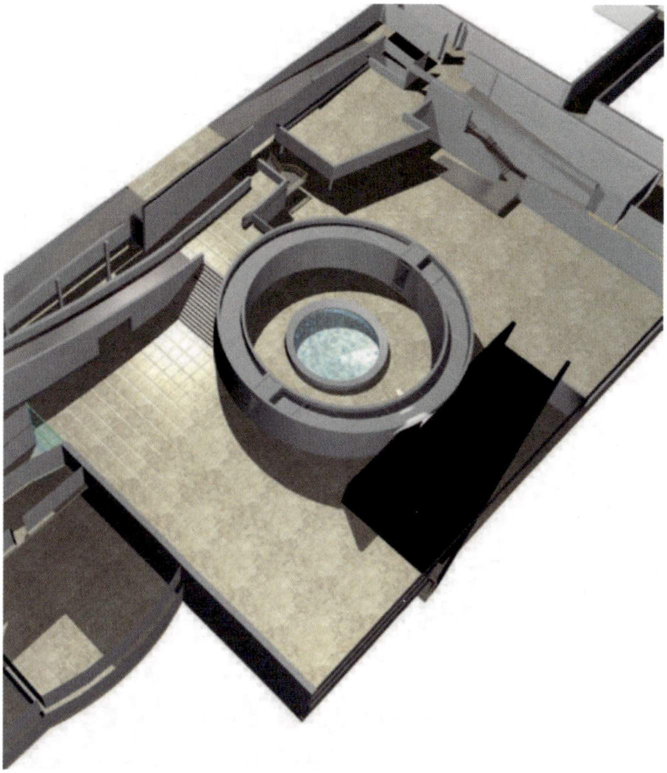

Urbana Architects (Kashef Mahboob Chowdhury and Marina Tabassum), Shadhinata Sthambha and Museum, Dhaka.

water ethos structures the social and territorial landscape from the delta of Bangladesh to the Chao Praya in Thailand and the Mekong in Cambodia and Vietnam.

Water cascading down from upland mountains brings pulverized remains to the flat flood-plains in the form of sand, silt and mud, depositing them in an unpredictable geometry of land-forms and waterways. In this complex choreography of land and water, delicate chars – land formation induced by the dynamics of soil-shifts and water flows appear one year to disappear the next, while more or less stabilized ones become sites of settlement. A char is thus a reminder of an earlier turn of a river and deposition of silt to form the new land-mass, demonstrating a geo-hydrological process in action. The char eventually offers a rich, arable land upon which grows a spontaneous settlement integrating habitation and occupation. It's a landscape in motion that thwarts conventional parameters of city building and architecture, in which site is hardly given or is reliable, and the architectural foundation is literally shaken or melted. Borne out of a fluid dynamic, in which the place-form is more important than object-forms, chars pose a conceptual challenge to the imagination of landscape norms, and to the relation between architecture and landscape.

Embracing water and wetness is a natural consequence of the deltaic milieu. From folk culture to modern literature, chars, lowlands and riverbanks continue to circulate as geographic sites of reference in the vastly "rural" Bengali imagination. But what of the city? In its positioning as a bastion of dryness, the contemporary city has not cooperated with the delta. Can the phenomenon of chars be instructive for a wet city?

Present Dhaka is being built from the fluid fabric of its surrounds. In Dhaka's inexorable expansion from its relatively higher grounds into the precious region of floodplains, wetlands and "lowlands," vast aquatic areas are being furiously filled up by a powerful coterie of developers in an unprecedented scale of urbanistic intervention. Every hour, as part of the operation, barges on various rivers and rivulets girdling Dhaka carry sand and soil from one location to deposit on another – typically, on a "lowland" that is marked for dry development with landfills eventually parceled off as building lots. In another method, an array of steel pipes, sometimes miles long, pump sand and silt from a river location onto a landfill site. This is the human version of landscape in motion.

Cape (Raziul Ahsan), SOS Village, Bogra.

And, it is precisely at this juncture, the edge, where the expansion of the city meets an aquatic matrix, a new kind of city-think is needed. What should be the perimeter of the city in such a nexus? How will the two sides of this fluid edge be planned? Dhaka cannot grow infinitely in every other direction, swallowing up wetlands and agricultural land with mind-numbing speed, and throwing off balance a precious ecological and hydrological system. If not, then, how will be the population growth and the appetite for urban land solved? The brilliance for urban designers and planners will be to show, in the framework of a wet urbanism, that growth can be addressed by sustaining and enhancing the city's crucial hydro-geographic system.

Building with the Land

If architects in Bangladesh were to take on a distinctive challenge today, it will have to be around a (hydro-)geographic theme, which is also deeply connected to future forms of cities and settlements in Bangladesh. While many successful practices are able to prove their forte in dealing with new global and urban types, and complex programs, it is to the persuasive wave of landscaped themed projects that one must turn to for a new phase.

Saif Ul Haque Sthapati, Govinda Gumolankar Hostel, Chittagong.

A perennial image of the Bengali landscape is that of modest-scaled detached structures tucked among foliage and ponds, in the larger background of rivers and ricefields. Such a scenario seems apt for a theoretical understanding of architecture as part of an environmental continuum. Going beyond the picturesque relationship between building and landscape, a new design intelligence is needed to address contentious and critical issues of the deltaic landscape: climate change, flood and flux, agricultural milieu, and social imbalance generated by the flux.

Responding to the alluvial land, Kahn had earlier intuited that in Bangladesh one is required to be a "land architect." While Kahn did not work out the idea systematically, he did indicate an

Khandaker Hasibul Kabir, Jol Jongol, Pubail.

architecture whose language will be conditioned by the physics of the delta – the mutuality of land and water, the malleability of earth, and precariousness of dwelling.

Bangladesh's hydro-geographical terrain changed Kahn's own attitude towards the relationship between architecture and landscape. It's a lesson Kahn adopted in his inimitable way and then abstracted as a broader philosophical principle that traveled to his other works. It is to Kahn's meditation on "how the buildings are to take their place" on the wetlands of Dhaka that one may locate the origin of the new wave of geography-responsive architecture.

Working in Bangladesh in the 1960s, Kahn intuited that in Bangladesh one is required to be a "land architect," by far the most insightful understanding of doing architecture in the delta. While Kahn did not work out the idea systematically, except to note that the perennial building principle has been to dig-and-mound, what is hinted here is a thought for an architecture whose siting and forming are both conditioned by the physics of the delta – the mutuality of land and water, the malleability of earth, and the tentativeness of dwelling.

In the delta, the most elemental but profound act of building is the "bhita," the raising or moulding of the ground to prepare a stage for dwelling, a solid earth platform on which the house rises. The SOS Village in Bogra is a most thoughtful and poetic elaboration of the "bhita." Raziul Ahsan's SOS Children's Village in Bogra (1994), a remarkable essay on placing and siting, where buildings sit effortlessly with the land without having to cry out "Look, I am architecture...," and yet offer a rich variety of compelling experiences. The architect, Raziul Ahsan, was working, in his random methods, on some of the most poignant themes of our architecture.

The Bogra complex consists of a school and houses for orphaned children, along with residences for staff. The first significant thing about the complex is that the huts, conceived of as simple brick structures with CI sheet roofing, are laid out on the site in a deliberate irregular manner. The overall arrangement is determined by the idea that architecture operates beyond a building, in this case, by the visual logic and kinesthetic dynamics of moving in and around the site. Moreover, the whole land of the site – the "bhita" – is reshaped into a completely new landscape of terraces, platforms, mounds, embankments, steps, and ramps. Passages and walkways are woven onto that created landscape. As Ahsan himself described, it is a "fantastic" landscape intended to take the inhabitants, the little children of the Village, into imaginative and wondrous journeys. The irregular layout of the buildings and the undulated land-form give a new expression to the concern for a land ethics. When many are quite happy treating a site simply as a flat base, Raziul Ahsan, while keeping the buildings rather straightforward, concentrated on the land-form, converting it into a complex and reconstructed topography. What was also evident in Ahsan's project was a new attitude of archaeological humility and geological impulse.

Atelier Robin (Salauddin Ahmed), residencce, study model.

Ana Herringer and Eike Roswag, Meti School, Rudrapur.

In a more recent project, Kashef Mahbub Chowdhury's Friendship Center in Gaibandha suggests land modulation as an architectural strategy in which a matted building complex with pavilions and courtyards is enframed by an "embankment" to keep the flood water out. Built on a flood-plain as a training center for people living in vulnerable areas, the project speaks of a new landscape-form even if it presents with the embankment a subdued opposition to the surrounding flood-plains.

Various projects, from social engagements to architectural and quasi-architectural creations, indicate new, innovative responses to the aquatic terrain. Bypassing the conventions of city generated forms, these projects are "soft" by their nature and comportment, and suggest a new language of quietude and commitment to social well-being.

A correspondence between boats and buildings seems to be an obvious answer to the diluvial delta. For his much featured educational and social program with floating schools, Mohammed Rezwan converted boats into classrooms that ply to where the students live if they are unable to come to school. Solar powered electricity and computer based education support the arrangement. Yves Marre and Runa Khan, of Friendship, have contributed considerably to restoring the disappearing culture and technology of boat building. In an economic environment in which developmental programs are dictated by the norms of a "dry" culture, a renewed attention to boats goes a long way. Springing from the deep riverine culture of the delta, in which boats have played a key part, restoring and reintroducing some of those beautiful boats may bring about a new ethic and appreciation of water-based practices.

For a special school on a flood-plain outside Dhaka, Saif Ul Haque has created a floating but anchored platform on which simple bamboo woven walls and roofs form a series of classrooms. Unfazed by volumetric flamboyance, the architectural language is one of restraint and adaptation. For a modest arrangement, the school is an important experiment on how to deal with the flux of water and not push it away, and how to carry on life when the water arrives.

Khondaker Hasibul Kabir has been carefully crafting a language of landscape arrangement in which ecology is the fundament of an aesthetic operation. In his "getaway" outside Dhaka, called "Jolo Jongol," Kabir has composed a cooperative landscape in which all elements participate in a delicate symphony, with none overwhelming the other. Buildings – more like lean-tos – become deliberately non-descript and unassuming as if they had been either always there or on the verge of dissolution; they straddle the edge of a wetland in precarious poise. In his now demolished "bamboo platform" in a slum in Dhaka city, Kabir arranged a similar situation in which an almost invisible architecture, garden, and community assembly sent a quiet challenge to the city's rowdy building culture.

Bengal Institute, Rendering of the transformation of Dhaka's Buriganga riverbank.

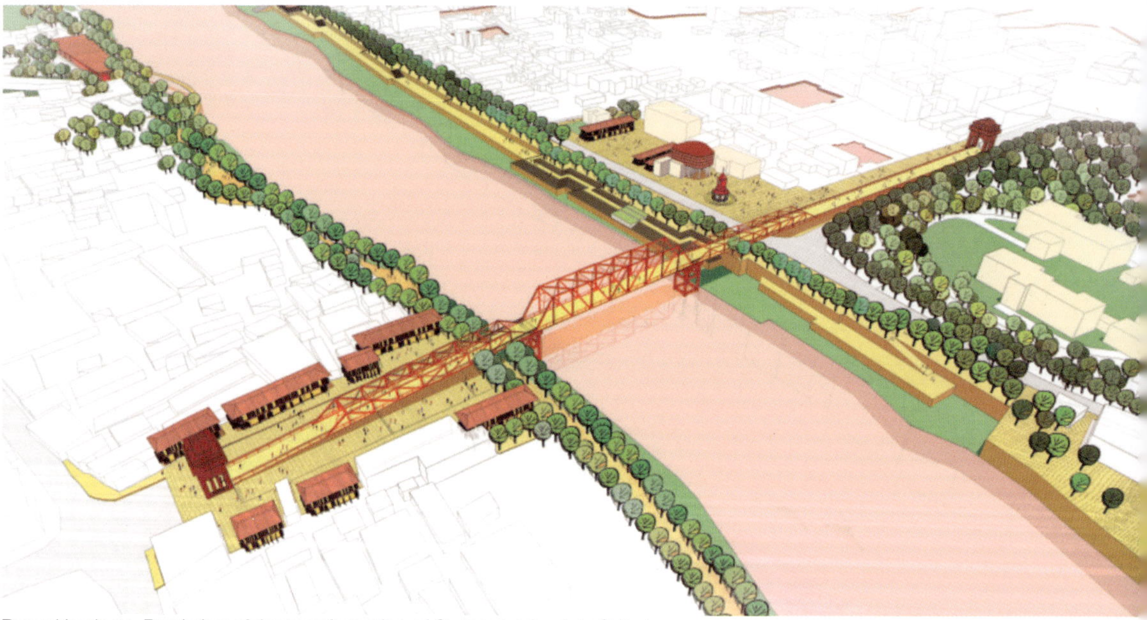

Bengal Institute, Rendering of the transformation of Surma riverbank in Sylhet.

At a more speculative and projective level, Kazi Khaleed Ashraf and his team at Bengal Institute for Architecture, Landscapes and Settlements are engaged in large-scale operations with water as a structural and organizational presence in the delta. Involved with urbanscape plans for Dhaka as well various small towns, Bengal Institute is defining the scope of the urban task as well as reassigning new significance to small towns.

With its aquatic-geological formation – *in flux* – and projected consequences of environmental changes, the organization of land, water and settlements takes on an urgency that is unique to Bangladesh. Settlements patterns, architectural types, and socio-economic life-world, that are dynamically inter-connected, also confront new conditions raised by accelerated economic, environmental and social transformations. It is frequently heard that: "Dhaka is the toughest city in the world." "Bangladesh is symptomatic of the gravest environmental challenges." It is in the neighborhood of such pronouncements that the Bengal Institute team finds necessary to rethink the scope of environmental design, and its pedagogy and practices.

With Bangladesh as a theorem for ecological actions, Bengal Institute thinks that the architectural agenda needs to go beyond problem solving and form creation in which the architectural task should extend its sights to the intellectual, ethical and creative issues facing the futures of human habitats. The question of systemic and integrated "landscapes," whether as habitats or place-forms, agricultural fabrics, flood plains, or natural wetlands, is at the center of new investigations and imaginations at the Institute, and form the theoretical core of a new design intelligence.

Motivations for this new architectural agenda are more about "place-form" rather than spectacular objects. It also becomes evident that developing this design intelligence requires a new kind of knowledge base, training and orientation that will uncover the original intimacy between architecture, habitation and landscape. In a sense, this new approach considered at Bengal Institute reveals a deeper coupling of the pavilion-form and landscape-form conflating the conventional boundary between architecture and landscape.

continent has been widely debated, it is difficult to ignore its overwhelming spectre even in contemporary times. Colonial rule constituted a great rupture in Indian societies, yet

anachronises the present. "The modern house is the house where I don't belong," Quetglas continues, "which I cannot claim as mine, where neither I nor my imagination

not only concealed the joints but also

hand, with Akbar's Diwan-i-Khas at Fatehpur Sikri.[26] Beyond this associational polarity it is the layout of the garden of the

sensitive to ideas and to beauty of form, let it prove its

immortality, in being-to-death." Thus, re-citing Seneca via Derrida, one could say destruction is imminent in building.

of the materials one is left to work with. In any case, both procedures are attempts at dematerializing either physically (by reduction) or virtually (by visual effects) the very fundamental conditions of architecture: materiality and presence.

exhibition in 1929 and placed in crates,

contradiction.

A structure was rebuilt on the same site in 1986. The original does not exist. The imagination is pervaded by the ruins of the original. What exists is a simulacrum. Or, a sarcophagus.

Why Did the Monk Burn the Temple?

and before proceeding to burn the temple, went on a drinking binge and visiting prostitutes. But that did not explain why he torched Kyoto's sacred monument.

Villas in Ahmedabad

in the age of industrial progress is justifiably ahistorical, acultural and international. It is more than coincidental that the reductive internationalism of the

Le Corbusier's "Prehistory"

tenuous and fragile requiring a frequent revision and reformation.

From the very beginning of Le Corbusier's entry into architecture, starting with his voyage to Eastern Europe and Turkey, a dual sensibility pervades his thought. In Greece, on the heights of the Acropolis, he perceives architecture

The Rafters Are Shattered

... before the 1930s, as in the Mundaneum project and the projects for Algiers, and as a more reconciled thrust in the ...

While young leaves twinkled like green stars at the gentle breeze, he sat under the bo tree determined not to stand up or open his eyes until what he sought has been found. Then at the end comes the brilliant moment, something ...

India and Le Corbusier: The Open Hand

... accommodated what Stanford Anderson calls the independent and ... richness.[8]

... home or house. And, second, there is the ushering of the dismantling of that structure. Two ...

India the Humane and Profound Civilisation

... imagery for the body? And, why is the event rendered in a cataclysmic manner?

... reduced to asking what is "Indian" about his work? The problem of framing such a question has its roots not merely in the dominance ...

... whose existing lineaments and ligaments must be shattered before the enlightened life can begin. Clearly this is a vivid body and ...

... powerful mill-owners, and two villas.

In Buddhist sense, the destruction of the "last" hut is an ideograph of nirvana, the climax of renunciation. The cataclysm, using the trope of the shattered hut, basically inaugurates a new life in the teleological narrative where the old ...

... a positive alternative.[9] In claiming the city as a social and urban disaster, some people have demanded: "Leave Chandigarh ...

The Temple of Doom and Enthusiasm

... the squabble over the appropriation of the new city as capital by the two states of Haryana and Punjab.[10]

... the stuff that drives all cities. Le Corbusier himself expresses the struggle: "There was anxiety and anguish in taking decisions on that vast ...

... wives, mothers and whores: wife of a senator, mother of a general, sister to a noble person, or just a plain prostitute from the shadier part of ...

... other. Since the 1960s, a different development ethos was introduced and encouraged. As part of that practice, landfills, ...

... kinds of intoxicants. The god dances through the streets, from one neighborhood to another, followed by his raucous retinue. The women run to the windows for a glimpse. Some run out of their houses, from their kitchen, from their afternoon nap, from attending to their children in the aulae. Some are young, some are old, dutiful wife of ...

Measures of Water

... architecture. There, meaning is not generated by the visual and symbolic relationships ...

... who came from nowhere and elsewhere, the women pounce on the temple. They climb and grab at the ropes tying the bundle of wooden posts that hold the roof rafters, they shake and pull in frenzy, their palms bruised and bloody in no time. The ropes come apart, and one by one, the purlins fall, crashing to the ground, and soon the roof tiles, often one by one and often in the loud ...

... would jump down and pounce on the poor, fallen woman, and pull and tug at her until her limbs are severed. Thus the temple and its builders and un-builders would enter a curious and volatile relationship of building and mayhem, of death and birthing, recalling the genealogy of the god himself, whether it is the mother figure Semele impregnated after drinking a potion made of the heart of Dionysis torn ...

... enthusiasm but more ...

The Matrix of the Delta

... and inverted the roles of citizenship and duty, ecstasy and responsibility, and the sacred and the sacrilegious.[The above tale ...

WATERNESS

The Origin of Architecture Is in a Slaughter

... hidden in its basement or concealed behind its walls, is a secret story told only ...

... and therefore what is architecture. *Chars* provoke a new thinking in the relation ...

Parasols and Silhouettes

... to matrix. While there are villages focused towards (dry) towns and cities, a vast part ...

... soft alluvium, cutting and twisting through hard ground. After making a broad ...

... slaughtered and dismembered, with each ...

... of air, it is the shade, and yet the sun must penetrate at the proper time, in the favourable seasons. The conditions of the problem are ...

... manifest. Thus on the dismembered body of the poor thing emerged a grid of order and measure, and for each grid appeared property and character, and upon that ...

... typological counterpart: the brise-soleil and the roof as an umbrella. From a tentative expression as in Villa Bezeau in Carthage, Tunisia (1928), the brise-soleil becomes a highly articulated "element poetique" in the office tower for Algiers (1939-1942). The separation of the roof from the more used volume of the building also dates as early as 1928 in the first sketch for Villa Bezeau, and 1939 in the pavilion at the exposition at Liege where the ...

... of the making of a worlding.

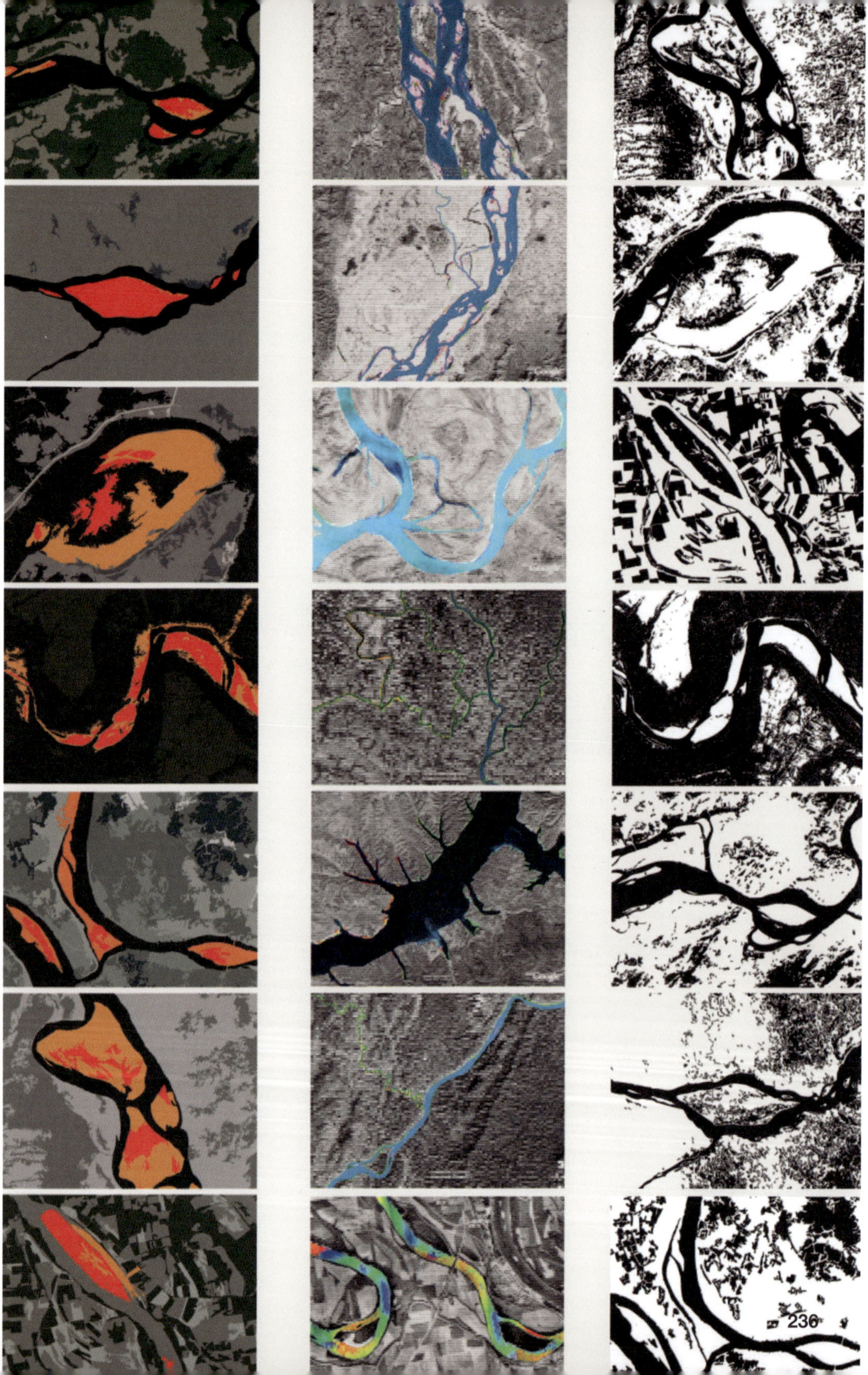

Fluid dynamics in the delta (study by Aarthi Padmanabham, University of Hawai'i).

Water as Ground

Published in *Design in the Terrain of Water*, edited by Anuradha Mathur and Dilip da Cunha (Applied Research + Design Publishing, San Francisco, 2014).

Once upon a place and time, the city of Dhaka emerged delicately from an irascible landscape called the Bengal Delta. Powerful rivers churn through this landscape constituted by rainfalls, cyclones, floods, silting and land-shifting of monumental proportions. In this fluctuating hydrological world, cities and settlements continue to be structured by an impromptu organization into a dynamic matrix of rivers, canals, wetlands, floodplains, agricultural fields, *chars* (silted landforms) and human habitation.

Yet Dhaka and the delta appear increasingly as two separate entities, antithetical and stranger to each other. Since the 1960s, a different development ethos was introduced and encouraged. As part of that practice, landfills, embankments and roadways supported the technology of a dry culture, pitting the city against the delta. Much of the current crises of Dhaka – lack of land, lack of housing, lack of civic spaces – stem from this opposition, at the center of which is the inability to incorporate the language of a dynamic aquatic landscape into planning mechanisms and policies. Planners and policy-makers glorify land, while water is exiled to the domain of poets and vagrants, and pitiful margins of the city. Indeed, what is wet is seen as a sign of backwardness and archaic practices.

Measures of Water

In one of the stories in *Invisible Cities*, Italo Calvino describes how one's perception of a city will depend on how one arrives there, whether by land or sea. It is an imperative now that a new design discourse consider a "water ethos" where water is the measure and instrument of spatial and social organization. A water ethos indicates a fundamental immersion in water with anthropological and sociological significance. A measure of water will have to consider the following:

Water creates a paradox, water is a paradox. There is, often in deltaic places, too much water, and there is often too little water. Again, water purifies, water needs to be purified. Once water was needed to purify everything, and now, Ivan Illich observes, water needs to be purified before doing anything with it.

Dhaka versus the delta.

Water disorients and reorients. Water is an agent of transformation, of fluctuations and inversions, and as a consequence, generator of ambiguities. The entry of water in the everyday dry domain can disrupt normativity, and produce new social and political realities.

Water assures neither terra nor firma. The reversibility induced by water disrupts the privilege enjoyed by terra firma as being the basis of the life-world. Water challenges the taking for granted that *land is ground*. In a new constitution of water/ground, where land coordinates or the firma of terra has been unsettled, we will have to develop new terms of references, such as the following:

Immersion. Buoyancy. Drift. Level. Depth. Fluidity. Flotation. Ebb. Tide. Rhythm.

The Matrix of the Delta

The singular emblem of the Bengal delta is the *char*, land formation induced by the dynamics of soil-shifts and water flows. Water cascading down from upland mountains brings pulverized remains to the flat flood-plains in the form of sand, silt and mud, depositing them in an unpredictable geometry of land-forms and waterways. Here, delicate *chars* appear one year to disappear in the next, while the more or less stabilized ones among them – it is always more or less – become sites of settlement and habitation.

Borne out of a fluid dynamic, *chars* pose a conceptual challenge to design imagination. They bear unsettling questions on what is site, what is fixity, and therefore what is architecture. *Chars* provoke a new thinking in the relation between architecture and landscape, even urging a re-thinking of the copula: *between*. *Chars* shift the thinking from object to situation, from form to matrix. While there are villages focused towards (dry) towns and cities, a vast part of the delta is structured by the *char* and consequently by shifting and emergent rivers and riverbanks.

Advaita Malla Barman, in his epic and autobiographical tale of life in the delta, *A River called Titash*, imagines the origin of the river Titash: "Once upon a time the restless Meghna, dancing along her way, slipped into a careless moment – her left bank strained and broke. Her current and waves flowed into that breach. The inflow there created its own course, finding and molding soft alluvium, cutting and twisting through hard ground. After making a broad sweep that held hundreds of villages along the two sides of its course and touched the edges of many forests and flatlands, this pride of the Meghna returned to the lap of the Meghna."

There are then hundreds of stories for hundreds of rivers and their hundreds of twists and turns. Their floods and emergent courses impart to the delta a corrugation of flat plains, ponds, muddy enclaves and lowlands. Architecture here does not prescribe an enclosed and delineated center, but a string of responses based on dig-and-mound, *ghats* (riverbank hubs) and elevated *machas* (impromptu platforms). These – an assortment of spatial typology – then become methods and practices of inhabiting the delta, often as a set of linked systems but quite often as isolated phenomena.

Liquid Urbanism

Chars, lowlands and riverbanks continue to populate popular narratives, from folk culture to modern literature. The vast matrix of the delta, typically "rural," has adopted techniques and practices for dwelling in that landscape. But what of the city? In its positioning as a bastion of dryness, the city has not cooperated with the delta. Can *char-thinking* offer another kind of urbanism for the delta?

People who dwell in the core of Dhaka city, walk its streets and live its urban doldrums may not be cognizant of it, but current urban development practices are based, literally, on liquid matter. Present Dhaka is being built, without a pause, from the fluid fabric of its surrounds. In Dhaka's inexorable expansion from its relatively higher grounds into the precious region of floodplains, wetlands and "lowlands," vast aquatic areas are being furiously filled up by a powerful coterie of developers in an unprecedented scale of urbanistic interventions. Every hour, as part of the operation, barges on various rivers and rivulets ringing and networking Dhaka carry sand and soil from one location to deposit on another – typically, to a "lowland" that is marked for dry development where landfills are eventually parceled off as building lots. In another method, an array of steel pipes, sometimes miles long, pump sand and silt from a river location onto a landfill site. It is precisely at this juncture, where the expansion of the city meets an aquatic matrix, a new kind of city-think is needed: liquid urbanism.

Liquid urbanism entails an epistemic shift. The norm in thinking about Dhaka has been to privilege a core. Liquid urbanism suggests that this thinking begin instead from its wet edge, ushering a conception of a city that is integrated with the delta. Here fluid dynamics structures the city and its infrastructure and hydrological issues serve as starting points and frameworks for future urban planning and design interventions.

A provisional manifesto for such an urbanism may yield the following approaches:

A platform in the delta. The production of platforms will remain a fundamental existential and functional objective in an aquatic terrain. This is poignantly evident during flooding, especially in monumental and turbulent deluges in Bangladesh. The design challenge will be to work with water and not against it. Innovations in the ideas of dig-and-mound, ghats and machas can be points of departure for a revised construction of platform architecture.

Fluid dynamic. Form does follow flow in the dynamic of the floodplain where horizontal and vertical movements of water organizes and directs architectural and landscape formations. Porosity and perforation thus become standard condition in the topography. An organized matrix of mounds and canals may create a new topographical and urban formation as an alternative to the troublesome practice of wide scale landfilling.

An embankment ecology. Following a series of devastating floods in the 1980s, Dhaka is now defined by embankments, a circular barrier and transport infrastructure that physically defines wet and dry. The norms of embankment mean cutting off wetlands and agricultural lands from conventionally prescribed developments, and posing unresolved questions for urban expansion. Instead of a sharp delineation, the embankment may be conceived as a fractured formation. It can be undulating or porous, multi-leveled or layered. The critical thing is to allow the passage of water. What that means is a redefinition of the embankment as an edge. It can be, instead of a barrier, developed into an integral landscape with boulevards, terraces, drainage systems and water reservoirs. Controlled fractures and openings may allow flow of water from both sides in response to wetlands, reservoirs, retention ponds, and agricultural parks.

Embankment is a barrier, how to deconstruct it? The given embankment can be reconfigured from a ribbon into a matrix. Instead of a single Bund along the river or other waterscape, a series of small embankments can be created to develop a matrix of spaces and functions throughout a certain area. The idea behind the size, direction and location of such mini-embankments is to intertwine the built and natural environments,

Dhaka on Buriganga River in the 1950s.

Flood plain, agriculture and housing as integrated landscape (G. Takahashi and L. Nakamine, Ashraf Studio, University of Hawai'i).

Khandaker Hasibul Kabir, Jolo Jongol.

River life. Photo: Ashraf.

Water and land alternation. Photo: Pavel Rahman.

Dhaka's riverbank in the 2000s.

Transformations, from Mathur and da Cunha, *Design in the Terrain of Water.*

as well as to control and retain water for agriculture, water table recharge, and everyday human needs. The embankments can also act as circulation paths. Producing these embankments will also help to restore the natural dynamics of the river and create recreational landscapes and gardens. On a more ambitious level, the embankment may be conceived as the basis for a linear city.

Elevated system. With the intention of bringing "the city into the flood-plain and the flood-plain into the city," a network of cautious and careful development – streets, walkways, housing and public places – that are mostly elevated either on stilts or non-continuous earth mound over agricultural fields, gardens and parks, each at different elevations and responding to different levels of flooding may be proposed. The porosity at the lower level will assure an unimpeded flow of water at different seasons.

Where there is water, floatation is not far away. In a terrain of constant water, floating decks and buildings are a natural response. People in the delta have developed responses through boat-houses, floating markets, floating vegetable gardens and other buoyant devices. Islam Khan, the Mughal governor of Dhaka in the 17th century, is known to have lived on a barge. Floating gardens and markets still continue in practice. Floating schools and hospitals are becoming known as part of various NGO operations. There are many areas in and around Dhaka that still retain a watery landscape, a vestige of an earlier wetland or agricultural condition as leftovers from the embankment intervention. Certain selected areas could be developed as "demonstration villages" to show how a community could live more effectively on water, utilizing its ecological resources and potentials. The settlement could be designed as floating or partially floating on water through innovative vernacular architecture amidst purposeful and productive bamboo groves, orchards and fish farms. A large segment of adjoining riverbanks could be planned for agriculture (rice-fields) in which the people of the settlement could be engaged. The reason to build such a community in and around the city itself is to make a strong rhetorical and visual example: that paddy-fields can be both an economic enterprise and a civic, public space, and part of the city's landscape. Water becomes a common denominator for agricultural urbanism.

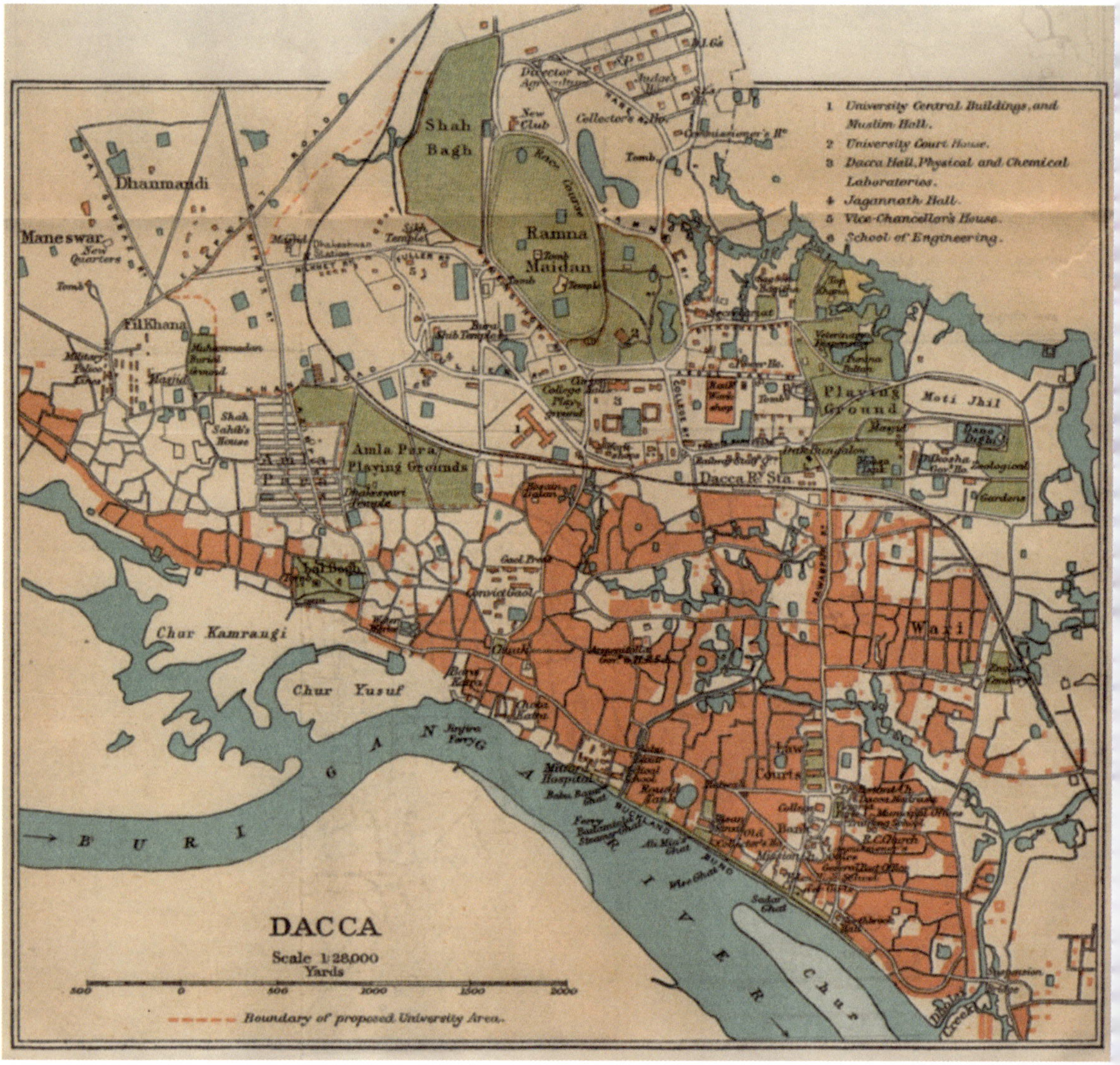

Dhaka as a perpetually porous city, permeated and defined by water, from a 1912 drawing.

Wet Narratives: Architecture Must Recognize that the Future is Fluid

Published in *The Architecture Review*, May 2017.

It goes without saying that water is the stuff of life, and if the levels of world waters rise, the stuff that will make life difficult. We are made of water, we drink water, we wash with water, we purify water, we purify things with water. There is too much water, there is too little water. Before water is somewhere, as landscape architect Anuradha Mathur and architect/planner Dilip da Cunha argue, it is everywhere. Be like water, Bruce Lee implores. Despite the ubiquity of water, its measure is diverse and polyvalent.

Whether framed through political ecology or literary devices, water remains an existential theme. If catastrophes and perils determine design motivations in the twenty-first century, water is up there – whether as threat of sea-level rise, depletion of coastal cities and communities, tidal surges, hazardous contaminations, or for that matter, as life-threatening scarcity. Besides channeling the discourse of disaster, a narrative of water is already inducing alternative strategies in design thinking. A wet narrative asks for a new design intelligence that is perhaps better conveyed by the term 'waterness' than a tagged-on qualifier like the 'aquatic', 'liquid' or 'hydraulic'. In overcoming the deep dichotomy of a wet and dry ideology, and a prejudice of the dry land codified, for example, as 'land use' in planning vocabulary, new motivations entail a phenomenological appreciation of 'water as ground', and an urban and landscape strategy: wet urbanism.

Once upon a place and time, the city of Dhaka – Bangladesh's capital and now a poster-city for wild urbanization – emerged cautiously from an irascible landscape known as the Bengal Delta. A 10-minute ride outside the metropolitan madness still shows the aquatic reality of the land – rivers, canals, waterways, ponds, floodplains and agricultural fields completely girdle the city. But few people recognize that Dhaka is a tender landmass, virtually an island framed by three rivers and a fluid landscape. From furious landfilling operations, motivated by real estate economy, to infrastructural interventions, precipitated by a perception of peril, the precious landscape remains savaged. Dhaka is symptomatic of most cities in powerful hydrological milieus (deltaic, riparian or coastal) and undergoing furious transformations, where practices of planning, whether official, private or impromptu, have succumbed to the regime of a dry ideology.

A deltaic geography is an immense force of flow. Water cascading down from upland mountains brings pulverized remains to the floodplains below in the form of sand, silt and mud, depositing them in an unpredictable geometry of landforms and waterways. Flows and overflows – more commonly understood as 'floods' – impart to this landscape a corrugation of flat plains, ponds, muddy enclaves and 'lowlands', all of which constitute the distinctive but amorphous topography. As 'delta urbanist' Kelly Shannon observes, in such an excruciatingly flat terrain a few centimeters matter in differentiating what is wet from what is dry.

Both mystical and cosmogonic as a phenomenon, the chars – land formations caused by the dynamics of soil-shifts and water flows – rise annually in the delta waters to inaugurate an Adamic landscape. Delicate chars appear one year in the complex choreography of land and water to disappear the next, while more or less stabilized ones become sites of settlement. A char is thus a reminder of an earlier turn of a river and deposition of silt to form the new landmass, demonstrating a geohydrological process in action. In this motile landscape, where a site is hardly reliable, and the architectural foundation is literally wobbling, the conventional parameters of city building and architecture are brought into question. Born out of a fluid dynamic, in which place-form is more critical than object-forms, chars pose a conceptual challenge to the imagination of landscape norms, and to the relationship between architecture and landscape. From the heart of the present city, Dhaka and the delta appear as two separate entities, antithetical and strangers to each other. Fed on dry ideas, planners and policy-makers remain befuddled about envisioning or even managing a city in such a toiled terrain; any deliberation begins with an assumption that a water terrain is unreliable for the city and must be thwarted. In the horizon of the contemporary city, the delta does not even appear in the consciousness until a deluge comes, like clockwork, annually and unmistakably. The past tense of Dhaka being a deltaic city marks both a failure to innovate planning positions and exacerbation of the 'natural' opposition between city and landscape.

Conventional urban planning has basically become the production of land, the manufacture of dryness. Landfills, embankments, bridges and roadways have supported the technology of a dry culture, pitting the city against the aquatic delta. In the schism between dry and wet, dominant planning practices have not only obscured immersive worldviews, but also enforced a limiting measure on an otherwise prodigious and unruly landscape represented by the delta, whether it be the Gangetic, the Mekong or the Mississippi. How can one find an urban and architectural relevance in such a fluid dynamic? Water has never been too far away in architectural and landscape operations, but it is clear that we are on the cusp of a new water discourse. From the technological utopia of the

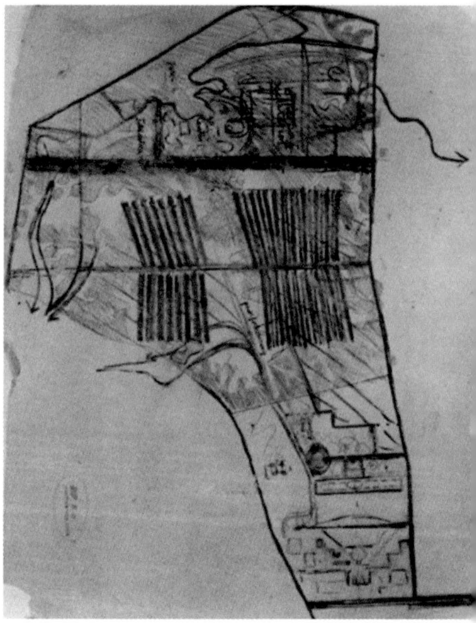

Kahn's sketch of the northern areas of the complex indicates the housing 'bridges' that traverse the floodplains. Image courtesy of the Louis I. Kahn Collection at the University of Pennsylvania.

Bulwarked and sustained by water, the Isle of Manhattan in a nineteenth-century map.
Image c. 1875 Parsons/Currier & Ives.

1960s that produced powerful images of floating cities and water machines, from Kenzo Tange's Tokyo Bay Project (1960) to Buckminster Fuller's Triton City (1966), we have entered new conversations that swing between the standpoints of hydrological technocrats and climate scientists (climate change is primarily a water and moisture issue) to landscape strategists and wet philosophers. Traceable to a reverie about water by Gaston Bachelard and a short but brilliant exposé by Ivan Illich, on how reverential water has now become chemical H2O, a shift has been precipitated in the design field by an abundance of writing and schemas, by architects, landscape architects, academics, and design professionals arguing from a wet perspective.

Italo Calvino's city by the water, in one of his oft-cited descriptions of invisible cities, constitutes pithy prescience of the perceptual, philosophical and ideological dichotomy between wet and dry: arriving there by sea or by land will result in a different city. A lesser known work outside the Bengali language, Manik Bandhyopadhyay's *Padma Nadir Majhi* (*A Boatman of the Padma*, 1936) centers on a river trader's scheme to create a utopia on a char island. The story also describes the life-world of a marginal riverbank community intertwined with the ebb and flow of one of the greatest deltas of the world in one of the densest places on earth, where hydrological intensity meets sociological density. Benh Zeitlin's film *Beasts of the Southern Wild* (2012) shows life on the other side, the Louisiana bayou or

Proposal for Artisanopolis shows what the infrastructure of a sea-based civilisation might look like. Image courtesy of the Seasteading Institute.

the 'bathtub', bringing to the foreground the differential politics of dry regimes and wet regions.

There is still much to learn about a water ethos. Even though water practices have existed for centuries in hydrologically charged places, from Suzhou (China) to Ayutthaya (Thailand), a deltaic geography is a heightened condition for producing new measures of water and new imaginaries in contemporary design discourse. In *Naga: Cultural Origins in Siam and the West Pacific* (1982), the Thai architectural anthropologist Sumet Jumsai takes a measure of the deep structure of such aquatic landscapes. Jumsai also recalls Buckminster Fuller's assertion that humans had spread not from Africa but from Polynesia, and people in the Pacific Rim still bear, what he calls, a 'nautical reflex'.

In its variegated properties, there are two kinds of water: water that we contend with which is everywhere – moisture, rain, puddle, pond, river and ocean – and water that we channel, pictorialize, enclose, pipe, distribute, or otherwise make subservient to infrastructure. While the channeling and canalizing of rivers (often employing a dubious term: 'river training') and the erection of embankments are all premised by the literate deployment of lines, water refuses lines. As an instrument of measure, representation and projection, lines construct edges.

If, as on the Rhodian shore, lines are attributes of the human intellectual endeavor to bring about clarity and control, in practice they always misrepresent the dry and the wet. Precisely articulated lines – Mathur and da Cunha tell us – confine water as 'rivers' and 'channels' when they would prefer to flow and overflow. Instead of being a line, the edge of water is always a zone of gradation of moisture from sparseness to submersion. Conventional methods in mapping and representation, in engineering, architecture and landscape operations, fail to register this nuance. We conceive the world in how we represent it, and if lines show a stark edge between dry and wet, we seek that in our realizations – we are already in a defective default mode.

Water is an agent of transformation, of fluctuations and inversions of the orientations of the world, producing ambiguity and reversibility. This is a recurrent motif in the cultural and literary imagination of the delta, as in *Padma Nadir Majhi*. In his fictional *The Stone Raft* (1986), José Saramago provides a more troubled depiction of a disoriented life after the Iberian Peninsula starts drifting away like a raft on the sea, making all land-based constancies fraught. Whether in a fictional or factual narrative, when water enters the everyday domain it can disrupt normality, and produce new social and political realities.

The reversibility induced by water and its flux interrupts an easy equation between water and ground. The term 'ground' continues to privilege terra firma as the fundamental basis of the life-world. Water not only challenges but also disturbs what we take for granted: that land is ground. In an alternative constitution, in which the firma of terra has been unsettled, one can think of three possible scenarios: water *versus* ground, water *as* ground, and water *is* ground. It is also necessary, consequently, to bring to the foreground a language of the phenomenon of water: Immersion. Buoyancy. Absorption. Drift. Level. Depth. Fluidity. Flotation. Ebb. Tide. Rhythm.

When floodwater comes and stays for weeks, it presents a fundamental architectural dilemma: the givenness of a solid platform, on which life happens, is disrupted. In extreme situations, as when floodwaters seasonally hit Bangladesh or Thailand, or for that matter New Orleans, people climb up on the roof with what matters most (in Bangladesh, cattle and poultry). The search for something that we take for granted and that has become disrupted – the horizontal as a fundamental architectural necessity, indeed something primordial and ontological – becomes a powerful imperative to reboot human and community life.

Embracing water and wetness is a natural consequence of a deltaic milieu. From folk culture to modern literature, chars, lowlands and riverbanks continue to circulate as geographic sites of reference in the vastly 'rural' Bengali imagination. But what of the city? In its positioning as a bastion of dryness, the contemporary city has not cooperated with the delta.
Present Dhaka city is being built from the fluid fabric of its surrounds. In Dhaka's inexorable expansion from its relatively higher grounds into the precious region of floodplains, wetlands, and 'lowlands,' vast aquatic areas are being furiously filled up in

an unprecedented scale of urbanistic drive. Every hour, as part of the operation, barges on various rivers and rivulets girdling Dhaka carry sand and soil from one location to deposit on another – typically, on a 'lowland' that is marked for dry development eventually to be parceled off as building lots. In another method, an array of steel pipes, sometimes miles long, pump sand and silt from a river location onto a landfill site. This is the human version of setting a landscape in motion.

Most of the radical transformation of this landscape is happening beyond the orbit of a master plan, and certainly without any deeply considered urbanism. In the meantime, the fluid margin of the city is increasingly inhabited by subaltern groups, vagrants, and other exiles upended by the furious city-making at the drier core, unable to partake in the fruits of the furious economy. It is precisely at this juncture, the edge, where the expansion of the city meets an aquatic matrix, that a new kind of city-thinking is needed. What should be the perimeter of the city in such a nexus? How will the two sides of this fluid edge be planned? Cities like Dhaka cannot grow infinitely in every other direction, swallowing up wetlands and agricultural land with mind-numbing speed, and throwing off balance a precious ecological and hydrological system. If not, then how will population growth and the appetite for urban land be resolved? The brilliant opportunity for urban designers and planners is to show, in the framework of a wet urbanism, that growth can be addressed by sustaining and enhancing the city's crucial hydro-geographic system.

Louis Kahn intuitively recognized the dynamics of water when he received the commission for the National Capitol Complex in Dhaka in 1963. Although water was a powerful compositional thematic in the design of the assembly complex, with the whole layout seen as a mirror of a delta topography, Kahn moved beyond compositional engagement after he received the commission for a large housing project in a functional floodplain. Kahn's unrealized sketches show a new investigation of water as ground, in which bridge-like housing hovers above fields and floodplains allowing the passage of water. Without naming it so, Kahn had already inaugurated the foundation of what we now call wet urbanism.

Wet urbanism entails a conceptual shift. What for the visionaries of the 1960s was an ideational exercise has now become an ethical imperative. Going beyond the norm of thinking about Dhaka, and similar cities, in which morphologies of the dry center are privileged, plans for such cities have to find terms of cooperation with an aquatic nexus. A provisional manifesto for such an urbanism might propose the strategies listed below.

Platforms and plates. In Nan Madol, on the Micronesian island of Pohnpei, built in the eighth century and abandoned six centuries later, is an enigmatic settlement built as a set of artificial islands on a coral reef at the edge of the island and sea. In designing a school on a site that doesn't quite exist as it lies submerged in monsoon waters for months, Saif Ul Haque, in his Arcadia school project outside Dhaka, created a bamboo platform and pavilion on simple floating devices harnessed to the submerged soil. As an architectural fundament, platforms and their production take on urgency in an aquatic place. Kahn, while working on the Dhaka Capitol, reflected on dig-and-mound as an architectural strategy in the delta. This could be a point of departure for new iterations of the platform.

Fluid dynamic. Form does follow hydraulic flow in which horizontal and vertical movements of water may direct architectural and landscape formations. The Mexican architect Alberto Kalach suggests the inundation of a vast area outside Mexico City, not only to recall an earlier pre-Hispanic hydrological setting, but to restructure the growth of the city, ensure water security and restore the depleting ancient Lake Texcoco. Kongjian Yu, the prolific landscape architect from China, is also known as the restorer of troubled waterscapes. In projects such as the Liupanshui Wetland Park in Guizhou Province, and the Tianjin Qiaoyuan Wetland Park, in Tianjin, Yu modulates landscape forms to generate new public realms and enriched ecology with flowing water as the structuring element. Porosity and perforation, flow and overflow, can be new leitmotifs in constructions. An organized matrix of mounds, canals, and water plains may create a new topographical and urban realm as an alternative to the practice of troublesome landfilling.

Embankment is a barrier, how can we deconstruct it? Embankments, bridges and landfills have become standard prescriptions for large-scale infrastructural operations for the modern environment. Following a series of devastating floods in the 1980s, Dhaka is now circumscribed by embankments that physically define wet and dry. Embankment structures have sliced through wetlands and agriculture, posing more questions for environmental justification, as well as urban expansion. Instead of being a ribbon, articulated from the concept of a line, embankments can take many forms. They can be undulating or porous, multi-level or layered, and fractured or disassembled: the critical thing is to allow the passage of water. Instead of being a rude barrier, embankments can be developed into an integral landscape with circulation paths, terraces, drainage systems, and water reservoirs, and perhaps even housing as a superstructure. Controlled fractures and openings may allow flow of water from both sides in response to wetlands, reservoirs, retention ponds, and agricultural parks. Producing such embankments would help to restore the natural ecology of the river and create new habitational spaces for the city.

Stilts and sticks. With the intention of bringing 'the city into the floodplain and the floodplain into the city', a network of cautious and careful development – streets, walkways, housing and public places – that are mostly elevated either on stilts or non-continuous earth mound over fields, gardens and parks, each at different elevations and responding to different levels of flooding, may be imagined. The porosity at the lower level will assure an unimpeded flow of water at different seasons. Le Corbusier's unbuilt hospital project for Venice remains unexamined as a possible source for such a model.

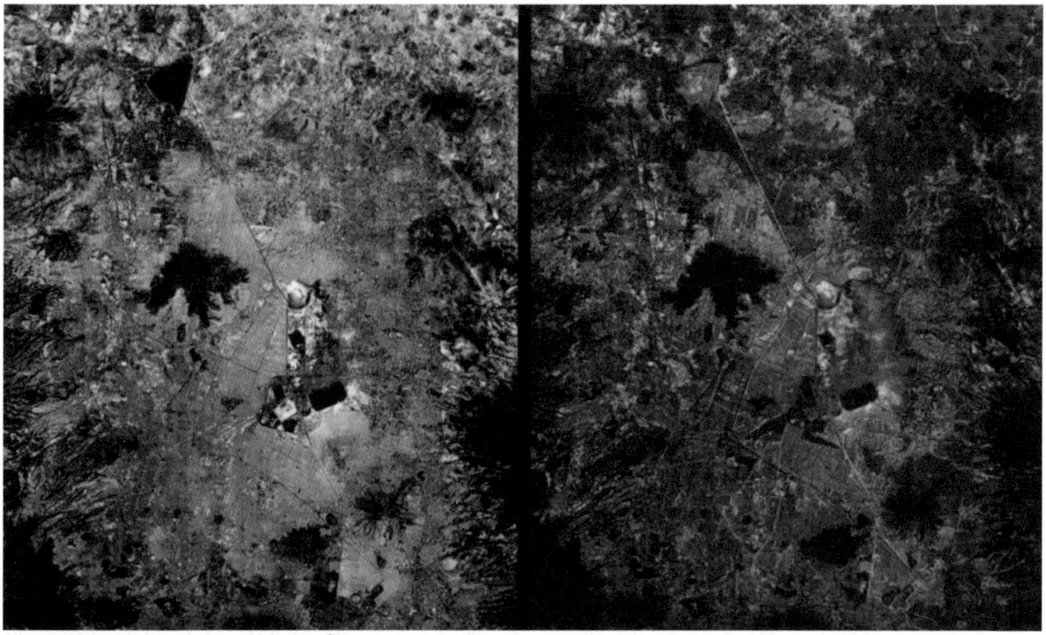

Alberto Kalach's inundation of Mexico City reconceptualises the growth of the city around it's central lake. Image courtesy of Taller de Arquitectura 'X'/Alberto Kalach.

Where there is water, flotation is not far away. Fuller's Triton City was conceived as an anchored floating city that would be located close to the shore and connected with bridges to the mainland. While the original project commissioned by a sponsor did not proceed, Fuller was invited by the US Department of Housing and Urban Development in 1968 to plan a series of neighborhood-sized floating communities between 3,500 and 6,500 persons. Perhaps the cruise ship has now become an exaggerated incarnation of Fuller's idea, but there are many modest and effective examples of floating architecture, such as boathouses, floating markets and floating vegetable gardens. Itsuko Hasegawa's proposal for the Yokohama Port competition suggests recycling anchored ships as a series of interconnected public spaces. Mohammed Rezwan's flotilla of floating schools in Bangladesh and Kunlé Adeyemi's Makoko Floating School in Nigeria are examples of revising received types that follow the flow rather than circumvent it.

Whichever of these strategies of perforation, inundation, elevation, and flotation are adopted to accommodate an increasingly blurred world, architecture must recognize that the future is fluid.

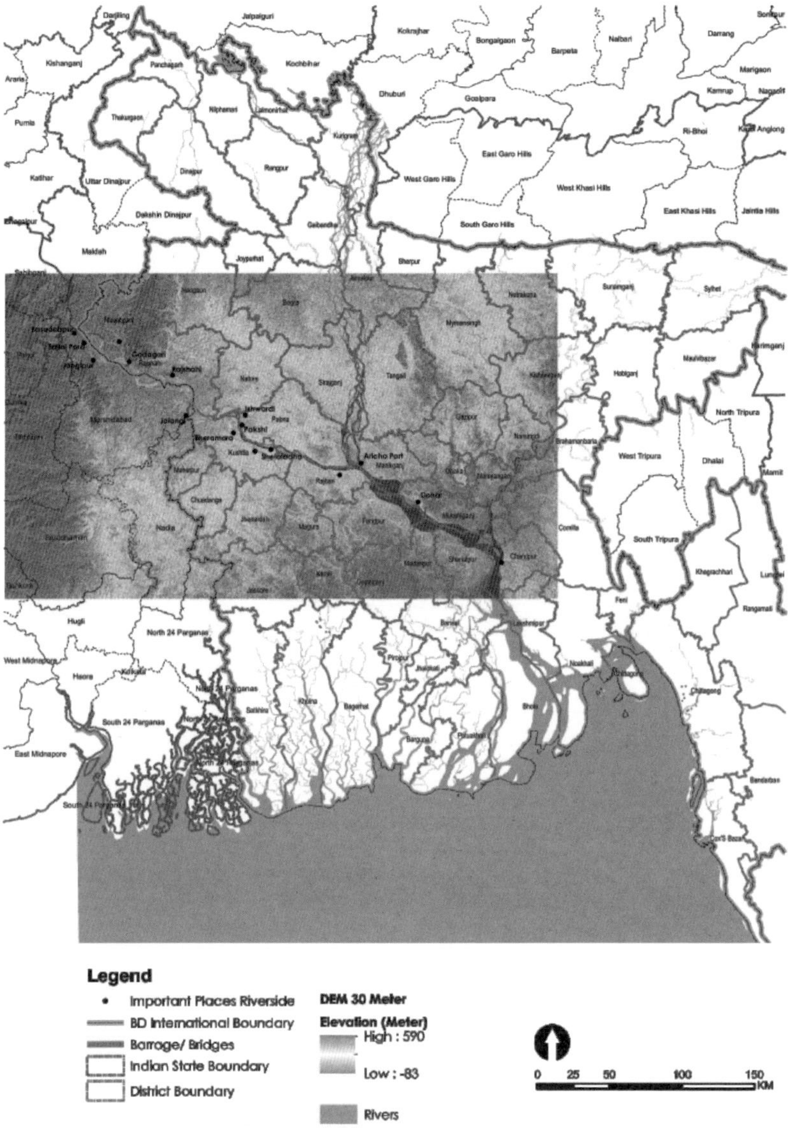

The flows of the Padma, the Brahmaputra, and the Meghna
Map by Arfar Razi, Bengal Institute.

When the Ganga becomes the Padma

Unpublished, 2017.

Flow

All things take a radical turn as the Ganga becomes the Padma. But it is not precise where the Ganga flowing over a vast part of the subcontinent, commandeering its historical and geographical imagination, all of a sudden is no longer a riverine flow but part of the largest delta in the world.

The Padma is the last leg of the river Ganges before it converts into a mush of foam and mud at the mouth of the sea. It is the final stage of Ganga's operatic metamorphosis, from a mountain trickle to an epic river, and to a grand finale in the flow of three rivers. The point from where the Padma begins, ambiguously from the stream of the Ganges, to the bowels of the ocean, is about 258 km of the total stretch of 2,600 km of the Ganges. Between where the Padma begins and where it dissolves, both ambiguously, describes an incredible phenomenon of geological and hydrological dynamic. By the time the Ganga is the mighty Padma, the water is an oceanic expanse – in the designation of Sir Charles Lyell who observed ocean currents: an "oceanic river" – whose banks are often so far apart that it is one is hardpressed to call it a river.

From the Ganga to Padma is not simply a name change but a qualitative shift, in which the Padma along with two other major river systems establishes the Bengal Delta. With 144,000 sq km area, the delta is also one of the most populated and densest, and with an ancient production of rice, perhaps the most fertile. With a population of 200 million (of which over 160 million is in Bangladesh), the delta is a "nation of water upon land,"[1] creating a highly precarious and contested environment that, writes the landscape architect Kelly Shannon, "is essentially a gigantic floodplain, with the Ganges (called the Padma) carrying the silt of India and the ashes of millions of Hindus, the Brahmaputra (called the Jamuna), principle river of the eastern Himalayas, joining in what is known as the mighty Meghna, which then flows southeast to the Bay of Bengal."[2] It is also the instance where the Ganges meets its other riparian protagonists, the Brahmaputra-Jamuna coming straight down from the north. Soon after meeting the Meghna river further east that comes down from the northeast, the Padma ends in the Bay of Bengal, or known as Bangoposagar from the second century CE.

[1] J. Novak, *Bangladesh: Reflections on the Water* (Dhaka: University Press Limited, 1993).

[2] Kelly Shannon, "Let it Flood," lecture at Bengal Institute, 2016.

Borne out of the hydrogeological chemistry of the three rivers, land is literally formed by silt deposits through a constant shaping and reshaping conducted by these three rivers and their many tributaries, which themselves are perpetually shifting and changing. This dynamic gives the land an amorphous nature, and characterizes the region's climate, topography, ecology, and eventually the social fabric.

The Ganga-Padma is a force of flow that carries with it materials that rematerialize as the alluvium of the delta (the annual average discharge of the river is 30,000 m3 and the bankful discharge is 75,000 m3). Stones and pebbles from the hills of the north, debris of humanity from the middle of India, and ashes of the deceased are all pulverized and agglomerated, and resurface as land and island formations – the *chars* – along the Padma.

Before trains and roads, it was the Ganga-Padma flow that linked Bengal with northern India. Giant boats with enormous sails, with names like Mayurpankhi, Aswamukhi, and Singhamukhi, plied on these waters. Visitors like Abul Faz'l, Tavernier, Hedges, and Rennell, and many others, must have traveled down this mighty stream to the heart of the delta, and returned the same way.

In this essay, I take a downward flow in a river narrative, from where the Padma may have begun in the west of the Bengal delta to the point where it vanishes in the great aquatic convulsion in the southeast.

Bhati

From the plains of Indraprastha or the Lal Quila of Delhi, the uniqueness of the eastern region, known variously as Vanga or Bangala, was recognized with a degree of apprehension, mixed with wonder and derision. The Vedic Aryans considered the region "impure," outside the pale of Aryavarta. Sanskrit texts mention that because of the impurity of the eastern land, anyone venturing out there will require ritual purification before returning.[3] Even the Turks, Afghans, and Persians who gained control over northern India considered the eastern region with mixed perceptions, describing it as *dozakh pur-i-niamat* (hell full of boons). In reference to its geographic constitution, the Mughals called the land *bhati*, the downstream of the river.[4]

The delta or *bhati* is where *hilsa* fishes spawn, rivers become rivulets, rivers meet rivers, rivulets become wetlands, rivers merge with the ocean, and land is held captive in a great rhythmic churning of mud, silt and sludge. Great nets are cast in the waters, and settlements small and large thrive and plunge in the treacherous waters. In a great alchemy that is part mystical and part tragic, land-forms arise again in some unexpected, unmapped waters, and thrive. In such an excruciatingly flat terrain, a few centimeters matter in defining what is wet and what is dry, which in turn describes two cultural paradigms: one organized by an aquatic life-world, and another by a dry ideology, so to speak.

[3] *Baudhyana Dharma Sutra*, 1, 2, 13-15.

[4] Abul Faz'l, in the *Ain i Akbari*, is of the opinion that the name Bangala was derived from the ancient name Vanga and *al*, which meant mounds raised by the rulers throughout the region.

[5] An example of valorizing terrestrial-aquatic cosmology is the veneration of the serpent as goddess/spirit "Manasa" in Bengali folk cultural practices irrespective of religious affiliations.

View of Padma River from Lalon Shah Bridge. Photo: Tarik Adnan Moon, Wikimedia.

Scene from the film *Padma Nadir Majhi* by Goutam Ghosh (1993).

A world of moistness and fecundity makes the *bhati* a predominantly water-based civilization where cosmological and valorized concepts are generated from riverine rhythms and agricultural rituals.[5] It is also a matrix of "rice culture," where rice is not something merely consumed but is the basis of value-construction, of a collective ethos and mythos. In the Bengal delta, rice cultivation is an existential occupation; the production of rice is the production of a worldview. Two paradigmatic figures populate the Bengali imagination: the man with the plough (*langal*), the farmer; and, the man with the fishing net (*jaal*), the fisherman. The boatman and the boat are also integral to the delta narrative; in their *bhatiali* songs, the boatmen provide the musical resonance to the landscape.

The Padma certainly belongs to the Bengal delta and has shaped the material and psychological imagination of its peoples. Who named the Ganga as Padma? In Bangla, *padma* is "poddo" meaning the lotus flower, another name for the goddess Lakshmi (Lokkhi). Does the name change indicate a shift that is perceptually cultural, but also fundamentally meteorological and material? The *Ramayana* mentions the transformation of three gods into riverine forms: Ganges as the male Bhagirathi, Lakshmi as Padma, representing feminine wisdom, and Saraswati as herself; it seems that from the start Ganges and Padma have always been two and different.[6] The *Ramayana* also mentions a muni named Poddo, who instructed the Ganges to flow in the east, and the name may have come from the muni, as was Bhagirathi from the muni Bhagiroth.

Modern texts describe the Padma from the point where the Ganges meets the downflow of the Brahmaputra-Jamuna up to Chandpur at the mouth of Meghna river. Popular perception however stretches the origin of the Padma further west from Chapai Nababganj district, which is almost coincidental to the political boundary of Bangladesh, or farther west in West Bengal where the Hooghly begins its tributary flow away from the Ganges, to Chandpur, the port-hub at the cusp of the oceanic river.

Another way to think about the Padma is the distinctive dynamic that the Ganges generates or encounters as it enters the geography of the delta – where river courses have shifted and widths have fluctuated and landscapes revised. The tumultuous Padma have shifted its course drastically in the last several hundred years. Once the Padma flowed much closer to Dhaka, but now lies about 46 km to the south of the city. Regions south of the Padma, all the way into the Sundarbans and the ocean, is a hydrological outcome of the Padma. The rivers and rivulets, emerging primarily from the Ganga-Padma flow, create that incredible weave of land and water that is the mark of the delta.

Barrage and Bridge
By the time, the river known as Ganga reaches Rajshahi, it is already the mighty Padma; it has entered the historical landscape of Bengal, and the political terrain of the nation-state of Bangladesh. Rajshahi is north of Ganga-Padma, a town of mango groves, picturesque riverbanks, and unique urban relationship with the river. It is the first big town that boldly faces the Padma highlighting the point that there is *also* urban life on the banks of the Padma. Organized riverside parks on *chars* that are adjacent to the city are a distinctive feature of the town. Very few towns have such an incredible adjacency to a dynamic oceanic river.

About 100 km upstream from Rajshahi is the Farakka Dam in western Bengal, completed in 1975 to tame and reorient the Ganges. Between Farakka and Rajshahi, an arbitrary weave of a political boundary takes hold, through which flows the uncertain, unruly flow of a riverway. Deceptive enterprises of certainties and containments spring up in the form of bridges, barrages, canals and embankments.

While the original purpose of the Farakka barrage was to divert water from the Ganges to the Hooghly in order to flush out sedimentation near Kolkata Harbor, the natural flushing has not been as successful as planned; additionally, riverbank conditions on the Ganges have been adversely affected due to the high level of back waters. A more critical consequence involves the *bhati*: the barrage affects the flow of the Padma that in turns impacts the ecology of fishes, mangroves, salinity, river tributaries, and human lives. A point of contention between Bangladesh and India has led to constant negotiations between the two neighboring countries that share a mighty river. In the meantime, Bangladesh has considered building the Ganges Barrage project with the projection that it will hold back water in lean periods, generate electricity, and reroute the waters of the Brahmaputra.

Barrages, bridges, canals and embankments are modern engineering responses to the management of the environment, but as with such large-scale infrastructural projects that intervene with river flow and its waters, unforeseen ecological and human consequences may emerge. Anthony Acciavatti describes the various modern engineering enterprises surrounding the Ganges that has transformed the landscape of central India as, what he describes, the "Ganges Water Machine."[7] Following the Farakka Barrage, the Padma Bridge may be the largest infrastructure construction planned across the Padma.

Initiated in 2010, with construction ensuing and originally expected to be completed by 2018, the Padma Bridge will be the most ambitious undertaking of the Bangladesh government. At 6.15 kilometers (3.8 miles) in length, being one of the longest river crossings in the world, the Padma Bridge will be a landmark structure. With a two level passageway, one for road vehicles and another for rail, and with cost of $3 billion USD, the Padma Bridge is also an engineering challenge. "One of the greatest challenges," writes Robin Sham of AECOM involved in the design of the bridge, "to long-span bridge engineering are the forces of nature. Recent catastrophic events around the world reinforce the fact that nature can be destructive to infrastructure."[8] Taking on that challenge, as well as controversies around funding by international agencies that stalled the project before it could start, the Bangladesh government is constructing the project mostly from its own resources with a special claim to building a bridge on one of the most dynamic rivers in the world.

Exchange

If the Ganges is the river par excellence in the Indian imagination, the Padma circulates similarly in Bengali imagination, in geographic, literary and mystical terms. Manik Bandhopadhay's novel *Padma Nodir Majhi* (*Boatman of the Padma*, 1936), on the life and travails of people along the riverbanks, becomes an allegory for humanity in the delta. Centered around the emergence of a mysterious island (*char*), a freshly brewed landscape, where a Muslim trader wants to establish a new community – a kind of a utopia – *Padma Nodir Majhi* depicts the tidal fluctuations in the precarious lives of Hindu and Muslim boatmen and fishermen, and an intertwining of their intimate lives. The Padma landscape is a constant reminder of dissolutions and emergences, both of the material landscape as well as human lives. In narrating the plebeian culture of the Padma, *Padma Nodir Majhi* represents the rhythm of the Padma, its oscillation from being a bountiful source to an untrusting phenomenon, and from inciting hope and submission simultaneously.

[6] Ashok Biswas, *Bangladesher Nodikosh* (Dhaka: Gotidhara, 2011).

[7] Anthony Acciavatti, *Ganges Water Machine: Designing New India's Ancient River* (San Francisco: Applied Research and Design, 2015).

[8] Robin Sham, "Padma Bridge: Design for Severe Earthquake and Deep Riverbed Scour," in *Structure* (August 2013).

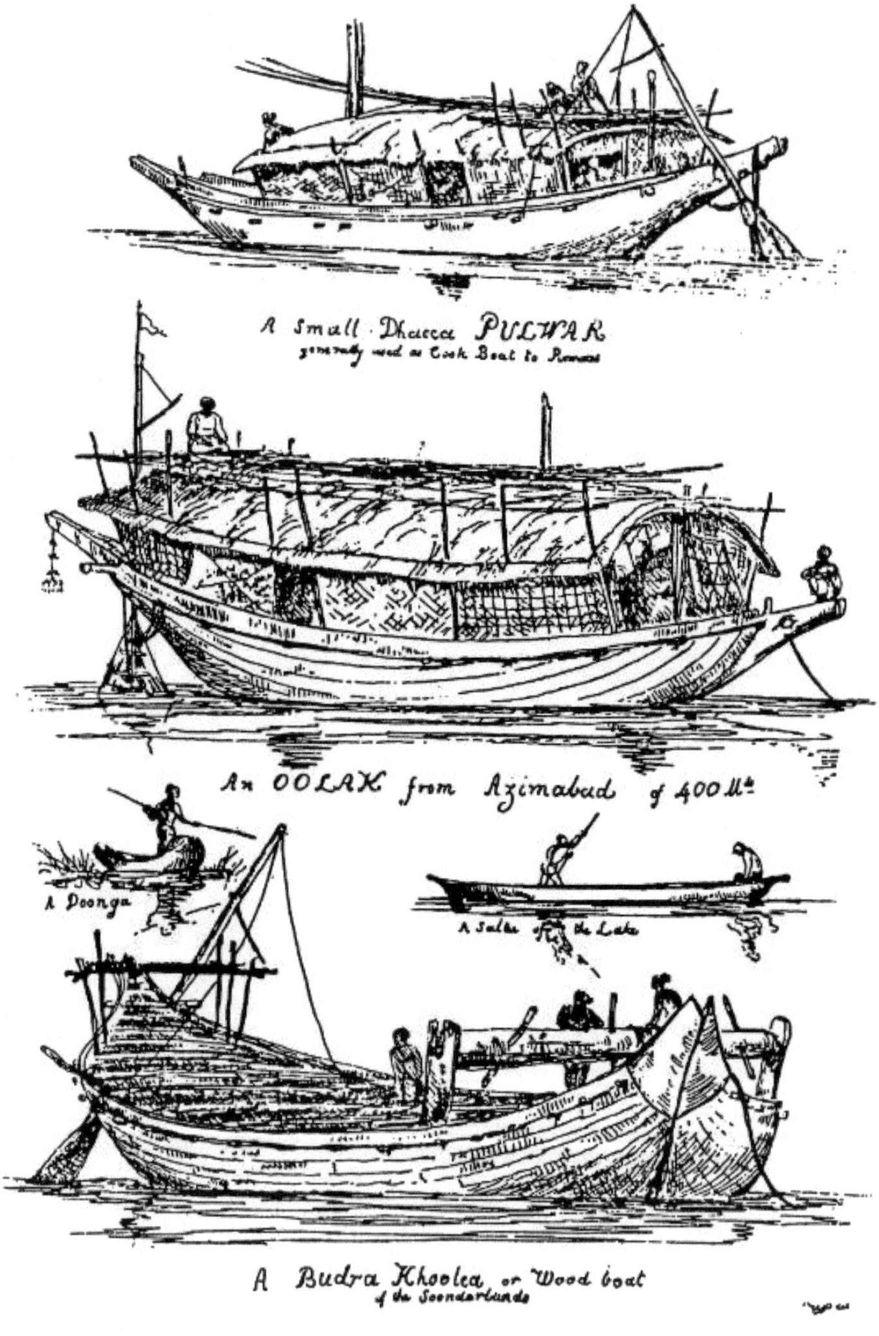

Boats of Bengal 4 (from Jean Deloche, *Boats and Ships in Bengal Terracotta Art*, 1991).

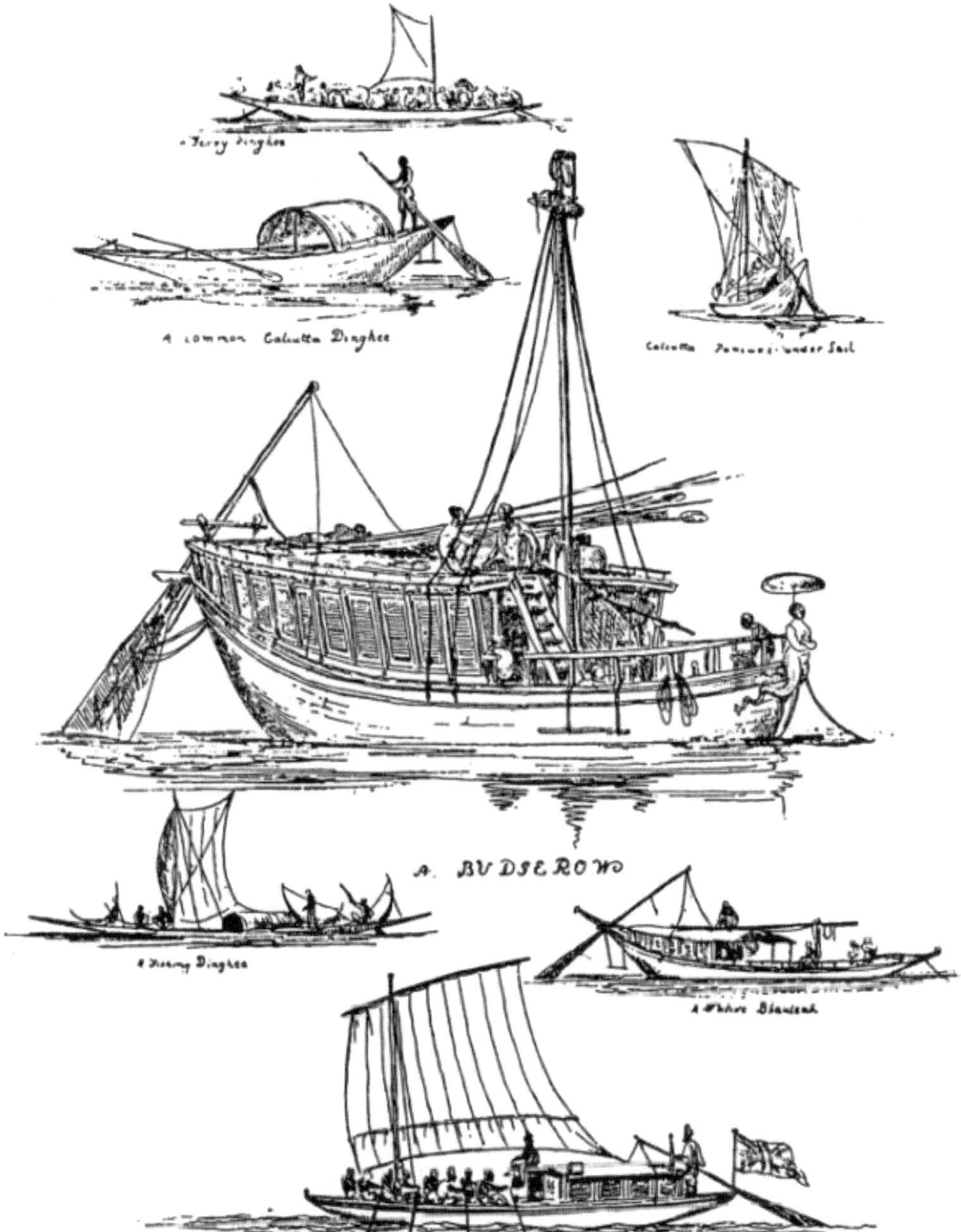

Boats of Bengal 1 (from Jean Deloche, *Boats and Ships in Bengal Terracotta Art*, 1991).

Sheliadah in Kushtia is a place 40 km (25 miles) south of the Padma, and the estate of the Tagore family of Kolkata; it is there, and on the nearby banks, a great exchange took place between an urban cosmopolite and a rural humanist. The poet Rabindranath Tagore stayed at Shelaidah and Shahjadpur in Pabna intermittently for nearly a decade from 1890. Rabindranath's father, Dwarkanath Tagore, had boat-builders from Dhaka build a boat that the poet used to ply on the terrain; it was called the *Padma*.

The Kolkata elite that Rabindranath Tagore belonged to and the people of the Padma – as represented in *Padma Nodir Majhi* – are worlds apart (amplified by the fact that the Tagores were landlords in the eastern delta), but the river, and the various canals and channels, had a lasting impact on the great poet. Rabindranath by then was already renowned for his work, having composed many songs drawing from Western, Hindi, and Asian sources, and having already created his inimitable musical genre. During his stay at the Padma estate, Rabindranath befriended disciples and friends of the baul mystic Lalon Shah, such as Gagon Harkara and Kangal Harinath, who with their folk mysticism and rural ethos, had a transformative impact on a poet already in a mature stage of creations. Rabindranath wrote some of his key works including *Sonar Tori* and translated the *Gitanjali* into English while staying in Shelaidah. Drawn so much to Lalon's ideals, Rabindranath Tagore often called himself "Rabindra Baul."

In a poem, Rabindranath writes: "*He had his poet's welcome from the river Padma/ and the morning star through the intervals of bamboo leaves on her bank./ The dark masses of cloud had spread before him/ a purple shadow on the distant rain-dimmed forest;/ his eyes had followed the track of noisy girls to the river/ along the shady village lane/ and enjoyed the duet of colours under the sunset sky/ in the blossoming field of mustard and linseed sown together./ He gazed and said, 'I love it.'*

What Rabindranath Tagore was to Calcutta-centric western Bengal, Lalon Shah of Kushtia was to the east. A mystic, singer, composer, and folk philosopher, Lalon's songs have often been described as the "lyrics of the Padma." It was in the southern landscape of the Padma, living in the zamindari of the Tagores, amidst the life-world of the people akin to that depicted in *Padma Nodir Majhi*, in the whittled and braided matrix of land and water, that Lalon developed his humanistic spiritual position. Avowedly neither Muslim nor Hindu, but both, and more, Lalon epitomized a spirituality and humanity that also broached on social reform in that rural universe. Lalon was deeply embedded in the ethos of rural Bengal, the everyday of common life particular to that landscape, but that combined Sufi mysticism, baul poetry and Baishnav spirituality. Ever alert to the call of the self against the self-centered politics of identity that pitted one religion against another, Lalon was to wonder: "Shob loke koi Lalon ki jaat shongsharey" (people wonder what is Lalon's identity in society). Rejecting classism, social hierarchies, and any kind of fractious ideology, Lalon used his music in the capacity of social transformation and to affect the individual psyche in understanding life anew.

[9] Sadya Afreen Mallick, "The multi-faceted influences in Tagore's work," *Daily Star*, January 13, 2013.

Rabindranath Tagore's boat, the *Padma*.

ir Lalon Shah as sketched by Gogonendranath on boat *Padma*.

Even if Lalon's direct meeting with Rabindranath is uncertain, he is known to have visited the Tagore family in their Shelaidah zamindari. The only portrait of Lalon, from 1889, was sketched by Jyotrindranath Tagore in his houseboat on the Padma.

Since Lalon worked orally, and in the language and mood of the common people, much of his work is not recorded. Kangal Harinath Majumdar, a disciple and friend of Lalon and a pioneering rural journalist from Kushtia, collected many of the songs that were perhaps shared with Rabindranath. Even if a direct meeting between Rabindranath and Lalon did not happen, something substantial did take place through the exchange with the disciples; Rabindranath's journeys in the Padma landscape also impacted his intellectual and spiritual position. What with his spiritual romanticism derived from the beauty of the aquatic landscape, Rabindranath became enamoured with the folk melodies that are part and parcel of that milieu. "During the monsoon," Sadya Afreen Mallick writes, "Tagore was drawn to the *jari, shari* and *bhatiali* songs of the boatmen. Many of Tagore's compositions came to reflect this period, depicting the life of the working class."[9] Supported by Kangal Harinath, Rabindranath collected a set of songs by Lalon, and published them in the Calcutta based monthly *Probashi*. Gagan Harkara's songs, especially "Ami Kothaye Pabo Tare" were also published. Rabindranath's song, "Amar Shonar Bangla," the national anthem of Bangladesh, was composed and based on the *baul* tune of Harkara's song.

There in the delta, along the shores of the Padma, where things are raw, elemental and primitive in the best sense, the intellect is thwarted if not subdued for either a romantic twist or spiritual turn for the Kolkata elite. This meeting of the elite and the elemental, with Lalon as the anchor for the latter, produced some of the finest works of Rabindranath. Even as late as the 1990s, Lalon's net caught the imagination of the American poet Allen Ginsburg to write:

It's true I got caught in/ the world/ When I was young Blake/ tipped me off/ Other teachers followed:/ Better prepare for Death/ Don't get entangled with/ possessions/ That was when I was young,/ I was warned/ Now I'm a Senior Citizen/ and stuck with a million/ books/ a million thoughts a million/ dollars a million/ loves/ How'll I ever leave my body?/ Allen Ginsberg says, I'm/ really up shits creek [After Lalon (1992)]

Land/Water/Wet/Dry

From where the Ganga becomes the Padma settlement patterns change and the precise calibration between dry and wet becomes uncertain. Kelly Shannon notes that topographic differences of a few centimeters define what is wet and what is dry, or what will be mostly wet or dry for most part of the year, and for that matter what kind of habitat, occupation or human activities will take place. In such conditions, cities and settlements, those stubborn edifices of dry practices, remain fragile.

This is clay country where the land is at the mercy of the water. Before clay, a product of moisture, can solidify into a crusty, soily substance, it is awash with water again, shaped and reshaped in a seasonal rhythm. Land has no self-defining ontology; it can only by hyphenated with water for water is everywhere and everything. How to make habitats here? How to build settlements? How to rethink the city?

That Bangladesh is rich in alluvium, and tragedy is a persistent narrative. Padma is the femme fatale in Tagore's poems, the "rakkhasi preyasi," the witching lover, one who cannot be fully trusted, but one who charms and delights, and draws us to its bosom like moth to fire. Borne of the bewildering dynamic of the delta, with its confounding flux and flow, and the seasonal gift of flood and the occasional scourge of cyclones and tidal waves, the people of Bangladesh demonstrates a resilience that others are mystified about. When Katrina hit New Orleans, that far away city at the edge of America, newspaper reporting the events suddenly found a kinship between people of the Mississippi with their tribulations and people of the Bengal delta with their resilience.

The people of the delta – the Bengalis – have an ambivalent relationship with cities. Poets and writers of the land sing the sweet songs of villages and versify the vileness of the city. Even when they live and enjoy the city, they dream of the little village through the poet of rural ethos Jasimuddin's comforting image of salubrious vegetation and that untranslatable sense of being wrapped in "maya-momota." Apu, in Satyajit Ray's filmic *Pather Panchali* (based on Bibhutibhushan Bandyopadhyay's novel) reclines wistfully in his hovel in a grimy neighborhood in Kolkata, playing the flute like a Krishna dislocated from his arboreal and aquatic habitat.

Dhaka city, once intimate with the Padma but now at a deceptive distance, is a poster child of a city that is at odds with its larger landscape. The transformation of Dhaka and its regions, along with its physical and social landscape, have been relentless and brutal. By creating one landfill after another, emaciating rivers and canals, and decimating floodplains and agriculture, Dhaka makes for a perfect candidate for an urbanization without urbanism.

An urbanism for Dhaka needs to be conceptualized from the hydrological property of the delta. The theoretical challenge is this: Surrounded and infiltrated by a labyrinthine and delicate network of rivers and canals, tissues of wetlands and floodplains, and organic formations of mounds and settlements, Dhaka needs a new approach to city-thinking and city-form. The biggest challenge in the recomposition of Dhaka lies in engaging its landscape reality – the dynamic hydrology of the delta. With an ever-expanding city, the dynamic also involves an ecology of the edge.

The edge of Dhaka city is a precious landscape where new patterns of space need to be organized in response to a hydrologically fluctuating condition that includes flood-plains,

Catching the Padma's hilsa fish (from bdnews24).

wetlands, and agricultural fields. Innovative ideas, with new visions for housing typologies, transport network, and civic spaces, will have to negotiate between the hard city and vast fluid landscape of the delta. What is particular with Dhaka is how landscape reorganization is happening at a rapid pace to create (dry) lands for industries and then residences for the upper class in a global chain of complicities and linkages.

Official planning is unable to conceptualize this edge, to recognize that the edge is its own ecology and a critical one. Without that realization it is easy to participate in the destruction of the city's hydro-geographical landscape. Dhaka is not alone in this urban upheaval. Following Dhaka's lopsided planning, other towns and settlements are also pursuing a dry paradigm.

A re-appreciation of the edge is critical to anyone deliberating on the city in the delta: The geography of the edge is determined by the built-city marching up to meet the "non-urban," a magnificent but precious terrain of land-water mass made of wetlands, flood-plains, canals, and agricultural fields, the matrix of the delta. The edge is where the dry meets the wet, the "developed" meets the "primitive," and infrastructure meets the structure-less. This is also where the urbanite meets the farmer, the land grabber discovers his opportunity, and the uprooted often makes her habitation. Site/s of the biggest battle in the city, the terrain of the edge is determined by the presence and flux of water. No planning scheme will work for Dhaka, or any other town, if this simple equation is not recognized.

Nothing short of imagining a new landscape of city-form will offer a salvation for cities in the delta such as Dhaka. The edge conditions of Dhaka presents the possibility of re-negotiating the social and economic, as well conceptual, separation between city and its conventional anti-thesis, whether the village, flood- or agricultural plains. The edge is where new forms of space organization in response to a fluxed landscape will have to be reorganized, along with newer types of economic and social opportunities. In the meeting of an older form of the city with agricultural landform and hydrological landscape, a new conception of a city will have to be developed that integrates urbanism, agriculture, infrastructure and flooding. Only then a plan for Dhaka will be commensurate with the dynamic of the Padmatic landscape.

Flow

The hilsa, the national fish of Bangladesh, literally a bone of contention between the two Bengals, is a pure product of the Padma. At soccer games between East Bengal and Mohun Bagan clubs in Kolkata, fans of East Bengal is known to wield hilsas as a mascot, and a sign of its prowess. On the other side, fans of Mohun Bagan flash the *golda chingri* (shrimp) as their team 'fish.'

This soccer chauvinism around fish is a reflection of a cultural fission between the two Bengals, with people from the bhati referred to as "bangals" in Kolkata parlance, and people on the western side of this arbitrary divide as "ghotis." "Now for the uninitiated," writes Shomini Sen in a newspaper article on the contest between hilsa and *chingri*, "Bangals are those whose roots belong to the other side of Padma River – now known as Bangladesh. While Ghotis are those whose roots are in western side of the same river. There has been an underlying rivalry between Ghotis and Bangals since time immemorial that has spilled on to the football field as well. While Bangals are known to support East Bengal Club, Ghotis are ardent supporters of Mohun Bagan." Depending on which team wins, fans and supporters will organize food festivities around their fish mascot. Such is the passion around hilsa that when East Bengal wins against Mohun Bagan, the demand for hilsa will shoot up in markets in Kolkata with even the fish running out of stock early in the morning. The price of the fish will also shoot up.[10]

Being the emblem of the Padma, the hilsa is also critical in the economic and ecological life of Bangladesh. Generating about 1percent of Bangladesh's total GDP, nearly a million people – fishermen and traders – are occupied with the hilsa. As an anadromous species, the hilsa breeds upstream in the fresh water of the Padma with the larvae hatching from free-floating eggs. A large sized female hilsa can produce up to two million eggs. After growing for a short period in the river water, the fish swims down to the mouth of the river-sea, south of the confluence of Padma-Meghna, feeding on planktons and algae to return to the river as mature fish to breed again. The cycle is completed in a flow and counterflow in a river-sea ecology.

[10] Shomini Sen, "East Bengal vs Mohun Bagan: The War Between Hilsa and Prawns," News18, http://www.news18.com/news/buzz/east-bengal-vs-mohun-bagan-the-war-between-hilsa-and-prawns-1290199.html.

A depleting hilsa production reflects a combined economic and ecological impact. Apparently, low water discharge from the Ganges due to Farakka Barrage and consequent increase in siltation is a principal factor. Catching of the juvenile fish when they are migrating towards the sea thus disrupting the cycle, loss in spawning and feeding zones in the Padma, and pollution of its waters, and disruption in migratory routes due to increased human and mechanized movement are some other causes for the adverse effect on hilsa production. Fishing regulations are being employed to counter the adverse practices.

It appears that while waters, silt, ashes, and debris flow downstream, hilsas move both upstream and downstream. The hilsa tells the story of an entire human and physical landscape that runs from the depth and flow of the Padma River, to the banks where fishermen and boatmen have led lives from immemorial times, to the traders and middlemen and their transport network on water and road that comprise of the modern economy, and to the markets and shops of big cities like Dhaka and Kolkata where the fish completes its economic cycle, and finally to the dinner plates where a national, cultural, and culinary life is fulfilled. But recent facts indicate that phenomenon of the *hilsa* is neither stable nor guaranteed. Neither are the formation and flow of the Padma, and in turn an entire cultural and geological landscape.

Afifa Razzaque, Arfar Razi, and Sanjoy Roy, all at Bengal Institute for Architecture, Landscapes and Settlements, provided research assistance.

Amulya meets muddy Bengal, a still from Satyajit Ray's film *Samapti.*

Shoes abandoned, Amulya walks barefoot on a muddy road, a still from Satyajit Ray's film *Samapti.*

Thinking about Mud

Published in the *Daily Star*, January 2019.

Mud is the bane of the Bengali middleclass. Yet, mud is all over the place. Mud – that gooey, gluey, brown muck – lies waiting in the dry dust and with a little sprinkling of water rises up in rebellion, and grabs the pumps, heels and sandals of the middle-class and makes them skid off balance.

The whole ground cover of Bangladesh is a blanket of mud, unsuspecting when dry and unforgiving otherwise. The ground under water, in ponds, paddy fields, canals, and wetlands, is mostly mud. In other geographies, it is swamp, bog, peat or fen, that muck we have abandoned as we donned the culture of cities (they literally bog us down, or put us in a quagmire). Salman Rushdie, in *Midnight's Children*, gives an animated picture of a landscape of 'chirring insects and croaking frogs' (he was describing the Sundarbans), where ripened fruits fall on the ground to be devoured by insects, bugs, and other miniscule creatures that throng the moist ground.

Mud's elusive behavior makes it unreliable to the urbanites. When dry, sans water, mud can be as brittle as biscuits, and crumble like dust at the slightest pressure. As winds whip up over such a terrain, mud floats around as dust. Here is the opening shot of a film that captures the conundrum vividly:

Amulya returns to his home village from the city educated and transformed into a petit babu. His boat glides into the mushy riverbank, and as he steps off the boat, bag and baggage, he slips and falls into the mud full body. A young girl, Mrinmoyee, watching the sad spectacle of the town babu breaks out in laughter. We will soon realize that Amulya falls in love as well. With this mud metaphor, Satyajit Ray's tender and beautiful movie *Samapti* opens up a narrative on that slimy substance as well. Based on Rabindranath Tagore's short story, the narrative is a reverse transformation of a sahib, willing to reconcile with the world of wetness.

Mud and muck are at the crux of development strategies, in what we consider as "cultured," and what we deem to be otherwise. There is nothing glorious about mud. When it clings to us, on our white pants, we immediately rush to clean it off. Advertising agencies are constantly selling detergents that get rid of mud and soil off rambunctious children, as if the slightest strain will mark the fall of society. While some mothers chastise their children for getting mud on their clothes, some mothers and others cake in mud for a more beauteous body. While urban dwelling calls for the banishment of mud from its premise, people in villages still lovingly layer the floors and walls of their houses in a most aesthetical way.

Muddy stuff is at the cosmic beginning of things, yet there is no philosophy of mud. No one has thought deeply about the ubiquity of mud in our progression as humans. Aristotle spoke about a certain "foamy matter" in a primordial world condition that allowed for the generation of new life, but we are not quite sure it is mud.

Borne out of the mixture of water with dirt and soil, mud is transformative, shifting from brittleness to a paste. In the hands of men and women, mud becomes clay, and the substance of Bengal's cultural products for millennia. Baked, mud can become brick and terracotta, and remains the fundamental material source for building edifices, such as cities. When barge loads of brick arrive at the periphery of Dhaka, and when trucks grumble along urban streets loaded with bricks, they are basically bringing in "banglar kada,"caked and baked.

Yet wetness remains an anathema to the urbanite. Frankly speaking, I myself am at odds with mud and water. My personal urbanisation is so complete that if I were to find myself in the shoes of Amulya, literally, my fate would have been no different than his.

With his new jacket and pumps, the emblems of the "shohoorey" sahib, Amulya (Apurbo in Tagore's story) relies on dry weather and grounds to maintain his new urban aplomb. Muddiness is despised as a condition of primitivity, the original cosmic chaos from whence order and civilization may have evolved. That wet, muddy and slushy condition can only be the domain of "backward" peoples.

There are other muddy predicaments for Amulya, one who has forgotten his rural manners. While walking a village road one day, he encounters that abhorrent stuff once again, and once again fails to negotiate it, and in desperation and frustration, kicks his shoes off, and walks on barefeet. Only Ray could portray that sweet and sour moment of a young babu in the midst of mud. There are quite a few occasions where mud is a protagonist in "Samapti" which so far has eluded most critics of the film usually fixated on romance and relationships.

While the urban class abhors it, the farmer and the fisherman cherish mud. Call it what you will – silt, sediment, "poli" – mud is the stuff of life. Mud is the opposite of dry and rough. While we are desperate to be dry, the delta refuses that, and presents us with giga-gallons of water and tons of mud, silt and slush every year. Life in the delta depends on that.

For the dry ideologue, mud is nothing but treacherous. It lies awaiting in the dry dust before the monsoon comes, and makes the elegant babu or *begum* sahib walking along a village path lose all their elegance, not to mention encounter embarrassing bouts of slips and falls. Cars get stuck on rural roads, and only helping villagers, barefeet, can salvage such a situation. Stories of Pakistani soldiers in 1971 stuck in a muddy bout and unable to maneuver still provide us glee.

Unfortunately, in vying to build brick and concrete houses with tin roofs, the beautiful mud houses of Bangladesh are fast disappearing. Centuries of refinement for a cool condition that came with mud walls are being disowned for climatically discomforting situation as long as there is no reference to the uncouth mud.

The American architect Louis Kahn made great use of bricks in his architectural masterpiece in Dhaka. Bricks become elegant walls, straight and curved, and arches open up as beautiful cuts. Kahn knew the transformative property of mud. In an apocryphal story from the 1960s, Kahn was meeting some engineers in Dhaka. Soon he went out of the room and returned with a bucket of mud and pointing to the content, demanded: "Make me brick." And they did… and thus the magnificence of Sangsad Bhaban arising from the water as a new song of modernity.

In the last scenes of *Samapti,* while a storm rages on, Amulya goes out barefeet and drenched, looking for his wife Mrinmoyee who is hiding herself, rain soaked and shivering, under a tree. In what most critics note as a tender story of romantic reconciliation, Amulya also comes to term with the material foundation of his rural life-world: the intractable blend of mud and water.

knowledge.” The highest function of a poet, or for that matter an artist or architect, or anybody involved in the act of production, is the invention of monsters. “An architect must subject the reality presented by nature to a host of legitimate

another. There is always something else.

than Hercules's ambiguous bivium.

Destruction is a beginning. The enactment of destruction has a contractual relationship with pre-established norms and practices. As with Edward Said's meditation on beginnings, one would suggest that there is intention and method in

that can only be dismantled and dispatched off. The pavilion is dismantled, Quetglas argues, because the modern house is empty, and the presentation of emptiness is the object of the representation. Since the modern

imagination is pervaded by the ruins of the original. What exists is a simulacrum. Or, a sarcophagus.

ideological polarity, and at the same time an approach to a reconcilement.

the sacred fire is one of humanity's most ancient existential activities. It brought humanity, divinity, earth and sky into a precarious and precious conversation. The burning temple too is a “fourfold,” as the famous philosophical reflection

ON LOUIS KAHN

stands apart from the Maison Monol and Maison Jaoul precedence, but also finds a place in the Indian situation.

house (*gaha*) again." That is when the young man known as Gautama Siddhartha becomes the Buddha.

in different instances in the trajectory of this paper, India brought a metamorphosis in Le Corbusier too, urging him to reorganise the strategy of his 'patient search' and engage in new dialogues. The spirit of 'with a full hand I receive, and

The Origin of Architecture Is in a Slaughter

Unnamed and unidentified, the thing appeared suddenly over a cerulean sky. The perturbed gods ganged up and brought the thing down on earth. They laid him/her/it on the ground, each god holding a limb or an organ. The thing had

architectural-typological counterpart: the brise-soleil and the roof as an umbrella. From a tentative expression as in Villa Bezeau in Carthage, Tunisia (1928), the brise-soleil becomes a highly articulated "element poetique" in the

consideration was purely plastic.

The place of beginning as a site of slaughter and blood sacrifice and eventual construction, is central to many ancient practices. Marcel Detienne describes such a cosmogonic murder scene, an infanticide from an Orphic account of the

Louis Kahn, sketch of Buriganga River, 1963.

The National Capital Complex: Louis I. Kahn's Architecture in Dhaka

Text in *Louis Kahn: National Capital in Bangladesh*, edited and photographed by Yukio Futagawa, GA 73 (Tokyo, 1994). An earlier version of the essay was presented at a paper at the conference "Shere-E-Bangla Nagar: Dhaka Capital Complex," at the Massachusetts Institute of Technology, Cambridge, 1991.

Assembly Building from South Plaza steps. Photo: Ashraf.

1

Louis Kahn's Capital Complex at Dhaka is an epic work. Next to Chandigarh it is the most important landmark to influence the architectural destiny of the region. In the Assembly Building of the Complex, major architectural streams, Roman, Renaissance, Mughal and Modern, seem to have converged – not in a synthesis but as a palimpsest – in one single architectural event. Well beyond its immediate architectonics, but primarily through it, and long before its programmatic purpose, the Assembly Building took on a haunting presence in the natural and cultural landscape of Bangladesh. Recalling both celestial and terrestrial energies in its architectural organism, and tapping the depth of Bengali dreams and mythologies, the Assembly emerged from land and water as a kind of cosmic phenomenon. Like an epic, which is no longer of its time, but of a cosmic time, and time and time again, it spoke of essential things, things around which life coheres and seeks meaning.

Eluding categorical statements of economic and cultural impropriety often made by some critics, the Complex continues to provoke an inspirational dialogue on the fundamental nature of architecture and human institutions. The significance of the Capital Complex has become inextricably linked with the national and political struggle of the Bengalis. Long before its functional occupation as a political "citadel," the Assembly Building became inscribed in the collective mind, paradoxically through its 'ruinous' image, as an emblem of things to come. This is often not comprehensible outside the Bengali domain, and whether Kahn participated in this is open to question, yet it is possible that Kahn's contemplations on architecture, especially the idea of Assembly as an Institution arising out of the fundamental desires of man, and consequently meeting as the origin of the city, found in Dhaka a coincidental meaningfulness. Between Kahn's ensemble and the Bengali collectivity, there arose an unforeseeable empathy.

Known as Sherebanglanagar, the Capital Complex is situated on an 1,000-acre site, originally a farmland to the northern outskirts of the old city of Dhaka but now engulfed by a burgeoning metropolis. The Complex is constituted by the Assembly group in the south, the unbuilt Secretariat in the north, the hospital

All drawings, unless otherwise mentioned, are courtesy of the Louis I. Kahn Collection, the Architectural Archives, University of Pennsylvania.

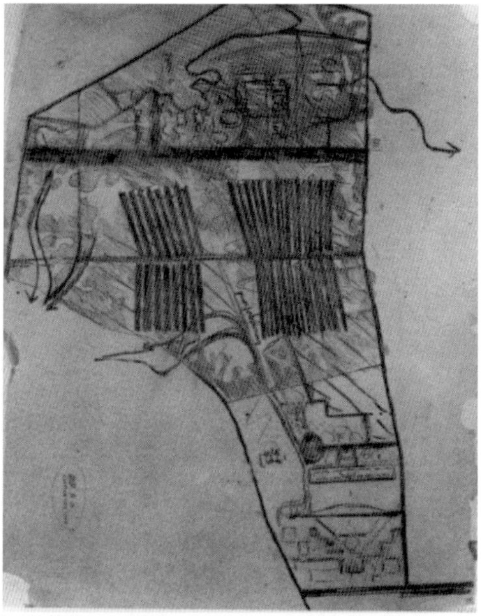

Louis Kahn, sketch for northern area of the Capital Complex.

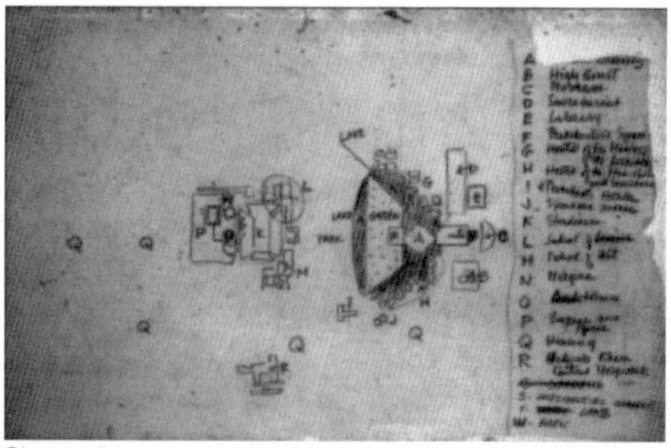

Site and program study, 1963.

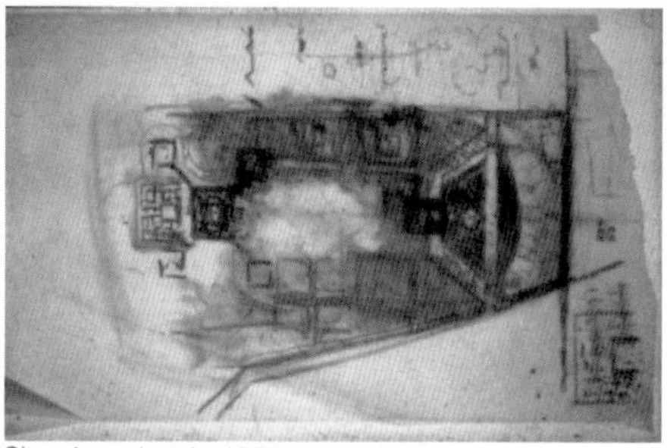

Site plan, sketch, 1963.

Site model, 1973.

Site model, May, 1963.

group in the northwest, and government housing around the Secretariat site – it is the Assembly group that forms the focus of the Complex. Set in the midst of brick buildings, public spaces, lakes, gardens and park, the Assembly building crowns the group by the gravity of its presence and its sculptural architectonics; it faces a public Plaza to the south and the more formal Presidential Square to the north. This southern group, earlier called the Citadel of Assembly, was set up at the end of a north-south axis, the other end formed by the Citadel of Institutions that included programs for "well-being,"[1] like a stadium, a museum, recreational buildings and markets. After the independence of Bangladesh, the northern Citadel was replaced in the master plan by the Secretariat, conceived as a 2,100-feet-long brick building as the center of bureaucracy of a national government.

[1] Kahn would consider three things as the "greatest desires of man: the desire to learn, the desire to meet and desire for well-being." They all serve the will to be to express and that is the reason for living. Quoted by Giurgola and Mehia, *Louis I Kahn* (Boulder: Westiew Press, 1975). p. 34.

Kahn received the commission for the project in 1962, and continued design until his death in 1974. Construction continued slowly, often with interruptions, but was substantially finished, at least as far as the Assembly group goes, by 1982. The project was initiated in a way by the improbable status of Pakistan, a nation divided both physically and culturally into two regions. The decision to make a 'second' capital at Dhaka in the eastern region (East Pakistan), and to install the National Parliament there, was taken in 1959 not out of a reverence for democratic institutions but as a bid to placate the growing discontent among the Bengalis against the hegemonic motives of western Pakistan. This would eventually lead in 1971 to the bloody onslaught on Bengalis by western Pakistan and the subsequent independence of the eastern province as Bangladesh.

By the early 1960s Kahn's complex architectural inheritances seem well-known. Genealogical analyses point to the Beaux Arts foundation, the Roman and Egyptian inspiration, a Piranesian fascination and the French connection, but often overlooking other major and minor tracts, for example, an affinity for Baroque plasticity, the architecture of Persia and Central Asia, and forms of castles and fortifications. At Dhaka, Kahn can no longer be contained within a single stream, and neither can his architectural form be explained only by historical linkages. If he is Roman, he is Mughal too. If he is modern, he is also primordial, and if he is a twentieth century architect, he is also an esoteric alchemist. Kahn's work at that stage bypasses straightforward criticisms of the tyranny of its geometry and the misconnections with the here and now. Vincent Scully notes that "his later buildings have normally remained eloquent expressions of space and structure that invoke traditional stabilities and are unconcerned with any symbolism of the immediate present or with the technology or the ambiguities of contemporary life."[2] Kahn proposed his own ambiguous dimension, the significance of which lies in the difficult co-existence of past and present, synchronous and diachronic, measurable and immeasurable, and by which, as Mario Bottero argues, Kahn managed to open a breach in the closed circuits of Wright's organicism and European rationalism.[3] By the early 60s, Kahn was poised for his great alchemical performance; he was ready to stir the depths of silence.

During the same time, Kahn found little success in the United States with the kind of architecture he was developing. The response that was not forthcoming in the United States came from Bangladesh and India. In Dhaka and Ahmedabad, "he found ambitions that were large enough and support that was deep enough to build on a scale nearly equal to his vision, despite the limited resources of his clients."[4] Kahn's commitment to the projects in the subcontinent in turn was extraordinary; Dhaka was particularly special to him. What Charles Correa had to say about Le Corbusier in India is equally true for Kahn: Bangladesh was lucky to receive Kahn as Kahn was to receive Bangladesh.

2

The natural and cultural landscape of Bengal complements the understanding of the Capital Complex. There is a degree of

[2] Vincent Scully, *Modern Architecture* (New York: Braziller, 1961).

[3] Mario Bottero, "Organic and Rational Morphology in Louis Kahn," in *Zodiac* 17, 1967.

[4] David B. Brownlee and David G. De Long, *Louis I Kahn: In the Realm of Architecture* (New York: Rizzoli, 1991), p. 103.

Assembly Building, sketch.

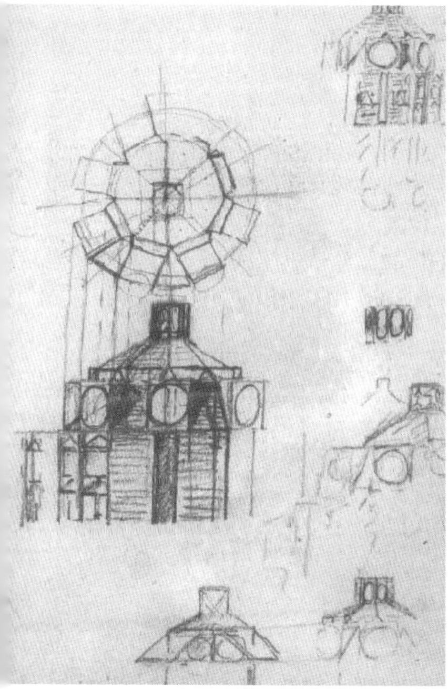

13
11
14
15
17
8
16
1
5
6
20

From Piranesi's Il Campo Marzio dell' Antica Roma, 1762.

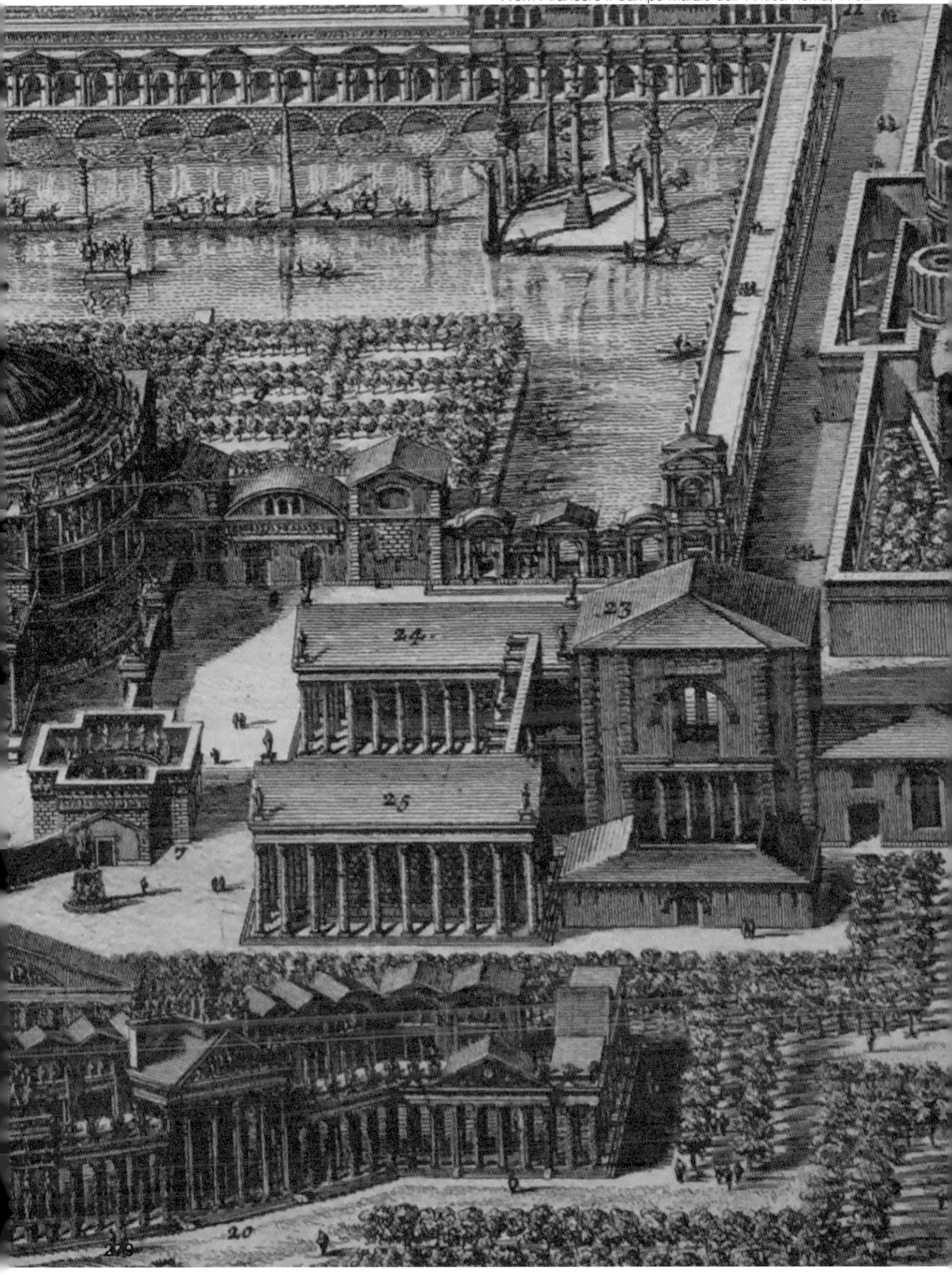

connection, often surreptitious and subliminal, between Kahn and Bangladesh (Bengal in the larger cultural sense) which is very much unexplored.

Bengal is located, geo-culturally, at the edge of two worlds. On the one hand, it has always been considered within the orbit of the larger Indian culture extending as far back as Sanskritic India. The orbit has also moved towards Persia, Arabia, and ultimately Europe, creating a western connection seen in most areas of explicit culture: language, liturgies, institutions, and the laws. On the other hand, at a level that can be termed variously as archaic, primordial or foundational, there is an irreducible stratum that delinks Bengal from its western appendage and thrust it towards the east, towards the matrix of "rice culture."

This matrix suggests a specific way of being-in-the-world, to be precise, being-in-the-delta. The Bengal delta is a pure chemistry of land and water, an excruciatingly flat terrain formed by one of the most dynamic river systems of the world. The Ganges and the Brahmaputra while pouring into the plains weave the incredible land-water mesh that has formed not only the life-providing richness of the soil (and its terror) but also the spiritual milieu to which one is still bound. In this milieu, the cultivation of rice is an existential occupation: the production of rice becomes the production of a worldview. This implies a special relationship with the cycles of nature, with the rivers, the rain, the overwhelming presence of water, with silt, with day, and the dense vegetation. All life-orienting rituals, folk stories and devotional creations echo this experience.

The entrenchment of Kahn's ideas in the modern Bengali domain is not something strange: it was anticipated in the intellectual climate created by the nineteenth-century movement called the "Bengal Renaissance." Rabindranath Tagore, as the most important figure of the movement, articulated the dilemmas of the face-to-faceness of modernity and tradition, of East and West, of India and Europe, and of the local and the universal. Kahn, being a member of the Tagore Society in Philadelphia in the 1950s, probably knew Tagore's work. There is, in any case, a great correspondence between Kahn and Tagore, particularly in the idea of what constitutes the human and where the creative personality of humanity lies. Tagore was to say that "men must find and feel and represent in all their creative works Man the eternal, the creator. Their civilization is a continual discovery of the transcendental humanity." For Tagore, art is humanity: it is that biological surplus, emanating as "luminous imagination," that characterizes the humanity of man, as for Kahn "art is man's only real language since it strives to communicate in a way that reveals the 'human,' and that the 'will to be' in a man is really the 'will to be to express.' "

If the task of rational and philosophic thinking is to dispel mystery, the purpose of mythic thinking is to deepen its depth. As poetic personalities, both Tagore and Kahn tapped the mythological consciousness to arrive at the gate of mystery, at the nexus of Silence and Light, of the measurable and the immeasurable. The

Study model of Assembly Building and South Plaza.

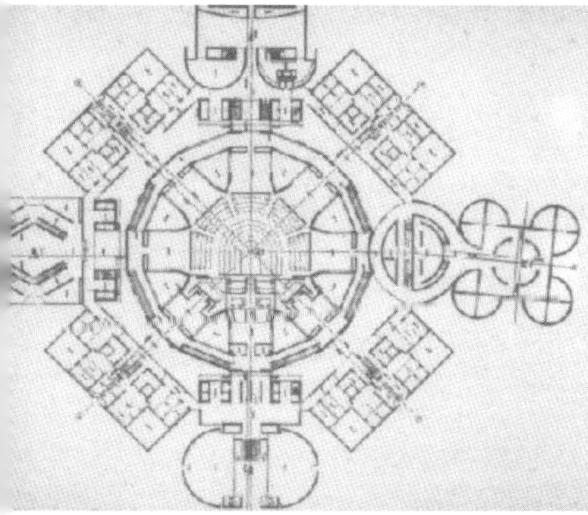

Plan, Assembly Building, final version.

Construction of South Plaza.

mythic also crosses path with the poetic; for, the poetic image, as Gaston Bachelard writes, "stirs the depth before it scratches the surface." From the standpoint of Indian aesthetics, this is experientially a fleeting discontinuity in the existence in profane time whereby an irruption of the extraordinary (alaukika) occurs. Kahn would claim this as wonder "which brought about the desire to learn, the profundity of which lay at the threshold of where the unmeasurable and the measurable met," for "it is from the sense of the incredible that all man's desire to make and establish comes."[5]

In the intensely spiritual atmosphere of Bengal, a spirituality that cannot be approached by official religions alone, the creative experience of the extraordinary has been homologized with the ecstasy of quasi-sacred experiences leading to what has been called "the deification of aesthetics." This phenomenon persists in most twentieth century creative productions, including Tagore's, maintaining for art a highly spiritual significance.

3

The beginning of the project has a biblical undertone. In narrating his struggle with the design, Kahn mentions that on the third day of dwelling on it, he fell out of bed and conceived the idea that assembly is of a transcendent nature. More intriguing ontologically is the question he had posed earlier: "How the buildings are to take their place on the land?" This two-fold theme – the transcendent nature of assembly and the way buildings are to take their place on the land – becomes Kahn's primary reflection on the project and the basis for the architecture. The first part stems from Kahn's contemplation on the nature of architecture, especially the understanding of architectural form as an aspect of immeasurable "Form" considered autonomous from the vagaries of circumstances. This sense of Form may seem to correspond with Platonic Idea, on the one hand, and archetype in a Jungian sense, on the other hand. If Form involves Kahn's quest for the significance of architecture beyond local specificities, the second part, a much less talked about aspect, is more about establishing, abstracting and revealing the particularities of a specific locale, and intensifying the experience of its landscape and natural milieu. The scope of the artifact to reveal the landscape is the breach in the closed circuits of Wrightian harmony and Rationalist contrast between building and nature that begins with Salk Institute and the Atlantic, and is continued up to Kimbell and Texas, but finds its most cogent expression at Sherebanglanagar.

During his very first trip to Bangladesh in 1963, Kahn recognized certain qualities of the land and of building. He made few sketches on a river cruise that record his impressions of the overwhelming presence of water in the land; he was to say that in Bengal one does "architecture of the land." Kahn also conceptualized building in the delta as a "dig and build" process that results in an earth mound on which the building is placed; the excavated pit becomes a pond. Besides observing "the religious way of life of the people," Kahn noted, "The two elements of nature most pervasive in the landscape of East

[5] In a letter for Iranian architect Nader Ardalan, dated November 1971, Box LIK 10, Louis I. Kahn Collection, University of Pennsylvania and Pennsylvania Historical and Museum Commission.

Pakistan are water and vegetation. They almost assert their presence. The examples of intelligent cooperation with these pervasive elements of water and vegetation in some of the best examples of Mughal Garden Architecture has been a great inspiration to me."[6]

The overall plan was conceived as two aggregations set on a north-south axis separated by gardens and lakes and ordered by a diagonally of architectural figures and roadways, within which varieties of changes and alternatives were studied. The configuration of the southern group – the Citadel of Assembly – took a centralized volume flanked by smaller attending forms, and the northern group a vast courtyard-like space around which smaller groups of buildings were arranged (a plan that shaped the Ahmedabad project). On the flat plain, the Citadel of Assembly assumed a mountainous topography with the Assembly Building as the highest peak consonant with Kahn's conceit of an originating marker and an axis mundi. Kahn was to note: "The simple structures of shelter seem like the markers only of a dominating desire to establish a claim out of the vastness of the land, a place from where to dream of anticipated enterprise full of the promise of a kingdom where the house or the castle yet is not in the mind."[7]

Although Kahn began with the idea that "the house of legislation is a religious place," his early sketches show a triangular relationship of the assembly, the mosque and the supreme court: a diagonally placed cubic assembly aligned with the supreme court with a free-standing pyramid-shaped mosque between the two. But, primarily it was the juxtaposition of the assembly hall and the mosque that gave meaning to the Assembly: it became the locus for the articulation of the sacred and the religious.

Their relationship – from separate equipoised status to the subordination of the mosque as a skewed prayer hall to the assembly whose iconography oscillates between fortification towers and the quatrefoil form of Sultanate mosques – is more than architectonics. Metaphorically, it is a dialectic between the sacred and the religious, between the mythic and the historical. This has acute relevance in Bangladeshi social dynamics as attested by the continuing tension between autochthonous spirituality and Islamic religiosity.

From the very beginning, the form-diagram of the assembly proceeded with the theme of centrality and concentricity. The centralized plan started predictably – within a taut orthogonal geometry, the main assembly chamber occupied the center ringed by smaller subservient spaces of various offices, meeting rooms, cafeterias, etc. In a progressive development as the plan also took a mandalic formation, elements of the outer ring gradually became detached from the main volume and gained figural autonomy; that is, the taut geometry was transformed into a Baroque play of concavity and convexity. The central volume was also increasingly articulated within the rings of an ambulatory apace and "hollow columns;" it irrupted into the skyline peering through gigantic perforations towards the city

[6] In a note regarding presentation, Kahn wrote: "All along our effort has been to evolve the new architectonic forms for a new civic order... to suit the personality of a great Islamic culture with glorious traditions of Mughal architecture." Box LIK 120, Louis I. Kahn Collection.

[7] In a letter to Clovis Heimsath, February 16, 1968. Box LIK 10, Louis I. Kahn Collection.

Interior view of ambulatory. Photo: N. R. Khan.

Assembly Building across the triangular lake. Photo: Ashraf.

Aerial view of Assembly Complex. Photo: Anwar Hossain, 1983.

and the horizon. This simultaneous attraction and repulsion between the center and the periphery, and the autonomy and integration of the figures became the ordering principle. In its planimetric and sectional iconography, as has been claimed, an immediate genetic connection can be made with centralized Mughal monuments, as can be made with various Renaissance structures,[8] and a number of Bengali temples. Imperial and Piranesian Rome served as the precedent for the connective system between various forms, and for the inspiration of the forms themselves, particularly the Baths of Caracalla, as Kahn himself points to, and the Domus Aurea, among others.

Kahn's own pre-history anticipates to a considerable degree the architecture of the Complex; it appears as if all of Kahn's earlier works were directed towards a conclusive moment at Dhaka. For example, the Unitarian Church at Rochester (the early version) strongly suggests the form-diagram of the Assembly. The double wall in the outer ring of the Assembly and in the brick buildings was explored earlier in two ways, as a climatic screen for the U.S. Consulate in Luanda, and as a second enveloping geometry at the Salk meeting house. The hollow "columns" of light – as a triangular shaft girdling the assembly chamber and the ambulatory, and as corner turrets of the Prayer Hall – has a more complicated history; it began as Kahn's reflection on Greek columns and as the expression of "servant" space at the Bath House in Trenton, but ultimately connected to Kahn's life-long preoccupation to integrate light, space and structure.

Construction of the Prayer Hall.
Photo: Louis I. Kahn Collection.

There are however moments specific to Dhaka. The horizontal and vertical band of marble, stratifying the wall of the Assembly and monumentalizing the seam between two poured concrete walls, is a human inscription; it both shows and exploits the scope of local construction techniques. The fabrication also resembles the white marble inlays of Mughal monuments, and to some, the lithified form of bamboo-framed walls.[9] Besides the dimensional control of distance and access, the architecture of water confirms a thematic use in many Bengali honorific buildings, from mosques and temples to feudal palaces.

Brick construction is an ancient tradition of the region, the terra-cotta color brick building amidst a deep-green foliage and neighbored by a dank tank of water provides a perennial image of the Bengali landscape. Kahn tapped this to new heights. He remarked: "I changed the buildings from their original design in concrete to that of brick, honoring thereby the advice that brick would prove to be more economical. Though I first resisted this change, I have now discovered, in the development of the design, some beautiful shapes that are true to the order of brickwork."[10] All structures other than the assembly building were constructed in brick. The order of this brick architecture – the geometry of the form, the architectonics of shadows, the earth-hugging ambiance, but particularly the "invention" of the arch with the concrete tie – introduced a completely new vocabulary in the repertoire of modern architecture.

[8] The Tomb of Humayun in Delhi and the Taj Mahal in Agra are commonly cited as examples of Mughal centralized forms having a correspondence with the form-diagram of the Assembly. Other Indian architectural elements are noted as sources of inspiration for Kahn or as parralels to various architectural features in Dhaka, see William Curtis, "Authenticity, Abstraction and the Ancient Sense: Le Corbusier's and Louis Kahn's Ideas of Parliament," in *Perspecta* 20 (1983), and Florindo Fusaro, *Il Parlamento a la nuova a Dacca di Louis I. Kahn* (Rome: Officina Edizione, 1985). Fusaro also documents affinity with the architecture of the Renaissance period, especially regarding the centralized form and shape of the roof over the Assembly Hall.

[9] William Curtis, "Cosmos and State: The National Assembly in Dhaka," in *A&V*, 44. November-December 1993.

[10] In a letter to Roy Vollmer dated May 24, 1965, Louis I. Kahn Collection.

4

If Kahn saw the house of legislation as a "religious" place, he considered centrality as the architecture of sacredness. Centrality however is a tricky condition; it verges, on the one hand, too closely to being the instrument of tyranny, and on the other hand, to being the vehicle of sacrality. Sacrality too is an uneasy theme. Is there a sacrality in secular existence? Is them an "other divinity" in modem life? Kahn's persistent evocation of another sacredness – the sense of the sacred outside liturgies but within modern existence, the sacred as something wondrous, extraordinary, *alaukika* in a Tagorean sense – is suspect from two opposed ranks: the secular intellectuals, who might consider this reactionary and regressive, and the religious guardians, who might perceive this as a threat to their entrenched position.

The Assembly Building attains its specific character within the genre of centrality because of the ambulatory space, a seven-story high interior "street" between the assembly chamber and the outer offices. Here, light – dark light, gray light and passing sun-light – materializing from mysterious sources fill the space, while stairs, ramps, walkways and various openings wrap around it as in a Carceri drawing. Programmatically it is only a circulation ring, and compositionally a mediator between the inner form and various geometric figures in the outer ring, but experientially it is a device. As a primary orienting (often disorienting) envelop before entering the inner sanctum, recalling the experience of *pradakshina* (circumambulation), it is a sacralizing device as ancient as the Buddhist stupa.

Construction of Hospitality Hall in the Ministers' Hostel.

But, what makes this architectural organism take its place on the land? It is not the planimetric geometry alone, the purely architectural correspondence with Buddhist or Mughal complexes, or with vernacular idioms, but the situational manner of the assembly: how it irrupts in and gathers all the paradigmatic elements of the Bengali landscape – the horizontal terrain, the terra-cotta ground, the deep-green foliage. the dark dank water, the brilliant sky – into one indivisible experience. This may be considered through two intertwined issues: the manner of grouping and the idea of the city.

Kahn's conception of grouping in the Citadel of Assembly may be linked to a number of sources, particularly to the hierarchic and diagonal order of Beaux-Arts planning, but it is possible that it was inspired by Piranesi's speculative drawing which shows the Pantheon as a fulcrum within a setting of supportive buildings, public spaces, gardens and lake. But, the Bengal delta also may help in understanding further the formation of the Citadel. It can be seen firstly in the appearance of the huddling, jostling masses of the assembly, with its raw, stratified surface appearing out of the earth/water like some crystallizing primeval thing, evoking further an Indian aquatic symbology of the beginning of things from a primordial fluid. Kahn's persistence in three-dimensional representation of architectural organisms coagulating out of the earthly plain says something about his conceptualizing methods on the origin and formation of architectural material. Mario Bottero sees this as a mysterious phenomenon in form selection in that instead of sort of descending from Platonic Forms "form rises out of a submerged world."[11]

Besides the aggregation evoking the assemblage on mounds, the delta *appears* in a second way. In the envelope of the assembly and the brick buildings, when Kahn makes those gigantic perforations, when he makes those cavernous spaces of shadow, he is surreptitiously "landscaping" the buildings. This is landscaping not in a botanical but in a phenomenal sense in how nature – the sun, the wind, the air – invades a man-made artifact, erodes its envelope, makes it porous, and finally repossesses it. Only then the sun (and the wind) realizes how wonderful it is.

Hostels at the National Assembly. Photo: Ashraf.

Of course, the invasion of the atmospheric aura in architecture is possible because Kahn does not use glass. When he does use it, as in most American projects, or in modifications at Dhaka, the box is immediately formed, creating a sharp disjunction with the elements. "Masonry masses and voids. That's what Kahn wants,"[12] that is, "an architecture of open forms, integrated with the *plein* air of the surrounding landscape."[13] In the elementalism of dwelling in nature in India and Bangladesh, Kahn's architecture finds a home.

The issue of grouping also leads to the problematic and paradigmatic case of Kahn's architecture of the city. It may seem problematic to construct a homogeneous self-referential urban order when the city is characterized by fragmentation and disjunctiveness at all levels, a result no doubt of the collapse of the pre-colonial singular world-view and the legitimate rise of various ideologies and group-interests. How much then does a centralized and self-absorbed urban institution relate to a dispersive nature of current urbanization? Is circumstantiality an adulteration of Order, or is there an order to circumstantialities itself? Moreover, the archaic symbolism of the center is anathema to progressive and pluralist ideologues who see in it only the representation of power and tyranny. Critics like Manfredo Tafuri consider this outmoded in the European discourse; it can now only be exported to "underdeveloped" nations.

Kahn arrives at the city through other routes, not through the thicket of the market economy nor through the melange of the ad hoc habitat. His thinking involves the distillation of institution-types to find the irreducible essentials of a city, a sort of backstepping to the "original" moment of assembly that is both the essence and source of the city; and, the disposition of institutions not only spatially and sociologically but as paradigmatic elements of the landscape. While Kahn's evocation of an "original" city is self-serving, it may be entertained by two conditions: in a western context, as Kenneth Frampton mentions, due to "the fatal degeneracy of all civilized institutions in the consumerist city," and in a non-Western context, due to the amnesia in which vital culture has lapsed into.

The image of the city at Sherebanglanagar may not coincide morphologically with the currently existing city nor with "the city of the figure-ground" derived from the urbanism of north India. If

[11] Mario Bottero, ibid.

[12] Scully, ibid.

[13] Bottero, ibid.

[14] Fumihiko Maki used the term to describe and distinguish the 'urbanism' of Japan and South-East Asia, at a seminar in New York in 1990.

View of Suhrawardi Hospital. Photo: Ashraf.

there is a correspondence it is with the city of the "rice culture" matrix, or what may be called "the city of figure-nature,"[14] in which the traditional city-country opposition is not abrasive, and where the idea of urbanism is not in building densification alone but in the special disposition of buildings, as pavilion types, their relation with each other and with other urban materials: ponds, waterways, trees, gardens and orchards. This was reflected in Dhaka, specially Mughal Dhaka, a city of gardens and canals with pavilion-like dwellings, before it was ransacked by 'development' planning.

At Sherebanglanagar, there is something abstract, and yet intensely immediate, about the "iconography of the landscape," in the configuration of the coagulating mass in the flat, aquatic landscape, as in the assemblage of dwellings on mounds signifying the family. It is here when the "buildings make the landscape speak" that one can think about a sense of place. At the Capital Complex, one can sense the silhouette of the phantasmal Bengali city, the utopic and at the same time primordial. Dhaka and Sherebanglanagar, through a mythic veil, glimpse each other.

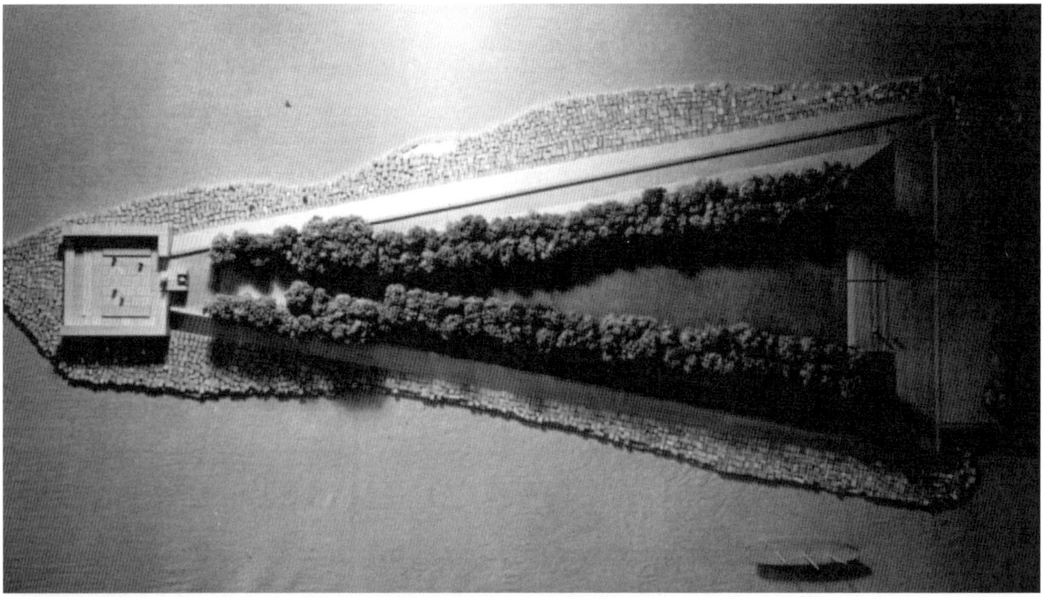

Model photograph, Franklin Delano Roosevelt Memorial, New York, 1973-74 (unbuilt). Louis I. Kahn Collection, Architectural Archives University of Pennsylvania. Photo: George Pohl.

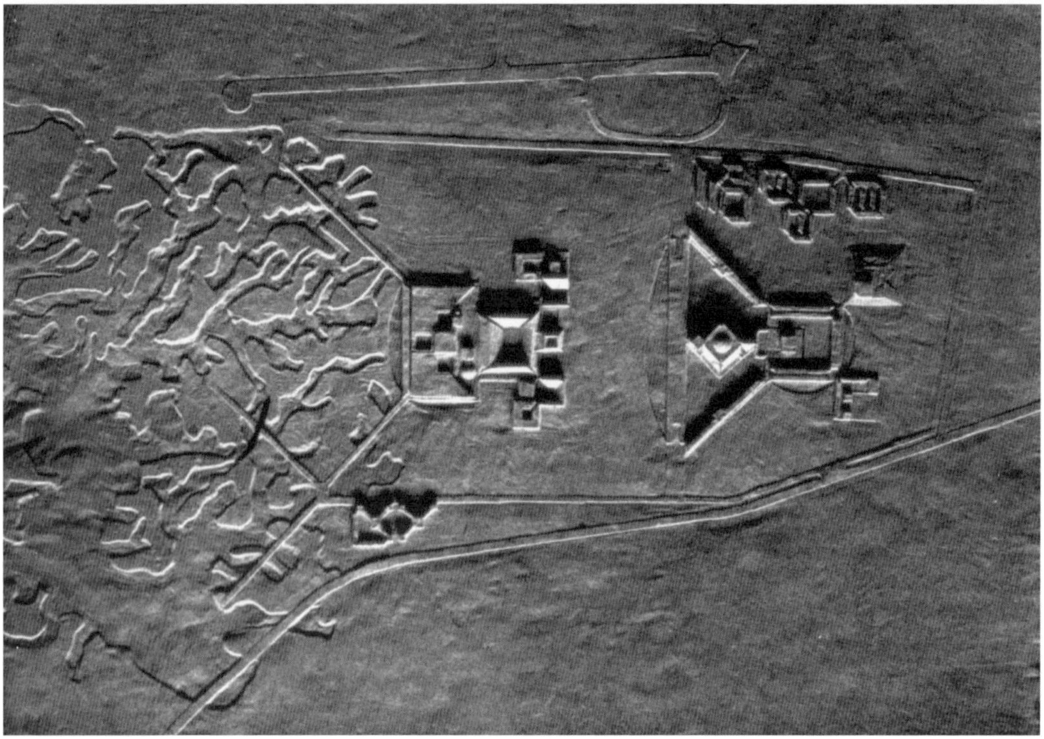

Site model, National Parliament Complex, Dhaka, Bangladesh (May, 1963). Louis I. Kahn Collection.

Taking Place: Landscape in the Architecture of Louis Kahn

Published in the *Journal of Architectural Education,* November, 2007.

Vincent Scully describes when he and Louis Kahn were visiting Moscow in 1965, and were walking around the Kremlin, he pointed out towards some of the famous towers in the area and said, "Look, Lou, how they point to the sky." To which Kahn replied immediately, "Look how they bring the weight down."[1] In Peter Kirby's documentary on Kahn,[2] Richard Saul Wurman talks about the AFL-CIO building in Philadelphia, and narrates how Kahn was overly fussy about the "look" of the foundation and was giving inordinate time to it by actually designing and making models of it. When some of the office people inquired about it, Kahn admitted a concern for how the building will look as a ruin.[3]

I think these and other visual and literary narratives, but more than stories, the buildings themselves, and what can be extracted from what Kahn said aligns him with a sensibility that cannot be easily located within what we commonly call modernism, and provides a more complex reading of his work than the predictable Platonist, mystical, genealogical or structural interpretations. While these interpretations are immensely relevant in the context of Kahn's work, I want to say that Kahn was also profoundly interested in the relationship of building and land in a very particular way. Provisionally, I would like to say that there is a recurrent and heightened notion of the intertwining of form and, for a lack of right word, landscape or environment in his thinking. This is what I would like to unravel in this essay.

When it comes to locating landscape in the context of the work and ideas of Kahn, there is however expected ambiguity. Although Kahn himself provides openings towards the realm of landscape, it is a-systematic and sporadic, and is superceded by a more persistent meditation on "Form." In any case, different notions of landscape could be posited from Kahn's work, from the conventional to more conceptual, from what Kahn himself remarks upon to what I extrapolate from my own orientation. My intention is two-fold that intersects: one, to recover from this diversity a distinct idea of landscape in Kahn that is generally bypassed in the scholarship on his work, and, two, use that understanding to propose a notion of landscape that I argue is inherent in architecture, that building in its essence is a landscape event. The second point may be seen as expanding the idea of landscape and at the same time revising an

1 Richard Saul Wurman, ed., What Will Be Has Always Been: The Words of Louis I. Khan (New York: Access Press and Rizzoli, 1986).

2 *Louis I. Kahn: An Offering to Architecture*, film directed by Peter Kirby (Media Art Services, 1992).

3 The ironic fact is that the AFL building was domolished, and one wonders about the concern.

Model photo, ca 1968, Palazzo dei Congressi, Venice, Italy, 1968-1974 (unbuilt), Louis I. Kahn Collection.

understanding of architecture. My thesis of seeing architecture as landscape gains particular insight from Kahn's work but refracted by the ideas of Maurice Merleau-Ponty, especially in seeking an analogy of architecture to the notion of "lived-body." This is the intersection that I alluded to above.

To begin with, Kahn did talk on occasions about a more conventional sense of landscape in the form of gardens. Landscaping does refer to a botanical or agricultural understanding that involves the particularity of places, the nurturing of plants, the precision of soil, moisture, etc. Kahn expresses admiration for the work of Gertrude Jekyll – a few places where Kahn mentions other designers – especially the work of Jekyll in intimate relationship with the architecture of Edwin Lutyens, bringing up the matter of building and site as garden.[4] On another occasion, Kahn sees an analogy between gardening and building, for the architect can learn from a farmer in not making the landscape pretty but "to preserve his crops by the logic of planting."[5] The attitude is not too dissimilar from what his friend the sculptor Wharton Esherick had to advise designers: Think like a farmer.

In Kahn's own work, a botanical or vegetal landscaping becomes an important element in the overall architectural plan in a number of projects, such as the grove at Salk, the [japonais] trees at the entrance of Kimbell, the linear cluster of trees for the Roosevelt memorial, the carpet of grass for the Dhaka Assembly, and the circle of trees on the unbuilt esplanade and meeting center in Dhaka. While commenting on Kimbell, Aldo Rossi notes an interpretation of the classical realm and mentions cryptically that there is something Grecian about the grove and entering the museum,[6] which, in my view, provides a scenario different from the usual Roman genealogy of Kahn's work. Kahn also came to know Mughal gardens directly from his sub-continental sojourns, and the expansive design of water in Dhaka and Ahmedabad (the latter was not carried out) is arguably derived from examples of lakes in North India.

While it may be useful to make a compendium of such landscape strategies in Kahn's work, it is not something that I plan to do here. When I say landscape in the context of architecture, I do

[4] Kahn considered Gertrude Jekyll an example of a sensitive person in regard to "human agreement." Kahn would note that Lutyens was a great architect, but he had his limit. "He responded so beautifully to the landscape architect Gertrude Jekyll that his porches that looked into her gardens had the feeling of satisfying a greater order sympathizing with the garden itself.... Gertrude Jekyll was also responsive to what would sympathize with his architecture." From a lecture at the University of Virginia, Charlottesville, 1972, in Wurman,*What Will Be Has Always Been: The Words of Louis I. Khan*, p. 137.

[5] At the First International Congress of Architects, Isfahan, Iran, in Wurman, *What Will Be Has Always Been: The Words of Louis I. Khan*, p. 99.

[6] *Louis Kahn: Silence and Light*, film directed by Michael Blackwood (Michael Blackwood Productions, 1995).

mean it beyond the botanical aspect, not ignoring it but rather subsuming it in a broader and perhaps more fundamental understanding of architecture, especially architecture in the sense of built work. In brief, a built work takes place, and it takes place in certain conditions and actualities. It is this taking place of architecture – being intertwined with the world above all – that I consider as the dimension of landscape.[7] I would like to think that the matter of the taking place of architecture opens up a rather unexamined prospect in Kahn's thinking, that I discuss through two conditions: the grounding of architecture, and the weathering or ambient dimension of architecture.

Taking Place

What did Kahn think about nature, something that ought to come up in any discussion on landscape and building? Certain notions of nature are certainly subsumed in his various oracular proclamations around Order, Silence and Light, and the processes of the universe, and yet at the same time, there is a recurrent idea with Kahn that juxtaposes nature and architecture.

First, Kahn proposes a commonality between human and nature. "nature records in everything it makes how it was made. This record is also in man and it is this within us that urges us to seek its story involving the laws of universe, the source of all material and means, and the psyche, the source of all expression, Art."[8] Second, there is a difference between the human-made and the natural environment, and that there is a proactive quality about humanity that was already obvious in the first description, that is, both humanity and nature are part of an eternal process but it is only humanity who is able to "express" that. Kahn, as we know, has spoken extensively on the desire for this expression. Kahn also notes: "One thing that occurred to me, that what nature can make, man cannot make. And what man can make, nature cannot make without a man." Humanity becomes an instrument in a crucial transformation. Kahn also realizes that he can improve "the constructiveness of what is being built by man" by drawing, for example, that he could not "the constructiveness of that built by nature."[9] It is not the idea of an immutable, unchanging nature that Kahn is subscribing to but to the primacy of constructiveness made possible by architecture.

The most important consideration for Kahn in juxtaposing nature and architecture then is that architecture completes what nature cannot make. He uses a parable to highlight this: "The desire to be to express comes to the mountain and tells the mountain about its inspiration to build a temple: Look, I won't hurt you, I am going to take you and treat you beautifully. I am going to cut your edges, I am going to put stone upon stone and I am going to build an enclosure, a place where I can try to express the greatness of eternity of which I am a part."[10]

In this quasi-theory of nature, Kahn sees nature as the essential bedrock of all things, or even a necessary "collaborator" in the expression of humanity, but he proposes a fundamental distinction between what nature can do and what the human does. Humans complete what is deemed as an inadequacy of

[7] I would like to think that this intertwined reality of building and the world as landscape has not been fully dealt with in a number of recent critical writings on landscape even as urbanism, land forms, and other kinds of planning strategies are considered. See, for example, James Corner, *Recovering Landscape*.

[8] In *A+U*, 1973.

[9] In a conversation with Jan Hochstim in *The Paintings and Sketches of Louis I. Kahn*, see ff...

[10] Lecture at Drexel University, Philadelphia, 1968, in Wurman, *What Will Be Has Always Been: The Words of Louis I. Khan*, p. 29. Kahn goes to the mountain on other occasions. At a lecture at the University of Virginia in 1972, he narrates: "A man goes to the mountain, saying, I need you because I feel you can express what I want to express. The mountain says, I am busy, I am basking in the sun, I am having a hell of a good time. What do you want from me? And he says, I tell you, it's quite marvelous. And out of his pocket comes a little something, with some columns and pediments. The mountain says,"What's that?" "It's you." The mountain becomes a collaborator as soon as you show him how beautiful he is in the form that man makes him."

Foundation of Hadrian Mausoleum, from Piranesi's *Le Antichita romane*, 1756.

nature. How else can one explain that much bandied aphorism of the sun never knowing how great it was until it struck the side of a building. Kahn himself explains: "The sun goes along. Man makes something: the sun is inspired."[11] What may be extracted from this poetic reflection is the consideration of a mutuality – an asymmetrical mutuality – between architecture and the world that persists in Kahn's thinking from the more abstract notions of nature and man to a more palpable condition of site and building.[12]

I would like to return to the idea of "taking place," to what it means for a work of architecture being situated. A building – a built work – is a situated, emplaced event, and this attribute of being emplaced means reckoning with certain inevitable or rather ontological "realities" or "actualities" that affect both openly and surreptitiously the life and form of architecture:

(1) A telluric reality indicates that the earth is the ultimate ground-basis for architecture, where architecture can be seen as another topographical manipulation of the earth's surface.
(2) A climatic reality is the most direct and visceral evidence of architecture's chiasmic relation with the elements. Architecture has to reckon with weather, and it itself weathers.
(3) A geologic reality stresses that architecture is a phenomenon of gravity, not so much in a technical sense but in a seamlessly affective way.

What we have in shorthand are earth, climate and gravity. Climate and gravity impinge on us imperceptibly even if inconstantly, two things we take for granted as being given, and yet are essential for where and how we are. What distinguishes lived and actualized architecture from say an ideational or digitized one is that it is literally and perceptually embedded in climate and gravity in a seamless manner, in the way Eugene Minkowski in his study of "lived time" describes the body being enveloped by "night."[13]

It is in this context that I invoke the idea of "lived body" from Maurice Merleau-Ponty. The issue of "situatedness," if I may use a word like that, indicates an ideological and strategic difference between the "what" of architecture and "where is architecture." "Where is architecture" brings up the nexus of architecture and the world, or landscape if you will, that I would like to describe as a chiasmic relation between two entities. Despite our habitual thinking of the autonomy of architecture which is perhaps the biggest visual deception that we contend with, architecture is always in a chiasm, and that is its unperturbed inevitability. My understanding of "where is architecture," and therefore the structure of architecture-place, commences to a great degree from Merleau-Ponty's phenomenological understanding of the body, the body as a lived, percipient spatial subject as distinct from the objective conception of the biological and seemingly independent entity.[14] The position of "what" presents an objectification of the body, no matter from what perspective it is coming from, whether empiricist or intellectualist, both of which Merleau-Ponty wished to supercede. As both ideas regard

[11] From a conversation with Peter Blake, 1971, in Wurman, *What Will Be Has Always Been: The Words of Louis I. Khan,* p. 128.

[12] Site can be transposed for a more concrete sense of nature. Kahn described the site as confirming the possible and encouraging agreement on the beginning in the making of man's place. "The builder seeking a beginning/ is primed by the feeling of commonness/ and the inspirations of nature/ just a fragment of knowing steers wonder to intuition/ and to the acts of expression./ In the presence of the mountain, the water, and the wind/ the desire to express feels the possible/ The site confirms the possible..." Kahn Studio, University of Pennsylvania, 1969, in Wurman, *What Will Be Has Always Been: The Words of Louis I. Khan,* p. 82.

[13] I find Eugene Minkowski's description of "lived space" particularly illuminating for an analogical rephrasing of building: "I look in front of me: I then see objects or people more or less distant from me. But I also see life unfolding around me ...it is the clarity of this visual space which forms the backdrop against which my own life and the life of other living beings come to unfold. But clarity is not the only substance of life; we also live in the night. But I no longer have the black night, complete obscurity before me; instead, it covers me completely, it penetrates my whole being, it touches me in a much more intimate way than the clarity of visual space. Certainly, the dark night is not taken here in the sense of absence of light or the impossibility of seeing; it is taken in its positive value - in its materiality, we would almost like to say - and as such it is much more material, much more tangible, and even more penetrating than the limpid clarity of visual space ...it will be given to it in a particular way, completely different from the way in which clear space is given, and the words "distance" and "touch" seem to bring out this difference very well. The dark night also has something more personal about it in relation to the ego: I remain face to face with it; it is more "mine" than clear space ...[also] auditory space envelops me and penetrates like black space; there will be neither free space nor a "next to," neither perspective, nor horizon, nor distance in it, as there is in lived space." Eugene Minkowski, *Lived Time: Phenomenological and Psychopathological Studies* (Evanston IL: Northwestern University Press, 1970), p. 400.

[14] Merleau-Ponty rephrases what it means to be human. "The lived body, although human, is not all-too-human because it is a phenomenal body, an organism that retains its inherence within the world." Focillon, p. 131.

onstruction photo of Assembly Building, Presidential ntrance plaza, Dhaka, Bangladesh. Louis I. Kahn ollection.

the body as something located in space whose fundamental structures are independent of it, Merleau-Ponty considers the ideas inadequate in regarding the body. What makes the concept of the objective body distinct from the lived body? It is the taking into question the embodiment, emplacement, or deployment of the body in space, in the world, and thus its various transactions with it. And, hence the inevitable condition of chiasma. It is this phenomenological understanding that the body is an emplaced being, a landscaped subject, that leads me to realize analogically the nature of the inherent "situatedness" of architecture.

The history and theory of architecture return again and again to the analogy between body and building, the body considered primarily as mentioned above as the imaginary or ideal autonomous body, be it defined biologically, mystically, metaphysically, or cosmologically. The lived-body is in constant engagement with the world, and consequently opens up very new criteria of understanding [15] Do we encounter a fundamental difference when we consider architecture as analogous to the lived-body?

For the lived-body, the environment is an indefinite extension of it, and not distinguished as standing over and against the living body, so that I am here and space is there, where actually as Heidegger might say that one is revealed through the other. Merleau-Ponty, in his major phenomenological work on perception, sees the environment as a "manipulatory area" for the lived-body, something potentially to be taken in and incorporated.[16] The lived-body appropriates certain objects in the world to the extent that these objects cease to be objects and become "incorporated," that is, become part of the lived-body. On the other side, the environment directly and indirectly regulates the lived-body. The environment conditions the body in such a way that the body is the expression or reflection of the environment. In living, the body not only lives itself but also lives the environment, making the body a landscaped subject. This is what Merleau-Ponty calls a "reciprocal insertion and intertwining" of the lived-body and the environment. As another writer explains it: "the limits of one are lost in the other."

While I should be careful in making this analogy as we are talking about a percipient body of consciousness, I also realize the importance of rephrasing the place of architecture in the scheme of things. Architecture as an analogy of the objective body would lead us to iconology and disembodied ideations, no matter what their efficacy is. The analogy of the lived-body, on the other hand, would reveal the manner of its situated presence, its corporeality, which is also its spatiality and emplacedness. This is how I see architecture as "taking place."

Groundwork/Landshaping

All built works are then analogically lived bodies. So what is special about the work of Louis Kahn? Does the work reiterate the taking place and the intertwined reality of building? I would like to consider that from two conditions: the grounding of a built work, and its ambient realm.

[15] As Merleau-Ponty was to describe, that the body is not merely one space among many, rather "it is the origin of the rest, that which projects significations beyond itself and gives them a place," *The Phenomenology of Perception*, p. 146.

[16] Maurice Merleau-Ponty, *The Phenomenology of Perception*.

Kahn's architecture, to begin with, can be understood in a major way as a meditation on grounding, as articulating the telluric reality of architecture. It is this, and not only a certain geometric preference or archaic aura, that runs counter to the modern avante-garde attitude going back to the 1920s. I particularly point to an "aerial opsis," a view of the world from above that permeates the architectural thinking of someone like Le Corbusier. A large aspect of Le Corbusier's conceptualization in the 1920s was possibly generated from the radically and strikingly new prospect offered by aerial flights that would amplify the idea of buildings as free, autonomous masses, something that would form a paradigm for much of modern architectural production.[18] At the same time, Le Corbusier, in his characteristic contradistinction in his work, would go on to do projects often simultaneously that had to do with a kind of "deliberate pact with nature," such as the Weekend House near Paris (1935), the Sarabhai House in Ahmedabad (1955), or the excavated Trench of Consideration at Chandigarh (1952), or for that matter the roofscape of the Unite and the Chandigarh Secretariat, where the grounding of the building, the shaping of land-form, or the explicit investment of landscape in architectural form becomes an integral part of the configuration.

Construction photo of Indian Institute of Management Ahmedabad, India. Louis I. Kahn Collection.

Mies van der Rohe's work presented a more precarious relationship with the ground, a sort of tentative accord with it. Mies did think about lifting the building from the ground as in a classical manner in the Barcelona Pavilion or the National Gallery in Berlin where the presence of the ground is rather neutralized, but perhaps more definitively in the Farnsworth House. The Farnsworth House is not lifted up enough to make a polemical point as the Villa Savoye, but enough to uproot the building without really redefining the ground (although carried out in response for the practical reason of flooding). Although lifting up establishes one relationship with the ground, the transparency of the house, as well as the reflectivity surrounding it, mysteriously diminishing the boundary between the man-made and the natural world,[19] or as Kenneth Frampton describes it, where the haze of nature is held horizontally in the house,[20] makes for a new uncertain relationship between architecture and nature.[21]

Perhaps the architect who comes closest to the grounding notion of Kahn is Frank Lloyd Wright. While Kahn might have built for Le Corbusier in that idealistic or inspirational sense (as when Kahn was to declare, "I dreamt I lived in a city called Le Corbusier," and on hearing the death of Le Corbusier, "Whom should I build for now?"), his notion of grounding is far closer but not quite similar to that of Wright. It is closer in the sense that both are interested in a more or less grounded disposition of their buildings. Kahn's grounding is anticipated in a deeper psychology of form however; the relationship of his buildings with the earth is ponderous compared to say the rooted but more free-footed stance of Wright's rather dynamic buildings. The grounded buildings of Kahn give him away as a rather a-modern, even archaic, architect, which doesn't work with the largely Anglo-American pragmatic attitude about land and nature, and that despite Wright's transcendentalist inheritance.

[18] Adnan Morshed, "Le Corbusier and the Aerial Gaze," *Thresholds* 13, (Fall 1996). Morshed points to the compressing of the geographic reality as well as the generation of modernist utopia from the detached view from the airplane, "a discovery of the world hitherto unknown from a privileged observation point in the sky." LC: "the airplane=philosophy/ thematic performance and no longer joy of the senses." Brings about a utopic turnaround. Privileged distance and surveillance... nomadic consciousness... Also, Charles Waldheim, "Aerial Representation and the Recovery of Landscape," in *Recovering Landscape: Essays in Contemporary Landscape Architecture*, edited by James Corner. (Princeton, 1999)

[19] Phyllis Lambert, ed., *Mies in America* (New York: H.N. Abrams, 2001).

[20] Kenneth Frampton, "The Glass House Revisited," in *Philip Johnson: Processes*, Catalogue 9 (New York: Institute of Architecture and Urban Studies, 1978).

[21] Although Mies was to say that "Nature should also live its own life. We should attempt to bring nature, houses, and human beings together in a higher unity." In America, ff. 32.

I might add here that two projects may be cited from Kahn's oeuvre that represent elevating a building from the ground: the Richards Medical Laboratories in Philadelphia and the unbuilt Palazzo dei Congressi for Venice. It seems to me that at Richards, markedly an early building, the elevation of a bulk of the building is mitigated if not overwhelmed by the groundedness of the service towers. For the unbuilt Palazzo, although the building volume is levitating over a canal, the tug of gravity is articulated by the catenary belly of the building, shaped also, I must point out, by the seating configuration inside.

What are the evidences of Kahn's notion of grounding? And what are their conceptual implications? As the opening anecdotes indicate, when it comes to Kahn there is an occupation, even a certain mild obsession, with foundation, echoing some of Piranesi's drawings that present a subterranean prospect, a meditation on the remains of a building left in the last bits of its foundations. After all, foundational remain is the material domain of architectural archaeology, and when it comes to Piranesi, his archaeological imagination. Piranesi illustrates that in many ways – his whole thinking being derived from "reading" the foundation ruins of Roman buildings – that include restored views of vanished buildings, hyper-real projections of incredulous buildings from some exaggerated foundation, or even the unseen prospect of such a thing as the continuation of an arch of a bridge under water. The foundation then is not a just a vector of load, but a sign of an absence, and absence is the domain of imagination, either of a promise of things to come, or in the case of ruins and Piranesi, of things than can now be imagined.

At the Indian Institute of Management in Ahmedabad, some of the buildings have their foundation literally exposed, as if a stratum of the earth has been hauled away to reveal a city that lay buried underground. As with the construction of brick buildings, the foundation to the walls staggers out with increasing dimension that is conventionally embedded into the ground. The dormitory buildings at the Institute are articulated with rhythmic parallel walls with diagonal footing expressing the transfer of load as they near the ground. For the academic buildings that are aligned to a pedestrian street, they have their tiered foundation literally revealed, something that is seen when the wall is going up from the foundation trench and which is then covered by earth. The exposition of the foundation of these buildings in Ahmedabad becomes an expression, and not merely an accidental occurrence. I want to describe the exposure of the foundation and it's taking part in the architectural language as the aestheticization of the foundation. In certain projects, such as Kimbell and the Center for British Art, while the foundation is not actually exposed, a pit is excavated below the normal grade to reveal, among other things, the lower depth of the building as it descends Orpheus-like into the ground, or if you will, emerges from it like Persephone.

Sketch of stepped pyramid, Saqqara Egypt, 1951. Collection of Sue Ann Kahn.

Kahn's travel drawings and sketches provide fascinating aspects about his predilection that have not been fully deciphered. The

Sketch of the Acropolis, Athens, 1951. Private Collection.

only book on the topic by Jan Hochstim wonderfully brings the sketches and drawings together, but at the same time a lack of a fuller discussion of the issue of landscape in the drawings is surprising,[22] for a review of the drawings will reveal that most are about landscapes and territorial scenes even if a building or a group of buildings is the subject. Many of the drawings are about Kahn's attempt to capture the elusive and changing atmospheric qualities of some of the architectural sites that he visited (especially highlighted in the drawings of Sienna and the Parthenon), but above all, to my view, some of them are visual essays, in a sort of provisional way as we are not sure that Kahn was thinking about it, about the nature of building and land.[23]

In the book, Hochstim makes mostly elaborate analysis of compositional and technical norms in the drawings, and offers certain descriptive understanding. Vincent Scully in the introduction, almost characteristically, is still looking for the "missing" drawings of Ostia, as he writes there, in order to establish his thesis that Kahn's resurrected architecture from the 1960s stems from his Roman visit.[24] Yet, something more important is overlooked especially when I study the sketches of the Egyptian pyramids and the ruins at Delphi from his trips in 1951. In one particularly striking drawing of the Saqqara pyramids, nearly two-third of the drawing is devoted to the foreground, a vast and blank landscape of brown and gray earthy mass with a dark sky, that make me speculate that Kahn is not only thinking about the Platonic, or if you like stereotomic aspect of the pyramidal form, but also the nature of their arising from the ground. There are other sketches of a similar quality.

Similarly, his sketches of Greece of the same period are not so much about the expected renditions of architectural figures than the landscape that surround them or from which they materialize. Many of the drawings of the Acropolis, like the pyramids, are also about the emerging of crystalline forms from a landscape, in this case a craggy one as Kahn gives inordinate attention to the slopes and buttressed walls of the Acropolis. There are also numerous sketches of the peak of Arakhova (Drawings 358-359) and the mountainous landscape of Delphi with the sanctuary of Apollo (Drawings 363-365) conducted in a stylized and abstract manner that are about consolidating in drawing the spectacular panorama.There is a stark drawing in crayon of a ruin with trees (Drawing 362), where the abstract forms of the two in sharp light and shadow reflect each other. In another pair of sketches (Drawing 381), Kahn draws a temple of Apollo in Corinth in clear sunlight in one, while in another he draws the same temple in silhouette with the sun casting deep shadows on the ground.[25] Hochstim does note that "the abstract quality of these sketches highlights Kahn's interest in conveying the very spirit of the subject, rather than its obvious external appearance."[26] There are also sketches of Egyptian buildings that are more about the ambient quality of light, shadow, heat and dust rather than solely the autonomous architectural form. It is important for Kahn to render the ambience of the ruins, as in his drawings of the sanctuary at Delphi, for it is also obvious that the spirit of the subject incorporates the landscape or landscape elements in an

[22] Jan Hochtsim, *The Paintings and Sketches of Louis I. Kahn* (New York: Rizzoli, 1991).

[23] In few sketches Kahn does an architectural form, they are mostly about capturing ambience, spent light, as in the following figures in the book: 117, 127 (coming storm), 140 (farming village), 253 (white church, Rockport), 329 (abstract planes in landscape), 340 (baptistery, Sienna).

[24] Scully comments, "It is disappointing that more drawings by Kahn of the ruins of Roman brick and concrete architecture have not come to light." Hochstim, *The Paintings and Sketches of Louis I. Kahn*, p. 15-16.

[25] Hochstim, *The Paintings and Sketches of Louis I. Kahn,* sketch 381, pp. 278-279.

[26] Hochstim, *The Paintings and Sketches of Louis I. Kahn,* note to plate 362 "Ruin with Dead Trees," p. 263.

[27] From a conversation with Robert Wemischner, in Wurman, *What Will Be Has Always Been: The Words of Louis I. Khan,* p. 121.

integral way. Drawings of the ruins of Delphi would be prescient of the later Adele Levy Memorial Park in New York.

There is also the philosophical, or at least, the poetic question of gravity. There are a few drawings in Hochstim's book that seem unfinished, but also clearly drawn from the top of the sheet (374, drawing of Arcopolis). Hochstim explains that as Kahn's intention of keeping the relatively unimportant foreground or lower part incomplete. While that may be so with some drawings, the interpretation does not work well with Kahn's own explanation in another context of the nature of drawing by say a painter and an architect.

Kahn explains what it means to draw like an architect: "I draw a building from bottom up because that's the way it is constructed. It depends on gravity. You begin with the way all the weights can be distribute on the land, and then you build up. If you do that, then you draw like an architect."[27] Drawing from the top, from where it gives to the sky, and then going down is drawing like an artist, like Marc Chagall. Kahn would say that it is drawing and not a building: "You have the same right as Chagall has. He can stop the building right in the middle of the sky and indicate ground. And say, The hell with it. I am not going to go any farther. You are conveying something which shows the prerogatives of a painter, one who know who can defy gravity."

This inscrutable relationship of building and land that Kahn had identified is revealed through another seemingly ordinary prospect, in the regular model making technique in Kahn's office. Clay was the ubiquitous material for producing site and master plans, a process that was introduced apparently after Kahn collaborated briefly with the sculptor Isamu Noguchi.[28] One could perhaps compare Kahn's clay city models with the aerial forms in a Corbusian model. In the latter, the cubic forms of architecture appear clearly designated as extraneous and autonomous from the ground plane of the model. One hesitates about how much can be extrapolated from the technique of model-making, but I would like to think that in the case of Kahn the same terrestrial clay lacking any entity congealing into crystalline architectural forms strengthens the idea about Kahn's sense of the fundamental rootedness of architecture at the same time that human-made form is being privileged.

Dormitory interior, Indian Institute of Management, Ahmedabad, India. Photo: Louis I. Kahn Collection.

Learning from the Delta

All this is to say that as early as the 1960s when, tentative at it may be, and as much as Kahn was working with crystalline geometries and modernist forms, he was inclined towards the grounding of architecture as a fundamental fact. And he began to consider this in a more persistent manner with a term that he had coined: "land architecture." It is not very clear from what period in time Kahn started to think of architecture and land in such an integral way with a conceptual rigor as promised by the term, but it is highly likely that his experience in Dhaka and Bangladesh was crucial in reinforcing that idea.

When Kahn visited Dhaka for the Capital Complex project (having arrived there the first time in 1964), and was taken around in the deltaic countryside, he was greatly transfixed by the landscape, especially the immensity of water, and the fluidity of land in the precarious hydrological chemistry of the delta. His earliest sketches of the Complex captured this particularity and continued that in the heart of the design. While this essay is not an occasion to discuss the overall architecture of the Dhaka complex,[29] I wish to point out towards one thing that intrigued Kahn the moment he landed in Dhaka, something that was also a point of entry for me into his thinking about landscape: "How are the buildings to take their place on the land." Kahn also intuited from the beginning that "the two elements of nature most pervasive in the landscape of [Bangladesh] are water and vegetation. They almost assert their presence. The examples of intelligent cooperation with these pervasive elements of water and vegetation in some of the best examples of Mughal garden architecture have been a great inspiration for me."[30]

Kahn was to comment that in the delta one does "an architecture of the land," meaning that the fundamental building fact is the molding of the earth to provide both platforms and proto-architectural shapes. He conceptualized this fundamental or primordial fact as the process of "dig-and-mound," something that involves an excavation of the ground to create an artificial earth mound on which the building is placed where the excavated pit becomes a pond (a sustaining fish pond). The horizontally sculpted earth mound is called the *bhita*, and when people refer to their homes, they refer to the *bhita*. The bhita is a more permanent than the bamboo and thatch superstructure raised there that has a tendency to disappear completely during cyclones and floods. In any case, the notion of dig-and-mound becomes the *de facto* basis for the articulation of buildings in Dhaka, although a question remains whether considering an assembly building from such a vantage point was superfluous to begin with. Kahn was also beginning to think about a set of "bridge-buildings" for a heavily flooded area north of the Complex just before his death, where a set of finger-like platforms would bridge over low lands, the platforms to be used as site for building while the area under it for agricultural cultivation during dryer seasons.

Kahn's conception of grouping – how the buildings are to come together, and how are they going to take their place on the land – may be linked to a number of other sources, particularly to the hierarchic and diagonal order of a Beaux-Arts plan, or an inspiration from Piranesi's speculative drawing of the Pantheon showing it as a fulcrum in a setting of supportive buildings, public spaces, gardens, and lake. The grouping and setting in Dhaka is also a remark on the delta topography. It can be seen in the appearance of the huddling, jostling masses of the Assembly with its raw, stratified surface appearing out of the earth/water like some crystallizing apparition as in some archaic myth of the beginnings from a primordial fluid. Again, is this a conceit? Kahn's persistence in the three-dimensional presence of architectural organisms coagulating out of the earth plain says something about his conceptualizing methods on the origin and formation of architectural material. Maria Bottero, as early as the

[28] This is Robert McCarter's thesis.
[29] I have discussed the Complex in two contexts: GA Monograph 74: *Louis Kahn's National Capital Complex in Bangladesh* (Tokyo, 1994) and *Sherebanglanagar: The Making of a Capital Complex* (Dhaka, 2002).

[30] Box LIK 120, Louis I. Kahn Collection, University of Pennsylvania.

[31] Maria Bottero, "Organic and Rational Morphology in Louis Kahn," in *Zodiac* 17, 1967.

[32] From a caption in MOMA exhibition model of Levy Park in 1966, noted by Isamu Noguchi in *Isamu Noguchi: A Sculptor's World* (Thames and Hudson, 1967), p. 177-178.

Louis Kahn, Kimbell Art Museum, Fort Worth. Photo: Ashraf.

1960s in a brilliant essay, saw this as a mysterious phenomenon in form selection in that instead of sort of descending from Platonic Forms "form arises out of a submerged world."[31]

A more literal expression of "land architecture" is the unbuilt Adele Levy Memorial Park in New York City carried out in collaboration with the sculptor Isamu Noguchi between 1960-65. The project is a sculptural landscape for children involving the shaping of land forms, what today one would describe as "land art." The project ended somewhat controversially but highlighted the contested realm of architecture and sculptural landscape. It is not clear who between Noguchi and Kahn contributed most to the idea of a land architecture for the park, but Noguchi, in a rather disappointed mood, notes a comment by a critic on "a scattered assault of Kahn's geometries upon Noguchi's hill."[32] Kahn, on the other hand, remarked about Noguchi's disparate, unrelated pieces in the landscape. But what Brownlee and De Long note is that right after returning from Dhaka, Kahn embarked on two strategies that would mark as new dimensions in his architectural thinking: one, the irregular linking of discrete architectural pieces that would find its most compelling expression in the unbuilt Dominican Motherhouse in Pennsylvania (1965), and, two, the intimacy between building-form and land-form.

Kimbell Art Museum. Photo: Carol Highsmith, Wikimedia.

The Notion of "Land Architecture"

Kahn would also take up his notion of "land architecture" in an academic context. In the teaching of architecture, Kahn did not quite agree to the difference between architecture and landscape architecture in the curricular division that is standardized now. He would simply admit his dislike for the term "landscape architecture."[33] He would suggest that architecture schools could have two courses for operational reasons, one called *architecture and land*, and the other called *land and architecture*. Kahn's simple but cryptic explanation was that one may be called landscape architecture because the emphasis is on land, and the other may be called architecture because the emphasis is on architecture.

Kahn basically criticized the academic divisions of architect, landscape architect, planner – the setting up of new fields – as marketplace conditions. The division, he argues, comes out of the contingencies of professions, and it is all right if one were to be satisfied by serving professional needs, but "profession is one thing and man is another, that if you think of serving the profession then you must think of serving the marketplace. And if you think of serving man then you are serving that which can

[33] In his words: "It sounds prissy to me... land architecture sounds great, nobody lives up to it... I hope they become land architects instead of land-scraping architects." Lecture at Drexel University, Philadelphia, 1968, p. 31.

[35] Interview in *VIA* magazine, Philadelphia, 1969, in Wurman, p. 38.

[36] Corner, *Recovering Landscape*.

[37] If it were to change to land architect, then Kahn "I would say that even the President of the United States would understand his role in the affairs of the world. As landscape architect he cannot, as land architect he can, and as land architect I showed him so many ways how nature can be the great partner of his work... and the architect is called in as the advocate of nature, and makes everything in the deepest respect for nature by not imitating it at all. He must plant the tree as a man, a choosing individual, and conscious man, which nature, not being conscious, makes."

set an example and be an interpretation in completeness, from all angles, meaning to say that an architect cannot entrust the land which belongs to his project to anyone at all but himself."[35] Is this simply a question of control of turf, or as Kahn would have like us to believe that one would treat land "as though it were a great conservation, as though you are taking a piece out of the whole?" It is, to Kahn, a recognition of oneness, not division.

So what are the theoretical consequences of the notion of "land architecture?" First, the land architect does not mimic the landscape architect for the former looks at land from his or her point of view, that is, from a condition of reconstitution. Second, a land architect is also like a building architect in the sense that bridges, highways and interchanges, for example, that is, the large-scale realm of a constructed landscape, are all part of his consciousness, thus foreseeing some of the landscape architecture thinking today.[36] Even the president of the United States, Kahn would insist, would understand his role in the affair of the world better as a land architect and not as a landscape architect, for he would be shown how nature can be the great partner of his work.[37]

The principle of land architecture would consider the rising of the building from the undifferentiated, non-conscious mass of the earth. In a converse sense, this is the matter of the inevitable grounding of architecture. While grounding is important, that does not restrict the physiognomy of the risen form for Kahn would insist, as I have noted earlier, that even while nature is a partner, "he must plant the tree as a man, as a choosing individual." There is then a complicated dialog between the grounding and the rising, as if the building – a fact of constructedness – rises from the muddy earth into crystalline forms even as the source is still the earth, materially, genealogically, and psychologically.

Still, the ponderous relationship of Kahn's buildings with the earth might be his bane, giving them away as rather a-modern, archaic, or just plain earth-bound creations. There is perhaps more: Kahn's ambiguous landscape is more pre-cultural and primordial, that is, certainly pre-modern. If Le Corbusier seems interested in a sort of Virgilian or arcadian landscape, thus placing him in a kind of picturesque realm, Kahn is taken in by the cosmological imagery of the muddy waters and the shaping of things to come from the oozy, dark mud of the primordial gumbo. That for Kahn is "beginning," conceited as it may be. By that token, the image of the Virgilian landscape is already historical, while the nebulous, formative landscape of Kahn is from a mythic realm, a rather pre-Socratic landscape prior to the distinction of building and land.

Exposing the foundation and ruminating on it seem consonant with Kahn's concern for beginning. Does this hint on anything about a possible nomadism that is inherent in Kahn, an idea that was put forward in the quest film by his son Nathaniel Kahn, that this could also be rephrased (or psychoanalyzed) as a longing for belonging? Kahn operated from a modern urban homelessness that was perhaps doubly signified by being Jewish and immigrant, both weighing in a desire to be anchored. Wright's Robie House, on the other hand, with its vertical solidity and sweeping roofs emblematized a simultaneous compulsion of being perfectly anchored but wishing to be mobile.

Kahn's sharing of an archaeological sensibility with Piranesi is fairly well known. The sensibility is not archaeological in the sense of digging up ruins, but to peel away layer after layer of circumstantial accretions to arrive at some fundamental, or rather foundational substratum. Is the pit in Kimbell emblematic for that reason? Is the aestheticization of the foundation in Ahmedabad narratival or revelatory, that is, part of a larger story? Does it in an unselfconscious way besides uncovering an architectural space reveals the architect's originary search, elusive as it may be, of human belonging that is being increasingly jeopardized by the inevitable instruments of modern life?

And, finally there is the question of form, of its emergence and its taking place in the world, which is surely a cosmogonic question. A large corpus of work is dedicated to interpreting the idea of form in Kahn's thinking to which he himself contributed to, often times in uneven ways. It would not be unreasonable to say that most interpretations see form in some Platonic way as "Idea," but Kahn had also began to think of the architecture-landscape continuum that throws a different light on form. Kahn is not only interested in the mathematical purity of the so-called archetypal form, but that such forms arise from a real-life phenomenal, material world. Also, the significance of the so-called archetypal forms, if they are to be seen that way, happens in their juxtaposition with the real, phenomenal, and the everyday. Despite the crystalline geometry, Kahn's conceptualizing saw forms as arising from the ground in some mysterious, metaphysical ways as Bottero describes it, placing it in a realm rather Aristotlean than Platonic.[38]

Kahn's treatment of form is therefore more geological than cultural. If the situatedness of architecture is an abiding theme in Kahn's architecture, at least since the 1960s, it happens not so much from a cultural vantage point but primarily a geographical and climatical understanding of place and situation, such that one could say that it was place rather than culture, the latter being more portable, that affected Kahn's architecture.

Spent Light, and the Weathering Narrative of Architecture
The simultaneously seamless and distinctive relationship between building-form and land-form proceeds from the matter of grounding to the ambient "flesh" of a building.

"You don't know how beautiful the sun is until it strikes a wall." What to make of this statement now over attended into a poetic triteness? Is there a possibility of extending an understanding? I think this meditation presents a strikingly different view than Le Corbusier's pronouncement of architecture as the play of masses under light, which also seems to me a matter of opsis (the directed gaze), of the retinal encounter of sculpturesque architectural forms in light and shadow induced by the sun. It

[38] Bottero, "Organic and Rational Morphology in Louis Kahn."

[39] Lecture at Drexel University, 1968, in Wurman, *What Will Be Has Always Been: The Words of Louis I. Khan*, p. 29.

The Yale Center for British Arts, New Haven, Connecticut. Photo: Gunnar Klack, Wikimedia.

also invokes the moment when Kahn tried to capture in drawing the atmospheric quality of Sienna.

Kahn literally turns the gaze around, from form to light (sun), and back to the form. More than being a fixed gaze, there is a fluctuation, a reverberation between the illuminator and the illuminated. The essence lies not in either end of a pole, but in a mutuality of the two, the intertwined reality of the sun and the wall, which is to say that this is not an utterance with a metaphysical implication, or with a cosmological consequence, but a profoundly phenomenological one. The statement underscores a phenomenology of material emplaced, matter situated, and the inevitable consequence of that, the striking of the sun on the wall. In fact, it is by the striking of the sun on the wall that the wall gains its being, and that is how the reality of the wall came to be designated by Kahn as "spent light." But for that matter, everything is spent light: "You are spent light, the mountains are spent light, the trees are spent light, the atmosphere is spent light, water is spent light. All material is spent light."[39] The significance that could be derived from here, aside the immediate reality of sensoriality and tactility, is that there are no "objects" in the classical empirical or rational sense, but all are situated things and beings.

But, at the same time, Kahn is also no romantic naturalist. In the mutuality of things, it is the wall that makes the presence of the sun beautiful, and to refer back to the efficacy of man-made architectural form in Kahn's vision, man makes what nature cannot.

If this crypto-poetic utterance makes greater sense, it is by a possible alliance with Merleau-Ponty's notion of "chiasm," the ineluctable intertwining of the body and the world, and by extension between the architectural body and the world. What I am trying to reiterate is that there is a seamless relationship between architecture and its situation in the world, an "ontological inseparability," so to speak. One could make a mute display of that seamlessness, one may not display it at all, as all general body of architecture does, or one like Kahn, in a heightened condition of material expressiveness make an event of that seamlessness. The sun, when it is daytime and it is not a gray day, does strike a wall when there is a wall. The wall does take care to keep the interiors cool, it works to take to hide the glare, etc. But Kahn does a little more, an excess perhaps. Where the sun strikes the wall, at that juncture where a mutuality is only potentially present, Kahn allows it to be pronounced, to have presence, to be poeticized in the sense of poeisis. It is the excessiveness that makes the difference.

This is what I mean by Kahn's original sense of landscaping a building, of allowing a building to be cloaked by the natural givenness where it has a presence, like Minkowski's night shrouding the body, or the orange shroud over Sienna. To allow the situational givenness to have presence in the architectural condition/construction is what I describe as the weathering narrative in architecture, of making weather, weathering, and a climatic chiasm part of an architectural epistemology. At this point, what has been described in the context of grounding may be taken up for the other perimeters of the architectural form; if grounding implies the horizontal incorporation of the world in the architectural body, weathering implies the vertical or ambient inclusion. It is in this context one can rethink the architectural components that Kahn dedicated to weathering: the porch, the arcade, and the double skin.

When in the envelope of the Assembly and the brick buildings at Dhaka, Kahn makes those gigantic perforations, when he makes those cavernous spaces of shadows, he is surreptitiously "landscaping" the buildings. This is landscaping in a phenomenal and visceral sense: how nature – the sun, wind, and rain – invades a man-made artifact, erodes its envelope, makes its porous, and finally repossesses it.

Of course, the atmospheric aura is possible because Kahn does not use extensive glass in Dhaka and Ahmedabad. When he does use it, for compelling reasons, in other projects, or even in modifications in Dhaka, the box is immediately formed, creating a sharp disjunction in the mutuality. "Masonry masses and voids. That's what Kahn wants," Vincent Scully observed but not really explaining why other than the allusion to robust archaic forms.[40] Again, Maria Bottero notices this early in one of the most perceptive essays on Kahn, and describes the phenomenon as Kahn wanting "an architecture of open forms, integrated with the *plein air* of the surrounding landscape."[41]

If opening up of the building, its perforations and cavities are a way of "landscaping," there are a few instances to consider. From the consulate in Lusaka to the unbuilt meeting halls at Salk via the buildings in Dhaka, the double envelope becomes an unambiguous instrument of the weathering narrative. While Kahn himself generated a contesting picturesque idea of the double wall as a ruin wrapping a building, he also notes: "All windows must recede to where the cool air can open to the rooms. The outside of the building belongs to the sun, the interior belongs to the shadows. It is the place where people live."[42] About the porch that would also characterize his buildings in Dhaka and Ahmedabad, but most dramatically at Kimbell where it would seem that the wind billows open the entry vault, Kahn would say that "the porch is a building… the porch is an offering to the sun."[43] The library at Exeter is the most compelling articulation of an arcade, another device in the chiasmic elements of architecture. And what is the nature of the arcade? "The arcade is a landscape thing. It belongs to the building, certainly, but it also belongs to the entrance and belongs to the ground."[44] The cavities in Dhaka, the arches in Ahmedabad, the arcade of Exeter, the vaulted porch of Kimbell, the diagonal studies at Salk, all are, to use a Kahnian phrase, of the same "order of landscape."

[40] Vincent Scully, *Modern Architecture* (New York: George Braziller, 1961).

[41] Bottero, "Organic and Rational Morphology in Louis Kahn."

[42] Lecture in Philadelphia, 1973, in Wurman, *What Will Be Has Always Been: The Words of Louis I. Khan,* p. 217.

[43] From interview with John W. Cook and Heinrich Klotz, *Conversation with Architects*, 1973, in Wurman, *What Will Be Has Always Been: The Words of Louis I. Khan,* p. 197.

[44] Comments at the Philip Exeter Library, Exeter, 1972, in Wurman, *What Will Be Has Always Been: The Words of Louis I. Khan,* p. 181.

Louis I. Kahn: The Making of a Room

Exhibition Review, published in *Journal of Architectural Education*, 2009.

Louis I. Kahn: The Making of a Room
George Marcus, Curator
Arthur Ross Gallery, University of Pennsylvania, Philadelphia
February 7–March 29, 2009

A room is a room is a room. Or perhaps there is more than that. Among the various subversive operations against modernism credited to Louis Kahn, a fundamental one is his embrace of the archaic notion of the room instead of the radical idea of the plan libre. The room, that most ancient of architectural ideograms and experiences, was central in Kahn's imaginary. But the room that appears in his drawings, built work, and oracular texts was neither archaic nor usual. It opened new meditations on the tectonics, phenomenology and anthropo-sociology of the room in modernist discourse.

The exhibition *Louis I. Kahn: The Making of a Room* with an operatic sub-title *Dramatis Personae: A Cast of Characters from the Architectural Drawings of Louis Kahn* casts some new light on some old characters. Professor George Marcus was responsible for selecting the drawings, along with students in the Halpern-Rogath curatorial seminar on modern design in the art history department at Penn. Marcus and his students selected forty drawings and sketches that charted a mythopoeisis of the room in Kahn's world, matching phrases from Kahn's cryptic repertoire with appropriate drawings (the characters) from Penn's archive.

The point of departure for the exhibition is Kahn's well-known 1971 image that combined drawing and text into a visual meditation on the room. This image, along with several compelling phrases derived from Kahn's consideration of the performance of the room, provided the thematic organization of the exhibition: "The plan [is] a society of rooms," "the room is a place of the mind," "a room is not a room without natural light." "Architecture comes from the making of the room" is perhaps the clearest indication of Kahn's reification of the room. The statement suggests a conceptual kinship with Adolf Loos's raumplan and the oneiric properties of certain spaces as observed by Gaston Bachelard.

As the drawings in the exhibition demonstrate, for Kahn the room is not a monadic thing; it also inspires the idea of family

Architecture comes from The Making of a Room
The Plan A society of rooms is a place good to live work learn
A great American Poet once asked The Architect 'What slice of the sun does your building have. What light enters your Room' as if to say the sun never knew how great it is until it struck The side of a building
The Room
is The place of the mind. In a small room one does not say what one would in a large room. In a room with only one other person could be generative. The vectors of each meet.
A room is not a room without natural light. natural light gives the time of day and the mood of the seasons to enter.

or society. The socialization of the architectural plan is seen in three ways: in the hierarchical assembly of individuated rooms, as in the Assembly Building in Dhaka; in a systematized matrix, as in the Kimbell Museum; in the free grouping, as in the unbuilt Dominican Motherhouse. Kahn's sense of urbanism was also informed by the room. This is made clear not only in his "a street is a room" sketch, but also in his well-known studies for a civic center in Philadelphia from the 1950s. In these drawings, streets become ideal spaces of sociality, made even more powerful by the fact that, in reality, American streets had already succumbed to a techno-functional takeover that rendered them spaces of sheer mobility.

The exhibition began with a simple investigation of Kahn's interiors, but it became obvious to Marcus and his students that Kahn's idea of the room was a modulated oscillation between the inside and outside. Kahn, in fact, rendered this seeming duality in his unbuilt Roosevelt Memorial. Here, the garden is truly an enclosure, presenting the first architectural ideation of the room in such a way that there is a greater kinship between the room and the garden than an antinomy.

In the sense of an anthropological ontology, Kahn's room was the setting for a fundamental human relationship, a unit of life-world where the space belongs to two humans defining social interaction. This designation is markedly different from the anthropocentric space of the single person. With respect to the inhabitation of the room, this relates to Kahn's distinction between an event and a performance. The former is precipitated by two people conversing; the latter is the prerogative of the single person. Kahn assigned the significance of the room to two people in conversation. The conversation or exchange is further affected by size and light.

A room's particularity is constructed by its size and conveyed by the light inhabiting it and this, in turn, has an impact on the thoughts exchanged within. The size determines the social modicums of the conversations and thus the various spatialities of the life-worlds: "In a small room one does not say what one would in a large room." For this reason, the Memorial for the Six Million Jewish Martyrs is a perplexing entry in the exhibition. Of the six glass structures that form the memorial, all but the central one (the chapel) are solid blocks with no suggestion of interiority. Can solid blocks be thought of as closed rooms where access is physically denied, but where interiority exists as an idea? While this was not particularly intimated by the exhibition, it certainly suggests another degree of habitation of the enigmatic room.

As an exploration of Kahn's social, architectural, and poetical "characters," the exhibition made clear the various topologies of the room in Kahn's oeuvre. What was less obvious was when, why, and how Kahn moved decisively into the room – with its elements of four walls, apertures, and a roof – in the midst of modernist openness and spatial fluidity. The exhibition circles around materials when the room is already at the center of Kahn's architectural theater.

Drawing courtesy of the Louis I. Kahn Collection, the Architectural Archives, University of Pennsylvania.

such a cosmogonic murder scene, an infanticide from an Orphic account of

a possible future." They are enigmas that can be interpreted only with a vague precision,

and went to the University of Oregon in the United States and to Yale University where he received a Masters

The Lost House

supervision of Paul Rudolph. It was upon his return to East Pakistan, and as part of his responsibilities within the ubiquitous Public Works Department (as no private architectural firms existed at the time) that

because it is the house of the Other." And Rudolf Otto has pointed

ther is either a divinity or monstrosity, or some kind of bewildering phenomenon.

The Eventful 1960s

important foreign architects like Louis I. Kahn, Paul Rudolph, Constantin

gloves of certain common characteristics. But today that range

at every instant. The imminence of a disappearance

house-set is burning. The house had to be rebuilt so it could be burned again). In Tarkovsky's driven meditation on the macrocosmic scope of human annihilation (in the film, nuclear catastrophe), and its microscopic reach into the lives

and presence.

are apparitions and haunting images.

contradiction.

Why Did the Monk Burn the Temple?

Le Corbusier's Prehistory

("a pact with nature"), Corbusier not only reverts his ambiguous conception of nature, but attempts to tap a earth-hugging sensibility, which he does more

House, it is the brazen animation, busy and diverse as a bazaar under a sheltering umbrella, the various brise-soleil and complex organisation of the terraces, which

Le Corbusier, the total affirmation of will and power over nature – a stark clarity borne out of intellectual reason – Istanbul is popular memory characterized by a pluralistic, malleable and passionate spirit.

ARCHITECTURE IN INDIA

India and Le Corbusier: The Open Hand

India the Humane and Profound Civilisation

The Temple of Doom and Enthusiasm

Measures of Water

The Origin of Architecture Is in a Slaughter

Parasols and Silhouettes

[illegible] domains, a spatial screen for filtering not only sun and rain, but also activities and territories. This is the element that gives houses in the sub-continent the [illegible]

[illegible] and corresponds to [illegible] Le Corbusier himself, time and again, confirmed his dualistic proclivity: "This prodigious spectacle has been produced by the interplay of two elements, one male, and one female: sun and water. Two [illegible] objectivity of forms, under the intense light of a Mediterranean sun: male architecture. In the other limitless subjectivity rising against a [illegible] shattered, the ridge-pole is destroyed, and the architect will no longer erect the [illegible] sources, even if a-historically: from Western Europe to Africa, from "high classical" to vernacular, from machine imagery to folk art, [illegible] becoming an architectural reality in the Corbusian schemata.[5] As a rule, the appropriated [illegible] his consistent cores. The strategy also permitted the retaining of the identity of elements even when they were contradictory,[7] and became effective when ideological and cultural collisions came to play. Such juxtapositions also led to an ambiguity producing [illegible] the Indian state of the categorized ideals of Hinduism, Buddhism and Islam. This question was [illegible] with more recent implications. As K.T. Ravindran notes: "The problem with seeking a national or regional diversity is that such efforts are basically [illegible] world, socially, familially and phenomenally. The Buddha's statement is the most vivid expression of the violent destruction of *gaha*. And [illegible] pursuit of the ascetic to literally de-construct the existing structure of [illegible] immediate responsibility–the design of Chandigarh, the new capital city for the state of Punjab and its key components. While the city plan was carried out by a team following an [illegible] mode of existence, akin to a "second birth," of dying to this world and being born again in order to create another "human," a body more purified and superior. The Buddha once used the example of a chick breaking out of the egg-shell as a "second birth." "To break the shell of the egg is [illegible]

[illegible] virtues, the town was an embodiment of Laws and Principles. On the liminal side of that illustrious town, on a site at the far outskirts where tall, green trees surrounded a dank, marshy land, lay the temple. It was a wooden temple, with stocky columns and tiled roof on a wooden frame held together by rope lashings. The [illegible] mechanisms and policies. Planners and policy-makers glorify land, while water is exiled to the domain of poets and vagrants, and pitiful [illegible] ged. The official gods, the gods from the sky, look elsewhere, and generals, senators and merchants appear helpless as the women grow [illegible] -five years of research through continuous attempts in his life to give expression to the collective ethos of "the new epoch" through its various [illegible] anthropological and sociological significance. A measure of water will have to consider the [illegible] time. The ropes come apart, and one by one, the purlins fall, crashing to the ground, and soon the roof tiles, often one by one and often in the loud rumble of a [illegible] fluctuations and inversions, and as a consequence, generator of ambiguities. The entry of water in the everyday dry domain can disrupt normativity, and produce [illegible] Semele impregnated after drinking a potion made of the heart of Dionysis torn apart by Titans, or dying before giving birth to baby Dionysos whence the impregnator Zeus sews the fetus to his leg for a paternal birth.

[illegible] Loire from a description by the geographer Strabo.]

[illegible] that intellectually [illegible] wards [illegible] Athens.[15] [illegible] ghna, dancing along her way, slipped into a careless moment [illegible] nor French, nor American but Indian of the second half of the twentieth century."[16] Those gods assigned for measurement and survey brought out their instruments, the thread, the chalk powder, the theodolites, and the tripods. On the ground where Vastupurusa lay slaughtered and dismembered, with each [illegible] current of air, it is the shade, and yet the sun must penetrate at the proper time, in the favourable seasons. The conditions of the problem are [illegible] easy," the point of the axis mundi around which things to come manifest. Thus on the dismembered body of the poor thing emerged a grid of order and measure, and for each grid appeared property and character, and upon that [illegible] typological counterpart: the brise-soleil and the roof as an umbrella. From a tentative expression as in Villa Bezeau in Carthage, Tunisia (1928), the brise-soleil becomes a highly articulated "element poetique" in the office tower for Algiers (1939-1942). The separation of the roof from the more used volume of the building also dates as early as 1928 in the first sketch for Villa Bezeau, and 1939 in the pavilion at the exposition at Liege where the [illegible] of the making of a worlding.

Still Life, 1920, Museum of Modern Art, New York.

Le Corbusier and India: An Osmosis

Unpublished text, 1988.

"…truth is not to be found at the extremes. The truth flows between two banks, a tiny rivulet or a mighty torrent… and different everyday…"
—Le Corbusier (1957)

"There was a time when human races lived in comparative segregation and therefore the art adventurers had their experience within a narrow range of limits, deeply cut grooves of certain common characteristics. But today that range has vastly widened, claiming from us a much greater power of receptivity than what we were compelled to cultivate in former ages. If today we are a living soul that is sensitive to ideas and to beauty of form, let it prove its capacity by accepting all that is worthy of acceptance, not according to some blind injunction of custom or fashion, but in following one's instinct for eternal value, the instinct which is a God given gift to all real artists. Even then our art is sure to have a quality which is Indian, but it must be an inner quality and not an artificially fostered formalism, and therefore not to be too obtrusively obvious and abnormally self-conscious..."
—Rabindranath Tagore, *The Meaning of Art*

"I do not want my house to be walled in on all sides and my windows to be stuffed. I want the cultures of all the lands to be blown about my house as freely as possible. But I refuse to be blown off my feet by any."
—Mohandas Karamchand Gandhi

"The march of time will wait for no man and these who cannot fall in step will perish, I do not intend to get India perish while I am around. She will adapt herself now as she has done many times before and she will survive."
—Jawaharlal Nehru

Uttered at various times, the above statements sum up the dominant political and intellectual context of India in the twentieth century. As the architect of the new capital of the Indian state of Punjab, Le Corbusier faced that ideational context. The political situation of that time involved the emergence of India as a new nation-state within the world economic and political matrix following the Second World War, and a dominant leadership that foresaw the future in the treasury of modernity: industrial progress, democracy and international fraternity.

At the same time, vestiges of an ancient civilisation remained deeply entrenched in the niches of the society along with anomalies that have accumulated over time. It was those anomalies, along with colonial consternations, that fanned contemporary progressive thinking in people like Jawaharlal

Nehru, the first prime minister of India. In being invited to plan for Chandigarh by Nehru, Le Corbusier was thrust into the heart of that contradiction.

In Chandigarh, at the foothills of the Himalayas, the plains trodden by waves of historical movements, where Buddhist culture once flourished with a Greek flavour, Le Corbusier was given the opportunity, so many times frustrated before – during the League of Nations, the Palace of the Soviets, and the UN Headquarters – to construct an epochal monument for a new nation-state. Chandigarh, the "temple of New India" became Le Corbusier's first real opportunity to concretise his idealisation of a new age. In Nehru, he finally found "a political leader whose outlook was in tune with his own architectural philosophy and whose authority was strong enough to put it to work."[1]

Even if Nehru's ideology became the dominant aspiration for post-war India, the Gandhian philosophy of returning to roots, finding self-sufficiency in verancular means, and perpetuating ancient myths, remained quite operative in the production of another reality, and against which Corbusier's architectural production in India will continually and finally be perceived. Le Corbusier's work in India also becomes significant in stirring certain fundamental issues in contemporary architectural consciousness. Even without really settling the matter whether his production in India is really modern/European, Indian, or purely Corbusian, the works jeopardise the homogeneity of that body of work called "modernism," and undermine the modernist idea that architecture in the age of industrial progress is justifiably ahistorical, acultural and international. It is more than coincidental that the reductive internationalism of the postwar years received its major contrapuntal twist in the Indian subcontinent, through the work of Le Corbusier in India and Louis I. Kahn in Bangladesh.

Le Corbusier's "Prehistory"

From the very beginning of Le Corbusier's entry into architecture, starting with his voyage to Eastern Europe and Turkey, a dual sensibility pervades his thought. In Greece, on the heights of the Acropolis, he perceives architecture as a rationally crystallised human artefact located in nature with a brazen disposition. While

Istanbul skyline, drawing, 1911.

[1] Stanislaus von Moos, "Notes on Le Corbusier and Nehru at Chandigarh," in *The Open Hand: Essays on Le Corbusier*, edited by Russell Walden (Cambridge: MIT Press, 1977).

The Acropolis in Athens, sketch.

in Istanbul, architecture appears to him in passivity, as sinuous shapes mediating between the spirit of the human and nature, and as part of mythic folk cultures nurtured through centuries.

While the Acropolis is, to Le Corbusier, the total affirmation of will and power over nature – a stark clarity borne out of intellectual reason – Istanbul is popular memory characterized by a pluralistic, malleable and passionate spirit. The Acropolitan mode is in sharp contradistinction with nature, while Istanbul seeks "closeness to the soil and the earthly sensuality." Whether mediative or conflicting, dualism becomes a recurrent trope in Corbusier's architecture at a number of levels in which the Acropolis and Istanbul remain as perceptual sources, and the Apollonian and Dionysian notions as intellectual motives. A tension of the '"pair" of concepts' may operate at the broadest scale, in the opposition of nature with geometry, or at a building scale within the frame of a form itself as in the distinction between rectilinear and curvilinear elements. Both as an artist and an architect, von Moos notes, Le Corbusier wants to include the element of contrast – the clash of thesis and antithesis, of order and disorder, of seriousness and humour – as a necessary factor in the formal whole. With dualism as a tool, an ideological tension runs as the main thread in Corbusier's philosophy and production, and may actually explain what appears to be shifts or oscillations in his position. The compositional and formal whole, for any particular time and project, depended on the positioning of either mode, whether of dominance and balance. Although such a mode often subsumed the finer nuances of places, Corbusier used this strategy to confront various conditions of his architectural undertaking, whether they came from program, site or cultural settings.

For Le Corbusier, the 1920s involved a closer relationship to the peer group of the European avante-garde and its vociferous claims for modernism. This situation brought to the foreground the Acropolitan mode and a suppressing of the Istanbul sensibility, although by that time Corbusier has given tentative architectural expression to both: the Citrohan project for the Acropolitan (1922), and the Monol houses for the Constantinopolitan (1919). There was always the tendency in Le Corbusier for the surfacing of heterogeneous sensibilities in various shades, sporadically before the 1930s, as in the Mundaneum project and the projects for Algiers, and as a more reconciled thrust in the 1950s. Such tendencies make understandable some of the primary aspects of Le Corbusier's work in India.

The seeming irreconcilability of dualism in Le Corbusier led to the adoption of juxtaposition as a compositional mode to accommodate the identity of each realm. Thus, while "Frank Lloyd Wright fused, Mies neutralised, and Corbusier juxtaposed leading to a kind of tension in his ensemble. It was almost the exteriorisation of his inner ideological polarities," as von Moos observed.[2] "No doubt that some of his paintings can be understood as reflections of strong and unresolved inner tensions." Le Corbusier himself, time and again, confirmed his dualistic proclivity: "This prodigious spectacle has been produced by the interplay of two elements, one male, and one female: sun and water. Two contradictory elements that both need the other in order to exist,"[3] and again, "in the one, strong objectivity of forms, under the intense light of a Mediterranean sun: male architecture. In the other limitless subjectivity rising against a clouded sky: female architecture."[4]

Juxtapositional composition allowed Le Corbusier to appropriate and invest ideas and icons from diverse sources, even if a-historically: from Western Europe to Africa, from "high classical" to vernacular, from machine imagery to folk art, and from archaic sensibility to contemporary ideology. The original source was

Small-holder's home in Algeria, study.

[2] van Moos, *Elements of a Synthesis*.

[3] Le Corbusier, *Radiant City*.

[4] Le Corbusier, *The Modulor*.

[5] Sunand Prasad, *Le Corbusier in India, Architect of the Century* (London: Arts Council of Great Britain, 1987).

[6] Stanford Anderson, "Architectutal Design as a System of Research Programs," *Design Studies* 5, no. 3 (July 1984).

[7] Peter Serenyi, "Timeless but of its time: Le Corbusier's architecture in India," *Perspecta* 1983.

[8] Robert Venturi, *Complexity and Contradiction in Architecture* (New York: The Museum of Modern Art, 1977), p. 56, 71, 82.

[9] Uttam C. Jain, in *A+U* (May, 1970).

always transformed and 'meaning transposed' before becoming an architectural reality in the Corbusian schemata.[5] As a rule, the appropriated source was always passed through the Corbusian filter to ultimately render its origin incomprehensible. The strategies of juxtaposition also accommodated what Stanford Anderson calls the independent and continuing "architectural research programmes" of Le Corbusier.[6] The evolution of his personal typologies (construction theme, architectural promenade, and climate control) allowed fresh inspiration to and newer dimension in his consistent cores. The strategy also permitted the retaining of the identity of elements even when they were contradictory,[7] and became effective when ideological and cultural collisions came to play. Such juxtapositions also led to an ambiguity producing eventually a multiplicity of meanings, and interpretative richness.[8]

"India the Humane and Profound Civilisation"

"She is waking up... intact at a time when all is possible ... But India is hardly a brand new country: it has lived through the highest and most ancient civilisations. It has an intelligence, moral philosophy and conscience of its own."
—Le Corbusier, 1950s

Le Corbusier arrived in India in 1951 to begin his immediate responsibility–the design of Chandigarh, the new capital city for the state of Punjab and its key components. While the city plan was carried out by a team following an earlier idea by Albert Mayer, the design of the Capitol and its buildings was executed solely by Corbusier. Besides the Capitol he also designed two museums, two colleges, houses for peons, and a clubhouse. Corbusier was also invited to Ahmedabad, a city of both past and recent significance in terms of commercial, cultural and political prowess, to design the city museum, a building for the powerful mill-owners, and two villas.

Chandigarh and Ahmedabad posed two very different priorities: one was for the state on a blank terrain, but resonant with overt political, ideological and mythical tones, and the other in an existent urban milieu with more modest pressures. Chandigarh was a high representational task, while Ahmedabad involved exploring the nature of dwelling and living. Chandigarh was heroism on a national scale, while Ahmedabad involved heroism, if it did, on a smaller and personal level.

Even if Le Corbusier participated as a member of a team in laying out the master plan of the city, he has to eventually bear the responsibility of the urban prospect of Chandigarh. After all, it was his urban visions that spurred off the planning and its realizations. In India, the mood about Chandigarh the city is highly polarised. While William Curtis may claim that the axes and sectors resonate with the plan of Jaipur, it is actually the quality of openness, greenery and sunlight–as an alternative to the grubbiness of cities like Calcutta and Bombay–that many perceive as a positive alternative.[9] In claiming the city as a social and urban disaster, some people have demanded: "Leave Chandigarh alone!" Some are less concerned about the

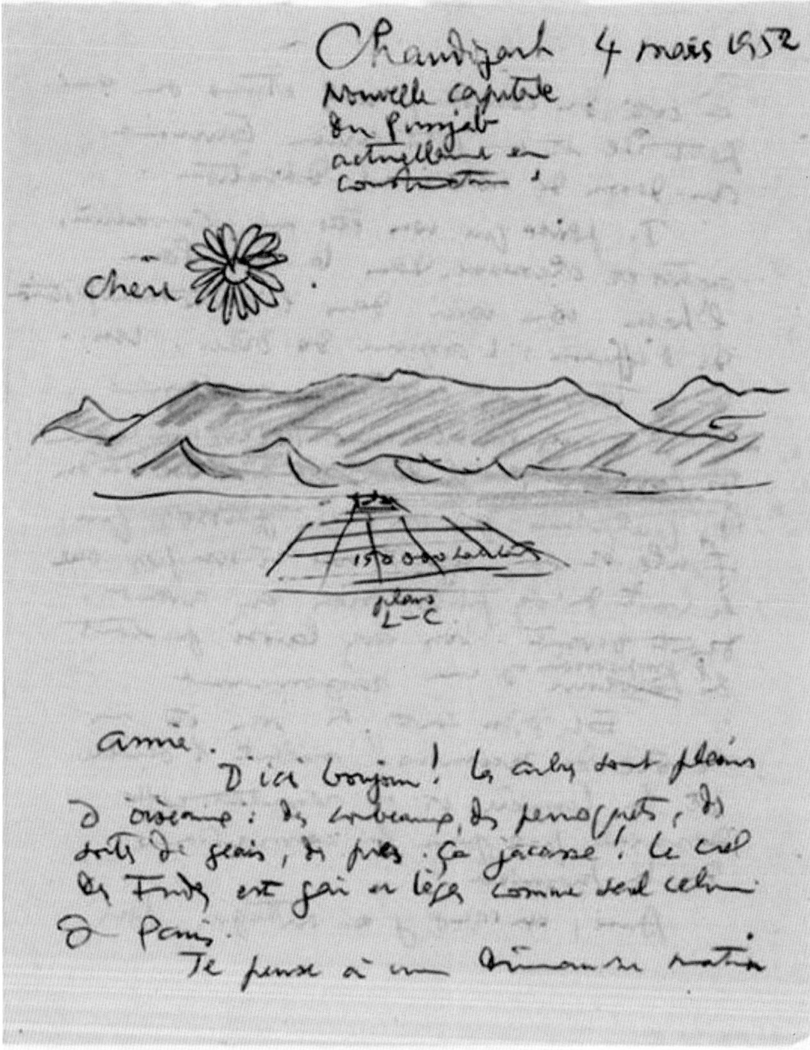

Governor's palace and site, sketch.

squabble over the appropriation of the new city as capital by the two states of Haryana and Punjab.[10]

In thinking of Chandigarh as an architectural ensemble, one is automatically drawn to the symbolic "head" of the city and the architectural tour de force: the Capitol. The compositional organisation of the Capitol had its fundamental problem – it had to be part of a city built instantly, and yet myths had to be provided, the stuff that drives all cities. Le Corbusier himself expresses the struggle: "There was anxiety and anguish in taking decisions on that vast limitless ground... The problem was no longer one of reasoning but of sensation."

The composition of the Capitol is informed by two sources: first, Corbusier's twenty-five years of research through continuous attempts in his life to give expression to the collective ethos of "the new epoch" through its various institutions: cultural, as in the case of the Mundaneum project; political, as in the League of Nations project; and, administrative and communitarian, as in St Die in France. In the Capitol at Chandigarh, functionally an administrative seat of the state, Le Corbusier brings forth the potency of all three institutions, and his typological instruments to sustain them.

Secondly, the geographical siting of the Capitol urges Corbusier to take an unprecedented strategy in constructing scale and meaning in his architecture. There, meaning is not generated by the visual and symbolic relationships of the architectural figures alone, but equally from the tension of their relationships with nature, the plains on one side, and the hills on the other. The consideration for the arrangement was more mytho-poetic than urbanistic. A convention is implied for that arrangement which is

Prasad, *Le Corbusier in India*.

[10] D. N. Dhar, *Thoughts on Architecture*

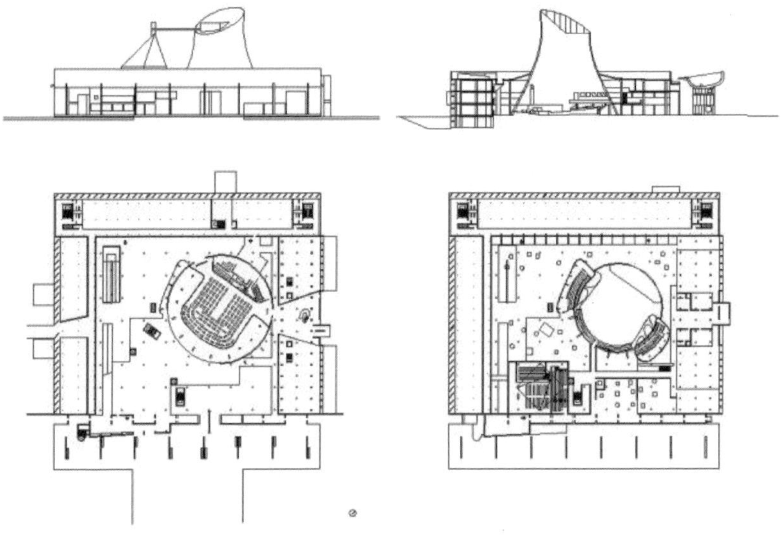

Assembly Building, plans and sections.

(Apt Books, 1987).

[11] Uttam C. Jain, in *A+U* (May, 1979).

[12] Uttam C. Jain, in A+U (May, 1979).

[13] William Curtis, "Authenticity, Abstraction and the Ancient Sense: Le Corbusier's and Louis Kahn's Ideas of Parliament," in *Perspecta*, Vol. 20 (1983).

[14] Anupam Banerji, "Conversation on Louis Kahn," in *Chetanar Patra* (Dhaka, Bangladesh, 1986).

[15] Anupam Banerji, "Learning from Bangladesh," in *The Canadian Architect* (October 1980).

[16] Le Corbusier letter to Fry, Drew,

neither Indian nor European, but totally Corbusian in the mythical engagement of a dialogue of the three colossi: the Himalayas, emblematic of nature; India, the ancient human civilization; and Le Corbusier himself, the protagonist of the new epoch.

In the Corbusian perspective, such an Olympian dialogue can only be enacted by an Acropolitan stance of the object-actors, by a deliberate over-scaling of dimensions and distances. Uttam C. Jain imagines the three main actors as Rama (the Assembly), Ravana (the Secretariat) and Sita (the High Court) in a grand staging of the epic *Ramayana*.[11] In his characteristic aplomb, Corbusier chooses to respond to the immensity, vastness, and awesomeness of man and nature: "It's precisely the presence of the term: *espace indicible* (inexpressible space). Impossible to dimension. The Himalayas are behind, the mountains, the hills, the site ...crushing. Not at all! The site united with the inexpressible, the imperceptible, and the inexplicable."

The final formation of the Capitol makes the visual drama take on an almost oppressive predominance over 'the humanisation of the space,'[12] "The vastness of the plaza has the effect of isolating the very elements of the monumental whole that it was meant to unify." (20) A connection to an Indian sensibility seems difficult except in a tangential way to the imperial-colonial ensemble at New Delhi. The allusion to Fatehpur Sikri, especially in the location of the Governor's Palace, is also tenuous;[13] the Himalayan distances at the Capitol at Chandigarh does not correspond to the subtler human dimensioning in Akbar's palace complex at Fatehpur Sikri.

In that "vast, limitless space," Le Corbusier does respond to the geo-physical sense of the place, as S. Prasad states, where "the Capitol is a highly charged place." But in the pulling apart of each institution to almost autonomous existence, giving them heroic yet 'pathetic' individuality by the great distances is a spiritual metaphor not understood in the social organisation and urban conventions of India. Ultimately a deeply Corbusian metaphor, the "pathetic soliloquy" relies completely on the expressive fragmentation of the institutions of power, an allusion that intellectually gravitates towards the heights of Athens.[14 15]

Parasols and Silhouettes

If an evocation of a sense of place becomes the struggle in the formation of the Capitol, a more architectonic means of connection with Indian culture is sought in the individual architecture. Corbusier had formulated the problem for himself: he described the architecture he wanted to create in India as "a fundamental organic architecture, unquestionable, which is neither English, nor French, nor American but Indian of the second half of the twentieth century."[16]

Like his predecessors before him, Lutyens and the hordes of British engineers and architects building in India, the first understanding of the place came through a rational interpretation of the geo-physical sense of place: the land, the climate, and the human condition. Although, in many instances, Le

Palace of Assembly, Chandigarh, from Wikimedia.

Corbusier admires the climatic innovation of the English people in India, he finds the rational simplicity of the undertaking an illusion in contemporary times: "An architect must adapt to the antagonistic requirements. Comfort is coolness. It is the current of air, it is the shade, and yet the sun must penetrate at the proper time, in the favourable seasons. The conditions of the problem are constantly dictated by a constant merciless sun with the state of temperature, humidity and dryness varying from one month to another – all contradictory factors. To play the role of a modem architect under these conditions is not easy."

Confronting the climatic conditions of hot-tropical regions was not new to Corbusier. In his long and inspirational relationship with North Africa, he had already developed the fundamental notions of control, and "invented" their architectural-typological counterpart: the brise-soleil and the roof as an umbrella. From a tentative expression as in Villa Bezeau in Carthage, Tunisia (1928), the brise-soleil becomes a highly articulated "element poetique" in the office tower for Algiers (1939-1942). The separation of the roof from the more used volume of the building also dates as early as 1928 in the first sketch for Villa Bezeau, and 1939 in the pavilion at the exposition at Liege where the consideration was purely plastic.[17]

Corbusier thus is already equipped in his personal typological cache to work with climate control in India. His association

quoted by S. Prasad.

Monument to the Open Hand, sketch.

Sketches of India.

with Maxwell Fry, who more than anyone else was concerned with the tropical conditions of creating architecture, facilitates that.[18] Corbusier fully exploits his two types in the formulation of his architecture in India: the brise-soleil for the vertical surface, and the parasol for the roof, in a unique "Indo-Corbusian" configuration. But the final significance of these types is not in their role as climatic instruments but as symbolic 'coding devices' in the hands of Corbusier.[19]

According to both Serenyi and Curtis, the notion of parasol came about probably after Corbusier's encounter with Mughal structures. The parasol as *chattri* (umbrella) had also a symbolic significance in earlier Buddhist architecture and ideology, attributing to them a mythic, cosmological content. Perceiving this significance quickly, Corbusier used the parasol as a constant coding device by exploiting the climate control gesture to stage a greater monumental drama.

There is then a fundamental and crucial difference between him and his English predecessors. While the English adapted imported European form to Indian climate, Le Corbusier invented Corbusian form out of Indian conditions. The response to climate 'transcended its utilitarian roots,'[20] and became an instrument of 'sculptural dramatization' and symbolic codification. Such poeticization did not help the fact that the preliminary necessity of climate control, more than often, failed to be delivered – the brise-soleil not only got heated up, but it in turn heated up the interior spaces it was supposed to protect.[21]

In the Assembly, the parasol becomes a signal for an entrance vestibule. On the roof of the High Court, the parasol monumentalises the otherwise simple, cubic building. For the Secretariat Building, the parasol becomes a signal for a special place for the governor's balcony. On top of the unbuilt Governor's Palace and the Mill-owners' Building, the parasol takes on a pure symbolic function in replacing the traditional dome as a communicative element in important public edifices. The

Villa Baizeau, Carthage, sketch, 1928.

[17] von Moos, *Elements of a Synthesis*.

[18] Maxwell Fry, "Le Corbusier at Chandigarh," in *The Open Hand*.

[19] Kenneth Frampton, *A Critical History of Modern Architecture* (London: Thames and Hudson, 1980), pp. 229-30.

[20] von Moos, *Elements, and Prasad, Le Corbusier in India*.

[21] Charles Correa, "Chandigarh: The View from Benares," in *Le Corbusier*, ed. by H. Allen Brooks, (Princeton: Princeton University Press, 1987).

[22] Alexander Gorlin, An Analysis of the Governor's Palace of Chandigarh, in *Oppositions* 19/20 (1980).

[23] Balkrishna V. Doshi, interview in TFC, date unknown.

[24] Le Corbusier, *Journey to the East*.

[25] William Curtis, "Authenticity, Abstraction and the Ancient Sense: Le Corbusier's and Louis Kahn's Ideas of Parliament," in *Perspecta*, Vol. 20 (1983).

[26] P. Serenyi, *Timeless*, S. Prasad, *Le Corbusier in India*, and W. Curtis, *Authenticity*.

physical shape may have been abstracted from the horn of the ubiquitous, sacred cow,[22] but the generative signal is certainly that of a dome. In the Shodhan House, the parasol is at its purest in functioning as a genuine *chattri*.

In discussing the "Indianness" of Corbusier's architecture, Balkrishna Doshi says: "The silhouettes, the skylines are Indian, the transparency is Indian. I am not talking about the sun breakers and all that, they are part of India, because you find verandahs, jalis and porches there. But his architecture, if you look at the Assembly or the High Court, and you look at those walls, you find that they are really the negative of the positive space. If you did not have the umbrella – the parasol which he put on top – of you remove that and you really imagine the transparent was really the dome, you find again another sort of skyline. It is almost as if you saw the building in black and white, reversed."[23]

Besides its symbolic justification, the parasol also serves a highly intense plastic role in the construction of silhouette in individual buildings and in the holistic composition of the Capitol. Corbusier wrote in Istanbul. "The walls of Byzantium, the mosque of Sultan Ahmed, Saint Sofia, the Grand Seraglio. Come, you town builders, note it down in your files: 'Silhouettes!!'" [24]

The lesson of the silhouette – the way human artefacts touched the sky – had remained registered in Corbusier's mind since his trip to Istanbul, and now in India, in the world of *chattris* and domes, he finds an analogous condition. In most buildings in India, the pristine geometric volumes and the undulating shapes crowning them bring forth perceptions gathered at the Parthenon and Istanbul.

The articulation of the silhouette is a part of a series of metaphorical gestures Corbusier makes to touch many levels of simultaneous readings. In almost all the buildings within the taut grid of modern rationality, Corbusier intersperses a number of disparate allusions; often, they are submerged together to render their identity and source ambiguous. Is the gigantic device on the High Court a monumentalisation of the Mughal parasol, or the image of a domical building in reverse (as Doshi notes)? Is the U-curve at the apex of the Governor's Palace (a device unseen in Corbusier's typology) the emblem of a dome, the diagram of a cosmological significance, or in the extension of the wheel motif "a metaphor for the long traditions and slowly evolving technologies of India?"[25]

In the Capitol, the Governor's Palace and the Assembly are the two most symbolically charged loci, both in their locational potency and plentiful metaphorical gestures. Besides its rooftop metaphors, the Governor's Palace has been associated, on the one hand, with the composition of Lutyens' Rashtrapati Bhavan, and on the other hand, with Akbar's Diwan-i-Khas at Fatehpur Sikri.[26] Beyond this associational polarity it is the layout of the garden of the palace that seemed to have the most unequivocal relation with an Indian tradition.[27] "...the way it (the Palace) takes possession of its territory and the way this territory is ordered must be his only indisputable debt to the Indian high architectural traditions." Here, Corbusier not only makes a direct correlation with Mughal gardens (he had visited and studied the Pinjore gardens near Chandigarh) but also outlines for the first time a more committed attitude towards the composition of the landscape as against his earlier ambiguous notion of mediating on nature.[28] It is clear that India prompted this definitive attitude.

A classic case of formal and metaphorical assemblage, the Assembly is a simple cuboid in which the sculptural parasol is contrasted with the hyperboloid and pyramidal volumes on the roof. The compacted relationship is more vivid in the interior where the regularity of the straight columns distinctively confronts the voluminous and curved envelope of the Assembly Hall.

In the operation of metaphors, almost all the signalling devices work at a number of levels. In a monumental way, the parasol indicates the entry as a semi-shelter before proceeding into the womb of the building. An allusion to the entry portico of a classically based building is not unfounded. Diagrammatically, the Assembly has a number of affinities with neo-Classical honorific building models, especially in British India. The parasol for the portico, the procession to the climax of the composition – linear and centralised in the classical model but deliberately asymmetric and displaced in the Assembly – and, finally, the climactic space itself, consciously dramatic and overtly expressive, with the dome for older models and the hyperboloid for the Assembly. In this sense, the Assembly does strike a kinship with Schinkel's Altes Museum in Berlin or Lutyens' Rashtrapati Bhaban in Delhi, both belonging to the same genealogy.

Despite relying on an Eurocentric tradition of composing honorific buildings, what Le Corbusier does in order to depart from the association is a deliberate distortion and displacement of the conventional sense, and the simultaneous overlaying of other diverse references.

In the Assembly, for example, the centrality is only allusive. The main Assembly Hall is not only physically displaced from the center of the overall plan but is set into a tension by the secondary hall housed under the pyramid. While the pyramidal shape implies an archaic/universal sensibility serving an honorific function, the hyperboloid shape from an industrial imagery is adopted by Corbusier to consciously subvert the convention of domes. With this semantic contortion he seems to be making two comments on contemporary conditions: the slipping into memory of recent institutions (Lutyens' Delhi), and the coming of a New Age (Nehru and industrialisation).

The psychological drama created in the interior of the Assembly Hall is probably derived from diverse sources: from the ocular in the Pantheon to the cosmological meaning of Jantar Mantar. In the fervour of modernity as generated by the new nation-state, Le Corbusier shifts from the dominant horizontal ideology of the twentieth century to a vertical one that seems to pander to a perceived mythic and cosmic content of Indian society.

[27] S. Prasad, *Le Corbusier in India*.

[28] Caroline Constant, "From the Virgilian Dream to Chandigarh," *The Architectural Review*, 1079 (1987).

[29] P. Serenyi, *Timeless*.

Villas in Ahmedabad

The two villas in Ahmedabad are significant Corbusian production because of two reasons: firstly, absolved from the overt symbolism and political overtones of the state project, the villas sited in existing milieu deal directly into the living conditions and traditions of India; secondly, both the villas are direct outcome of Corbusier's architectural pre-history, and by the nature of the transformation and displacement which they undergo, reveal in a more decipherable way his understanding and admission of the new cultural conditions he faces in India. Also, the simultaneous design and construction of two architecturally diverse villas, Shodhan House and Sarabhai House, bring forth more acutely the ideological polarity, and at the same time an approach to a reconcilement.

A partial archaeology of Shodhan House links it immediately with Corbusian houses of the 1920s, all rooted in the Citrohan/Parthenon mode, and all dominant gestures on the landscape in a contradistinction with nature. But although we may find in Shodhan House a shadow of Villa Savoye, Corbusier makes a number of important reassessment there that could be construed as shifts.

Unlike the Citrohan type which is raised on stilts (in deference to the famous five points), Shodhan House grows directly from the ground thus "imbuing it with a sense of rootedness,"[29] and actually beginning a conversation with the landscape. By establishing a closer relationship with nature and site ("a pact with nature"), Corbusier not only reverts his ambiguous conception of nature, but attempts to tap a earth-hugging sensibility, which he does more unequivocally with the Sarabhai House. Secondly, unlike his earlier work like Villa Savoye, where the spatial and organisational complexity is camouflaged behind a comparatively restrained exterior, Shodhan House makes explicit its internal tension and complexity, thus attaining a richer and more animated expression, and as a whole, a more dynamic sculptural mass. Animation on the exterior is another strategic shift that Corbusier makes fully after the War, although it goes back as far as his projects for Algiers. This is seen in the Unite d'Habitation, and more elaborately in his buildings in India. Accentuating this aspect was also the reversal from the machine imagery to a more rustic expression in the materials and construction. However, in the Shodhan House, it is the brazen animation, busy and diverse as a bazaar under a sheltering umbrella, the various brise-soleil and complex organisation of the terraces, which creates a distinct identity.

If Shodhan House ultimately seems unmediated as it 'does not sit easily in the genteel unostentatiousness of its social context,'[30] it is Sarabhai House that comes closest to being the most Indian of Corbusier's Indian projects. The distinctiveness of this project with its other Indian counterparts is a lack of deliberate virility, and its greater coherence with the context and place.

Sited in a wooded estate in the city, the Sarabhai House was designed for a widow with two sons, all members of a prominent

Ahmedabad family. The basic components of the house are its sprawling form, the parallel load-bearing walls, and the Catalan vault ceiling. What was tentative in Shodhan House, in terms of 'a pact with nature,' becomes thorough and unequivocal in Sarabhai House. The earth-hugging forms, the undulating ceiling, and a closer agreement with nature link this work to the Weekend House of the 1920s which again is a descendent of the Monol model and an architectural formulation of the Istanbul sensibility. At Sarabhai House, Corbusier does not excavate his own architectural prehistory out of caprice but out of poetic deference to site and programmatic demands.

Villa Shodhan South-West Facade.
Photo: Lucien Hervé, Public Domainse, 1958.

From the Indian perspective, the Sarabhai House evokes the nature of a dwelling in multiple manners. Its exterior nondescriptness and comfortable co-existence with nature prepare the primary ground rule for the abstract Indian house-type. The interior spatial organisation of Sarabhai is its tour de force. While by replicating the spatial drama of Ville Savoye, Shodhan House introduces a radical space-type in the Indian scene, the spatial quality of Sarabhai prods a spatial-psychological need in the Indian context. In most Indian dwellings (except those in the desert region), interior space is never completely contained; it spills out and almost overflows to the "outside" whether it is nature or an urban public realm. There is the mediating space between the outer and inner domains, a spatial screen for filtering not only sun and rain, but also activities and territories. This is the element that gives houses in the sub-continent the traditional "sheltered openness."[31] This sheltered porosity as a mediative space, the spatial directionality and the categorical 'pact with nature' become the distinctive qualities of Sarabhai House. With those qualities, the Sarabhai House not only stands apart from the Maison Monol and Maison Jaoul precedence, but also finds a place in the Indian situation.

Shodhan House, plan.

India and Le Corbusier: The Open Hand

"When we talk of Indian art it indicates some truth based upon the Indian tradition and temperament. At the same time we must know that there is no such thing as absolute caste restriction in human cultures; they ever have the power to combine and produce new variations, and such combinations have been going on for ages proving the truth of the deep unity of human psychology."
-Rabindranath Tagore, *The Meaning of Art*

"India was lucky to get Le Corbusier; Le Corbusier, too, was lucky to get India."
-Charles Correa, "Chandigarh: The View from Benares"[32]

Le Corbusier's interjection in India raises many questions, but none of them can be sufficiently reduced to asking what is "Indian" about his work? The problem of framing such a question has its roots not merely in the dominance of European culture and in its colonial extensions, and the subsequent dilemma of identity, but substantially in the repeated overlaying on the Indian slate of the categorized ideals of Hinduism, Buddhism and Islam. This question was probably not asked in a premodern period as it is a fundamentally contemporary problem with more recent

Sarabhai House, plan.

implications. As K.T. Ravindran notes: "The problem with seeking a national or regional diversity is that such efforts are basically reactionary in spirit. Historically, they have been an important cultural manifestation of fascism."[33]

When Le Corbusier built for India, one could ask: which (or what) India was this? In the 1950s, in the post-colonial euphoria, it was the India of Nehru, poised implacably towards a vision he truly believed in: development through industrialisation, knowledge through science, and modernity through international fraternalization. Thrust into that visionary moment, Corbusier conveniently "delivered."

In the projects at Chandigarh and Ahmedabad, Corbusier's architectural roots are diverse; they are vastly Mediterranean, and some Indian. The final synthesis is undeniably Corbusian, completing and continuing more of his own history than that of India or Europe. India was historically ruptured and ideologically fragmented to assert an all-Indian production, much less from somebody alien to the culture. India extended another strata to Corbusier borne out of a distinct alchemical reaction with her. For India, even with the subsiding of the euphoria, it was the beginning of a new strata, as historically radical, and yet planted in its soil, as its new social and democratic institutions which spurred the architectural episode in the beginning. Despite the built-in barrier of cross-cultural operations, Le Corbusier in India "acted as a decisive catalyst, triggering off our nascent sense of architectonic form and syntax."[34] And, as probably evident in different instances in the trajectory of this paper, India brought a metamorphosis in Le Corbusier too, urging him to reorganise the strategy of his 'patient search' and engage in new dialogues. The spirit of 'with a full hand I receive, and with a full hand I give' could not have been said more conclusively for *both* as in the monument of the Open Hand – a true metaphor of osmosis.

[30] S. Prasad, *Le Corbusier in India*.

[31] P. Serenyi, *Timeless*.

[32] H Allen Brooks (ed.), *Le Corbusier* (New York: Garland, 1987).

[33] K.T. Ravindran, "Architecture and Identity," in Rewal, R. (ed.) *Architecture in India* (Paris: Electa Moniteur, 1985).

[34] Charles Correa, *Vistara: The Architecture of India* (The Festival of India, 1986).

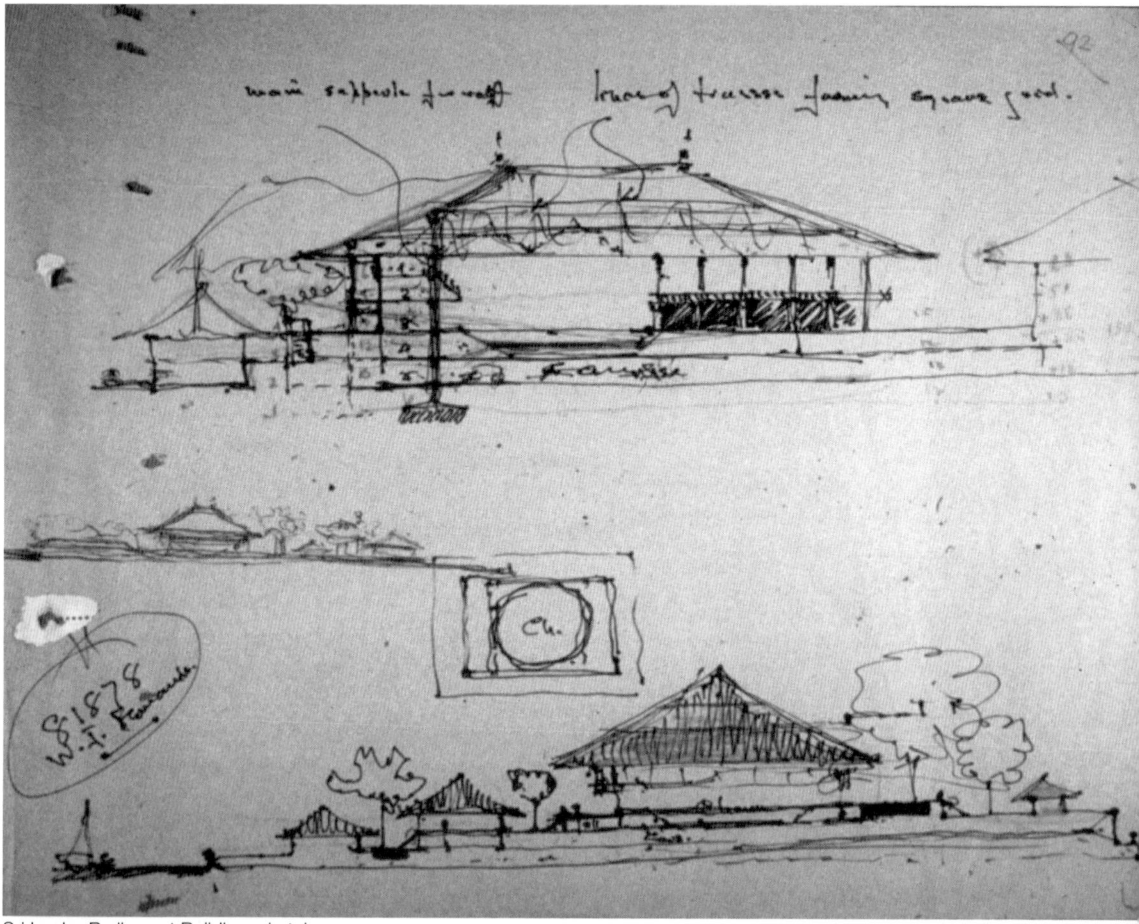

Sri Lanka Parliament Building, sketch.

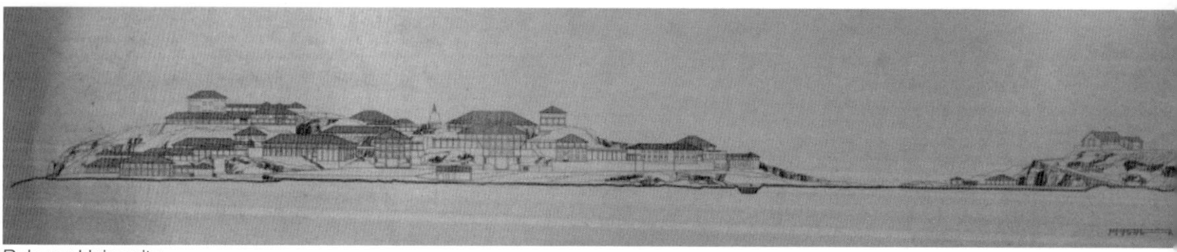

Ruhunu University.

Geoffrey Bawa: An Alternative Architecture

Published in MIT student newspaper, 1988.

The prominence of Geoffrey Bawa coincides with the collapse of the modernist worldview in global architecture. Although Bawa has been building consistently since the 1960s, mostly in his native country Sri Lanka, it is only in the last few years that his work is being highlighted internationally with a special appreciation and enthusiasm. Cutting through the labels of vernacularism and back-to-the-past, Bawa's work presents a cogent alternative in in the post-modern debacle.

In countries like Sri Lanka, the struggle for an architecture alternative is not an easy one considering how traditional cultures there have succumbed to the various manifestations of Euro-American influence. As in many Asian cultures, the situation in Sri Lanka is critical, where paradoxically, the past lives into the present, "as a woman drapes her sari," as Charles Correa is to say, and yet the question of an architecture of the place remains suspect.

A kind of schizophrenia still persists in most countries of the so-called non-Western world, especially those with a colonial experience. A rich legacy of diverse but deeply rooted practices confronted with imported ideas and ideals, multiple layers of often contradictory realities, and lures of the technological miracle mark the contemporary scene in places like Sri Lanka. All these make the production of a decent situational architecture even more complex and demanding.

Geoffrey Bawa is certainly a foremost sage in resolving some of the contradictions, and actually synthesizing a new architectural order of a place. Bawa's achievement not only highlights a seminal contribution in shaping contemporary Sri Lankan architecture but also inspiring other cultures undergoing a similar metamorphosis.

Born in a well-placed Sri Lankan family with diverse affiliations, Bawa was first trained as a lawyer in England. His passion, however, got reoriented from the manipulation of human beings to rearranging the landscape and the environment. Two years later, at a late age of thirty-six, it was that passion that took him to the Architectural Association School in London. Bawa's maturity and developed cultural notions may have prevented him

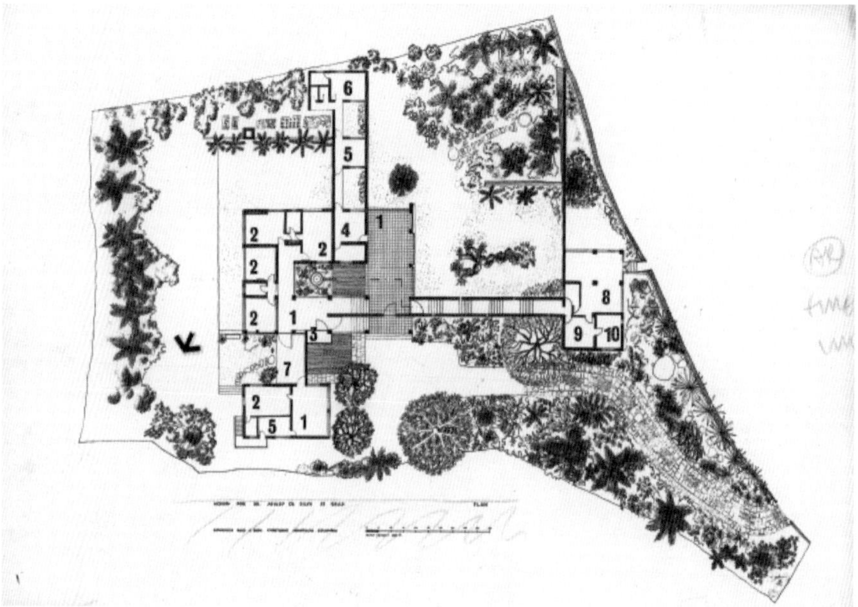

ASH de Silva house, plan.

Ena de Silva house, section.

from being totally absorbed in modern currents of architecture but that did not stop him from learning from various cultures in his wide travels.

As Bawa himself says, "All the time I was absorbing – like a piece of blotting paper... medieval hill-towns... their splendid instinctive massing of buildings which, often totally varied in purpose and age, making a magnificent total picture; great English country houses and their essential compliment of park and garden: Greek, Roman, Mexican and Buddhist ruins, the Alhambra in Granada, the chapel in Ronchamp, the Mogul forts in Rajasthan and the marvellous palace of Padmadbabapuram built in the 18th century by the Maharajah of Travancore [S India]."

Sri Lanka's critical geopolitical position made it an ideal crosscurrent of cultures. Since the flourishing of Buddhism 2500 years ago, the shores of Sri Lanka have been trodden by such diverse peoples as Arabs, Chinese, Tamils, Dutch, Portuguese, and the English. Geoffrey Bawa is an embodiment of that cultural potpourri.

Bawa acknowledged the deep infiltration of various cultural idioms in Sri Lankan traditions, including colonial ones as long as they served a sincere architectural purpose. Adding those to his lessons from other cultures, he attempted to synthesize something like a new Sri Lankan expression. How does Bawa arrive at this juncture? On what aspect does his architecture pivot?

The most important clue to understanding Bawa's work is the lyrical, yet powerful, dialogue it establishes with nature and "history." "A house is a garden, and even more. It is almost nature itself," as Bawa claims. Brian Brace Taylor notes. "Rarely do his designs allow the architecture to preempt the primordial importance of the natural surroundings, either by their scale, use of materials or sitting."

The beauty and power of the Sri Lankan landscape are extraordinary. The pallet of the intense green vegetation, the palm trees and the beach, the terraced paddies and mountains, and the monsoonal landscape appear to be so strongly composed

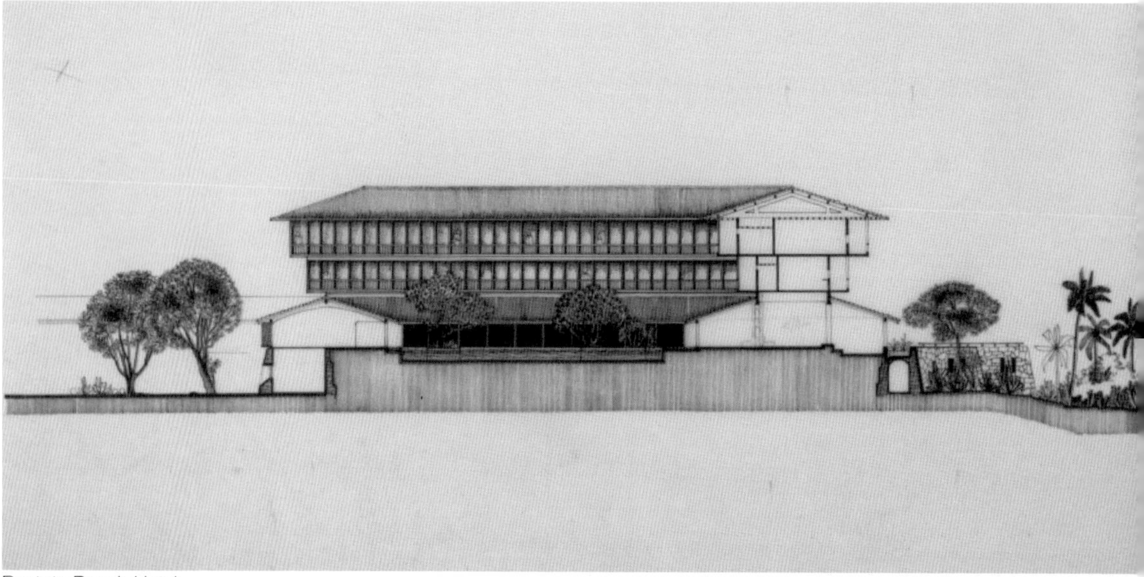

Bentota Beach Hotel.

as to preclude any human intrusion. In that overwhelming natural ambiance, the appropriate architectural answer is the most direct and simple one, almost devoid of any overt theory, deliberate irony or contrived posture. Bawa's intervention in such a precious landscape attempts to, and succeeds in, doing just that. He attains an ensemble that is as composed, sensuous and balanced as the landscape itself. By being sensitive to the natural ambiance, and citing and improving on the traditional and age-old responses to it, Bawa establishes a rapport simultaneously with nature and history.

A preoccupation with nature actually began prior to Bawa's architectural education, in the early 1950s, in the poetic rearrangement of that marvellous garden at Lunuganga. A more developed architectural language is found in his Ena de Silva house (1962), through an original version of a classic colonnaded, courtyard house, with tiled roofs and shaded courtyards. By transporting a well-known form into a new context, Bawa elevates it from neglect and decay to an imitable position. This becomes a persistent theme in all later designs, gaining more sophistication and refinement in his sensitive hands. It is probably due to Bawa's successful evocative versions of this neglected form that Sri Lankans are now more willing to favor this form over the banal boxes, the fictitious symbol of progress.

This significant shift may somewhat offset criticism of the extravagant and sensuous, and non-urban, disposition of most of Bawa's work, such as the Bentota Beach Hotel (1969), the Serendib Hotel (1969), the Triton Hotel in Ahungalla, and

many high-end residences. Even in more practical buildings on a low budget, such as the St. Bridget's Montessori School (1964), the farm school in Hanwella (1966), and the Piliyandala Adult Education Center (1981), Bawa achieves heightened architectural experiences and displays his versatility in dealing with details. In large-scale projects, he incorporates the building's functional purpose in realizing compelling and original architectural expressions in a tandem with the landscape, as in the University of Ruhunu in Matara (1980), and the new Parliament buildings at Kotte (1981).

Another feature of Bawa's work is on-site design, that is, how design decisions are made after the initial drawings based on his first-hand encounter with the site, rather than the detached and abstracted situation on the drawing board. This is particularly effective in bringing the forces of the proposed and the existing landscape together, and in composing richness and delight in the Bawa ensemble.

The work of Geoffrey Bawa thus demands to be looked at more intensively. Deep in the heart of Bawa's creation is the germ of a profound and projective architecture. It will be limiting to see merely the picturesque in his work or an anti-urban temperament. In this time of search for relevance and meaningfulness in one's own architecture, following the period of blind imitation of the west, Bawa's work brings back a resurgence of cultural productions. By rediscovering the virtues of the age-old ways of building, and interrupting progress and modernity, Bawa's work has shown a cogent alternative to the gross caricatures we often see today.

Street view of Mumbai. Photo: Ashraf.

Reincarnations: Modernity and Modern Architecture in South Asia

Published in *Constructing New Worlds*, Proceedings of the Association of Collegiate Schools of Architecture International Conference at Rio de Janeiro, 1998. Originally published in *An Architecture of Independence: The Making of Modern South Asia*, ed Kazi K Ashraf and James Belluardo (The Architectural League of New York and Princeton Architectural Press, 1997).

India's tryst with modernity has been a complex one. While architectural modernism might have begun in the Indian subcontinent in the late 1940s, the roots of modernity are much older. Although modernity is intimately tied to the colonial experience, there is a fundamental difference between the two. While colonialism flourished on maintaining a categoric difference between the East and the West, modernism was articulated about an ideal of blurring boundaries, and creating a universal civilization and history. The galvanizing call was for the commonality of the human tribes, a single trajectory for mankind.

But the fundamental character of modernism, its monolithic nature and its premise that a single international mode is not only possible but imperative, turned out to be its biggest enigma. Scepticism would emerge around the function of flattening those cultural topographies that bestowed identity and character. Paul Ricouer saw this project as a subtle destruction of the "creative nucleus of great cultures." Other interpretations would indicate a dubious relationship between modernity and globalization, and between the enchanting image of a universal civilization and the ominous reality of a single global economy.

There is a further complexity about the east-west conundrum. In the transaction between the two, it is not quite clear what transpires: who sees, who lends, and who borrows. When Edmund Husserl, the leading German philosopher, announced sometime in the late 1930s the historical inevitability of "the Europeanization of all foreign parts of mankind," he was restating an earlier perception: that Europe alone can provide other traditions with a universal framework of meaning and understanding, and the context and the categories for the exploration of all traditions of thought. These other traditions, Husserl pronounced, will have to Europeanize themselves, whereas "we, if we understand ourselves properly, will never, for example, Indianize ourselves."

Is the Europeanization of the planet the true telos of mankind? Wilhelm Halbfass, who introduced this poignant discussion in *India and Europe* (1988), thinks that in fact Europe itself has been superseded and left behind by the modern Westernized world; as he puts it, it is not the master and protagonist of the process of Europeanization anymore. Curiously, European culture has remained restrictive, seeing the world only through its own eyes and denying other possibilities, while the "others" appear to be in a more dynamic situation, where seeing the world is not exhausted by European categories.

In recent studies, Ashis Nandy brings up this critical theme observing that the West does not incorporate India in its battleground, whereas "in the East the battle has involved the West ... India has tried to capture the differentia of the West within its own cultural domain, not merely on the basis of a view of the West as politically intrusive or as culturally inferior, but as a subculture, meaningful in itself and important, though not all-important, in the Indian context."

The noted Indian thinker Jarava Lal Mehta responded earlier to the notion of the "Europeanization of the Earth" by accepting the challenge of "belonging, irretrievably and inescapably to this 'one world'," to the global presence of Western science and technology. He insisted that "there is no other way open, to us in the East, but to go along with this Europeanization and to go through it. Only through this voyage into the foreign and the strange can we win back our own self-hood; here as elsewhere, the way to do what is closest to us is the longest way back."

An Indian Modernity

Raja Rammohun Roy (1772-1833) inaugurated the journey into the foreign that would lead to the idea of selfhood – the basis of the "modern project" in India. Learning from Arab philosophy, Unitarianism and Vedic scriptures, Rammohun, in his various writings and reformist enterprises, unambiguously proposed the primacy of rationality and inquiry over habitual slavishness, and opened a modern quest of the self through the world of reason and comparison. Although his teachings influenced contending groups, it nonetheless became the basis of establishing a humanist worldview and rational dimension to modern India, Rammohun Roy's immediate influence was on the major movement that came to be known as the "Bengal Renaissance." Although generated by an elite class in Calcutta, the movement encompassed a whole array of creative activities in the social and religious realm, in literature, theater and art, that began in the mid-nineteenth century and continued into the first half of this one. Bankim Chandra Chaterji, RabindranathTagore, Aurobindo Ghosh, Ananda Coomaraswamy, Abanindranath Tagore, Nandalal Bose, Stella Kramrisch, and later Satyajit Ray, in one way or another, belonged to this movement. The Bengal Renaissance did not prescribe a single coherent objective; in fact, there was much ideological conflicts among various groups. But by the turn of the century, however, a modern ideal was strongly propounded through a diverse set of concepts and aspirations: from rationalism and scientific objectivity to liberal humanism and internationalism, and from Upanisadic spiritualism and Vedic metaphysics to Indian nationalism and social realism.

The movement, in essence, was a complex dynamic of acceptance and resistance. Indian intellectuals resisted both the

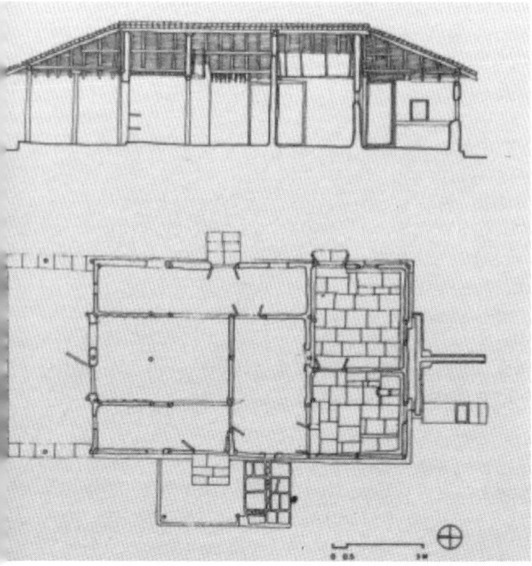

Gandhi's House in Wardha, Central India.

trauma of colonialism and the tyranny of tradition. It involved a rejection of the alien intruder/dominator who is however to be imitated and surpassed by his own standards, and a disavowal of certain ancestral ways that did not conform to newer notions of humanism. Simultaneously, acceptance involved embracing, from a global repository, anything that assured a new degree of social and intellectual liberation. It also involved an inward journey, a rediscovery of the "self," a conscious archaeological excavation of one's own assumed cultural strata in order to find a mooring in the turmoil engendered by colonialism.

This inward journey, the awareness and understanding of "self," was however double-edged. While it was a moment of self-discovery, it was also a moment of distancing oneself from the familiar and the habitual. Self-discovery presupposed a sense of alienation and remoteness from tradition, as Jarava Lal Mehta remarked; it does not happen so long as "we unreflectively live under its domination, or fail to see the novel present as it actually is and claims It is from this condition, where tradition is no longer available unreflectively, that the idea of cultural identity, be it national or architectural, ultimately emerges."

The Swadeshi Ideology

Art was one of the earliest sites of the fabrication of a modern Indian identity. Engendered by the movement around the Partition of Bengal, the rise of Swadeshi (pro-indigenous) ideology would generate a strong feeling for the idea of a nation, and in turn create a search for "national" elements in literature, music, theater, and above all in the realm of art and painting. It was through the ideas and activities of E.B. Havell, the famous educator at the Calcutta Art School, and the paintings of Abanindranath Tagore, that art became a site for nationalist discourse. Abanindranath's work was projected as the rediscovery of the aesthetic ideal of India. The implication was broader; it was no less than the political project of national rediscovery. Through the Havell-Abanindranath discourse, art – Indian art as well as Indian ethos – came to be regarded as "essentially idealistic, mystic, symbolic and transcendental."

The longing for a spiritualized Indian art was, however, sharply criticized from various directions: from the historian Akshay Maitreya, who commented that one does not produce Indian painting just by painting in India, to Benoy Sarkar who, writing from Paris in 1922, extolled the necessity if not the inevitability of a "truly International modem style of art." It was also argued that, in their attempt to confront the colonizer, the Swadeshi traditionalists took refuge in a fabricated pre-colonial past, never questioning which or whose past was being recovered, whose past suppressed. This invariably led to eulogizing "a pre-capitalist social order" while ignoring "the grim realities of a people striving under sub-human conditions."

Rabindranath Tagore, the poet-philosopher, also moved away from the agitational ideology of Swadeshism to seek more "universal" values. Although, he appears disengaged from social realities, and actually comes close to the idea of the spiritual-artistic figure, he remained sharply critical of what he saw as a contrived Indian art. "When in the name of Indian art," Tagore wrote, "we cultivate with a deliberate aggressiveness a certain bigotry born of habit of a past generation, we smother our souls under idiosyncrasies unearthed from buried centuries. I strongly urge our artists vehemently to deny their obligation carefully to produce something that can be labelled Indian Art according to some old world mannerism." Tagore was quite categorical about the universality of human creativity, in "the truth of the deep unity of human psychology" which would urge the breaking down of caste restriction in human cultures and the capacity to combine and produce new variations.

All these would mean a sharp criticism of Swadeshi ideology. What appeared to be a return to an Indian ethos could also be contested as a selective and exclusive cultural formulation. In the end, it seemed that Swadeshism was tragically Janus-faced: It formed a virile articulation of the nation and was the first aggressive intellectual search for independent genres, but, ironically, it also consolidated the religious divide and the partition process.

An Indian Architecture

The project of aesthetic and national recovery also laid claim to the idea of an Indian architecture. Predominantly practised and professed by English architects until Independence, architecture was either in the romantic-domestic or the archaeological-monumental mode. The architect Claude Batley in Bombay and the art educator Havell in Calcutta were instrumental in the early part of this century in installing different ideas of tradition in education and practice.

Batley's research into the domestic tradition served as a basis for a projected resurgence of an Indian architecture. Otherwise, tradition was primarily defined in the stylistic synthesis known as Anglo-Indian. Although there was some illuminating work, it was confined to palace architecture. Edwin Lutyens' capitol at Delhi (completed in 1930), remains the most monumental example of this synthetic creation.

A deeper approach was taken by the Austrian-born art historian and theorist Stella Kramrisch. While she introduced modern European art and art theories into the Calcutta circle, Kramrisch made the strongest theoretical interpretation of India's ancient sastric architecture. In her magnum opus, *The Hindu Temple* (1946), she argued for a metaphysical substratum to India's sacred architecture that integrated architectural form, sculptural iconography, symbolic image, myth and metaphysical conceptions, which she substantiated through interpretations of texts, rituals and architectural form. She was one of the earliest interpreters of the mandala, seeing in it simultaneously a ritual diagram, a cosmic model, and the basis of temple construction. This was a very different approach to Indian architecture from the earlier descriptive archaeological methods of James Fergusson, Percy Brown, and John Marshall, and even the romantic model of Batley.

Chaman Lall, Mubarak Mahal, Jainpur, 1900.

Claude Bately, Lalbhai Residence, Mumbai, 1941.

Meanwhile, both Mahatma Gandhi and Rabindranath Tagore made reference to building as part of their larger philosophical and social vision. Gandhi's consciously simple buildings, particularly his house built in the ashram at Wardha in Central India, embodied his ideology of self-reliance and indigenous craft and ecological principles. Tagore's "academic village" in Santiniketan was an architectural manifestation of his poetic ideal of harmony with nature. Although laden with moral and ethical lessons, both ideas remained more or less marginalized from the chaotic, vital social conditions of the 1930s and 40s, and from the enthusiastic orientation of an increasingly powerful group towards building a modern industrial state.

A Modern Vision

It was Jawaharlal Nehru, the first prime minister of independent India, who would articulate the spirit of the time, and define a brave new world unfettered by tradition and medievalism. Although Nehru would attempt to describe the "spirit" of India as it had persisted over thousands of years, he would declare that "India must break with much of her past and not allow it to dominate the present. Our lives are encumbered with the dead wood of this past; all that is dead and has served its purpose has to go." In close proximity to the rational dimension of the Bengal Renaissance, Nehru would pledge his allegiance to what he would see as the two ideals of his age, humanism and the scientific spirit. The orientation unmistakably was towards a secular and democratic order combined with an industrial and scientific spirit. The heroic optimism of the 1950s was concretized in architectural terms by Le Corbusier in Chandigarh (1951-1965), the capitol of the Punjab.

In post-Independence India, and in almost all South Asian nations, the name Chandigarh reverberated, despite the controversy it created, as the most powerful Asian version of the modernist vision. In Islamabad, Pakistan also built its future-oriented alternative. Although both Chandigarh and Islamabad originated in the traumatic history of Partition, both remained for a while shining models of a new urban and architectural possibility. The state endorsement of architectural modernism was rooted not only in industrial technology and the new trans-geographic realities, but also in the notions of universal history and free society.

Modernism was then seen not just as an aesthetical device, but as part of an ethical, visionary and conceptual approach to confronting social realities and dealing with the deprivation and discord of humanity in general. By the end of the 1950s, architectural modernism seemed quite established in South Asia, dramatically changing the landscape of the region. The proponents of modernist ideas were making their mark everywhere, from Delhi, Ahmedabad, and Bombay to Dhaka, Karachi and Colombo. Since the 1930s various modernist architectural and urban models were being proposed for South Asia, from the early Pondicherry Ashram by Antonin Raymond (1938) to the intervention of numerous foreign architects, including Otto Koenigsberger, Richard Neutra, Edward Durell

Stone, Constantin Doxiadis, Gio Ponti, and Paul Rudolph. However, it was the work of Le Corbusier and Louis Kahn, in India and Bangladesh, that left the deepest impression on an incipient modern architectural culture.

Achyut Kanvinde, Balkrishna Doshi, Charles Correa, Joseph Allen Stein, Habib Rahman, Jeet Malhotra, Laurie Baker, and, a little later, Ranjit Sabikhi, Raj Rewal, Uttam Jain and quite a few others began to define a contemporary tradition in India. In Sri Lanka, Geoffrey Bawa and Minnette de Silva, and, in Pakistan, Abid Ali Mirza in his brief career, and Muzharul Islam (later in Bangladesh) became the most notable architects to articulate the language and scope of a new architecture.

Climate and Identity
Climate was the first dimension through which abstract modernism attempted to find its place. The genre of "tropical architecture" established a climatic, material and constructional rationale for planning and building in most Asian countries. Since the 1950s, when climate was addressed primarily in a quantitative sense (temperature gradient, heat loss, physical comfort zone, and so forth), climate and culture have now become more intertwined. We are acutely aware today how the persistence of a type in a particular geographical and cultural milieu might indicate the synthesis of ecology, mythology, and sociology.

Climatic features would also come to be reified. Doshi, echoing the pensive reflection of Hassan Fathy, would see the courtyard of the hot-dry climate as related to Brahmand. In Sri Lanka, Geoffrey Bawa would explore the pavilion-in-the-garden as the paradigm for dwelling in a hot, humid, and vegetal milieu. In 1983, in a momentous essay that established "regionalism" as an enduring idea in architecture, Kenneth Frampton noted how site and climate, among other things, offered resistance to a homogenous adaptation of modern principles, and could actually inflect them towards a more critical production of architecture. "The fundamental strategy of Critical Regionalism," Frampton writes, "is to mediate the impact of universal civilization with elements derived indirectly from the peculiarities of a *particular place*." [italics added] In fact, it is possible that the peculiarities of a particular place – the air, wind, water and topography for example – are its particularities, that they define the character of a place, and form its irreducible matrix, its life-world.

New Cosmologies
Le Corbusier, like Louis Kahn somewhat later, derived a whole new architectural vocabulary out of reflections on climate. Le Corbusier's climatic rationale, matched by a powerful architectural oeuvre offered a new family of forms with which one could build the "brave new world." But it was not only the infectious inventiveness of Le Corbusier and Kahn that distinguished their work; more importantly, it was their insistence on giving a quasi-sacred dimension to architecture within the modem secular and functional context that probably established their work in the South Asian milieu.

Both Le Corbusier and Kahn, one in Chandigarh and the other in Dhaka, conceived the parliamentary assembly as a hallowed congregation within the secular world. Both brought their architectural resources to bear on giving form, shape, and space to, what they prescribed as, this new cosmological phenomenon. In deliberate riddles and puzzlements, Le Corbusier suggested the making of a modern mythology where the sun-path diagram became the emblem of a cosmic rhythm, an industrial flue became transformed into an honorific form, and various cosmological curios, icons and emblems were presented as mysterious signs.

Kahn's expression was more categorical. At the Assembly Building in Dhaka, he chose an unambiguously honorific typology, a centralized volume with hierarchical rings of space. The plan itself could be seen as a mandalic formation, an order of a nine-square grid, where the explicit forms, the spatial concatenation, and the artifice of light are orchestrated as if to express the inexpressible, the sublime "emptiness" of the center, or what Kahn conceived of as the "transcendent nature" of the act of assembly.

The evocation of the sacred is both dubious and compelling though. This sense of the sacred as something wondrous, extraordinary, *alaukika* in a Tagorean sense, is an uneasy theme. Suspicion naturally arises in this regard from opposite quarters: secular intellectuals find this to be reactionary and regressive, on the one hand, while guardians of religion perceive it as a threat to their entrenched theological positions, on the other hand. The persistence of spirituality nonetheless introduces the profound question: Is there a sacrality in secular existence? Is there an "other divinity" in modem life?

Ideals and Ideologies

The "sacred" has re-emerged in a significant way in architectural discourse through the work and thoughts of Balkrishna Doshi and Charles Correa, for example. Doshi articulates the sacred as the central essence of architecture and well-being. In a critique of straight-laced modernism and the mechanistic condition of contemporary world, which he sees at the root of today's frustrations and insecurity, Doshi argues for reinstating the dimension of the sacred, for it is the link to the "inner-self" which is ultimately the "seat of our true happiness."

In Doshi's recent architecture, the key feature is the combination of ambiguous, plural spaces and the routes of movement that are articulated there. These ambiguous spaces, Doshi writes, "activate the human psyche and induce it to sink toward the centre, the mythical world of man's primordial being. Time and space are internalized, and a deeply rooted personal identity with the built form gets established." The route of movement is another way of engaging rituals. And, "when space is a place for observance of rituals, it becomes sacred. At this point, I think, architecture emerges; the built-form becomes timeless and has a quality which goes beyond the obvious, a meaning and profoundness which go beyond the particular person or action."

Doshi's recent projects are also telluric offerings in some form or another: An ode to the dark, vital earth to claim a sort of metaphoric return to more terrestrial cosmologies. At Sangath, building and earth intertwine, and, at the Husain-Doshi Goofa, the structure rises from the dank bosom of the earth as a subterranean creature (in perhaps an allusion to the mythological creature Vrtra, slain by Indra, complete in the sinuous serpentine form with the vertebral anatomies). It is a contemporary reflection on a primordial architectural paradigm, the cave, and on the irrational subconscious dimension of man.

Correa's re-discovery of the sacred realm is also clear from the themes of his recent projects and the way he often narrates them. At the State Assembly in Bhopal and the Jawahar Kala Kendra in Jaipur, Correa makes unequivocal reference to a cosmo-astrological basis of architecture. The mandala plan in a nine-square grid, the reification of the central space as "sunnyata," and the whole panoply of Buddhist sacral iconography, Tantric emblems and astrological signs in one very witty conflation serve to represent a metaphysical schema. The condition of arraying different plastic and utilitarian forms all along the periphery is to emphasize a rhetorical point: the center as "emptiness." "Emptiness is infinitely satisfying to the human mind. Art and architecture are simply the concrete externalizations of our attempts to understand that void." It appears that Correa has taken up the recurrent challenge of Indian metaphysics: The paradox of how to express the inexpressible, to manifest the non-manifest through the world of formal and material creations.

On the other hand, architects like Muzharul Islam, Achyut Kanvinde, and Joseph Allen Stein, for example, remain somewhat suspicious of explicit metaphorization, and focus on what they claim to be the "real" in architecture: the tectonic and the constructional. Distancing itself from symbols and metaphors, their architecture instead employs tropes of rationalism, of mass-forms assembled in the clear light of reason and necessity. The materialist claim is, first, that metaphors are deceptions, that they are construed and not constructed, and, second, that they might still embody some old history of repression. "Whose symbols? For whom?," as Muzharul Islam would sharply respond when questioned about the downplaying of symbolism in his work. His materialist ideology finds a definite rationale in the political conditions of South Asia. He consciously distances himself from symbolism of any kind, and for that matter any religious evocations (the two being intricately linked together in South Asia), for the simple reason that both are premised and practised on the basis of dividing humanity, and both are implicated in some way in the tragic political events of the subcontinent. In a modern multi-cultural egalitarian definition of society, there is always the possibility of exclusion in re-evoking ancient symbols and signs. Kanvinde stays away from symbolism out of a deep respect for it; there is, he insists, an appropriate place and occasion for symbols. Even when Kanvinde designs a religious building, as in the ISKCON temple at Delhi (1997), where he adapts Nagara temple elements to

Antonin Raymon, Aurobindo Ashram, Pondicherry, 1936-1948.

Minnette de Silva, Karunaratne House, Kandy, 1947-1951.

Geoffrey Bawa, The Garden, Lunuganga, Bentota, 1950-.

modern materials and technology, there is more concern about tectonics and spatiality rather than the creation of a mystifying condition.

In this sense, architecture – in the work of Kanvinde, Muzharul Islam, Joseph Allen Stein – tries to find its significance in itself, asserting what one might call the autonomy of architecture: the realness of building, the art and mark of construction, the well-built thing, on the body of which, if need be, meta-architectural things might gather. The focus is on the tangibility of tectonics, as elaborated by Kenneth Frampton in *Studies in Tectonic Culture*, and the "realness" of presence, as explored by Michael Benedikt.

What "real" architecture aspires to is a sort of ascetic condition, where the goal is to gradually filter out everything conditional and extrinsic, to arrive at an irreducible stratum where there is a simple coincidence of appearance and reality, where nothing needs to be qualified by something else. An ascetic ideology might be valuable in its own right, but what would he lacking in the architectural experience is a certain exuberance, even play, as this is often seen in folk creation. This does not need to be other-worldly at all times but it certainly serves to expand our experience of the "real." As Correa remarks in respect of the sacred, reductiveness might actually diminish the experience of life.

Geoffrey Bawa celebrates the dimension of the sensorial and the sensuous in his work. This is based primarily on the situation of the body in space, in heightening the awareness and experience of the different senses. Shades and shadows, and winds and air. Become substantial rather than ephemeral things. One needs to listen to Jun'ichiro Tanizaki on the Japanese perception of shadows to realize how intangible things often form the reality of a particular place. The real, if it is fully addressed, also then involves the sensorial and the phenomenal.

The architects, however, do not always operate in a world neatly sub-divided according to the categories of the metaphysical, the rational and the sensorial. Doshi's Sangath is wondrous both in its architecture-earth reference and in its innovative tectonic dimension. Sangath is also a strong example of the aural, tactile and peripatetic experience of architecture. Correa at the Bhopal State Assembly and the Jawahar Kala Kendra has tried to systemize the signs, icons, and emblems of the sacred towards building a metaphysical center, while also incorporating the dynamic spatial experience of the meander and the exuberance of "folk" art. Muzharul Islam, while steadfastly adhering to his materialism, has, almost grudgingly, invoked the metaphorical, if not the metaphysical in the centralized plan of the National Library.

References

Paul Ricouer, *History and Truth* (Evanston, IL: Northwestern University Press, 1965).

Edmund Husserl, *The Crisis of European Sciences and Transcendental Phenomenology: An Introduction to Phenomenological Philosophy,* translation (Evanston, IL: Northwestern University Press, 1970).

Wilhelm Halbfass, *India and Europe: An Essay in Understanding* (Albany: SUNY Press, 1988).

Ashis Nandy, *The Intimate Enemy: Loss and Recovery of the Self Under Colonialism* (Delhi: Oxford University Press, 1983).

J.L. Mehta, *Martin Heidegger: The Way and the Vision* (Honolulu: University of Hawaii Press, 1976; first ed., Benares: 1967).

V.C. Joshi, editor, *Rammohun Roy and the Process of Modernization in India* (Delhi: Vikas Publishing House, 1975). The complex landscape of the "Bengal Renaissance" movement, from the rational scientific temper to the development of Hindu nationalism, is discussed here.

Tapan Raychaudhuri, in *Europe Reconsidered: Perceptions of the West in Nineteenth Century Bengal* (Delhi: Oxford University Press, 1988) writes: "All responses to the West in colonial India were not within the two polar limits of slavish admiration and xenophobic rejection. There is an extensive area of rational and scholarly assessment untouched by hangups of one sort or another," p.5.

"The need for new capitals was precipitated by the consequences of Independence – the partition of India, and furthermore the division of the provinces of Punjab and Bengal." Charles Correa, "A Place in the Sun," in *Royal Society of Arts Journal*, Vo1.131 (May 1983), and Places (Fall, 1983).

Kenneth Frampton, "Towards a Critical Regionalism: Six Points for an Architecture of Resistance," in *The Anti-Aesthetic: Essays on Postmodern Culture* (Port Townsend: 1983). Florindo Fusaro, Il Parlamento e la nuova capital a Dacca Louis I. Kahn (Rome: Officina Edizioni, 1985).

Balkrishna Doshi, "Between Notion and Reality," in *Souvenir* published in conjunction with the 1987 IIA Convention.

Kenneth Frampton, *Studies in Tectonic Culture* (Cambridge, MA: The MIT Press, 1985), Michael Benedikt, For an Architecture of Reality (Lumen Books, 1987), and Jun'ichiro Tanizaki, *In Praise of Shadows* (New Haven: Leete's Island Books, 1977, original 1933).

Building the Nation: The Architecture of Achyut Kanvinde and Muzharul Islam

with James Belluardo, published in the *India International Centre Quarterly*, Vol. 24, No. 2/3, Crossing Boundaries, Monsoon1997.

The 1940s and '50s were both a turbulent and optimistic time for the subcontinent. The period spanned the end of colonial rule and witnessed the granting of independence to India and Pakistan. With Independence also came Partition—not only a political one but also the breakup of a civilizational unity.

Yet at the same time there was a vision, an optimism, and a faith in the radical transformation of society for a collective well-being and common good. Science, rationalism and secularism became the most visible medium and expression of this idealism. Chandigarh, and the partnership of Nehru and Le Corbusier make a most compelling example. Modernism was proposed as an alternative civilizational unity in a fractious time. Achyut Purushottam Kanvinde in India and Muzharul Islam in then East Pakistan and later Bangladesh, shared a critical time in the history of the subcontinent.

Kanvinde began his architectural practice in 1947 after returning from the U.S., while Muzharul Islam's practice began in 1953. In their respective countries, both were the earliest proponents of an architecture of modernism; and, both engaged in their work the issue of nation-building with a social purpose.

Even today, despite the gradual weakening of social idealism and the faltering stature of modernism, Kanvinde and Islam have remained more or less steadfast in their commitment to a rationalist rigour and a modernist vocabulary. They have continued to define modernism not only as a formal creation but in its ethical and existential dimensions, to articulate the exigency of time but often to counter the tyranny of tradition.

The Modern Movement in architecture spread rapidly throughout the world in the years immediately following the Second World War. Its intellectual approach was functionalism, and its aim was to make architecture accessible to all. As a style, it dominated architecture in Europe, North and South America, Australia and Japan from the late 1940s until the 1970s. Using modern technology the movement allowed for rapid rebuilding of the industrialized nations devastated by the War's destruction.

The Movement offered India the possibility of meeting its needs and participating along with the industrialized nations in a common future that would restore India's greatness. However, it met with strong opposition by some in India, including Claude Batley at the J.J. School in Bombay. Moreover there was pressure in the mid-1950s for legislation that would have meant that India adopt a national policy for architecture, similar to what was adopted in the Soviet Union and China. Proponents advocated an architecture that would make use of traditional Indian motifs, so that an easily understood Indian identity could be given to all buildings. Even Nehru, who strongly believed in the present, appreciated art and architecture as belonging to the past. Chandigarh was seen as part of his program for a twentieth century India, respected for its efficiency and challenge to the past, but not for the greatness of its architecture. While Nehru was not concerned with modern art or architecture, he was an enlightened leader and open to ideas.

A group of modernist architects were well aware of the proposed mandate for a national policy on architecture, and they were disturbed. One of them arranged a meeting with Nehru to convey his strong opposition to such action. At a seminar on architecture convened at the Lalit Kala Akademi in New Delhi, the opening remarks appealed directly to the Prime Minister:

> Our problems concerning architecture have changed entirely from the past age because of our changing cultural outlook, namely the political institutions, scientific and technological development, our knowledge about human sciences, and our new ideas of aesthetics which developed as a result of the visual arts. Almost all past periods of architecture came into being as a result of desire for glorification, as an expression of the vanity of the ruling class and the dominant religious sentiments. Thus the architecture of the past was essentially feudalistic in approach. Contrary to this, the present political institutions are democratic in their approach where the stress is on the economic and social values related to the common man.[1]

Nehru's inaugural address was his only direct reply and statement to the architects.

> You cannot isolate architecture from the age, from the social conditions, from the thinking, from the objectives and ideals of that particular age. In an age which is rapidly changing, like our present age, in fact since the industrial revolution came, that necessarily has a powerful effect on architecture.[2]

To those who favored the use of historical elements, Nehru pointed out that the past was good when it was the present, but that it cannot be brought forward when the world had entered a technological era.[3] Nehru was firmly aligned with those who

[1] Seminar on Architecture, March 1959, Lalit Kala Akademi. Jaipur House, New Delhi (1959), p. 12.

[2] Ibid. p. 5.

[3] Ibid. p. 5.

[4] Ibid. p. 9.

[5] Walter Gropius, *The Scope of Total Architecture* (New York: Collier Books, 1962), p. 59.

[6] Walter Gropius, *The New Architecture and the Bauhaus*, trans. P.M. Shand and F. Pick (Cambridge, MA: MIT Press, 1965).

supported modernism—in the ultimate analysis he felt that a thing that fits with its function is beautiful.[4] He saw modern architecture as a way to bring India into the contemporary world. The Prime Minister expressed confidence that India's young profession of architecture would be able to meet the needs of its time in providing new forms. India would not have a national policy of architecture.

The architect who met with Nehru, convened the seminar and delivered the opening remarks was Achyut Purushottam Kanvinde. Born in 1916, the son of a landscape painter, in a small coastal village, south of Bombay, Kanvinde enrolled in the J.J. School in 1937. Under the direction of Claude Batley, the J.J. School provided training in Beaux-Arts principles with decorative elements that relied on Indian motifs extracted from measured drawings of historic buildings.

In 1945, Kanvinde was sent by the government to study architecture at the Harvard Graduate School of Design, which was headed by Walter Gropius. Here he absorbed the design principles inherited from the 'Bauhaus' which were based on an aesthetic that was in revolt against the past. Gropius proclaimed that a *breach has been made with the past, which allows us to envisage a new aspect of architecture corresponding to the technical civilization of the age be live in; the morphology of dead sales has been destroyed; and we are returning to honest y of thought and feeling.*[5] *He defined the New Architecture as simply the inevitable consequential product of the intellectual, social and technical conditions of our age*.[6] For the young Kanvinde, these remarks were aimed directly at his lessons from the J.J. School, which he now jettisoned. Like many of his generation, and especially those who passed through the Graduate School of Design, his course was set. He had found a direction for architecture that would serve him for a lifetime. After graduating from Harvard, Kanvinde came back to India in September 1947—barely a month after independence.

Under obligation to work five years for the Council of Scientific and Industrial Research, he based himself in Ahmedabad. With few architects available in India at the time, he was immediately assigned such major commissions as the Ahmedabad Textile Industry's Research Association (ATIRA) and the Physical Research Laboratory. It was there that Kanvinde made important contacts with the powerful and enlightened textile millowners who would, with Kanvinde's guidance, become important patrons of modern architecture along with its social concerns. Leaders like Vikram Sarabhai and Kasturbhai Lalbhai would consult Kanvinde on such matters as the merit of inviting Le Corbusier and Louis Kahn to Ahmedabad.

A great deal had to be built within a short period of time; there was a sense of urgency and little time for debate, or to set a theoretical basis for Indian architecture after Independence. Modern architecture gave India a vision of the future based on a functionalist language that was free of colonial reference, and easily understood by the technocrats who made decisions for the state, which prioritized industry, commerce and science. Traditional ways of building could not meet the needs of a nation anxious to participate in a new world that was rapidly industrializing. The manual trade of building would have to be transformed into an organized industry.

Well equipped with the language of functionalism, Kanvinde legitimized the modem movement in India years before the arrival of Le Corbusier and Kahn. His buildings during his tenure with the Council of Scientific and Industrial Research were typically long slab structures, each an object in itself set on an open site, and the logical result of an individual idea which embodied the universal language. Kanvinde firmly believed that buildings were an expression of their time, and that modern technology presented new possibilities that architects should exploit.

In 1955, released from his government contract, Kanvinde entered into private practice in New Delhi with Shaukat Rai and Morad Chowdhury. He organized their private professional office into a discipline driven by modern technology. Most of their commissions were for projects of large scale on tight schedule that address India's industrial possibilities. They required an organized construction industry similar to the construction process throughout the industrialized world.

Their first major commission was for the Indian Institute of Technology at Kanpur in 1960. While the overall layout of this campus makes reference to Gropius planning principles, and in particular to the Graduate Center at Harvard University, the buildings themselves represent a significant departure. Kanvinde's superior handling of local red brick within a concrete frame acknowledges not only Le Corbusier's and Kahn's work at that time and the first buildings of the New Brutalists in England, but also recalls several large projects, including St. Stephen's College (1938) in New Delhi, designed by Walter Sykes George.

Kanvinde's involvement with the National Dairy Development Board began in 1968 with the construction of their campus at Anand. This cooperative was set up by the government to allow small dairy farmers, mostly those with less than four cows, to sell their milk to collective so that it could be processed into powder, ghee, cheese, and other dairy products that required substantial facilities with highly regulated sanitary standards that these farmers could not provide for themselves. This is an example of how a large-scale industrial project, dependent upon modern technology, has been able to help sustain a traditional way of life for small farmers by guaranteeing them a market for their production and a steady income. Here two very different Indias, appearing to contradict each other, find themselves in mutual support.

In the 1970s. there was a global questioning of "progress," and of architecture that had made use of advanced technology. Kanvinde, as one of India's foremost modernist architects, found himself out of fashion. In India, the presence of Le Corbusier and Kahn made the Bauhaus principles seem obsolete to many.

Achyut Kanvinde, Balkrishna Harivallabhdas Residence, Ahmedabad, 1962. Photo: J. Belluardo.

Muzharul Islam, NIPA Building, Dhaka University.

The newly found interest in contextualism became a call for an architecture with a specific Indian identity.

Kanvinde remained true to his search for an architectural expression that responded to new idea transforming if not all, a prominent segment of India. He saw modernism as a way to advance social goals that were not part of India's past; he believed in the concept of modern democratic India, and Nehru's egalitarian and socialist policies. Modernism, solidly rooted in the present, was still relevant.

In an effort to popularize India's great investment in science, the government commissioned two major museums. These were to display not only scientific discoveries, but also enable a scientific understanding of all India and its vast natural resources, and make these accessible to a larger public. Visitors were to be involved as active participators in a series of experiments and especially young students were to be encouraged to pursue a career in the sciences. These museums have proved highly successful in attracting a large number of visitors from all strata of Indian society.

In 1976, Kanvinde was asked to design the Nehru Science Centre in Bombay, and in 1586, the National Science Centre in New Delhi. Free from his functionalist training at Harvard, he considered these projects an exercise in providing visual excitement through volumes that could be used to create abstract patterns. The repetition of multidimensional hexagonal modules juxtaposed to create a dynamic space maintains a unifying structural system. Columns act as shafts that utilize roof fans to blow and extract air on all levels, and project beyond the roof to give the centre its distinctive profile.

Both museums, strongly identifying with science, rely on a powerful geometry to give them architectural clarity and strength. Unlike Kahn, who also utilized a forceful geometry, Kanvinde does not monumentalize his architecture. Instead, he searches for ways to scale even his large buildings to the human dimensions. Yet he does this without making the work look timid. As part of an historic precinct in New Delhi, and mediating between the trade fair grounds and the adjacent fortress of Purana Qila, the National Science Museum asserts itself as a strong modern building that can stand next to the powerful architecture of the past—with more credibility than one which relies on historic images.

For most Asian societies, modernism is conveniently seen as the perpetrator of a disruption, set against a 'pre-modern' condition: tradition. It is necessary to rethink this demonization characterizing most contemporary criticisms. A different claim may be presented: that Muzharul Islam, in his work and thinking, adopts the principles of modernity in order to *overcome* what has been perceived as colonialist rupture. Modernism, in this sense, becomes an attempt to "return home."

The idea of modernity in Bangladesh—by extension the ideology of Muzharul Islam—can best be understood by that broad sweep of cultural and intellectual upheaval ushered in Bengal by the "Bengal Renaissance" movement. It was a complex intertwining of resistance and acceptance; a resistance to both the traumatic results of colonialism and to the tyranny of tradition. The condition of acceptance was also two-fold: It involved embracing from a global repository anything that assured new degrees of social and intellectual liberation—as for example, what the scientific and progressive institutions of European Enlightenment seem to promise; and an inward journey, a conscious "archaeological" excavation of one's own taken-for-granted cultural strata.[7]

Self-awareness however is double-edged: while it is a moment of self-discovery, it is also a moment of distancing from the familiar. Self-discovery presupposes a sense of alienation and remoteness from tradition and does not happen so long as "we *unreflectively* live under its domination, or fail to see the novel present as it actually is and claims us."[8] Both Charulata and Bimala, characters from two of Rabindranath's novels, portray this. At the moment of their self awareness, when they become conscious of their one identity, the familiar is made foreign; one is made a stranger to the comfort of habitual setting. And, yet, it is within this condition, *where tradition is no longer available unreflectively,* that the idea of identity—gender, cultural or national—arises.[9]

What is the historic root of this alienation from "home"? The colonial experience still remains the point of departure for understanding contemporary conditions. For Muzharul Islam, the idea of return emerges through interpreting colonialism as a "rupture", a fatal and irreversible condition created by its disruptive mechanisms. In Bengal, as in the rest of India, the "rupture" was experienced as conflicts between pre-colonial and colonial conditions. In the context of Bangladesh, especially after 1947, the aggressive Islamic ideology of Pakistan introduced a second and a more deadly wedge. Religion was used, often deviously, to undermine Bengali cultural consciousness.

The events of the 1971 War of Independence marked a violent form of Pakistani intervention and a critical moment of Bengali resistance. Bengali culture faced a trichotomy with European traditions and Pakistani Islamic ideology.[10] It is in the context of these various disruptions—from political to psychological and spiritual—that Muzharul Islam speaks of *mone-prane-karmokande khati Bangali houa*, that is, to be a 'true' Bengali in mind, spirit and praxis. The metaphor of "return" assumes that one is displaced from where one was once *mone-prane-Karmokande Bangali*, and the return there is prior to any ethical and creative behavior.

Modernity, for Muzharul Islam is as much a returning as going away. It is a going away from the immediate colonial past, and a returning to an "essentialist" condition, free from exclusivist religious ideologies, traumatic inheritances, propagandist

[7] Tapan Raychaudhuri, in *Europe Reconsidered: Perceptions of the West in Nineteenth Century Bengal*, writes about the perceptions of the West among the Bengali intelligentsia, whose productions, mostly literary, affected and continue to affect the thinking of the larger public. "All responses to the West in colonial India were not within the two polar limits of slavish admiration and xenophobic rejection. There is an extensive area of rational and scholarly assessment untouched by hang-ups of one sort or another," p. 5.

[8] J.L. Mehta, "World Civilisation: The Possibility of Dialogue," on *Heidegger, Hermeneutics and Indian Tradition*, edited by William J. Jackson (Leiden: E.J. Brill, 1992).

[9] Tapan Raychaudhuri calls this an "anxious and neurotic effort at cultural self-assertion," a major trait of the late nineteenth century milieu in Bengal. In *Europe Reconsidered*, p.11.

[10] This antagonism, between a Bengali Islam and a pan-Islamic ideology, has older roots. Pakistan, in the context of Bangladesh, tapped this as a major political instrument. Much literature exists on this, but for a synoptic view, see Rafiuddin Ahmad, "Conflicts and Contradictions in Bengali Islam: Problems of Change and Adjustment," in *Shariat end Ambiguity in South Asian Islam* (University of California Press , 1988).

symbolizes and pretentious iconographies. As much avowed to a Bengali political identity, he would not immediately translate this iconographically by adopting traditional motifs and other such tell-tale signs. Architectural modernism seemed to be a convincing way of arriving at an essentialist condition. It is this move that is not to go away further but towards an essentialist condition, encircling both the past and the present that may be understood as the metaphor of "return."

It is apparent though that one can now only return to a transformed or constructed locus. Once self-awareness begins, one is forever fated to a "re-construction." But what distinguishes this from the facile method of instant traditionalism? What might give it a greater degree of authenticity?

Muzharul Islam's position is dialogic. Although it is hinged to a specific place, it does not falter in engaging in a "world dialogue," that is, in recognizing "the mode of existence of present-day man, who has his sojourn in a region where civilizations, cultures and religions touch each other, where times and places flow together;" it is also not daunted that this might necessitate a different or new way of making. Muzharul Islam wants to operate within the nexus of a cultural particularness and the humanist idea of "the-world-as-my-village."[11] This is what brings him close to a Rabindrik ethos.

In Bengal, "aesthetics" and the idea of the nation have historically formed a kinship. It was through the Bengal School movement, constituted primarily by the writings of E.B. Havell, the famous art educator, and the paintings of Abanindranath Tagore that art becomes a site for nationalist discourse. The development of 'modem' Indian art becomes the most vivid record of the triangular tension of traditions, nationalism, and modernity.[12]

The attempt for "aesthetic and national recovery" was countered by another camp that was critical of the pretentious "Indianness" of the ideal and spiritual art as envisioned by Havell, Coomaraswamy and Abanindranath. A group of younger Calcutta artists emerged who declared in their manifesto that the "Bengal School paintings lacked vitality and that the false sense of Indian art and the propaganda for the eastern art should be resisted." They argued that the so-called "traditionalists" in their attempt to confront the colonizes, took refuge in a 'recovered' pre-colonial past—or more correctly, in a fabricated past, never questioning which or whose past was being recovered and whose past was being suppressed. This invariably led to sentimental spiritualizing which eulogized "a pre-capitalist social order" ignoring "the him realities of a people striving under sub-human conditions."[13]

An important figure in this debate is Rabindranath Tagore. Although he appears like his nephew Abanindranath disengaged from social realities, and actually comes close to the idea of the spiritual artistic persona, he is sharply critical of the "narrow-mindedness" of an 'Indian' art:

[11] Interview in *Sthaptya O Nirman* (January-March 1992).

[12] A number of recent studies treat this important period in Bengali cultural history: *Tapati Guha-Thakurta, The Making of a New 'Indian' Art: Artists, Aesthetics and Nationalism in Bengal*, c.1850-1920 (Cambridge University Press, 1992), and *Ratnabali Chatterjee, From the Karkhana to the Studio* (New Delhi: Books and Books, 1990).

[13] R. Chatterjee, *From the Karkhana to the Studio*.

[14] Pritwish Neogy, *Rabindranath Tagore On Art and Aesthetics: A Selection of Lectures, Essays and Letters* (Calcutta: Orient Longmans, 1961).

[15] From the mid-1960s, Muzharul Islam became increasingly involved in matters political, accelerated in 1970-1971 by the Bangladesh liberation movement, and formalized by the mid-70s by his joining of political organizations.

> I strongly urge our artists vehemently to deny their obligation carefully to produce something that can be labeled as Indian Art by conforming to some old world mannerisms.[14]

The debate focuses, on the one hand, on the figure of the truly artistic persona such as Rabindranath and the architect Louis Kahn, who are suspicious of political rhetoric, and, on the other hand, on the impossibility of political aloofness particularly in nations like Bangladesh. Political ideology and architecture enter an impasse. While political consciousness, in the nation-building context, is about drawing boundaries whereby nations are articulated, architecture cannot be contained within political perimeters.

Although these two strands—commitment to the idea of a nation, and to the realm of architecture-are tied up in Muzharul Islam's thinking, his architecture remains adequately distanced from nationalistic polemics. He understands that nationalistic posturing does not automatically lead to the spirit of architecture. Yet, through political engagement he is gradually led to the confirmation that architectural form is inadequate in addressing immediate social problems and therefore he himself moves towards the realm of politics.[15] While he adheres to a Rabindrik idea of a Bengali cosmopolitan spirit, he remains, in the light of Marxian materialistic rigor, suspicious of talks on artistic spirituality.

In his 1944 essay *Our Heritage*, Humayun Kabir notes that "in all modern manifestations of Indian art, the one form which is absent is architecture." If literature, paining, and somewhat later, cinema, were thematically confronting the existential question of 'what it means to be a Bengali in the twentieth century,' architecture remained far behind as a mere activity of construction. An architectural discourse was clearly missing from the "Renaissance" movement, despite the stimulating debates on aesthetics.

It was in this imbalanced situation that in 1953 Muzharul Islam began his career. After training in engineering at Calcutta University, he went to Oregon University in the United States from where he received an architectural degree in 1952 and later a master's degree under Paul Rudolph at Yale in 1981. As a thirty-year old and the only formally trained architect working in Dhaka, he began with an enormous task: an architectural production which involved, at one level, a challenge to the entrenched practice of the engineers, and, at another level, the making of a Bengali building paradigm.

From the very first projects, his work raised a two-fold concern: the question of the house and the question of the city. Throughout the 1950s and most of the 1960s, Muzharul Islam experimented with a number of house types, compositional configurations and construction methods. The early houses, in articulating the paradigm of the pavilion in modem bungalows, incorporated the spatial and planar dimensions of the classic houses of early modernism.

The idea of the 'pavilion' was also behind large buildings, from the Public Library and the Science Laboratory to the NIPA building at Dhaka University. The Public Library (1953) was organized in a clearly Corbusian mode, but for Dhaka it was a fresh approach to urbanism. The NIPA building at Dhaka University (1967) signified the pavilion with its array of concrete piers girdling the building, the 'usable' space being recessed behind. The hovering plane of the roof as a *chattri* (parasol) completed the imagery.

The Art College, designed at the same time as the Public Library, stands apart. It comes closer to mediating with the sensorial conditions of place. Sprawling, low building volumes, the use of exposed fired brick which always has such a magical resonance with the "greenness" of Bengal, the natural garden setting on an urban site—all went to form the atmosphere of a campus ideal for the contemplation and learning of the arts. More importantly, it indicated a spatial environment evoking the architectural poetics of the land.

The 1960s remain his most prolific period of building in a practice affected by many discontinuities. He was involved in the development of the Institute of Architects, and influential in drafting its constitution, for which he is still well remembered by architects in Pakistan.[16] Besides his own contribution to architecture culture, he was also instrumental in bringing Louis Kahn, Paul Rudolph and Stanley Tigerman to Bangladesh.

His early projects from the 1950s up to works like NIPA and his own house in the '60s owe much to Frank Lloyd Wright, Le Corbusier and Paul Rudolph. This is evident, in varying degrees, in the basic skeletal configuration of the works, in the innovation of climate control; in the sculpturesque quality made by varying reliefs, deep shadows and juxtaposition of materials; in the spatial composition; and, finally, in the manner the buildings confront the landscape with an assertive stance.

His later phase the late '60s—saw the commissioning of two university projects, involving large-scale organization. While the theme, as in Jahangirnagar University (1967-1971) and the housing for Jaipurhat Limestone Factory (1979), is an *a priori* geometry, the concern is to generate an 'urbanized' order by the formation of spatial enclosures, streets and continuous facades. The buildings are constructions in brick, where spaces and voids seem to be carved out of masonry solids, and which, despite their often curious geometrical purity and unlike the skeletal nature of earlier projects, form a more earth-hugging ambience.

The shift in architectonic configuration is most explicit in the National Library project undertaken in 1978. Gone is the stark clarity of his earlier skeletal work; there is now a ponderous presence accentuated both by the centralized form and the use of brick-mass. The building presents a convincing response to the neighboring ensemble by Kahn, which has by now formed an important context in the north of Dhaka. While geometric abstraction and a consummate skill for crafting constitute a continuity in all his work, the iconography of the National Library

[16] Zaigham S. Jaffrey's comments at the Aga Khan Award for Architecture seminar "Regionalism in Architecture," Dhaka, 1985.

[17] From Muzharul Islam's unpublished essay, "Re-Designing and Re-Building of Cities."

is a world removed from the Public Library of 1955. The National Library is a surreptitious triumph, almost against Muzharul Islam's own rational rigor, of the accidental over the planned, and of the *a posteriori* over the *a priori*.

The plans for Jahangirnagar University and Jaipurhat Housing are also Muzharul Islam's closest effort to move away from the conventional morphology of either the city or the country. Muzharul Islam has arrived at a kind of 'alternative' city—collectivized, yet receptacles in sun, light and air—after a Marxian reading of the difference between the city and the so-called rural hinterland as social disparity. Here a Marxian perspective comes to an agreement with a Rabindrik vision. Finding the difference unacceptable, and, echoing Rabindranath's 1928 essay "City and Village," he believes that "old ideas of society divided into haves and have-nots are no longer valid.... The world has advanced sufficiently in science and technology to help remove the difference between the city and the so-called rural hinterland."[17] While the vision of this city has a strong moral and economic underpinning, Muzharul Islam recognizes that "the cities should provide the environment for civilized life within the context of our own culture." Moreover,

> the city can develop only as a part of the physical environment of the country—with the ultimate aim of abolishing all differences between the city and the rural areas. The traditional relationship with nature (still existing to a certain extent in the villages of Bangladesh) should be continued in the cities.

Old landscape, new typology - farmhouses sans farming. Rajeev Kathpalia, Vastu Shilpa, Arjun Farmhouse, Ahmedabad, 2004.

Masala City: Urban Stories from South Asia

Published in *Architectural Design*, September/October, 2005.

Even on wintry mornings, Anurag Tripathi cycles through the virtual decay of Varanasi. Slicing through the thick fog, he stops at a brand new hotel on the Ganges, one built around a temple and brightly lit with Christmas tree lights, and parks his rickety bicycle there... The he goes down Assi Ghat below, ignoring teeming hordes of beggars and sadhus. He makes a bundle of his white shawl and unwashed clothes, keeps it on his books and plunges into the filthy, toxic river. Shivering and humming Hanuman Chalisha, he emerges from the water, puts on his clothes and pedals down to the Benaras Hindu University Campus. Tripathi spends the day on experiments in the physics laboratory, reading science journals, making notes, and dreaming of going to the MIT one day... When the evening mist begins to blanket the sprawling campus, he leaves the lab, cycles up to the Lanka Gate and orders a burger at a small, squalid roadside hole. Hundreds of flies buzz around him as he eats his burger – a thick, greasy potato chop in a droughty bun with some rotten onion and a thin slice of stale tomato. Finishing his grub, he picks a 'Miss Lewinsky' ice-cream from another vendor and moves into a narrow lane where they teach you to speak English in the American way. As darkness thickens, Tripathi gets out of the institute and moves into a damp, cold cybercafe, assumes an oxymoronish identity – coolfire21- and begins chatting with 'serenesoul80', a 24 year-old girl in Scottsdale, Arizona.
—Shobhan Saxena, "America in Our Lives," *Tehelka, The People's Paper* (January 15, 2005)

"Amar, Akbar, Anthony"

Mix, in urban configurations and architectural syntactics, is not new; it is an evident reflection of social and cultural formations. Hovels and *havelis*, domes and *shikhara* spires, nuclear reactor and pyramidal forms (the roofscape of Le Corbusier's Assembly in Chandigarh) emblematize the tenacious hybrid nature of architecture and urbanism in South Asia/India, indicating an inherent resilience to the making of economic, religious, and cultural monoliths. While Anurag Tripathi, like millions of young subcontinentals, gets a high dose of Americana now, history attests to various forms of inadequacies to unitary formations.

Mix can take on different profiles, from the cinematic sense of collage and montage, to the obvious culinary concept of *masala* and *chutney* (as well as melting pot and salad bowl), and from the biological idea of miscegenation and hybridity to the pharmaceutical techniques of concoction and amalgamation. What ideas of "mix" inaugurate in the contemporary context, since Homi Bhabha's seminal discussion of hybridity and difference, is to turn asunder the proposition of a unitary notion/nation, and bring the dissolution of "coherent identities, conceptual purity, and cultural unity."[1] A new battleground is laid out, as Bhabha notes, not so much between east and west, or modernity and tradition, but between essence and fragmentations. This is revealed paradoxically in the tussle among the various fragments and constituencies themselves. When it comes to sub-continental societies, mix represents a kind of invisible truce between the different classes, castes and communities, that is, when difference does not become pronounced viciously and lapse into a bloody apocalypse. The armistice, as depicted cinematically in the popular film of the 1970s "Amar, Akbar, Anthony," where three brothers who were lost as children grow up as Hindu, Muslim and Christian respectively, has now devolved into virulent exclusivities, most notably the Hindutva variety.

In the sphere of architecture and urbanism, mix exposes a natural fluidity that is bound to happen in a condition of strong cultural co-valencies, as represented by the Mughal emperor Akbar's city of mélange Fathepur Sikri. At the same time, an architectural fusion may just be gestural, such as Charles Correa's theatric montage at the Bhopal State Assembly, where the selective iconic pieces are hardly commensurate with various social constituencies. Mix in contemporary urban environments is symptomatic of a guerilla strategy that surreptitiously and unpredictably thwarts the surveilling nature of the Master Plan, as in the production of the "illegal" slums, and the continuous bending of urban rules and regulations that make up the Master Plan. Without the disciplinary deployment of the Master Plan, and even within it, a city will always rearrange itself to ever new arcs of desires, to new tribal, economic, and cultural orientations. Lutyens' New Delhi and Le Corbusier's Chandigarh share a common criticism that they disavow the inherent mix of Indian cities, and curtail any impromptu, hybridizing intervention (although the architecture of both Lutyens and Le Corbusier are better understood as synthetic work).

Every epoch brings its own poetry of mix, and every hybridity is distinctive. A new interfusion is certainly redefining the contemporary urban landscape in South Asia in ways that are unprecedented and not fully predicated on home-spun norms. If an earlier amalgam was of the Hobson-Jobson variety, triggered either by colonial infraction or metropolitan-rural polarity, the new mix is engineered by a triad of forces – transnational culture, new media and intoxicating consumerism. The former is emblematized in the figure of the Anglicized "babu sahab,"[2] while the latter in the poly-placed NRI (the non-resident Indian), already a quasi-mystical figure in the Indian imagination, as one popular film after another attests.

While all Indian/South Asian cities are undergoing paroxysmic changes (but not quite as the Shanghai phenomenon), it is far from clear if the new landscape, with new works of architecture, is a culturally liberating condition or a surreptitious profit-driven product. Is the mix only spectacular, or does it promise social

[1] Homi Bhabha, *The Location of Culture* (London and New York: Routledge, 1994).

[2] This is explored by Tabish Khair in *Babu Fictions: Alienation in Contemporary Indian English Novels* (New Delhi: Oxford University Press, 2001).

[3] The term was derived after a conversation with Michael Meister.

[4] Film-makers outside of India apply both euphoric and ironic contemplations of *masala*. Mira Nair in "Mississippi Masala" alludes to the new racial and cultural coagulation on the banks of the Mississippi. The Canadian film "Masala" follows the displaced god Krishna from the bowery of Vrindaban to a video shrine amidst the discordant coordinates of diasporic Indians in Toronto. Gurinder Chadha's "Bride and Prejudice" renders motleyism and stereotyping derived from both Bollywood and the NRI scene into a subdued farce.

justice? Is it truly a mix, or a juxtaposition of attitudes and desires that are tangential to each other, in reality maintaining a wedge between the various constituencies? Will the triad transcend the deep cut of the religious divide, and offer a new promise for Amar, Akbar and Anthony as the metrosexual metropolis?[3]

Mixed Blessing

Masala, originally a culinary term for spewing spices, has now entered the Anglo-Indian vocabulary as an ideogram of amalgamation. What the "melting pot" is to the American sensibility, *masala* is to the South Asian imaginary, alluding both to a mix and a potent, spicy content. This culinary sensibility has now traveled to a wider body of work. The film industry in Mumbai – Bollywood, which perhaps should now be called Mollywood with the change of name of the city – employs the term as a tool for concoction and exaggeration.[4] Salman Rushdie, in his various novels, employs the *masala* mode, in his characterizations, imageries, but especially in the spoken language, as a postmodern vitality. It is this vitality and hybridity that threaten the grip of the classical and the thoroughbred traditional, as well as the squeaky, clean modern.

Urban phantasmagoria and its profiles. Hafeez Contractor, Noida Tower, Noida, Delhi, 2005, Project.

Fusion is now the cultural engine from Mumbai to Macao, especially as they are spewed out non-stop through the omnipresent TV channels. The infinite mixing capability of the camera and the digital media – like the fast output of a TV commercial that in three seconds will flicker thirty images of diverse provenance – has taken collage or montage to a new height. In music, new genres are being configured by an invigorating and sometimes unabashed miscegenation in the form of "remix." Musical remix may be a metaphor for a larger reality where life or culture is no longer whole; it is composed of the simultaneous existence of multiple realities, of bits and pieces of both the familiar and the strange, and it does not matter whether they add up to a whole, and whether the bits and pieces are themselves constantly in flux.

If mix and hybridity are the new mantras that will dislodge the power of the pure and unitary, we are not yet sure if it is eventually going to be redemptive or simply disruptive. The term hybrid still refers to some kind of originary pureness, although it gets its current valorization by sullying that purity. Where the new heterogeneity differs from Bhabha's idea of hybridity is that it is not necessarily situated in the interstices and fissures of official spaces but constitutes it own spatial matrix. The new mix presents its own terms of reference.

A Place Called Elsewhere

In the 2003 film *Mein Prem Ki Diwani Hoon*, the setting is a fictional town eponymously called Sundarnagar, or the city beautiful. It is a town of idealized dreams and bourgeois opulence, of houses belonging to the purveyors of traditions, with living rooms the size of a small stadium, populated by pampered patriarchs, gullible grandmothers and servile servants, all in their proper places. The lawns to the houses are wide, and the driveways regal, while the riot-free, languorous town harbors

Life in Sundarnagar, the make-belief Indian town in the film *Mein Prem Ki Diwani Hoon*, which was actually shot in New Zealand.

manicured parks, quaint telephone booths, gardens, outdoor spaces to run away to, and that includes quite inexplicably snow clad mountains, lush streams, sandy beaches, all at the same time. In the film, Sundarnagar is depicted as a town in India, but the fact of the matter is the entire film is shot in New Zealand. The Indian city of Sundarnagar may be fictive, but it is depicted in a real place, and that place is elsewhere, and that is the fixation in Hindi-Bollywood films: the relentless flight towards elsewhere.

This flight to elsewhere is structurally embedded in the song-dance numbers – "chansons d'amour," the raison d'etre of Hindi-Bollywood films. I call the location of these "chansons d'amour" *song-sites*. The "song-site" in the Hindi-Bollywood filmic imagination weaves in music, dance, couture, urban and landscape imagery, not to mention hip-hop and catwalks, into a phantasmagoria of dreams and desires. The literal space of the "song-sites" has always been an exotic, far-away place, somewhere that the amorous protagonists could be transported to instantly without a cue. The lush valley of Kashmir was a ubiquitous site of that dream topography, as also places like Manali, Kanyamumari, Goa, and Simla. But now more and more, since Kashmir descended into political chaos, the "song-sites" exist subliminally in imported places from Switzerland, Germany, and even New Zealand. Charming, urbane, or just generally well-formed places, as National Geographic exoticas, are grafted onto the body of an extremely predictable and hyper-theatrical narrative that may have a generic setting in some village in Punjab, or a *chawl* in Mumbai. What makes *Mein Prem Ki Diwani*

Hoon striking is that it is in its entirety a "song-site"; it takes the elsewhere of the "song-site" to the entire film.

What to make of the manufacture of this cinematic urban imagery without being facetious? Can one make a Italo Calvino-like catalog of these grafted places, as a kind of modern fable of urban imagination? Or, can they be treated as a cryptic enumeration of the collective fetish of the Indian urban middle class as it encounters, experiences and succumbs to (new) global coordinates? Are these sites a symptom of a latter-day postmodern hybridity (a New Mix) manufactured, distributed and consumed filmically? Is Bollywood, surreptitiously, unwittingly or unselfconsciously, writing alternative visions for urban India? Is cinematic Sundarnagar, as Thomas Pynchon did with the medium of TV in his fictional work *Vineland*, a "quixotic cognitive enterprise" that converts a postmodernist space into a tool for thinking about an otherwise elusive and unrepresentable system?[5]

These places from elsewhere, real and actual, become fictive in the Hindi film narrative because the places are not named, and they are not located with any amount of precision; they are literally framed to be "foreign," to be *elsewhere*. It is this admixture of actuality and alienness that make these sites hyper-real places. In the generic Hindi films, the sites of the songs are hyper-real because they are seemingly real. The sites are not unreal by themselves. A city like that exists somewhere in Germany. A landscape like that exists in Switzerland. And yet they become profoundly unreal, or seemingly real, and hence hyper-real, by the nature of being grafted on the cinematic body, when they are collaged, montaged, cut-and-pasted alongside a familiar and urbanistically messy landscape, a real city in India. The significance is in the juxtaposition, in the being side by side.

What is being side by side is the usual and the ideal, the place here and now and a place elsewhere, the messy city and a dream topography. The former is of a native and the latter of a transnational provenance. It is also in this sense that spaces of Hindi film represent a mix. And despite what is perhaps conceptually a jarring hybridity, the satisfied audience takes it as a "flow," a flow through diverse, unrelated, discontinuous spaces, not unlike negotiating an actual city. Sundarnagar is not an isolated cinematic place, and yet Sundarnagar is not an Indian town that could be located with precision for it is part of the longing of the urban upper/middle-class, refracted by the NRI phenomenon, to approximate an "elsewhere." It is not clear though if that longing is therapeutic or psychotic.

What distinguishes Sundarnagar from another well-known fictional town – R.K. Narayan's literary Malgudi – is the transnational divide, the frame by frame embodiment of intercontinental utopias on a native set of references, of the presence of the idea of a globally charged site that replaces (or at least contests) the vestiges of the empirical here. Is Sundarnagar then a premonition of Indian cities happening in the simultaneous collapse of either Nehruvian or Gandhian ideology, and the proliferation of a global, transnational indulgence?

[5] Brian McHale uses Thomas Pynchon's Vineland to understand the postmodern ontology of television. "Much in the same way… that [Fredric] Jameson has sought to convert the spaces of postmodernist architecture into a tool for thinking about ("cognitively mapping") the otherwise elusively unrepresentable system, Pynchon may be seeking to convert TV into a tool for cognitively mapping the place of death in a postmodern culture. And much as Jameson has strangely, and controversially, redeemed even so unlikely a building as John Portman's egregious Bonaventure Hotel by appropriating it in this way to his (and our) cognitive use, so Pynchon has, perhaps more strangely still, "redeemed" TV," p. 141, Brian McHale, *Constructing Postmodernism* (London: Routledge, 1992).

[6] Fredric Jameson, *Postmodernism, or The Cultural Logic of Late Capitalism* (Durham, NC: Duke University Press, 1991).

Developing a dream topography, Hafeez Contractor, Dheerja Dreams Development, Bhandup.

The Metrosexual Mantra

The longing for "elsewhere" is now embodied in new building configurations that are radically altering the urban landscape: malls and shopping centers, cineplexes and flyovers, and exclusive apartment or residential complexes. The shoppers and strollers at Connaught Place in New Delhi have literally gone elsewhere, abandoning the old commercial center for more exclusive, air-conditioned enclaves that are spread out as a matrix of hyperspace in the familiar cityscape. Billboards of upcoming shopping centers in and around Calcutta rise from the ashen and smoky landscape of the city like some divine apparition. The gigantic Basundhara City, which is not a city but touted as Asia's largest mall, has replaced the traditional site of open-air promenade and assembly for the people of Dhaka. At Nagpur Airport, a model with rendered images of a sleek apartment complex canvasses not so much a bourgeois dwelling as we know it but an enigmatic collective and selective future. Fredric Jameson's rumination on the hyper-spatial quality of certain postmodern spaces, such as the atrium of the Bonaventure Hotel in LA, comes to mind. While these spaces are here upon us, for us to travel to and enter, most of us do not possess "the perceptual equipment to match this new hyperspace."[6]

In this new, urban admixture, the self-reflective architect seems exiled in Malgudi, in a pre-transnational ethos, while a newer generation takes on the mantle of translating the desire of elsewhere in an outpour of exhilarating architectural images. Balkrishna Doshi's vision for New Jaipur, a city premised on a pre-consumerist urban mixture, now seems overly "real." Hafeez

Contractor, and a number of emerging architects in the region, on the other hand, addresses the paroxysmic present by their embrace of exuberant materials and manners.

In this exuberant context, the mall is a paradigmatic space borne out of a transnational breeding that, on the one hand, represents the shopping cult of America, and, on the other hand, embodies the surreal city of Sundarnagar. The mall model pervades other building types also, from offices and hospitals to even dwellings. While South Asian malls are typologically derivative of American malls, the internal coding of the latter are reworked in the South Asian context. While the former is a populist, mass destination, the mall in India/South Asia has taken on a unique upscale and exclusive aura that is codified by architectural and other means, including goods that are disbursed there. While older shopping complexes, including Connaught Place, offered a degree of shop and street interface by being tropically porous realms (even allowing a little paan shop to flourish in the cracks), most malls are hermetically sealed interiorized enclaves that are in complete visual and attitudinal denial of its surroundings, where, to recall Walter Benjamin's observation regarding glass, no dust can collect. The city is held at arms length through a series of barriers, by the visually resplendent architecture, by restricting interaction with the surrounding city, by the inevitable motorized access, and by the spectacular security befitting a maharaja's palace, all of which work towards intimidating groups that are not participants in this new urban experience. The residential enclaves are also similarly policed and truncated off from the continuum of the city. The metrosexual citizen can now travel from home to mall, bypassing the rest of India.

If mix and hybridity are operative mechanisms for mass engagement, a vast mass is still held at bay, making the new mix a double-edged phenomenon. While the spectacular, cinematic means present a virtual access to anyone to the above arc of desire, spaces in the city are being fabricated that are distinctively the prerogative of a privileged party where access for other groups in the larger community is severely curtailed.

The farmhouse is the site of a new architectural exuberance. Rajeev Kathpalia, Arjun Farmhouse.

Architectural Design special volume, "Made in India," 2007.

Raga India: Architecture in the Time of Euphoria

Introduction to the *Architectural Design* special volume, "Made in India," 2007.

The Empty Bottle

In a setting of an allegorical pickle factory – the pickle or chutney is a virulent postmodern trope and decisively Indian – Saleem Sinai marinates another story of national and autobiographical destiny in Salman Rushdie's *Midnight's Children*. Rushdie's alter ego both refigures the present and prefigures the upcoming India in clairvoyant pickle jars. There are thirty bottles on the factory shelf. Twenty-nine bottles are full, and each one makes up each chapter/episode of the tumultuous and fabulous history of India after its independence in 1947. The thirtieth bottle is empty, waiting to be filled and written in. What will the next vessel contain?

Vrtra's Ghost

The Husain-Doshi Gufa in Ahmedabad, that houses the work of the irrepressible artist M.F. Husain, was built in 1994 as a collaborative project between the artist and the architect Balkrishna Doshi. Dug cave-like into the earth, blurring the edge of building and landscape, the undulating structure of the Gufa has the unmistakable physiognomy of a terrestrial creature with its vertebras, ligaments and eyes (Husain also painted a black serpent on the wall). The Gufa is also Doshi's counter-homage to Corbusier's paean to the right angle. With every square foot, including the floor and columns, warping every other way and not offering a horizontal plane of repose, the Gufa is a perceptual tour de force. It marks a departure towards suppressed depths of the unconscious, as it were, from the rational, technocratic modality represented by crystalline and cubic forms, upraised in the sun. The uncanny resurrection at the Gufa also coincides with India's increasing embrace of the fabulous and meta-rational.

Vritra lay very dead, and not unlike Vastupurusa upon whose dead and dismembered body a new episode and edifice might rise.[1] Vritra, a terrestrial dragon, held on to the waters of the world, as the story goes, until the celestial and luminous Indra ("smasher of enclosures") arrived to destroy the ninety-nine fortresses of Vritra, kill the dragon, and release imprisoned rivers. On the destroyed ramparts and ligaments of a telluric structure arose a brave, new world. And in Ahmedabad, a catatonic creature is resurrected by an inconoclast artist and a mystical

[1] In an idea where ritualized death is conflated with the production of the mandala, Vastupurusa is an undefined being who was seized by the gods and pinned down to the earth, and whose dismembered body is distributed across the gridded mandala before building and habitation can begin. Vritra is mentioned in ancient Vedic texts as a terrestrial creature who controls the water and must be annihilated – in this case by the celestial Indra – before a proper socialized beginning. Both myths perhaps circulate the pre-historic subjugation of terrestrial and locational symbolism by the predominantly celestial and abstract ideology of Vedism.

architect as a terrestrial architecture arising mysteriously and ominously from the ground.

From Raga to Ragas

August in Bombay: a month of festivals, the month of Krishna's birthday and Coconut Day; and this year – fourteen hours to go, thirteen, twelve – there was an extra festival on the calendar, a new myth to celebrate, because a nation which had never previously existed was about to win its freedom, catapulting us into a world which, although it had five thousand years of history, although it had invented the game of chess and traded with Middle Kingdom Egypt, was nevertheless quite imaginary; into a mythical land, a country which would never exist except by the efforts of a phenomenal collective will – except in a dream we all agreed to dream; it was a mass fantasy shared in varying degrees by Bengali and Punjabi, Madrasi and Jat, and would periodically need the sanctification and renewal which can only be provided by rituals of blood. India, the new myth – a collective fiction in which anything was possible, a fable rivaled only by two other mighty fantasies: money and God.

—Salman Rushdie, *Midnight's Children,* 1980

The pan-Indian edifice for whose mythical soul a French-Swiss architect wrote an urban epic at the foot-hills of the Himalayas, and which ironically has now been usurped by a (Hindu) religious right, exhibits multiple fissures. The tryst with destiny, as Nehru scheduled, gives away to a hundred trysts, and a million destinies. Architects now hesitate to talk of an Indian value as a debate rages between an essentialist and differentiated positions. A quasi-nationalist articulation of an "Indianism" was premised in most work even until the late 1980s; the Bhopal State Assembly by Charles Correa is the last operatic assemblage of that vision. In the context of Bangalore, an epicenter of new tensions, this time between a Malgudian anonymity and rapacious globalism, Prem Chandavarkar proposes (in his essay in the volume, "The Background in Bangalore: Architecture and Critical Resistance in a New Modernity") the palpability and specificity of places in lieu of a singular spatiality of the nation, and a critical post-nationalist practice that now must adopt a triple resistance – to both Indianism and globalism, and at the same time not appear or be "backward."

Sundarnagar, a Place Called Elsewhere

Urbanism is the Achilles' heel in the rush for euphoria. An avalanche of houses, malls, IT campuses, and condominiums mark the architectural landscape in market-driven India, yet there is little attention to how the individual creations come together as a social and spatial matrix amongst themselves and with the existent. Ramesh Biswas writes that a paradigmatic thinking in architectural urbanism is needed for this unprecedented urban phenomenon (in his essay in the volume, "One Space, Many Worlds"), notwithstanding forms of media, broadcast and cinematic urbanism. The urban utopia of Chandigarh that was criticized for its alienating features has been superseded by a greater phantasmagoria: of a Gurgaon in Delhi or Hirandani in Mumbai which are at best exclusive places in relation to the larger context, or more questionably, in Gayatri Spivak's rephrasing of global capital behavior, "secessionist."[2]

[2] Gayatri Chakravorty Spivak, "City, Country, Agency," presented at the conference "Theatres of Decolonization," Chandigarh, 1995. Spivak was referring to a statement on electronic capitalism by the US Secretary of Labor.

[3] The "song-site" is a literal space of the exotic and far-away in popular Indian filmic imagination that weaves in music, dance, couture, urban and landscape imagery into a phantasmagoria of dreams and desires.

Popular Hindi films provide a vicarious view of this new translocation. The setting of the 2003 film *Mein Prem Ki Diwani Hoon* is a fictional town called Sundarnagar, or the city beautiful. It is a place of bourgeois opulence, of resplendent houses populated by patriarchs and purveyors of tradition. The lawns to the houses are wide, and the driveways regal, while the riot-free, languorous town harbors manicured parks (obviously water supply is not a problem), quaint telephone booths (no sign of the ubiquitous ISD-NSW-Local), and lush outdoor spaces for cavorting (no vestige of the pulsating mob either). In the film, Sundarnagar is depicted as a town in India, but the fact of the matter is the entire film is shot in New Zealand. The Indian city of Sundarnagar may be fictive, but it is depicted in a real place, and that place is elsewhere, and that is the fixation in the Hindi-Bollywood imagination: the relentless flight towards elsewhere.

This flight is embedded and encoded in multiple realms, from the "song-site" numbers in Bollywood filmic productions to new building configurations.[3] This presents a juxtaposition of the place here and now and a place elsewhere, the messy city and a dream topography, where the former is of a native and the latter of a transnational provenance. The places from elsewhere in the "song-sites," which are real and actual, become fictive in the Hindi film narrative because the places are not named, or located with precision; they are literally framed to be "foreign," to be *elsewhere*. What makes *Mein Prem Ki Diwani Hoon* striking is that it takes the *elsewhere* of the "song-site" to the entire film. The longing for elsewhere – or for that matter, the desire to secede – is increasingly being embodied in new building configurations that are radically altering the urban landscape.

Despite the exhilarating lightness of arbitrariness, the relentless dissolution of geography, and the adoption of mimicry as an economic policy (Meenakshi in Mangalore presenting herself as Monica to a housewife in Minneapolis), many architects return to the intractable and redemptive theme of architecture's specificity in the geology of places. The critical question still – whether it is for Bijoy Jain in the humid swamps of Bombay, Prem Chandavarkar in a temperate and verdant Bangalore, or Rafiq Azam in the terracotta terrain of Dhaka – is "where is architecture" and not "what is architecture."

House Works

Housing is out, houses are in. If one allows for some more divine apparitions, gods are now in small things, in residences, shops, and small campuses, and in the their meticulous crafting, where the condensed poetics and tectonics negotiate the pendulum of the inevitable here-ness and the tantalizing elsewhere.

Since the 1960s, housing was a major domain of the Indian architectural enterprise that reflected a communitarian concern of the post-Corbusian/Nehruvian period. The emerging economy and radical shift in the lives of the middle class have now opened up new desires for articulating the house. The Turkish novelist Orhan Pamuk writes that the way to understand the people who have been part of the transformation in the astounding expansion of the middle class of India and China is to see "their private lives reflected in novels." In India, a vast part of that transformational imaginary is being narrated through the house, from opulent *havelis* and fictive "farmhouses," to elegant constructions of Bijoy Jain, Rahul Mehrotra, and others, and delectably delirious propositions of Michael Sorkin.

The once dialogical continuum of house/home with the world is being refashioned according to the emergent "secessionist" tendency to Home versus World. It is also in the context where the public building recedes in the social horizon, on the one hand, and unprecedented atomization proliferates socially, on the other hand, house/home is now a major site of the architectural exegesis in India. Whether it is merely another object in the consumerist cosmos (K.K. Birla, of the famous industrialist family, points out that what was once a symbol of attainment, the brick house, first shifted to the motor scooter, and to the car now),[4] and whether it retains the *gravitas of dwelling*, remains unclear, but projects presented in this issue return to the house as an embodiment of situation and materiality.

[4] Dr. K.K. Birla, "India 2020," in *Hindustan Times*, May 9, 2007.

Reincarnating the Courtyard and the Pavilion

The Orchard House outside Ahmedabad by Rahul Mehrotra recalls both the courtyard paradigm of hot-dry climates and a reactive interiority that may stem from the raucous urbanism of Indian cities (Mehrotra explains that his architectural vocabulary hinges on the reading of his city of practice, Bombay). The interiority is defined by the reification of preponderantly long and solid walls. While courtyard houses are by nature exclusionary (socially and visually), the redemption is in the itinerary, in the arrival and passage through the various articulated thresholds into the ecstatic focus of the house: the open-to-sky court.

An obverse of that model is the pavilion where the inner court gives away to a canopy, and the predominantly solid wall dematerializes into perforations, membranes, lattices and *jalis*. Much of the architecture of Bijoy Jain (Studio Mumbai Architects) is a delightful celebration of the pavilion, approximating the Sri Lankan architect Geoffrey Bawa's consideration of the house-as-a-garden in the hot-humid milieu. Whether in tactile-rich wooden slats (Jamshyd House in Alibag near Bombay), or a diaphanous luminous screen (the Reading Room addition to his house in Alibag), Jain's architecture amplifies the phenomenal and spatial continuum between the house and landscape in a moisture saturated environment. However, such singular typologies are not always possible as one confronts inevitable complexities, either programmatic or urban. Samira Rathod, in her Mariwala House (also, in Alibag) creates a horizontal symphony through an ensemble of disparate pieces that are tactile, colorful and voluble. Mathew and Ghosh, for their studio and residence on a small lot in Bangalore, produce a compacted bricolage of diverse pieces as an urban essay. In their attempt to reconfigure the contemporary urban box, in a context where a purity or unity is no longer possible, the architectural body is composed of fragmentations and a patchwork of memories and events. Rafiq

Azam, in Dhaka, rearranges the conventional location of building, garden and landscape, and in doing so boldly devises a house of landscape layers even within the city. Many of these works share a material and expressive language with a trans-Asian tropical modernity, practiced by architects as Bedmar and Shi, Kerry Hill or Chan Soo Khian.

A transformation is also happening where architects fear to tread – rural houses or dwellings of the economically disadvantaged, both of which constitute a significant number in South Asia. Adnan Morshed, in a sort of subaltern narrative, traces the anthropological metamorphosis of rural dwellings touched by the Grameen Bank housing program. He argues that even as architects are largely uninvolved in affecting homes in such areas, a quiet revolution is happening to those "timeless" villages, something that needs to be incorporated into the story of Indian and South Asian architecture, especially as the axis of contention in the new economy is increasingly between the city and village.

Gandhi in Exile

Our strategy should be not only to confront empire, but to lay siege to it. To deprive it of oxygen. To shame it. To mock it. With our art, our music, our literature, our stubbornness, our joy, our brilliance, our sheer relentlessness - and our ability to tell our own stories. Stories that are different from the ones we're being brainwashed to believe.
—Arundhati Roy, 2003

Our architecture?

I was not wholly surprised, on a visit a year ago, to see Gandhi's ashram in Wardha (Nagpur) rather desolate like a residue of an abandoned village. A few Japanese tourists sat down for a lesson in the *charka*, while giggling couples from the neighboring areas roamed the yards in oblivious frivolity. If the *charka* is an emblem of sustainability – and Gandhi is to be credited for that much fashionable architectural term now – it is now as alien as Buddha's *dharma-chakra*. I was more surprised to find the name of the venerable Ivan Illich on a dusty, monotyped pamphlet on Gandhi's house. Written in 1978, as an ethical and sociological explanation of the emblematic *bapukuti*, the pamphlet predicted the challenges of the coming decades, on the onrush of accumulation and consumption that "shining and incredible" India now revel in. Both Nehru and Gandhi represented modernist self-reflectivity, but while Nehru professed what was then an internationalist position, Gandhi appeared parochially nationalist. The matter has flipped now. If Nehru is the modernist of the industrial-socialist makeover much discredited now, Gandhi's experiments with himself align with the radical modernist project of transfiguration: through the ascetic body in the minimalist space. I have often speculated how Gandhi would be sitting on the floor of the sparse Farnsworth House, and I see him rather at home there especially if it is an autumn month in Chicago, the trees not yet bare right outside the large plate glass walls. The once national is now the irrefutable international, but in his own ashram he is ironically absent.

A far cry from Illich's prognosis, an accelerated consumerism proceeds at warp speed (pun intended) that throws caution to the wind and revels in the febrile architectural outpour India has ever seen. What to make of this all?

Anthologizing India

India is a giant squid that every now and then must be wrestled to the ground to make sense of. And in the melee, one tentacle does not know what the others are doing. Is India poised for an economic lift-off the likes of which has not been witnessed before, or perched on the precipice of an urban and ecological cataclysm? Is India about the irrefutable phantasmagoria of Bollywood or the timeless poise of a Bharatnatyam? Is the Indian an argumentative one or a meditative one? Is India in the end really about India itself, as understood by notions of nations, or the much more fluid, elusive and yet definitive subcontinental substance? And when you have the giant squid finally pinned to the ground, all tentacles flailing, you realize it's not a multi-tentacled squid after all but a hydra-headed creature.

With the task of presenting a survey of contemporary architecture, I wanted to see what analogy can be drawn from literary anthologies, an area characterized by a vibrant output. Among various anthologies, including Rushdie's *Mirrorwork: Fifty Years of Indian Writing* (1997), Amit Chaudhuri's *Picador Book of Modern Indian Literature* (2001), and *The Granta Book of India* (2004), an early collection edited by Adil Jussawalla (1974) is very prescient. Jussawalla opens the collection with an excerpt from Qurratulain Hyder's reflection on statelessness from her trans-historical fiction *The River of Fire*.[5] While a Himalayan view of India is always a dubious project, Hyder's River speaks of the "Indian" state of mind that overflows the imperviousness of new nation-states. Within an effluent history, the River charts the cultural fluidity, geographic porosity, and transnational mobility that describe the South Asian subcontinental phenomenon.

Is the vitality in literature matched in architecture? I wasn't sure when I began the gathering, but as this issue will show that there is a definitive inauguration of new latitudes and energies in Indian and subcontinental architecture. The enigmatic empty jar of Saleem/Salman that portended an archaeology of the future is now and here. And if that bottle were filled, would it look like the present issue of *AD*, a raga of indelible vitality?

[5] Adil J. Jussawalla, *New Writings in India*, Penguin (Hamondsworth: Penguin, 1974). Qurratulain Hyder's *River of Fire* was first published as *Aag Ka Dariya* in 1957.

Palmyra House.

Night view of the North block with its reflection in the pool in the foreground. Palmyra House, Alibagh, India.
Photo: AKAA / Rajesh Vora.

Reading the Wind and Weather: The Meteorological Architecture of Studio Mumbai

Published in *Architectural Design*, June 2012.

A building is like a tree. Unfolding into the environment, incarcerated in it and incarnating it too, buildings by Studio Mumbai dwell in the space between architecture and landscape.

In most projects by Studio Mumbai, the first thing one notices is the crafting of the building in a kind of poetic and situational economy. A building emerges effortlessly as if it has been there all along, without the conceit of artifice. Kengo Kuma thematises such an act of building as "weak architecture" following Gianni Vattimo's program of "weak ontology" as a non-hierarchical, non-dominant condition. The Bangalore based architect Prem Chandavarkar approximates that through the notion of "architecture of background," when the test of a building is not its spectacular presentation, but the accrued experiences and memories of its everyday inhabitation.

Such a position is driven by a profound act of building: the architect's perennial art of putting things together as a condensation of the landscape. For the practice's resort in Leti, up in the Himalayas, Studio Mumbai's Bijoy Jain describes the act of building as "a passive reworking of the landscape through gathering, moving, condensing native materials into cohesive but temporary structures." Jain understands that a built work takes place, how it is inscrutably situated, and how it is environed or enveloped by the world in a manner where, in the language of phenomenology, "no cleavage is possible" between the work and the world.

Taking place invokes two perennial truths: the inevitability of situatedness, and building from a site. The environmental analogy of the tree suggests care and an exact understanding of the science of geology and moisture, and the rhythm of the seasons. When students inquired of the Philadelphia-based wood sculptor Wharton Esherick how they should proceed, the Modernist craftsman is supposed to have replied: "Think like a farmer." Louis Kahn, who designed one of Esherick's studios, also understood that an architect can learn from a farmer in not making the landscape pretty, but rather "to preserve his crops by the logic of planting." It is in the logic of planting that Studio Mumbai frames its work, as a kind of cultivation. A building – or a tree – emerges in the horizon from the material potentials and

Workplace, Studio Mumbai Architects.

possibilities of the world, from their numerous combinations and assemblages, and from the natural laws and systems that dictate their production.

The inevitable situatedness of architecture indicates an ideological and strategic difference between the "what" of architecture and "where is architecture." The question of "where" brings up the obvious nexus of architecture and the world; but one that is increasingly opaque to most architects inordinately beholden to the seduction of "what."

Despite our habitual thinking of the autonomy of architecture (which is perhaps the biggest visual deception with which we contend), architecture is always in a kind of "reciprocal insertion and intertwining" with the environment, where the limits of one are lost in the other.

Such an intertwined identity positions Jain's work in, as Kuma observes, the relationship between architecture and landscape. Disagreeing with the division of disciplines into architecture and landscape architecture, Kahn proposed the term "land architect" as someone who looks at land from an indivisible point of view, from a condition of oneness. The principle of land architecture suggests a complex dialogue between the grounding and a rising of a building, as if the building – a fact of constructedness – rises from the ambiguous earth into a precise form even if the earth is still the material and genealogical source of the unfolding. Such a reasoned consideration of the simultaneity of distinctiveness and seamlessness – of architecture and landscape – is expressed in the articulation of subterranean gravitas and atmospheric lightness in Jain's work. A section drawing through the Tara

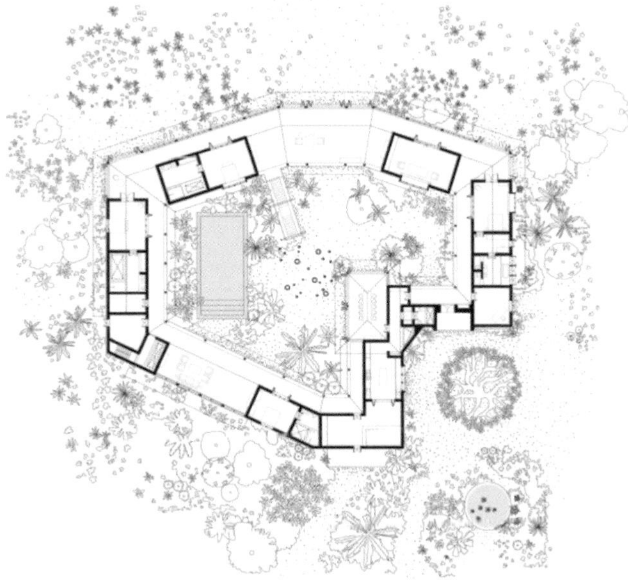

Tara House, Kashid, Maharashtra. Plan.

House in Kashid, Maharashtra (2005), with the well as excavation and building as construction, reveals his predisposition towards architecture as a manipulation of the topographic continuum.

Appearing as an emblem of dwelling in the Copper House II in Chondi, Maharashtra (2011), Palmyra House in Nandgaon, Maharashtra (2007) and Tara House, the deep, dark well confers on these projects a subterranean sensibility that is both ecological and mythical. Excavated spaces, deep wells and stone-walls form a lexicon of grounding in Jain's work. The Copper House begins with the new excavation of an artesian well forming the organising core of the project. The curb of a dank well covered with moss sits amid the coconut grove of the Palmyra House. In Tara House, a secret room under the courtyard/garden forms a reservoir of water for the house, drawn from an underground aquifer. The courtyard and garden rise above it, and the house spirals out as an ensemble of pavilions.

The stolid mass of the earth is contrasted by another language defining the arisen building: diaphanous membranes, floating planes, skeletal frames and delicate slats form a tectonic configuration for most of the houses. Palmyra records the architect's earliest articulation of an architecture of porosity formed simply by slatted envelopes as an analogue of the filigree of coconut-tree leaves. Formed over and along low basalt walls rising from the ground, the tectonic assemblage of the Utsav House in Satirje, Maharashtra (2008), utilises the porous property to complete the intertwined relationship.

"I am alert to the weather," claims Jain. Learning from the nature of being exposed in the moisture-laden landscape, especially the

Tara House, Kashid, Maharashtra. Photo: Studio Mumbai Architects.

Tara House, Kashid, Maharashtra. Section.

Hiremath House pool.

monsoons, largely in the region of Mumbai, he has developed a typological vocabulary (the pavilion-like disposition) and a refined language of materials and details. House pavilions are woven through coconut groves (Palmyra) or mango trees (Belavali House, 2008, and Copper Houses). In a kind of apostolic succession to Sri Lankan architect Geoffrey Bawa, Jain has invigorated the promise of tropical architecture, taking its ecological ethos towards a new poetic prospect.

Few architects in India seem to have patience for either the phenomenology of situatedness or the care of crafting. The former requires a listening to the wind, so to speak, and the latter a tactic of delay best relayed by that wonderful Latin phrase *festina lente*, 'make haste slowly.' Jain emphasises an attention to the process of making and the patient evolution of things. He speaks of *riyaz*, the practice or discipline of doing architecture every day with both attentiveness and repetition.

These are best represented in his workshop practice, placing craftsmen and artisans in the middle of the process, doing life-size mockups and prototypes, and material innovations, and eventually weaving a tapestry of sensorial experiences out of the constructed materiality.

Jain's close collaboration with artisans and craftsmen recalls what noted Egyptian architect Hasan Fathy developed with the master mason Aladdin Mustafa, or what Bawa and British-born Indian architect Laurie Baker practised with their builders. In the highly disciplined practice of Studio Mumbai, there is also room for instinctiveness. Jain lets the building 'respond to the instincts of the craftsmen and the evolving challenges of construction, with predictably surprising results.' It is this combination of the tactical and instinctual that will produce an empathy for the language of unauthorised architecture from the niches and interstices of Mumbai's official fabric and their plastered reincarnations at the Victoria and Albert Museum.

In maintaining a consistent sense of situational particularity and tectonic poetics, Jain's architecture approximates the act of resistance that Kenneth Frampton put up as a provocation in an environment of devastating sameness. Delicately poised between the contemporary and the traditional, and Zen minimalism and delightful elegance, Jain's work cannot be described as regionalist either. Not avowedly staged as a resistance, Jain's work nonetheless represents an alternative to India's double trouble: the raucous architectural phantasmagoria serving the neoliberal economy and the hyper-aestheticized extravaganza surrogating for tradition. Jain tiptoes towards a more precious and patient position. Like a farmer, he scans the sky for a meteorological intuition, treads the earth for secret semaphores, and then gathers with carpenters, masons, architects and artisans for cultivating the building-tree together.

Site with building shown in a miniature painting by Doshi.

Sangath as a Landscape Event

Published in *Balkrishna Doshi: Architecture for the People*, edited by Mateo Kries, Jolanthe Kugler and Khushnu Hoof (Vitra Design Museum), 2019. An earlier version appeared in *The Companions to the History of Architecture*, Volume 4, edited by David Leatherbarrow and Alexander Eisenschmidt, 2017.

As twin projects, although separated by about ten years, Sangath (1979-1981) and the Husain-Doshi Gufa (1992-1994) heralded a new fantastic dimension in modern Indian architecture, and a turning point in the oeuvre of the master architect Balkrishna Doshi. Similar to the awe and intrigue generated when Ronchamp was first unveiled, the two projects presented a new plastic language and building ethos, reincarnating ancient and phantasmagoric sentiments in an India that was then positioning itself for a new global and corporate trajectory. Both projects are also powerful essays on architecture's inscrutable relationship with the landscape, a theme that eluded most architects until then. Deliberately produced and articulated as an "event" in the landscape, in which architecture is intimately implicated, the projects mark a new synthesis of building, topography, planting, and landscaped elements.

Sangath sits between two phases in the oeuvre of Doshi: between cubic masses raised aloft in the landscape, and a crustacean creature lying embedded in the ground. The former belongs to a group of projects from the Institute of Indology in Ahmedabad (1957-1962) to the Indian Institute of Management in Bangalore (1977-1985), and the latter is expressed singularly at the unusual Husain-Doshi Gufa (1992-1995), a progeny that followed Sangath. Sangath is a key project that inaugurates the mythopoeic dimension in Doshi's work that takes him from an explicitly rational and objective approach to architecture towards an openly oneiric and phantasmagoric realm.

As a stalwart among the first generation of Indian architects following the national independence in 1947, Doshi took on that enormous task of graduating India towards a "brave, new world" as imagined by the first prime minister Jawaharlal Nehru. Since then, through a powerful body of work, Doshi was instrumental in framing a modern architectural idiom and ethos for India. This was made possible through his personal commitment to nation-building and a unique background of working with two foremost form-makers of the modern period. The experience of working with Le Corbusier in his Paris studio (1951-1957) for the buildings in Chandigarh and Ahmedabad already destined Doshi to take on bigger challenges. Doshi set up his practice

Section.

in Ahmedabad (1958), a city that had already positioned itself, with work by Le Corbusier and later by Louis Kahn, as a site for demonstrative modern architecture. Doshi also founded an architectural school (1962) that he directed and established as one of the distinguished institutions in India.

Besides his intimacy with the mission of modern architecture, Doshi has remained deeply aligned with the ethos of India's ancient civilization. Doshi continues to reflect on and draw inspiration from the vast repertoire of Vedic and Hindu traditions. It is this presence of two civilizational and philosophical strands in Doshi's work that has always offered new possibilities and excursions, as well as debates, in the evolution of modern Indian architecture.

In line with his expanded commitment to architecture involving professional practice, research and teaching, Doshi conceived his practice in a wider term, as a laboratory for the creation of new architectural paradigms. Beginning in the 1970s, Doshi designed and created a miniature complex on a parcel of land at the outskirts of Ahmedabad that came to reflect his synthetic vision of practice and research. Doshi gave that expanded practice the title of Sangath, or "moving together through participation," that includes his architectural office and the Vastushilpa Foundation for Studies and Research in Environmental Design. Sangath was conceived, as William Curtis notes, as Doshi's version of an architectural laboratory in the likeness of Corbusier's atelier at 35, Rue de Sevres, or Frank Lloyd Wright's Taliesin.

In characterizing Sangath as a turning point that marks both a crystallization of earlier experiments and deliberate movement towards a new stage, three principal themes stand out: an intimate conversation between architecture and landscape, a constructional assembly derived from a climatic imperative, and a choreographed movement in a spatial matrix.

Grounding

The dominant imagery of Sangath is a group of vaulted shapes oriented in one direction that rises from a constructed landscape of planes, terraces, walls and steps. Water runs along the interstices of the vault, on channels and troughs, often cascading down, to create a pool. While the interiority of the building is a mystery from the exterior, a subterranean possibility is already indicated in the overall ensemble. The "miniature" drawing series generated by Doshi following the construction shows the site with a veritable catalog of architectural and landscape motifs: wall, steps, terraces, trees, artifacts, architectural fragments strewn in the larger landscape.

What immediately characterizes the physiognomy of Sangath is the proposition of architecture as a topographical manipulation. Producing an ambiguity between building and landscape, the configuration is better understood as something evolving from the ground as if sculpted from it.

While the compact ensemble sits on the site as if it has been there for a long time, architectural critics have suggested a few metaphors for it: a group of buildings on a hill, a small village, or a traditional building grown from the ground. A reference to traditional Indian architecture invoking an earth building or domical architecture is only allusive and without any particularity. However, a suggestion for a village is possible which one encounters in a path on a hilly terrain as an ensemble of buildings. An Indian context is more compellingly present in the climatic responses and peripatetic experience on the site. Some of the textural modulation, although suggestive of the work of the Spanish-Catalan architect Josep-Maria Jujol (1879-1949), with whom Doshi has expressed a new kinship, may also be found in certain vernacular traditions of India.

Sangath's figural alignment may be closer to the other repertoire of Le Corbusier that involves a deeply imbricated mutuality between building and landscape rather than the polemical antitheticality represented in the Swiss-French master's cubic projects. Two residences designed at the same time by Le Corbusier for Ahmedabad represent this dual and divergent strands: Villa Shodhan as a tropical reincarnation of the cubic Villa Savoye, and the Sarabhai House as recalling an earth-hugging Mediterranean vernacular. Sarabhai House, especially with its Catalan vaults, structural parallelism, grass-covered roof, and clear "merging" with the landscape exonerated the territorially detached ideology through, what Le Corbusier described as, a "pact with nature." The grounded physiognomy of Sarabhai House can be traced back to Le Corbusier's consistent attention to translating vernacular types, works that were carefully left in the background in the prime-time of his cubic ideology in the 1920s. The strand of this series of work proceeds from his own Weekend House with the vault and grass roof (1920s) to the radical post-war design of Maison Jaoul (1951).

Sangath, in bringing to the foreground the ancient relational theme of architecture and landscape, and challenging the "twoness" of the two, also remains an homage to the other Le Corbusier.[1] Doshi's new propensity for a collaboration between architecture and landscape in which the continuum of the land-form dilutes the autonomy of the building-form creates a deliberate and rich ambiguity. Realizing the ontological inevitability of a building sited and emplaced, Doshi presents Sangath as an affirmation of architecture as a "landscape event."[2]

Doshi's subterranean quest, and a profound mutation of the cubic paradigm inaugurated at Sangath, turns towards the mythological – the realm of ruins and monsters – finding its explicit expression for the gallery designed for the iconoclast artist M.F. Husain, the Husain-Doshi Gufa at a site not far from Sangath. Starting from Sangath, Doshi increasingly seeks mythological verification in the grounding of architecture, and valorizing a primordial relationship with the earth. While at Sangath, embedding part of the building into the ground was carried out as a tectonic and climatic strategy, the Husain-Doshi Gufa was conceived as some kind of reptilian creature slithering in the ground.

One had to enter that part-reptilian and part-cave-like project through a mouth-like orifice. Doshi himself speaks of dream encounters of divining the site and figuring out the form-shape. The elaboration of a subterranean creature-form is not unlike a resurrection of Vrtra, an aquatic-terrestrial monster in Vedic mythology who was once slayed by the celestial god Indra. This is not unlike Pythia slaughtered by Apollo in Greek imagination to inaugurate a new imperium of the celestial over the terrestrial. Such imagery points to Doshi's engagement with ancient Vedic and Hindu narratives, and his own deeply personal oneiric imagination in form conception. With the deep and ancient symbolism of the cave, the Gufa provokes a rethinking of the original conditions of architecture submerged in the onslaught of a marketplace dynamic and the displacement of sacrality in the everyday life.

A disposition for an earth-bound configuration is also displayed in other projects whenever an opportunity offered itself. Even for a project with pragmatic currency such as the National Institute of Fashion Technology in New Delhi (1997), and one dressed up a little with postmodern paraphernalia, Doshi was intensely attentive to discovering and digging up an ancient well that produced an excavated parti in the courtyard of the project site.

Doshi's Sangath phase speaks of his attempt to literally dig down into some primordial depth for a new foundational and ontological verification for architecture in India. "I tried to listen to the vibrations and activities that lay deep in her womb," Doshi confesses. "The earth always rekindles many dormant ideas in me."[3] Even though Sangath does not speak of any particular architectural tradition of India, it proposes a new mythos in the tradition. While none of the themes at Sangath match up to a particular tradition or practice, it appears to be in an easy and natural collaboration with the site, as if it has been there for a long time.

[1] In interviews, Doshi has likened Sangath as an homage to Le Corbusier, and his later Gufa to Kahn, two architects with whom he worked closely and enjoyed a unique symbiotic relationship. Interviews conducted with writer, 1994.

[2] The idea of "architecture as landscape event" is discussed in Kazi Ashraf, "Taking Place: Landscape in the Architecture of Louis Kahn," in *Journal of Architectural Education* (November, 2007).

[3] Doshi, in "The Revelation," from James Steele, *The Complete Architecture of Balkrishna Doshi* (Mumbai: Super Book House, 1998), p. 146.

Exterior view of amphitheater and lawn.

The "Vault"

Sangath also displays a rigorous plan, or one that began as a rectilinear parti on a rectangular plot constituted by two bays of vaulted space, a part of which gets skewed into a diagonal motif to receive a layered land-form shaped as an amphitheater. The amphitheater becomes the linchpin on the site around which a circulatory rotation is articulated. An earlier plan shows the site organized through four parallel rows of vaulted spaces alternated by a sliver of "servant space." Such a plan diagram recalls the intertwined spatial and structural articulation of both Le Corbusier's Sarabhai House, and Kahn's Kimbell Museum at Fort Worth, Texas, making possible for a rich tapestry of layered and overlapped spaces.

The vaulted roofscape – an inhabitable landscape – is a defining element for Sangath. Although a structural shell that is shaped as a vault, the "vault" is a carefully wrought iconographic device that complements the landscape narrative considering that the natural tendency of a risen vault is to return to the ground. Doshi's vaulted orientation has a number of possible sources: from the Sarabhai House to Doshi's early work with brick vaults for the housing for ATIRA (1957-60) and Bhandari House, New Delhi (1966). Doshi talks about appreciating the visual and material economy in roofing an outhouse on the site with bent corrugated sheets.[4] His sketch of a museum in Egypt by Wissa Wassef, an associate of Hasan Fathy, is telling of discovering an architectural idiom for a hot and dry milieu (1978).

After the adoption of the vault as a principal structural and spatial organizing element in the design schema, its shape and geometry was studied closely through drawings and various models. While the geometry of vaults required a structural and volumetric discipline, the rigor was allayed by a largely irregular distribution of walls and piers from which the vaults emerge. Since the vault is actually a shell structure, techniques of its construction were tried even with participation by local communities, again leading to new possibilities that were carried out in a more plastic way in the Gufa.

Sangath is also a catalog of cooling practices, in which the vaulted shell structure is a key performer. Doshi realizes the sensibility of locating the habitable space in Ahmedabad's unforgiving hot and arid climate in a sheltered cocoon. Besides the vaulted canopy, digging into the ground provides another means of finding a cooler environment. Doshi speaks of a suggestion made by the artist M. F. Husain in the early 1970s of going underground for climatic reason.[5]

In Doshi's climate-centered investigations, the "vault" is conceived as a shell structure created by two thin hand-layered ferro-cement concrete with hollow terracotta tubes in-between. The vault-like shell with its hollow layer provides an insular envelope for the interior spaces in Ahmedabad's harsh hot climate. The shell is finally layered by a mosaic of white broken china with the intention of reflecting off the sun. Openings are minimal and when they do occur, the entry of light and view is very much modulated. Water channels and troughs form the

[4] Steele, *The Complete Architecture of Balkrishna Doshi*, p. 90.

[5] Doshi, "Revelation," in Steele, *The Complete Architecture of Balkrishna Doshi,* p. 146.

shallow area between the vaults that provide another insular layer to the roofscape. In some instances, the channelized water cascades over a window opening, invoking a vernacular practice of cooling an interior by spreading moistened fabric over a window.

With the vaults produced out of terracotta tiles in ferro-cement layers and broken ceramic tiles laid piece by piece, Sangath is also an artisanal building made by local hands rather than specialized professionals.

The Itinerary

A choreographed movement is the third distinctive feature of Sangath. Upon arrival at the entry court that faces the vaulted end of the building-form, one is immediately directed towards the left, away from the building to encounter a series of shifting axes, crossing of thresholds, and panoramic views of the main building across a garden. The choreographed journey from the entrance, from the ruckus of the street, through the garden to the inside of the vaulted space is a phenomenological experience of the distance and near, surface tactility, and precisely located objects (earthen jars and sculpture) conducted through an *architecturale promenade*.

The diagonal is a key device in this experience. With the aim to activate surprising views and encounters, "the approach is never axial but diagonal," as Doshi himself notes, "to make one discover and absorb the building before entering it." Along this itinerary, one experiences earthen jars as markers, metal sculpture, passage by trees, view from under trees, landscaped grounds, water pool, low walls and layered plinths, pavings with pebbled textures, a grass-stepped amphitheater, and a canopy under which a conversation can be held. Located like a little plaza in a hillside village, the amphitheater is used for meetings and performances.

Axial shifts in movement make it possible for exploring the terrain through various techniques of landscape design. Akin to the order of movement in a Japanese garden, shifts are accompanied by textural changes and moments of pause and reorientation. The construction of pauses – transitional spaces and thresholds – in the spatial matrix becomes for Doshi a mark of Indian architectural experience. Describing the spatial quality created at the Indian Institute of Management in Bangalore (1977-1985), where in concept a monolithic block has been disaggregated to create a matrix of spaces and volumes with various degrees of inside and outside, Doshi proposes that "supreme among architectural experiences are ones which occur in spaces which could be characterized as pause or ambiguous, plural spaces." In terms of a corporeal experience, pauses initiate a breaking down of the scale for a more humanized encounter. Such spaces, Doshi further argues in more mystical terms, "activate the human psyche and induce it to sink towards the center, the mythical world of man's primordial being."

From one of the farthest point, in the diagonal arrangement, the building is presented in its skewed disposition revealing as in a picturesque tradition coordinated relationship of things far and near, the modulation of landscape and building, and the anticipation of getting there. It is at this moment, the elongated building-form is exposed in its fullest on that long property. It is almost as if Doshi had crafted that axial turn as the perfect moment to take in the full panorama of Sangath: a visually controlled vantage point that establishes the image of the vaults risen from the ground modulated by terraces, plinths, walls and steps, with grassy surface and water pools in the foreground.

The final progression to the building occurs through a tight entry, almost an inadvertent opening in the folds of the building. The itinerary continues into and in the interior landscape as one proceeds through a maze of layered spaces that often connect the various levels creating experiences of compactness and openness, different heights to the vault, and stairs going up or down mysteriously in a kind of tightly packed spatial drama. The condensed and rich overlay of architectural pieces is a snapshot of some old city in North India. Ultimately the itinerary climaxes towards a long vista along the vaulted studio space where windows are few, but the most prominent ones are the half-circle under the vaults that give a glimpse of the Ahmedabad sky, bringing the itinerant to the heart of Sangath: the long row of architects' desks in a kind of near-monastic setting not unlike Le Corbusier's Paris studio.

Sangath, in its vacillation between an urban and un-urban model, for that tension seems not to have been resolved, between paying homage to an old master and attempting to transcend that, between a structural logic of building and a dream-like inner journey, and between being an architectural ensemble and landscape form, still constitutes a dense example for inventions in modern Indian architecture.

A cross-view towards Sangath.

Muzharul Islam's Residence, East Pakistan (Bangladesh), Muzharul Islam (1923-2012), Plan Oblique, Muzharul Islam Archive.

Barbara Sansoni (b.1928), *Yakadagala* (1964), hand coloured print, Barbara Sansoni Archives.

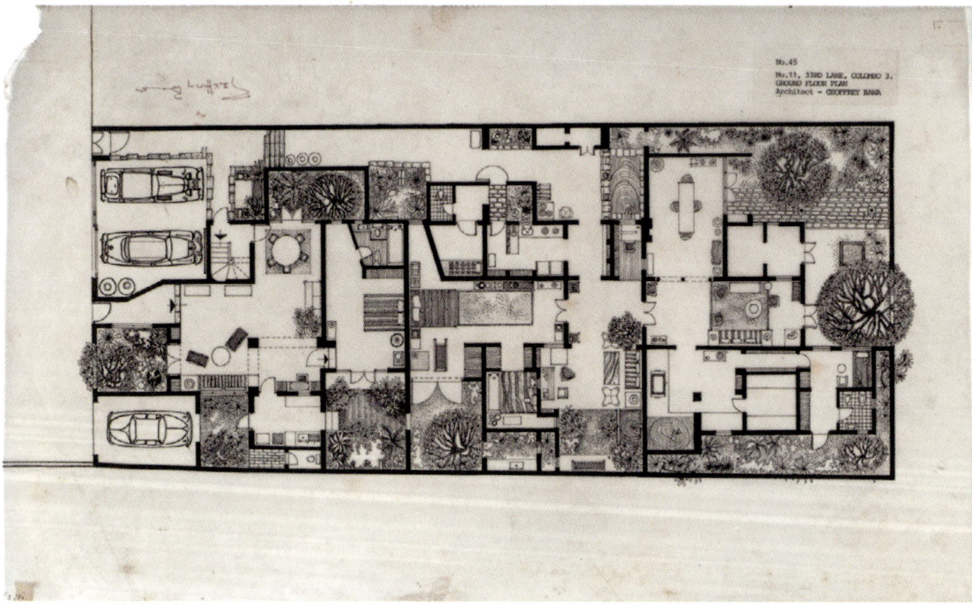

No.11, 33rd Lane House, Colombo, Ceylon (Srilanka). 1960-98TK. Geoffrey Bawa (1919-2003). Ground-floor plan. Ink and pencil on tracing paper. The Lunuganga Trust.

"Sheltered Openness": The Modern House in South Asia

Published in *The Project of Independence: Architectures of Decolonization in South Asia, 1947–1985*, edited by Martino Stierli, Sean Anderson and Anoma Pieris (Museum of Modern Art, New York, 2022).

Modernity appeared in South Asia in a slow, simmering process entangled with both the marauding enterprise of European colonialists, and a commercial as well as intellectual resurgence among a new native elite. While the progressive groups of Bengal and India were eager to embrace European modernity in episodic changes focused on institutions, their enthusiasm stopped literally at the doorstep of the house.

Venerated as well as repudiated, home has always been a contested category in the subcontinent. While the traditional home in South Asia is considered an introspective place, erected both tectonically and ritually, "homelessness" as practiced by ascetics and renouncers was also glorified. With multiple households living in each home, it is also a place in which the individual is subordinated to deep-rooted norms. If modernity signifies the celebration of the self, the traditional home appears antithetical to the modern project. All of these conditions perhaps account for the fitful development of the modern house in South Asia.

Iohandas Gandhi (1869-1948) at his hut Bapu Kuti, hmedabad, India. 1946.

Other than sporadic examples—from Claude Batley's neotraditional residences in Bombay in the early decades of the twentieth century to Rabindranath Tagore's historically styled houses in Santiniketan—colonial-period experiments in private housing design are few. The bungalow, on which more below, is an exception. On the other hand, the "home" in the village of Sewagram (outside Nagpur), where Mohandas Gandhi lived from 1936 to 1948, was deliberately constructed as a hut in a rural ethic and now appears as a prescient rethinking of the house paradigm.[1] A manifestation of a political and spiritual discourse, and of a contrapuntal modernity, Gandhi's home, popularly known as *bapukuti*, recalls the ideological shift from *grihya* (home/household) to *kuti* (hut) as practiced in ancient renunciatory traditions.

In maintaining the vast machine of the colonial empire through relentless building projects, European architects and engineers presented to middle- and upper-class Indians the image of the "modern home" encapsulated in that now universalized building type, the bungalow. Adopted from the vernacular architecture of Bengal and configured out of climatic concerns, metrics of comfort, as well as fear of tropical "miasma," and providing prototypes for various economic groups, the evolution from *bangla* (or village hut) to bungalow is perhaps the biggest and most underrated architectural event triggered on the subcontinent.[2] While the primary impetus was pragmatic, the bungalow created the most pervasive residential paradigm in modern South Asia—from ubiquitous villas and suburban houses to dubious "farmhouses" dotting the fringes of the contemporary metropolis. Two aspects of the bungalow paradigm would keep modern architects in thrall: climatic parameters in configuring a house, on the one hand, and in situating a building, on the other.

Although superseded by a high architectural poetics, climate was a primary driver in Le Corbusier's iconic residences in Ahmedabad, the Shodhan Villa and the Sarabhai House (both 1951–1955). A major influence on residential design for the upper class, both houses quickly transcend their "utilitarian roots,"[3] and become examples of architectural virtuosity. Shodhan Villa, by replicating the spatial drama of the Villa Savoye (1928–1931), introduces a radical type of architectural volume in the Indian scene, while Sarabhai House, with its sprawling character and intimate relation with the site, prods a deeper spatial-psychological sensibility.

Villa Shodhan, Ahmedabad, India. 1951–1956. Le Corbusier (Charles-Édouard Jeanneret, 1887–1965). Interior view. Photographer unknown. c. 1956. Architecture & Design Study Center, The Museum of Modern Art, New York.

In most South Asian dwellings, across various social strata and geographic contexts, the living space overflows to the "outside," producing a mediating realm between the outer and inner domains, and giving houses a perennial property of "sheltered openness."[4] Charles Correa would conceptualize that quality as a "place in the sun," integral to "open-to-sky" interior courtyards and ambulatory spaces.[5] Such tenets for dwellings also offer a convenient alliance with the modernist intertwining of exterior and interior spaces.

Moving away from the pragmatism of the bungalow, the house by the late 1950s became an architectural statement, an ensemble expressing transparency, porosity, and openness under a parasol. Achyut Kanvinde's Harivallabhdas House in Ahmedabad (1964), Correa's Umbrella House (Parekh House) in Ahmedabad (1966), Muzharul Islam's own house in Dhaka (1968), Balkrishna V. Doshi's Tejal House in Ahmedabad (1994), and Geoffrey Bawa's Jayewardene House in Mirissa (1996), all fall under the "parasol house" type.

Sarabhai House, Ahmedabad, India. 1951–1956. Le Corbusier (Charles-Édouard Jeanneret, 1887–1965). Interior view. 1955. Photo: Lucien Hervé. Architecture & Design Study Center, The Museum of Modern Art, New York.

The Sri Lankan architects Minnette de Silva and Geoffrey Bawa, inspired by the documentation of vernacular architecture carried out by the designer Barbara Sansoni and artist/architect Laki Senanayake, developed a distinctive regionalist mode. An early articulation of the "tropical modernist" house, and a laboratory for a regionalist expression, is the Karunaratne House in Kandy (1950) by de Silva, considered to be among the first modern houses in the country.[6] Writing in the magazine *Marg* in 1953, de Silva described the house as an experiment in "modern regional architecture in the tropics."[7] In that building, and others that followed, de Silva assembled the ingredients that were to define architecture in Sri Lanka: relating building and landscape,

Balkrishna Harivallabhdas Residence, Ahmedabad, India. 1962–1964. Kanvinde, Rai & Chowdhury (est. 1970). Achyut Kanvinde (1916–2002). Exterior view. c. 1964. Kanvinde Archives.

overlapping inside and outside, and rejuvenating the vernacular courtyard (*midula*) in modern form. In Bawa's work, the bungalow/house received two distinct conceptual revisions: the "house in a garden" as in his magnum opus, the garden estate Lunuganga, and the "house as a garden" seen in his Colombo home on 33rd Lane, in which, as historian David Robson argues for the Ena de Silva House (1962), the bungalow is refashioned to become "inward-looking," dismantled and reassembled in a tight urban setting.[8] As "meta-bungalows," Bawa's houses transcend the pragmatic parameters of the bungalow to be more akin to sensuous artifacts operating in tandem with landscape conditions.

Symptomatic of a rising middle class but reflecting diverse aspirations in different cities, houses were defining a new lifestyle in a Westernized milieu as a fusion of the old colonial *babu* culture (the upper middle-class adaption of English norms), European modernism, and, from the 1960s onward, Americanization. The result, as a successor to the bungalow model, was the generic villa in an open lot, a house type that was supported by urban planning dictums. Noteworthy works were produced under those conditions. In what was then East Pakistan (now Bangladesh), Muzharul Islam designed a few hundred houses between 1960 and 1970 as various tectonic, spatial, constructional, and expressive experiments. The socialist enterprise of the Indian government in the 1950s and 1960s also produced some remarkable housing designs. Propounding the dictum "form follows climate," Correa conducted innovative experiments with climatic parameters, most notably with the concept of the Tube House (1960), aspects of which were taken up in the sectionally organized Ramkrishna House in Ahmedabad (1962–64), as well as his own house with a solar parasol (unbuilt, 1968).

The interiors of many of those houses were also indicative of a new aesthetic; their furnishings ranged from ethnic and traditional accoutrements to a quasi-Gandhian sparseness.

Kanvinde Residence, New Delhi, India. 1965–67. Kanvinde, Rai & Chowdhury (est. 1970). Achyut Kanvinde (1916–2002). Interior view, with the architect seated at center. c. 1967. Kanvinde Archives.

Such interiorscapes, conceived as a *raumplan*, with fluid spaces, steps going up and down, low walls, and visual overlays are best expressed in Kanvinde's own house in New Delhi (1966).

Configured as a concrete and brick assemblage, with cantilevered elements, many houses of the 1960s and 1970s, from Doshi's Chinubhai House (1959) to Hasmukh Patel's Indubhai Sheth House (1973), of the Ahmedabad circle, to the Yasmeen Lari House (1973) in Karachi, presented a quasi-Brutalist framework. On the other hand, Kamil Khan Mumtaz's early projects in Lahore, the Kot Karamat farmhouse (1970) and his own residence (1969); Bashirul Haq's own house-studio in Dhaka (1979); Nayyar Ali Dada's Shakir Ali House (now museum, 1982) in Lahore; and the "eco-friendly" buildings by Laurie Baker in the Indian states of Kerala and Karnataka introduced a new brick ethos as well as a new take on the meaning of the home. In a deliberate program of resituating the traditional thematic of the house in a modern framework, brick is adopted in the work of these architects as a redemptive material seen as conducive to creating an architecture closer to the ground and to its site, and darkened ambience in contrast to the skeletal or planar aesthetics of previous decades.

Chinubhai House, Ahmedabad, India. 1959–60. Vāstu Shilpā (est. 1955). Balkrishna V. Doshi (b. 1927). Exterior view. Vāstu Shilpā Foundation Archives.

In the larger global debate of the 1980s between "universalization" and "local culture," in which ideas of postmodernism and regionalism surged, a more social concern for housing dampened a glorified narrative for the house. The house, in fact, became a site for the restoration of older cultural typologies and values, and in some cases a flamboyant demonstration of the excesses of a neoliberal economy, which is especially evident in the Antilia in Mumbai (2003–10), the world's most expensive private home, a twenty-seven-story tower. By shifting from the ideology of a modern dwelling to a spectacular theater, the house now espouses a contrarian prescription to modernism.

Mumtaz Residential Complex, Lahore, Pakistan. 1977–1980. Kamil Khan Mumtaz (b. 1939). Exterior view. 1987. Photo: Kazi Khaleed Ashraf. Aga Khan Documentation Center, MIT Libraries.

References

[1] Gandhi's ideological hut was bypassed in most architectural narratives other than a cameo in Charles Correa's traveling exhibition *Vistāra: The Architecture of India (1986)*. With the parameters of building materials and how they can be accessed, the hut is now discussed as emblematic of a sustainable practice.

[2] See A. D. King, *The Bungalow: The Production of a Global Culture* (Oxford, UK: Oxford University Press, 1995).

[3] With the brise-soleil and parasol roof, Le Corbusier developed an architectural-typological language for climate control from his early work in North Africa, as in the first sketch for Villa Baizeau Bezeult in Carthage, Tunisia (1928). See Stanislaus von Moos, *Le Corbusier: Elements of a Synthesis* (Cambridge, MA: MIT Press, 1979), 128.

[4] Peter Serenyi, "Timeless but of Its Time: Le Corbusier's Architecture in India," *Perspecta* 20 (1983): 108.

[5] Charles Correa, "A Place in the Sun," *Journal of the Royal Society of Arts* 131, no. 5322 (May 1983): 328–40.

[6] Shiromi Pinto, "Minnette de Silva: The Brilliant Female Architect Forgotten by History," *The Guardian*, December 14, 2018; and Amy Sherlock, "Born 100 Years Ago, Remembering the 'Tropical Modernist' Architect Minnette de Silva," *Frieze Masters*, no. 7 (September 2018), https://frieze.com/article/born-100-years-ago-remembering-tropical-modernist-architect-minnette-de-silva.

[7] Minnette de Silva, "A House at Kandy, Ceylon," *Marg* 1, no. 3 (1953), 4–11,

[8] David Robson, *Geoffrey Bawa: The Complete Works* (London: Thames and Hudson, 2002),

a possible future." They are enigmas that can be interpreted only with a vague precision,

further study in architecture, and went to the University of Oregon in the United States and to Yale University where he received a Masters

The Lost House

supervision of Paul Rudolph. It was upon his return to East Pakistan, and as part of his responsibilities within the ubiquitous Public Works Department (as no private architectural firms existed at the time) that

radically absent from it, because it is the house of the Other." And Rudolf Otto has pointed

The Eventful 1960s

ther is either a divinity or monstrosity, or some kind of bewildering phenomenon.

the important foreign architects like Louis I. Kahn, Paul Rudolph, Constantin

ves of certain common characteristics. But today that

stant. The imminence of a disappearance

house-set is burning. The house had to be rebuilt so it could be burned again). In Tarkovsky's driven meditation on the macrocosmic scope of human annihilation (in the film, nuclear catastrophe), and its microscopic reach into the lives

gility and presence.

left are apparitions and haunting images.

contradiction.

Why Did the Monk Burn the Temple?

Le Corbusier's Prehistory

("a pact with nature"), Corbusier not only reverts his ambiguous conception of nature, but attempts to tap a earth-hugging sensibility, which he does more

Shodhan House, it is the brazen animation, busy and diverse as a bazaar under a sheltering umbrella, the various brise-soleil and complex organisation of the terraces,

Corbusier, the total affirmation of will and power over nature – a stark clarity borne out of intellectual reason – Istanbul is popular memory characterized by a pluralistic, malleable and passionate spirit.

CITYNESS

A language for a canal front, Ashraf, 1998.

Fifteen Points for Making Dhaka a City: A Manifesto for a Civic Place

Published in the *Daily Star*, August 8, 2003. Written with Saif Ul Haque.

Dhaka is not a city, yet. Dhaka has transformed tremendously in the last fifteen years or so sporting more sparkling buildings, larger number of swanky automobiles, a greater sense of urban hustle and bustle, and yet, Dhaka is not a city. It is only a gigantic, bursting agglomerate of buildings, bazaars, and glorified bustees. A more popular imagery projects the city as an environmental time-bomb where sewage bubbles, fumes spew, vehicles run amok, parks vanish, and lives perish wantonly. We don't need an Amartya Sen or some Japanese research team to tell us how horrible things are; if we had a little self-respect, we should be able to confront the mayhem ourselves.

A city is not easy to define. All cities are alike and yet each city is different. A good place to understand a city is its meaning in different languages, revealing something of the dream and desire of its people. Of the Bangla terms "nagara" and "shahar," the former of Sanskrit and the latter of Persian origin, "nagara" relates to a place of buildings and structures, and also describes what is clever and cunning (things that are in abundance in our own city). The "nagarika," for example, is someone adept in the pursuit of "kama" and "artha." Suffixes in names like "pur," as in Gazipur, refers to a fort, while "ganj" to a market.

None of these terms suggest the idea of a civic polity, the ethical and spiritual basis of collective living in a modern city. In the grand sweep of our agricultural rhetoric, our deep and ancient sentiment for the soil, we continue to see the city as a curse when in fact it is now as essential and crucial as the paddy-field.

The English term "city" derives from "civitas," a Latin word with a cluster of meanings: citizen, civic, and civilization. As the city draws people from various ethnic, racial, and social categories into one space, and becomes a place where differences and complexities occur by definition, the most critical need for a city is a civilized mode for addressing differences. New York City or New Delhi works superbly with its multiethnic complexities (and when they do not, it is apocalyptic). We with a more or less homogeneous society, on the other hand, have elevated disagreement to a national institution, where conflicts and confrontations, and indifference and intolerance have become main modes of our social interaction. Our civic commitment and civil responsibilities lie completely abandoned.

When we raise 15 points for making Dhaka a city, we would like to maintain that Dhaka lacks fundamental ingredients that make a city a city. And unless an agenda for a civic life is advanced, Dhaka will continue to spiral down into more and more anarchy.

Here are then fifteen wishful points for a better, livable, and decent city:

1. A "good" city does not just happen; it is envisioned, planned in a professional manner, and then implemented with meticulous dedication. Before anything else, we need an understanding on what makes a good city: What kind of urban life and culture will deliver the most collective good to most of its citizen (something that hasn't been discussed in our plentiful seminars and symposiums). This is followed by a vision, a comparatively clearer articulation of what a city wants to be. Finally, the "Master Plan" of a city becomes a concrete document of that vision: recommendations for urban policies and forms. So far, Dhaka has had no vision whatsoever but a spate of mediocre plans produced by some unexceptional international consultants. The contribution of local institutions and experts has been hopelessly useless. Why should we not receive the best? Let our governments have the vision and the audacity to go and seek the best professionals in the world, if that is necessary, but let us entrust the future of the city to people who understands cities, knows how they work, and how they can be reorganized. As ever newer forms of modernization and globalization hit the horizon of Dhaka, it needs a more informed and dynamic attention.

2. In the meantime, Dhaka is growing, if it can be called growth, through a worst spurt of ad-hocism; the only planning technique that exists is "jokhon jemon, tokhon temon." The institutions empowered to manage the city have failed most miserably in their role. In fact, much of the woes of the city can be traced back to the corrupt chambers of these institutions. Everyone knows that but nothing is done. The present structure and method of operation of these urban institutions will not – WILL NOT – produce anything productive and progressive for Dhaka. First things first. If we really desire a better city, all those dysfunctional and diseased institutions should be thoroughly overhauled, transformed, or even disbanded if need be. Next, we need a mayor – a Teddy Kollek who transformed a sleepy Jersusalem into a modern city, a Kadir Topbas, an architect who changed dreary parts of his city, someone who loves his or her city dearly and wishes to see it bloom, and not a political toady whose idea of development is to legally vandalize the city by mindless markets and tottering over-bridges.

3. Dhaka is a traffic nightmare. That is perhaps the biggest understatement about the city of Dhaka. Our street manner is a vivid manifestation of our deeper urban behaviour: self-centered, undisciplined, and life-threatening to others. Only by a radical restructuring of the traffic network can Dhaka function as a truly cosmopolitan place. 50% of Dhaka's traffic problems emerges from a lack of traffic and civic sense, and the other 50% from

lack of roads. The same surface of roads that existed in the 1960s is servicing Dhaka now while traffic volume has increased ten-fold. The city of *ba-anno* bazaar and *teppanno* goli, the capital city of a nation, has only two premier roads (Airport Road and Mirpur Road) running north and south along the axis of the city's development. What about a water bus system circling the city, following the natural course of rivers framing Dhaka? What about a mass transit railway that both circles and intersects the city, but in both cases gets people off the clogged inner streets and into a faster way of moving? Is anybody noticing? Is anybody listening? Roads, roads, we need more roadways! We just need more ways of getting around.

4. People in Sao Paolo say about their polluted city that one of the best things about it is you can at least see the air you breathe. If Sao Paolo is up there, Dhaka is not far behind. To the title of "one of the top twenty populous cities of the world" we can add another glorious one for Dhaka: One of the, if not the, most polluted cities in the world. The malaise is monumental: Air pollution. Water pollution. Noise pollution. Visual pollution. And then there is the perennial problem of garbage clearing and disposal in our le nagari tilottama. An idea: How about organizing a rally, gather all our trash in rented trucks, go in a colorful procession, and dump it in the lobby of Nagar Bhaban? How about doing that every month?

5. Urban spaces are the most important ingredients of a city. Buildings alone never make a city, but buildings and spaces in a well-knit fabric. The spaces - lungs, if you will - include large areas of assembly, parks, gardens, lakefronts, riverfronts, etc. Dhaka one time had an enviable resource of such spaces; now they have either vanished or are vanishing in an avalanche of greed and manipulation. "Light, Green, Air!" that old modernist slogan that produced cities like Chandigarh and Brasilia is not as defunct as one thinks. Dhaka was, and is no longer, but again can be a place of light, green, and air. An immediate and water-tight moratorium should be set on all open spaces. And spaces that have been brutally violated should be recovered without mercy. The mayor of Istanbul in the 1980s bulldozed his way through industries and warehouses that clogged up the banks once gardens at the edge - of the Bosphorus, and recovered the open spaces again. It's possible!

6. The sidewalk (or the footpath) is the supreme mark of a civility of a city; it belongs to the culture of walking, strolling and promenading. The quality of sidewalks gives evidence to what the city managers think about a fundamental human condition:

The pedestrian and his humanity. Dhaka shows no such conceptions. How can it? It's a city where driving a car is a symbol of status, and the poor pedestrian is just a pitiable creature at the bottom of the totem-pole. Such urban pedestrian devices as boulevards, promenades, riverwalks, just simple sidewalks with various activities that are the hall mark of all livable cities - Paris, Florence, New York, Istanbul, even our neighboring Mumbai, Kuala Lumpur, and Kolkata - are

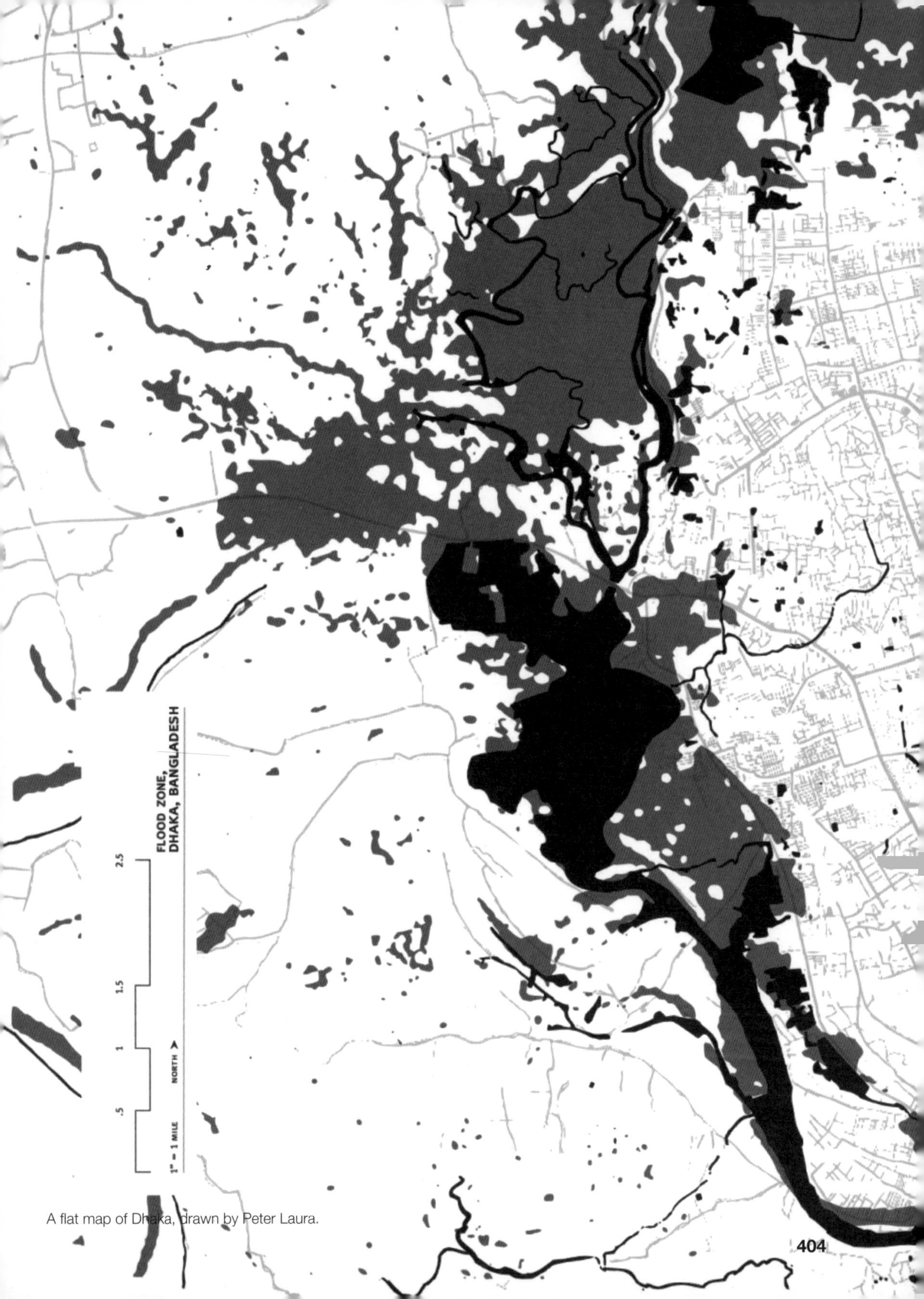

A flat map of Dhaka, drawn by Peter Laura.

Riverbank view of the Buriganga, by De Fafeck, 1861.

Riverbank view, from *the Panorama of Dacca*, published by Messrs. Dickinson, 1850.

completely non-existent in Dhaka. The only decent sidewalks are in Sherebanglanagar, and that because it was conceived by a humanist American architect. All other sidewalks in this city of 10 million are but an extension of the open drain, and whatever is there - two feet or three - are occupied by vendors, bovines, and the debris of urban negligence.

7. “A city is a place where a child walking on the street decides one day what he wants to do with his life.” The architect Louis Kahn made that observation about the vitality of a city, about its institutions that cater to the mental well-being of its people. Active institutions like cultural centers, libraries (the only inspiring library in the fine city of Dhaka belongs to a foreign council), museums of all kinds, athletic centers, movie theaters... are essential like oxygen to the future of a city (and in turn the nation). Think of your ten-year old. Where can you take her for a spark of inspiration, for a possible magical moment that just might change her life? It should not be acceptable that we leave things to fate in Dhaka, and let that child grope around for an elusive destiny. We need to manage and maneuver our fate. We need catalysis for our imagination, and challenges to our cocoon-like existence. We have every right to participate in a world culture, as we should have the imperative to contribute to it. So, why not few movie theaters that show the finest films from every corner of the world (and we find out how even countries like Iran and Vietnam are producing world-class films)? Why not outdoor theaters where we invite to perform a flamenco group from Spain, a qawwali ensemble from Pakistan, a jazz band from New Orleans, a No theater from Japan, a rai singer from Algeria, a fusion band from Mali? Why not a truly dynamic museum (unlike the morgue at Shahbag) where we see art from

Mexico, Japan or Rajastan, or find out why dinosaurs vanished from the earth, or why quasars are the most fascinating objects in the universe? Why shouldn't Dhaka - like any other civilized city - be a conduit to the wealth of the world? Think why the "world-shattering" French philosopher Jacques Derrida comes to a book fair in Kolkata, and what that signifies, while we remain excited by the flaunting belly of a cheap Mumbai starlet.

8. How many of the younger generation know that there used to be canals crisscrossing old Dhaka, somewhat like Venice? How many realize Dhaka is an island framed by three rivers? Well, how many know that there is actually a river in Dhaka? The choking of Buriganga is the most tragic event in recent times, something that continues shamelessly despite the continuing uproar. A similar fate awaits Asulia and other wetlands around the city. A radical overhaul of Buriganga river and its banks is crucial for an economic, transport and cultural revitalization of Dhaka. The river can again become a major life blood, and the riverfront a much more organized area providing renewed recreational, civic, economic, and transport facilities for the residents of the vicinity, and the city in general. Like the horse-racing in Sienna, the bull-chase in Spanish towns, or the Sanja Matsuri festival in Tokyo, the now lost boat racing (*nouka baich*) could be revived into a spectacular event for Dhaka.

9. "Trees." Just that single word changes the perspective on a city. A model in the mind is the street in front of Dhaka Medical College, or what it used to be, a most dignified row of shadow-giving, corridor-creating trees, or a street intersection in Becharam Dewry with a banyan tree creating a cool space-defining public square. But that was then, when we were a bit more civic-minded, and concerned about the larger scheme of things. Now we have simply become urban bandits, pillaging and raping all things good about the city. Dhaka could have been a garden city, a city like Philadelphia or Honolulu where the rush to build did not stop the civilized and healthy need for trees and vegetation at every available nook and corner of the city, where buildings could be seen as pavilions in a garden. Perhaps in that wishful scenario we could claim Dhaka as a truly Bengali city.

10. The proper imageability of a city is given by all those things that add up to the total urban visual environment - benches, sculptures, fences, light-posts, signages, billboards, bus stands, newspaper stands, the whole paraphernalia that falls under "urban art." Every little thing matters. And being a poor country who shouldn't we be concerned about that? Why then should we endure those ugly concoction out of bathroom tiles, those horrific things that sell for art and get constructed for money, that cartoon of an Islamic architecture in the form of arches at ZIA VIP terminal, or that ungainly bird sculpture in a city crossing that neither inspires nor edifies, or those obnoxious boxes set up as newstands right in the middle of a footpath? Perhaps an Urban Arts Commission made of seriously committed lovers of Dhaka who knows the art of urbanity might be entrusted to monitor such imageries for the city.

Aerial view, near the Kuril area.

11. Housing is the fabric of the city. How we define and conceive housing is finally how we see our cities, and vice versa. Housing is not just a numerical and fiscal matter; it can enhance the quality of life, both the life of the immediate dwellers and the life of the city. And yet housing is Dhaka's greatest failure. One reason for the city's chaotic condition is that we have not been able to create suitable large-scale residential models for the many different communities that inhabit it. The public sector housing, catering to government and corporation employees has no innovative models unlike say New Delhi and Karachi with similar financial and social resources. The limited and lower income groups have been completely ignored in whatever housing programs we have. In short, our platoon of housing experts has not been able to provide any vision of how we should live as a group in new urban conditions. They are still floundering with two dull-witted models: the individual plot with the independent bungalow-style house, and the individual plot with a clunky apartment building. The two does not add up to a wholesome whole, nor create any fabric of a residential complex, a cohesive community with an admirable quality of life. The brainless strategy of making "new" housing areas by plotting and subdividing land should be ceased immediately, and alternative imaginative models of mass housing should be explored. In

Dhanmondi, for example, instead of building up a whole plot in an individual manner, 7 to 8 plots could be pulled together and developed as one single housing complex with various internal facilities including generous open spaces for the whole complex. Similar strategies may be taken for Uttara, Purbachal and other so-called planned towns.

12. The general form of a city - its physical and spatial configuration is capable of nurturing or disrupting the nature of communities. Dhaka has seen a gradual deterioration of its communities, seen in the collapse of the idea of the moholla and tattering away of the cohesiveness that defined it earlier. Dhaka has become a city of fragments, broken down to the individual households living in their walled enclaves. Notice how the biggest investment in the city is walls and fences, none of which fare in our rural dwellings... so much for civic polity! The reasons may be fodder for sociologists and anthropologists, but it is possible that the development of a thoughtless physical fabric is affecting the social one.

13. Certain areas in the city – "urban treasures" – should be immediately marked as special zones, and every means should be adopted with the utmost urgency to preserve them through regulations. If there are few places left in Dhaka that could be labeled as urban treasures, Sherebanglangar is one of them. But in our urban illiteracy we do not realize that Sherebanglanagar is a masterpiece in world architecture, created by one of the greatest architects of the twentieth century. With the buildings in a setting of lakes, gardens, orchards, and parks, it is perhaps the closest modern vision for a "Bengali city." Sometimes it's a mystery how that chemistry was possible in this city of mediocrity. But fear not, souls braver than you and I, greater than Kahn and Michelangelo combined, are fully active in their intent to "civilize" Sherebanglanagar. They are building mind-boggling boxes all around the complex, they are converting Kahn's brick buildings into glorified slums, they are driving away people from the plaza, they are building over lakes, they are even "beautifying" spaces within the Assembly, all these in their sly process to steal from this hapless city one bit of world-class phenomenon. Forget special zone, why not paint the damn building pink and get it over with?

14. Architecture – building as a catalytic event – has often been an occasion to give new impetus to a city. The building of Sherebanglanagar was such an occasion; it oriented the growth of Dhaka to the north but also provided an urban anchor for the city beyond the old railway lines. If Sherebanglanagar was a spark produced in the 1960s, Dhaka needs another one. Like the inspiring architectural showmanship in Berlin where the best architects of Europe were invited to build exemplary buildings, or the Pompidou Centre in Paris that converted an anonymous area into an urban mecca, or the Asian Games Village in New Delhi that provided a new model of urban housing. What is needed is to take a large area in the city and develop it in an exemplary way to inspire and edify people. The old airport area is right there under our nose waiting to be used as a talisman for the city.

Sketch for a new Buriganga riverbank. Ashraf, 1998.

We should invite ten top architects of the world to provide their visions for Dhaka using that area, and perhaps implement one of the ideas. Even if the process costs a fortune, it is nothing compared to what priceless gift it will bear for the future of the city.

15. In the absence of any solid tradition of civic urban culture, Dhaka city is the sole model, the city par excellence in the country. It is ironic that every small town, every nook and corner in the mofussil wishes to mimic a dysfunctional Dhaka in some form or other. The future of the country depends on what we make of Dhaka city.

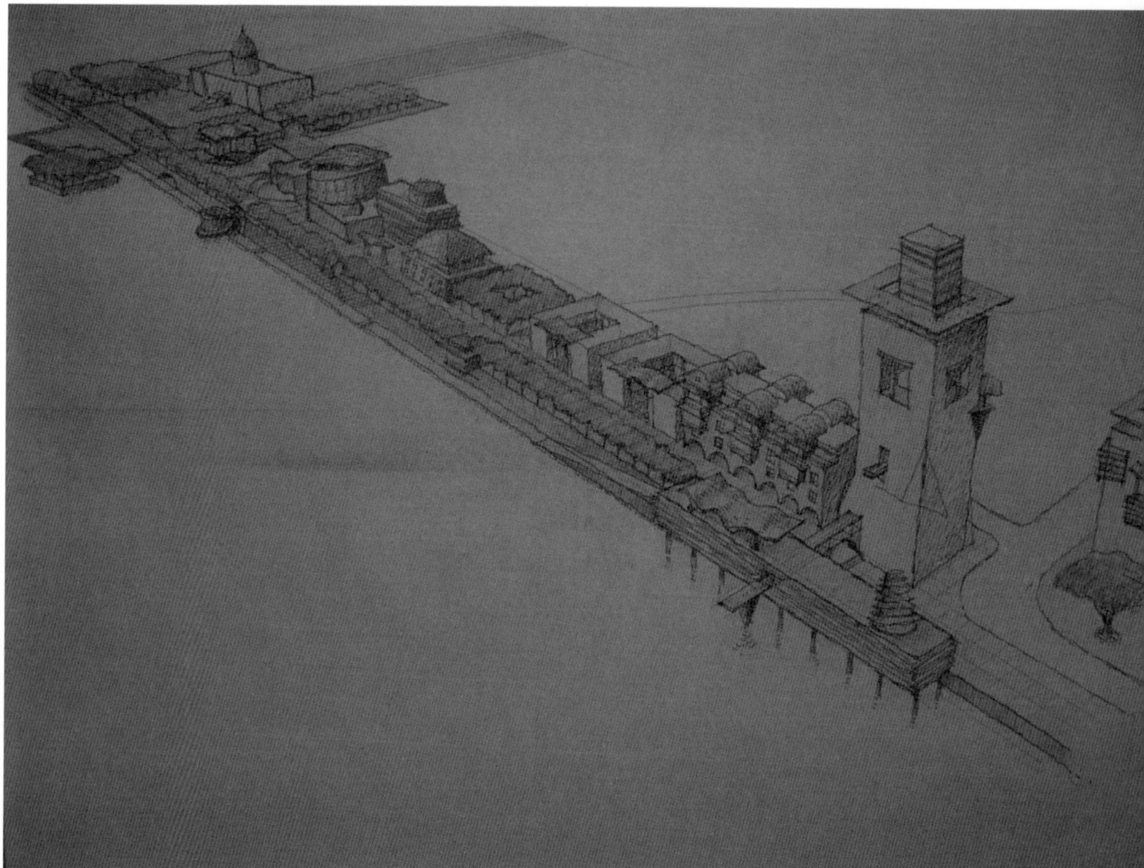

A Plan for Sadarghat. Ashraf, 1998.

Designing Dhaka: History of a Future[1]

Published in *400 Years of Capital Dhaka*, edited by Sharif Uddin Ahmed (Asiatic Society of Bangladesh, Dhaka, 2012).

Cities are strange things; they are neither given to us as found objects like a shell on the beach nor are they conjured up in a dream out of thin air. Cities are the destination of an assiduous search or a meticulous plan. We are not certain of finding them, yet we know that they can't be found if we don't start to *found* them. In the Latin classic *The Aeneid*, Aeneas, the hero of Troy, leaves home with an entourage to found a new city that came to be known as Rome; the journey for the city becomes the odyssey. The Aztecs wandered over mountains and forests following a sacred sign before they founded the city of Tenochtitlan on a lake (that later became Mexico City). And, in the *Candi-mangal*, Kalaketu builds a new city following carefully a visionary plan, and the city becomes a successful experiment in sociological formation. These narratives indicate that to find a city that one is looking for may take a prolonged wandering or bit of a sustained effort.

Even as we celebrate four hundred years of the city of Dhaka, we wonder whether we have found the city that we have been looking for, or whether at all we have started a journey. For such a journey is preceded by a vision or a utopia. Where is Dhaka's utopia?

The term utopia retains negative connotations affixed either to a fantasy of the bizarre or pathology of the unobtainable. But utopia is primarily generative, based on critiques of the present to propose a better future. From Thomas More's humanist society and Renaissance ideal cities to modern urban visions, the image of the city and social utopia have been inseparable in imagining a promised and future landscape. Realism is usually invoked as a counter-thesis of utopia, but realism itself is a fiction we prop up to maintain and benefit from a debilitating status quo or hide our inability to come out of the shadows. Daniel Burnham, the 19th century American architect who designed parts of Chicago and Washington, DC, said decisively: "We need to dream lest we become like owls accustomed to the night and thinking there is no such thing as light."

Well-meaning detractors will ask why clamor for the city when apparently more crucial things are at stake. Bangladesh continues to be seen as a rural civilization (with some bursts

[1] Segments of this article were co-written with Saif Ul Haque, and published at various times in the *Daily Star* and *Forum*. The images are drawn from planning and design studies conducted with students at the University of Hawai'i, Honolulu, and Temple University, Philadelphia.

of industrial islands at best), and therefore much of the cultural discourse, including political and institutional programs, champions the ideology of an eternal "gram bangla." But in the last thirty years or so, something dramatic has happened: an urban movement has taken hold of the country.[2] More and more people now live in cities, and if they do not, they participate in its dynamic, making cities and towns no longer minor parties in the national project but vigorous sites of human habitations, relationships and economies (the result places a big question mark on the "eternal" nature of "gram bangla"). If cities are the battlegrounds of our anxieties, they are also the decisive locus of our imaginations and capabilities. And that is why cities require a more imaginative and critical attention; they cannot be addressed through technical or legislative considerations alone. Cities do not begin from policies, but from dreams and visions.

The future of Dhaka city is the future of the country. While it is imperative to plan the urban landscape of the whole country, from primary cities to small towns, from the *mahanagar* to the *mofussil*, Dhaka will continue to play a vital role in impacting places far and wide. In the absence of any solid tradition of civic urban culture, Dhaka city remains the sole model of urban development in the country. It is ironic that every small town, every nook and corner in the *mofussil*, wishes to mimic a dysfunctional Dhaka. Buildings, grouping of buildings, roads, institutions and commerce in the small towns are all beginning to look like some pale imitation of things Dhaka. It is in that sense the future landscape of the country depends on what we make of Dhaka city. Cities, therefore, require the boldest thinking, especially when our cities – again Dhaka as 'role model' – continue to exemplify the ignoble conditions of a malfunctioning system. Why should we then not demand from the political elite a clearer vision for the future of our cities and towns, recognition of the importance of planning cities in the national agenda, and more definitive plan for Dhaka.

What a City Is

The city continues to taunt us as we have not yet made peace with it. The notion of the city has not yet settled comfortably in our cultural imagination, as a result of which our urban discourse remains naïve and undeveloped. We see the city nothing more than a cauldron of crises and problems. But before we proceed to solve the city's myriad problems, it is crucial to gather a consensus on what we mean by the city.

A city is civilization. The city today has become harder and harder to define, yet that persistent, ancient idea is still conveyed by the popular English term. The term "city" is linked to the Latin word *civitas* and to civilization and citizen, and therefore describes the finest form of civic, collective life.[3] To Jaime Lerner, former mayor of the miraculous Brazilian city of Curitiba, the future is in cities and cities can be the most beautiful collective dream.[4] He rejects the notion that the city is a problem; it is, in fact, the solution to collective existence.

The city is the most obvious spatial condition of how we should live as social group in a civic and humanistic manner. Cities

[2] The urban population of Bangladesh will be 45 percent in 2030, up from 10 percent in 1951 and 25 percent in 2000, see Ness and Talwar, *Asian Urbanization in the New Millennium* (Singapore: Marshal Cavendish International, 2005).

[3] Of the Bangla terms "nagara" and "shahar," the former of Sanskrit and the latter of Persian origin, "nagara" relates to a place of buildings and structures, and also describes what is clever and cunning. The "nagarika," for example, is someone adept in the pursuit of "kama" and "artha." Suffixes in names like "pur," as in Gazipur, refers to a fort, while "ganj" to a market. None of these terms suggest the idea of a civic polity, the ethical and spiritual basis of collective living in a modern city.

[4] When architect Jaime Lerner took over the Brazilian city of Curitiba as its mayor in the 1970s and 80s, it was afflicted by all the familiar "third world" ills. Lerner changed the living conditions of the city, its ailing economy, the poor transportation system, and the polluted environment, making him quite rightly an urban wizard.

Promanade along the river. Ashraf and M. Islam, 2012.

require buildings, but buildings alone do not make a city. Cities are socio-psychical facts; they express, according to the French sociologist Henri Lefebvre, our being and consciousness (which led Lefebvre to write "the right to cities," a manifesto for a transformed city and egalitarian participation in urban life). The first tag – socio – is comparatively easier to address, but the psychical facts are irksome to many trying to unravel the mystery of the city.

The comprehension of our own cities is far more rudimentary. In the grand sweep of our agricultural rhetoric, our deep and ancient sentiment for the soil, we continue to see the city as a curse, a sentiment that is old as the Vedic suspicion of the city Most of our poets and writers sing only the song of the village, producing an unrelenting imagination around the mythic village; no wonder that most of the political elites are in a perpetual tension with the city. We fail to acknowledge the emerging truth that for the first time in human history nearly half of the planetary population is now urban dwellers, and in the context of Bangladesh, the city is now as essential and crucial as the paddy field.

What Dhaka Can Be

Dhaka is not a city, yet. What is touted as "growth" in Dhaka is actually the pillaging of the city in the name of progress and development. Dhaka has no cohesive plan and proceeds only with bursts of ad-hoc decisions, usually taken by bureaucrats, ministers or half-baked professionals with no deep knowledge of and abiding love for the city. The city is being built furiously but without a language for building, that is, without a language for streets, a language for open spaces, a language for the river's edge, a language for housing. The end result is the same as elsewhere where the city is left to such dysfunctionalism:

Riverwalk at Keraniganj. Ashraf and M. Islam, 2009.

remorseless development, curse of pollution, heightening social inequality, unpredictability of services, increasing break-down of community (*moholla*), wretched transport and road system, blatant occupation of land and waterways, ravaging of open spaces, and lack of models of how people should live collectively. Being in the top ten populous cities of the world, and one of the most densely inhabited places on earth is not an accolade but a passage towards an ecological and social cataclysm. Unless that is stemmed by desire and design.

The poet Shamsur Rahman wrote about Dhaka, "This city daily wrestles with the wolf with many faces." Nearly thirty years of relentless greed, political nonchalance, and administrative inefficiency has positioned the city towards a calamitous future. From what was truly a garden city on water, Dhaka now faces a certain civic and environmental deterioration. With failures in urban planning and management, development has fallen largely to private interests, which often act without regard to natural resources, urban context, or community benefit. As a chaotic urban development places increasing strain on its social and environmental fabric, the people of Dhaka must negotiate a civic deterioration that is, ironically, aggravated in the name of progress and growth. Thus the paradox of city-building: one can destroy a city by building it.

A well-functioning city is designed and meticulously planned which then is diligently implemented; it simply does not happen on its own. While there should always be latitudes in design, a city begins and proceeds with a plan, one that has both poetry and pragmatism. Dhaka dearly needs a vision of what it can be, what is possible, and what is more profitable in every respect. Development and investment should follow that plan.

And the plan should be based on urbanism, on the quality of urban culture, and not urbanization, a set of abstract statistics and economic parameters. The term "urbanization" describes the dark side of the modern city: migration, malfunction and misery; it does not show how a city can be lived in its fullest human, social, aesthetical and ecological potential. Those ideas are taken up by the term "urbanism." We have to overcome our ambivalence of the city, and declare a positive and proactive manifesto about our urban destination.

Dhaka needs a bold and creative plan that addresses its tropical, hydrological, and civic conditions. We need to conceive, first of all, the idea of a tropical city in the twenty-first century. Far from being a situation of calamity, Dhaka can become a tropical model that responds to the particular geological and environmental conditions of a deltaic place. Even until the 1950s, with its spacious green spaces, majestic trees, crisscrossing canals, civilized riverbanks, and boats plying through the heart of the city, Dhaka promised to be both a garden city and a place by the water. With buildings in a setting of lakes, gardens, orchards, and parks, Dhaka can still set the model for a tropical city. Only then it can be billed as a Bengali city, and a truly sustainable one.[5]

And, secondly, any vision for Bangladesh will have to consider the emerging urban landscape not as a cause for crises but as vast opportunities. Dhaka can be a city for change, a smart city positioned globally in the age of trans-nationalism. Cities are not merely dire sites of institutional and social failures that need constant remedial attention; if properly organized, they can be economic, social, and cultural dynamos. Bangladesh's potential for utilising its human resources in the new era of global economy remains largely untapped, and yet there are ways by which Dhaka (and other towns and cities) can be oriented towards a unique development programme merging urbanism and economic growth.[6]

For all that is wrong and all that is calamitous, Dhaka can still be a laboratory for a balanced urban dynamic. The profile of a new Dhaka may emerge from the following considerations:

A Liquid Landscape

Dhaka is a child of the Buriganga, and yet it turns its back to the fundamental reality of being part of the world's most dynamic hydrological system. Too few planners, no city fathers, and even the people of the city remember that Dhaka is a tender land-mass framed by three rivers and a fluid landscape. This is the most central issue for beginning any discussion on the future of Dhaka. Dhaka cannot forget its genealogy, for that forgetfulness will be reciprocated by dreadful environmental effects. An audacious vision for Dhaka has to begin from where Dhaka

[5] Louis Kahn's Complex at Sherebanglanagar, with the buildings in a setting of lakes, gardens, orchards, and parks, is perhaps the closest modern vision of a "Bengali" city. While the Parliament Building poses a monumental architectural presence, Kahn gave extensive thought to how the various buildings may be grouped in a setting of water and vegetation evoking imageries from the Bengali landscape. One preponderant reflection for him was "how the buildings are to take their place on the land," that is, in what ways the buildings can be grouped together so that they reveal the qualities of the place. Kahn wanted to heighten the idea that buildings also come together in a particular way in the delta, and that the age-old deltaic practice of "dig-and-mound" could generate a modern interpretation of a hydrological architecture.

[6] Many cities of the world are now bypassing the national state in order to forge extra-national linkages with other urban centers around the world through new economic network. For example, readymade garments, textiles, light manufacturing, and computer/information and medical outsourcing can be part of global industries in a far more energetic and productive way. New urban nodes set up as model townships can be designated for a particular purpose complete with work places, training centres, residences, recreational facilities, etc. Some of the nodes can also be set up as experimental, vertical farms and centers of energy production and, as described in the election manifesto of a major political party, as "high-tech park, software technology park, ICT incubator and computer villages."

began at the edge of the water: To think about Dhaka not from the center but from the edge. The edge is where the solutions are. The Dutch urbanist and architect Rem Koolhaas considers the edge (of the city) as a beautiful urban form. Although Koolhaas meant the ambiguous edge of the post-industrial European city, the important implication is that the edge is the new urban challenge.

What is that "edge" that will help us to re-conceptualize the city? The edge describes the rivers and the hydrological and aquatic landscape that frames Dhaka. The first task is to consider carefully how the edge should be defined and what should be the language of that edge condition even if it is a fluctuating one. We need to re-think that Dhaka is a precious land-mass surrounded by rivers, canals, wetlands, and agricultural landscape; how Dhaka, in fact, is like an island. It is clear that the battle for Dhaka is being fought over the edge, what with encroachment of rivers, filling up wetlands, buying off of agricultural lands, and the wholesale transformation of a precious ecological system (in the name of "housing societies"). New models of urbanism that respect the ecological requirements of Detailed Area Plan (DAP) of the master plan and embrace the economic desires of development are possible through creative propositions. It need not be an either/or situation; there could be options that do not see the ecological ethics in simple conflict with development models.

Dhaka is a deltaic city, and water forms the matrix of the city. It is not a simple image of a picturesque landscape; it implies communication, drainage, economic life, festivity, and a certain way of being. Working with water and embracing wetness mean working with a total environmental relationship: The rivers, the wetlands, the flood plains, the eighty inches of rain per year, the drainage are all tied in an intricate relationship. A deltaic city cannot be developed by economic desires alone. We have to evolve our desires and imaginations from the mathematics of the delta.

Planning around land and water (and not land versus water, which is how conventional planning thinks) could give Dhaka a very unique characteristic distinguishing it from the other cities of the world. As co-writer and architect Saif Ul Haque notes: "Water could provide inexpensive transport solution for the city, it could serve as reservoirs for containing monsoon rains, it could provide for valuable protein for the city dwellers by fish farming, and it could help in keeping the underground water table stable by way of percolation and other methods." A new vision for Dhaka has to begin from the precious landscape of wetlands and agricultural terrain, ushering a conception of a city that integrates urbanism, agriculture, and flood. We need to realize that we can try to take the city out of the delta, but we cannot take the delta out of the city.

A City That is Dispersed and a City That Is Contained

The foci of Dhaka need to be radically reorganized. Dhaka is "growing" in its own happy rhythm, tickled every now and

A reimagined footpath from *Designing Dhaka*, 2012

then by fragmentary official initiatives. This "growth" is neither relieving pressures at the centers nor creating a liveable urban development. The whole city and its peripheries should be brought under an active and aggressive planning net and coordinated development spurs. New urban nodes as townships should be created, and existing and congested centers revitalized so that selective commerce, institutions, and government offices may be dispersed across the urban region in a uniform way.

It is not a contradiction to say disperse the existing city, while at the same time contain its unbridled expansion. The idea suggests that a metropolitan Dhaka needs to be framed within a regional Dhaka. It means the axis and locus of development should be identified in the wider Dhaka region after examining the regional landscape. Once the footprint of the expanded city is identified, the perimeter and in-between zones should be carefully delineated so as not to affect more agricultural areas and wetlands. A rigorous balance should be established between Dhaka's urbanization needs and ecological obligations (which is what DAP has set out to do but without provisions for creative planning).

A thorough balance should be established between needs and obligations. Once that is done, it should be maintained with rigorous vigilance. A wider Dhaka can be conceived by creating new nodal and satellite towns within the administrative reach of Dhaka but also expanding to regional towns as Manikganj, Munshiganj, and Gazipur. The first circle could be developed as nodal townships within Dhaka, and the second ring of existing towns could be energized to create a network of satellite towns. The new nodal towns should be high density developments with selective commerce, institutions and government offices. Such reorganization depends on a new network of movements that connect the nodes, and this is where the much talked about circular water and rail routes come in.

The following should be the manifesto for Dhaka's planning: (a) Selective decentralization: Spreading out the pressures from the existing city. (b) Creating a network of nodal and satellite towns. (c) Restoring the older city, and revitalizing it. (d) Creating new urban nodes, and revamping existing ones. (e) Delineating the built periphery of the city, and maintaining it. (f) Creating a new network of movements connecting the nodes.

City = Mobility

It is obvious that Dhaka's future is in a de-pressurized regional city made of a matrix of a new and revitalized nodes and towns. For Dhaka to spread out and yet remain connected requires a successful transport system.

Dhaka requires a radical restructuring of its transportation network to sustain itself as a city. There are three responses for Dhaka's traffic trouble: Mass transit! Mass transit!! Mass transit!!! The only rapid solution is to introduce systems that will bring in and move as many people as required in as less number of vehicles as possible. We identify three crucial sectors – rail, bus, and waterway – where new transportation modes may be implemented without facing too many infrastructural and constructional challenges.

A river, rail, and transport hub.

Dhaka has a perfect condition for a circular rail (and road) system that rings the city with cross-city links. The circular rail (conceived along the embankment) could also be an opportunity for creating new and revitalized urban nodes along its line. For the cross-city rail system, Dhaka's main train hub may be shifted from Kamlapur to Tongi. There is no particular locational benefit to Kamlapur as all train destinations pass by Tongi. By shifting the station to Tongi will free the train line from Tongi to Naryanganj for a faster and frequent commuter train system serving the city. The Tongi-Naryanganj Line may be the start point for more elaborate commuter system that is present in current transportation planning strategies. At a future phase, an elevated track may be constructed over the existing lines for a faster, express line.

Buses continue to be the accepted mode of urban mass traveling but are hardly effective mass transit. A thorough revision of bus network and travel mode is needed where eco-friendly vehicles carrying large number of passengers may be introduced on dedicated routes. This will require a few things: Freeing left lane as dedicated routes for special and designated buses, and creating special designed bus stands for faster transfer and passenger loading. To implement the system quickly and effectively, tax benefit and other incentives may be provided to private investors and operators.

Water-based transportation system for Dhaka is a natural choice in a water-borne geography. Regularised and extensive water-transport system will also be a way of ensuring the effective use and control of rivers and canals, and their edges. The way Dhaka has turned its back to its rivers may be reversed by implementing a strong riverine transit system. For the riverine system to be effective, multi-modal stations need to be created that are conveniently linked with other transportation loops. As river stations can be hub of riverside development and spur for energetic growth, the planning of such hubs should be done carefully in order to control haphazard development. The waterway system can also be extended into the heart of the city after clearing up and deepening some of the encroached canals. With the completion of the Hatirjheel and Gulshan Lake redevelopment projects, water-taxis will be able to link, for example, Gulshan and Kawranbazar.

Urban Spaces
Urban spaces are the most precious ingredients of a city considering that buildings alone do not make a city, but buildings and spaces in a well-knit fabric. Spaces could be varied and wide-ranging, from formal to informal, from large-scale to intimate, from South Plaza at Sherebanglanagar to space outside Gausia Market. Large spaces include areas of assembly, maidans, parks, gardens, lakefronts, riverfronts, etc., while small spaces may just be an intersection of two lanes, space under a tree on a sidewalk, or just a broad sidewalk. Dhaka one time had an enviable resource of such spaces; now they have either vanished or are vanishing in an avalanche of greed and manipulation.

The city of Dhaka used to be synonymous with trees: flower-bearing, scent-giving trees, trees that marked the passing of the seasons, trees that gave shade, and trees that added to a healthy environment. A model in the mind is the street in front of Dhaka Medical College, or what it used to be, a most dignified row of shadow-giving, corridor-creating trees, or a street intersection in Becharam Dewry with a banyan tree creating a cool space-defining public square. But that was then, when we were a bit more civic-minded, and concerned about the larger scheme of things. The climate of Dhaka desires it to be a garden city, a city of trees, flowers and foliage. “Light, Green, Air!” that old modernist slogan that produced cities like Chandigarh and Brasilia is not as defunct as one thinks.

The sidewalk (or the footpath) is the supreme mark of the civility of a city; it belongs to the culture of walking, strolling and promenading. The quality of sidewalks gives evidence to what the city managers think about a fundamental human condition: The pedestrian and her humanity. Dhaka shows no such conception. It’s a city where driving a car has become

[7] Hong Kong is a good example where an integrated planning approach has succeeded in maintaining low automobile dependency despite Hong Kong's high per capita income and population density. The success of Hong Kong's pedestrianization was possible due to the integrated network of pathways that separate car and pedestrian, and allow those pathways and sidewalks to be spaces of their own.

an essential symbol, and the poor pedestrian just a pitiable creature at the bottom of the totem-pole. Such urban pedestrian devices as boulevards, promenades, riverwalks, and just simple sidewalks that are the hallmark of all livable cities are completely non-existent in Dhaka.

The pedestrian and the sidewalk is ultimately an indictment on the car, on its ultimate effect of the automobile on the natural environment (through pollution, etc.), urban exchange (disruption of the public realm), and social interaction (segregation of classes). A successful pedestrian infrastructure means relying mostly on a set of public transportation such as railways, buses, vans, trams, ferries, and such public spaces as elevated and moving walkways, tunnels, footbridges and regular sidewalks. If we could walk, many of us would not need to drive cars.[7]

Housing Is the Fabric of the City

Housing is the material and social fabric of the city, and yet housing is Dhaka's greatest failure. Despite what seems like a developer's boomtown, Dhaka has not been able to create suitable residential models for the many different communities that inhabit it. There simply has been no vision of how we should live as a group in our emerging urban conditions.

Housing is more than a numerical and fiscal matter; it is the key to enhancing the quality of life, both that of the immediate dwellers and the overall city. The platoon of housing experts has not been able to provide any vision of how we should live as a group in new urban scenarios. The public sector housing, catering to government and corporation employees still continues along the defunct line of building one block after another with no thoughts for social spaces.The limited and lower income groups have been completely ignored in the housing equation. The middle-class is making do with what it can in the brutal housing and rental market. The planners and experts are still floundering with two dull-witted models: the individual plot with the independent bungalow-style house, and the individual plot with a box-style apartment building.

The unimaginative strategy of making new housing areas by plotting and subdividing land should be ceased immediately, and alternative imaginative models of mass or group housing should be explored. Dhanmandi that started off as a "model" residential area using the plotting mechanism has now been disfigured beyond recognition by new living and economic imperatives. Dhanmandi could be better. Instead of building up on a plot, for example, in an isolated manner, Eight to Ten plots could be pooled together and developed as one single housing complex with various shared internal facilities including generous open spaces, gardens. meeting and play areas, a shop or two for the whole complex. Similar strategies may be taken for Uttara, Purbachal, and other so-called planned towns. Loan and tax incentives may be offered for initiating projects like this in existing built conditions such as Dhanmandi and Banani. For newer areas under planning, such group housing should be introduced by regulation.

High-density group housing. E. Khan, S. Haque and Ashraf, 2010.

The idea of "housing for all" by 2015, as declared by the Awami League government in its election manifesto, along with the "growth-center centric village housing" in every union and upazila, is certainly a powerful one but remains vague if no hint is given on what kind of housing, how it will be delivered and how it will first constitute a human settlement and social habitation.

Housing is ultimately about building communities. This is critical in the context of Dhaka today when older structure of communities (*moholla*) is fast disappearing, and the current patterns of residential models is not encouraging community building. Dhaka has become a city of fragments, with its social cohesiveness tattering away, broken down to the individual households living in their walled enclaves. The truth is that the general form of a city—its physical and spatial configuration—is capable of nurturing or disrupting the nature of communities. The current framework of plot-based residential "development" will not lead to community building.

A housing manifesto for Dhaka should be based on the following: (a) Stopping the planning of plots. (b) Developing group housing complexes, and building exemplary housing and housing complexes. (c) Providing housing incentives at all economic levels, especially the lower income. (d) Innovating mechanisms for private developers to supply housing at all income levels.

Urban assets

A city thrives when it values its assets, and those could be buildings, natural spaces, built open spaces and urban districts. While this may be obvious, sometimes the obvious is not that obvious in Dhaka.

In this city, there are indeed many Dhakas. Dhaka has given rise to several urban morphologies, each of which represents a particular social, economic and environmental destiny. In the older city, hugging the river, colorful mixed-use buildings are crowded cheek-by-jowl along narrow, winding streets in tradition-bound neighborhoods. Further from the river in the Ramna area is the old colonial quarter, studded with bungalow-and-garden type governmental, cultural and residential buildings, many of which were built during the colonial rule. Louis Kahn's

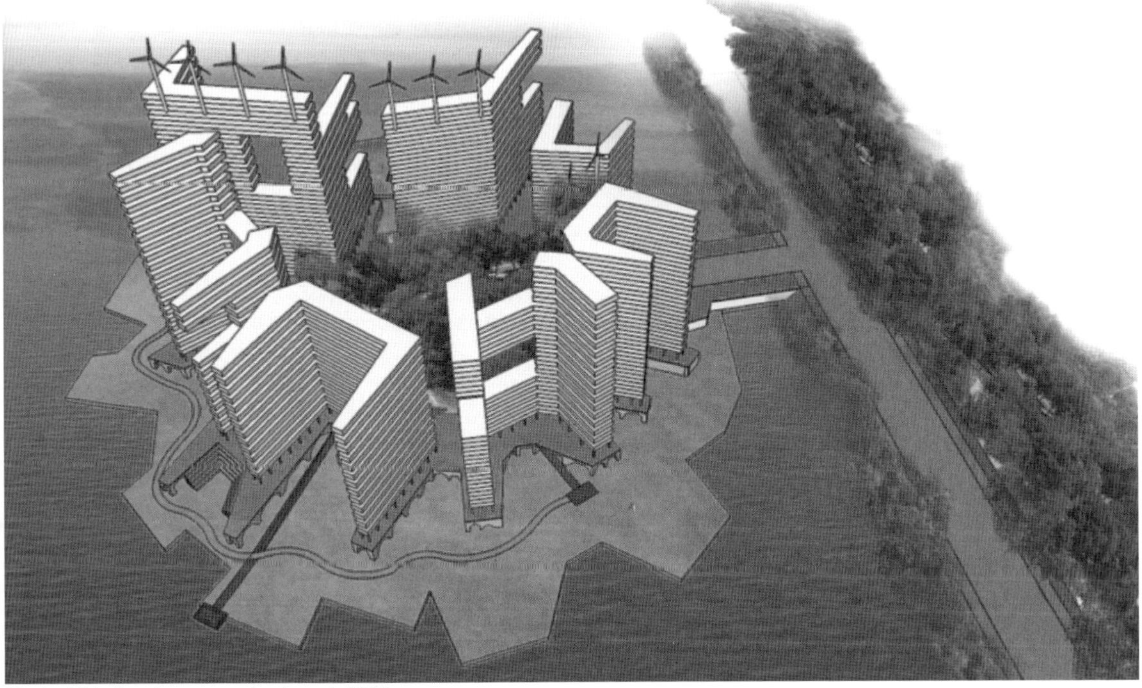
Cluster high rise along an embankment, 2009.

An urban palette around a wetland. Alex Maly, University of Hawai'i, 2007.

Streets for pedestrian uses. Arghya Bhattacharjee, 2012.

Parliamentary Complex is another distinctive area in the city's urban and social fabric that represents a world-class urban ensemble of buildings, lakes, orchards and parks. The so-called planned residential areas created as plotted properties with individual buildings were the most distinctive development of the 1960s and later (a morphology that is now undergoing radical transformation). Alongside these formal areas, however, are vast, amorphous swaths of largely unplanned residential and commercial growths that are glaring symptoms of planning failure in addressing the rapid transformation of the city.

It would be a pity if all of Dhaka began to look the same because of uniform development orientations and planning regulations. Certain areas in the city—"urban treasures" or heritage-rich areas—should be immediately marked as special zones, and every means adopted to preserve them through differentiated regulations and uses. Such areas include Wari, Chowk, Shakhari Bazar, Alia Mia Talao, Balda Garden, etc.

Building as a catalytic event has often been an occasion to give new cultural and economic impetus to a city. What was once a dreary urban environment has often been turned around at the physical, psychological and economical level by the creation of a new and inspiring work of architecture. Such is the power of good architecture: a single building or complex that can change the life of a city.

If Sherebanglanagar was a spark produced in the 1960s by Louis Kahn, Dhaka needs few more impetuses now. There are critical areas in the city that need to be addressed in the most creative way before they are vandalized by illegal invasions or officially by poor planning. Such areas should be developed in an exemplary way to inspire and edify, as well as open them up for new urban experiences. The old airport area is waiting patiently to be used as a new gift to the city (until that happens one cannot understand why that area cannot be enjoyed as a public park). The central jail could be relocated at a new location and the area opened up for new park, cultural, recreational and selective residential uses for the people of old Dhaka. The BDR area at Peelkhana could similarly be renovated. The totality of such catalysis could go towards a dynamic transformation of the city.

All these understandably may take time and resources, and that is why it is imperative for the government to form an Urban Task Force, empowered with the proper authority and manned by the right expertise that begins to address some of these things. The Urban Task Force should take a stance on the following (to create short-term and long-term goals): an overall intelligent plan for Dhaka; and, urban strategies for the whole country. The latter suggests a coordinated and managed development of a network of primary cities and smaller towns with precise ideas about the constitution of such cities keeping in mind interlinked issues of housing, transport, public spaces, wetlands and waterways, and their regional impacts. As I have claimed elsewhere, and I truly believe, if there is a political will, there will be a way out of perdition. And if the political parties who claim authority over our destiny have set us up on a dream time with calls for social justice, environmental protection, economic equality, good governance and human rights, why should we not add to that life in the city that is truly civilized and modern, and Bengali.

Epilogue: Three Catalyses
Dhaka needs critical interventions in selected sites that will be models for transforming of the city. The projected developments will be urban catalysts, acupuncture in the miasma-ridden body of the city in order to develop a clear and distinctive language for exemplary developments.

A satellite view of Dhaka clearly reveals the immensity of the water system that surrounds Dhaka and penetrates the edges like a vascular tissue. The satellite view also makes it obvious that amidst that watery landscape, Dhaka is surrounded by a region of undefined settlements, some of which are established, while others are in the throes of a helter-skelter evolution. They are a product of both planning callousness and development abuse; that is, whatever planning exists for some of those areas is poor both in conception and implementation, and whatever development goes on is short-sighted and simply troubling. I hold the view that a condition of dystopia is also an occasion for imaginative renovation. Such sites of urban disarray provoke a strategy where pockets of intervention can be identified for creating new paradigms of city-building.

I identify three areas as potential sites of critical interventions for the remaking of Dhaka city:

Revitalizing Sadarghat
The redevelopment of Sadarghat could be a catalyst for an economic and social rejuvenation of not just old Dhaka but the whole city. Sadarghat remains one of the most dynamic areas in Dhaka, but its fullest potential has not yet been realised. In fact, from being a historic civic space and an energetic urban place, the area has now become the symbol of sharp physical, social and environmental deterioration. With thoughtful and imaginative planning, Sadarghat could be transformed befitting the riverfront of any decent city.

A "riverfront district" with a new authority can be designated with Sadarghat as the epicenter for the purpose of producing and maintaining a clean river, a civic riverfront and a sustainable and exemplary riverfront district enjoyable for and accessible to everyone. The district will exhibit model public spaces and civic buildings designed especially for a riverfront condition.

The single goal of the riverfront development is to return the riverbank to the city. That would simply mean that the banks (to a certain clear width) should be decreed as public space allowing uninterrupted access for people where no private encroachment and building of any sort will be allowed. The whole length of the riverbank in the district should be developed as a tree-shaded promenade, largely a pedestrian public space that is linked to other open and green spaces, historic sites, and special purpose buildings creating a clear and legible pedestrian network. Parks and gardens, even floating ones on the river (on barges), could be part of that network. One foresees dynamic activities on and along the river through the systematic promotion of boat racing, water pageants, floating restaurants and various tourism related enterprises.

It is obvious that to have riverbanks, one needs to have a river. The dynamicity of the river, along with its canals (whichever are remaining), should be recovered and maintained by eliminating adverse features and modifying some of the existing conditions (a drive that is ongoing). A re-planned and reconstituted Sadarghat can be a more powerful economic engine than what it is at present catering both to the vibrant economy of the old city and new economic bonanza. This may be achieved through new commercial generators, such as well-planned shops and markets, modern business centers, hotels, restaurants, eateries and other enterprises, including large scale cultural and entertainment centers.

Intensifying the City: Tongi

Despite a seemingly dense and overbuilt reality, there are areas in and around Dhaka that suffer from low or poor urban intensity. While some of these areas have designated urban administration,

Tongi Bridge area reimagined. Ashraf, 2012.

they are in fact far less than being urban. From Tongi in the north to Savar in the west and Keraniganj in the south, there are "para-urban" pockets that await a systematic urban intensification than the pell-mell urbanization taking place.

There are many such opportunities in this city of a reckless future. Take Tongi for example, a curious urban configuration that one would be hard-pressed to call even a "township." Tongi is divided blatantly along the Dhaka-Gazipur Road. On the western side, there is a somewhat disciplined layout of industrial lots, while on the east is a wild melee of dwellings, factories, industries, shops, markets, vestigial lands that do not come together to forge an efficacious urban community. Tongi is a good example of how old agricultural lands have tumbled

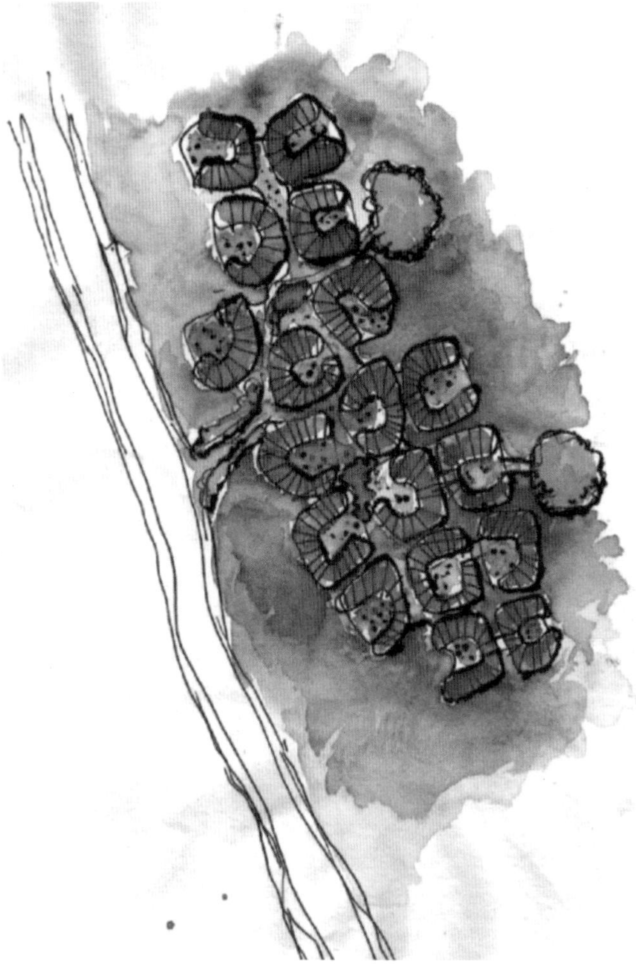

Housing in the floodplain. Ashraf, 2009.

pell-mell into ad-hoc land divisions and usages without an urban identity and coherence. Tongi is but one example of such areas in Dhaka: settled, populated, urbanised but without urbanism. There still remains a great opportunity for converting Tongi, and areas like that, into a highly planned and effective urban fabric. I describe such a development as an urban "acupuncture" as it not only affects, positively, the immediate area but also offers multiple dividends for the rest of the city. Such a development is also an opportunity to plan the "outer ring" of Dhaka city that can give new impetus to developments in those rings.

The whole of Tongi area can come under a special planning action that can systematically convert it into a denser, planned and truly urban place that is socially and economically richer. Reorganization of a vast part of Tongi is easily possible that might create new garments factory district with demarcated areas for factories, offices and warehouses, and housing and amenities for the workers with efficient transportation network. Similarly, an IT district may also be conceived where people can be trained in the emerging industry and setup of outsourcing stations. Only then, Tongi may be reincarnated into a modern industrial town, and a proper gateway to Dhaka.

Tongi can also become the model of an "eco-city" that maintains a balanced relationship of development and ecology with the use of river and its banks. The area around the bridge, along the banks of the Turag, can be developed as an arts district with carefully designed buildings in a setting of parks and public places. The arts district may house a set of civic buildings such as a convention center (along with a hotel complex) that can become a new urban focus for the city. The edge of the river can be a long promenade that connects the bend of Turag in Asulia in the west to the railway crossings in the east.

Building on the Floodplains

The touchiest topic in Dhaka is the business of building on the flood-plains, that is, the refiguring of the city's edge. A land-water form that was characterized by an intricate network of canals, ponds, agricultural fields and wetlands all ultimately linked to the river is being aggressively changed simply by land-filling and creating dubious "housing societies," a process that marks the so-called urbanization of Dhaka all around its edge.

There are two set of questions, one is on the flood-plains: Is building on the floodplains a contradiction? Does this conspire against the ecological principles embedded in DAP? How to resolve the pressure of building and the ethics of the environment? The other questions involve the edge: What should be the perimeter of the city? What will happen beyond that edge? What will be the relationship between two sides of the divide? Dhaka cannot grow infinitely in every other direction, swallowing up wetlands and agricultural land with mind-numbing speed and greed, and throwing off balance a precious ecological and hydrological system. If not, then, how will be the population growth and the appetite for urban land solved? That is the challenge. The brilliance for urban designers and planners will be to show that sustaining and enhancing Dhaka's geographic life system can address growth.

The conceptual question is: How does one dwell in an aquatic landscape? How does one inhabit the water? We have to bring a paradigmatic shift to how we see the environment at the edge, which is primarily and fundamentally a liquid landscape. It appears that we do not have the conceptual framework for dealing with such a landscape; the planning designation "land-use" may not be quite appropriate. We might have to coin a new term: "water-use" or "land-water use." We have to confront the challenge of how "to bring the city into the floodplain and the flood-plain into the city."

In such a fluid landscape, the question of "site" has to be revised, as sometimes there is no site in the conventional sense, and "building" may have to happen on water itself. In one prospect for such a situation, a new network may be conceived that is made of cautious and careful development – streets, walkways, housing and public places – that are mostly elevated either on stilts or non-continuous earth mound over agricultural fields, gardens and parks, each at different elevations and responding to different levels of flooding. A new urban morphology is suggested where the porosity at the lower level will allow an unimpeded flow of water at different seasons, and a more or less stable urban form overlaid on that.

One edge of Dhaka is defined by a controversial engineering monument: the embankment (the built western edge and the anticipated eastern one). The embankment itself could be the generator of a wholly different building and landscape morphology that makes new matrix for settlements, transportation, use of wetlands and agriculture. Ribbons or clustered development could be conceived at strategic locations along the embankment that will contain primarily high-density housing and commercial spaces (the embankment will double as a transportation corridor). The floodplains will also be reorganized for designated areas of rice cultivation, elevated fields for perhaps orchards and rose cultivation (that will also be accessible as parks via boat or bridges from the ribbons), and permanent canals for boat-ways.

The embankment itself needs to be re-conceptualized. Instead of being a stark divide that has often compounded than solved problems, the embankment may be deconstructed into a series of interlocked walls, planes and platforms, creating a grid of bounded areas. The result could be a new framework where water from either side–city or river–could be allowed passage in either direction in a controlled way. The gridded spaces controlled by locks and sluice gates will create retention ponds, water reservoirs, water filtration areas, natural parks, or agricultural fields as needed. The new interlocking "walls" could be a platform for creating housing structures over a continuous pedestrian or vehicular movement system.

An imagined canal bank. Ashraf with Arghya Bhattacharjee, 2012.

The flood-plains require a new investigation of the place of agriculture and fishing in relation to urbanism. This involves a more uneasy issue in social and topographical utopia: The possibility of reorganizing scattered homesteads in the flood-plains into clustered and close-knit settlements served by proper infrastructure while dedicating the plains for planned, intense agriculture and fishing in response to the rhythm of flood. This is perhaps the next big challenge for our planners and policy-makers: Can this be a model of settlement and economic production in the future catastrophic scenario of climate change?

An almost empty Mirpur Road, a result of the mass exodus ahead of Eid-ul-Fitr, is seen in this photo taken on Thursday, May 13, 2021 Syed Zakir Hossain, *Dhaka Tribune*.

Another road in Dhaka during Eid. Photo: Syed Zakir Hossain.

Hometown: The City in the Postnational Landscape

with Jyoti Puri, published in the *Economic and Political Weekly*, Vol. 45, No. 41, October 9, 2010.

The nation is under siege, and the attrition comes from both without and within. The cross-border flows of capital, communication, and people produce a trans-national dynamic across the horizon of the nation, while the various regional, local, and subaltern upsurges pose a sub-national wave. This double vortex generates what has been proffered as a postnational condition.

The sociological and political critiques emerging from a postnational framing argue that the nation has not quite lived up to the promises of its originary dream. Envisioned as unique, unified, and egalitarian political communities, postcolonial South Asian nations, not unlike nations elsewhere, are marked by fragmentation, repression, and ambivalence. Even as South Asian nations fiercely resist movements for autonomy and sovereignty through indescribable violence, the fractures of regional, ethnic, religious, class, linguistic differences are more evident than before. Concurrently, contrary to the decline of the state, states in South Asia are simultaneously expanding and retracting, or in short, being reconfigured. Even as they expand in unprecedented ways through militarization, states are retracting and realigning in a vast complex of relations with Non-Governmental Organizations (NGOs) and other regional, national, and transnational private constituencies.

What are left unresolved in scholarly framings of the changing dynamics of national states are considerations of "home," or meaningful existential, cultural and political affiliations to space. Our point of departure is to foreground questions of what makes specific places a "home-space"; how do we begin to think about affiliation and belonging to space in a way that does not privilege the national?; what is the nature of affiliation to the city in particular that presents an alterity to the nation. We are interested in both the emotive as well as the political aspects of such affiliations, and in the existential, cultural and political forms of belonging to specific places. Postnational interventions have been useful in noting the limitations of nationalisms but less effective in positing alternatives. The postnational is spoken of as a new ethical condition or a political practice but its spatial structure is hardly addressed, especially when the discourses of the nation, homeland, and region are essentially socio-spatial constellations.[1] Our interest is in exploring the dynamics of belonging and cultural-geographic spaces, which may include the nation but are not, in fact, contained by it. Cities, especially in South Asia, may open up alternatives, or at least, *an anotherness*, within what is claimed as the postnational landscape.

Attention to cities is not justified simply by the rising trends in urbanizations in contrast to the "eroding" nation (even though more than half the world's population is now urban for the first time in human history),[2] but by renewed claim, following Henri Lefebvre's persuasions, about the city as expressing and symbolizing "our being and consciousness." We seek to bring the declining relevance of the nation and increasing significance of the city within the same field of exploration to present the city as another viable site of affiliation and engagement in light of the nation's predicaments. It seems that we have been too quick to concede to the romance of homeland and nation as sites/spaces/containers of attachment and belonging (as well as loss), for subsumed in the extrapolations of such "homes" are the rich and complex textures of places such as the city. However, with the contradictory characterizations of "home" in common parlance, it is not clear how that resonates in/with the city: While cities are home to vast millions, the predominant discourses are about unmanaged growth, sprawl, migration, struggle for survival, and, in effect, "unhomeliness."

To identify and unravel the lived, affective, and affiliative properties of the city, we deploy the term "hometown."[3] The phenomenon of hometown, despite or because of its highly charged and gauzy sensibility of "home," offers a particular way of understanding the nature of the city. By bringing hometown to the foreground, we are emphasizing a distinction between the abstraction of homelands and nations and the lived spaces of belonging and embodiment. The important point here is that an abstract spatial coagulation (whether at global, continental, regional or national scale) is always negotiated through the specifics of a social habitus. What the recalcitrant presence of the city, in various narratives and representations, indicates is that even the attachment to nation or homeland takes shape through the particular, everyday textures of place—the call of the fish vendor at a neighborhood in Dhaka, the neon signs at an intersection encountered daily in Karachi, the smell of exhaust and the puttering of an auto-rickshaw in Delhi. When one returns from travel abroad, one does not return to an India or Bangladesh per se, or for that matter an Africa or Asia, but to a specific city or place, a Lucknow, a Chittagong or a Kathmandu. A place that is perhaps a hometown.

The Apocryphal Space of the National State

In the discourses of national states, the combination of space and scale normalizes the national state as the legitimate, overarching authority and primordializes the relevance of territoriality and sovereignty while subsuming and obscuring the significance of the local and particular (Ferguson & Gupta, 2002). Indeed, as Aditya Nigam (2009) notes, the national works

[1] While the essays on the postnational condition in the special issue of *Economic and Political Weekly* are provocative and instructive, the specificity of space or place is neglected in theorizations of the postnational.

[2] The statistics for the urbanization of the planet is staggering: By 2030, 60 percent of the world population will be urban, of which "developed regions" will have 84 percent of the population living in cities and towns, and for "least developed regions," about 56 percent. Figures for South Asia show that the urban population of India in 1951 was 17 percent, in 2001 it was 27 percent, and it is projected to be 40 percent in 2030. For Pakistan, it is 17.8 percent in 1951, 33 percent in 2000. For Bangladesh, it was less than 10 percent in 1951, 25 percent in 2000, and will be 45 percent in 2030. From Gayl D. Ness and Prem P. Talwar (2005).

[3] The term "hometown" seems to resist a South Asian tenor. It appears that despite thousand years of urban culture in South Asia, the circulated terms for home-places, as with the ubiquitous *des*, is the home village, or at best, the *mofussil* town. The city or town does not seem to proffer any such terminology.

by erasing the presence of notions of belonging that circulate within South Asia, *des*, *vatan*, and *nadu*. Maps are especially potent spatial representations that help colonize places into the spaces of national states. Not just spatial depictions of national states, continents, and landmasses, maps continually capture and shape our imaginations of what counts as space and our relationship to it. Speaking to the shift from place to abstract space, sociologist Craig Calhoun (1997) notes how maps before the eighteenth century were either local, for city plans or charts, or meant to give directions to travelers, or, we might add, aimed toward military encounters. Calhoun suggests that it was the influence of the Napoleonic wars in the early 19th century that encouraged the proliferation of the "national" model, which was reflected in and facilitated by maps that divided the world into discrete nations and their territories. Maps-as-logo (after, Benedict Anderson) help literalize and opticize territory, augmenting the pre-occupations with borders, and sovereignty, the defining characteristics of the national state. The result is the flattening if not obliteration of the cognition of places.

No wonder, then, that national states are frequently willing to sacrifice innumerable lives and wreak unaccountable havoc in order to retain national territory or regain territory believed to rightfully belong to the nation. The several wars between India and Pakistan over the contested terrain of Kashmir, the inexhaustible injustices committed within the Indian-controlled parts of Kashmir and Pakistan's attempts at recuperation of territory derive from the ontology of national spaces. Just as the space of nation and state is no longer separable, territory and sovereignty are fully inflected with affect. As Michael Billig (1995) notes, national geography has to be imagined as total, unified, and unique; there can only be one Macedonia, just as East Pakistan had to be renamed Bangladesh following the 1971 War of Independence.

The particular spatial configurations of the national state reproduce a powerful set of discursive-material claims that continually normalize the national state as our spatial coordinate, the locus of cultural and political belonging, and that which completely and fully contains us. Space and affect, the material and representational constantly work together to appropriate the grammar of belonging and attachment to the national state. The predominant notions of belonging and attachment emerge from a synthetic relationship of affect and politics that is reproduced in the mundane as well as the spectacular spaces of the national state. Belonging connects us to something, giving us membership within a group or collective, but insofar as belonging connotes possessions and property, we are also the things that belong to something larger than ourselves. Thus, as much as home and nation belong to us, we belong to them. Belonging also connects us to other people and relates us to others through descent and kinship. It bridges putative distinctions between the intimate and the public spheres. Not surprisingly, then, the affective idioms of national state, much like homeland, are wrought through metaphors of gender, kinship, and heterosexuality.

Belonging brings together multiple affective valences of the national state—allegiance and affiliation in the politico-legal sense with affinity and attachment at an emotive level. The space of the national state is more open to such valences in comparison to the fabric of homeland with its implicit exclusionary structure. What emerges from here is a critical differentia of allegiances and affiliations. It is possible to be naturalized as a citizen-member even if one is never quite fully accepted within the fold of the nation. At the same time, the racialized and religion-based exclusions that mark more than one nation of South Asia are painful reminders that some groups are excluded despite their equal claims to soil, blood, and a common past. The particular mix of affect and politics plays out in a number of different ways, mediated by hierarchies and differences engendered and nurtured by ethnicity, religion, gender, sexuality, language, and social class. Despite and, in fact, through these differences of belonging, spatial and affective idioms of the national state claim not only our political attachments but attachments of the heart. Nation, home, and heart are used interchangeably, just as are rights, citizenship, and state.

What forms of belonging to a socio-spatial matrix are available that are not contained by the discourses of homeland and national space? It is a question shared with scholars such as Mary Layoun who ends her book Wedded to the Land? Gender, Boundaries, and Nationalism in Crisis with the assertion that alternative ways of conceptualizing and living difference, an "otherwise," has always existed alongside the hegemony of nationalism (Layoun, 2001). Layoun's strategy regarding the unsaid and unmarked, however, poses a problem. Perhaps the problem is not so much in terms of what lies unsaid but the ability of scholars and researchers to pay attention to what is actively lived, experienced, and desired alongside and outside the framework of nationalism. Layoun is right to note the fissures and fractures in dominant accounts of nation and homeland that are revealed through the storytelling of the marginalized and the dispossessed. Yet, the focus on the interplay between dominant narratives and silences, between nationalisms and its alternatives, obscures something particularly critical: that accounts of belonging, of cultural, political and spatial affiliation are by their nature multiple. Accounts of homeland, nation/state, home, community, origins exist simultaneously where they are sometimes neatly aligned, sometimes in irregular lines, but always numerous.[4] To ignore the very existence of multiple accounts and to focus on the other-wise of nationalisms, or the silences and the interstices, ironically, is to leave intact the structure/edifice of nationalisms. Instead, we suggest fresh and richer articulations around the particularities of space and the spatiality of the city.

The City in Spatial Imagination

Salman Rushdie's rambunctious de-construction of the nation in *Midnight's Children* begins with this line: "I was born in the city of Bombay… once upon a time." A later collection of essays, *Imaginary Homelands*, written as a cartography of journeys also begins with Mumbai, with an old photograph of the house

[4] No matter how deceptively straightforward the question—and the question is almost always deceptive—of "where are you from," or for that matter "who are you," the answer is multivalent and multi-directional. Consider the response by the noted litterateur U. R. Ananthamurthy: "If somebody asks me in London, who are you? I would reply I am an Indian. If in Delhi, someone asks who are you? then I would say, I am from Karnataka. In Bangalore, if somebody asks me who are you? then I would say I am from Shimoga, I would say I am from Melige (a village). In Melige, nobody would ask me who are you. Because they know not only my caste, but even my sub-caste."

[5] Spivak characterizes postnational talk as "Northern radical chic."

[6] Orhan Pamuk's (2005) admission is relevant here: "For a time, when I was thirty-five and dreaming of writing a great novel about Istanbul along the lines of *Ulysses*." (p. 97).

in which Rushdie was born (Rushdie 1991). Dating it to 1946, Rushdie pauses to describe the peculiar house, with its red tiles and bougainvillea creepers, captured in the photograph and his emotions of an estranged present and a homely yet removed past. Rushdie ruminates on the haunting of loss experienced by those exiled from home and nation but also of the generalized nature of this condition that renders the past itself a country from which everyone is more or less banished (1991,12). Still, the disjunctions of time and space are most acutely felt by those for whom ties to homes of past and present are rendered incommensurable, even contentious.

Rushdie appears preoccupied with the project of the nation and its mythical derivatives in order to understand how we form affiliation to such constructs, and how they define our subjectivities. But, the opening line of *Midnight's Children* and essays in *Imaginary Homelands* give away clues for other forms of affiliative practices than what Rushdie is explicitly dismantling. While Rushdie remains relentless in de-normalizing the nation as homeland, he has spoken more than often in agreeable terms about Mumbai ("my lost city") and New York as sites of his domicile, and even perhaps as loci of desire. It appears that for one as cynical about allegiances and affiliations as Rushdie, the city is a more viable destination than the nation.

The silhouette of the city also appears reluctantly in sociological critiques. Gayatri Spivak perambulates the city while "de-singing" the national state. Spivak sees the national state ambivalently, as a problematic but also as a possibility. She reaches beyond the national state in an effort to theorize Asia as a "critical regionalism" but invokes it as a buffer to the emergence of the Asian megacity (Spivak, 2008).[5] What is striking, and particularly significant for us, is Spivak's begrudging admission of two cities that she considers as hometowns, New York City and Kolkata, in this larger discussion. And she detects moments of such resistances in these hometowns. Spivak admits: "I continue to feel a clandestine comfort that the megacity-effect is resisted in New York and Kolkata is somehow resistant to it" (Spivak 2000, 2008). Here, an intimacy of the national state and hometown is indicated in their mutual contra-position to the global megacity.

It is at those moments of the phantasmal appearances of the city in the nation-think (as Spivak calls it), we are left to wondering: Why is the city discussed so tentatively in South Asia? Where is the city in spatial imagination and theorizing in the way it circulates from James Joyce to Henri Lefebvre, and from Italo Calvino to Saskia Sassen? The work of a number of South Asian (or South Asia-born) writers invokes the spatial landscape of the city in the content and structure of their fiction (the textual form of *Midnight's Children*, like James Joyce's inscription of Dublin in *Ulysses*, is an analog of the rambunctious city of Mumbai), but again it remains mostly undesignated and unmapped.[6] Works of fiction, from *Midnight Children* to Amitav Ghosh's *The Shadow Lines* and Qurratulain Hyder's *A River of Fire*, and certainly R.K. Narayan's stories of Malgudi, all of which have been incorporated overwhelmingly within postcolonial conversations of the nation, can be re-read within a South Asian city thematic. And if read closely, perhaps a hometown or two might appear there in the textual interstices. And it is that city that we are trying to recover.

But what is that city? What is the scope of city-think in South Asia when the discourse has not gone beyond seeing the city, first literally as an urban landscape, and then either as a catalogue of catastrophes or capitalist-consumerist bonanza? The pragmatic or politico-economic discourse on cities is a far cry from considering the city in existential terms. Cities become distinctive or "enlivened" not only by topographical features, urban morphology or civic enterprises, but by imbrication of one's self in the fabric of the city whereby one becomes a dweller or inhabitant besides being a politically constituted "citizen." Joseph Rykwert (1976), in describing this blatant gap in contemporary studies of cities, recalls the words of the fourth century. BCE Athenian general Nicias to his colonizing soldiers: "You are yourselves the town, wherever you choose to settle... it is men that make the city, not the walls and shapes without them (1976, 23)."[7]

The implication of Nicias is that there is a mutuality of self and space that is not fully engaged in political or sociological interpretations of the city. While humans may live in cities, cities live in them as well. It is this obvious but elusive mutuality that we wish to bring forth through the claims of hometown. Hometown represents a charged relation to a particular place, which is shaped by human emplacement, affiliation, and imagination. Despite being under-theorized in socio-political critiques, spatial narratives of "home-ness" perpetuate in deeply compelling ways, because they articulate a "life-world," or the fundamental human condition of being-in-the-world. The point is not that hometowns are perfect, immutable or foundational places but that we are always emplaced in a specific locus, and we seek, as much as possible, to make ourselves at home in those places, and we do so in lived and practiced ways—routinely, emotionally, and psycho-geographically[8] (In *Imaginary Homelands*, Rushdie's nostalgia wells up as he discovers that the listing for his father still exists in the city's telephone directory).

How then to think of the city within a home thematic in modern South Asia where it remains constrained by developmental or sociological parameters, where the city is conceived either as a financial matrix or demographic constellation?[9] Ashis Nandy's (2001) "psycho-analytical" treatment of the modern city is a point of departure for a historiography of homeness in South Asian cities. In South Asia, home is caught up in a singular narrative with the city and modernity: the silhouette of one and the anxieties of the other are like warp and woof of the national fabric. Ashis Nandy proposes "journey" as the principal trope in understanding how the making of home – or more likely the thwarting of one – constitutes the modernity of South Asian cities. The modern South Asian city, which is the colonial city catapulted into a post-colonial connurbation, is constituted of two such journeys, and they are also decidedly ambiguous ones: movement from the village to the city, and from the city to the

[7] While traveling in India, Mark Twain wrote back: "All the me in me is in a little Missouri village halfway around the world," in Richard Lingeman (1980: 483).

[8] Although the Situationists used it in innovative ways in their exploration of and encounter with the city, the term "psycho-geography" refers to its original usage by Guy Debord and the French Situationists as the effects of the geographical environment on the behavior of individuals. The term is genealogically related to Charles Baudelaire's notion and practice of urban wandering in the *flaneur* to Walter Benjamin's expansion of the idea, and the Situationist strategy of "derive" (another version of urban encounters). The term has now expanded to multiple derivations of psychological and kinesthetic awareness of urban spaces.

[9] Henri Lefebvre's point that the city is an "*oeuvre*, closer to a work of art than to a simple material product" might seem to be a natural proposition in Europe's dense urban meditations, but in South Asia, despite a 4000 year old urban history, the city remains very much ambiguous, still haunted by Vedic indictments around the evils of the city.

[10] The journey to the city is both literal and physical (migration to cities), psychological (an inner evolution of the self from fidelity to freedom), and metaphysical (city as emblem of the nation-state, of development and "progress" of the nation towards modernity, etc.), Nandy, 2001: 7. We note that this oscillation is analogical to earlier historical or mythical journeys, such as the Buddha's departure from the city to the forest and his subsequent travels through urban places, and the protagonists of the Mahabharata in their "travel" from the city to the forest and from the forest to the city.

[11] It may be noted that Gandhi made an effort to end that ambivalence by proposing an alternative destination that was neither city nor village. Having arrived from the city, Gandhi located himself at the fringe of a city – Ahmedabad or Nagpur – and invented for himself a quasi-village ethos and practice. Made in the image of a village (or ashram), located at the fringe of a city, but calibrated by a national significance, Gandhi's habitation remains as part utopia and part heterotopia.

[12] The constructed otherness appears in multiple ways, particularly in an unwitting way in cinematic imagination as in the fictive Sundarnagar in the commercial film *Mein Prem Ki Diwani Hoon* where a whole projected city space is occupied by Indians as if in India when the actual spaces of the city are of a distant New Zealand. See Kazi Ashraf (2005).

village.[10] The two journeys constitute more of an oscillation, and, it is this oscillation, and its various fluctuations and tensions, that describe the quandary of the modern national state. The trope of journey can also be used for the Partition narrative where the journey can seen as relocating from a specific town to an abstract nation, from the reliability of a home-world to the ambiguity of the nation-home, perhaps best emblematized by Sadat Hasan Manto's Toba Tek Singh.

Even as Nandy works through a binary spatiality – the city and the village – an important conclusion is reached, that the modern Indian city, borne of the lofty songs of the nation, of which Chandigarh is the greatest composition, instead of providing a new home, offers a "planned homelessness" (2001, 25).[11] This is a critical indictment that describes the unsettling nature of the modern city. If the asymptotic oscillation between the two spatial loci is the character of the modern city, a transnational exchange characterizes the neo-liberal convulsions of the contemporary city. To the earlier binary oscillation between the city and village now must be added a transnational movement and transcontinental spatialities. Homeness is now caught in a trialectical conundrum and the city occupies new spatial coordinates.

A key aspect of the transnational exchange is the global megacity phenomenon where contentiously constructed spaces, the office parks, malls, entertainment complexes, in the matrix of the existing city embody an instantaneous "otherness."[12] While these atolls of spaces are selectively blanketing the landscape of South Asian cities, the program is premiated on the projection that the whole city will be transformed into a global space. The new social and spatial formation of otherness is far less studied as a crisis of home-world. Spivak (2008) describes this tendency in South Asian metropolises as "secessionist," that is, the manner how global coordinates functions in those cities through local capital and a compliant socio-economic class to dissociate from the existing matrix. The built simulacra of "elsewhere" as in Gurgaon in Delhi and Hirandani in Mumbai, and multiple smaller incarnations all over South Asia, is not a merely a fabulous imagination; these spaces, imagined or built, are enumeration of the collective desire of the powerful urban elite as they encounter, experience and succumb to (new) global coordinates, and remain pointedly "homeless."

The contemporary city is no longer the representation of the national state, as Chandigarh was in an earlier dream-time, but the site and agent of its vigorous attrition. The role of the city is now double-edged. On the one hand, it is the collaborating site of globalization and an agent of the erosion of the national state, and on the other hand, it is an inherent location of "home-world," and a mode of resistance to the megacity, and thereby somewhat of a redemptive factor to the faultlines of national state.

Proposing Hometown as a Counter-Discourse

The idea of hometown is considered, especially against the twin foils of homeland and national state, to be potentially a deeply political one. It is obvious from these discussions, and from the numerous nuanced accounts of hometown in literature and popular culture, hometown does not immediately lend itself to romanticization despite the frequent gloss. Hometowns, like homelands and nations, can be as exclusionary, parochial, and sites of violence. Hometowns are places that some seek to flee as much as others seek to arrive into them.

Violent exclusions, more typically inherent in the discourses of homeland and nationalism, are oftentimes borne by particular communities in urban areas making hometown a chauvinistic fortification. In recent years, Mumbai has witnessed the resurgence of violence against "North Indians," at the hands of Maharashtra Nirman Sena (MNS). Although the Shiv Sena's first staging of violent exclusions was directed to migrants from southern India, specifically people from the state of Tamil Nadu, MNS has been increasingly aimed at the expulsion of northerners, especially migrants from the states of Bihar, Uttar Pradesh, among others. The common underlying refrain is that Mumbai is for Mumbaikers.

The point of departure for hometown is not that it supersedes the limitations of space/place or the exigencies of culture and politics, but that it opens up different possibilities of subjective attachments. First of all, it presents a kind of intimate allegiance with places that is possible to forge, modify, replace, and re-forge as only in a situation of fundamental embodiment; hometown is mine, my construction, my experience. In short, what is particular to hometown is that it is one's own. By intimate, we do not imply the personal and the individual, although we are interested in how individuals create these subjective attachments to place because of one's fundamental, lived embodiment and emplacement. The claim of spatial "my-ness" can also be an anxious one, often disrupted, alienated, or even challenged, for the intertwining of self and space is not merely corporeal-spatial in a mechanical way but contains psychological, affective and oneiric contents.

Secondly, beyond self-embodiment, hometown is about belonging and attachment. Given the enduring draw of the homeland and the hegemony of the national state, these belongings to hometown and to homeland or national state are not mutually exclusive but may, in fact, work in and through each other. Nonetheless, belonging to hometown foregrounds the nuances and specificities through which attachments are forged and revised on the terms described above and earlier.

Thirdly, and this is a crucial point that characterizes narratives of hometown, that attachments to places are quite frequently multiple. Unlike the relative exclusivity of homelands and national states (notwithstanding the possibility of more than one passport), hometowns can be and often are simultaneously plural. The manner in which we form attachments to places – subjectively, intimately – inherently allows for a plurality of such attachments, making possible more than one hometown. These attachments may be organized along the temporalities of the past and the present, but more frequently in a synchronic manner. Even though one dwells physically in one place, hometowns may be elsewhere, just as much as one may be living in one's hometown while holding equally dear two other places. It is therefore that Fowzia, a newly married Pakistani woman who was interviewed for this project, emphasized her attachment to Boston, alongside Lahore and Kingston, Canada. Despite the fact that she has lived in Boston for only six months, she counts it among the places to which she belongs, because this is where she started her married life, became familiar with the neighborhood of Brookline, and knows the streets, restaurants, and cafes. As she also puts it simply, "I get very emotionally attached to places." Or, as Emiko, an anthropologist from Paris living in Phnom Penh describes her latter home-making: "I made a life there."[13]

The Topography of Hometown

If hometown defines in a basic sense one's relationship to a city or town, it remains as an understated and unexamined sociological and anthropological phenomenon. Although part of a lived experience, and a personal and public imaginary, hometown is yet to be located within a materialist, existential or phenomenological framework. While song-writers, novelists and film-makers have approached urban or hometown affiliations in a lyrical vein, social scientists, urban geographers or anthropologists have not developed any particular approach to study the phenomenon. The episteme of hometown has remained dubious because that social landscape never found itself promoted from, what John Hollander describes, a mere geographical middle into a representational center. Hollander makes the observation while reviewing Morris Wright's photo-textual narrative on the American Midwest, *The Home Place.* Only a "powerful imagination" as Wright's, Hollander notes, could open up such geographic middle of anonymity for the active consciousness as "concentric circles of significance."

A basic understanding of hometown comes from considering a place that is home due to generational or familial reasons. Michael Ondaatje, in his narrative of return to home-places, describes that familial milieu as the "original circle of love" (Ondaatje 1984). One is committed by dint of being there, being born there, or growing up there, with a kind of commitment without choice. One could preliminarily speak of hometown as a generational continuity in a contiguous space, but that integrity may be ruptured by dislocation or movement away from it with subsequent reorientation of affinities and commitments. There is a commitment that comes out of a conscious choice (or as part of conflicting choices), a decision making when one is away from hometown, and for a number of reasons – political, personal, professional, economic, nationalistic, a combination thereof – one opts to be associated with hometown, to return to it, even as return and home-space may be reconstituted, or to create a new one.

What also needs to be recognized is – and we have noted this earlier – that whether gained for the first time or gained anew,

[13] Conversation with one of the authors, Honolulu, 2010.

hometown is not just a sweet place of giddy belonging; it is also frequently the source of a tense relationship. As hometowns are gained, they are lost too, and sometimes, ironically, it is precisely when they are lost that they emerge cognitively. The columnist Kuldip Nayar writes about such a tragedy of losing hometown to a vanishing point, equating his and his family's loss of Sialkot during partition and the recent loss of Harsud to its residents because of the state's forced development project (the submerging of the original town due to the Narmada dam).[14] Loss of hometown can also be experienced without a physical dislocation. Feminist writer Urvashi Butalia recounts her trip from Delhi to Lahore to locate an uncle who did not migrate to India with his other Hindu family members following the 1947 dislocations of partition (Butalia 2000). The uncle, Ranamama, opted to stay back in Lahore with his aging mother with the purpose of retaining their ancestral home until the trouble died down. Butalia locates him thirty years later, still in Lahore, the city which belonged to the family for generations and to which they belonged. Ranamama is in the same house, has converted to Islam, married, raised daughters, and buried his old mother per Muslim customs. Although the uncle has remained in the same spatial coordinates, he reveals strong feelings of disjuncture and otherness.

The principal epistemic question regarding hometown is how a city is rendered or perceived as socially, materially and existentially significant, which is to say, when does it become officiated as a hometown. Walter Benjamin made a distinction between two options for writing the story of a city, one that could be described as a documentary mode which is the prerogative of the foreigner and visitor to the city who is immediately drawn more to its spectacular side, and the other as an autobiographical one, a privileged possibility for the native writer, an in-dweller to the city. If there is a true cartography of a city, as Mike Davis notes, it requires thousands of maps, each resident of a city with his or her own "psycho-geography." From the vantage point of hometown, a city or town needs to be understood from both lenses of the abstract and the particular, which is to say, the set of the conceptual, affective, empirical and narrative categories that we outline below.

Place and Space. Hometown represents a charged relation to a particular place, which is shaped by human emplacement, affiliation, and imagination. Place has always played second fiddle to the more conceptually sturdy and resolute space. And that simply may be the primary reason why notions of place, including hometown, are under-theorized. The debate around place, especially in philosophical circles, is two-pronged: one is about the relation between space and time, and the other between space and place. Even though place has been represented in various discourses, from *Chora* to *Heimat* and *Desh*, it remains analytically obscure. The general neglect of a systematic study of place, notes the historian of philosophy Edward Casey, is not because it is a controversial or embarrassing topic but because "place is so much with us, and we with it" (Casey 2009) A theory of hometown has to

[14] Wikipedia's description of a contemporary town as "Harsud *was* a town" is both striking and disconcerting.

reinvigorate the discussion of place but without retracing its sentimental quagmires.

Livedness. The "lived" nature of hometown is one of its defining features. We refer to the lived quality of hometowns in at least two ways that are not easily extricable from one another. The terms of human geography, the lived-world as *umwelt* and the socio-spatial surround as a matrix, help elaborate the first aspect of how hometowns are predicated in the condition of livedness. *Unwelt* refers to the lived aspect that comes from being embodied in a space (as well as time), or what may be described as the lived-body in space, for to live, in the phenomenological description, is to be in space. There is an intrinsic mutuality between self and space that Maurice Merleau-Ponty describes as "intertwining" and "flesh." The lived-body is a particularly useful notion that also offers a mapping of the horizons of "experience" and "reach" in the various spatial orbits, from the house, to the neighborhood, the town, the region, and beyond, to the nation. The construction of hometown takes place in specific horizons of "reach," and the spatiality of the city describes that "reach."

This is the second aspect: Hometown is the spatial horizon of the corporeality of the body; anything else is "outside," not home, even perhaps an alien or "other" space. Hometown is the spread of a space that a body traverses, not that it has traversed all parts of that town, but they form part of the horizon of one's corporeality. Hometown thus constitutes what Hannah Arendt describes in a different context, as "the horizon of reach." What we are calling into play here is the experiencing and sentient subject, the lived-body. Such a subject-oriented consideration is not indicative of a self-centered world projection but an understanding of the subject in its sociological and spatial internment in the lived world, *umwelt*. The term matrix connotes the social and material context in which this livedness occurs. It is "a place or medium in which something is bred, produced or developed" (Casey 2009, 24). The lived life implies that I am here, and my life revolves around the rhythm of the day and night, and that my lived experience is seamless in the social-spatial matrix I find myself.

Practices of Habitations. The everyday city is also a practiced city. One encounters the city or one is of the city in all kinds of nondescript and ordinary ways that run the gamut of strategies and practices that Michel de Certeau (1984) has elaborated in *The Practiced Life.* Hometown thus is not merely a sentimental production but sedimentation of the social practices in an (urban) spatial matrix with an array of engagements including negotiations, mediations, agreements, subterfuge, camouflage, alternations, etc. The practice of the everyday, in large part, is characterized by a repetition, the reproduction of habits and rhythms that are most often anonymous and unselfconscious. Rhythms and repetitions produce certain conducts that manufacture hometownship: riding the bus to work, the city newspaper, Ganpati celebrations in Mumbai, local licensing procedures, and various other paraphernalia of city associations and rituals. We literally become linked to our habitations through habits, through the ritual repetition and reproduction of the everyday practices. While in most cases we seem to be the arbiters of reproduced practices, that is, in charge of the vicissitudes of life, we are, more accurately, embedded in a world of socially constructed situations.

Temporalities. Livedness inevitably raises the question of temporality. Exigencies of travel and migration structure the temporal dynamics of affiliations. Travel, voluntary and involuntary migrations, mean movement away from an earlier city, the city of in-dwelling, whereby one's relationship to that prior city is now open to reconsideration. For those who have traveled from an earlier spatial locus to a new one as an immigrant, diasporic, transient or exilee, hometowns have to be constructed afresh. If hometowns can be lost, they can also be reconstructed or gained anew, and what was the space of actual time can pass into time past. Perhaps the most curious aspect of hometown is that one continues to establish new affiliations and attachments with places throughout one's life. This is to say, new hometowns may and do emerge. In brief, mobility as a mode of temporality mediates in the arrangement of more than one hometown.

****

As we point toward alternative/another affiliations and ways of belonging, those that do not toe the line of either state structures or nationalisms, it would be impetuous to herald the coming demise of nations, especially in South Asia. While we do not deny the fragility of nationalisms and nations we are invoking hometown as a way of a rethinking attachment alongside and beyond the national framework, rather than as an elixir for the pathology of nationalism. The alternative/another way of belonging/affiliation is not necessarily in a contentious relationship with the national state for sometimes hometown narratives emerge from a national discourse. At other times, they may be at loggerheads with each other (consider once more the federated state of India and the urban chauvinism of Mumbai's Thackerites, which in any case, is a good example of the political and even ideological production of hometown), but in general, the state or the nation is not visible or operative in the everyday practice of hometown. On more dramatic and usually tragic moments, such as the 2008 attacks in Mumbai, the city and nation collapse into the same space and narrative. Hometown then becomes the body where the specter of the nation finds tangibility.

While we identify the potential of hometown to deepen what Homi Bhabha describes as the "ambivalence" of nations, we also emphasize the capacity of hometown, despite its popular, sentimental inflections, as a political practice. The "silence" of hometown as such a practice does not confirm its weakness but rather its qualitative disposition as an exemplar of what Gianni Vattimo considers as "weak ontology," as something working around dominant and non-negotiable systems. Further, we ask whether hometown thinking holds up to the promise of Jürgen

Habermas' "postnational constellation" even though he is thinking of models that transcend the nation. Wary of political identity based on shared cultural characteristics, Habermas advocates a new frame of community, one that is formed by a civic mode of national attachment in distinction to an ethno-centric one. Habermas' description of a "civic mode of national attachment" returns the political to civitas and its original reference to the space of the city, and perhaps a fresh consideration of the older concept of city-state. Considering Jacques Derrida's conception of the cosmopolis as a "city of refuge" that offers humanist counterpoints to the mechanism and structure of the traditional state, the notion of hometown offers a fresh way of expanding postnational critiques, and opens a new space of political practice (Derrida, 2001).

References

Ashraf, Kazi K. (2005). "Masala City: Urban Stories from South Asia," in *Architectural Design*, Vol. 7, No. 5, September.

Billig, Michael. (1995). *Banal Nationalism*. London, Thousand Oaks, New Delhi: Sage Productions.

Butalia, Urvashi. (2000). *The Other Side of Silence: Voices from the Partition of India*. Durham and London: Duke University Press.

Calhoun, Craig. (1997). *Nationalism*. Minneapolis: University of Minneapolis Press.

Casey, Edward. (2009). *Getting Back Into Place: Toward a Renewed Understanding of the Place-World*. Bloomington: Indiana University Press.

Mike Davis. (1990). *The City of Quartz: Excavating the Future in Los Angeles*, London: Verso.

Derrida, Jacques. (2001). *On Cosmopolitanism and Forgiveness*. (M. Dooley and M. Hughes, Trans.). London, New York: Routledge

Ferguson, James and Akhil Gupta. (year). "Spatializing States: Toward an Ethnography of Neoliberal Governmentality." *American Ethnologist*, 29 (4), 981-1002.

Layoun, Mary. (2001). *Wedded to the Land? Gender, Boundaries, and Nationalismin Crisis*. Durham and London: Duke University Press.

Lingeman, Richard. (1980). *Small Town America: A Narrative History*. Boston: Houghton Mifflin.

Nandy, Ashis. (2001). *An Ambiguous Journey to the City: The Village and Other Odd Ruins of the Self in the Indian Imagination*. New Delhi and New York: Oxford University Press.

Ness, Gayle D. and Prem P. Talwar. (2005). *Asian Urbanization in the New Millennium*. Singapore: Marshall Cavendish International.

Nigam, Aditya. (2009). "Empire, Nation and Minority Cultures: The Postnational Moment." *Economic and Political Weekly*, Vol. XLIV (10), 57-64.

Ondaatje, Michael. (1984). *Running in the Family*. New York: Penguin Books.

Pamuk, Orhan. (2005). *Istanbul: Memories and the City*. New York: Knopf

Rushdie, Salman. (1991). *Imaginary Homelands: Essays and Criticism 1981-1991*. London: Granta Books.

Rykwert, Joseph. (1976). *The Idea of a Town: The Anthropology of Urban Form in Rome, Italy and the Ancient World.* Princeton: Princeton Architectural Press.

Spivak, Gayatri Chakravorty. (2008). *Other Asias*. Malden, MA: Blackwell Publishers.

The edge is the center. Photo: Ashraf.

We Are the City

Published as an editorial in *Jamini* issue on "Making Cities," 2010.

I dream of a city called Calvino where turning the corner of an alley, in front of a shop of curios and old books, I decide *what I want to do for the rest of my life*. As I gaze upon the street, on whose brick paved surface, millions have walked on and been swallowed, I hear the hum of stories. *Cities are millions of stories*. I see signs signaling that the city is both monumental and ephemeral, and elusive yet irresistible. I sense that even if *there is no there there*, there is a here where I stand: *I am the city.*

In Italo Calvino's *Invisible Cities*, when the Kublai Khan and Marco Polo exchange stories of places, I come to understand the city as an existential theater of actions, practices, dreams and imaginations. *Our* actions, practices, dreams, and imaginations. A city is neither hell nor heaven; we make cities in the shadow of our selves. *We are the city*.

As a theater of social action, the city "fosters art and is art." It is in the city, as theater and one that creates the theater according to the urbanist Lewis Mumford, "man's more purposive activities are focused, and work out, through conflicting cooperative personalities, events, groups, into more significant culminations."

One cannot proceed into the heart of a city without a mytho-poeitic imagination. A city is not mere buildings, streets and spaces; it is, first and foremost, an idea in which buildings, streets and spaces play key part. In considering Dhaka as the toughest city in the world, the challenge is not one of solving energy, transport and infrastructure crises but in producing the idea of how one should live as part of a collective. People do not arrive at the gate of a city with just an economic impetus; they arrive with an image of the city, with an *idea*.

A narrative of cities cannot be contained only by techno-functional notions around urbanization and economy. Talks of urbanization distract the discourse of cities with number games, not taking into account that a city is shaped, bit by bit, not only by policies and ordinances but imaginations and practices. Statistics do not show how a city can be designed and lived in its fullest human, social, aesthetical, and ecological potential, a dynamic that is approached best by the term "urbanism." A *city* is about material and spatial facts, and *urbanism* is about social relations staged there. Urban sociologist and thinker Henri Lefebvre argues that the two notions overlap even if they appear to be different.

I dream I live in a Dhaka for a "total experience of life," where the antagonism between the city and the landscape is not brutal, where the cliched opposition between city and village has been overcome, where wide sailed boats ply in the heart of a downtown, and when the waters come from the mountains people do not escape to the roofs of their huts but embrace the bounties of the delta. And, where, in the vision of master architect Muzharul Islam, there is no presence of "haves" and "have-nots." I dream that such a Dhaka is possible.

*

As the most ancient artifice, older than the making of shrines and monuments, the city reverberates with a greater poignancy as a human collective. New practices of the city are now challenging the certainty and dominance of the nation-state as the unilateral spatial container of our experiences.

An unprecedented urban phenomenon in a global theater is opening up a new conceptual and political scope of the city. With Venice voting recently to secede from Italy, and Hong Kong struggling with China, territorial boundaries of the nation are being redefined, and spatial obligations rearranged. The German philosopher Hans-Georg Gadamer's argument for a "post-national constellational" as an antidote to nationism is becoming more reasonable. Jacques Derrida speaks of another possibility in his proposal for making Paris a "city of refuge" in the ancient theme of a place of hospitality for those who arrive there despite the nation-state's obstruction.

At one level, the city as the generator of numerical gains is a principal player in the neo-liberal economic game, but at another level, it is the core of our existential being and consciousness. Henri Lefebvre talks of that specificity of the city, and how affiliative and affective relationships are practiced for individual and social destinies. Our designation of the city has to be revised, and planners have to learn to engage with the existential quotient of the city.

Cities can be the most beautiful collective dream, as the urban wizard Jaime Lerner claims. Rejecting the notion that the city is a problem, Lerner insists that cities instead are solutions to our nature of collective existence. In transforming the Brazilian city Curitiba as its mayor, Lerner proved that the city is not defined by smog, crisis, and deluge but as an exemplar of how we should live as a decent society in which the fruits of urbanism are available to all citizens. More recently, another South American city – Medellin – for long a poster child of a city gone terribly awry (drug, murder, and mayhem!) has shown that meaningful changes can happen through, as Alex Warnock-Smith notes, "visionary leadership, tough politics, and experimental urban design" (*Architectural Review* 2014).

If there is a doubt to why an art journal like *Jamini* should adopt the city as a theme, writers from Lewis Mumford to Henri Lefebvre have articulated the city as an art, a production. "The city," to Lefebvre, "is an oeuvre, closer to a work of art than to a simple material product. If there is production of the city, and social relations in the city, it is a production and reproduction of human beings by human beings, rather than a production of objects." As an *oeuvre*, a French word denoting an ensemble of distinctive work in art, music or literature, the city is contrasted with the "exchange" value that money and commerce generate. The city above all has "use" value such that streets and spaces, and edifices and monuments, have the preeminent purpose of being used or consumed "unproductively," something that may not be estimated through monetary value alone.

*

As incubators of our futures, cities are not simple manifestation of social formation, but prognosis for emerging social and cultural forms. Again, whether delirious or dubious, there is a new city in the horizon even if its contour remains largely unmapped. While the fabric of Euro-American cities remains mostly stable (or, in some cases, dwindling, like Detroit), migratory dynamic and entrepreneurial and predatory economics are fast changing the Asian urban landscape.

Clearly, there has been a quantum leap in the urban phenomenon of Asia. Ushered by economic and climate migration, and administrative impetus, more people now live in cities. China is literally building twenty cities every year, and India proposes spending $20 billion in seven years for its National Urban Renewal Mission. Despite the fact that contemporary cities are responsible, according to Warnock-Smith, for "history's greatest disparity between the wealthy and the poor," cities are the key catalyst for the future of the planet, its transformation, but most importantly, the destiny of subsequent generations.

*

From the deluge of the late 1980s to the unforgettable tragedy of Rana Plaza, Dhaka can be easily written off as an evidence of an apocalyptic city-site. Blood springs from the pillars of a garments factory, a tattered shirt is all that remain of a young man who toiled in a stitching section, a delicate foot of a young woman protrudes between slammed slabs, the sad anklet on her foot a sign of a thwarted hope. Such is the landscape of an unruly industrial globalization.

Borne of the bewildering dynamic of the Bengal delta, people for centuries have learned to live with the extremism of nature that has tested their mettle, creativity, and fortitude. The people of the delta, however, do not know how to live with collapsing and burning buildings, of which they do not have any collective memory or folk knowledge. This is the dark side of urban development, the conundrum of magical economic growth and consumer capitalism centered on major cities.

Death in the plaza is also a consequence of Dhaka's irresponsible planning, part of an abysmal failure by city fathers to establish what should be built where and how. Along the way to Gazipur in the north of the city, on the riverbanks towards Naryanganj, and on the road past Savar, concrete and steel rods replace the vernacular of bamboo and thatch. Multi-storied buildings—six to ten-stories high—hum with the music of a far-off Gap or Walmart. Freshly laid sand-beds announce the arrival of an upcoming housing society. The transformation of Dhaka and its regions, along with its physical and social landscape, has been relentless and brutal. When an agricultural milieu at the fringe of the city rapidly transforms into a hodge-podge urbanization, strange things will happen when nobody is taking notice. *Nalas, dobas,* and *pukurs* – the lowlands – will get filled to shore up tottering towers, without any basic recourse to safety and buildability, and petit goons with the blessings of political leaders will become *crorepatis*, and enter the mystical chain of globalization.

By creating landfill after landfill, emaciating rivers and canals, and decimating floodplains and agriculture, Dhaka makes for a perfect image of an urbanization without urbanism. But it is in this conundrum, a new narrative of Dhaka is being composed. Even if dubbed the worst city to live in and the toughest city in the world, we are already in an unprecedented urban dynamic. If a new and better Dhaka is possible, we have to start from here.

*

"Leave Paris and Amsterdam – go look at Atlanta, quickly and without preconceptions" urges the urbanist-architect Rem Koolhaas in his note on the contemporary city (1989), in an attempt to wean focus away from the usual city discourse based on classical European models. I would rephrase that and say: *Leave Paris and Amsterdam – go look at Dhaka, carefully and without preconceptions*. Dhaka presents not simply a catastrophe for the usual reasons of urbanization but a new theorem for city-thinking.

An urbanism for Dhaka, I have argued, has to be conceptualized from the hydrological property of the delta. The theoretical challenge is this: To conceive an urbanism that embraces an aquatic milieu. Surrounded and infiltrated by a labyrinthine and delicate network of rivers and canals, tissues of wetlands and floodplains, and organic formations of mounds and settlements, Dhaka needs a new approach to city-thinking that generates an aqueous urbanism.

A sociopolitical program is also aligned with the physical fabric of the city. "Cities should provide the environment for civilized life within the context of our own culture," Muzharul Islam wrote in 1968. "The city can develop only as a part of the physical environment of the country, with the ultimate aim of abolishing all differences between the city and rural areas. The traditional relationship with nature (still existing to a certain extent in the villages of Bangladesh) should be continued in the cities." This is not a plea from a romantic advocate nor a modern incarnation of Ebnezer Howard but someone wary of configured differences between "haves" and "have-nots."

*

Bengalis have an ambivalent relationship with cities. Poets and writers sing the sweet songs of villages and versify the vileness of the city. Even when they live and enjoy the city, they dream of the little village through Poet Jasimuddin's comforting image of salubrious vegetation and that untranslatable sense of being wrapped in "maya-mamata." Apu, in Satyajit Ray's filmic *Pather Panchali*, sits redolent amongst a grimy neighborhood in Kolkata, playing the flute like a Krishna dislocated from his arboreal habitat. Ashis Nandy talks of the troublesome oscillation between the village and the city in the course of which both emerges dystopic. Yet, the city thrives in its catankerous ways. Thousands arrive at its shore, suffering the insufferable, and not giving up the promises of an upcoming destiny.

Dhaka's primary urban crisis is one of imagination, of not being able to think of the form of an appropriate city even when there are inspiring clues.

Louis Kahn's designs for the Capital Complex at Sherebanglanagar are known far and wide, but primarily as examples of a high architecture. Few people recognize that Kahn thought through and demonstrated what a tropical city might look like in the form of a civic forum. The Complex is not only about the stunning architecture of Sangsad Bhaban but the way varieties of buildings, parks, gardens, orchards, and lakes are arranged in a kind of garden city to form a place of well-being. In an analogical way, Kahn's design continues to invoke the idea that a properly planned Dhaka can be à model tropical city.

With spacious green spaces, majestic trees, crisscrossing canals, civilized riverbanks, boats with unfurled sails plying through the heart of the city, Dhaka can actually be the garden city and a place by the water it always was. Instead of a total innovation, one could pursue a reformed restoration. The idea of a city as a garden is not a fantasy but an ideology of a city-form. Muzharul Islam imagined "the whole country as a concentration of population in certain areas in a certain way, but even then within gardens." He perceived Dhaka from such a vantage point: "Not only larger gardens but Dhaka city itself as a garden." "If you can do this [tall buildings] utilizing the highlands of Dhaka city," he suggested, "even now, you can place here a population three times its current number, and, at the same time, keep the lowlands as lowlands, keep the water bodies, and create gardens." (1992)

*

The biggest challenge in the recomposition of Dhaka lies in engaging its landscape reality – the dynamic hydrology of the delta. With an ever-expanding city, the dynamic also involves an ecology of the edge.

Koolhaas also introduces the notion of the "edge" in his cartography of the contemporary city. But where the clever Dutch urbanist meant the fringes of the Euro-American city defined by a frazzled fabric of the post-industrial condition or the tattered terrain of suburbia, a place like Dhaka confronts the edge as the new "center."

Most urban planners and policy-makers focus on the core or center city. Even when they are dealing with the edge, they see it in the image of the core. Official planning is unable to conceptualize this edge, to recognize that the edge is its own geography and a critical one. Without that realization it is easy to participate in the destruction of that landscape. An audacious vision for Dhaka has to begin from the edge that meets the precious landscape of wetlands and agricultural terrains. In short, the norm of planning for Dhaka by thinking from the core has to be reversed. This is valid for planning any deltaic town.

The geography of the edge is determined by the built-city marching up to meet the "non-urban," a magnificent but precious terrain of land-water mass made by wetlands, flood-plains, canals, and agricultural fields. The edge is where the dry meets the wet, the "developed" meets the "primitive," and infrastructure meets the structure-less. This is also where the urbanite meets the farmer, the land grabber discovers his opportunity, and the uprooted makes her habitation. Site/s of the biggest battle in the city, the terrain of the edge is determined by the presence and flux of water. No planning scheme will work for Dhaka if this simple equation is not recognized. It is a battle because it is in that terrain the instruments of landfill and embankments are in play. A new imagination and creativity are needed to address this phenomenon in which neither the stilted ecological ethos of DAP (Detailed Area Plan) nor the aggressive pragmatics of developers has risen to the task.

Nothing short of imagining a new landscape of city-form will offer a salvation for Dhaka. The edge conditions of Dhaka presents the possibility of re-negotiating the social and economic, as well conceptual, separation between city and its conventional anti-thesis, whether the village or agricultural plains. The edge is where new forms of space organization in response to a fluxed landscape will have to be reorganized, along with newer forms of economic and social opportunities. In the meeting of an older form of the city with agricultural land-form and hydrological landscape, a new conception of a city will have to be developed that integrates urbanism, agriculture, infrastructure, and flooding.

Review of Messy Urbanism

Messy Urbanism: Understanding the "Other" Cities of Asia, by Manish Chalana and Jeffrey Hou (Hong Kong University Press, 2016), review published in the *Journal of Architectural Education (JAE) Online*, June 18, 2021.

Messy urbanism is almost alright. This is perhaps the unwritten dictum of *Messy Urbanism: Understanding the "Other" Cities of Asia*, in which fourteen writers explore a dynamic and an emergent urban phenomenon. The book argues that Asian cities from Delhi to Tokyo attenuate an existing system in which order is not so much abandoned as scavenged, refracted, or mutated. There is a tenuous truce between what is claimed as the necessary order of things, predicated on cities' strategic plans, and the simultaneous promotion of contrary or divergent tactics. Occupy Wall Street and Arab Spring, even Black Lives Matter riots on American streets, all demonstrate inequities and pathologies lurking within the "system." The nineteenth-century European city is the classic urban mess that needed to be cleared, cleaned up with public spaces and social policies in housing, education, and health. But then there are other messes—the messes in this book—which call for a reverse action: planners, policy makers, and architects ought to embrace the life-world practices that arrive as unforeseen forces and unpredicted events, rich with new possibilities. José Edgardo A. Gomez Jr. writes that there is indeed a differential mess within all Southeast Asian cities—"a recurrent, if inelegant logic" (p. 77)—and that is perhaps the takeaway of this book.

In short, *Messy Urbanism* posits the city as an oscillation between two destinies. Editors Manish Chalana and Jeffrey Hou begin by describing a scene from Wong Kar Wai's film Chungking Express, set in the notorious chaos of Honk Kong's Chunking Mansions, inviting us to the abyss, so to speak, and challenging us to see what constitutes the production of such concatenated conditions. In discussing Tokyo, Ken Tadashi Oshima points out that messy has many meanings, which hints that each city is fabricated in the language of its place (103). Such linguistic notions as informality, impromptuness, inclusivity, and insurgency that characterize the messy city need to be assessed in the framework and nuances of local languages.

There are therefore as many *messinesses* as there are cities. We learn that Shinjuku is polyphonic rather than messy. Koompong Noobanjong writes that Bangkok's Royal Field is a "polysemic urban palimpsest" (83), like the Indian *maidan*. Annette M. Kim argues that the "desire to control" the sidewalks of Ho Chi Minh

Little Manila, Seoul, Korea. Photo: Jeffrey Hou.

City is a critical emblem of messy urbanism (25). Jose Edgardo A. Gomez, Jr. claims that the "syncopations" (77) of Manila have a pattern distinct from Chinese, Indian, and Western notions of order-making. Hou and Chalana assert that in Taipei's Shilin, as in Bangkok's Siam Square (3-4), urban life entertains two fluctuating rhythms: "order/disorder, formal/informal, legal/illegal" (3).

It is understandable that a modest book (252 pages) cannot take on the full panoply of Asian cities. Nevertheless, Western Asia, from Kabul to Aleppo and Beirut, where convulsed cities have become a norm, begs for a distinctive reading of messy urbanism. Also missing are Dhaka, where the transgression of gender boundaries within the messy garment factories has upended civic corridors, and Karachi, where ethnic factions have created miniature cities within the city. There is a necessity to apply the parameters raised in this book to small or midrange towns that are overlooked in the study of Asian cities. Is messy urbanism a megalopolitan phenomenon, the inability of the megacity to come to terms with the burgeoning frontiers of its own making?

The "other" of the subtitle is the least explored topic in the book. Daisy Tam's analysis of Little Manila in Honk Kong looks at the othering of Filipino workers. But the unexplored other in this case is in the context of the reception of Asian cities in global discourse, whether it is a World Bank argument to better what it assesses as a debilitating condition, or a *New York Times* article shining light on what its correspondent deems to be a dark aspect, or a Hollywood film celebrating the underdog life, as in *City of Joy* or *Slumdog Millionaire*. Indian cities especially seem to be natural sites of the urban "other." Istanbul, too, serves merely as an exotic film location, perfect for motorbike chases on the roofs of old buildings or through the crowded souks.

The book would have benefited from some introspection into one's complicity in participating in the dominant order and entering the circle of mess. As Abidin Kusno writes, messiness is a perception as well as a product of knowledge (41). Who will identify and write about the mess? Is there a conundrum about self-representation here, akin to the lack of voice for the subaltern to speak? Those who live within the mess and navigate its channels, like fish in water, do not theorize about it. Is then the theorizing of messiness a prerogative of those who are outside the fish tank, so to speak, or sitting on its rim, one leg in the water?

If the modernist city—the antagonist in this narrative—has arrived in Asia, it is in bits and pieces, contentiously and reluctantly, and in the historic horizon of each city. Messy urbanism in Asia is the failure of the modernist city to find a home; in that sense, the city is perpetually under construction. Messy urbanism is Asia's aspiration for the contours of a new city that is inclusive and evolutionary, although each city is evolving according to its own trajectory. Whether it is Neo-Tokyo in the manga-inspired film *Akira* (1988), or whether the mess is a post-apocalyptic nightmare or a bundle of atomic fire, there is still redemption and reconciliation. In three separate movies, the monster Godzilla arrives to terrorize Tokyo and destroy Shinjuku. In 2015, the Shinjuku Ward awarded residency to Godzilla and made him a special ambassador for tourism. No matter how big the mess is, or in whatever form it comes, there is hope after all.

beholden in a kind of a catatonic grip to something we understand vaguely. And whatever we seem to understand, we hardly acknowledge.

thereafter, on earth is to be considered a dwelling act, the making of a world. It was first and foremost existential. "I call monsters all original inexhaustible beauty," writes Alfred Jarry. Marco Frascari traces the designation of mostri sacri

opted for further study in architecture, and went to the University of Oregon in the United States and to Yale University where he received a Masters degree under the supervision of Paul Rudolph. It was upon his return to East Pakistan, and as part of his responsibilities within the ubiquitous Public Works Department (as no private architectural firms existed

The Lost House

Quetglas continues, "which I cannot claim as mine, where neither I nor my imagination may

house dethrones the fundamental citizen of the house, the dweller, for "the modern house… excludes me, because I am radically absent from it, because it is the house of the Other." And Rudolf Otto has pointed

The Eventful 1960s

architects like Louis I. Kahn, Paul Rudolph, Constantin Doxiadis, Richard Neutra, Stanley Tigerman produced their works here. It was at Dhaka, in 1968, that the most important conference of the Institute of Architects Pakistan was organised, proclaiming a new spirit of architecture.

visited and studied the Pinjore gardens near Chandigarh) but also outlines for the first time a more committed attitude towards

classically based building is not unfounded. Diagrammatically, the Assembly has a number of affinities with neo-Classical honorific building models, especially in British India. The parasol for the portico, the procession

of the materials one is left to work with. In any case, both procedures are attempts at dematerializing either physically (by reduction) or virtually (by visual effects) the very fundamental conditions of architecture: materiality and presence.

in 1929 and placed in crates, put on a train and shipped back to Germany. En route, the crates containing the dismembered house were lost in toto. A house that begins in disappearing can only disappear in full. No trace. And what is left are apparitions and

contradiction.

A structure was rebuilt on the same site in 1986. The original does not exist. The imagination is pervaded by the ruins of the original. What exists is a simulacrum. Or, a sarcophagus.

Why Did the Monk Burn the Temple?

Le Corbusier was given the opportunity, so many times frustrated

Sarabhai House, bring forth more acutely the

It is more than coincidental that the reductive internationalism of the postwar

Le Corbusier's Prehistory

Istanbul is popular memory characterized by a pluralistic, malleable and passionate spirit.

CONVERSATIONS

…as Von Moos observed.[2] "No doubt that some of his paintings can be understood as reflections

…other in order to exist,"[3] and again, "in the one, strong objectivity of forms, under the intense light of a Mediterranean sun: male architecture. In the other limitless subjectivity

…At the same time we must know that there is no such thing as absolute caste restriction in human cultures; they ever have the

…has been found. Then at the end comes the brilliant moment, something that

…and 'meaning transposed' before becoming an architectural reality in the Corbusian schemata.[5] As a rule, the appropriated

…what Stanford Anderson calls the independent and continuing "architectural

…led to an ambiguity producing

…some of them can be sufficiently reduced to asking what is "Indian" about his work? The problem of framing such a question has its roots not merely in the dominance

…Ravindran notes: "The problem with seeking a national or regional diversity is that such efforts are

…manifestation of fascism."[33]

…the enlightened life can begin. Clearly this is a vivid body and

…strata to Corbusier borne out of

…rhetoric may be, but a radical reconstitution or transformation, in which "something" remains, although the old measures of identity are no longer valid. The so-called destruction of the hut is comparable to attaining a "non-conditioned" mode of existence, akin to a "second birth," of dying to this

…the squabble over the appropriation of the new city as capital by the two states of Haryana and Punjab.[10]

The town was a luminous artifact, an ideal representation of upright citizens, celestial gods and the institutions of man. Emblem of Apollonian Virtues, the town was an embodiment of Laws and Principles. On the liminal side of that

…of Nations project; and, administrative and communitarian, as in St Die in France. In the Capitol at Chandigarh, functionally an administrative

…architecture. There, meaning is not generated by the visual and symbolic relationships

…came from nowhere and elsewhere, the women pounce on the temple. They climb and grab at the ropes tying the bundle of wooden posts that hold the roof

…by a deliberate over-scaling of dimensions and distances. Uttam C. Jain imagines the three main actors

…are severed. Thus the temple and its builders and un-builders would enter a curious and volatile relationship of building and mayhem, of death and birthing, recalling the genealogy of the god himself, whether it is the mother figure Semele impregnated after drinking a potion made of the heart of Dionysis torn

…[12] "The vastness of the plaza has the effect of isolating the very elements of the

…of the god who transgressed the customs of the city and inverted the roles of citizenship and duty, ecstasy and responsibility, and the sacred and the sacrilegious. [The above tale

…in its basement or concealed behind its walls, is a secret story told only

…the origin of the river Titash: "Once upon a time the restless Meghna, dancing along her way, slipped into a careless

…own course, finding and molding soft alluvium, cutting and twisting through hard ground. After making a broad

name. They simply proceeded to dismember it. After the deed was done, then they had a name for it. They called it Vastu…

The navel was in the central grid, the source of things to come. It was the point of emergence for Brahma, the master deity of creation. The navel connected to the origin. The navel was the mundus, the omphalos, center of the

…(1939–1942). The separation of the roof from the more used volume of the building also dates as early as 1928 in the first sketch for Villa Bezeau, and 1939 in the pavilion at the exposition at Liege where the consideration was purely plastic.[17]

Such is the origin of a mandala, of the making of a worlding.

"Signs and Symbols. For Whom?" A Conversation with Muzharul Islam

Original interview conducted in 1992. From the book *An Architect in Bangladesh: Conversations with Muzhaurul Islam*, edited by Kazi Khaleed Ashraf, Loka Press, 2012.

Kazi Khaleed Ashraf: You have worked with concepts of space in your own house (at Road No. 25, Dhanmondi). A wonderful discovery for me was your design for the Executive Engineer's Residence?

Muzharul Islam: Why?

Ashraf: It is mainly because of the brick vaulting, although you have worked with it earlier.

Muzharul Islam: There is something about us. We try to explore by working in different ways, and by doing so, we try to find our own nature. What is the best medium to work with? How best to conduct the work? You might be able to produce the best in one particular way. But I feel that for architects the most difficult thing is to find oneself. There is a lot of struggle. Even after finding oneself through the struggle, one cannot remain stuck to it. It does not work. It remains a theoretical thing. Take the case of the vault. I feel that the vault is a beautiful thing for our country. By beautiful I do not mean only the architectural quality, I mean the nature of dwelling, the construction means, etcetera. I had always meant to work in brick, to know about brick, how brick makes a transition – from brick to brick – without coming across another material, or without adopting another construction means. [The Engineer's Residence] was a later work. I remember designing a few other projects with vault. None of them was constructed.

I have tried to avoid one thing while talking to you. I have tried not to embellish anything with language, with an emotional effusion [*moner madhuri mishiye*, a favorite phrase of Muzharul Islam]. I am trying to bring clarity to something. How to organize brick and vault in our contemporary condition? That is what I have tried to do.

Ashraf: Something different was happening in your own house in Road No. 25. We see a clean, free roof under which all the volumes and spaces are organized. I am thinking of the pavilion type.

Muzharul Islam: It began with the intention of doing a pavilion type structure. But ultimately there remains a remote connection with the pavilion as you call it. I don't know what your readings are but there were all kinds of funny reactions in laypeople. They used to come and tell me that it appears like a fortress from outside because of the mostly solid facing walls, "But, Mr. Islam, how is it possible? Inside, it is all open, filled with sunlight, air." Inside, there was the feeling of a pavilion.

Ashraf: You have worked largely within abstraction in these projects. When I say the pavilion, it is the conceptual pavilion you are working with. Can we say that you have tried to avoid one thing in your work – the aspect of symbolism?

Muzharul Islam: I have terrible objection to that.

Ashraf: That's what we would like to know about.

Muzharul Islam: I have heard so much about [symbolism] that I think there is a lot of falsity about it. There are two things here. There are people who have claimed symbolism in a work after its creation. The other thing is to produce symbols. This has been derived mostly from religion. Even where it has appeared culturally, there is the force of religion at the back. I am always cautious because of this.

What I have tried to see in a work is the simple geometric form and whether one can derive a simple visual enjoyment from it. Hundreds of things appear when you get into symbolism. This has been derived from that, this represents that, etcetera, etcetera. I am working at a slightly "cruder" level.

Ashraf: On the one hand, "crude," and, on the other hand, it is a filtration of symbols, such that they cannot be recognized anymore. Is that possible?

Muzharul Islam: There is an issue here. Say I want to cover a space. For whatever reason, I make the space with vaults. The vault is a traditional element; it comes from a thousand year old practice.

Ashraf: Instead of symbol, if we call it cultural motif, that is also not present in your work.

Muzharul Islam: There's not even a question of its arising. Let me tell you why. There is also the motif of the overall total design. If you consider that as a motif, then it is there. But, I am not sure about motifs for details and elements. I was very afraid that this will take place. For this reason, I have consciously avoided it. Let me say this too. If you consider the jali as a motif, it was done as an absolutely different thing, through a different logic, different material, different form. The jali in the Art College has some semblance to traditional ideas, it was a space divider. Jalis in the [Public] Library was done with great care, so that there was a clear flow of south-north air from one side to the other. It was a wholesale jali.

Saif Ul Haque: I am thinking about the expression of a building. The structural elements – wall, roof, pillars, beams – are derived logically without the issue of surplus. The walls are located here, the roof is supported on four posts, I need an opening here, I need light from outside, I need air, I will enter here. Was there a reductive thinking like this working there?

Ashraf: Let me add to that. What Saif [Haque] called reductive, can we describe that as minimalist or purist? Are you rejecting something by adopting this approach? Are you denying the impulsive desire [for those who will see, use or experience it]? By "impulsive," I also mean what is not pure or ideal.

Muzharul Islam: Yes, I understand. There was obviously an idea. This is Bangladesh. You are given a program. There is a budget. You are trying to arrive at a solution employing all your ideas and thoughts. And while solving, you are considering a purist attitude that I will work with the most simple things, I will organize a comparatively decent thing. Not that you might not want to do something interesting time to time, it is possible. That is called "flourish," to add "flourish." But isn't it a major responsibility to restrain that [impulse]? One or two small "flourishes" may be [entertained] but I always had a hesitation about large-scale "flourish." [I wondered,] am I playing around with other people's money?

There is something fundamental in the context of Bangladesh, that I will work with minimum things. The reason is simple: To do the most economic structure and form in the real sense of the term. In the case of [European] aesthetics – what they may call purist, minimalist – it's a question of the brain functioning in a way to produce certain things. Here, my whole world is like that. If I can produce something in two takas, why should I spend five. [You won't even get five takas.]

Ashraf: I was trying to bring it up in a different way. By thinking in a minimal, essentialist way, I come to the decision that I need a roof. The roof is the most important element. There are a few decisions after this, whether the roof is going to be like this or in another way. I think these are important issues, not only about aesthetics or style, or visual enjoyment.

Muzharul Islam: That is right. The roof is not merely a roof. It's part of the whole thing, what you are trying to do with the whole thing. On the one hand, it can simply mean a shelter, a shelter from rain, sun, etc. It may be flat, it may be curved, it may have multiple curvatures.

There's one more thing. When I say cultural background, I mean both world culture and one's own culture. There maybe a number of things in world culture that is not here. Can I impose some of that? What happens if I do? Is that appropriate?

Crudely, what I have tried to say repeatedly is the search for one's own ground, which is something enduring, not fashion or style, but some basic principles from which all forms of art of all periods evolve. This cannot be explained easily, it is an extensive issue. The whole aesthetics of form creation is involved here. It is not the job of one person, it needs the tremendous collective energy of a huge number of people.

Ashraf: Let me bring up another matter, in continuing the discussion another way. You talk about taking up kurta-paijama [traditional outfit for men]. Does that not fall within the range of signs and symbols?

Muzharul Islam: In one way, if perceived that way, it can be part of that range. When I mention standing on one's own soil, the issue of signs and symbols can come up in that sense. But it is different. It's to find oneself, but not to find oneself and become stagnant. What I am seeking is to stand one one's own feet and then to proceed forward. If for that reason I have to take two steps backward to go one step forward, I have no problem with that. I think that there is no other way of moving forward.

In this sense, certain principles – not form, the copying of which would be most shameful – could be absorbed, and for that reason if I have to go back, and if you place it within the realm of signs and symbols, it's up to you, but what I am saying is to move beyond, forward. When I say, by the by, the wearing of kurta-paijama, it is to mean that now one can proceed. This is for the reason of collective identity.

Ashraf: Collective identity. We are made collective through signs and symbols.

Muzharul Islam: In a sense, it is always so. I object to signs-symbols only then when it implies supernatural things.

Ashraf: Supernatural, or fascist or ultranationalist?

Muzharul Islam: Right. I object to both. For that reason, I have always repeated that one needs to be a Bengali. One needs to be a world man. You have to be a world man and a Bengali. It's impossible otherwise.

Ashraf: Is there a reason here to consider the human experience holistically? There are perhaps two things. One the one hand, there is the question of restraints when impulsiveness is involved. And, on the other hand, there is the matter of various desires that confront pure, idealistic work.

Muzharul Islam: I am trying to solve a problem. By employing minimum elements I am trying to produce a decent thing. The minimum remains as an idea, it does not stay like that afterwards. It is possible in painting, in sculpture, to put something together with few things, but it is quite difficult in architecture. The matter of "flourish" comes in a different way, in a subtle way. It comes in organizing the minimum, the whole thing with one or two small details. A whole thing can be transformed by a small element. Time to time, there has been an intention for doing this. In few places, I have also done this. I sometimes feel uncomfortable saying this...

Let me give an example. There was a good designer at Yale. A first-class draftsman. He produced something, a nice building, and in front of that, he placed a 40 ft-50 ft pillar. A sheer concrete pillar. Paul Rudolph came and asked, "What is this?" "It is nothing..." There was silence, and then Rudolph said it was good. A pillar changes a whole building. Am I making the issue of "flourish" clear? It does not mean it is something gaudy.

Ashraf: It is possible that the whole form may be of an impulsive character, as in expressionistic work. I really didn't mean that. Certain elements may be introduced within a largely purist format that may please at another level, call it sensuous level or something else.

Muzharul Islam: It is sensuous level, exactly.

Ashraf: I am thinking of the work of the Czechoslovakian architect Joze Plecnik. He was prolific in the 1920s. I enjoy his work because it can be approached at a number of levels. At a distance, many of his work have the appearance of a neo-classical building. A pure volume. As you draw closer, you notice numerous other things. A whole wall may be composed of very irregular rubblework, all the columns are not in the expected configuration.

Muzharul Islam: Every architect has his or her own uniqueness. Certain codified aspects were also present in various cultures. In China, a building facing a courtyard might not have all its columns regular, it might have one askew. This became codified. What you are suggesting I now see that differently once it is codified.

I think the most difficult task is to make a thing simple. It is quite possible to produce a complicated composition, to engage the brain in great many exercises. But it is truly a difficult task to excite the brain by producing a truly simple thing. Not simplistic, but simplicity. There is an ocean of difference between simplistic and simplicity. It is the most difficult task to bring excitement in simplicity. I don't think it is possible by me.

Ashraf: You have not spoken about one particular project of yours, the National Library [and Archive]. We can interpret the National Library as a pure form has been deformed to create a complex entity. Overall, it began as a pure square, then the corners were sliced, and then the four sides were organized in four different ways for reason of the site, climate, function or program, and visual reasons. This brought up "complication" at a different level. And that brought a level of richness to the work.

Muzharul Islam: But that was not produced crudely.

Ashraf: Certainly not crudely.

Muzharul Islam: Neither for the purpose of "flourish." It can be an ultimate success when the total thing is successful. But isn't this a bit unfair to demand it from me?

Ashraf: Another issue is related here. Our education. We all undergo a largely purist sort of training, to do the minimal things. And since it is divorced from construction, from the tactile sensibility, how materials are arranged in a concrete way, how the brick is being laid, etc., we approach the whole business in a kind of naive straightforward way. But the real experience is not so straightforward. When the building is erected, people expect and experience a lot more, rather holistically... including the impulsive matter.

Muzharul Islam: I suppose a lot is being said today about this by many people.

Ashraf: Sometimes things are happening in the other extreme [as with "postmodern architecture"]: How to make the work deliberately contradictory or eccentric. I am not talking about that.

Muzharul Islam: There is a beautiful description of this from long ago. Say a building. I enjoy seeing it first from a distance, it's overall treatment. This increases as I come closer. And everything is linked. [Ultimately, how the screws are going to be set, you have to design that too.] I am talking about the eye of the architect, not that of the layperson. When I come closest, I feel like touching it, for I wonder why is it so beautiful. You will see that in almost all the works of Lou Kahn. It is coming from a consciousness that everything is linked, that in my work every item be beautiful, and every piece be enjoyed [by people].

The flourishes that are here, and I have tried to explain that... there are certain limitations. The limitations are not due to intention. There may be intention, but it is monitored by two things. First, there is a danger in working within limitation. The danger is... it may ultimately become uncouth. I don't know what your reactions are about certain buildings but I really feel uncomfortable about a lot of European buildings.

You are creating a sculpture, you are thinking about each space so that everybody enjoys every square inch. Every space is thought out. Not only the spaces, but every square inch of surface areas. It is a tremendous thing. I have no problem.

Ashraf: There are certain unbuilt works of Kahn where he seemed to have catered to impulsive qualities as opposed to a geometrically rigorous formation. In some projects such as the Dominican Motherhouse, Kahn wanted to create an accidental arrangement, an ad-hoc formation.

Haque: Are you worried that the work might be deformed or destroyed?

Muzharul Islam: There are a number of things related to [deformation]. No, it is not a game. I can do that in painting. I can do that in sculpture. The difficulty with building is that it is being done with someone else's money. This is a big responsibility. Certain experimental things can be carried out in places like your own house. There are certain intellectual issues here. I want to describe something. Now whether I want to introduce certain flourish in this description or not. Will this introduction [contaminate] the whole thing or not, even if the flourishes by themselves are beautiful things? Even if I can totally control flourishes, they invariably add to the cost. I am repeatedly bringing in cost but not negatively. If you can do this, if the client agrees, certain flourishes can be allowed.

You create a new kind of ceiling which no one has done anywhere in the world. There is a cinema-house in Mexico City that has floating clouds. They are free, and the air-condition ducts, etc., are linked to them, but they are geometrically organized. I have designed a small house where I created windows with triangles and other things. I broke the whole concept of windows. You can try it. I am not setting any limitation. Even there, I had to be conscious about cost and other things.

Even with the room, you can do all sorts of flourishing things. They are in Corbu's work, like the Meeting Hall in the Mill-Owners' Association Building. The whole wall is twisted and curved in different ways. There is of course [the chapel at] Ronchamp. You can try. People did it before. They did flourishes in thousands of ways.

Timmy Zamir Aziz: We can see this in a different way. Whatever we do, whatever we build, becomes more or less symbols. However we try to avoid 'childishness,' ultimately the situation is we must play. Since we are making, we are playing. We cannot but not play. Then the matter of doing itself becomes the making of symbols.

Muzharul Islam: Then please explain to me what you really mean by symbol? Symbol for what? Symbol of what? Symbol for whom? You raise the issue of symbols. The hesitation in my mind has deep roots. I feel that human society has been kept in darkness for thousands of years by the use of symbols. I revolt against it. By raising the issue of symbols, in the name of symbols, my perspective has been kept limited.

Aziz: Well, personally, I try to avoid the discussion of symbols not because it is irrelevant but because it gets tied up in semantics.

Muzharul Islam: Absolutely.

Aziz: But, at the same time, most of the work of the modernists never relapse into abstraction, they are very concrete.

Muzharul Islam: No, abstract design is not meant in that sense. Again, there is a semantic problem. The meaning of abstract design lies in its original roots. It does not mean it is either in the brain or the heart. The particular methodology of design is known as abstract concept. Design concept is abstract. But what is held together with material is a material object. The matter of concept, the matter of composing and configuring, the intellectual operation of the brain is described by some as process. We have discussed this here at Chetana [the architecture study group founded in the late 1908s]. When we say something (in language), it is a very abstracted idea, very much removed from reality. When we say "chair," the word "chair" means no particular object. I have to do a number of things with "chair," it has to be described, it has to be measured, the wood has to be shown. Despite all these I am unable to describe to you that this chair has a life of its own, an independent existence. The idea of a chair is an abstraction. The next step (in abstraction) is to make a copy of this, you can draw it or you can construct it in a small scale. There is literally no limit to this abstraction. When it is carried out in language, it becomes a sort of a boundless phenomenon. Here lies the biggest problem. The problem is related to design. We verbalize, as we are doing now. We are talking about various things, as you are raising numerous questions. I am sure all of you do a lot of complicated thinking. This thinking is an abstract phenomenon. It is not real as a material thing.

Haque: (laughing) Then are you saying that your work cannot be explained in words?

Muzharul Islam: No work can be grasped in words. I want to [possess] real things. When you say symbol, what does it mean, for whom, for what. Let me say one thing. I'll show you heaps of books where Islamic architecture is flaunted as a symbol of this, a symbol of that, symbol of heaven... I think it is absolute nonsense. People have tried to link two things later. In my view, the intention is not honest. The architect does his work from a completely different idea, with very beautiful things - ripple of water, the murmur of water flowing, these are all very significant things in some cultures. This may be the basis of the work. But then linking this distant symbols, calling it heaven, etcetera, is all absurd. There is an intention to this absurdity, to keep you shackled in religion. Think of a Gothic church, in Paris. An incredibly exciting thing. Then they say it is a heavenly matter. Or if you go to St. Peters. It's exactly the same thing. The most beautiful space, created by some of the greatest people on earth. But then claiming the rest as symbolic, you want to convert me into a Catholic, I certainly don't accept that. We have Lou Kahn's symbolism here – the water, earth, the buildings rising... We don't have to say how close it is to Bangladesh. Exciting and close. I have no objection to this symbolism. But what I terribly object to is what is generally implied as symbolism in European and American culture. I have a great fear.

Aziz: I would like to pose a different question. Many now claim that we don't have an existence, no space outside language. When you are saying that the plan is an abstraction, I believe the opposite. I think it has a "truth-value." For example, the Art College for me now is a symbol of certain time and place, of what I understand to be Dhaka city. When something is built, it attains a symbolic content.

Muzharul Islam: Yes, now you have come to the core. This is something different. And that is doing something exemplary. A work in vault has an identity in a certain sense, what you may call symbol. You are only using a word, I don't object to that. I am saying that the [Art College] maybe identified as a particular work of the transition period. If you use symbol in this sense, I don't have a problem with it.

Aziz: Would you still object if I begin to play with this symbolic value with the best of intentions?

Muzharul Islam: I do have an objection. A big objection. The reason is that easily identifiable cliches are used as symbols. There is a great danger here, particularly in a country like Bangladesh which is in a formative stage. Now if you start this... you see Dhaka city is full of it. During the Ershad regime, certain ugly things were created with bathroom tiles in the name of Islamic art. Completely ugly things that were peddled off as symbols. I have fought against this my whole life. I have mentioned it before that during the Pakistan time, we put up a tremendous fight. The Pakistani government officially wanted to establish an Islamic architecture that we resisted strongly. And because of that it could not be carried out even in Pakistan.

Haque: Are symbol and motif getting mixed up?

Muzharul Islam: It is to some degree because it is a question of a symbol of this or a symbol of that. Notice here the problem of language. This is the reason I am so apprehensive. This had happened in the 1920s, 1930s, in Germany. They tried to identify certain types of buildings with Fascism and Nazism. During the time of Stalin in the Soviet Union. And in Paris, for imperialism: the emperor lies at the center of the light. Islamic architecture! I am really fearful of such expressions. Rather I would accept what you were saying how society by its own merit and judgment can ultimately decide, this is a good building, an example.

Ashraf: Let me try to return to a fundamental issue. Architecture is such a thing that various games can be played with it.

Muzharul Islam: You are right.

Ashraf: It can even be played in dubious ways. The Fascists have played that. The imperialists at Delhi. In Berlin. What is happening here? We work with form, but does things end there? What is content? This word wasn't raised before, but could we use it instead of symbol?

Muzharul Islam: I have responded to this at the very beginning. And I am not saying anything unique, there are many other architects with me. The meaning of architecture has now completely changed. Now the task of the architect is to make better and beautiful the environment where humans dwell and work.

Ashraf: And the rest will follow?

Muzharul Islam: Yes, it will. This is deeply related. That is the realization of our modern times. There is no other way than this. To continue culturally, to survive individually and for the survival of the city, there is no other way. Western culture has also no other alternative. However they may try, they know very well that they have created monsters.

Haque: In our discussion, various descriptions of symbols are cropping up. At Sherebanglanagar, Kahn talked of a symbolic relationship, especially when he was composing elements of the plan – the Supreme Court, the Assembly, the Mosque.

Ashraf: In the Kahnian sense, form has some significance that goes beyond material facts. What happens when I make this building higher than that. A significance develops the moment I do that. Whether I should make this a square or a rectangle, a pyramid or a cube. And with the understanding that in a particular culture certain meanings have developed over thousand years. Kahn had always pondered about these things.

Haque: That is why I would like to return to your work, particularly the National Library project. It is situated within the extended perimeter of Kahn's work at Sherebanglanagar. Was there an attempt for any [symbolic] dialogue with Kahn's building? There is the open-to-sky terrace on the front side. Was one to stand there to engage in the dialogue?

Muzharul Islam: (laughing) I think that is taking it a bit far. The existence of Lou Kahn is so overwhelming there that no architect can ignore it during design. It becomes absurd if anyone tries to work there by ignoring it unless one wants to destroy it deliberately. When you know what Kahn has done, then when you are working [there], certain things, which are mental and not formal, appear automatically. It is not about taking a form and doing this or doing that. The influence of Lou Kahn on my work is possible if I have not deliberately rejected him. And I see no reason to reject him. I think he has produced a most beautiful work, a successful work for Bangladesh. It is only possible for a [foreigner] when he works with extreme sympathy, after giving consideration to everything in the country. The Indian architects are not completely pleased with Chandigarh. There is a lot of conflict with climate, and lots of problems have arisen about its use. And the concept is also not acceptable to many. Lou Kahn approached with great care, with a lot of understanding and patience.

Ashraf: There are certain projects which are inherently of a symbolic nature where content is significant. They involve how they stand, how they are to be "read," and understood. It is difficult to understand such projects without addressing this. Projects like the Assembly Building in Dhaka. Or, Chandigarh.

Muzharul Islam: Of course. In your sense, that is symbol. [What Kahn said that] this is a symbol in the sense that this is the place where decision is taken about the fate of a country.

Ashraf: Kahn also avoided those symbols that you are also concerned about, such as those used purely in religious or liturgical sense. Kahn made sure that such readings do not take place with his symbolic repertoire. He carefully bypassed those.

Muzharul Islam: But he said a few things… He loved speaking, he spoke a lot. And he spoke about symbolism. For example, he said a street is a building. These things can be difficult for the general people. He used to speak in such manner more and more near the end of his life.

And that is not the only thing. When you are preparing a brief for the client, there is no mention of such things. It's not even in the thinking. But it can grow gradually. It's also possible that the idea might develop after the building is done. Many architects have made fun of this. No, not about Lou Kahn, but others. This is what critics are all about, this is what they do.

A Philadelphia Architect in Dhaka

Published in the *Daily Star*, Dhaka, 2003.

The following are excerpts from a conversation between Nathaniel Kahn and Kazi K. Ashraf. Nathaniel Kahn, an upcoming film-maker from New York, has just completed and released a film, "My Architect: A Son's Journey," on his father, the illustrious architect Louis I. Kahn. The film is actually a genre-bending masterwork, a spell-binding story that weaves architecture, life of a creative personality, and the emotional landscape that connects people around him. The film is already receiving rave reviews in such publications as *The New York Times*, *the New Yorker*, *Variety*, etc. The film critic Leonard Matlin describes the film as "the best this year… any year." The Parliament Complex project in Dhaka takes a prominent place in the film for Nathaniel believes that in his search for who his father really was, which is also centrally what the film is about, he found him in Dhaka. The conversation was taped in Philadelphia in August 2003 especially in the light of recent and unwarranted building interventions in the Parliament Complex.

Kazi K Ashraf (KA) The Parliament Complex takes a very special place in your film. It is in fact the climax to your film. What made you realize the importance of this group of buildings in Dhaka?

Nathaniel Kahn (NK) There are a few things that come to mind. One is the importance of Lou [Kahn] and his work to the world of architecture, and also the importance of this project in the process of his work, and also thirdly, my perception of what Lou did with the government of Bangladesh. My first access to it is because I've been traveling around the world seeing the places that my father built. I saved Dhaka for last because I remember as a little boy the passion he had for this project, and as a little boy in his office seeing the way he worked on this project for years and years, even when the war [of 1971] was on. The great story is when the war was on everybody said, stop working because we don't know what's going to happen, we don't know if there is going to be a government after this, and you're not being paid. His response was: there will be a time when there is peace again and they will need this building. And I think for two years with very little communication he kept working on this project because he knew how important it was for the future of this country that was going to emerge. Lou was somebody who believed in the ability of architecture to transform the world and to create a better society. We would consider him here an idealistic person. But I think he found in Dhaka a commission to design a center of government, really his dream project because it was a new country and he knew if he did it right and if he was able to get his vision done it could change the world.

KA Let me ask you this way, because other people will raise it, so why should we now be concerned about this man coming to Dhaka from Philadelphia with his dream project?

NK Well I think that's a good question. There are several answers. One, I found in the people of Bangladesh tremendous respect for what someone has given, more respect there than we have here. This is about a man who really gave his life for this project. And I think that so many times people have given their lives for something and maybe it hasn't turned out that well. What amazed me is how wonderfully this project turned out not only as a national treasure but an international treasure. This isn't just my father's dream project, it's also an example for the world… It is considered by architects around the world to be an absolute masterpiece of modern architecture. It is now going to be the subject of several books. It's an amazing place. I didn't know how wonderful it was until I went there.

KA Is it too premature to mention the Hollywood film here?

NK No, not at all. Hollywood is what Americans look to for what's important and who's important. A number of famous producers in Hollywood have seen my film and they were totally blown away by this story of this man from Philadelphia, who came from poor beginnings, who found his greatest achievement in this far away land called Bangladesh. And the buildings that he created there absolutely knocked them out, and they said, look, we want to make a feature film about this, about this man. It will be a huge Hollywood production because they were so impressed by the passion this person had to reach across the boundaries that separate east and west, different languages, different cultures and yet somehow a universal language was found between this architect from Philadelphia and the people of Dhaka, Bangladesh. And the building that was built is nothing short of the great pyramids of Egypt. I think Hollywood realizes that this is the kind of story that dreams are made of and that people go to see movies about. I think people will fly to Dhaka once they see this building, there will be tourists coming to Dhaka just to see this building. They will realize that it is a timeless piece of architecture and as time goes by the perception of his importance as an architect will continue to rise. He is one of the greatest architects of the 20th century along with Le Corbusier, Frank Lloyd Wright, and Mies van der Rohe.

KA People seem to return to Louis Kahn, his philosophy, his work, recurrently no matter what kind of fashionable things that are going on, and what rises and falls.

NK It's interesting, you're reminding me of a great friend of Lou's, the Indian architect Balkrishna Doshi who thought of Louis Kahn as a guru or yogi because he said he felt he was from here, he was from India, he was from this part of the world. I asked why, and he said because the things he was concerned with are the timeless things. He wasn't concerned with money, he wasn't concerned with fame. He was concerned with making something that would last forever. Now you have in the middle of Dhaka city the single most important creation that Louis Kahn ever made. You have it. It's in your country. It is of international value, it's of value for all time and the most important thing with a building like that is you've got to preserve the space that's around it so that it can be seen and be understood.

KA This project is an offering to the city of Dhaka, to the people of the city... it's not just a parliamentary complex. This is something that people in Dhaka should really value, should realize it as an infinite gift. I think they do... but you have this story, this beautiful story about your first experience of the Complex.

NK You know I had traveled around the world to see my father's buildings for this film. And I saved the Parliament Complex in Dhaka for last because I knew it was his greatest and also it was the one that had the most emotional impact for me because I remember as a little boy his passion for this project... and also it was from here, not exactly from Dhaka but from India, that he never returned really. He died on the way home. So when I went to Dhaka I was almost afraid because I knew it would be the last building I would ever see for the first time of my father's and that has great significance for a son. In a way this is the last piece of him on the earth that I can see. I wanted to see it in the right way. I didn't want to just arrive and suddenly have it be there. I wanted to really be in the right place. I wanted to be on that south lawn... looking at it. So I was with a friend an architect from Dhaka, Nurur Rahman Khan, and I said look I want to see this thing the right way, I don't want to see it in an accidental way, I want to see it in a really emotional way. So he suggested why don't we blindfold you and I'll drive you there. And so Nurur blindfolded me, and we drove through the streets and as you know Dhaka is very noisy. The sound of the baby taxis, the sound of the trucks, the constant honking and yelling and shouting and rickshaws and everything, it's very exciting but it's also very, very loud. And we drove through the streets… So we pulled up front and I got out from the taxi and suddenly there was soft ground under my feet. And we started walking up, I was being led blindfolded into this area. I didn't know what it was yet. And it was soft ground under my feet and sounds of the city started to recede and Nurur said, "Are you ready to see this building?" And I said "I'm not ready yet, not ready I just want to stand here for a moment and feel this place." I have to say that standing on that lawn you could feel the building, you could feel the space around the building. It was as if something was breathing there, it was air around it, it was space. It's really being in the presence of something spiritual. It's like being in the presence of a great temple. You feel it. You can feel a great monument by the silence around it and my father talked about the silence...

KA You need a silence like that in the city.

NK Absolutely, a city must have silence. And of course you can call it a park, you can call it whatever you want to call it but a city must have silence somewhere in the core because that is a place of calm from which action comes. You can't have action if it's all just nervousness and energy. You have to have a calm space. So there I stood in the calm space, breath deeply, and I said, okay, I'm ready and he took off the blindfold and there was the south lawn in front of me, the south plaza and the building rising above it with the flag, the Bangladesh flag, and I burst into tears. I actually burst into tears and it is the only building of my father's that has ever made me cry because I felt this was worth everything he gave, giving up obligations to family, giving up worldly goods that he could have had, money he could have had, all kinds of things he gave up for this. It was worth it because this building is a timeless work of great spiritual power. My immediate impression was, I didn't see anything else around it but this building, this form. There was nothing encroaching upon it. It was a pure, very pure view, and that view also talks about how a government has to act with great clarity and definition and be a symbol for its people. That's something that deserves space around it. You can't just shove that in the middle of buildings in a city…

KA Yes, one has to realize that architecture is not just buildings, the material physical objects. The space around it, that's architecture too. We should realize that we need those spaces. A city is a matrix of buildings and spaces.

NK Absolutely, and the Parliament building is the centerpiece of that matrix, no matter what happens in the rest of Dhaka City. Let them build elsewhere if there are needs... progress is good but it is not progress if you squeeze the Parliament by building all around it.

KA I like that.

NK That is not progress, this is actually going backwards. Think of what New York City would be without Central Park. The city would not exist. I live in New York, the city would be utterly unlivable if we didn't have Central Park. It is the only place where the city breathes, and the city can stop and collect itself and remember who it is. You take a run through that park and you remember this is a wonderful city. I live in the middle of this din but I can get away from it. I was also deeply impressed by the fact that everybody I've met in far flung places of the world, Bangladeshis, everybody has a story not just about the parliament building but the space around it. Everybody has a story about meeting a friend on the plaza, playing a game on the lawn, being a child on the lawn, walking around the Crescent Lake, exploring the area that the streets go past the hostels. Everybody has a story about it, and they're wonderful stories. Some of them are romantic. "I met my wife there." Some of them are dramatic. "I had a political confrontation, an important political discussion there." Some of them are artistic. "I had an idea for a book while walking around that lake every morning." A very famous American architect, I.M. Pei, told me before I went there, "Look, I've seen pictures of this building but I've never seen how it's used by people…" I was there for a week, two weeks actually, and every time I went I saw the building being used in different ways and that is a sign of a great space.

KA There is something else I would like to bring up, Kahn's interest in landscape. I don't know when he really became involved with that idea, although he was thinking about how buildings emerged from the landscape as a profound relationship between the two. His buildings look very crisp and crystalline, but they arise from the ground in a sort of mythical manner. I think especially in Bangladesh Kahn was really amazed by the aquatic landscape and talked about how he should do "an architecture of the land" here, what I call a hydrological architecture. I know that your mother is a landscape architect and she worked with him for a while even on this project. I would think, and people would say too, that Lou Kahn brought his own American, western ideas, and what have you, but at the same time he engaged very poetically and in very imaginative ways with what's already there, with the landscape of Bangladesh. The result is a very new creation in Dhaka, especially the matrix not just the buildings.

NK Beautifully said. A couple of things come to mind. When the Aga Khan Award was given, they said that the Parliament building is a universal kind of architecture but it could only exist here, it could only be in Dhaka. It is a timeless building but it is also very specific to this place. My father's first response when he came to Dhaka was to go on the river because he realized flying in that this is delta country. It is a land that is floating on water. And he took a boat on the river and the first thing he drew was – there's a beautiful little series of drawings – little boats... When we were figuring out how to get to the building in the film, we decided it has to rise out of the water. It is like an impossible, wonderful castle that lives in the middle of the water. The fact that Lou put it in water is very significant for several reasons. There's a practical reason, the water rises and falls. Yes, it's on dry land but really this whole place is floating on the water. And so I think his specific response to the place, to the landscape was very, very strong, and that building was not something he just kind of stuck there. It was something that grew out of his experience of the land of Bangladesh. And I think that it was very clear to him, he actually said this which is interesting that his dream more than anything else than designing individual buildings was to design the basis on which buildings would be built. So you're worried about matrix. That's a plan, that's a master plan. It's something he couldn't do anywhere else in the world. He tried in Philadelphia, he was denied. And Philadelphia now is suffering the consequences… Anyway I think his response was very strong: I want to create not just a building that serves a parliamentary purpose but a building in a landscape, a building in a landscape that responds to and expresses the actual landscape that is native.

KA And at the same time it's a city. So there is a twin thing, to live with the landscape and being in a city. It's not an anti-city, that landscape and city are not antithetical. That I think was a challenge.

NK I'm sure. And he didn't impose the western grid. It is a much freer, more like the delta country. It is not rigid, it's canalled, it's meandering. The river goes this way and it goes that way.

KA Even through the geometry.

NK Sure. It has a porosity to it. Water passes through, air passes through and this is space. So it's taking a chunk of space and defining it.

KA I have also been saying that if there is a model or a paradigm of a so-called Bengali city, it is perhaps this. Even though it has been proposed by a Jewish architect from Philadelphia, it is a model of a Bengali city. One doesn't have to be a Bengali to do that.

NK Absolutely, and this raises something wonderful which is that what Lou was after... an architecture that came from before the beginning of history. He was interested in creating an architecture that was so ancient that it was more ancient than anything you've ever seen and I think in Dhaka he did that. And this is part of what people respond to from all over the world. They go there and they think, God, where is this from? It belongs here yet it has this resonance of something enormously ancient. Was it built ten years ago, was it built 10,000 years ago? You don't know. And that is something, that wonderful ambiguity and that reach for something very ancient and very fundamental.

KA You know this idea of a Bengali City could be entertained in two ways. This sense of very archaic as you just mentioned, this idea of Volume Zero that Lou talked about. That sort of Bengali City could have been there 2,000 years ago. But at the same time it could be the Bengali City that could be 2,000 years from now. We're getting into wild speculation but it's that sort of a model Kahn gave the foundation to. From the foundation any kind of building can come up in any style and material, glass, aluminum, steel, brick... that is not important, what is important is the way the matrix is set up, that's what he gave here and what we really need to appreciate.

NK I think this raises the question of what is the edge of this creation...

KA He was really getting into something quite exciting. He was commissioned to look at the low lying area in the north which used to get flooded during the monsoon and he was thinking of buildings on bridges where you could cultivate at the lower level and you could have houses on the upper level. A new kind of building typology on the water.

NK You know there have been many assaults on Central Park. People have tried to say we need more housing. We need to build something in the bottom of the park and many times things have gotten close to being built and they've been stopped and every time people have breathed a sigh of relief, and five or ten years later they say, boy, with this temporary gain what we would have lost. So, if you start encroaching upon what exists there in the Complex your dream of the Bengali City, which is really a city on the water, is totally lost. And you just get more of the same, yet you get what you already have...

KA Which you are getting in the rest of the city.

NK The other thing is that there is an issue of national pride and identity. The people that I talked to when I was filming, they said this is our national symbol, we are very proud of this. But I am thinking when those people said to me this is a symbol of our country, we're proud of it, what exactly are they saying? Is it just the building? No, it's also the whole space around it... it is a little city in a park. It is a calm space which brings people together and from which you make policy about everything else but you don't let the petty concerns of the day, needing a house here and a house there, encroach upon the big vision.

KA Let me come back to his urban visions for Philadelphia. Lou Kahn was not just an architect he was also an urban visionary. He had some very significant ideas for the city.

NK He started in public housing.

KA That too, plus his idea for a civic downtown but then some of the ideas trickled down and...

NK ...became Dhaka.

KA And sure became Dhaka. This is the interesting twist that despite his great plans for Philadelphia, the drawings of which are studied even now by architects and urban planners all over the world, some of that got built in Dhaka

NK This is interesting because it reminds me of a story that he was very fond of telling about his city Philadelphia. People asked him why do you love Philadelphia? And he'd say a city is a place where a small boy when he walks through it can find what he wants to do for the rest of his life, and for him that city was Philadelphia, and I also think for him that city could be Dhaka, but in Philadelphia I think at the time when he was growing up there were great institutions of learning, great schools that were free to people no matter where you came from. There were beautiful art museums, there were fantastic government buildings, and a child could wander through the parks and think about things, and as time went by other things happened... people were going to the suburbs and soon there was a need to rejuvenate the cities. Lou Kahn had some magnificent ideas for Philadelphia... one of the greatest ones was to leave the cars outside of the city and you walk in the center. In every step of the way he was prevented from building these visions of the city of the future. Instead they built Philadelphia like every other city in America. It's all the same. It's clogged with traffic. It's got these high rises that you wish you could tear down. And now, it's not a city of the future, it's a city of yesterday. All the problems we have with crime, with overcrowding, with noise, with depression among the people, all these things that we could have avoided and that he was trying to design about... places where a little boy wandering through them could find what he wanted to do for the rest of his life, whether it was to be an architect, a painter, a naturalist, a filmmaker, or a business man. The interesting is that in Philadelphia he was basically given mostly projects to design individual buildings. In two places he was given the chance to design more than just a building, actually a plan for a small city, the two places in India and the greatest one absolutely in Dhaka. And I think it's significant that this is not a complex of art galleries, it is not a school, it is the center of government which is the central symbol of the entire country. So I think he brought many of the best ideas that he had that should have been implemented in Philadelphia and that now people here are wishing that they had done but it's too late. He brought to Dhaka those visions and those experiences of how a city can be screwed up. Let's learn from the mistakes we made in America. Don't make the same mistakes we made here.

KA We don't want to be Philadelphia.

NK Believe me you don't want to be Philadelphia, you don't want to be New York, you don't want to be those things. And I can tell you right now that in the Complex there is a place where a small boy wandering through it can find what he wants to do for the rest of his life. Don't lose that. That's it. You've got it there. And it's not an American city, it's a Bengali City but it comes with tremendous knowledge of what went wrong in America.

KA So, Lou has a vision of what will happen in the next forty, fifty years. I'm sure he was looking at cities and he didn't want cities to be like that. So in a sense he has given a vision for any city.

NK You raise an interesting point here which is: you were talking about a city being buildings and spaces. Now basically what we have in our cities is buildings and then a park. We have very poor integration of landscape and buildings. We don't put them together very well. We have to designate areas. This is a park, you can't build here. But what you've got in the complex in Dhaka is this perfect combination of buildings and space ,and the way they interact with each other is the best of both worlds. It's kind of what you were talking about, this matrix.

KA One last thing… about the film. We are already seeing that your film is going to be a major event in the next few months opening all over the US. The Parliament Complex is so important in your film. You end the film with it. But really what I am interested in finding out is how do you think people are perceiving the Complex as you show the film?

NK Well, I can tell you what they've already seen. There's no question that everybody loves the part of the film that takes place at Dhaka. It has been mentioned in reviews, in the New York Times, in Variety magazine. Many people have never seen the building before first of all which means there's a PR problem. People need to know more about these buildings. But they cannot get over the building and the people who we encountered in Dhaka. Their vision of Bangladesh is floods literally and then they see this and they say, oh, my god, that's the capital of Bangladesh and Kahn built that? And that's what it looks like? I want to go. Their response really is what a spiritual building, what an incredible place, what beautiful people. We want to go, how do we go? And their response also is how my father was thwarted in his dreams in America. They say we missed out and Bangladeshis got the cream of the crop. I wish we'd done it. And I think they also are completely knocked out by another aspect that is very touching for me and that is my mission to try to find out who my father was. Many people in America treated me as "here comes this nearly middle-aged man...get over it" and their response is in the film. Not all of them were that way. There was more openness with people in Dhaka. It's almost as if for a Bengali it's completely normal that you should try to find out who your father was and you should honor the quest. When people watch the movie they say, you really found him there, didn't you? You found him in Dhaka. You looked for him all over the world and you got pieces of him but you found him there. And I say in the movie if my father was going to be anywhere, he was here (in Dhaka). My father has a grave outside Philadelphia. It's in a cemetery with a lot of other people. I know that his body may be there but his heart was in Dhaka.

Metrophilia: A Love of the Horizon Line

A Conversation between Kazi Ashraf and Dimitri Kim
Published in *Prototropic: Tales and Speculations under the Sun*, Issue 0.1, November, 2014.

"It is the year 2015. There is an unprecedented building boom in Hawaii. The construction of the new rail has just begun. The district of Kaka'ako in Honolulu is brimming with youth, arts, new business, and chaos..."

Dimitri Kim. What is your perspective on all the changes that are taking place in Hawaii?

Kazi Ashraf. I think this is a very interesting time. Some architects now describe it as a new renaissance. The first time I came here some 12 years ago, I saw different things. I read a piece in the weekly "City Paper" that was titled "10 most ugly buildings in Honolulu."

D. I think I do recall that article.

K. I was kind of stunned seeing that article, after having lived in New York, Philadelphia, and Boston. I haven't encountered media really taking a hard look at ugly buildings. The piece in the weekly made me think, is that the core of the conversation here? There was no discourse but only a conversation on ugly buildings. And that was kind of a gloomy thing to think about.

So I think the conversation now is shifting with all the new things that are happening right now, with Kaka'ako especially, with the rail project, and other developments in town. Whether it is a "Renaissance" and all that, I am not sure. But certainly there is a new building momentum, and also along with it a conversation around it. I think interesting conversations are happening.

I am going to add something else. On the one hand, there is this conversation around the new developments, as well as heated debates around the rail projects. Whatever the different views are, it is a good debate, about the nature of the city, about the form of the rail projects and the stations, and the stations as the new epicenter of developments and new loci of energy for the city. But before we cite Kaka'ako, or similar developments in town, especially the two towers of the Design Center that was completed 6-7 years ago, before claiming them as new renaissance of sorts, we need to talk about them a bit more. Because I have a question about these sort of tall buildings as representatives of a building boom. Unless we are careful, just tall buildings by themselves, no matter how stunning they are, I am not sure how deeply effective they will be in the urban environment. At the end, they might look like a lot of Titanics drifting around aimlessly in a sea of unremarkable-ness.

D. Yes, despite all the boom and what it has created (sea of tall buildings), they are more or less unremarkable and does not necessarily add value to the city. Time will tell if much of these additional buildings would have any lasting, positive effect on the island. I suspect negative.

K. What I am saying is that tall buildings by themselves, however stunning they are, cannot claim to be a measure of contribution to the urban environment. I will say this in a different way. The city is a relentless battle between private profit making and civic obligations. We know that. It's not news. And tall buildings clearly manifest the profit making motive. Formally, it is a visible representation of profit making and I am not against that. That is how the economy operates.

The tall building versus the city. It has come down to that. I see this as a conflict that has not really been resolved, not in Honolulu, not even anywhere in the world. Maybe in some degree Hong Kong was able to deal with it in a more resolved way, maybe Manhattan in its own way has dealt better with the conflict between what I would call "metrophilia," my term for a love of the city, for a horizontal experience of the city, how I walk the city, how I engage with civic and urban offerings, versus what I call "Phallophilia." Yes, the love of things erect and stand alone! So Metrophilia versus Phallophilia, and that is how modern city has come down to and that is an old debate and has not been resolved.

In Honolulu, as you walk by these huge parking garages, they are totally dissociated from street life. Metrophilia involves the street. Tall buildings, in its kind of most basic way, do not care about street-life… you drive into your parking garage and you go to your unit. Unless this is resolved via design, we are going to see this as a conflict.

D. I think much of the intensities going towards the real estate developments in high rises are driven by financial speculations and short-term profit. An immediate discussion is needed to determine the long-term impacts of these developments.

K. Well first of all, I am not quite sure about the full ramification of new developments centered around high-rises. I don't know of any complex being built, something developed and integrated as a district. The whole thing is about high rises, their impacts have not been discussed much. Are high rises going to be the only discussion regarding economy and urban development?

Are there other models that doesn't include high-rises right away and that is something we need to discuss, and that leads us to another topic which you have laid out as the tilt of your journal itself, the tropic, the "tropical city." I think the whole question of tropical city is key… because the kind of model of the city being reproduced in Honolulu, have been built elsewhere, like Dubai or Shanghai, so that's one kind of model and that mode is generated by economy, and not quite driven by civic obligations.

So going back, what kind of city Honolulu is, that is the question.

D. Vladimir Ossipoff's legacy played a significant role in the establishment of modern architecture authorship in Hawaii, do you feel that he's work was an exception or has his influence crated a distinct imprint that is still relevant?

K. Well definitely we have not encountered anyone of the stature of Ossipoff after Ossipoff. Although Ossipoff has designed mostly residences, and few civic and institutional buildings, he has produced a fantastic language in combining modern Hawaiian tropical and Asian traditions that have not been surpassed. So after Ossipoff, shall we say we have little to show? Well, there has been decent architecture, but they are not significant in the sense of Ossipoff nor have they taken on the challenges of our times.

D. It's interesting because one of the project in this issue is David Rockwood's tropical case study house. The TCSH Program (by Rockwood) challenges architects to build within limitation and opportunities of a tropical environment. It has always been my view that only real requirements for the design of a house in Hawaii is a roof and a floor. Yet the vast majority of architecture in Hawaii are built with the same tradition and construction techniques used in cities with seasonal weather conditions. Yet, despite his sensitivity to regionalism, Ossipoff did not embrace environment heartedly.

K. Well Honolulu is not a small city. And it has many districts and neighborhoods and building types. I am sitting here in the neighborhood of Makiki, in a much older house, with a porch, lawn, lot of vegetation, lot like living in a pavilion. Which is what you want – the pavilion type, as a building model for hot, humid, tropical places, because in a pavilion, you allow breezes to pass through, you have views, green vegetation. But that does not mean you can build a pavilion in all urban situations because of tighter lot sizes, parcels, and what have you, and therefore, it's a challenge, which is what David is trying, which Ossipoff in a more sort of generous site and land was able to do in a beautiful way.

The challenge is when you are working in a tighter urban condition, how do you translate a pavilion in such situations. I don't see any examples that has taken that up.

D. In regards to Honolulu within a global context, do you think that the perception of Hawaii gives an unrealistic or negative expectation about the city?

K. Well that is an interesting question that could take different direction.

D. Well the most common generalization about Hawaii is that it is an isolated island, beautiful, but devoid of any real city and lacks contemporary and modern conveniences. And these are some of the more milder speculations I have heard throughout the years. There was a recent, Chicago Tribune article, stating a similar view about Hawaii's bid for Obama's presidential Library.

K. Well, that opens up a big question, whether it is in a geopolitical sense or the geographic location of Hawaii, we are one of the most isolated spots on the planet, but does that matter in our present day nature of mobility and connectivity. Why does it matter? I don't know if that is a problem of isolation, but I wouldn't call it a negative connotation of Hawaii, but how Hawaii has been imagined, invented, and circulated for the last hundred years or so. The present perception of Hawaii falls into that pattern, and that is the view of a landscape of paradise, and paradise is translated immediately, architecturally speaking, with a coconut and palm trees, and all that stuff, you know the 'exoticization' of the primitive.

If you want Hawaii to claim a distinctive position in the community of cities, it is a dichotomy. Meaning that you want to be considered as another kind of a city, say like Singapore, a major economic destination, etc. And then you want to make Honolulu distinctive and contemporary, and really understand city form, social equality, civic obligations, no, that is missing in the conversation… not only missing in the conversation but missing in the production.

Architecture in Bangladesh and the legacy of Muzharul Islam

A discussion with Kazi Khaleed Ashraf
Dhaka, November 2015.

From the *Dhaka Art Summit 2016 Exhibition Guide*.

If the present exhibition, taking place as part of the Dhaka Art Summit, is a journey through modern and contemporary Bangladeshi architecture, then the recurring task of this journey is the search for a "nation building architecture". Although today the word of "identity" may seem difficult to use due to its loaded connotations, we see nevertheless, in Bangladesh, from modernism to regionalism, from independence and liberation, into the current era of globalization, that the primary challenge of architecture here is one of finding a common cultural identity.

– Aurélien Lemonier

***Aurélien Lemonier:* When and how do you identify the origin of modernity in Bangladeshi architecture?**

Kazi Ashraf: The question of modernity, modernism and identity depends on what time frame we are talking about. Should we start in the 1950s when architectural modernism arrived here? I tend not to identify "modernity/modernism" with that time right away. The original time frame, as far as political and cultural practices are concerned, is older, rooted in the colonial presence here in Bengal and in India. As you know, the British enterprise largely took place in Bengal: it is here that the British landed first and from where they began their operations that started with commerce leading to establishing an imperial power. Afterwards, the English went to Delhi and ruled the rest of India. The idea of modernity has to be seen in the light of colonial history, different than the practice of modernity seen through the lens of globalisation now.

We can highlight three phases if you like: modernity as part of a colonial history, modernity as emerging in the field of architecture beginning in the 1950s, and modernity refracted through globalisation. Each phase has its own complexity. Even now, we really have to rethink the relationship with the colonial West, which ironically brought the culture and practice of modernity in terms of rationalism, individualism, education, laws and institutions. I say ironically because colonialism enabled Bengalis to adopt those institutions and practices, and begin the question of "who are we"? The question of identity didn't emerge before this. It arose when major transformations were taking place culturally, individually, and existentially within the period of colonial turmoil.

I would describe the whole experience as a very complex relationship between acceptance and resistance. Some people accepted the British, working with them, some people resisted, struggled strongly; it's a complex interplay between acceptance and resistance. On the one hand, accepting the major transformation caused by the colonial power led to a lot of enlightening things as well as disruptions. On the other hand, the colonial period led to looking at things broadly, globally. The nineteenth century was the time when an international and world civilisation was strongly introduced. And we felt this world civilisation in every aspect of Bengali culture, such as literature, paintings, and later on architecture.

Here lay the foundations of Bengali modern culture. Fantastic events came about from that situation. A key one was the founding of the Bengal School of Art that broadly became the foundation of modern art in India, one of the main streams of what some people call the "Bengal Renaissance." In a certain way, being aware about ourselves, asking the question of identity… nobody attended to this question two hundred years ago. But this happened in the complex interaction with the British and the West. Because of their presence, we were beginning to look at ourselves, at how we were constituted. That led to a productive output, a worldly openness…

The Bengal Renaissance is often critiqued because it was led by a Hindu elite in Calcutta. Nevertheless, it had a strong impact on an overall Bengali culture. It was led by the reformer Raja Ram Mohan Roy. The movement can still be considered the basis of the modern formation of Bengali identity, all of which may also explain a lot of things about Muzharul Islam in the 1950s. I would like to argue that Muzharul Islam is the architectural representation of the "Bengal Renaissance", though he figures certainly quite late in the time span. In cinema, it is the same with a major figure like Satyajit Ray…

Let me tell you a story that will highlight what I am talking about. If I remember well, when Simón Bolivar liberated what became Bolivia, Raja Rammohan Roy arranged a big feast in the streets of Calcutta. Just think about that: we are in the nineteenth century, and a remote country, which became Bolivia, liberated from its colonial rulers, and that was being celebrated in Calcutta. This is what we mean when we say being part of a world civilisation. This also illustrates Muzharul Islam's ideology: being part of the world as well as being Bengali. Each architect has to figure out how to play this double obligation: acceptance and resistance. That is how I would describe the road to modernity.

Is modernity a construction of the self?

If I have to understand modernity, I would say it starts when you become conscious of yourself which is not necessarily a wonderful thing. We could describe it as looking at yourself in a mirror, like the story of Narcissus: he sees himself in the reflection of the water and he falls in love with himself. But he cannot touch his reflection, make it palpable. That could be about identity: once you become conscious of yourself, you have to face a split, the distance between yourself and the reflection you have of yourself. If I use that imagery in our discussion, modernity may suggest we will never get back to tradition reflected over there, we can never retrieve the past, we can never get our "fantastic" golden age in history because a rupture has happened. And if modernity produces this rupture, it allows you to accept it and as well to claim it. But you can't claim it in copying things from the past, or by adopting things from outside. The solution is to reconstruct. This is the condition from where Muzharul Islam started. He did not copy any kind of elements from tradition. If he allowed himself to be called a regionalist, it is because he was strongly devoted to the spirit of the place, its political history, and its cultural legacy. So there is an awareness of identity, but an identity that needed to be constructed. And that is the struggle.

This struggle, which Muzharul Islam began in the field of architecture, was carried out in a new architectural language, the language of abstraction, which had nothing to do with symbolism, iconic reference, or even figuration. Was abstraction, as an architectural language, a strategy to deal with this struggle?

Absolutely. That is a very important point. There were various streams among the artists of the Bengal Renaissance; one was literally and directly inspired by folk art, pre-modern traditional art, another experiment was what we could call abstraction adopted from European modernity. Muzharul Islam was very clear about architecture. Even until the 1950s, the main reference in architecture was the language of colonial architecture, especially those of neoclassical imperial buildings. One other option would be deriving a language free of European references, one that may have been available from buildings in rural areas or monuments of the past. The third option was to adopt a modernist language. In the 1950s, nobody would, nobody could adopt a colonial language for obvious reasons – we threw them out! Certainly, it was the same with traditional architecture, much of it was a thing of a stilled past. Muzharul Islam was skeptical about tradition, because some of it contained a history of repression and tyranny. That is why Muzharul Islam chose abstraction as a language. It was not adopted for stylistic reasons but from an ethical and political viewpoint. It was also climactically very viable. That was a second reason. Modern architecture works well in tropical climates.

How would you describe the situation of Bangladesh at the beginning of the 1950s and its link with other countries of the subcontinent?

As you know, during the 1950s, Bangladesh was part of Pakistan. It was a new country, a new nation with its own agenda and plans for new institutions and buildings. It was the same for India, which commissioned the plan for Chandigarh. New institutions had to be made. In India, they were supposed to express a socialist, secular, and industrial worldview. A little bit of that circulated in Pakistan, but in a subdued way. Pakistan was established as an Islamic state on a religious line. This became more and more problematic moving from the 50s toward the 60s. At the beginning, Bengalis were accepting of the state of Pakistan, but by the mid-1950s, they realized that they may have struck a bad deal. Being part of this religious state would mean suppressing the pluri-secular culture of Bengal. Muzharul Islam was part of this political consciousness and became more and more involved politically. 96 This was basically part of the larger political and cultural movement of the 1960s in Bangladesh against the increasing oppression by West Pakistani authorities, resulting in the Liberation War and Independence in 1971.

Going back to the question of architectural expression, the West Pakistan commissions for public buildings were asking for motifs recognized as "Islamic": domes, arches, whatever. Neither Muzharul Islam nor Louis Kahn would have anything to do with those demands. For instance, when Louis Kahn was asked to design the Presidential residence in Islamabad, he declined to use Islamic-Persian motifs, and at the end lost the commission. In Bangladesh, things were different.

We are talking about the social involvement of architecture. It is not only about constructing buildings, it is about how to build a society. Muzharul Islam understood this. How then did the idea to organize the Chetena Society come about?

From independence, Muzharul Islam single handedly innovated a modernist language in his buildings. We must recognize that he tried to establish, to the largest degree, a norm for a modern culture in architecture, which is about discourse, investigation, rational practices and finally about being aware of the contribution of architects in society. Architecture is not only about corporate or commercial buildings. Muzharul Islam was able to bring about the notion of self-critique to the role of the architect. He was president of Institute of Architects of Bangladesh, and by his activist work he transformed the culture of being an architect. Maybe Bangladesh is a small country, and probably, even today, people only see the disasters. But Bangladesh was also a theatre for important events in South Asian modernism. During the 1960s, Bangladesh played a significant role, notable because of Louis Kahn obviously. Kahn brought up so many questions, including the question of spirituality. This was perhaps too problematic to put forward in the US at that time, but in India and in Bangladesh, it did make a lot of sense. At the same time, Muzharul Islam brought Paul Rudolph and Stanley Tigerman to work here. Constantin Dioxidis came as well because he was commissioned by Pakistan to establish the master plan of Islamabad. Richard Neutra came on his own and built a couple of buildings. So in the 1960s, there was a fantastic group of architects working in Bangladesh who made exemplary buildings, which we might call "tropical architecture."

By the 70s and the beginning of the 80s, the track of the architectural journey seemed to have been lost. For the young architects – we had just graduated – the question was what to do now? The old debate on, if you call it "identity" – I don't use that word anymore, but in the 80s, yes, we did use this word and we questioned its consequences or lack thereof. What about appropriateness? What about culture? Globalization had not yet come but architects seemed to have already lost the authentic sense of responsibility to culture and community that fundamentally led us to a different kind of wondering. First, how would we be able to build a new kind of consciousness about the obligation of the architects toward society? Secondly, how could we rethink history and tradition? Those questions came in order to establish a new "conversation" between architecture and the other cultural disciplines like literature, poetry, archaeology, history. Muzharul Islam was able to reconnect the younger generation of architects with major intellectuals in those cultural fields, because he knew most of them. For us, it was a fantastic opportunity to share a platform of debate and discussion. Before that – if I can say so– most of us would have asked why should we be listening to Bengali music to do architecture? We were able in a way to reintegrate all that in a kind of new "renaissance" if you want. Chetana could literally translate as "consciousness." It brought a new consciousness for re-integrating all these areas that perhaps can have a huge impact how you think and do architecture. And I do personally believe that Chetana did have a huge impact in terms of developing a new sensibility and awareness of place, geography, and culture.

What happened after the fall of the Soviet Union, regarding the spread of globalization and the liberalization of the economy? In just a few decades in a city like Dhaka there seems to me to have been a huge impact. How would you explain this new challenge over the last twenty years?

That is a huge question.... there are two issues here, the first is about contemporary challenges, and the second is how Dhaka has transformed.

The German sociologist Ulrich Beck has described the contemporary phenomenon as a "second modernity," and as a new paradigm compared to what we call the first or European modernity, which was an ideology for transforming society into a better world. Architecture, and more generally modern culture, was looking for a universal language that could be understood and adopted by anyone; roughly speaking, it was a kind of salvation for humanity. The second modernity does not particularly care about a societally better world. It is really about, as Beck describes, risks and speculations, based on monetary flow, new technology and information systems. We can't focus on culture anymore rooted only into geography and history; it has to be rephrased from the condition of transnational exchanges. Yes, boundaries do still exist, yes nations are still there, but porosity is shaping our societies more than ever. Look for instance what is happening in Europe with Middle Eastern refugees... The transnational flow became the term of reference. Historians used to describe migration from rural countryside to cities during the first Industrial Revolution as a major historical event, but for the last thirty years, people have been moving from country to country in an intense way; this is unprecedented. You can find large communities of Bengalis in London, New York, and San Francisco for instance. And there are Bengalis living inside Bangladesh. Identity is no longer defined by the country from where you are, it is also about where you will be heading.

In this situation, people have new desires, new requirements. Architects are also in this game and their obligations have changed. This is a long discussion, but I will make it simple. I would say that the dark side of the current transformation is in the widening of inequality, which we see especially in more explosive ways in cities like Cairo, Mumbai, Karachi or Dhaka, for instance. So, risk and speculation, the globalized economy, transnational migration, these are all triggered by a consumerist culture and wealth formation. Some will reach it, some will not, and that will compound problems. Radical transformation of the landscape, of cities like Dhaka or Chittagong, is happening not only because of things inside Bangladesh but also because of a global chain of forces. We are part of the global network. And transformations are happening in such an accelerated way that you can't even follow what is going on. Thirty or forty years ago, we had policy makers, planners, industrialists, to organize our state of affairs, but today we cannot figure out how to deal with the complex transformation that is going on.

In a way, it is out of control and you cannot even conceive it properly. Beck has provided one idea. In a way, challenges for the city were much easier in the 1950s than today. We need to have a new kind of intelligence to handle contemporary evolutions. We are still thinking about a much more fixed, manageable kind of destiny, but Dhaka is moving on to new fluctuating terrains. I am not going to make a list, but Dhaka faces challenges. Having looked at many cities, I describe Dhaka as the toughest city in the world. Still devoted to this topic, some of us feel obligated to do something. The challenge is huge and eventually traditional intelligence will not help us. To handle a situation like Dhaka, we need to reposition our understandings, what we know and what can be done.

What do you mean when you are talking about a new kind of intelligence? According to you, what kind of shift do you think needs to be made to deal with the complexity of contemporary life?

From my point of view, it is not enough to note what is wrong in our city, the traffic, social inequality, lack of public facilities. We know these. The challenge is elsewhere. To me it is how a city like Dhaka is going to be reorganized with the landscape. It could sound like a nice phrase around a picturesque condition, but working with the landscape involves new political, ethical, and environmental agendas. First of all, I think that the European idea of the city will not completely work here. Everybody is talking about organization and urbanization in a very negative way. But we must describe the growth of the city in a much more positive manner. We don't have a proper translation of the beautiful French concept of 'urbanisme.' To think about the city in a positive and dynamic way, we should look at the new pulse and tempo of the city. The city can be an economic generator, and actually it is, but if I talk about a new intelligence that means a new way of thinking about the inner dynamic of the city. It is not only a new language, but rather a new set of concepts. And this must engage the landscape – the aquatic, wet landscape. Dhaka has decent regulations. But a typical way of thinking through these regulations is to push the water away and make a big division between "dry" and "wet": the city and society is dry, while the countryside, the farms are wet... such conceptual division cannot work in Bangladesh. Wetness and dryness should be interactive in a new urban dynamic. Urbanism should include this condition of intertwining; it could bring about a new kind of morphology that has not been thought of yet.

As architects, we have to produce new ways of thinking. We cannot give up and hand over this responsibility to engineer or planners or policy-makers. It is the job of the architects to do that. We know that in the past many architects did just that. Look at Le Corbusier who articulated the image of the modern city. My point is architecture is bigger than architecture. By that I mean that, architecture is not about single buildings, it has to go beyond that to a larger sphere. To rethink the morphology of the city, the landscape orientation has to engage with water instead of pushing it away. That is the next frontier and that is what I am devoted to. I think, yes, that is the continuation of the legacy of Muzharul Islam.

Legacies That We Leave Behind: An Interview with Balkrishna Doshi

Interview conducted in Ahmedabad, 1994, published in *Locations: Anthology of Architecture and Urbanism*, 2016.

Excerpted from a longer text.

Kazi Khaleed Ashraf: There is another story that Stanley Tigerman narrates. He is supposedly the last architect Kahn met on his way to New York and to his death. They met at Heathrow Airport. Tigerman was coming to Dhaka. You were saying how in the later stage Kahn was thinking about what he is to be, what he has to do. He is sort of assessing himself in a certain way. Tigerman says somewhat the same thing. They were talking for a couple of hours while they were waiting at the airport. One thing that seemed to bother Kahn was about [the Bangladeshi architect] Muzharul Islam. He was asking Tigerman, why did Muzharul Islam leave architecture for politics? Kahn seemed very disturbed about that, and was saying, "I could never do that." Probably, Kahn was asking, how does someone ultimately relate to society, to a larger whole? What is one's contribution after all?

Balkrishna Doshi: His trips to India and Bangladesh must have given him another message. That message is very simple. This is a question [that is] probably raised in everybody's mind. There is something in the air, and that is, what is the purpose? What do you leave behind? Kahn was never fascinated by money either, so the question of money is not there. So, if not money, what else? The question that what is left is eternity. What stays? What cannot be questioned will stay. What cannot be altered will stay. What is natural, what will naturally flow, will stay. What is inherent will stay. And, therefore, the Upanishad is talking about the air, the water, the sky, and then the soul, the moving soul, the non-local mind. This will stay, and that is all pervading. And that is what Lou was always talking about: the psyche. What it is.

I think he was looking for those things always, because, as he says, if he has to find the architectural expression of a brick wall, what is the difference between his brick wall and somebody else's brick wall? Then, he is talking about the slice of light, which comes and just touches that. That means what kind of little vibration the bricks must give or the joints must give, the little projections must give so that the bricks begin to sparkle and smile, so that little slice, that light, that breeze which comes with a fragrance, but it is actually what is. You don't know where the breeze is, and you can't hold the fragrance, either. It is only the sensation that is left, and I think good architects are looking for those sensations. I think that is what is Kahn does. He always talked about silence; he talked about the ruins. To him, finally, it was that meditative silence: How does one make a building, which exists and yet doesn't want to say anything and yet says everything everybody wants to know?

So the building in Dhaka stands there. If you look at them in the evenings, if you look at them in the early mornings, it is almost as eternal as the rocks of the Himalayas. He makes the statement that "I have no Himalayas around, but my buildings stay there as long as this sun rises because it is so simple from the outside, from the distance." How do you make that opening unless you make a circle, that opening from where you see very simple things? Hardly any extra thing has been done, and also, the scale has to do with that. The scale is big. If there were small holes, it won't be the same. They had to be big enough to make them look infinite. The power is in the scale in which he makes the apertures and the box.

I think from that point of view of the base is very important for him. You should go in the early morning and walk around the houses, go around, and then you see this base; it is almost like a banyan tree, which comes up with the roots coming out and covering the whole ground, as if it is all pervading. It is stretching its arms at the ground level, and the ground level stretches far beyond because all the houses are at the same height so that everything becomes part of that, and then this rises up like this.

I was struck by the way of his model making. The buildings always seemed to rise from the clay base. They are not boxes thrown from the top to the ground.

Yes, it was like a mesa. It was very much like a stupa. I would say Dhaka is like a stupa, as in Sanchi.

Before he even started thinking about the Assembly, there was something else that intrigued him. He asked himself two questions: One, how do buildings take their place on this land? And, the other thing, how are buildings to be grouped together? Also, he began to talk of a new way of thinking about architecture, which he called "an architecture of the land." He was saying that for Bangladesh, the primary way to think about is architecture of the land. In that context, I see his buildings as land-sculpted.

All studies with diagonals, triangles, and geometry really become part of the land, part of the wall. The land and the wall do not change. You see, Wright made a wall and then made the roof in such a way that the whole wall continued, his studio as a shell, and his other buildings go like this with an inclined wall, and he brings the roofline right up to the wainscot, so the whole building really hugs the ground. Kahn is trying to do it from the ground up, to go up like this, to reverse this.

Here, can we also discuss the importance of water? Before Dhaka, I don't see any significant presence of water in Kahn's work.

In Dhaka, it [water] is the whole question. You are on the plains, and the water is going to be there, anyway, so the Dhaka landscape cannot be without the Ganges, without the rivers around, and so the flooding, the delta, has to be there. It is the reflecting element but also water, an integral part of your culture. The whole of Bangladesh is made of lakes and rivers. To me, it is a country that is floating.

I am curious to know what places he visited in Ahmedabad or elsewhere in India?

He went to Ranakpur. It is a Jain temple about ninety miles from Udaipur. He also went to Abu, the Delawara temple. Delawara is before Udaipur. These are all Jain temples, and Kasturabhai [Lalbhai] had asked him to come with him. The Jain Abu Temple is made of marble, exquisitely carved, translucent. Ranakpur is very geometrical, again in a valley, a solitary temple with an axis and raised plinth with a huge number of columns. You can see the gods from anywhere. When he came back, I asked him which one did he like. He said Ranakpur, and I asked why. He said Abu is very decorative and asked me back which one did I like. There [at Abu Temple], the marble has been totally transformed into wax. You talk of marble as marble; we in India talk of dematerializing things. And I said that when you can spiritualize a matter, it is quite different. I said this body, which is material, has to be spiritualized, and that's what the message is. And he said I didn't know that, but I prefer the other one. This is really where you asked me a question yesterday: How do I see Kahn as an "Indian" architect? Well, there are only a few great architects who came to the sub-continent, Lutyens, Corbusier, and then Kahn. There are not many like them because people like that are not born every day. But what one is looking for is what is it one can do so that the material really moves, the material begins to become something else. Can we learn about ourselves as a vehicle of the spirit moving, and can we infuse this vehicle into bricks and concrete and stones so that the material also melts away in the process and just emerges as it should be?

And as I told you last night, I invited you here [the Gufa] only because here is one building which I tried to do. You can say that partly, it is an influence of Gaudi; partly, it is from other places, I don't know where, but I feel one is trying to do here is really to infuse things so that finally, you know only the experience, and I think in this building, you get that "Silence," not my other buildings, so what I have learned from Kahn is this search for silence; what I learned from Corbusier is the lyricism; what I learned from Wright is the point of hugging the ground, and what I learned from Gaudi is the great quality of flowing inward and outward. And so what I am doing really is trying to find these because that's the only way I cannot only pay my respects to them, but I can also learn. Slowly, I am trying to learn the silence, the act of silence through the ruins of above ground, relating the surfaces. And then one is still trying to say that in the content of their work that if you still want to get this, then there are these paradoxes in India, in Bangladesh, where different cultures stay together; different religions stay together; you find a mosque and a temple next to one another; you find a big palace and a haveli and shacks together. [There are] people [who] are well dressed and people with no clothes. There is a car, and there is a buffalo on the road. There is a cycle-rickshaw, and there is a jet plane. These are all contradictions that we have accepted. We know that without the disparity, true existence doesn't work. There is no existence without disparity. It is only when we see it in a short span that there is a disparity. Actually, it is the same process; you see only one end, and you see the other one, but [they] depend upon the suitability of one and the other. It is like an insect; the fly has only one hour of life, and the mountains have thousands of years of life. So, we consider temporary and permanent. It is not there at all. It is all permanent and all temporary because we also go away. So, these are relative terms, and I think if we can learn these from those people that they knew this relativity and felt them, and that's why you will find all the great architectures of the world, including the work of today's masters, you will find there are a lot of things, but the experience is very similar; it touches us the same way as we can smell the fragrance of a flower or look at the mountains or go to the sea. That is because this kind of continuous phenomenon is there; that is what is beautiful. This is the great lesson to me working with these masters, including Bucky Fuller, whom I met several times.

I am finding that there is a thread. They want to find out what will last. What will disappear? How can you make things without a strain? The most important thing is, is there a strain in that building? Is there a strain in that triangle which hits the opening, and, therefore, the opening looks as if it is very natural? In a circle, there is no strain; in a square, there is no strain.

It seems to me, if I am not mistaken, that you are looking at these major figures, especially Kahn, that he is moving in a continuum, almost autonomous from specific experiences related to [coming to] India and Bangladesh.

Yes, yes ... because they are made to sense things; they are made to smell, feel. They don't feel superficially; they feel deeply within themselves. Actually, they are themselves. The whole reason of their being what they are is because they know themselves, and they work within their own self. They are very alive within; we are very alive outside. To them, the body has no meaning because their presence is inside. That's why they are yogis, and that's why they cannot be communicated in a normal way, because they are only manifestations of [what they are doing on this earth]. But manifestations come, as if like a spring, from within. It is a surge, which tells them to do this. It is a manifestation, and they become instruments. That's what Kahn talked about, that's what Corbusier talked about, and that's what Bucky talked to me about: that we are only instruments. And that's what our yogis talk about. It's not man conquering this, man doing this, and man doing that. [That's how normal people talk.] That's why humility becomes very natural to them. You can see one doesn't seek publicity, one doesn't want things, one doesn't copy ... why? Because one is looking within, and he knows everything will be available to him in the long run. To them, the game was continuous.